Third Revised and Updated Edition

Basic Computer Course

made simple

(Based on NIELIT (DOEACC) Revised Syllabus)

by

Satish Jain

B.Sc., B.E.(IISc), M.E.(IISc), M.Tech.(IIT Kanpur),
Ex-Professor of Information Technology,
Institute of Information Technology & Management
GGS Indraprastha University, Delhi.

Dr. Shalini Jain

M. Geetha

B.Com., Diploma (IT)

THIRD REVISED AND UPDATED EDITION 2016

SECOND REVISED AND UPDATED EDITION 2014

REPRINT 2024

FIRST EDITION 2011

ISBN: 978-81-8333-459-4

Distributors:

BPB PUBLICATIONS
20, Ansari Road, Darya Ganj
New Delhi-110002
Ph: 23254990/23254991

DECCAN AGENCIES
4-3-329, Bank Street,
Hyderabad-500195
Ph: 24756967/24756400

MICRO MEDIA
Shop No. 5, Mahendra Chambers,
150 DN Rd. Next to Capital Cinema,
V.T. (C.S.T.) Station, MUMBAI-400 001
Ph: 22078296/22078297

BPB BOOK CENTRE
376 Old Lajpat Rai Market,
Delhi-110006
Ph: 23861747

Published by Manish Jain for BPB Publications, 20 Ansari Road, Darya Ganj, New Delhi-110002 and Printed by him at Manipal Technologies Limited, Manipal

www.bpbonline.com

Dedicated to

Sri Raja Rajeshwari and *Sri Sai Baba*

whose blessings overcome all hurdles in life

PREFACE

The objective of writing this book is to cover the entire revised syllabus of the "Basic Computer Course (BCC)" designed by NIELIT (DOEACC), in simple English and user friendly style.

The book is divided into eight chapters. Each chapter covers specific topic as per the syllabus outlined by NIELIT (DOEACC). Each chapters contains diagrams and screens are used to explain each concept clearly. It is hoped, that a person with some understanding of elementary English language would be able to use this book and work on a personal computer (PC) for Internet access, word processing and create presentation, etc. The reader of this book need not be from science or commerce background. This book will be able to generate interest in a reader for using PC for letter writing, sending e-mail, doing accounts work and accessing Internet.

The last chapter contains Financial Literarcy for Banking Scheme and Applications. This chapter discusses in particular, how to use Internet for financial banking services, such as saving, banking service and Bank on your mobile and wallets.

We have included Solved and Unsolved Sample Question Papers for practice. We hope this book will prove to be simple and very useful for answering the questions asked in the Online examination.

We shall feel obliged to the readers if they send us their critical opinion regarding the presentation, readability and coverage in this book and request them to mail their suggestions, if any, to improve the subject matter. The suggestions may be e-mailed to *bpb@vsnl.com*.

9Th July, 2016

Authors

BOOKS by Prof. Satish Jain

'O' Level made simple Books (According to NIELIT (DOEACC) Syllabus effective from July, 2010 Examination)

- **IT Tools and Business Systems** *(covering M1-R4, A1-R4 and B1.1-R4 papers)*
- **Internet Technology and Web Design** *(covering M2-R4, A2-R4 and B1.2-R4 papers)* *(**Also available in Hindi**)*
- **Programming and Problem Solving through C language** *(covering M3-R4, A3-R4 and B1.3-R4 papers)* *(**Also available in Hindi**)*
- **Application of .Net Technology** *(covering M4.1-R4 paper)*
- **Introduction to Multimedia** *(covering M4.2-R4 paper)*
- **Introduction to ICT Resources** *(covering M4.3-R4 paper)*
- **BPB O Level Course** (Covering: IT Tools and Business Systems, Internet Technology & Web Design and Programming and Problem Solving through 'C' Language) (Also covering A1-R4, A2-R4, A3-R4 as well as B1.1-R4, B1.2-R4 and B1.3-R4 papers)

'A' Level made simple Books (According to NIELIT (DOEACC) Syllabus effective from July, 2010 Examination)

- **Computer System Architecture** *(covering A4-R4 and B1.4-R4 papers)*
- **Structured System Analysis & Design** *(covering A5-R4 and B1.5-R4 papers)* *(**Also available in Hindi**)*
- **Data Structure Through C++** *(covering A6-R4 and B2.1-R4 papers)* *(**Also available in Hindi**)*
- **Introduction to Database Management Systems** *(covering A7-R4 and B2.2-R4 papers)*
- **Basics of OS, Unix and Shell Programming** *(covering A8-R4 and B2.3-R4 papers)*
- **Data Communication and Network Technologies** *(covering A9-R4 and B2.4-R4 papers)*
- **Introduction to Object Oriented Programming through Java** *(covering A10.1-R4 and B2.5.1-R4 papers)*
- **Software Testing and Quality Management** *(covering A10.2-R4 and B2.5.2-R4 papers)*

'O' & 'A' Level BPB's Golden Solutions for NIELIT (DOEACC) Examination Question Papers

- 'O' Level–**IT Tools and Business Systems** *(Also covering A1-R4 and B1.1-R4 papers)*
- 'O' Level–**Internet Technology & Web Design** *(Also covering A2-R4 and B1.2-R4 Papers)*
- 'O' Level–**Programming & Problem Solving through C language** *(Also covering A3-R4 and B1.3-R4 Papers)*
- 'O' Level–**ICT Resources** *(covering M4.3-R4 paper)*
- 'O' Level–**Introduction to Multimedia** *(covering M4.2-R4 paper)*
- 'A' Level –**Data Communication and Network Technologies** *(Also covering A9-R4 and B2.4-R4 papers)*

For B.E., MCA, M.Sc.(IT), B.Sc.(IT), BCA, PGDCA, and other IT Related Examinations for leading Indian Universities and Engineering Colleges

- **Introduction to Database Management**
- **Systems Analysis, Design and Management Information System**
- **Computer Networks**
- **Principles of Electronics–Analog and Digital**
- **Computer Organization and Architecture**
- **Data Structures** *made simple*
- **Advanced Computer Networking**
- **Wireless Communications and Networking**
- **Software Testing and Quality Management**
- **PC Software** *made simple*
- ***Guide to* Digital Electronics and Devices** *(Ques. & Ans.)*
- ***Guide to* Computer Networks and Data Communications** *(Ques. & Ans.)*
- ***Guide to* Systems Analysis, Design and MIS** *(Ques. & Ans.)*
- ***Guide to* Data Structures** *(Ques. & Ans.)*
- ***Guide to* Database Management Systems** *(Ques. & Ans.)*
- ***Guide to* Advanced Computer Networking** *(Ques. & Ans.)*
- ***Guide to* Computer Organization and Architecture** *(Ques. & Ans.)*
- ***Guide to* BPO and IT JOBS** *(Ques. & Ans.)*

For MBA, PGDBM and other Business Related Examinations for leading Indian Universities and Management Colleges

- **Computers in Business Management** *Principles and Practice*
- ***Guide to* Computers in Business Management** *(Ques. & Ans.)*
- **Information Technology Concepts** *(2nd Revisied and Updated Edition)*
- **BPB s Computer Course** *made simple (2nd Revisied and Updated Edition) [Windows 7/XP with MS Office 2007]*
- **BPB s Computer Course** *[Windows 7 with MS Office 2010]*
- **BPB s MS Office 2010 and Windows 7 Course**
- **BPB s DTP Course**

'O' Level CHM (Computer Hardware Maintenance) made simple (According to NIELIT (DOEACC) Syllabus)

- **Electronics Components and PC Hardware** *(covering CHM–O1 paper)*
- **PC Architecture** *(covering CHM–O2 paper)*
- **Computer Peripherals and Networking** *(covering CHM–O3 paper)*
- **System Software, Dignostics and Debugging Tools** *(covering CHM–O4 paper)*

Basic Computer Course (BCC) ***made simple*** (According to NIELIT (DOEACC) Syllabus of year 2011 Examination)

Course on Computer Concepts (CCC) ***made simple*** (According to NIELIT (DOEACC) Syllabus of year 2010 Examination)

Training Guides for Application Software Packages

- **CorelDRAW 10** ***Training Guide***
- **CorelDRAW 12** ***Training Guide***
  CorelDRAW Graphics Suit X3 (Version 13) ***Training Guide***
- **Photoshop CS3/CS5/CS6** ***Training Guide***
- **PageMaker-6.5/7.0** ***Training Guide***
- **MS Office 2007/2010** ***Training Guide***
- **MS Word 2007/2010** ***Training Guide***
- **MS Excel 2007/2010** ***Training Guide***
- **Internet** ***Training Guide***
- **Windows 7/8** ***Training Guide***
- **Dreamweaver CS5** ***Training Guide***
- **Flash Professional CS5/CS6** ***Training Guide***
- **Illustrator CS5/CS6** ***Training Guide***

Detailed Syllabus

Contents

Basic Computer Course

CHAPTER 1

Knowing Computer

1.0 INTRODUCTION

Computer is general purpose machine designed to automatically accept and store data, manipulate them, and produce output results under the direction of a detailed step-by-step stored program of instructions. It is actually a combination of both hardware and software that transforms data into information and performs calculation. It is an electronic device used for storing and processing data, information.

1.1 OBJECTIVES

The reader will be able to understand the following:

- What is a Computer?
- Components of Computer System
- Concept of Hardware and Software
- Concept of Computing, data and Information
- Applications of Information, Electronic and Communication Technology (IECT)
- Bringing Computer to life

1.2 WHAT IS A COMPUTER?

A computer is a digital electronic device that can perform a variety of operations according to a set of instructions called *program* and then displays or prints the result. A computer (See Figure 1.1) is a general purpose machine that manipulates raw facts according to a set of instructions that are fed into it. A computer performs five major operations or functions irrespective of its size and make. These are:

- it accepts data or instructions as input,
- it stores data and instruction
- it processes data as per the instructions,
- it controls all the operations taking place inside a computer, and
- it gives results in form of output.

Figure 1.1 Computer System

Computers work through an interaction of hardware and software.

Now before proceeding further there are few terms that need to understood:

- **Data:** Raw facts or figure that need to be processed.
- **Information:** Meaningful data which is processed, organized and presented in an understandable form.
- **Instruction:** Command that tells computer what to do.
- **Processing:** Sequence of action taken on data to convert it into information.
- **Hardware:** The physical components of computer.
- **Program:** The instructions that tell the computer what to do, either in sequential or non-sequential manner.
- **Software:** A sequence of instructions given to computer to perform a particular task.

Classification of Computer

Computers are classified according to their size, basis of work and the purpose of work, which are described as follows:

On the Basis of Size

- **Microcomputer/Microprocessor/Portable Computer:** These types of computer are widely used by single user and are small in size and cheaper (see figure 1.2).

Figure 1.2 Classification of computer on the basis of size

Types of microcomputer:

- *Desktop Computer/Personal Computer:* Input, processing, memory and output unit are self-contained, and are housed within a horizontal or vertical case called the system unit.
- *Notebook/Ultra Book/Laptop:* An extremely lightweight computer having integrated screen or keyboard, which uses flat panel technology, and can be moved from place to place. These types of computer consume less battery.
- *Handheld Computers/Palmtops:* Extremely small computer, having smaller screen and stores programs and data within the unit or on a memory card. They have no keyboard and the screen serves both an Input device and Output device.
- *Tablet Computers:* These are lighter notebook computer having a smaller screen, in which input is given either by touch screen or by pen called stylus. For example, Ipad.
- *Smartwatch:* A smartwatch or Watch phone is a computerized wristwatch or a wearable computer, which offers full mobile phone feature capability thus allowing a user to

make or answer phone calls, Send or receive text/Wats app messages. It is used to perform some basic tasks, such as calculations, translations, game-playing. By using a mobile operating system one can also run mobile apps on it. Smart watches can be customized according to one's need.

Smart watches function as portable media players, thus offering a playback of FM radio, audio, and video files to the user via a Bluetooth headset. It also supports wireless technologies like Bluetooth, Wi-Fi, and GPS.

Smart watches are used to upload data onto a computer or online to create a log of activities for analysis or sharing. It serves as full GPS watches, which displays maps, current location, and record tracks. It is also called as Fitness tracker as it tracks the daily activity of the user, including Lap times, speed display, Route tracking, Monitor heart beat rate.

Some of the widely used smart watches are:

  - *Motorola:* Motorola Motoactv, Moto 360
  - *Samsung:* Samsung Galaxy Gear, Gear 2, Gear 2 Neo and Gear Fit, Gear Live, Gear S
  - *Apple:* Apple Watch

- *Workstation:* It is mainly used by an individual as it is faster and more capable than a personal computer. It is used by small engineering companies, architects, graphic designer who requires a faster micro-processor and a large amount of Random access memory.
- *Minicomputer:* These types of computer are smaller in size and are faster than micro computers, and it is a multi-user (multi-processing) device, supporting from 4 to about 200 users simultaneously, and are used to carry out some specific task in engineering and Computer Aided Design (CAD). Examples Digital Alpha, Sun Ultra.
- *Mainframe:* These are large, powerful, expensive computers used by organizations to connect thousands of users simultaneously. Mainframe are just below supercomputer in computer hierarchy and in some ways are more powerful than supercomputer as it supports simultaneous programs. This computer contains specialized hardware and software, for processing millions of transactions. Examples IBM 370, S/390.
- *Super Computer:* It is the fastest, powerful and the most expensive machine available today, used to carry immense amount of mathematical calculations. Super computer is used in weather forecasting, scientific simulation, nuclear research and petroleum exploration, etc.

☞ *Supercomputer channels all its power into executing a few programs as fast as possible, whereas a mainframe uses its power to execute many program concurrently.*

On the Basis of Work

- *Analog Computers:* These types of computer use continuous physical phenomena having specific magnitude such as electrical and mechanical quantities to model the problem being solved. Operations are performed on it by manipulating and processing the data. Examples: Thermometer, Speedometer etc.
- *Digital Computers:* Digital computers process information which is in a binary or two-state form, namely zero and one. Digital computers fall into ranges called microcomputers, minicomputers, mainframes and supercomputers. It can produce desired graphics, sound.
- *Hybrid computer (Analog+Digital):* This type of computer is capable of inputting and outputting data in both analog and digital form. It is basically a digital computer that accepts analog signal and convert them into digital form for processing. It offers a cost effective method of performing complex simulations.

On the Basis of area of applications

Computer are either general purpose or specific purpose.

- *General purpose computer:* These are designed to perform a wide range of tasks. They can store numerous programs, but are lack in speed and efficiency. Example: Microcomputer
- *Specific purpose computer:* These are designed to handle a specific problem or to perform a specific task. Instructions which are needed to perform the given task are permanently stored into the internal memory, so that it can perform the task on single computer.

1.2.1 Basic Applications of Computer

A computer is a general purpose tool, which can do a variety of jobs. You can use a computer for different application by changing various kind of software packages.

Some common uses of a computer are shown in Figure 1.3 which are discussed below.

- **Scientific Research:** Computer was first used in scientific research. The speed and the accuracy of a computer enabled scientific analysis carried out very fast. Computers are now became an integral part of teaching techniques in Universities, and research institutes. Without computers, researchers find themselves in a very difficult situation to carry out their studies.
- **Office Management:** Almost every organisation (business or non-business) are moving towards making paper-less office so that computers are widely used today.
- **Internet:** It is a network of computers in the world. You can browse through much more information via Internet than you could do in a library. You also have very fast and convenient access to information. Through E-Mail you can communicate with a person sitting thousands of miles away in seconds.
- **Books Publishing:** With desktop publishing, you can create page layout for the entire books on your personal computer. Nowadays, newspapers, magazines/books are designed by using DTP, printed at one place and distributed so that we can get them every morning.
- **Computers in Hospital:** It is used for keeping the records of patients, help surgeons in controlling robots during surgery, to monitor heartbeat, blood pressure and to maintain patient's history.
- **Mathematical Calculations:** Thanks to computers, which have computing speeds of performing over a million calculations per second also we can perform the biggest of mathematical calculations.
- **Banks:** All financial transactions are done by computer software. They provide security, speed and convenience. The use of a computer has allowed the banks to improve many of the facilities offered by them. One can use the **ATM (Automated Teller Machines)** to deposit and withdraw cash 24 hours a day throughout the year.
- **Travel:** One can book air tickets or railway tickets and make hotel reservations online. It reduces the time wastage and travel time for everyone.

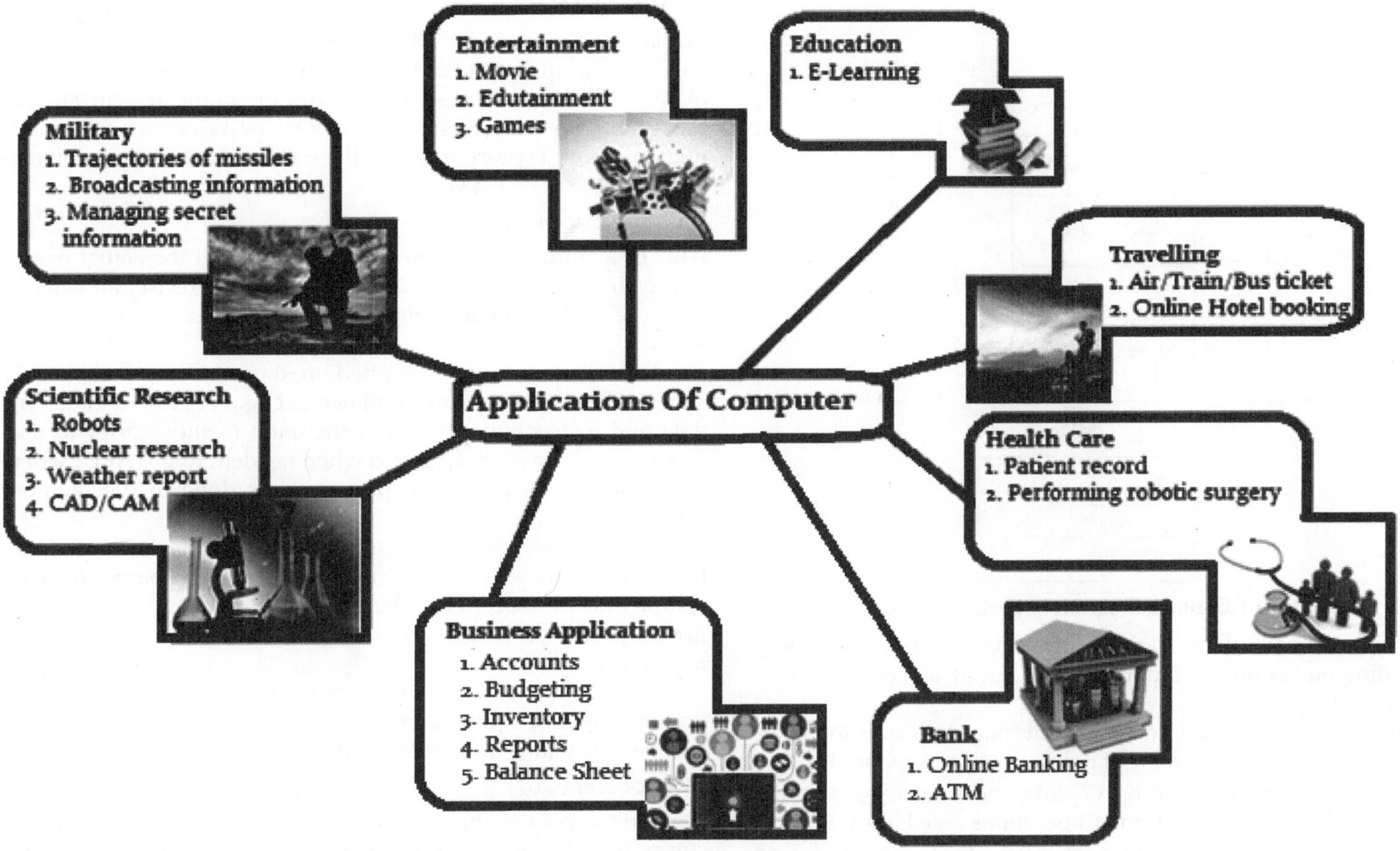

Applications Of Computer

Entertainment
1. Movie
2. Edutainment
3. Games

Education
1. E-Learning

Military
1. Trajectories of missiles
2. Broadcasting information
3. Managing secret information

Travelling
1. Air/Train/Bus ticket
2. Online Hotel booking

Scientific Research
1. Robots
2. Nuclear research
3. Weather report
4. CAD/CAM

Health Care
1. Patient record
2. Performing robotic surgery

Business Application
1. Accounts
2. Budgeting
3. Inventory
4. Reports
5. Balance Sheet

Bank
1. Online Banking
2. ATM

Figure 1.3 Picture showing different jobs where computer can be employed

- **Telecommunications:** All mobile phones have software embedded in them for maintaining customer details and also sending message, audio and video through the mobile software. Now a day's Internet is available in the mobile phone itself.
- **Defence:** There is software embedded in almost every weapon. Software is used for controlling the flight and targeting in ballistic missiles. Software is used to control access to atomic bombs.
- **E-Learning:** Instead of a book it is easier to learn from E-learning software. It not only contains text but contains image and animation so it is very easy to understand every thing.
- **Examinations:** We can give online exams and get instant results. You can check your examination results online.
- **Computers in Business:** It is used for billing, budgeting, accounting purpose, inventory, taxes and payroll.
- **Entertainment:** Movies, animation films, advertisement in newspapers and TVs, etc., use computers extensively. The entertainment industry uses computer even to plan the production of movies, as well as to create various special effects.
- **Communication:** Use of **email** or **Electronic-mail**, where one can use a computer to pass long messages, reports, etc., to many persons all over the world for a very low price.
- **Accounting:** Specialized programs, such as Tally.ERP 9, are available to handle company financial accounts and inventory management.

1.3 COMPONENTS OF A COMPUTER SYSTEM

The five major functional units of a digital computer (See Figure 1.4) are:

(a) Central Processing Unit (CPU)
(b) Input Device (Visual Display Unit(VDU), Keyboard and Mouse)
(c) Output Devices
(d) Computer Memory

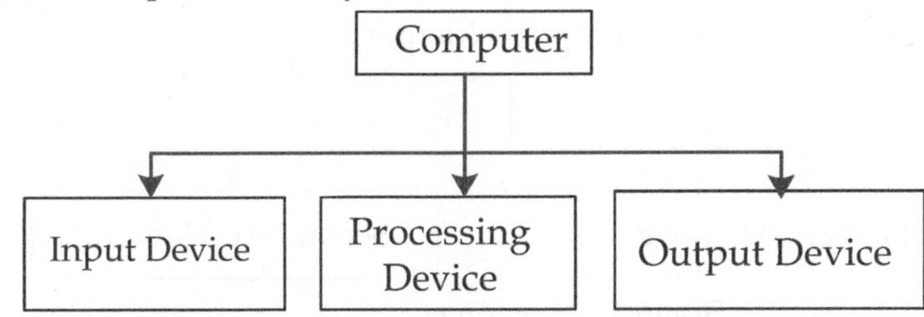

Figure 1.4 Components of Computer System

1.3.1 Central Processing Unit (CPU)

The CPU is the brain of a computer. Its primary job is to run program and control the operation of all the other components, such as memory, keyboard and printer.

A block diagram of the basic computer organization is shown in Figure 1.5.

The Figure shows the basic arrangement of different units of a computer. It depicts the five major building blocks or functional units of a digital computer system. These five units correspond to

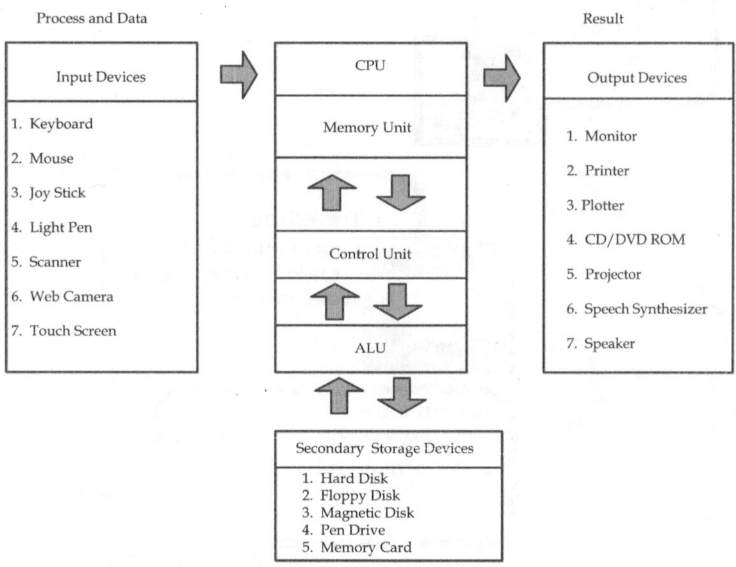

Figure 1.5 Block diagram of the computer

the five basic operations, namely inputting, storing, processing, outputting and controlling data, carried out by all computer systems. The five units are:

Inputting: Refers to the process of entering data into the computer, by the user using an input device, such as keyboard.

Storing: Refers to the holding of data and instructions in the computer's main memory, for manipulations (See Figure 1.6).

Processing: Refers to performing operations (both arithmetic and logical) or manipulation of data entered into the computer so that useful information may be taken out of the entered data.

Outputting: Refers to the process of showing the information or result to the user either on screen (monitor) or on paper (through printer).

Controlling: Refers to directing all the above processes, in coordination. This controlling is done by the Control Unit (CU) in a CPU.

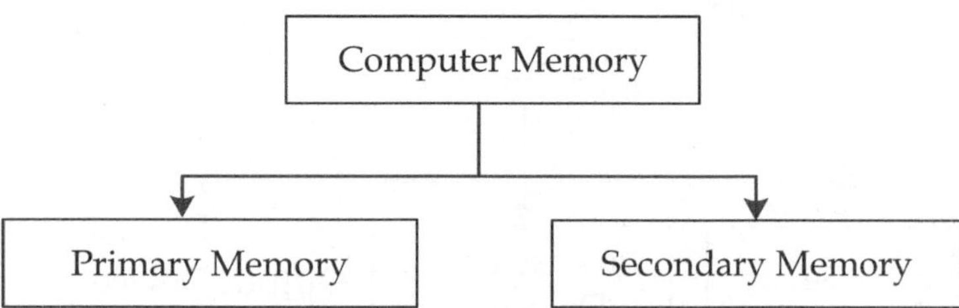

Figure 1.6 Computer Memory

The CPU of a small computer has a single microprocessor. The CPU of a large computer may contain a number of microprocessors and every microprocessor does one specific job.

A microprocessor contains a control unit and an Arithmetic and Logic Unit (ALU). When main memory is added to a microprocessor, it becomes a CPU.

The major sections of a CPU are:

(a) Primary Memory
(b) ALU
(c) Control Unit

Primary Memory

Primary memory or the Main memory unit is one of the major parts of a computer. It holds data which is currently manipulated by the CPU. It also keeps the necessary operating system, such as MS Disk Operating System (MS-DOS) or Windows. Since Primary memory is present within the CPU itself, it is also known as *internal memory* or RAM.

Arithmetic Logic Unit

ALU of a computer system is the place where the actual execution of instructions takes place. To be more precise, all calculations are performed and all comparisons (decisions) are made in the ALU.

Intermediate results generated in the ALU are temporarily stored in the memory unit until needed again at a later time. The data and instructions, stored in the main memory prior to processing, are transferred, as and when needed, to the ALU, where processing takes place. No processing is done in the memory unit.

Data may move from primary memory to ALU and back again to memory many times during the processing operation. After completion of processing, the final results which are stored in memory unit or RAMs are sent to an output device, such as monitor or printer.

All ALUs are designed to perform the four basic arithmetic operations–add, subtract, multiply, divide–and logic operations, such as less than, equal to or greater than.

Control Unit (CU)

This unit is responsible for controlling the entire working of the computer. The timing and control signals are generated by this unit and sent to other units for execution of the program for proper control. It also controls the transfer of data between memory and input/output devices.

1.3.2 VDU or Monitor, Keyboard and Mouse

Input/Output (I/O) devices are those devices which are used to enter information into a computer or display results of data processing devices. These devices are discussed below.

VDU (Visual Display Unit) or Monitor

A computer monitor, technically termed as a VDU, can be described as an electronic device that transmits information from the computer onto a screen, thereby acting as an interface and connecting the viewer with the computer.

At present, computer monitors are available in a variety of shapes, designs, and colors. However, based on the technology used to make computer monitors, they can be broadly categorized into three types. (See Figure 1.7)

Figure 1.7 Types of monitor

Cathode Ray Tube (CRT): These monitors employ the CRT technology which is most commonly used in the manufacturing of television screens. A cathode ray tube is basically a vacuum tube containing an electron gun at one end and a fluorescent screen at another end. From this electron gun, a process called thermionic emission generates a strong beam of electrons.

There are several advantages of using CRT monitors. These are:

- These monitors are highly reliable and efficient, and are capable of generating a resolution of up to 2048 x 1536 pixels, thereby providing a clear picture quality. Also, CRT monitors that are now available are capable of producing thousands of different colors.
- CRT monitors are affordable and cost effective.
- In modern technological advancements have resulted in the development of flat screen CRT monitors that reduce the glare and are good for the eyes.

Liquid Crystal Display (LCD): It is also known as liquid crystal diode, is one of the most advanced technologies available at present. Typically, LCD monitor consists of a layer of color or monochrome pixels arranged schematically between a couple of transparent electrodes and two polarizing filters.

At present, there are two types of LCD technology available. These include the active matrix or TFT and a passive matrix technology. Among these, TFT technology is more secure and reliable, and generates better picture quality.

Some major advantages of using an LCD monitor include:

- These monitors are compact, lightweight, and do not consume much desk space.
- These monitors do not consume much electricity and can even be operated by using batteries.

However, LCD monitors have certain disadvantages. These monitors are very expensive. Image quality is not constant when viewed from different angles. LCD monitor's resolution is always constant.

Light-Emitting Diodes (LED): LED monitors are the latest types of monitors available in the market today. Like LCD, it has a flat panel display making use of light-emitting diodes for back-lightning instead of Cold Cathode Fluorescent (CCFL) back-lightning used in LCDs. Primarily, the display is of LCD only but the back-lightning is done by LEDs. LED monitors use much lesser power than CRT and LCD.

Some advantages of LED monitors are:

- They produce images with higher contrast
- Lifespan and durability of LED monitors is more than CRT or LCD monitors
  Because of the technology, the monitor panels can be made very thin.
- Do not produce much heat while running.

Keyboard

Programs and data are entered into a computer through a keyboard which is attached to a computer. A keyboard is similar to the keyboard of a typewriter. It contains alphabets, digits, special characters, function keys and some control keys. When a key is pressed, an electronic signal is produced which is detected by an electronic circuit called *keyboard encoder* (See Figure 1.8).

Types of keys on keyboard:

- *Alphanumeric keys:* It includes all the numbers and letters on the keyboard. e.g., A-Z and 0-9.
- *Functions key:* Keys from F1 to F12.
- *Punctuation keys:* These include comma, semicolon and brackets.

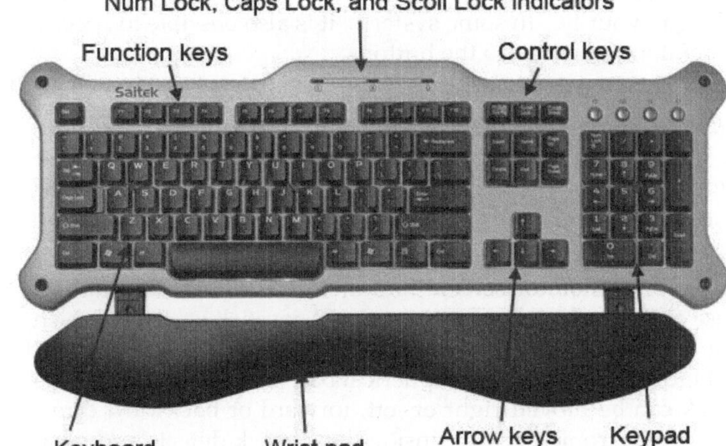

Figure 1.8 Keyboard depicting different keys' functions

- *Special keys:* These includes controls keys, Arrows key, Caps lock key, Delete key.

☞ *At the top of the keyboard are function keys (F1 to F12). Their functions depend upon the program being run. F1 key is used to get help from the program.*

Mouse

A mouse is a pointing device. It is held in one hand and is moved across a flat surface Figure 1.9.

The mouse can also be used to draw sketches, diagrams, etc., on the monitor screen. It is also moved on the graphic tablet for drawing work. The mouse is also used to edit text. For editing a text on the screen, the cursor can be quickly placed close to the desired point of the screen by moving the mouse.

Types of keys on Mouse

- *Mechanical mouse:* Movement of cursor is relative to the movement of ball present at the bottom of mouse.
- *Optical mouse:* It uses light emitting diode for detecting movement.
- *Wireless mouse:* It relay signal to base station, which is wired to computer's mouse port.
- *Laser mouse:* It uses infrared light emitting diode.

One type of mouse uses a rolling ball; others use optical sensing techniques. They are linked to the PC by using a cable or by using infrared light. A typical mouse has two or three buttons.

Figure 1.9 Mouse

What the mouse buttons do depend on the application program running in your PC. In some systems, it is also possible to specify independent functions to the buttons.

1.3.3 Other Input Devices

Input devices are those devices which are used to enter information into a computer or other data processing devices. These devices are:

Joystick

A joystick is also a pointing device. It is used to move the cursor position on a monitor screen. Its function is similar to that of a mouse and is used for playing games. A joystick is a stick which has a spherical ball at its lower end as well as at its upper end (See Figure 1.10). The lower spherical ball moves in a socket. The joystick can be moved right or left, forward or backward direction. The electronic circuitry inside the joystick detects and measures the displacement of the joystick from its central position. This information is sent to the processor.

Figure 1.10 Joystick

Light Pen

A light pen is a pointing device. It is used to select a displayed menu option on the monitor. It is a photosensitive pen-like device. It is capable of sensing a position on the monitor screen when its tip touches the screen (See Figure 1.11).

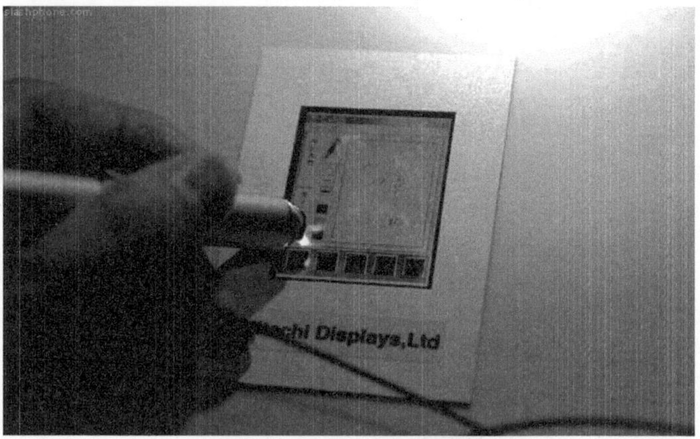

Figure 1.11 Light pen

Touch Screen

A *touch screen* is a computer display screen that is sensitive to human touch, allowing a user to interact with the computer by touching pictures or words on the screen. Touch screens are used with information kiosks, computer based training devices and systems designed to help individuals who have difficulty to control a mouse or keyboard. Some tablets on Smartphone comes with a small object which looks like a pen, called as stylus. By using which you can select something or draw on your screen with it. Some touch screen use transparent plastic protector to protect them from scratch. (See Figure 1.12).

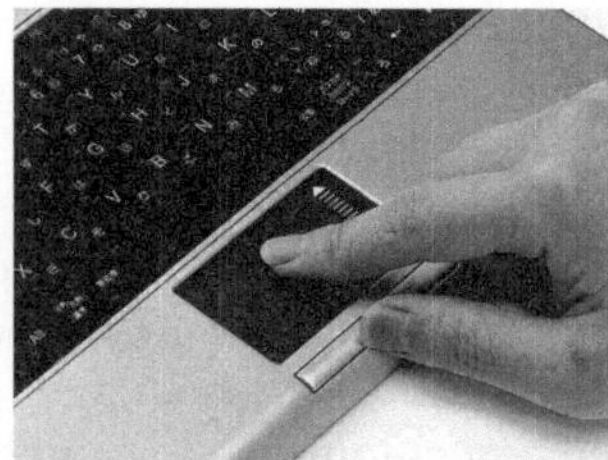

Figure 1.12 Touch Screen and Touch pad

Touch Pad/Track Pad

It has a special surface which understands the position of your fingers relative to the position of the cursor on the screen. It mainly translates the motion and position of user's fingertip to the relative position on the screen. It is widely used in laptops, notebooks, mobile devices. Some of the new touchpads can understand more than one finger and you can give commands like zoom in and out with just a gesture.

Graphics Tablet/Digitizer

A *graphics tablet* is a graphic input device that functions like a drawing tablet. The user makes contact with the graphic tablet with a device called a cursor, which is a pen-like instrument that is connected to the tablet by a wire or without wires (See Figure 1.13). For sketching, the user draws with the tablet cursor and the screen cursor "draws" a corresponding image. For tracing an existing image, the screen cursor is often not required.

Figure 1.13 Graphics Tablets

Microphone

A microphone, is a sound capture device which allows you to record voices or sounds convert them into digital form and then place them onto computers, generally as a wav file. Microphones can also be used with other applications such as a voice dictation program or a voice conference program and it is used in smart phone, video recorder, movie production etc. (See Figure 1.14) When connecting the microphone to the back of the computer, the microphone will be placed in the hole which generally has Mic or Microphone written next to it. While chatting you use microphone to speak and headphone to listen.

Scanner

Scanners are a kind of input devices which can captures an image or document and then import it to your computer. They are capable of entering information directly into the computer. The main advantage of direct entry of information is that users do not have to type the information. This provides faster and more accurate data entry (See Figure 1.15). Scanners are of three types. They are:

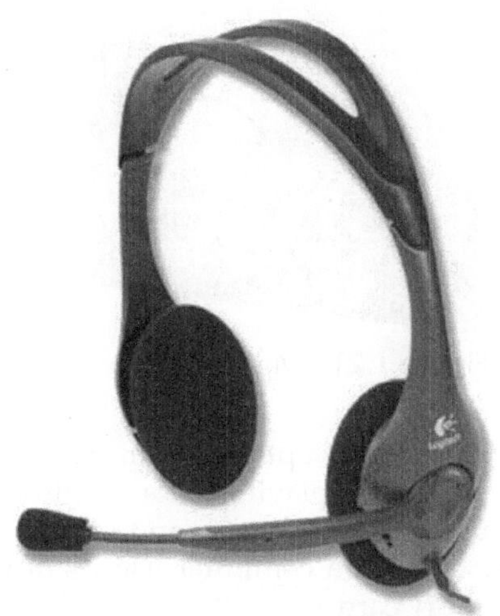

Figure 1.14 Microphone with earphone

Figure 1.15 Scanner

Type of Scanner

Scanner	Handheld Scanners	Flatbed Scanners	Drum Scanners
Size	Small in size and can be held in hand	Large, create high quality images	Medium size, and has rolling drum
Cost	Less expensive	More expensive	Expensive
Passes	Multiple passes are required to scan single page	Can scan page in a single pass	Scan in a single pass
Surface	They can be held in a hand	It has flat surface on which the image to be scanned is placed	Drum rolls over which the entire sheet to be scanned is placed

Voice Input and Recognition System

Voice input and recognition system is an input device, consisting of a microphone or telephone that converts human speech into an electrical signals. A signal pattern obtained in this manner is sent to the computer where it is matched against pre-stored patterns to identify the input. When a close match is found, a word is recognized by the system. The set of pre-stored patterns is known as the vocabulary of the system. To build up this vocabulary, the system has to be trained to recognize the words and phrases that are to be present in the vocabulary.

OMR (Optical Mark Reader)

Optical mark readers are special scanners used for recognizing a pre-specified type of mark made by pencil or pen. For example, in the objective test paper of competitive examinations, you mark your answers on a special sheet by darkening a small square, using a pen or pencil. These answer sheets are fed into the computer using the optical mark reader. The computer can then evaluate the answer sheets. The use of OMR is not limited to the grading of objective type tests. In fact, any input data that is in the nature of a choice or selection can be recorded for OMR input.

OMR focuses light on the page being examined and the light pattern reflected from the dark marks is then detected. Figure 1.16 shows the OMR characters.

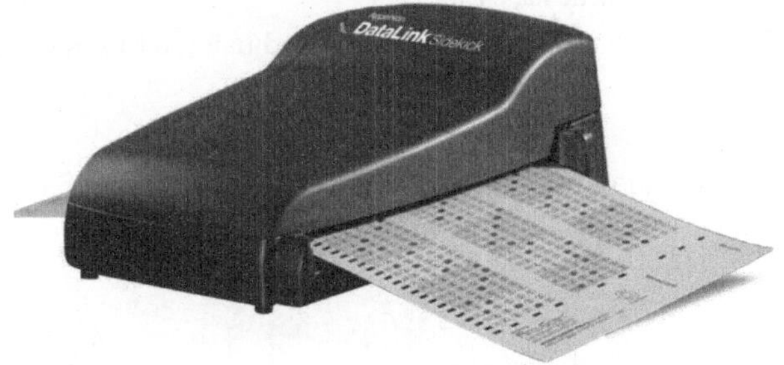

Figure 1.16 Optical marks in an answer sheet

Bar-code Reader

Bar-code readers are special devices used to read bar coded data. Bar code is a specialized code used for fast identification of items. It consists of a series of small lines, known as bars. The actual coding of the bars is the width of the bar, not the height. These are primarily used for identification of goods, such as books, postal packages, badges, etc., (See Figure 1.17).

Figure 1.17 Bar codes

MICR (Magnetic Ink Character Recognition)

MICR detects the special encoded characters on bank cheques and deposit slips. After detecting the encoded characters, the MICR converts them into digital data for the computer. Figure 1.18 shows a bank cheque which will be processed using a MICR device.

Trackball

A trackball is also a pointing device, contains a ball in the middle, which can rotate in any direction. It looks like an upside down mouse. The user spins the ball in different directions to move the cursor on the monitor (See Figure 1.19). The associated electronic circuitry detects the direction and speed of the spin. The information is sent to the processor. This type of pointing device is normally used in a CAD (Computer Aided Design).

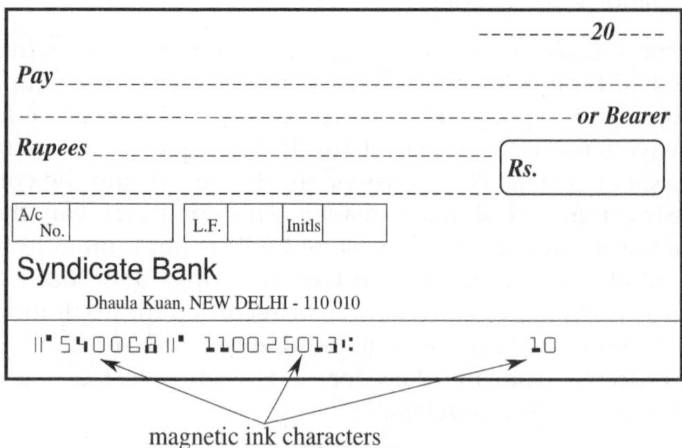

----------20----

Pay ______________________________

______________________________ or Bearer

Rupees ______________________ Rs.

A/c No. | L.F. | Initls

Syndicate Bank

Dhaula Kuan, NEW DELHI - 110 010

540068 110025013 10

magnetic ink characters

Figure 1.18 A bank cheque that is processed using a MICR device

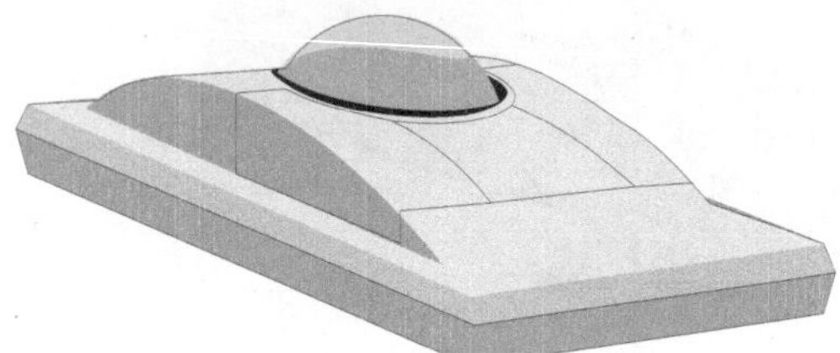

Figure 1.19 Trackball

Web Cameras

A web camera is a video capturing device which, allows a computer to accept input just by focussing on an object in real time. The camera is focussed on the input object to take a picture of the object. Image can be saved and transferred over network to a distant place by email or uploading them to the Internet.

Figure 1.20 Web Camera

The image of the object can be seen on the monitor of the distant computer connected through a network or through Internet. Voice can also be transmitted over the network. Thus, two or more persons can talk and see each another in this way. This method is used in video conferencing. By using web camera one can make video call by using Skype or any other video calling program. (See Figure 1.20)

Digital Camera/Digicam

It is an image capturing device which is used to take high definition photos. It does not use film and displays photos/ videos on LCD screen and saves them on memory card. From memory card images/ videos can be transfer to your computer and you can store them safely over there. You can also use a photo editing software e.g. Photo editor to edit photos on computer. Digital cameras, nowadays are integrated into mobile devices such as tablets and smartphones (See Figure 1.21).

Figure 1.21 Digital Camera

Video Camera

It is a recording device which capture continuous motion picture and generate a signal for displaying on a monitor. Nowadays, memory cards are used to store images and make it very easy to transfer and save videos on a computer. Hours of video can be stored on a tiny memory card.

Video cameras are used to capture daily moments, celebrations. It is also used by scientist to examine a scientific event and by astronauts to equip a spacecraft.

Biometric Sensor

Biometric Sensor is the device that is used to identifies finger prints, DNA identification, eye retinas and voice patterns, facial patterns, hand measurements, face shape and signature verification (See Figure 1.22). They are used for security purposes to identify the persons who are permitted to enter the organization.

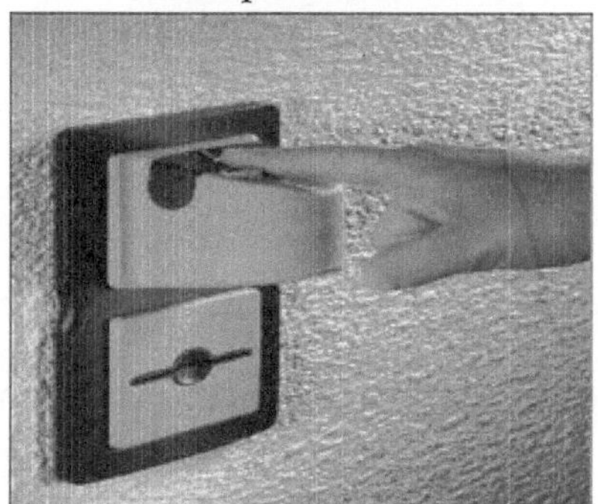

Figure 1.22 Biometric Sensor

1.3.4 Other Output Devices

Output devices are those devices of computer system that supplies information or results either in the form of hardcopy (printer) or softcopy (monitor). Some of the common output devices are as follows:

(a) Printers
(b) Plotters
(c) Multimedia Projector
(d) Speech Synthesizer

Printers

Printers provide information in a permanent readable form. They produce printed outputs of results, programs and data. You can print text, numbers, images and photos. The printer is usually connected to the computer through a USB cable. Before printing you must check your computer is connected to the printer and the printer is on. Apart from printing on plain paper you can also print on envelopes, stickers.

The printers can be classified as:

(a) Impact printers
(b) Non-impact printers

Impact printers use an electro-mechanical mechanism that causes hammers or pins to strike against a ribbon and paper to print the text. The impact printers are further classified into the following categories:

(a) Line Printers

(b) Character Printers

Line Printers: A line printer prints one line of the text at a time. Printing speeds may vary from 300–3000 lines per minute. Different types of line printers are–*Drum printer* and *Chain printer*.

- **Drum Printer:** A drum printer consists of a cylindrical drum on which the characters are embossed. The printer receives all characters to be printed in one line of the text from the processor. The hammers hit the ribbon and paper against the desired character on the drum when it comes in the printing position. Its noise level is high and speed varies from 200 to 2000 lines per minute. They are expensive also.
- **Chain Printer:** A chain printer uses a rapidly, rotating chain which is called print chain. To print a line, the characters in the line are transmitted from the memory to printer buffer. The band is rotated at a high-speed. The noise level of the printer is high and its speed lies in the range of 400-2400 lines per minute.

Character Printers (Serial Printer): A character printer prints one character of the text at a time. They are low-speed printers. Their printing speed lies in the range of 30-600 characters per second. Different types of character printers are–*Dot matrix printers* and *Letter quality printers*.

- **Dot Matrix Printer:** A dot matrix printer is the oldest and the most popular serial printer (See Figure 1.23). The printhead contains a vertical array of pins. As the printhead moves across the paper, selected pins fire against the ribbon to form a pattern of dots on the paper.

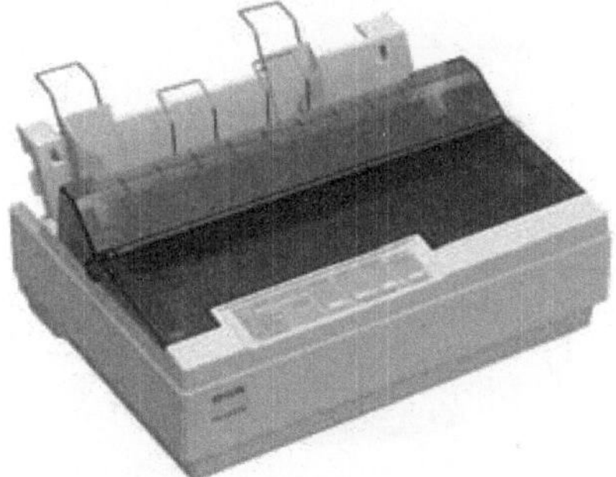

Figure 1.23 Dot matrix printer

A dot matrix printer is faster and can print many copies than a letter quality printer. These printers operate at two or three speeds. The lower the speed the better is the printing quality. Higher speed is for draft printing and lower speed is for Near-Letter Quality (NLQ) printing.

- **Letter Quality printers:** These printers print full characters, which means that a character is not made up of dots. The most popular printer of this type is daisy-wheel printer. In a daisy-wheel printer, the printhead resembles a daisy flower, with its print arms appearing like the petals of the flower. The daisy-wheel printer has a speed up to 90 characters per second. These are no more in use today.

Non-impact printers use thermal, chemical, electrostatic, laser beam or inkjet technology for printing the text. Usually a non-impact type printer is faster than an impact type. These printers are categorized as:

(a) Electromagnetic Printer

(b) Thermal Printer

(c) Inkjet Printer

(d) Laser Printer

Electromagnetic Printer: This printer uses magnetic recording techniques. By using this technique, the required output is written on a drum surface. Then this surface is passed through magnetic powder which adheres to the charged areas. The powder is then pressed onto the paper.

Thermal Printer: This type of printer uses special heat-sensitive paper. These papers have a special heat-sensitive coating. When a spot on the paper is heated, it becomes dark. A character is printed with a matrix of dots. These printers have a speed of 200 characters per second.

Inkjet Printers: Inkjet printers are more efficient than dot matrix printers. The print quality is good because the character is formed by the dozens of tiny ink dots. These printers produce better quality of text and graphics and are faster. Almost all ink-jets offer a colour option (cyan, yellow, magenta and black) as standard, in varying degrees of resolution. Inkjet printers are capable of producing high quality print which almost matches the quality of a laser printer. A standard ink jet printer has a resolution of 300 dots per inch, although newer models have improved on that (See Figure 1.24).

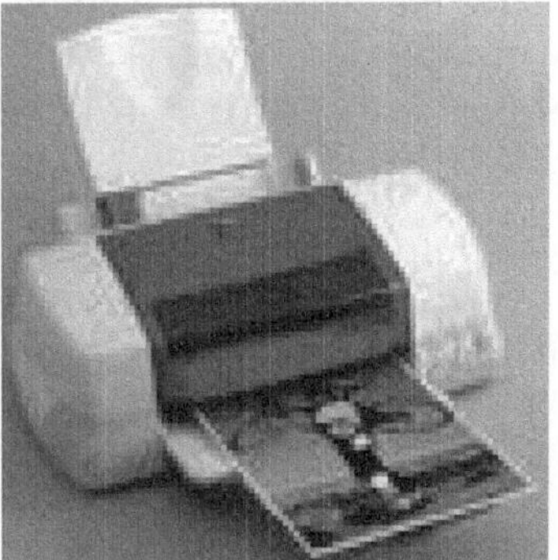

Figure 1.24 Inkjet printer

Laser Printers

Laser printers are non-impact type printers. These printers are expensive and require periodic maintenance. Low-speed laser printers produce 10 pages or more per minute and are used with microcomputers. High-speed laser printers produces upto 300 pages per minute and they are used with mini and large computers. Laser printers have become popular for voluminous printing work. They are mainly used for desktop publishing work. Figure 1.25 illustrates a laser printer.

Laser printer vs Inkjet printer

The laser printer is different from an inkjet printer in a number of ways:

(a) The toner or ink in a laser printer is dry. In an inkjet printer, it is wet.

(b) Inkjet printer is about ten times more expensive to operate than a laser printer, because ink needs replenishing more frequently.

(c) The printed paper from an inkjet printer will smear it wet, but a laser printed document will not.

(d) If your printing needs are minimal, an inkjet printer is sufficient. But if your printing volume is high, consider buying a laser printer.

Figure 1.25 Laser printer

3D Printers

3D printing is a form of additive manufacturing technology where a three dimensional object is created by laying down successive layers of material. It is also known as rapid prototyping, is a mechanized method whereby 3D objects are quickly made on a reasonably sized machine connected to a computer containing blueprints for the object. This method for creating 3D models with the use of inkjet technology saves time and cost by eliminating the need to design; print and glue together separate model parts. Now, you can create a complete model in a single process using 3D printing. The basic principles include materials cartridges, flexibility of output, and translation of code into a visible pattern.

3D Printers are machines that produce physical 3D models from digital data by printing layer by layer. It can make physical models of objects either designed with a CAD program or scanned with a 3D Scanner. It is used in a variety of industries including jewellery, footwear, industrial design, architecture, engineering and construction, automotive, aerospace, dental and medical industries, education and consumer products.

Plotters

Plotters are output devices. They are used to produce precise and good quality graphics and drawings under the control of the computer. They use ink pen or inkjet to draw graphics or drawings. Either single colour or multicoloured pens can be employed. It is used for architectural plan and large advertising banners. Figure 1.26 shows a plotter.

Figure 1.26 Plotter

Multimedia Projector

Multimedia Projector is an output device connected to a PC and used to project information from a computer on to a large screen (a cloth screen or wall). The information is thus viewed by a large number of people. It is widely used for giving presentations. The presenter can directly point to, mark or edit the displayed information to make it more understandable. Audio, video, image and animation can be prepared on a PC and by using a multimedia projector the presentation can be made more lively and interesting (See Figure 1.27).

Figure 1.27 Projector

Speech Synthesizer

Speech Synthesizer is an output device that converts textual data into spoken sentences. To produce the speech, basic sound units called *phonemes* are combined. The sequence of words in a text is combined into phonemes, amplified and outputted through a speaker attached to a computer (See Figure 1.28).

Figure 1.28 Speech Synthesizer

Speakers

Speakers are the hardware devices connected to a computer's sound card that outputs sounds generated by the card. A speaker makes sound by being fed on electrical signals which is changed or modulated, corresponding to the sound that is to be made. The speaker converts the changes or waves in the electrical signal to matching sound waves, which we hear.

There is no volume control in the PC, since it was not intended to produce sophisticated sounds. Speakers are further attached to the system to enhance the sound quality. (See Figure 1.29)

Head phones/stereo phones/headsets: These are the small pair of loudspeakers, which are placed closer to user's ear so that only one person can hear the output at a time (See Figure 1.30).

Figure 1.29 Speakers

Figure 1.30 Head Phones

1.3.5 Computer Memory

A computer needs memory to store data. It also needs memory to perform arithmetical operations and storing programs and pictures. Computer memory is of two types (Figure 1.6):

(a) Primary Memory
(b) Secondary Memory

Primary memory is a part of the CPU whereas the secondary memory is external to the CPU. The secondary memory stores the data and keep it even when the electricity to the PC is cut off whereas the primary memory looses its contents immediately.

Primary memory is made up of electronic circuits and keeps data as long as voltage supply is on. When power supply to a PC is switched off, the data is lost.

Primary memory can be divided into the following two types:

(a) RAM
(b) ROM

RAM (Random Access Memory)

RAM stands for Random Access Memory and it is a read/write memory. Information can be written into and read from a RAM. It is a volatile memory. It retains the stored information as long as it is supplied with power. Types of RAM is shown in Table 1.1.

ROM (Read Only Memory)

ROM stands for Read Only Memory and it is a permanent type memory. Its contents are not lost when power supply is switched off. The user cannot write into a ROM. Its contents are written at the time of manufacturing. ROMs store permanent programs and other types of information which are needed by the computer to execute the programs. ROMs store functions, such as sine, cosine, logarithm, square root, exponential and code conversion tables, etc. Types of ROM is shown in Table 1.2.

Secondary Memory/Auxilary Memory

Secondary memory is employed for bulk storage (mass storage) of programs, data and other information. It has much larger capacity than the main memory. It stores system software, assemblers, compilers, useful packages, large data files, etc. The secondary memory is non-volatile in nature. The magnetic memories, such as hard disks and floppy disks are the most common secondary memories used in computers.

Random-access devices are direct access devices. In such devices the information is available at random, i.e., it is available in any order.

☞ *A random access storage device is one in which any location in the device may be accessed at random and retrieval of information stored is direct.*

Magnetic disks and magnetic drums are typical direct access storage devices.

Magnetic Tape

Magnetic tape was one of the most popular storage medium for storing large volumes of data that are needed to be serially accessed and processed. The tape is a plastic ribbon usually 1/2 inch wide that is coated on one side with an iron-oxide material which can be magnetized. The tape ribbon itself is stored in reels of 50 to 2400 feet. It is similar to the tape used on a tape-recorder except that it is of higher quality and more durable. The magnetic tape can be erased and reused again and again (See Figure 1.31).

Table 1.1 Types of RAM

Static RAM/SRAM	Dynamic RAM/DRAM	Enhanced version of RAM
Requires constant power flow to hold information	It stores its information in cell called capacitor and transistor	EDORAM: Extended data output random access memory.
Expensive and faster	Less expensive and slower	SDRAM: Synchronous dynamic random access memory.
More power is required	Less power is required	DDR SDRAM: Double data rate synchronous dynamic random access memory.

Table 1.2 Types of ROM

PROM	EPROM	EEPROM
Programmable read only memory	Erasable programmable read only memory	Electrically erasable programmable read only memory
Information cannot be altered once written	Information can be changed by exposing to ultraviolet light	Information can be erased and reprogrammed by using electric charge.

Figure 1.31 Magnetic tape

1.4 CONCEPT OF HARDWARE AND SOFTWARE

Let us discuss the concept of hardware and software in brief.

1.4.1 Hardware

The physical components of a computer are called hardware. Such items may be electronic, electrical, magnetic, mechanical or optical components. Examples of components are microprocessors, ICs, hard disks, floppy disks, optical disks, monitors, keyboard, printer, plotter, etc.

1.4.2 Software

It is the set of computer programs, procedures, and associated documentation related to the effective operation of a computer system.

Role of Software in Computers

A set of instructions that perform a particular task is called the program or software program. The instructions in the program direct the computer to perform input operations, process the data and output the results.

Types of Software

The software are classified into the following categories (See Figure 1.32).

1. System Software/System Packages
2. Application Software /Application packages

System Software/System Packages

It is the sets of one or more general purpose programs designed to control the operation of a computer system. These programs are written to assist the users of the computer system by performing tasks, such as controlling all the operations, moving data in and out of a computer and all the other steps in executing the application program.

Types of System Software:

- *Operating Systems:* An operating system is a master control program that runs the computer and acts as a scheduler. It controls the flow of signals from CPU to various parts of the computer. It is the first program which is loaded (copied) into the computer's memory after the computer is switched on. Popular operating systems include MS-DOS, Linux, Windows and UNIX.

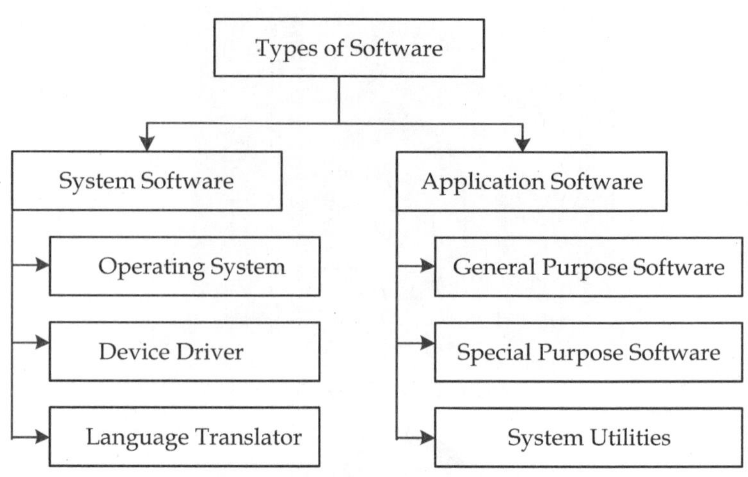

Figure 1.32 Types of software

- *Device Drivers:* A device driver controls a particular type of device that is attached, such as keyboard or a mouse.
- *Language Translators:* Translates programming language into machine language, translated programs are called as Object code.

  The types of language translators are shown in Table 1.3.

Application Software /Application packages

These are the sets of one or more programs designed to carry out operations for a specified application. For example, every month a payroll package produces the pay-slips for the workers of a company. Similarly, an inventory package may produce the list of different parts/equipment available in an organization.

Typical software applications that you might use are:

- **Word processors**–MS Word.
- **Spreadsheet software**–MS Excel
- **Graphics and Web Designing software**–Corel Draw, Photoshop, Picasa, Dreamweaver, FrontPage.

Types of application software

- *General purpose software:* Used to perform simple task, e.g., Word processing, multimedia software.
- *Special Purpose Software:* Used to perform specific task, as they target on a very narrow solution to a problem. e.g., Inventory management, Payroll system.
- *System Utilities:* These are used to support, enhance and secure the existing data in computer system. System utilities consist of:
  - *Disk Fragmenter:* It is used to arrange unused space on hard disk.

Table 1.3 Types of Language Translators

Assembler	Compiler	Interpreter
Convert assembly language to machine language	Convert source code written in high level language into machine language.	Convert high level language into machine language
Code consist of mnemonic code	Code consist of high level language	Code consist of high level language
Reads the whole page in single go	Reads the whole source code in single run and traps the error	Reads or convert the source code line by line.

- *Disk Compression:* It is used to compress the information stored on hard disk, so that more information can be stored on it.
- *Backup Utilities:* It makes the copy of all information stored on disk.
- *Disk Cleaners:* It is used to find files that have not been used for a long time and delete them the speed of slow computer can be increased.
- *Antivirus:* Program which scans the system and prevent the files of computer system from getting corrupted. e.g., Norton.
- *Clipboard Manager:* It is used to increase the clipboard capability of operating system.

1.5 CONCEPT OF COMPUTING, DATA AND INFORMATION

Computing is usually defined as the activity of using and improving computer hardware and software. It is the computer-specific part of information technology. Computer science (or computing science) is the study and the science of the theoretical foundations of information and computation and their implementation and application in computer systems.

☞ *In a general way, we can say that computing includes designing and building hardware and software systems for a wide range of purposes; processing, structuring, and managing various kinds of information. Doing scientific studies using computers; making computer systems behave intelligently; creating and using communications and entertainment media; finding and gathering information relevant to any particular purpose, and so on.*

1.5.1 Definition of Data and Information

Data is a general term used to denote any or all facts, numbers, letters, symbols, etc., that can be processed or manipulated or produced by a computer. However, all types of information stored in a computer are stored internally in the simple format: a sequence of 0's and 1's.

Technically, data are raw facts and figures, such as order and payments, which are processed into information, such as balance due and quantity on hand. However, in common usage, both data and information are used synonymously.

1.5.2 Basic Data Types

There are two types of data, namely, *integer* and *floating point.* From these two data types we can further derive two others — *character* and *double precision* (precision means how many digits can be used in the number). If you attempt to store a number with many digits, such as 2.1234543, (as a floating point variable, only 6 digit 2.123454) will be retained.

The bytes occupied by each of these types of data in memory of a computer as well as the names given to them are shown in Table 1.4.

If we need to store integer values less than –32,768 or greater than 32,767, then we should use long int. If we need to store integer values in the range –32767 and 32767, then we can use *short int.*

There are a number of cases where a variable will have to hold only non-negative values. For instance, variables that are used to count things are often restricted to non-negative numbers. C++ language allows us to declare the variable that take non-negative values or numbers only (or unsigned). This doubles the range of values a variable can take. Thus, a *signed short int* has a range from –32,767 to 32,767, whereas an *unsigned short int* has a range from 0 to 65,535.

The data type *char* can be used to hold either characters or numbers. For instance, after making the declaration

```
char c;
```

we can make either of the following assignments;

```
c = 'A'; or c = 65;
```

Note that characters having constant values are enclosed in single quotes. The quotes tell the compiler to get the numeric code (ASCII code value) of the character.

☞ *In the ASCII character set, character codes are ordered alphabetically. For example, ASCII code value of an upper case 'A', is 65, 'B' is 66,... 'Z' is 90. ASCII code value of lower case letters i.e. 'a' starts at 97 and runs through 122.*

int: Int is the basic integer data type. It is treated as an integer in that it cannot hold fractional values.

float: Integers are not adequate for representing numbers that have very large value as well as that have fractional values. For this, we need floating-point types of data representation. The simplest method is to place a decimal point in the number as seen below:

```
0.356
0.000001
```

In order to declare a variable capable of holding one of these values we use the keyword *float* or *double.*

Table 1.4 Typical Range and Size of Basic Data Types

Type	Range		Bytes	Represents
	From	*To*		
char/short	ASCII –128	127	1	characters
unsigned char	ASCII 0	255	1	characters
int	–32,768	32,767	2	whole numbers
unsigned int	0	65,535	2	whole numbers
long	–2,147,438,648	2,147,438,647	4	whole numbers
unsigned long	0	4,294,967,295	4	whole numbers
float	3.4×10^{-38}	3.4×10^{38}	4	fractional numbers
double	1.7×10^{-308}	1.7×10^{308}	8	fractional numbers
long double	3.4×10^{-4932}	3.4×10^{4932}	10	fractional numbers

double: The keyword double stands for double precision. It is capable of representing a real number ranging from 1.7×10^{-308} to 1.7×10^{308} which gives twice as much precision as represented by a float.

☞ *The precision refers to the number of decimal places that a number can be represented in.*

void: The data type void has two important purposes. The first is to indicate that a function does not return a value and the other is to declare a generic pointer.

Number system

A number system of base, or radix, r is a system that uses distinct symbols for r digits. Numbers are represented by a string of digit symbols. For example, Binary 0, 1 and base is 2. Decimal 0, 1,2-9 and base is 10. Octal 0, 1,2-7 and base is 8. Hexadecimal 0,1,2-9,A,B,C,D,E,F and base is 16.

1.5.3 Storage of Data

Data now a days are stored in hard disk, CD-ROM (Compact Disk Read Only Memory), Digital Video/Versatile Disk (DVD), pendrive and portable hard drive.

Data stored on hard disk and CD-ROM, etc., can be accessed directly. Thus, these storage devices are faster, and can also be used to transfer data from one computer to another or between a computer and a smartphone.

Hard Disk

A hard disk is a device used for mass storage of data needed for direct access. It is more stable, rigid and also it is contained in a dust-free environment. It stores more information.

The data and instructions that are entered into the computer system through input units must be stored inside the computer before the actual processing can start. Similarly, the results produced by the computer after processing must also be kept somewhere inside the computer system before those can be passed on to the output units. Moreover, the intermediate results produced by the computer must also be preserved for ongoing processing (See Figure 1.33).

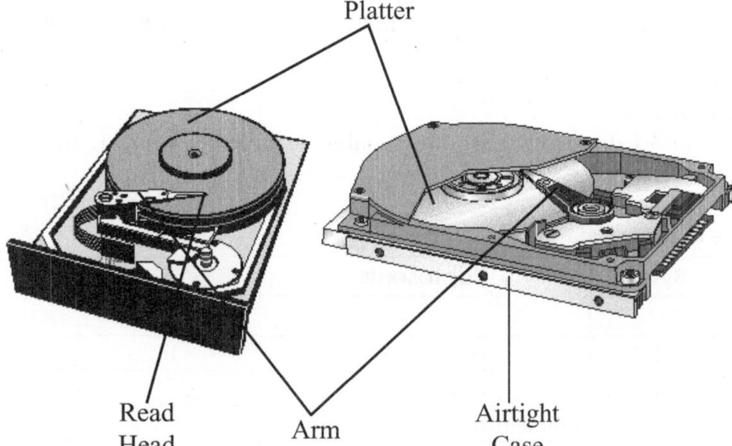

Figure 1.33 Hard disk

The specific functions of the storage unit are to store the following:

(a) All data and instructions to be processed,

(b) Intermediate results of processing, and

(c) Final results before sending them to output devices.

Never scratch CD/DVD surface as your data will be lost.

☞ *Computers also provide the facility of dividing the main memory into words or bytes. A byte usually consists of 8 bits of information.*

Compact Disk (CD)

It is an optical read (CD-R) and write (CD-RW) memory. The disk is made up of a resin, such as polycarbonate. It is coated with a material which will change its reflecting property when a high intensity laser beam is focused on it. The coating material is highly reflective, usually aluminium. The high intensity laser beam forms a tiny pit along a trace to represent '1' and the surface without a pit known as 'land' represents '0'. Figure 1.34 shows a compact disk.

Figure 1.34 Compact disk

For reading data, a laser beam is employed. In some cases, separate laser beams are employed: one for writing and the other for reading. The reflected laser light is sensed by a photodiode to read data. The intensity of the reflected light of laser changes as it encounters a pit. A pit spreads the light so that the photodiode receives less reflected light. But land reflects sufficient light to the photodiode. Thus, this change in reflected light is sensed and converted into electrical signals for data reading purposes.

Optical disks are of two types, namely compact disks or CD-ROMs and WORM (Write Once and Read Many) disks.

CD-ROM can store about 700 MB of data, making it an excellent medium for storing massive amount of data, higher capacity software, such as electronic reference books, business and entertainment software.

Digital Video Disk/Digital Versatile Discs (DVD)

Digital Video Disk (DVD) is introduced by Philips and Sony in 1995. It is an optical storage device that looks the same as a CD. A DVD has the same dimensions as a standard CD but cannot be read by a CD player, although a DVD player can read standard CDs. A DVD can store up to 4.7 GB of data.

Pen Drive/USB Flash Drive

A thumb drive, also known as flash drive, pen drive, memory stick or USB drive is a small portable device in the shape of the thumb, which can be connected to the USB port of a computer, which stores, transfer data quickly and easily. The main components of a thumb drives is flash memory. Flash memory is a special type of memory which can retain data even when there is no current passing through it. It is somewhat like an external hard drive. They are cheap resistant and came in different size. (See Figure 1.35)

Figure 1.35 Pen drive

Memory Cards

A memory card is a device offering an easy, fast and reliable way for storing and transferring digital files. It works like a portable hard disk drive but comes with some superior advantages, since almost every memory card is based on flash memory technology, of having much smaller form factor and being non-volatile and solid state. Making flash memory cards much more durable and reliable than hard disk drives. Memory cards are made by a variety of manufacturers and can be found in different storage capacities and transfer speeds.

MiniSD Memory Card The microSD card is even smaller than the miniSD card. The microSD card is designed for use in cellular phones and small mobile devices. The microSD card can accessed in a SD card slot via an adapter (See Figure 1.36).

Figure 1.36 SD card

Portable Hard Drive

Portable hard disk drive that is plugged into an external port on a computer, such as USB or FireWire are used for backup. For laptops, the PC Card slot may be used to connect a cable to a full-size drive, or the hard disk that may be contained entirely inside the PC Card (See Figure 1.37). The portable size available in the market are 320 GB, 500 GB and 1 and 2 Tetra GB.

Figure 1.37 Portable hard drive

It allows the user to back up or store important information separate from the main internal hard drive, which could become compromised by online or offline activities. Documents such as music files, DVD images, movies, disk images, and even a backup of the contents of your main internal hard drive, can all be kept securely and safely on an external hard drive.

Comparison among Floppy, CD and DVD

Storage Device	Floppy Disk	CD	DVD
Storage Capacity	1.44 MB	700 MB	4700 MB

By comparing the storage capacity of floppy disk, CD and DVD, one can say that 1 DVD can store data of approximately of 7 CD and 1 CD can store data of approximately 466 Floppy disk.

i.e. 1 DVD = 7CD

1 CD = 486 Floppy Disk

Memory Units

All information in the computer is stored using electronic components such as integrated circuits. Two symbols used to represent the two binary states are 0 and 1. These are known as BITS (an abbreviation for BInary DigiTS). In this, 0 represents the absence of a signal, 1 represents the presence of a signal. A BIT is, therefore, the smallest unit of data in a computer. Some memory units are described in the following sub-sections.

Byte: A byte is a unit of data that is eight binary digits (0 and 1) long (1 byte = 8 bits). A byte is the unit most computer use to represent a character such as a letter, numeral or typographic symbol. For example, g, 5, #. A byte can also hold a string of bits that need to be used in some larger unit for application purposes.

Kilobyte(KB): A Kilobyte (KB) is actually 2^{10} = 1024 bytes. Or 1 KB = 1,024 bytes (Apprx. 1,000 bytes and hence the name)

Megabyte (MB): A Megabyte (MB) is 2^{20} byte or 1,048,576 bytes in decimal notation. Or 1 MB = 1,024 KB (Approx. 1,000 KB)

Gigabyte (GB): A gigabyte (GB) is 2^{30} byte or 1,073,741,824 bytes in decimal notation. Or 1 GB = 1,024 MB (Apprx. 1,000 MB)

Terabyte (TB): A Terabyte is a measure of computer storage capacity and it is equal to the 2^{40} bytes. Or 1 TB = 1,024 GB (Apprx. 1,000 GB)

Petabyte (PB): A Petabyte is 2^{50} byte or approx. 1,125,899,900,000,000 bytes in decimal notation. 1 PB = 1,024 TB (Apprx. 1,000 TB)

Exabyte (EB): A Exabyte is 2^{60} byte. Or 1 EB = 1,024 PB (Apprx. 1,000 PB)

Zettabyte (ZB): A Zettabyte is 2^{70} byte. Or 1 ZB = 1,024 EB (Apprx. 1,000 EB)

Yottabyte (YB) : A Yottabyte is 2^{80} byte. Or 1 YB = 1,024 ZB (Apprx. 1,000 ZB)

1.6 APPLICATIONS OF INFORMATION ELECTRONICS, AND COMMUNICATION TECHNOLOGY (IECT)

1.6.1 e-Governance

e-Governance is the application of modern information and Communication Technologies, such as Internet, Local area networks, mobiles, etc., by Government to improve the effectiveness, efficiency, service delivery and to promote democracy.

It is also to use technology to enhance the access to and delivery of government services to benefit citizens, business partners and employees. Focus of these definitions range from those focusing on Information and Communication Technologies (ICTs) to those focusing on ICT-enables government and governance transformations. Some examples of such definitions include:

(a) The use of ICTs, and particularly the Internet, as a tool to achieve better government.
(b) The use of information and communication technologies in all facts of the operations of a government organization.
(c) The continuous optimization of service delivery, constituency participation and governance by transforming internal and external relationships through technology, the Internet, etc.

Why E-Governance?

E-Governance can transform citizen service, provide access to information to empower citizens, enable their participation in government and enhance citizen economic and social opportunities, so that they can make better lives, for themselves and for the next generation.

☞ *Governments are specialized institutions that contribute to governance. Representative governments seek and receive citizen support, but they also need the active cooperation of their public servants. Governance is the outcome of politics, policies and programs.*

Difference between e-government and e-governance

While E-Government has traditionally been understood as being centered around the operations of government whereas, E-Governance is understood to extend the scope by including citizen engagement and participation in governance.

Activities of e-Government using e-Governance

The primary delivery models of e-Government can be divided into:

(a) Government-to-Citizen or Government-to-Consumer (G2C)
(b) Government-to-Business (G2B)
(c) Government-to-Government (G2G)
(d) Government-to-Employees (G2E)

Within each of these interaction domains, four kinds of activities take place

(a) Pushing information over the Internet, e.g., regulatory services, general holidays, public hearing schedules, issue briefs, notifications, etc.
(b) Two-way communications between the agency and the citizen, a business, or another government agency. In this model, users can engage in dialogue with agencies and post problems, comments, or requests to the agency.
(c) Conducting transactions, e.g., lodging tax returns, applying for services and grants.
(d) Governance, e.g., online polling, voting, and campaigning.

Risks and Benefits of e-Governence

Risks There are many considerations and potential implications of implementing and designing e-government, including disintermediation of the government and its citizens, impacts on economic, social, and political factors, vulnerability to cyber attacks, and disturbances to the status quo in these areas.

Hyper-surveillance Increased contact between government and its citizens goes both ways. Once e-government begins to develop and become more sophisticated, citizens will be forced to interact electronically with the government on a larger scale. This could potentially lead to a lack of privacy for civilians as their government obtains more and more information on them. In a worse case scenario, with so much information being passed electronically between government and civilians. When the government has easy access to countless information on its citizens, personal privacy is lost.

Cost Although "a prodigious amount of money has been spent" on the development and implementation of e-government, some say it has yielded only a mediocre product. The outcomes and effects of trial Internet-based governments are often difficult to gauge or unsatisfactory.

Inaccessibility An e-government site that provides web access and support often does not offer the potential to reach many users including those who live in remote areas, are homebound, have low literacy levels, exist on poverty line incomes, suffer from chronic illness, are single parents or older adults.

Benefits

It is convenient and cost-effective for businesses, and the public benefits by getting easy access to the most current information available without having to spend time, energy and money to get it.

E-government helps simplify processes and makes access to government information more easily accessible for public sector agencies and citizens. For example, the Indian Bureau of Motor Vehicles simplified the process of certifying driver records to be admitted in county court proceedings. The anticipated benefits of e-government include:

(a) Efficiency
(b) Improved services
(c) Better accessibility of public services
(d) Transparency and accountability

Democratization One goal of e-government will be greater citizen participation. Through the Internet, people from all over the country can interact with politicians or public servants and make their voices heard. Blogging and interactive surveys will allow politicians or public servants to see the views of the people they represent on any given issue. Chat rooms can place citizens in real-time contact with elected officials, their offices or provide them with the means to replace them by interacting directly with public servants, allowing voters to have a direct impact and influence in their government. These technologies can create a more transparent government, allowing voters to immediately see how and why their representation in the capital is voting the way they are. This helps voters better decide who to vote for in the future or how to help the public servants become more productive. A government could theoretically move more towards a true democracy with the proper application of e-government. Government transparency will give insight to the public on how decisions are made and hold elected officials or public servants accountable for their actions. The public could become a direct and prominent influence in government legislature to some degree.

Environmental Bonuses Proponents of e-government argue that online government services would lessen the need for hard copy forms. Due to recent pressures from environmentalist groups, the media, and the public, some governments and organizations have turned to the Internet to reduce this paper use.

Speed, Efficiency, and Convenience E-government allows citizens to interact with computers to achieve objectives at any time and any location, and eliminates the necessity for physical travel to government agents sitting behind desks and Windows. Improved accounting and record keeping can be noted through computerization, and information and forms can be easily accessed, equaling quicker processing time. On the administrative side, access to help find or retrieve files and linked information can now be stored in databases versus hardcopies stored in various locations. Individuals with disabilities or conditions no longer have to be mobile to be active in government and can be in the comfort of their own homes.

Public approval Recent trials of e-government have been met with acceptance and eagerness from the public. Citizens participate in online discussions of political issues with increasing frequency, and young people, who traditionally display minimal interest in government affairs, are drawn to e-voting procedures.

1.6.2 Entertainment

Media and Entertainment industry are a major benefactors of multimedia technology. Images, animation and sound are widely used for making animation movies. Capability of computer is widely used by musicians to record, edit and mix sounds. Entertainment CDs, games, comics and stories for children are used for education and training.

Video editing, mixing, 3D animation and morphing are some of the techniques widely used for creating video films for various purpose.

Entertainment Software

Entertainment software allow computer system to be used as an entertainment tool. A few examples of such applications are:

- **Video Games**–Thousands of video game applications are available on computer systems. Special audio and visual effects are used in these applications to make the games thrilling and exciting the users.
- **Interactive Television**–Two way cable TV system that enables the viewer to issue commands and give feedback information through an electronic device called a setup box. The viewer can select which program/movies to watch, and what time, and can place orders in response to commericals. New Setup boxes also allow access to email and ecommerce applications via Internet.

  Its an approach to TV advertising and programming that creates the opportunity for viewers to communicated with advertiser and programming executives by responding to a call to action.

1.7 BRINGING COMPUTER TO LIFE

Over time, every PC will begin to slow down. Following are some simple ways to get a computer back to life.

Regular Maintenance

Do some basic maintenance on your PC. Clean Windows Registry , Run Disk Defrag, a scan disk, a virus scan, a malware scan, and clear your recycle bin. An unusually slow Internet connection experience is often the only sign that your computer is infected with viruses or other malware. Delete old files and temporary files. Never allow the free space on your C: drive to be less than 10% of the total size or twice the installed RAM (which ever is larger). A well maintained PC will operate much better than a PC that has never had any maintenance. For this, do the following:

(a) Before you start trying to clean up your PC, remember to take the usual precautions to prevent against data loss by performing a full backup.

(b) You should also run a complete anti-virus and anti-spyware scan before taking any other action. There is no point trying to improve performance on a PC that is being slowed down by malicious software. Another important step is to ensure your hard disk has no errors.

(c) The files and directories on your PC can be corrupted by power cuts. Windows crashes or by turning your PC off at the mains. It is worth checking these before defragmenting a drive, which allow the computer to reorganize files so that it can access and retrieve them more efficiently.

(d) Right-click the C: drive icon and choose Properties from the menu. Click the Tools tab and press 'Check now'. In Check Disk dialog box, click the check mark '*Automatically fix file system errors*'. Click **Start** and Windows will ask if you want to schedule a check the next time your PC Starts. Click Yes.

(e) Shut down Windows and restart your PC. Before Windows starts, you will see a screen in Windows 7 that runs the disk check automatically. It can take quite a while to complete, depending on how fast your PC is and if any problems are found. Then it will restart your PC automatically and go to the usual Windows login screen.

(f) The more applications you have opened at the same time, the slower your computer will perform. If an application hangs up, be patient and let it recover; if it is hung up for more than a few minutes, use Ctrl+Alt+Del or Force Quit to shut it down.

(g) **Get the Latest Updates:** Windows Update service is a free, regular service that will send updates to your computer for the OS and Internet Explorer.

(h) **Bodywork:** Two of a computer's biggest enemies are heat and dust. When dust clogs up fans or piles up on circuits inside, it can overheat your computer, which can cause malfunctions. If possible, keep your computer off and keep in a well-ventilated area.

(i) To clean the monitor, use a moist wiper first, followed by a dry dusting cloth. Always be careful wiping down Liquid Crystal Display (LCD) screens and other monitors. Next, clean your keyboard by blowing out dust that is in-between the keys and in the crevices. Use the canned air blower to get dust from the fans and Input/Output (I/O) ports on the back of the computer.

(j) **In the future:** With more self-activating diagnostic tools, next-gen computers will be able to alert users to potential problems and recommend solutions. Next-generation users will be alerted ahead of time to spyware and virus threats identified and tracked from online databases.

☞ *Software is also getting more self-aware in terms of updating itself. As soon as you launch an application, it will typically check with online services to ensure you are using the latest, greatest, bug-free version of the software.*

1.7.1 Connecting to Keyboard, Mouse, Monitor and Printer to CPU

After connecting the internal components, you can close the system case and then connect the external components, such as keyboard, mouse, monitor and printer.

Connecting to Mouse

Depending on the type of mouse, you can connect it to the appropriate port on the back of the computer.

A mouse can be connected to a computer system in one of the following ways:

- Using a serial port, • A bus connection
- PS/2 mouse port • USB port • Wirelessly

Let us understand these mouse connections in detail.

Serial Mouse

A serial port is the most common method of connecting a mouse. A serial mouse is connected to either Communication Port (COM1 or COM2), i.e., to any one of the available serial ports on the computer.

Connecting a serial mouse is very easy as one just needs to plug in the connector attached to the mouse wire to the vacant serial port.

Sometimes, one needs to configure the mouse drive to specify the COM port used for the mouse, but most of the new mouse drive software can auto-configure themselves.

Bus Mouse

While, serial mouse is connected to a serial port, a bus mouse is connected to a special cord made just for the mouse.

This special mouse adapter board is installed into the PC's expansion slot and then the mouse is connected to the connector provided at the back.

PS/2 Port Mouse

Now a days, many computers come equipped with a special mouse port for connecting the mouse. This method is similar to the bus mouse approach except that the mouse control circuitry is directly built into the motherboard of the PC and not connected as a separate card.

This type of mouse is called PS/2 mouse because these connectors are common with IBM/s PS/2 range of computers.

USB Port Mouse

The USB port can be used to connect a mouse. As the mouse is not required during power on/bootup process, no special BIOS is required for handling USB mouse.

Hardware installation of the USB mouse requires just plugging in the mouse to the USB port. Windows 7 Operating System can automatically install it in the PC.

Wireless Mouse

In a wireless mouse, no cable is used to connect the mouse to the computer system.

Basically, there are two types of wireless mouse:

- Infrared Wireless Mouse
- Radio-controlled Wireless Mouse

Infrared Wireless Mouse

An infrared mouse communicates with the receiving unit connected to the main system unit using infrared light. As the infrared light cannot pass through objects, it requires an infrared mouse to be in direct line of sight with the receiving unit connected to the main system.

Radio-controlled Wireless Mouse

When the radio-controlled wireless mouse is moved, radio signals are transmitted by it to a special receiver unit connected to the main system. The radio signal received is sent to the computer as any normal mouse signal received through the cable is sent.

As the radio signal can pass through objects, the radio-controlled mouse need not be in line of sight with the receiving unit.

In case more than one wireless mouse is being used at one place, they cause different radio frequencies, so one need not worry about signal from one mouse getting disturbed by the signal from another mouse.

☞ *Before connecting the mouse, it is safest to turn the computer off and unplug it. If your mouse is a USB device, your computer may be kept on.*

Connecting to Keyboard

Depending on the type of the keyboard, you can connect it to the appropriate port at the back of the computer.

➡ **To connect a PS/2 keyboard, do the following:**

(a) Connect the keyboard cable to the PS/2 port. Be careful to connect to the correct PS/2 port, as the keyboard and mouse PS/2 ports look identical.

➡ **To connect a USB keyboard, do the following:**

(a) Connect the USB keyboard to the USB port on the PC. If there are other USB devices, connect the keyboard to the USB hub. You will have to install the drives for your keyboard if it has additional advanced features. You will also have to install the software for the keyboard in this case. If need be refer to the keyboard manual (See Figure 1.38).

Serial port, used to connect the mouse

Parallel port, used to connect the printers

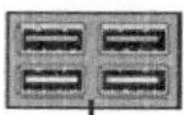

USB port is used to connect the mouse, pen drive, printers, etc.

Figure 1.38 Ports for connecting

Connecting the Monitor

Monitor is an output device which is used to display information on screen. The monitor must be installed by attaching the signal cable to the system and the power cord to the power outlet.

➡ **To connect the monitor, do the following:**

(a) Connect the one end of power cables to the power port at the back of the monitor.
(b) Connect the other end of the power cord to the power outlet or the system power supply case.
(c) Check the monitor using the built-in Power On Self Test (POST).
(d) Connect one end of the signal cable to the video port at the back of the monitor.
(e) Connect the other end of the signal cable to the video adapter.
(f) Turn the hard screws of the signal cable to lock the signal cable to the system case.

Connecting the Printer to CPU

To connect a printer directly to your computer

Most new printers support Plug and Play, while many older printers do not. The steps involved in installing a printer that is attached to your computer differ depending on whether it supports Plug and Play.

➡ **To connect directly to a Plug and Play printer do the following:**

1. Connect the printer cable to the appropriate port on your computer according to the printer manufacturer's instructions.
2. Plug the power cord of the printer into a wall outlet and turn the printer on.
3. Windows detects your Plug and Play printer and, in many cases, installs it without requiring you to make any selections. The printer is ready to print.
4. If the Found New Hardware Wizard appears, select the Install the software automatically (Recommended) check box, click Next, and then follow the instructions.

You can also add a printer by clicking **Add a printer** under **Printer Tasks** on the left side of **Printers and Faxes.**

Using the Add a Printer Wizard

Windows 7 provides the Add a Printer Wizard to simplify installing printers. The Printers folder for running the wizard and for managing printing processes. You open the Printers folder in the following ways.

1. Click **Start** menu, or click Control Panel and choose **Devices and Printers**. The Devices and Printers folders gives you a quick view of devices connected to the computer.
2. Click **Add a printer** to open the Add printer wizard, and then click **Next.**
3. Select the option that describes the printer you want to use.
   - Add a local printer, or
   - A a network, wireless or Bluetooth printer
4. Select the port you want your printer to use.
   - Create a new port or
   - Click Local port and then click Next.
5. Follow the instructions on the screen to finish adding a printer with the Add Printer Wizard.

☞ *The only difference between installing a network printer and a local printer with the Add Printer Wizard is that you must specify the path to the network printer or browse to find its network location.*

1.7.2 Checking Power Supply of PC

The power supply's job is to convert the power provided from the outlet into usable power for the many parts inside the computer. The power supply is mounted just inside the back of the case.

The side facing outside the case has a male, three pronged port that a power cable, connected to a power source, plugs into. There is also often a power switch and a power supply voltage switch.

Large bundles of colored wires extend from the opposite side of the power supply into the computer. Connectors at the opposite ends of the wires connect to various components inside the computer. Some are specifically designed to plugin to the motherboard while others have connectors that fit into fans, floppy drives, hard drives, optical drives, and even some high powered video cards.

Power supplies are rated by wattage to show how much power they can provide to the computer. Since each computer part requires a certain amount of power to function properly, it is important to have a power supply that can provide the right amount.

Testing a power supply is an important step when troubleshooting many issues, most obviously when your computer is having trouble starting.

You can test a power supply yourself manually using a multimeter or you can purchase a power supply tester to perform an automatic Power Supply Unit (PSU) test.

Here is some more information on how to test your power supply with each of these methods and some help deciding which method is best for you.

Testing a power supply manually with a multimeter is one of two ways to test a power supply in a computer. A properly executed PSU test using a multimeter should confirm that the power supply is in good working order or should it be replaced.

Important steps to test power supply are the following:

1. Manually testing a power supply unit involves working around high voltage electricity.

☞ *During a power supply test with a PSU tester and there are several points you should be aware of before beginning.*

2. **Open your case:** turn off the PC, remove the power cable, and unplug anything else connected to the outside of the computer.
   To make your power supply test easier, you should move your disconnected and open case somewhere you can easily work with it, like on a table or other flat and non-static surface.
3. Unplug the power connectors from each and every internal device inside the computer.

☞ *An easy way to make sure each power connector is unplugged is to work from the power cable bundle coming from the power supply inside the PC. Each group of wires should terminate to one or more power connectors.*

4. Group all of the power cables and connectors together for easy testing.
   As you are organizing the power cables, route them and pull them as far away from the computer case as possible. This will make it as easy as possible to test the power supply connections.
5. Confirm that the power supply switch located on the power supply is properly set.
6. Turn on your multimeter and turn the dial to the VDC (Volt DC) setting.
7. First we will test the 24 pin motherboard power connector.
   Connect the negative probe on the multimeter (black) to any ground wired pin and connect the positive probe (red) to the first power line you want to test. The 24 pin main power connector has +3.3 VDC, +5 VDC, -5 VDC (optional), + 12 VDC, and -12 VDC lines across multiple pins.

You will need to reference the Advanced Technology Extended ATX 24 pin 12V Power Supply Pinout for the locations of these pins.

8. Document the number that the multimeter shows for each voltage tested and confirm that the reported voltage is within approved tolerance.
9. Turn off the switch on the back of the power supply and unplug it from the wall.
10. Reconnect all of your internal devices to power.
11. Plug in your power supply, flip the switch on the back if you have one, and then turn on your computer as you normally do with the power switch on the front of the PC.
12. Once your testing is complete, turn off and unplug the PC and then put the cover back on the case.

Assuming power supply tested good or you have replaced power supply with a new one, you can now turn computer back on.

1.8 SUMMARY

This chapter is based on *Knowing Computer*. Chapter begins with computers and its characteristic and basic applications of computer by using various kinds of software packages. It also discusses various components of computer system, such as CPU, keyboard, mouse and other input and output devices. The later part of the chapter describes hardware and software. *Hardware* means physical components of a computer system which we can see and touch. The term *software* refers to set of computer programs. Software is divide into two major categories - System software and Application software. System software is a set of one or more programs designed to control the operation of a computer system. Application software is a set of one or more programs designed to solve a specific problem or to do a specific task. Concept of data and information has also been discussed. Connecting peripherals is the easiest task you will tackle when building a computer. Finally, this chapter explained entertainment software allow computer systems to be used as an entertainment tool.

MODEL QUESTIONS AND ANSWERS

1. Multiple Choice

1.1 The term LPT is related to

a. Serial port b. Centronics port
c. Parallel port d. None of the above

1.2 Which of the following holds the ROM, CPU, RAM and expansion cards?

a. Hard disk b. Floppy disk
c. Mother board d. None of the above

1.3 The language that a computer can understand and execute is called:

a. Machine language b. Application software
c. System program d. None of the above

1.4 To write, erase, rewrite data on a CD ROM what type of CD ROM you should use?

a. CD-RW b. CD R
c. CD-W d. None of the above

1.5 CD-ROM is a

a. Temporary memory b. Permanent storage
c. Optical memory d. None of the above

1.6 Information retrieval is fastest from

a. Pen drive b. CD ROM
c. Hard disk d. All of the above

1.7 RAM means

a. Random access memory
b. Read also memory
c. Read access memory
d. Random also memory

1.8 Which one of the following is a secondary storage device?

a. CD-ROM b. RAM
c. ROM d. OMR

1.9 In computer terminology, information means:

a. Raw
b. Data
c. Data is more useful
d. Alphanumeric data program

1.10 During data processing, the actual execution of the instructions takes place in the

a. Output unit b. Control unit
c. Hard disk d. Arithmetic logic unit

1.11 Indicate which, of the following best describes the term 'software'

a. Operating system programs
b. Application programs
c. Both (a) and (b)
d. None of the above

1.12 A mouse can be connected to computer system through

a. USB port b. Parallel port
c. serial port d. only (a) and (c)

1.13 Which one of the following is not an input device?

a. Microphone b. Mouse
c. Scanner d. None of the above

2. State whether the following statements are True or False

2.1 Computers cannot help in decision-making processes.
2.2 ALU is a part of CPU.
2.3 Never repair your computer when the power supply on.
2.4 The main advantage of computer graphics is that it substantially increases productivity.
2.5 Data stored in a ROM cannot be changed by user of a computer?
2.6 VDUs can be used both as input and output devices.
2.7 OCR is a device that scans written or typed text and transforms it into computer readable form.
2.8 The processing of one program after the other without user intervention is an example of batch processing.
2.9 Access to data stored on magnetic tape is random.
2.10 Computer software is normally classified as system software and application software.

Answers

1.	1.1	c	1.2	c	1.3	a	1.4	a	1.5	c
	1.6	d	1.7	a	1.8	a	1.9	b	1.10	d
	1.11	c	1.12	d	1.13	d				
2.	2.1	F	2.2	T	2.3	T	2.4	T	2.5	T
	2.6	F	2.7	T	2.8	T	2.9	F	2.10	T

CHAPTER 2

Operating Computer Using GUI-based Operating System

2.0 INTRODUCTION

An operating system is a program that acts as an intermediary between a user and the computer hardware. The purpose of an operating system is to provide an environment in which a user can execute programs in a convenient and efficient manner. The operating system must ensure the correct operation of the computer system. To prevent user programs from interfering with the proper operation of the system, the hardware must provide appropriate mechanisms to ensure such proper behavior.

2.1 OBJECTIVES

The reader will be able to understand the following:

- Basics of Operating System
- User Interface of OS
- Operating System Settings
- File and Directory Management
- Types of files

2.2 BASICS OF OPERATING SYSTEM

An Operating System (OS) is a set of system software programs in a computer that regulates the ways an application software programs use the computer hardware and the ways that users control the computer. For hardware functions, such as input/output and memory space allocation, operating system programs act as an intermediary between an application programs and the computer hardware. Although application programs are usually executed directly by the hardware. Operating System is also a field of study within Applied Computer Science.

The job of an operating system for a computer is to manage the hardware and software resources of the system. In desktops or laptops, the hardware resources include processes, hard disk, memory, disk space, mouse, printers, other peripherals, etc., whereas the software resources are the various software applications used on that desktop/laptop. Operating systems also play a very important role in providing a consistent interface for the applications irrespective of the hardware or peripherals used. There may be different drivers used along with the operating systems for this purpose.

2.2.1 Operating System

Operating system works as an interface between the user and the computer and all other programs need an OS to start them. It is software that controls the internal activities of the computer hardware and provides user interface. It is the first program loaded into the computer's memory and states the computer authentically when the power is turned on. Popular operating systems are Windows XP, Windows 10, LINUX and UNIX.

Operating systems

- Controls and coordinates the operation of computer.
- Controls input and output devices.
- Controls execution of computer programs.
- Does all the interaction between user and the computer.
- Helps you to manage and manipulate files and the use of main memory of computer.

An operating system performs the functions:

- *Processor Management:* It assigns processors (if a computer has more than one processor) to the different tasks that must be performed by the computer system.
- *Memory Management:* It allocates the main memory and secondary memory to the system programs, user programs and data.

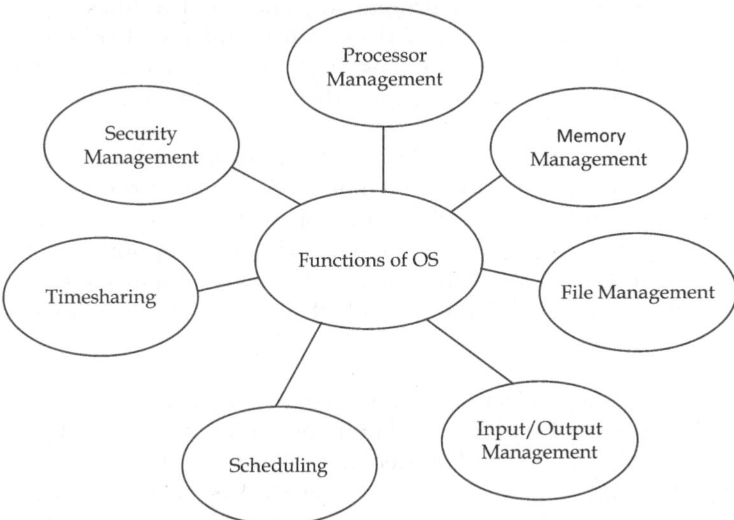

- *Input/output Management:* It carries out the input/output management, co-ordinates and assigns different input and output devices.
- *File Management:* It manages files on various storage devices and transfer these files from one storage device to another.
- *Scheduling:* It establishes and enforces the job priority.
- *Timesharing:* It co-ordinates and assigns compilers, assemblers, utility programs, and other software packages to various users working on the computer system.
- *Security Management:* It establishes data security and integrity.

All operating systems can be classified into following categories:

- *Single User Operating System:* It allows only one user to work on a computer at a time, e.g., Windows XP.
- *Multiuser Operating System:* It allows a number of users to work together on a single computer by providing a terminal connected to a single computer, e.g., Unix.
- *Single Tasking Operating System:* It executes a single job/program at a time, e.g., MS-DOS.
- *Multitasking Operating System:* It supports the execution of more than one job at a time, e.g., Windows 2012.
- *Multiprogramming Operating System:* In this several programs can be run at a same time via time sharing mechanism, e.g., Linux.
- *Real Time Operating System:* It responds to an event within a predetermined time, e.g., Windows CE.

- *Batch Processing Operating System:* Similar types of job are grouped under batch and then jobs are executed without any user interruption, e.g., MS-DOS.
- *Multiprocessing Operating System:* It uses more than two CPUs within a single computer system, e.g., LINUX, UNIX.

Windows 8 and 10 are the later versions of Windows desktop operating system for the PC. Windows 7 brings a new, more personalized look to the desktop that will also make it easier for users to scan or import images. It is meant to acquire music files on the Web and transfer them to portable devices. Windows 7 will allow different family members to use their own desktop and personal set of files.

Windows 8

Windows 8 is the eighth version of MS Windows, released on October 26, 2012. It includes several improvements to Windows 8, but the most notable feature is an updated user interface, which displays a grid of tiles on the home screen. These tiles provide one-click access to programs, games, and utilities. For example, it includes Photos, Videos, Music, Internet Explorer, Maps, Weather. Several of the tiles, such as the Maps, Weather, and custom social networking tiles, display information that is updated dynamically.

The tile-based interface (called "Metro") optimized for touchscreens as well as mice makes Windows 8 a suitable operating system for both traditional PCs and tablets. It also functions on hybrid systems that include a touchscreen but also support traditional input devices. While the tile-based interface is a major part of Windows 8, but did not get rid of the standard Windows desktop interface.

Windows 10

Windows 10 is a personal computer operating system released by MS as part of the Windows NT family of operating systems. On June 1, 2015, MS first announced that Windows 10 would be released on July 29, 2015. Windows 10 expanding on Metro-style apps and these apps can be designed to run across multiple MS product families including PCs, tablets, smartphones, embedded systems, Xbox One, Surface Hub and HoloLens. The Windows user interface was revised to handle transitions between a mouse-oriented interface and a touchscreen-optimized interface based on available input devices - particularly on 2-in-1 PCs; both interfaces include an updated Start menu that blends the elements of Windows 7's traditional Start menu with the tiles of Windows 8. The first release of Windows 10 also introduces a virtual desktop system, a window and desktop management feature called Task View, the MS Edge web browser, support for fingerprint and face recognition login, new security features for enterprise environments, and DirectX 12 and WDDM 2.0 to improve the operating system's graphics capabilities for games.

2.2.2 Basics of Popular Operating System (Linux, Windows)

Windows

One of today's most common operating system is MS Windows. It is the world's largest selling operating system for PCs.

Windows belongs to the category of software called a GUI (Graphical User Interface). The user interface determines how you interact with your computer. The hardware part of the interface consists of your *screen* monitor, the *keyboard* and the mouse. The software part of the interface determines what things look like on the screen and how you give commands to your PC to get your work done. With the advent of Windows environment, many of day-to-day computer tasks, such as *running programs, opening files, choosing commands,* etc. are done by using a graphical approach that is very intuitive to new users of computers. Further, Windows programs use the same command structure and graphical items on the screen, so if you have mastered one Windows program, learning other programs becomes very easy.

As soon as you switch on the power supply, Windows operating system program gets loaded in PC after initial checks and takes the PC's control. It provides the communication link between your computer hardware and the software that you use. For example, when you tell your spreadsheet software to save a file, the operating system tells the computer system how and where to save it.

However, Windows is more than an operating system. It provides functions that let you manage many programs simultaneously, customize PC, and do many of the maintenance tasks associated with a PC. It also comes with many accessories, software programs, such as utilities and media player, etc.

Windows takes care of PC and does many things in the background that are not visible to you. It keeps busy behind the scenes managing your software packages and hardware working. Windows does the following jobs:

- Provides ways for you to start application programs.
- Runs more than one program at a time. This is called *multitasking*. It means that you can have both a word processing program and spreadsheet program opened at the same time can easily and switch between them.
- Provides a way for you to manage files. Files are documents that you create, namely, letters, memos, and worksheets. Use Windows Explorer, the file management program that comes with Windows, to *copy, move, organize, delete,* and otherwise work with the files.
- Helps you to set up the Internet access.
- Windows comes with Outlook Express which is an e-mail program. Use this program to send and receive electronic mail, via Internet.
- Windows comes with a number of useful accessory programs, such as WordPad a word processing program. It has a text editor called Notepad for typing notes, etc.
- It provides a way for you to customize the desktop and other screen areas of the monitor.

Linux Operating System

Overview of Linux Linux is a multiuser, multitasking operating system first developed by Linus Benedict Torvalds. Linux is a 32-bit operating system. It runs on a wide variety of platforms, such as Intel, Sparc, Alpha etc. It can be considered in every sense as a full-blown implementation of UNIX. But it cannot be called as UNIX because UNIX is a registered trademark product owned by American Telephone & Telegraph company (AT&T). Linux is distributed as a free software under a free software licence called the GNU General Public License (GNU/GPL).

Advantages of Linux over Windows The advantage of Linux operating systems are:

1. **Low Cost:** The majority of Linux variants are available for free at a much lower price than MS Windows.
2. **Stability:** Linux does not need to be rebooted periodically to maintain performance levels. It does not freeze up or slow down over time due to memory leaks .

3. **Performance:** Linux provides persistent high performance on workstations and on networks. It can handle unusually large numbers of users simultaneously.
4. **Network friendliness:** Linux was developed by a group of programmers over the Internet and has therefore strong support for network functionality; client and server systems can be easily set up on any computer running Linux. It can perform tasks, such as network backups faster and more reliably than alternative systems.
5. **Flexibility:** Linux can be used for high performance server applications, desktop applications, and embedded systems. You can save disk space by installing the components needed for a particular use.
6. **Compatibility:** It runs all common UNIX software packages and can process all common file formats.
7. **Fast and easy installation:** Most Linux distributions come with user-friendly installation and setup programs. Popular Linux distributions come with tools that make installation of additional software user friendly.
8. **Full use of hard disk:** Linux continues work well even when the hard disk is almost full.
9. **Multitasking:** Linux is designed to do many things at the same time; e.g., a large printing job in the background would not slow down other work.

Disadvantages of Linux over Windows

1. Linux has more then three hundred version and all version can not be installed on a single computer system.
2. There are so many distributions of Linux that new users may get confused.
3. Some hardware devices and software may not be compatible with a particular version of Linux.

Basic Linux Elements The basic elements of Linux are discussed in the following sub-sections:

Kernel The kernel is at the core of Linux system and is loaded into the memory as soon as the system starts up. It manages main memory, files and peripheral devices. Maintaining the time and date, launching applications, and allocating system resources are the functions of this part of the operating system.

Shell Shell is a program which interprets commands given by the user. The command can be either typed in through the command line or contained in a file called *'shell script'*. Commands in 'shell script' files are interpreted by the shell.

File System Linux treats everything as file. Even a directory is treated as a file that contains entries for several other files. All the hardware devices, such as I/O devices, storage devices etc., are treated as files.

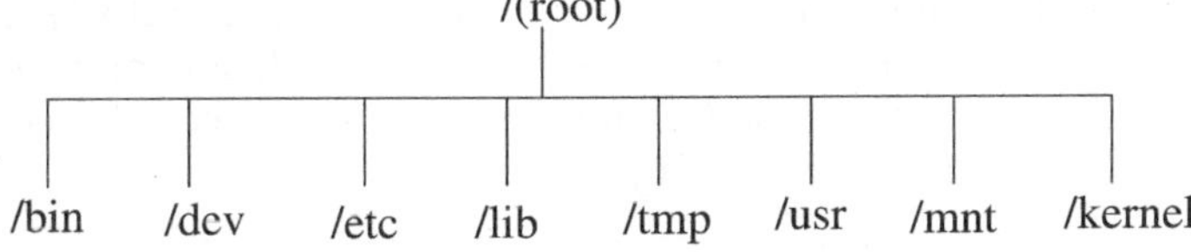

Figure 2.1 Linux file system

The Linux file system is organized in an hierarchy which starts with the *root* directory. The root is represented by a forward slash (/). Under the root directory several system directories and the home directory are there. Figure 2.1 lists the standard system directories in Linux.

Linux uses forward slash (/) as a separator (Windows or DOS uses backslash (\) as a separator). For example, a subdirectory *mydir* of the directory *usr,* will be shown as /usr/mydir. The slash (/) before the *usr* represents the root directory.

/bin This directory contains executable program files (**bin**ary files). In this directory, one can find the files for the Linux commands. (Similar to command.com file in DOS).

/dev This directory contains the special **dev**ice files. For example, the printer may be a file known as *prn* in this directory, the hard disk may be *hda* file and its first partition would be *hda0.*

/etc This directory contains all the system-wide configuration information as text files.

/lib This directory contains the **lib**rary files. Library files contain the reusable functions and routines for the programmer to use.

/tmp This directory contains all the **temp**orary files, which will eventually be deleted from the system. This is similar to the C:\windows\temp directory in Windows 98.

/usr This directory contains the home directories of the users, source text for the online manual (man) pages, games and other directories. There is one home directory for each user. For example, for a user called "mini", there will be a directory with the same name in usr directory. The directory *mini* will contain, all the files and sub-directories created by the user "mini".

/kernel This directory contains all the kernel specific code. Kernel is the heart of the Linux system. It is responsible for resource allocation, security and low-level hardware interfaces.

/mnt This is the directory where the storage devices other than hard disks (floppy disks and CD disks) are mounted. This directory contains the sub-directories "floppy" and "cdrom" which when mounted show the contents of the CD-ROM or floppy disk respectively.

Commands

A Linux command is a series of characters that you type. These characters consist of words separated by white spaces. The first word is the command itself and the rest are the command's arguments. The arguments provide information that the command may need for its execution. Linux commands are case-sensitive. That is, cp is different from CP and cP.

☞ *You must type all Linux commands in lowercase letters.*

Commands are issued to the shell at the command line. A command line comprises of commands, the line of instructions, options and any command line arguments that you may provide. For example, the following is a command line:

```
$ man cp
```

Commands are entered at the shell prompt ($, #). Prompt is merely a symbol that appears at the start of a command line. This lets you know that Linux is ready and waiting for your command.

Device Drivers Device drivers are software packages that form a major part of the kernel. They control the interaction between the hardware devices and the operating system.

Utilities Utilities are software tools included with the Linux operating system that lets you do miscellaneous jobs, such as text editing, programming and communications.

File Handling in Linux

Each directory or file in Linux is referred to, by using its pathname beginning from the root directory. For example, the directory **usr** is referred to as /usr (/ or root is its parent directory); mini is referred to as /usr/mini, where usr is the parent directory of mini directory.

There are two types of pathnames. These are:

(a) Absolute Pathname

(b) Relative Pathname

An absolute pathname tells you the complete path of a directory starting from the root, as explained above. Root is represented by a forward slash (/). For example, absolute pathname of "Delhi" directory is /usr/mini/sales/north/Delhi.

Relative pathname gives location of a directory, relative to the current working directory. For example, suppose your current working directory is /usr/mini/sales/north. Then the relative pathname to the "Delhi" directory is Delhi. Relative pathnames do not start with a "/".

☞ *If you do not start a pathname with "/", Linux assumes that you are using relative pathname.*

Identifying the Current Working Directory

To find out which directory you are currently working in, type the following command.

$ pwd Enter

The pwd command prints the absolute pathname of your current working directory. It takes no arguments. For example, in Figure 2.2[1], the user "mini" got the result as /usr/mini.

Making New Directories (mkdir) To create a new directory, use the mkdir command followed by the directory name. For example, suppose user mini (who is currently in the home directory /usr/mini) wants to create a directory named "sales", user need to give the following command (See Figure 2.2).

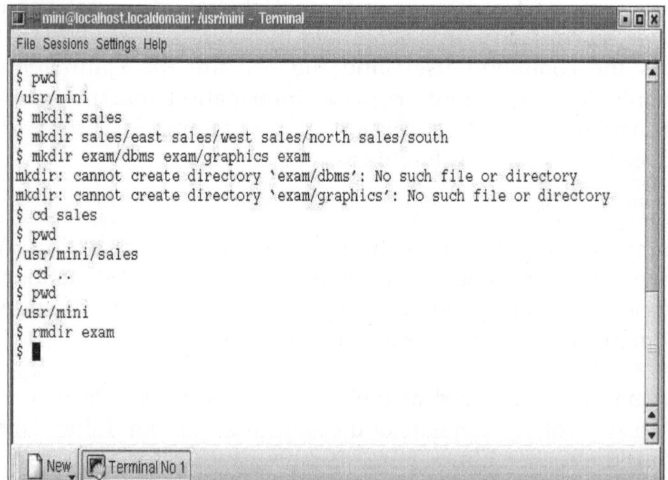

Figure 2.2 A sample Linux session using various commands

$ mkdir sales Enter

The sub-directory "sales" is created under the current directory (i.e. /usr/mini).

1 The screens shown in this book are taken from a Linux terminal.

To create a number of directories with one mkdir command, separate the directory names with spaces. For example, the following command creates various directories (See Figure 2.2).

$ mkdir sales/east sales/west sales/north sales/south Enter

The above command will create four directories under the sales directory.

☞ *The order of specifying the arguments is important. Note that we cannot create a sub-directory before creating its parent directory.*

If we enter the command as:

$ mkdir exam/dbms exam/graphics exam Enter

In this case, the system will fail to create the two subdirectories dbms and graphics, but it will create the exam directory.

Moving to a Different Directory (cd) You can change your working directory by using the cd command followed by the pathname (absolute or relative) to which you want to move.

For example, to move to the sales directory, type the following command:

$ cd sales Enter

Note that in the above command, we have made use of the relative pathname. After giving the above command, if you give the pwd command, you will see the result as /usr/mini/sales (See Figure 2.2).

☞ *The cd command without any following pathname always takes the user back to the user's HOME directory.*

☞ *Linux uses a single dot (.) to represent the current working directory and double dots (..) to represent the parent directory of the current working directory. For example, typing* `cd..` *will take user "mini" to her HOME directory (/usr/mini), since that is the parent directory of sales.*

Removing a Directory (rmdir) The command rmdir is used for deleting a directory. The directory to be deleted must be empty for this command to work. For example, to remove the "exam" directory, type the following command (See Figure 2.2):

$ rmdir exam Enter

You cannot remove a directory if you are placed in one of its sub-directories.

☞ *We can also delete more than one directory by separating the multiple directory names with spaces:*

Listing the Contents of Directories (ls)

To list the files and sub-directories of the current directory, **ls** command is used. Its function is equivalent to the DIR command of DOS. For example, to list the contents of current directory, user "mini" should type the following:

$ ls

following result will get displayed:

east
north
south
west

The order of display is numerals→uppercase characters→lowercase characters. That is, the list is displayed with numerals having precedence over alphabets and in alphabets, uppercase has precedence over lower case.

If the names of files and directories under a specified directory (say north) are to be listed out, then we need to specify the directory name with ls command, as follows:

```
$ ls north
```

The above command will give the result as shown in Figure 2.3.

Usually, a directory contains many files, and user may be interested in knowing whether a particular file is available or not. In that case, he/she just has to use **ls** with the filename, as follows:

```
$ ls March
```

The above command will prompt–File Not Found error, since there is no file called "March" in our current directory. Had the file existed, *ls* would have displayed the filename.

The command *ls* can be used along with a number of *options*. Options are nothing but predetermined arguments used along with a minus sign (-). The different options forces the command to work differently.

For example, the following command will display file and directory names in multiple columns.

```
$ ls -x
```

The result is:

```
east        north        south        west
```

Table 2.1 lists the different options of **ls** and their uses.

Table 2.1 Options of the command ls

Option	Used to
-x	Get multi-columnar output.
-r	List files and sub-directories in reverse order.
-t	List files and sub-directories with time order.
-a	List all files, including the normally hidden files.
-A	List all files excluding . and .. .
-c	List files by inode modification time.
-i	List the inode for each file.
-l	Display permissions, owner, size, modification time, etc., along with file and directory names.

```
$ ls -1
```

To list the names of files and sub-directories of the current directory, **ls** command is used. Its function is equivalent to the DIR command in MS-DOS. For example, to list the contents of current directory, user "mini" should type the following:

The purpose of -1 is that along with file and directory names. It will display names of hidden files also.

```
$ ps
```

It will display information about a selection of active process.

```
$ kill all
```

It sends a signal to all processes running any of the specified commands.

Creating Files (using cat) To create a file, type the command **cat** at the shell prompt, followed by > character and the filename. For example, to create a file called January, enter the following command.

```
$ cat > January
```
[Enter]

After you press Enter key, you will be prompted to enter the contents of the file. Type the data and press [Ctrl] + [D] keys together to terminate the command line (See Figure 2.3).

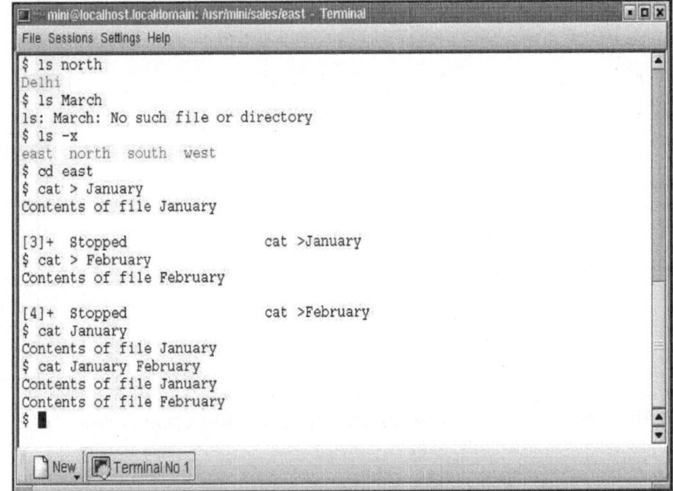

Figure 2.3 A sample Linux session using ls and cat commands

Listing the Contents of Files (cat) To list the contents of a file, use the command **cat** followed by the filename. DOS has TYPE command for this.

For example, to list the contents of file January type the following:

```
$ cat January
```
[Enter]

Absolute pathname can be given to display a file in another directory. The cat command can also display more than one file by separating different filenames with spaces, as shown in the following command:

```
$ cat January February
```
[Enter]

The above command will display the contents of the two files in different rows. Use of cat command to create and display the contents of files is shown in Figure 2.3.

Copying Files (cp) The command cp is used to copy a file into another. DOS equivalent for cp is the COPY command. Like in DOS, the cp command requires two arguments – a source filename, the contents of which are to be copied and a target filename, to which the contents are to be copied.

For example, to copy the file January into another file, say March, type the following (See Figure 2.4):

```
$ cp January March
```
[Enter]

Note that the *ls* command will now show three files, namely January, February and March.

☞ *Use cp with -i option if you want the system to ask for confirmation before copying the files.*

Here, the file January is copied to a new file called March.

☞ *If March file already exists, its contents will be destroyed and replaced by contents of January file.*

If you want to give more than one options along with command, you can use either of the following:

```
$ ls -l -a -t
$ ls -lat
```

Both the above methods will work.

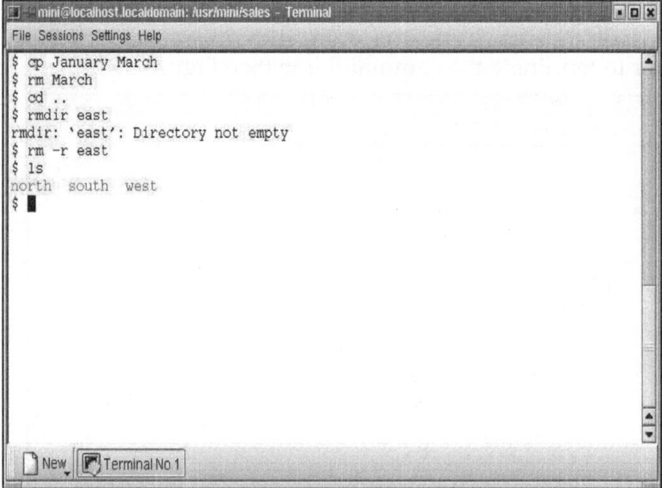

Figure 2.4 A sample Linux session using cp and rm commands

Deleting Files (rm) To delete or remove a file, the rm command is used. This is equivalent to the DEL command in DOS.

For example, to remove the file March, type the following command:

$ rm March [Enter]

This is shown in Figure 2.4.

☞ *Use rm with -i option if you want the system to ask for confirmation, like in cp.*

To remove a directory, use rm with -r option. Here -r stands for recursive deletion. For example, the following command will remove the directory accounts.

$ rm -r accounts [Enter]

☞ *Unlike rmdir, rm -r will remove directories even if they are not empty.*

In Figure 2.4, the system did not delete the directory "east" when *rmdir* command was given, but did so with the *rm -r* command.

Moving Files (mv) A file can be moved, using the mv command. Equivalent command in DOS is MOVE. The following command will displace the directory north from "sales" directory to the directory "/usr/mini".

$ mv north /usr/mini/north [Enter]

The above command does not create a copy of "north" but displaces it.

Now if you type the ls command, you will only see two directories, south and west (See Figure 2.5). The directory "east" was removed using *rm -r* command and "north" is moved to a different directory. The directory "/usr/mini" now contains the north directory and all its sub-directories and files as shown by the ls command in Figure 2.5.

Perform mv operation again to bring back the directory.

$ mv /usr/mini/north.

Note that the dot (.) represents current directory.

Files and directory can also be renamed by using the **mv** command. For example, the following command will rename the directory "west" as "bombay" (See Figure 2.5):

$ mv west bombay [Enter]

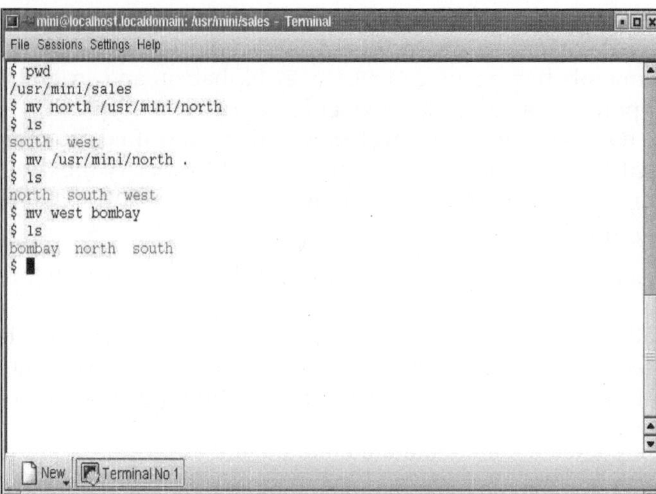

Figure 2.5 A sample Linux session using commands discussed till now

Files can also be renamed in the same way. If the destination exists, it will be overwritten and if it does not exist, it will be created.

☞ *mv also has the -i option like cp and rm commands and works in the same way.*

Installation of Linux

We will be discussing about the installation of popular Red Hat Linux 7.2 in this section. Before listing the procedures to follow for installing the Linux operating system, let us see what are the hardware and software requirements of Linux.

Hardware Requirements Red Hat Linux can be installed if the following basic hardware requirements are met:

(a) x86 platform namely 80386, 80486 etc.
(b) Intel, Sparc, Alpha or Advanced Micro Devices (AMD) processor
(c) x386 CPU family or above
(d) Minimum 128 MB RAM
(e) Minimum 2 GB free hard disk space
(f) Input devices such as keyboard, mouse etc.
(g) Controller cards, such as Small Computer System Interface (SCSI), Integrated Development Environment (IDE), Firewire etc.
(h) A Network card such as Internet Security and Acceleration (ISA), Peripheral Component Interconnect (PCI) or Universal Serial Bus (USB) etc.
(i) Sound card compatible to LINUX

Software Requirements Software requirements for LINUX installation are listed as follows:

(a) A partitioning program, such as fdisk or disk druid supplied by Red Hat.
(b) Linux Software package.

Preliminary steps before Installation

The first step is to create an installation disk.

➡ **To create the installation disk, do this:**

1. Copy the "boot.img" file from the Red Hat CD-ROM disk into a floppy disk. This file can be found in the /images directory of the CD. The file can be created using either the DOS rewrite command (in a DOS/Windows system) or the Linux

dd command (in an existing Linux or UNIX system). For example, to create an installation diskette using the dd command, do the following:

(a) Insert and mount the CD-ROM and then insert a blank floppy into the floppy drive of your computer.

(b) Now give the following command
# dd if=mnt/cdrom/images/boot.img
of=/dev/fd0 bs=1440k Enter
The above command will copy from the input file ("if") mnt/cdrom/boot.img onto the output file ("of") /dev/fd0. It is assumed that floppy drive is accessible from /dev/fd0.

To create an installation diskette using the rawrite program, give the following command (it is assumed that CD-ROM is accessible as drive D):

D:>cd images dosutils\rawrite Enter

For the source file enter "D:\boot.img" and for destination enter "A:".

The bootable installation disk is now ready and you can use it to install your Linux system.

Red Hat Linux can also be installed by booting using any of the following methods:

(a) booting using a floppy diskette (created as explained above).
(b) booting directly from the CD-ROM (your BIOS should support this).
(c) using a hard drive partition to hold the installation software.
(d) booting from a DOS command line.
(d) booting from across a network using HTTP or FTP protocols.
(e) booting from an NFS (Network File System) mounted hard drive.

2. The next step is to plan a partitioning strategy. This step is based on the knowledge of existing hardware. The planning process should also take into consideration the future expansion of the system. Knowing how to allocate the hard disk space for each of the Linux software is a real big challenge which every Linux system administrator has to take. He should find answers to the following questions:
   (a) How much of the disk is required presently and in future?
   (b) Is any other operating system also required?
   (c) How many application software packages are expected to be installed in future?
   (d) How much data needs to be backed up?
   (e) How many users will the system have?
3. If you require that the system should boot any other operating system also along with Linux, the next step is to choose a boot loader. Boot loader is a software that is responsible for booting Linux along with any other operating system. Examples include LILO (LInux LOader) and GRUB (GRand Unified Boot loader).
4. Now insert the floppy disk (the installation diskette you have created if you are using floppy to boot your system) into a floppy drive and power-on your system. After a few moments, the Red Hat installation program screen will appear.

Hard Drive Partitioning

A hard disk must be partitioned taking into consideration the present and future requirements. For example, let us consider that we have a given hard disk of 40 GB capacity. The different partitions can be as follows:

/swap directory	About double the main memory size. For example, a system having 128 MB memory should get 256 MB swap space.
/ directory (root)	About 60% of the available space.
/bin directory	About 20% of the available space.
/usr directory	Remaining space

The size of /usr should be the largest one. This is because all the users' directories and files, installed application softwares, Web pages, log files etc., will be stored here only.

Booting a Linux system

The general booting procedure involves checking of the basic subsystems of your computer, such as amount and validity of RAM, CPU time and speed, presence of floppy, CD-ROM or hard drive, keyboard and other attributes. The Linux may fail to boot if it detects a hardware failure, missing hardware or hardware mis-configuration.

Next the BIOS will look for the bootable disk, in the order given in the settings (such as search floppy first, then CD-ROM and then the hard drive). Following this, it will look for the boot code in the *Master Boot Record* (*MBR*) of the first hard disk. This area of the disk (MBR) contains the boot sector which loads the boot loader (viz. LILO, GRUB or BootMagic).

When the Linux kernel is loaded, the kernel will carry out the following:

(a) Initialize and load a RAM disk image.
(b) Perform timing tests.
(c) Parse for any boot time kernel arguments.
(d) Recognize, set-up and initialize the CPU.
(e) Set up kernel memory and process handling.
(f) Open a console for displaying kernel boot messages.
(g) Initialize configured system devices.
(h) Start memory handling (paging etc.)
(i) Set up and mount the file system.
(j) Start the init command.

The entire sequence of events that take place when the Linux kernel is loaded can be found in the file usr/src/linux/init/main.c.

☞ *If all goes well, you will see a "login" prompt. You can now login using your username and password.*

2.3 WINDOWS 7 OPERATING SYSTEM

There are various types of Windows. A type of Windows is referred to as a version. Windows 7 is the version of Windows desktop operating system for the PC. It is more advanced and robust operating system than any other operating system of MS Corporation.

2.3.1 Different Versions of Windows 7

MS Corporation of USA provides multiple versions of Windows 7 with a mixture of features and capabilities intended for different hardware platforms, personal preferences and business needs.

Versions of Windows 7 are discussed as follows:

- *Windows 7 Home Premium:* This edition is mostly used in new PCs. It includes entertainment features as its predecessor, Window Vista Home Premium.
- *Windows 7 Professional:* This edition is a superset of Home Premium and includes all features including Windows Media Center.
- *Windows 7 Ultimate / Enterprise:* These editions are identical. Ultimate is available on retails and Original Equipment Manufacturer (OEM) editions. But, Enterprise is distributed only to large-sized customers. This edition contains all features found in the Home Premium and Professional editions with some advance networking features, BitLocker encryption and support for multiple languages.

All of these editions are available in 32-bit and 64-bit options. Today Windows 7 64-bit is commonly installed on new computers, especially on systems with 4 GB or more RAM.

☞ *Windows 7 has a good antivirus program. You can download a free antivirus program called MS Security Essentials that works well with any editions of Windows 7.*

Features of Windows 7 Operating System

Windows 7 offers many new features over Windows XP. Some vital features of Windows 7 are as follows:

- *Libraries:* Libraries make it simple to pull documents, music, pictures, etc., from various places (folders) and have them shown up together. Note that while the files are displayed together, they are actually stored in their original folders, so the same file may be in multiple libraries.
- *Windows Aero:* 3D Graphical User Interface (GUI) with translucent "glass-like" window to view a thumbnail of programs when pointed on the taskbar.
- *Instant Search:* It is much faster and more diligent than other Windows OS. Search is integrated into every folder, making it simple to find a file from anywhere without having to use the Start Menu.
- *Windows Defender and Firewall:* Advanced anti-spyware and two-way firewall have been incorporated within the Windows 7 operating system to protect the OS, services, programs, Internet Explorer, and other parts of the computer from spyware.
- *Internet Explorer 8:* It is an improved Web browser, which is more secure and comes with a tabbed interface.
- *Windows Media Player 12:* Big work is done here with a new interface for the media library, photo display and organization, search-as-you-type capabilities, and music sharing.
- *Windows Live Mail:* A replacement for Outlook Express, this offers better stability, real time search, junk mail filtering and anti-phishing.
- *Ease of Access Center:* Ease of Access Center is same as Accessibility Options available in earlier versions of Windows. It now comes with several improvements and new features that you can use to get suggestions for accessibility features.
- *Taskbar Improvements:* Taskbar in Windows 7 makes it simple to rearrange icons on the taskbar and have them to stay where they are placed. It is also easy to review recent documents visited, Web sites, playlist, etc.
- *Jump Lists:* With Jump Lists, you can quickly find files that you have recently worked with. With this feature, you can right click the icon and select it from the list.
- *Parental Controls:* Parental Controls option makes it easy for parents to select games for their children to play. Parents can restrict specific game titles, control their children to play the games that are below a certain age level, or block games with certain types of content that they may not want their children to see or hear.
- *BitLocker Drive Encryption:* It encrypts the contents of the computer's system drive (C: drive) or any other internal hard disk or removable hard drive or (USB) flash drive to make it unreadable. Security can further be enhanced by requiring a USB key to be inserted with decryption key.
- *User Account Control:* It asks for permission whenever administrative tasks are requested to make sure that you asked for them, rather than a virus or spy-ware application. This is true even if you log on with a user name that has administrative rights. It can be customized to be as obtrusive or secure as desired.
- *Home Group:* Home group make it easier to setup a home network and share files, videos, photos, etc., with other using network. A wizard is used to set up the feature and a password is used by other computers wishing to join the group. Home groups are only accessible when the network location is set to "Home" and does not interfere with a domain that the computer may belong to at work.
- *Other Features:* Windows XP mode in Windows 7 provides the ability to run applications with compatibility issues with Windows 7 via a Virtual Machine (VM) running XP SP 3. Application installed in the VM appear in the Windows 7 Start Menu and runs like any other application. It is available as a free download from MS Web site. It requires AMD-V or Intel-VT enabled in the Basic Input Output System (BIOS).

  Battery life has been extended on laptops due to updated drivers, allowing more sleep features for devices and providing Adaptive Display Brightness, which automatically dims the display if the computer has not been used in a while.

  Touch screen support is available via Windows Touch if display supports it, allowing menu selections, scrolling media playing, etc., all possible without using a keyboard or mouse.

Windows Terminology

Windows terminology has very specific meaning. Various terms used are given below. Whenever indoubt, you should refer to the help for meaning of each term.

Choose: Executes a command.

Select: Selects an item to activate it so that it can be changed. Selecting a command or option turns it on but does not complete it. Selected *text* or *menu names/items* appear in reverse type or a different colour. Selected options show a dot (•) or an (×). Also the selected graphics appear enclosed by a dashed line or enclosed in boxes known as *handles.*

Point: Move the mouse so that the arrow pointer is on the desired *menu* name, *command* name, or *graphic* object.

Pointer: Pointer is the on its screen symbol controlled by the mouse. The pointer changes its shape to indicate the current status and the type of functions and selections available.

I-beam: When the mouse pointer is in a text area that you can edit, the pointer appears as a vertical I-beam.

Mouse Buttons: MS mouse has two buttons and other makes may have three. Clicking the *left* button completes an action and clicking the right most button changes to *shortcut* menu.

Using the Mouse

The *mouse* is a very convenient hand-held pointing device which is used to control the position of the on-screen pointer. As you move the mouse on your desk or mouse pad, the pointer moves on the screen corresponding to the mouse movement. Using the mouse, you can *select menus, commands, text, graphic objects,* or *window.*

☞ *You must make sure that the surface must be smooth and clean on which you move the mouse. You must avoid using the mouse on paper or cardboard surfaces.*

The main mouse actions are:

Click: Press and release the left mouse button quickly as you point to an item. Clicking is used to reposition the insertion point in text, select a menu, choose a command from a menu, or select an option from a dialog box.

Double-click: As you point to the pointed item on the screen, press and release the left mouse button twice quickly. By double-clicking an icon or file name, you can open an application or window related to that icon or file name.

Right click: Position the tip of the mouse pointer in the desired location on a document or toolbar and then click the right mouse button.

Shift *+click:* Press and hold down the Shift key as you click. You use this method to select many consecutive file names, or to select text between the current insertion point and the location where you press Shift+click keys together.

Ctrl *+click:* Press and hold down the Ctrl key as you click. This is used to select many nonconsecutive file names or item of choices.

Dragging: Dragging is moving objects on the monitor's screen. It is similar to moving objects on a desk. For example, clicking and dragging an icon is like physically picking up a pencil with your hand on a desk and putting the pencil in a new location. Similarly, to move object on your monitor's screen, you first position the mouse pointer on the object. Next, you "pick up" the object by pressing and holding down the *left* mouse button. While you are still holding down the mouse button, move the mouse pointer to where you want to "drop" the object, and then release the mouse button.

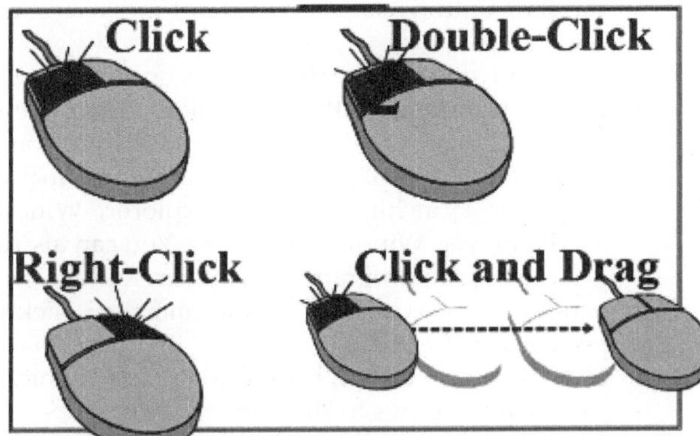

➡ **To select an object or menu item using the mouse:**

1. Move the mouse so that the tip of the pointer on the screen is on the *command, graphic object,* or *text* that you want to select.
2. Now without moving the mouse, press and release the left mouse button quickly.

➡ **To *drag* with the mouse:**

1. Move the mouse so that the tip of the pointer is on the object or at the beginning of the text to be selected. (Note that over text, the pointer appears as an I-beam).
2. Press and hold down the mouse left button.
3. Holding down the mouse button, move the mouse slowly to the right or left and up or down. This is called *dragging* (See Figure 2.6). Notice that while dragging a graphic, the object moves as you move the mouse. However, when you are selecting text, the highlighted text area expands as you move the mouse.
4. Release the mouse button.

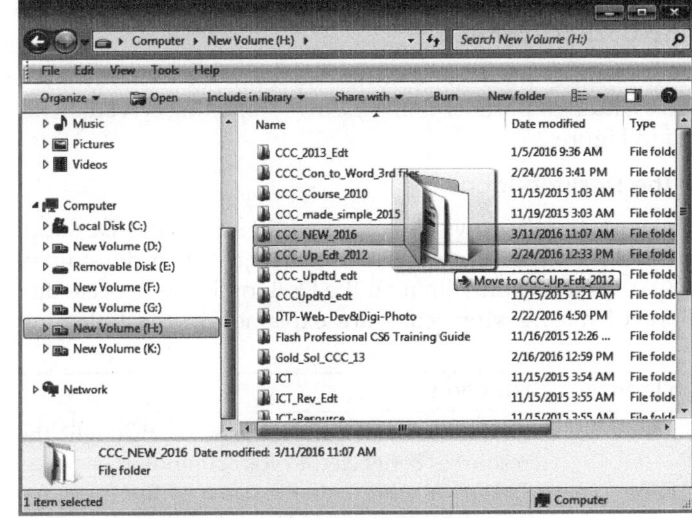

Figure 2.6 Moving an Icon by dragging

Using Right Button of the Mouse

Using the right mouse button you can perform several actions on the document. These are:

- Selecting documents by clicking them to highlight them.
- Copying selected files to a disk.
- Cut or copy selected text to the Clipboard.
- Deleting documents.
- Renaming documents.

Right-clicking a folder's name will produces a menu. It will enable you to perform all these actions.

Right-Clicking to Copy and Move Documents

A file icon's right-click menu allows advanced copying and moving of files. Use the Windows Clipboard to do all Windows copy, cut, paste and move operations.

☞ *Copying means to make a copy of the selected file or folder and insert it in another location, leaving the original file unchanged.*

➡ **To copy file from one location to another, do this:**

1. First, select the file that you want to copy.
2. Click the **Edit** menu and choose **Copy**. Or Right-click the button, the pop-up menu appears. Now select Copy. The selected file will be placed on the Clipboard.
3. Now place the location where you want to position the file.
4. Click the **Edit** menu and choose **Paste**. Or Right-click the button. The pop-up menu appears. Select Paste.

If you move a file from one location to another, Windows 7 performs a cut operation. That is it deletes the file from its current location and sends the file to the Clipboard. As you find the location to which you want to move the file, Windows copies it to the new location (such as different disk drive).

➡ **To move file from one location to another, do this:**

1. Select the file which you want to move.
2. Click the **Edit** menu. Choose **Cut**. Alternately, Right-click the button, the pop-up menu appears. Now, choose Cut. The selected file will disappear from the window and it will be placed on the Clipboard.
3. Now position the location where you want o place the file.
4. Click the **Edit** menu. Choose **Paste**.

2.4 The USER INTERFACE

Windows 7 user interface is different from the Windows XP interface. Different parts of the Windows 7 opening screen are as marked in Figure 2.7.

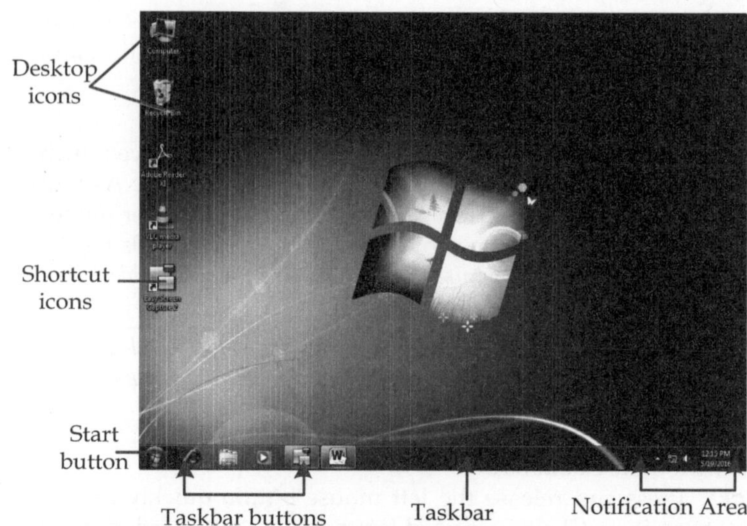

Figure 2.7 Different parts of the Windows 7 screen

2.4.1 The Desktop Icons

As you work in Windows 7, you move items on the Desktop, retrieve and put away items and perform many other day-to-day tasks. By default, the only item on the Desktop is the Recycle Bin. Functions of the Desktop icons are explained in the following Table.

System Icon	Function
Computer	This icon lets you to browse through the resources connected to your computer.
User's Files	This icon represents the name of the (personal user who logs on to the computer). Its folder contents are unique for every user on the computer. This folder contains files that belong to the user.
Recycle Bin	This icon provides temporary storage for files and folders that you want to delete.
Network	This icon opens a Window displaying the names of each server or computer in your own work group.
Control Panel	This icon opens a window containing system configuration and management tools.

Computer Icon

Computer is the gateway to resources stored on your own system. Computer icon on desktop allows you to browse through all the resources attached to your PC. When you click on Computer icon, a window appears as shown in Figure 2.8. The computer's information is divided into three parts:

(a) *Hard Disk Drives:* Display the hard disk drives of the computer.

(b) *Devices with Removable Storage:* Display floppy disk, CD-ROM, Zip drive, etc.

(c) *Network Location:* In the left pane of the Computer window, it displays the location of any disk drive or folder which is connected to the computer.

Rest of the features, such as shortcut icons and Recycle Bin will be explained later.

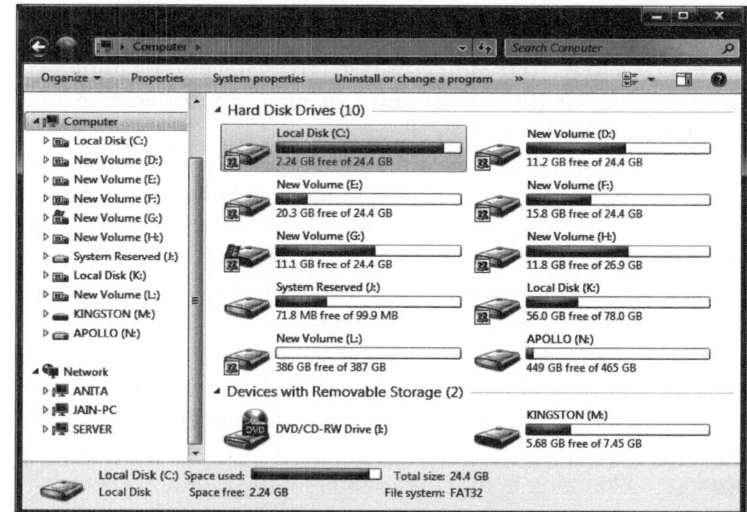

Figure 2.8 Computer window

2.4.2 The Taskbar

Taskbar is the horizontal bar at the bottom of the screen (See Figure 2.7).

Taskbar Elements	Function
Start button	It is located at the left end of the taskbar. Clicking the start button brings up the Start menu as seen in Figure 2.9.
Taskbar Icons	Taskbar Icons represents a set of icons. It lets you to launch programs with single click. When clicked, these buttons or icons activate certain functions or tasks. For example, the Taskbar Icons includes icons for launching Internet Explorer, Windows Media Player, Windows Explorer. You can also add your favourite programs in Taskbar. Right click the program that you want to add and then click this program to Taskbar.
Show Desktop button	Show Desktop button is used to temporary hide all the open windows to show the desktop.

(Contd...)

Taskbar Elements	Function
Task buttons	Task buttons are displayed in the center portion of the Taskbar. A button appears for each program you have started or each document you have opened. You can click these buttons to move from one open Program or Folder to another (See Figure 2.7).
Notification area	The right corner of the Taskbar has the notification area in which Windows provides information about the status of your system. It displays the time and also contains shortcuts that provide quick access to programs, such as Volume Control. Other shortcuts can appear temporarily. For example, the printer icon appears after a document has been sent to the printer and disappears when printing is complete.

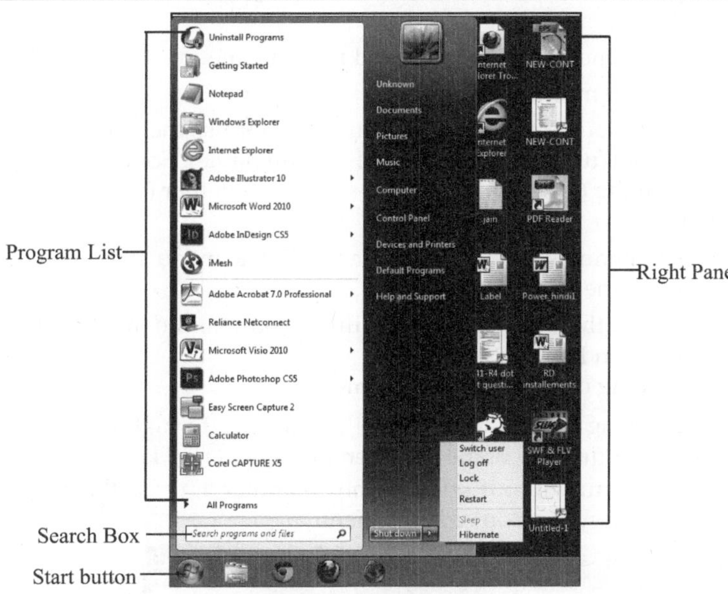

Figure 2.9 Start menu

2.4.3 Icons on the Screen

Windows place icons in columns on the left side of the desktop. But if you do not place with that arrangement, simply you can move an icon by dragging it to a new place on the desktop.

You can also have Windows automatically arrange your icons. Right-click an empty area on the desktop, click **View**, and then click **Auto arrange icons**. Windows place icons in the upper-left corner and locks them in place. To unlock the icons so that you can move them again, click Auto arrange icons again, clearing the check mark next to it.

2.4.4 Start Menu in Windows 7

Start menu appears when you click on the Start button on the Taskbar as seen in Figure 2.9. The Start menu provides you with more customization options. It shows you who is logged on. It automatically adds the most frequently used programs to the top-level menu. It enables you to move any programs which you want to be in the Start menu. Start menu is divided into three basic parts. These are:

(a) Program List
(b) Search Box
(c) Right Pane

Program List (Left Pane)

Left pane of the start menu shows recently used programs and those programs that have been pinned to Start menu. Program list shows up to eight recently used programs. If you want to see the complete list of programs installed in your computer, then click on the All Programs (Figure 2.9).

Search Box (Lower Left Pane)

Lower left pane of the Start menu is the search box which allows computer to search files, folders, programs or computer that are connected to your computer (Figure 2.9). To search any files or folder, type the name of the file or folder in search box and then press Enter key. To clear the search result, click on the Clear button [X].

Right Pane

Right Pane of the start menu gives access to commonly used folders. These are shown in Figure 2.9 which are discussed below.

Current User–It opens the folder of the user who is currently logged on to Windows. This folder contains files such as Documents, Pictures, etc.

Documents–It opens the Document Folder where you can store files.

Pictures–It opens the Picture Folder where you can store pictures and graphic files.

Music–It opens the Music Folder where you store and play the music files.

Games–It opens the Game Folder from where you can access the games which are installed in your computer.

Computer–It opens a computer from where you can access hard disk drives, printers, scanner, CD Drive and other hardware connected to your computer.

Control Panel–It opens window that allows you to install software and change different setting of Windows such as Date, Time, Keyboard, Mouse, Password, Display, Sound settings, etc.

Devices and Printers–It opens a window where you can see information about the printer, mouse, and other devices installed on your computer.

Default Programs–Opens a window where you can choose which program you want Windows to use for activities such as web browsing.

Help and Support–It displays help which is a set of screens of information about Windows itself where you can browse and search Help topics about using Windows and your computer.

At the bottom of the right pane is the Shut down button. Click the Shut down button to turn off your computer. Clicking the arrow next to the Shut down button displays a menu with additional options for switching users, logging off, restarting, or shutting down as seen in Figure 2.8.

Elements of a Window

When you start a program, it appears on the Windows 7 desktop. You work with a program by manipulating the various elements of its window. These elements of a program window are shown in Figure 2.10.

Borders The four edges that define the perimeter of a window are known as borders. Borders also give a way to change the size of the window.

Title Bar Just below the top border of the window is the Title bar. It displays the name of the program or the document. It is also used for moving the window.

System Menu Icon System menu icon is the small icon located on the left side of the Title bar. The System menu icon performs two functions (See Figure 2.10). These are:

- It opens the menu whenever you click this icon. In most of the programs, the command on a System menu lets you control the size of the window. But some programs may have special items on their menus.
- System menu icon for a program or document will close the window that terminates the program or closes the document when you double-click it.

Close Button At the right edge of the Title bar is a square containing an × called the Close button. Clicking the Close button closes a *document* or folder, or terminates a program (See Figure 2.10).

Minimize, Maximize and Restore Buttons The three small buttons at the right end of the Title bar as shown in Figure 2.10 with small graphics are *Minimize* button, *Maximize* or *Restore* button, and the *Close* buttons. These are control buttons with which you can quickly change the size of a window or close it.

- Clicking the *minimize* button reduces the window to a button on the Task bar. Once *minimized*, the window no longer takes space on the desktop but the program in it continues to run.
- Clicking the *maximize* button enlarges the window to occupy the whole desktop. When the window is *maximized*, the *minimizes* and *restore* buttons appear.

Scroll Bars, Scroll Boxes and Scroll Buttons If a window is not long enough to display its contents completely, you can scroll the *vertical scroll bar* which appears along the right edge. Similarly, if the window is not wide enough, a *horizontal scroll bar* appears along the bottom of the window.

☞ *Scroll bars offer an easy way to navigate through a window with the mouse. They also provide useful information about the contents of the window.*

Scroll bars have small rectangular boxes called scroll box (See Figure 2.10). The position of this box within the scroll bar tells you where you are within the window itself. If the scroll box is at the top of the scroll bar, it means you are at the top of the document.

Scroll buttons appear along the top and bottom edges of the vertical scroll bar, and along the left and right edges of the horizontal scroll bar.

Using Menu Bar

The row of words just below the Title bar constitute the *Menu bar* (See Figure 2.10). *Menu bar* appears only in an application window and not in a document window. Each word on the Menu bar represents a menu which opens up when you click it (See Figure 2.11). The names of the menus may vary from program to program but they have some common headings, such as File, Edit, Window and Help.

☞ *In Windows 7, Menu bar is hidden by default, such as in Control Panel. To display the menu bar, you have to press Alt key. Menu bar is displayed above the toolbar. If you want to permanently display the Menu bar, Select Layout from the Organize tab of that window and then select Menu bar. Menu bar appears on the screen.*

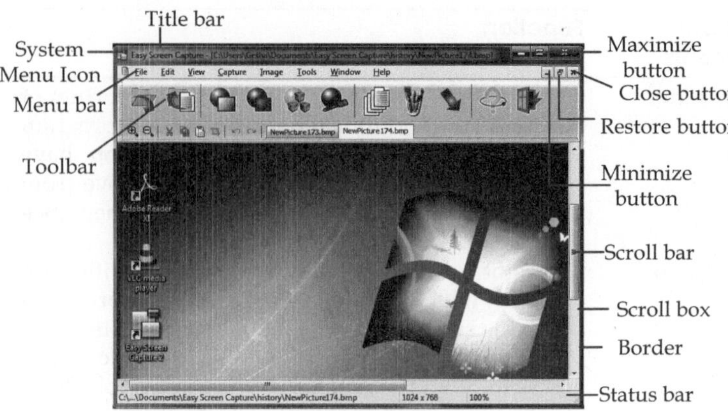

Figure 2.10 Elements of a program window

Using Menu Selection

By using menu selection involves two steps:

- Click to open it.
- Selecting the required command from the menu.

➡ **To open a menu:**

1. Use the mouse click on the menu name. Or use the keyboard, press Alt+(underlined letter in the menu name). For example, to open the Edit menu press Alt+E keys together (See Figure 2.11).

After a menu is opened, you can select a menu command either one of the following ways:

- By typing the underlined letter in the command name (e.g. P for Paste in Figure 2.11). Or
- By clicking on a command's name.
- By pressing the ↓ arrow or ↑ arrow keys to highlight the desired command name and then pressing Enter key.

To close a menu without selecting any command, press the Esc key or click anywhere outside the menu.

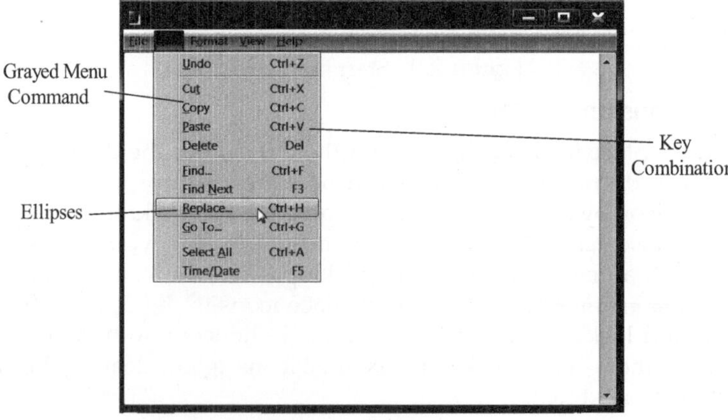

Figure 2.11 Edit menu open

Special Indicators in Menus

When you open a menu you would notice that many of the commands have additional words or symbols next to the command name (See Figure 2.12).

These additional words or symbols next to the command name indicate the following:

Grayed (Dimmed) Command Name When a command is displayed as grayed, or dimmed as shown in Figure 2.11, it means that this choice is not currently available for selection. A command can be dimmed for many reasons. For example, if a window is already Maximized, the Maximize command on the System menu will be dimmed because this choice does not make sense.

Ellipses(...) Ellipses as shown in Figure 2.11 next to a command means that you will be asked for additional information before it is executed on selecting such command. A dialog box appears on the screen, asking you to provide additional information.

Check Mark (✔) A check mark preceding a command as shown in Figure 2.12 means the command is a toggle that is activated (turned on). A toggle is a command that is alternately turned *Off* and *On* each time you select it. Each time you select one of these commands, it switches from *On* to *Off* or *Off* to *On*. If there is no check mark, then the command or setting is *Off*.

Figure 2.12 Special Indicators in Menu

Triangle A triangle to the right of a menu command as shown in Figure 2.12 means that the command has additional choices to choose from. This is also called a *cascading menu*. You can make selections from a cascaded menu in the same way as you would select from a normal menu.

A Key Combination Some menu commands list keystrokes that can be used for opening the menu and choosing that command (See Figure 2.11). These are also called *shortcut keys*.

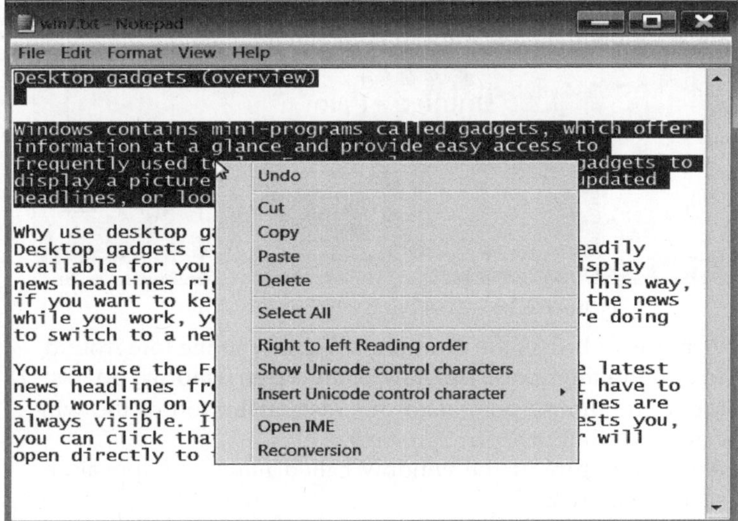

Figure 2.13 Shortcut/Popup menu

Shortcut Menus

Pressing the right mouse button brings up a small menu related to the currently selected object or the one the mouse is pointing to. This menu is also referred to as *popup* menu. For example, if you right click the Taskbar, you will get a menu of commands related only to the Taskbar (See Figure 2.13).

Dialog Boxes

A dialog box as shown in Figure 2.14 is a special type of window that asks you a question, allows you to select options to perform a task, or provides information. A dialog box will appear when you select a command with ellipsis(...) after it. Dialog boxes appear when Windows or its application program needs more information to execute the command. The various dialog box elements are as follows:

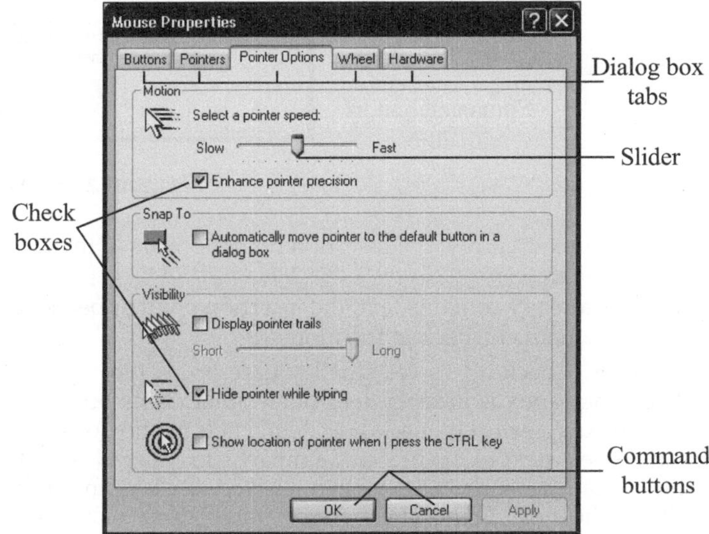

Figure 2.14 Dialog box Tabs

Dialog Box Tabs

Some of the dialog boxes have multiple option pages (See Figure 2.14). You need to select the page of your choice by clicking its icon at the top of the dialog box. Using the keyboard, press Ctrl+tab to flip through the option pages.

Moving between Dialog Box Elements

Dialog boxes often have several sections in them as seen in Figure 2.14. You can move between the sections in two ways:

- By clicking on the section that you want to change.
- Using the keyboard, you can press the Tab key to move between sections and press the Spacebar to select them.

Entering Information in a Dialog Box

The dialog boxes have following eight different types of sections where you need to enter information (See Figures 2.14 and 2.15).

- Text boxes
- Check boxes
- Option buttons
- Command buttons
- List boxes
- Sliders
- Spinners

Text Boxes Text box is also called an *Edit box* and it is where you type in the information (See Figure 2.15). To enter information on the text box, click the text box. The insertion point appears in the text box. The insertion point indicates the place where the character you type will appear.

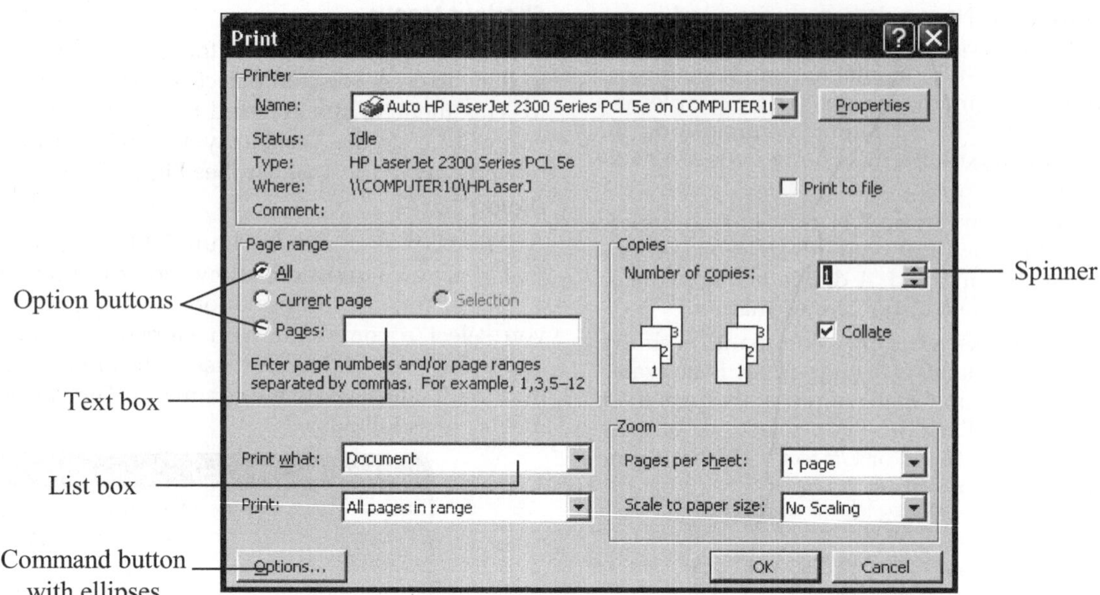

Figure 2.15 Dialog box elements

- If the text box is empty, the insertion point appears at the left side of the box.
- If the box already contains text, the insertion point appears at the point where you clicked the mouse.

Check Boxes Check boxes are small square boxes (See Figure 2.14). Each check box is independent of all other check boxes in the dialog box. To select a check box item, click the box or anywhere in the text next to the box and similarly, to deselect repeat the same procedure. A check box when selected displays an (×) or (✔) within the box. Some check boxes have three states — *checked, unchecked*, and *partly checked*. A gray (in place of a black) check mark means that certain condition applies to it and some of the selections do not apply.

Option Buttons Option buttons are also called *radio buttons* and present a set of mutually exclusive options (See Figure 2.15). Option buttons are always presented in groups of two or more and may either be round or diamond shaped. You may select any one option from the group, but not more than one. To select the option click the button or any where in the text next to the button.

Command Buttons Command buttons are like option buttons and are used to execute a command immediately. They are rectangular and not square or circular in shape. An example of a command button is the OK button which is found on almost every dialog box (See Figure 2.14).

Drop-Down List Boxes A Drop-down List box presents a list of options or items from which you can select. To make a selection from a list box, using the mouse, click on it or using the keyboard highlight the desired option and then press Enter to choose it (See Figure 2.15).

Sliders A slider works like a sliding control. Moving it in one direction increases some value, moving it in the other direction decreases the same value (See Figure 2.14).

Spinners A spinner is a pair of arrows used to increase or decrease the value in a text box (See Figure 2.15). To increase the value in the text box, click up arrow and to decrease the value click down arrow.

2.4.5 Running An Application

You may have different Application windows open at the same time. In such a case, the window on the top is called the *active window* i.e., window in which you are working and it is also called the foreground window. Active window's title bar is normally displayed in one colour, while the title bars of all inactive windows are displayed in another colour. In addition, Taskbar button for the active window appears to be pressed in the taskbar.

➡ **To change the active window, use any one of the following methods:**

1. Click the *Taskbar* button for the window you want to switch to. Or
2. Press and hold the Alt key. Then press Tab key to bring up the *Taskbar Switcher window* (See Figure 2.16).
3. The *Task Switcher window* displays an icon for each running program and draws a box around the icon of the active window. Continue holding Alt key and pressing Tab key until the window that you want to keep active.

Figure 2.16 Taskbar Switcher window

4. Windows 7 brings the program's window to the foreground.

➡ **To see the thumbnail preview of the open window, do this:**

1. Move the mouse pointer to the Taskbar button of the window you want to see the preview.
2. A small picture of the window called *thumbnail* appears as seen in Figure 2.17.

Figure 2.17 Thumbnail preview of window

➡ **To see the Windows Aero 3D Flip view of the open windows, do this:**

1. Press the *Windows logo* key + Tab key to open Aero Flip 3D (See Figure 2.18).

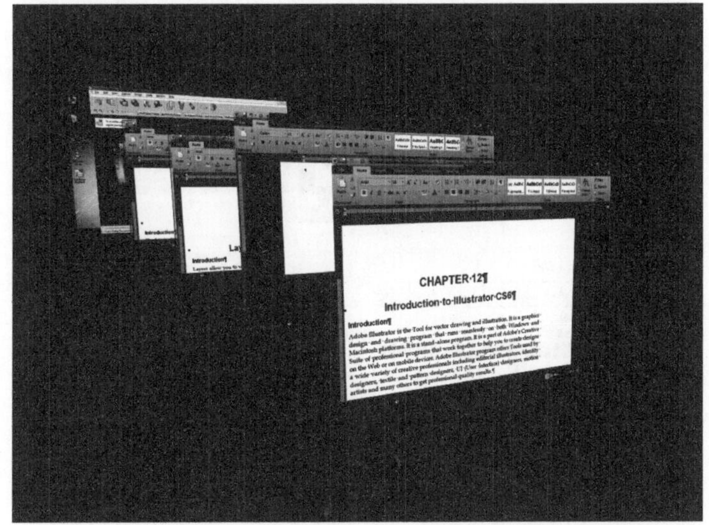

Figure 2.18 Aero 3D Flip view of the open windows

2. While holding down the *Windows logo* key, press Tab key repeatedly or rotate the mouse wheel to cycle through open windows.

☞ *Aero Flip 3D and thumbnail preview would not work in the computer unless your computer is running Windows Aero.*

2.5 OPERATING SYSTEM SIMPLE SETTING

Most of the changes you will make take place using the Widows **Control Panel**, which is a special folder that contains many small programs called *applets*. Each applet is designed to let you adjust setting for a particular part of your system.

To use Windows 7 effectively, you have to configure or reshape Windows and the other programs that you run to work with your computer's hardware. You do this using the following features:

Feature	Function
Properties	These are the settings for many different objects in your computer's hardware and software.
Control Panel	This lets you to see and change many properties and other settings.

2.5.1 Changing System Date and Time

You can change your computer's date and Time by double-clicking your notification area's clock.

➡ **To change the Date and Time, do this:**

1. Double-click the notification area's clock. The Date and Time Properties dialog box appears as shown in Figure 2.19.

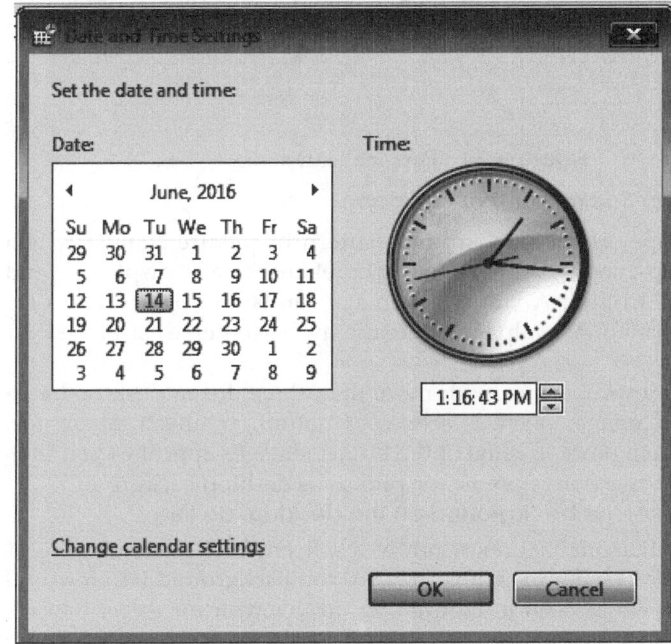

Figure 2.19 Shortcut Menu to change the property of an object

2. To change the month, click the arrow in the month list, and then click the correct month.
3. To change the year, click the arrows in the year list.
4. To change the day, click the correct day on the calender.

2.5.2 Changing Display Properties

The settings which are related with computer or desktop is the display properties. The display properties include wallpaper, screen saver, colour, font, etc. The display properties can be set through Display Properties dialog box.

The Personalization window is one of the most powerful and useful features of Windows 7. The settings which are related with computer or desktop is the personalize properties. These properties include desktop background, screen saver, colour, font etc. Personalize properties can be set through Personalization window.

➡ **To show the Personalization window, do this:**

Click on the **Start** button then click on **Control Panel**. In Control Panel window, double click on Personalization icon to open it. *Alternatively*, right click at an empty space on the desktop and then choose **Personalize**. This will show the Personalization window on the screen as shown in Figure 2.20.

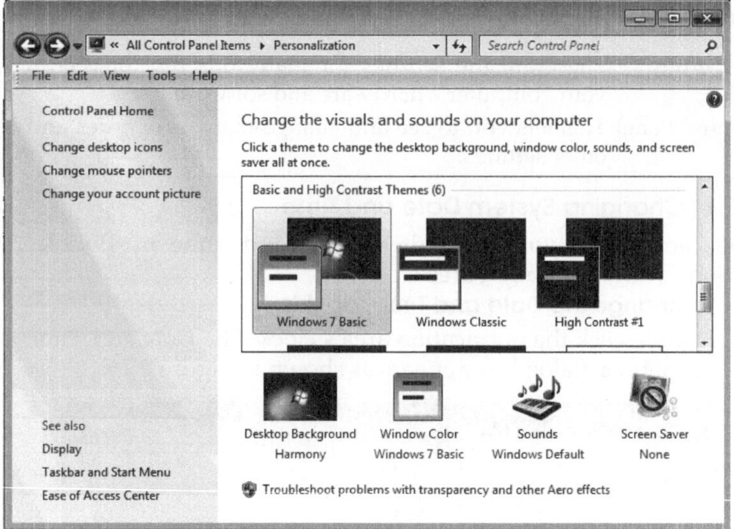

Figure 2.20 Personalization dialog box

Desktop Background or Wallpaper

Wallpaper is the background pattern or picture against which desktop menus, icons and other elements are displayed and moved around. A wallpaper image can be in `jpeg` format or a `gif` format. A wallpaper image may be centered, stretched, or tiled.

Windows 7 comes with more than three dozen desktop background images such as scenes of nature, architectural photos, and much more. If none of the built-in images appeal to you then you can use one of your own photos as desktop background.

➡ **To set the background on the desktop, do this:**

1. In Personalization window, click on **Desktop Background** link (See Figure 2.20). The Desktop Background window will appear as seen in Figure 2.21. In this window select the picture or any solid colour from the Picture Location drop down list box which you want to use.

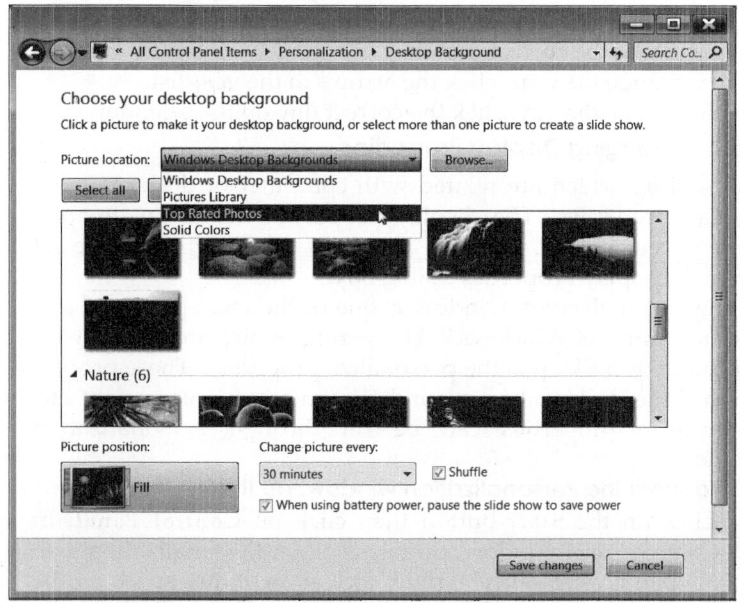

Figure 2.21 Setting the wallpaper in Desktop

2. Click on the Browse... button if you want to use your own image from the different drives.
3. Select the position of the wallpaper from the Picture position drop-down list.
4. Then click Save changes to accept the changes and close the window.
5. The picture or colour you select will be applied as desktop background.

Screen Saver

Screen saver is an animated image that is activated on the PC monitor when user walks away from the computer and leaves the monitor on. The main purpose of the screen saver is to prevent the burning of an image into the phosphorus material inside the monitor.

➡ **To set the screen saver, do this:**

1. In Personalization window, click on select Screen Saver link (Figure 2.20). The Screen Saver Settings dialog box appears as shown in Figure 2.22.
2. Select the desired screen saver from the drop down list from the Screen Saver section.
3. Click the drop-down list and choose the desired Screen Saver option. You can also set the time in Wait: section under the Screen Saver section.

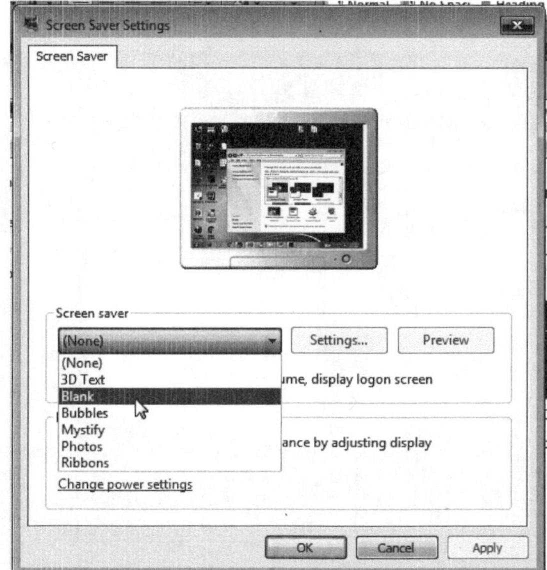

Figure 2.22 Screen Saver Settings dialog box

4. To see the preview of the selected screen saver click on the Preview button.
5. Click the On resume, display logon screen check to ensure that anyone who interrupts the screen saver can see your work only if he/she know your password.
6. To apply all the settings, click on the Apply button and then click on the OK button to close the dialog box.

☞ *In Windows 7, you can also use personal pictures as a screen saver. For this, you have to select Photos from Screen saver group.*

Working with Desktop Gadgets

Windows 7 contains mini-programs called Desktop gadgets. It keeps information and tools readily available for you to use. Gadgets are used to display a picture slide show, view continuously updated headlines, or look up contacts. For example, you can use the Headline gadgets to show the latest news headlines.

You do not have to stop working on your document, because the headlines are always visible. If you see a headline that interests you, you can click that headline, and your web browser will open that headline.

Adding Gadgets

By default, gadgets are not displayed on the desktop. But, you can easily add or remove gadgets whenever you feel the need for something new on your computer screen. The gadget gallery that comes with Windows 7 includes about a dozen offerings but has a handy link to a much larger online gallery.

➡ **To add a gadget on the desktop, do this:**

1. Right click an empty area on the desktop and then choose Gadgets.
2. The Windows Gadgets Gallery window opens, displaying various gadgets as shown in Figure 2.23.

Figure 2.23 Windows gadgets gallery dialog box

3. Double-click the selected gadget that you want to add to the Desktop or right click the gadget and then click Add button.
4. The Clock gadget appears on the desktop as shown in Figure 2.24.
5. After adding the gadgets, you can close the Windows Gadgets Gallery window by clicking the Close button.

Figure 2.24 Adding gadgets on the desktop

2.5.3 To Add or Remove a Windows Component

In Windows 7, you can install and uninstall programs, you can add or remove parts of Windows 7 to suit your needs. For example, if you only want to use iTunes for you media files, you can remove the Media Player.

To see what parts of itself Windows 7 has left off your computer or to remove unwanted components that Windows 7 has installed, follow these steps:

➡ **To add or remove Windows Component, do this:**

1. Click the **Start** button and then choose **Control Panel**, and click **Programs** icon.
2. In the **Programs and Features** area, choose **Turn Windows Features On or Off** as shown in Figure 2.25.

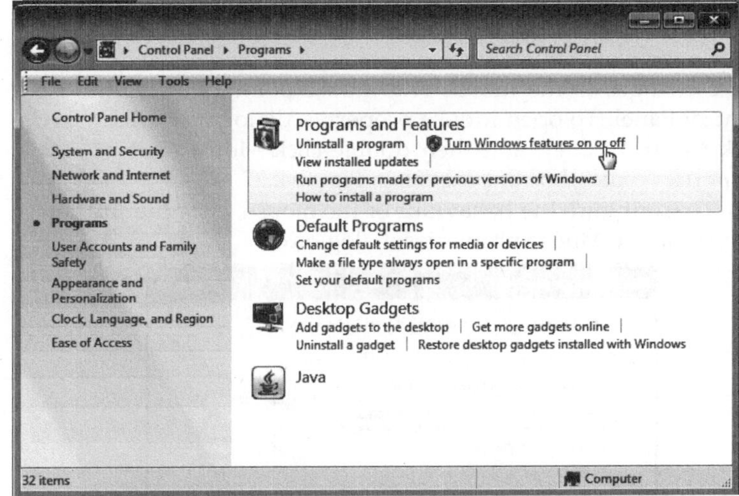

Figure 2.25 Selecting Windows Features on or off

Windows brings up a window listing all its features. The features with check marks by their names are already installed. If you see a box that's filled – neither empty nor checked – double-click to see what's installed and what's left out.

4. **Windows Features** dialog box appears as shown in Figure 2.26.
5. To add a component, click in its empty check box. To remove an installed component like Windows' Games, deselect its check box.

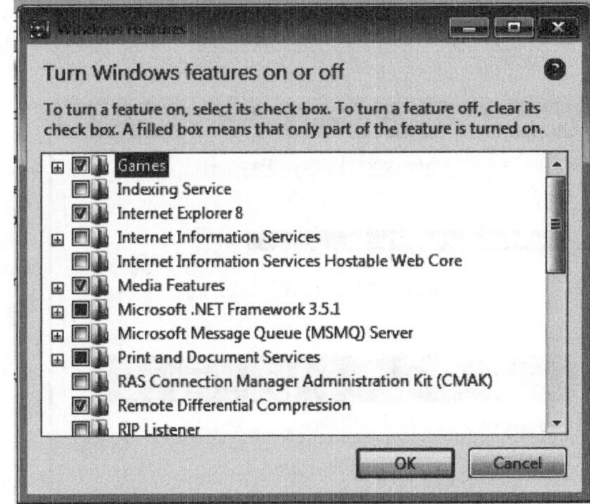

Figure 2.26 Windows Features dialog box

6. Click the OK button.
7. Windows 7 adds or removes the program.

2.5.4 Changing Mouse Properties

Use the mouse to interact with items on your screen as you would use your hands to interact with the objects.

While your mouse should just work when you start up your computer, you can make some changes to its functionality and to the look and behavior of your mouse pointer on the screen. For example, you can switch the role of the buttons on your mouse, or adjust the speed of double-clicking. For the mouse pointer, you can change its appearance, improve its visibility, or set it to be hidden when you are typing.

Button Tab of the Mouse

Make changes to the mouse and mouse pointers in the Mouse Control Panel. To open Mouse properties dialog box, click **Start**, click **Control Panel**, and then double-click Mouse. The **Mouse Properties** dialog box appears as in Figure 2.27.

1. To Configure the behaviour of the mouse, click the **Buttons** tab in the Mouse properties dialog box.

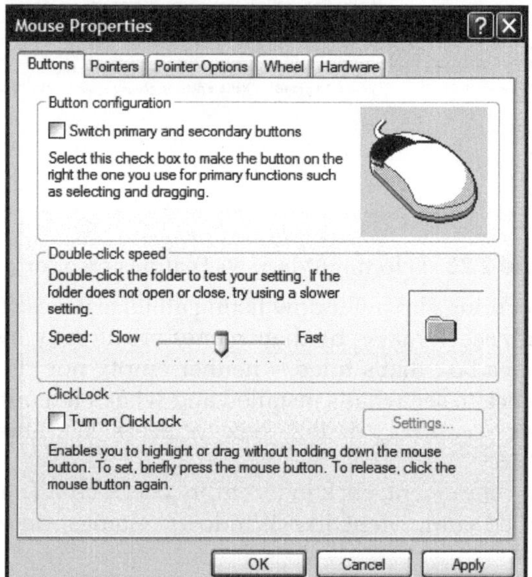

Figure 2.27 Mouse Properties dialog box of Button tab

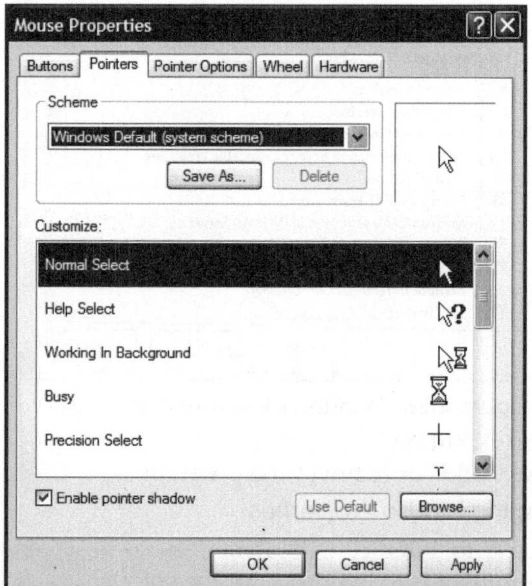

Figure 2.28 Mouse Properties dialog box of Pointers tab

Pointers tab of the Mouse

2. To Configure the behaviour of the mouse, click the **Pointers** tab in the Mouse properties dialog box (See Figure 2.28).

   To change the appearance of your mouse pointer, select **pointers** tab and do one of the following options.

   - To change all of your pointers at one time, select a new scheme, under Schema.
   - To change a particular pointer, select it in the **Customize** list. Click **Browse...** button. A list of selected cursor files appear. Select the name of the new pointer file you want to use for that task.

Pointer Options Tab of the Mouse

3. To Configure the behaviour of the mouse. Click the **Pointer Options** tab in the Mouse properties dialog box (See Figure 2.29).

   In the Motion section area, drag the slider to adjust the speed of your mouse. It causes the pointer to respond more quickly or slowly to the movements of the mouse. Or

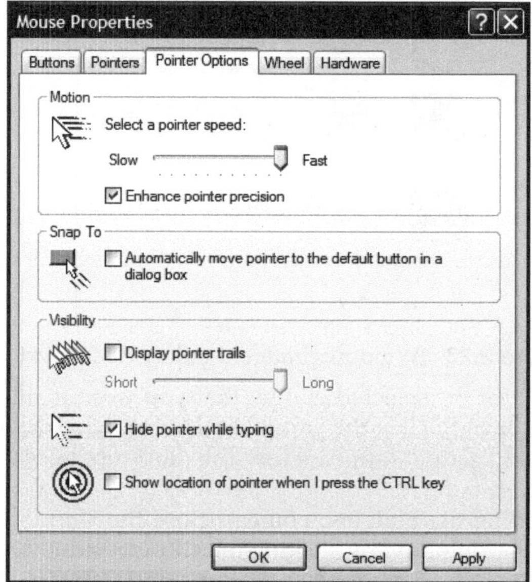

Figure 2.29 Mouse Properties dialog box of Pointers Options tab

Select the *Enhance pointer precision* check box to provide finer control of your pointer at short distances without closing the ability to move the point quickly across the screen. Clear the check box to turn off this feature.

In the Snap To section area, you can get the mouse snap to default buttons (such as OK or Apply) in dialog boxes by selecting **Automatically move pointer to the default button in a dialog box** under Snap To.

In the Visibility Section Area

- If you select the *Display pointer trails* check box, you can adjust the length of the pointer trail by moving the slider below the check box.
- To make the pointer invisible while typing, select the *Hide pointer while typing* check box. The pointer disappears when you are typing and reappears when you move the mouse.
- Select the *Show location of pointer when I press the* Ctrl *key* check box to find the pointer more easily when it is not in motion.

Wheel Option Tab of the Mouse

- To Configure the behaviour of the mouse, click the **Wheel** tab in the Mouse properties dialog box (See Figure 2.30).

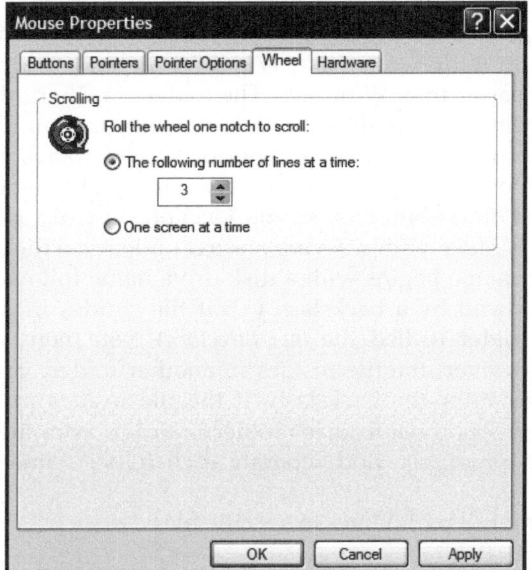

Figure 2.30 Mouse Properties dialog box of Wheel tab

In the Scrolling Section Area

- Select the number of lines to scroll with each notch on the wheel.
- Or click scroll one screen at a time. It means (scrolling one screen at a time is equivalent to using the page up or page down keys on your keyboard).
- If your mouse does not have a mouse wheel, the wheel tab may not appear.

Managing Documents with Right Mouse Button

Using the right mouse button you can perform several actions on the document. These are:

- Selecting documents by clicking them to highlight them.
- Copying selected files to a disk.
- Cutting or copying selected text to the Clipboard.
- Deleting documents.
- Renaming documents.

On right-clicking a folder's name it will produces a menu, which enable you to perform all these actions.

2.5.5 Adding and Removing Printers

Windows 7 provides Add a printer to simplify installing printers. The Printers folder for running the wizard and for managing printing processes. You can open the Printers folder in the following ways.

➡ **To add a printer, do this:**

1. Click **Start** menu and choose **Control Panel** or click **Devices and Printers**.
2. Click **Add a printer** from the **Devices and Printers** dialog box.
3. Select the option that describes the printer you want to use.
   - Click Local printer
   - A network printer, wireless or Bluetooth printer.
4. Select the port you want your printer to use.
   - create a new port or
   - click Local port and then click next.
5. Follow the instructions on the screen to finish adding a printer with the Add printer wizard.

☞ *The only difference between installing a network printer and a local printer with the Add Printer Wizard is that you must specify the path to the network printer or browser to find its network location.*

➡ **To remove a printer, do this:**

1. If you will not longer be using a printer, you can remove it from the Devices and Printers folder.
2. Click to open Devices and printers.
3. Rigth-click the printer that you want to remove, click Remove device, and then click yes.

☞ *If you can not delete the printer, right-click it again, click Run as administrator, click Remove device, and then click Yes.*

2.6 FILE AND DIRECTORY MANAGEMENT

The main function of computer is to manage data and information. The stored data and information on your computer, can be considered as file. File includes text, photos, and video. Each type of file has its specific icon, that makes you understand the type of file.

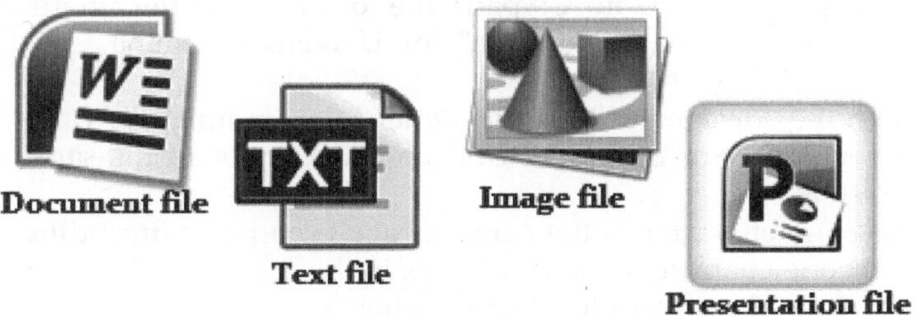

Types of Files

Everything on your computer is made up of files on your hard disk. Windows itself is just thousands of different files that interact with one another. The applications you use from day to day are also collections of many files that interact with one another and with Windows files. All the documents you create are themselves files that are loaded by the applications you use to create them. For example, when you save a document in MS Word, that document is saved as file on your disk.

What is a File?

A collection of data or information that has a name, called the filename. Almost all information stored in a computer must be in a file. There are many different types of files: data files, text files, program files, directory files, and so on. Different types of files store different types of information. For example, program files store programs, whereas text files store text.

In any computer system, especially in personal computers, a file is an entity of data available to system users (including the system itself and its application programs) that is capable of being manipulated as an entity (for example, moving file from one file directory to another). The file must have a unique name within its own directory. Some operating systems and applications describe files with given formats by giving them a particular file name suffix. (The file name suffix is also known as a file name extension.) For example, a program or executable file is sometimes given or required to have an ".exe" suffix.

Naming Conventions

A number of TSD (time sequence data) naming conventions are in use today. These formats are organized in three classes. The classes are called associated, coded, and sequenced. The filename extension defines the type of data storage format. For example, the extensions "HDR", "CFG", "DAT", and "INF" are used to indicate that the file contents are compatible with the IEEE COMTRADE standard. The non-extension part of an associated filename or the name is left at the discretion of the user and could be assigned in a coded or sequenced way.

The following fundamental rules enable applications to create and process valid names for files and directories, regardless of the file system:

- Use a period to separate the base file name from the extension in the name of a directory or file.
- Use a backslash (\) to separate the components of a path. The backslash divides the file name from the path to it, and one directory name from another directory name in a path. You cannot use a backslash in the name for the actual file or directory because it is a reserved character that separates the names into components.
- Use a backslash as required as part of volume names, for example, the "C:\" in "C:\path\file" or the "\\server\share" in "\\server\share\path\file" for Universal Naming Convention (UNC) names.
- Volume designators (drive letters) are similarly case-insensitive. For example, "D:\" and "d:\" refer to the same volume.
- Use any character in the current page for a name, including Unicode characters and characters in the extended character set (128–255), except for the following:

  The following reserved characters:
  - < (less than)
  - > (greater than)
  - : (colon)
  - " (double quote)
  - / (forward slash)
  - \ (backslash)
  - | (vertical bar or pipe)
  - ? (question mark)
- Integer value zero, sometimes referred to as the ASCII NUL character.
- Any other character that the target file system does not allow.

File Extensions

A file extension (or simply "extension") is the suffix at the end of a filename that indicates what type of file it is. For example, in the filename "BPB.docx," the .docx is the file extension. It indicates the file is a document. Some other examples include .txt, which is used for Notepad files, notepad and .PSD, which is the standard file extension for Photoshop documents.

By having file extensions you can quickly identify the type of file and have a better idea of how that file may be opened.

Directory Management

A *pathname* gives the exact computer system location of a file. The document and folder concept in Windows makes working with paths much easier than Windows. The folders in Windows used to be called *directories*. A directory is just a collection of files and other directories. In file listings, Windows OS displays a folder icon with a name to represent a directory that holds other files. Folders can hold subfolders, so the location of a file, the file's path, might be deep within several nested folder on a disk drive.

A full pathname begins with a disk drive name followed by a colon (:) followed by a backslash (\). If file resides in the disk drive's top folder (called the *root directory*), you then type the filename. However, the file resides in another folder, you must list the folder after the backslash. If the file resides in several nested folder, you must list each folder in order, from the outermost to the innermost, and separate each folder name with a backslash.

The following full pathnames to specific files:

c:\autoexec.bat

d:\Sherry\WordProc\Home\Insure\Fire and Casualty.exe

The first filename is autoexec.bat located in the root directory. The second filename is Fire and Casualty located within a series of nested directories.

Windows Explorer program, displays entire computer system graphically including all its files, in a tree structure form. With Explorer, you can access every data inside computer hard disk.

Elements of Folder or Library Window

When you open a folder or library, you see it in a window. The various elements of this window are designed to help you to navigate around Windows or work with files, folders, and libraries more easily. Elements of folder or library window are marked in Figure 2.31 which are explained below.

Navigation Pane Navigation pane appears at the left side of window. It shows four or five nodes, such as **Favorites**, **Libraries**, **Computer**, **Network** and **HomeGroup** (visible only if

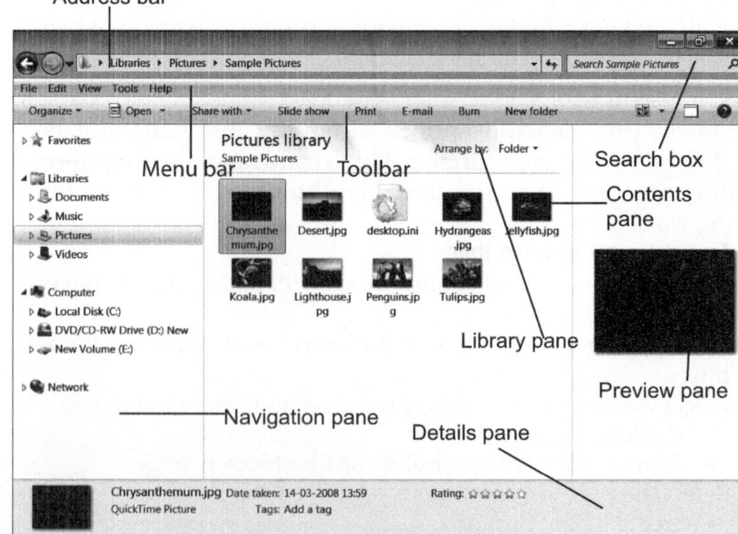

Figure 2.31 Elements of folder or library window in Windows 7

the network location is set to Home). You can hide the *navigation pane*, adjust its width, or change its content to include only the Favorites node and hierarchical folders list. You can also use the navigation pane to access *libraries, folders, saved searches*, and *even entire hard disks*.

Address Bar Address bar is used to navigate to a different folder or library or to go back to a previous one (See Figure 2.31). It also shows you where you are and helps you get where you want to go.

Back and Forward buttons are used to navigate to other folders or libraries you have already opened without closing the current window.

History drop-down list lets you to revisit the addresses you entered in previous sessions.

The *new breadcrumb trail feature* is used to help you in navigating to the *address bar*. To use this feature, click any folder name to move straight to that location or click down arrow next to the folder to display other subfolders at the same level (See Figure 2.32).

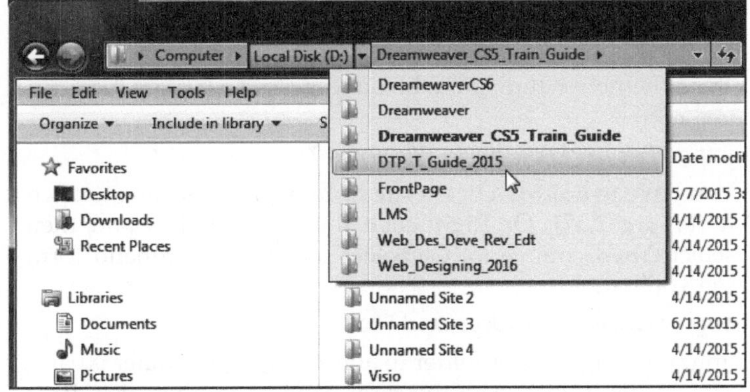

Figure 2.32 Breadcrumb trail feature to navigate in the address bar

Toolbar Toolbar is used to perform common tasks, such as changing the appearance of your files and folders, burning files to a CD, or starting a digital picture slide show. A few elements on the toolbar are always available, including the Organize menu on left and three buttons on the far right, which change views, show or hide the preview pane, and open a Help window (See Figure 2.32). But, the other buttons on the toolbar vary depending on the current selection.

Library Pane Library pane appears only when you are in a library, such as Pictures library (See Figure 2.32). It is used to customize the library or arrange the files by different properties.

Search Box Type a word or phrase in the search box to look for an item in the current folder or library (See Figure 2.32). The scope of search is restricted to the current location and displays search results immediately in the contents pane. The width of the search box can be adjusted by dragging its left edge in either direction.

Details Pane *Details pane* displays the properties associated with the selected file (See Figure 2.32). File properties provides information about a file, such as author, date you last changed the file, and any descriptive tags you might have added to the file. You can adjust the height of Details pane by dragging the top border up or down.

Preview Pane Use the preview pane to see the contents of most files. If you select an e-mail message, text file, or picture, for example you can see its contents without opening it in a program (See Figure 2.32). If you do not see the *Preview pane*, click the *Preview* pane button in the toolbar to turn it on.

Menu Bar By default, Menu bar is hidden. If it is seen, it is placed above the toolbar shown in Figure 2.32. If the menu bar is not displayed, you can make it appear temporarily.

➡ **To display menu bar:**

1. Click the Organize menu, choose Layout and then select Menu bar. Or alternatively, press Alt or F10 keys.

Selecting Files and Folders in Windows 7

➡ **To select a single file:**

1. Open the folder or Windows Explorer window containing the file.
2. Click the file.

➡ **To select multiple files:**

1. Open the folder or Windows Explorer window containing the file.
2. Click the first file.
3. Then press and hold down Ctrl key and then click the other files you want to select (See Figure 2.33).

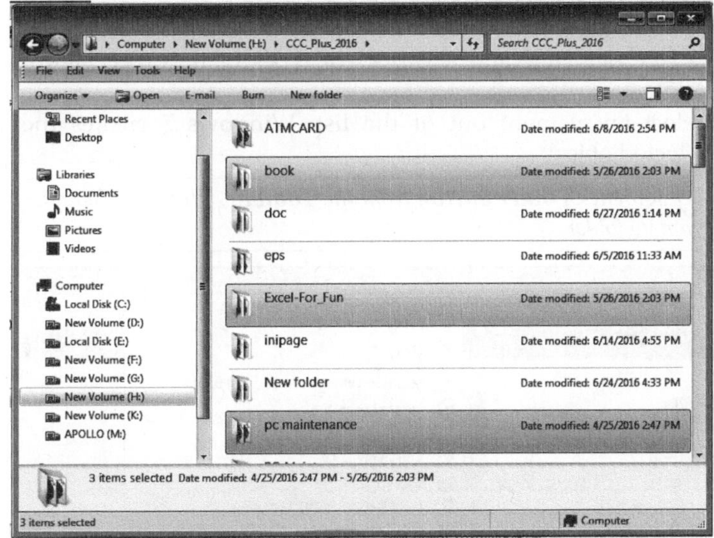

Figure 2.33 Selecting multiple files

➡ **To select a group of files:**

1. Open the folder or **Windows Explorer window** containing the file.
2. Move and position the mouse to the left of the first file you want to select.
3. Then click and drag mouse to the right until all the files you want are selected. (See Figure 2.34).

➡ **To select all the items in a folder:**

1. Open the folder or **Windows Explorer window** containing file.
2. Click the **Organize** menu and choose **Select all**. Or press **Ctrl + A** keys together.
3. Windows Explorer selects all the files in the folder.

Figure 2.34 Selecting group of files

2.6.1 Creating Files and Folders in Windows 7

➡ To create a new File/Folder:

1. In the **Folder window**, click the **File** menu and choose **New** or right click an empty area of folder window and choose **New**.
2. In both cases, a submenu lists the new objects you can create: *folders, shortcuts*, and a variety of types of files (See Figure 2.35).
3. Select an element out of the list. Windows 7 creates the selected object.

☞ *If you click **Folder button** from the **Toolbar**, Windows 7 creates a new folder.*

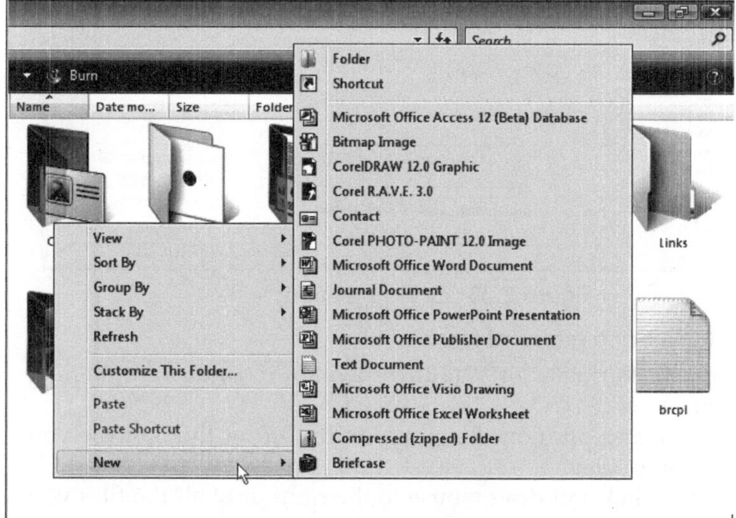

Figure 2.35 Creating new file or folder

2.6.2 Naming and Renaming Files and Folders in Windows 7

➡ To rename a file or folder:

1. Select the file/folder you want to rename.
2. Click the **Organize menu** and choose **Rename**. Or press F2 key (See Figure 2.36). Or *alternatively*, right click the file/folder and choose **Rename** from the context menu.

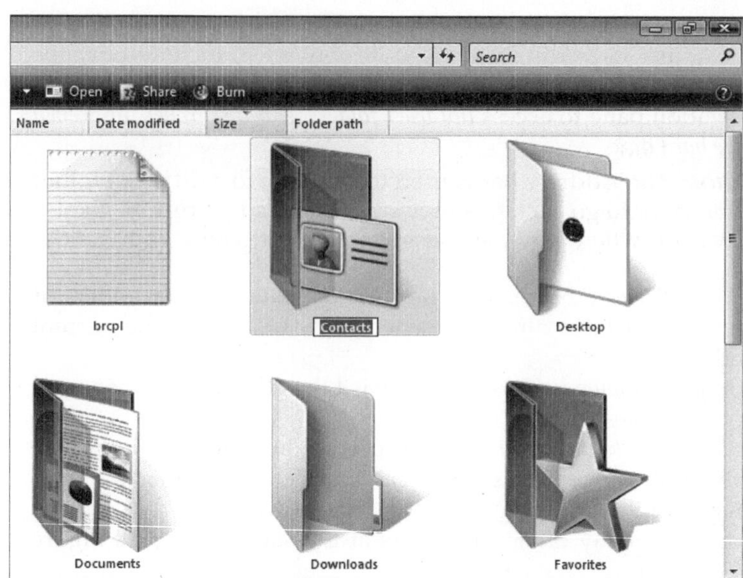

Figure 2.36 Renaming a folder

3. A box appears around current name, with its details selected. Type the new name in the box and press **Enter** key (See Figure 2.36).

Opening Files and Folders in Windows 7

1. You have to **double-click a file** or **folder** in this pane to open it (Figure 2.37). Or Right-click the selected files and then select **Open** command. Or Select the **Open** command form the Toolbar.

Moving or Copying Folders and Files

Moving/copying a file or folder to another drive or folder is easy. Just drag a file/folder from the right pane to another disk drive (or a folder on another drive) to copy/move it there.

➡ To move a file or folder to another drive or folder:

1. Select the file or folder you want to move.
2. Point to the selected file or folder, and then press and hold down the left mouse button.

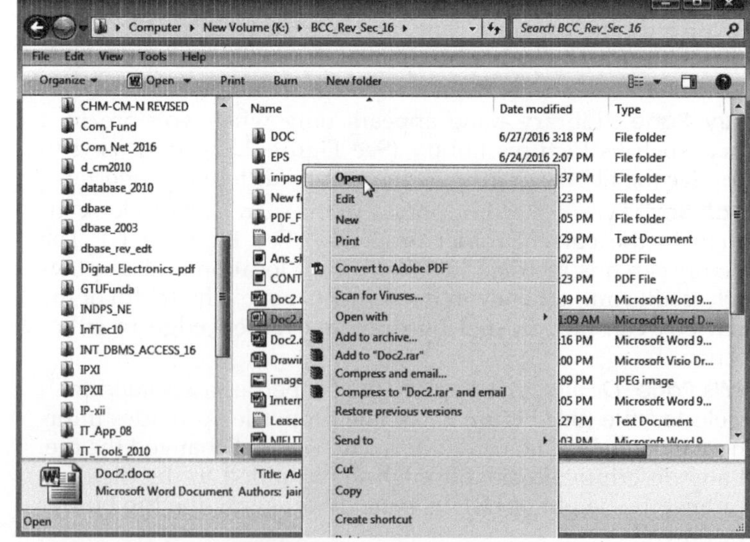

Figure 2.37 Opening a file

3. Drag the file/folder from the right pane to the left pane and drop it into the selected folder or drive where you want (See Figure 2.38).

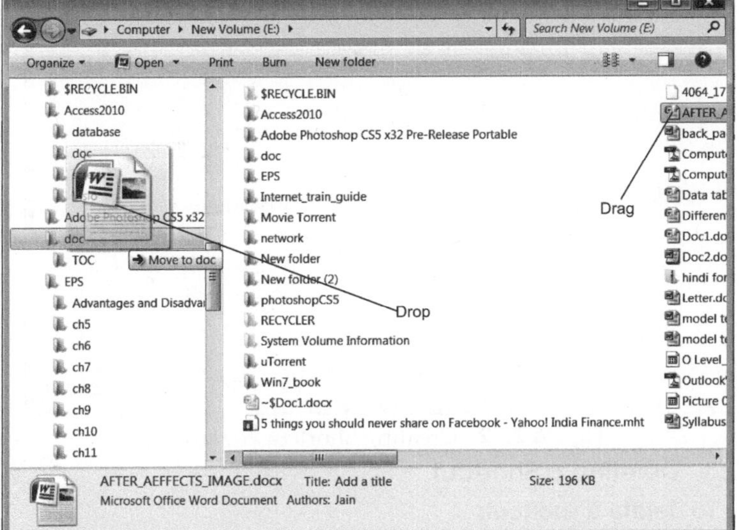

Figure 2.38 Moving a file or folder from one location to another

4. A Move button as shown in Figure 2.38 indicates where the file or folder will be moved.
5. Release the mouse button to move the file/folder into desired place.

➡ **To copy a file or folder to another drive or folder:**

1. Select the file or folder which you want to copy.
2. Point to the selected file or folder, and then press and hold down the left mouse button.
3. Press Ctrl key while dragging the file/folder from the right pane to the left pane and drop it into the selected folder or drive where you want (Figure 2.39).
4. A **Copy** button as shown in the Figure 2.39 indicates where the file or folder will be copied.
5. Release the mouse button to copy the file/folder into desired place.

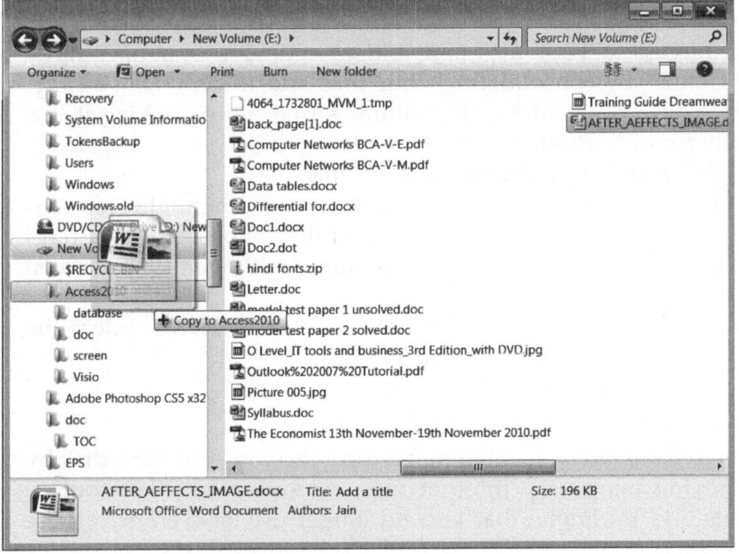

Figure 2.39 Copy a file or folder

Deleting Files and Folders in Windows 7

➡ **To delete file(s) and folder(s):**

1. Select the file or folder that you want to delete.
2. Click the **Organize** menu and choose **Delete** . Or *alternatively*, right click the file/folder and choose **Delete** from the context menu.
3. The **Delete File** dialog box appears. Click **Yes** in this dialog box.
4. The selected file get deleted from the folder.

☞ *Objects deleted from your computer are sent to the Recycle Bin. You can recover them by double-clicking the Recycle Bin folder, if desired.*

Opening and Closing Different Window

There are three types of window openings namely, *application window*, *document window* and *folder window*. Document window contains a document you are working on *within* an application window. Most of the applications allow you to have multiple documents window open at a time. The document window is also referred to as child window.

➡ **To open a document window:**

1. Click **File** menu and choose **Open**. The Open dialog box appears, click the file in the look in: drop-down list box and choose the file you want to open.

➡ **To close a document window:**

1. Click **File** menu and choose **Close**. *Alternatively*, click the × close button in the upper right corner of the window. Or
2. Right click the document in the taskbar and choose Close or press Alt+F4 keys together (See Figure 2.40).

☞ *Many of the features of Windows XP are also included in Windows 7.*

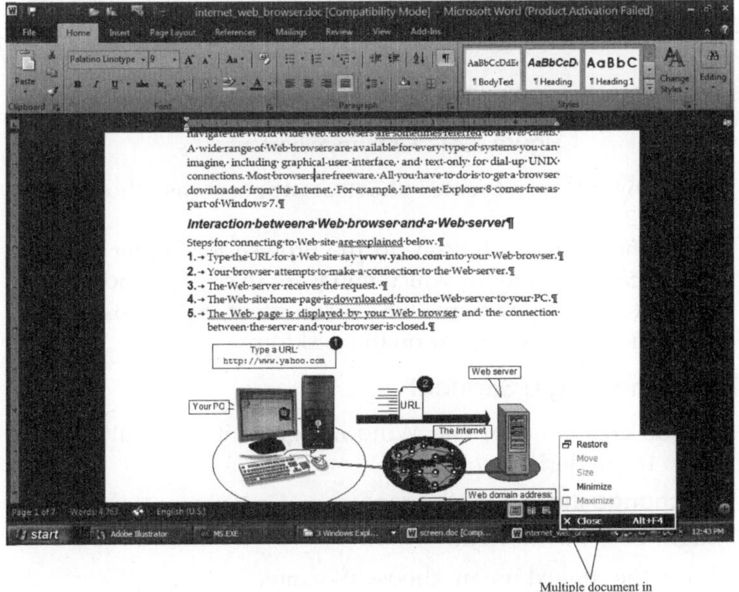

Figure 2.40 Closing a document window in the task bar

2.7 SHORTCUTS

A shortcut is a small file that is linked to a *program, document, folder* or an *Internet address*. The file is represented by an icon with an arrow in its lower left corner.

Shortcut is linked to a file or folder, which can be located anywhere–on a local hard disk or CD-ROM drive or on a floppy disk.

2.7.1 Creating a Shortcut

A shortcut can be created in the following two ways:

- By using cut and paste or
- By using the Create Shortcut wizard.

☞ *A shortcut is a pointer to an object, and not the object itself. This means that you can create and delete shortcuts without affecting the object which is linked to a file.*

➡ **To create a shortcut using copy and paste:**

1. Right click the items for which you want to create a shortcut.
2. From the **context** menu, choose **Copy**.
3. Now right click on the desktop and choose **Paste** from the context menu.

➡ **To create a shortcut using the create shortcut wizard:**

1. Right-click the desktop, from the **Context** menu choose **New**, and then choose **Shortcut** as seen in Figure 2.41.

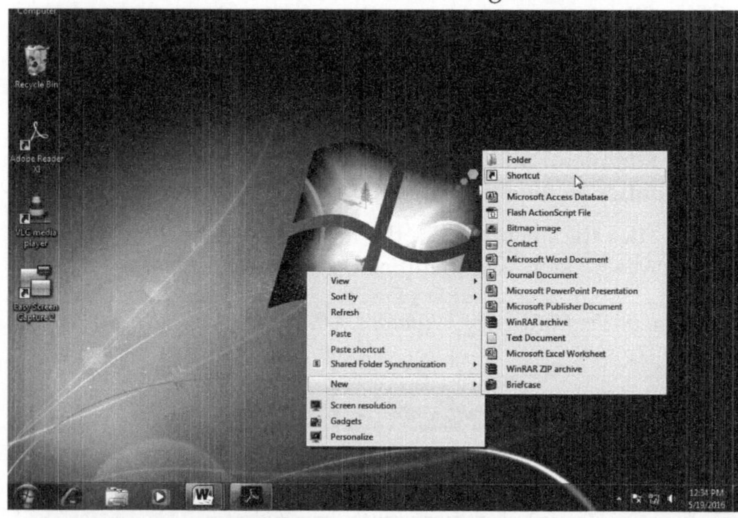

Figure 2.41 Creating Shortcut

2. The wizard for **Create Shortcut** appears as shown in Figure 2.42.
3. Click the Browse... button. In the Browse for Folder dialog box, locate the item for which you want to create a shortcut.
4. Click Next → type a name for your shortcut, click **Finish**, and your shortcut will appear on the desktop.

2.7.2 Renaming a Shortcut

When you create a shortcut, Windows gives it a default name based on the underlying object.

➡ **To change the shortcut name:**

1. Right-click the shortcut.
2. From the context menu, choose **Rename**.
3. Type the name that you want to use.

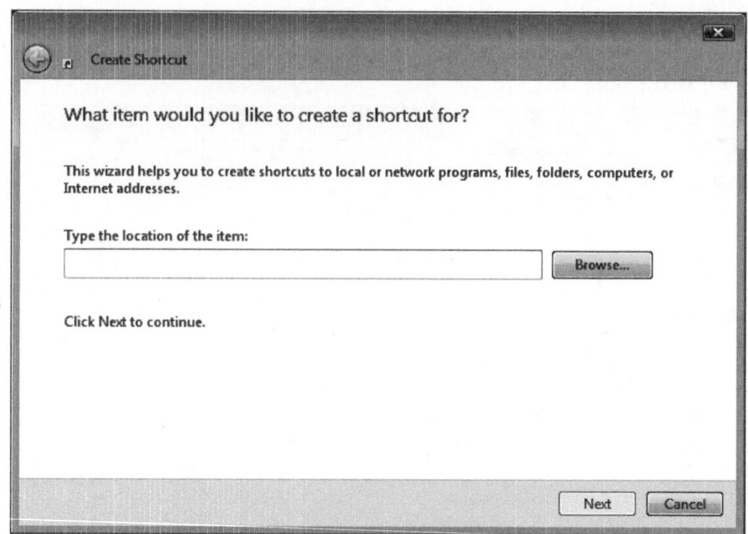

Figure 2.42 Creating Shortcut wizard

2.7.3 Deleting a Shortcut

➡ **To delete a shortcut:**

1. Select the icon and press the Del key. *Alternatively*, right click the shortcut which you want to be deleted and choose **Delete** from the context menu.
2. Windows prompt you for conformation before deletion.

2.8 COMMON UTILITIES

Windows 7 provides some utility software packages, such as Calculator, Notepad, Paint, Entertainment, Snipping Tool, Sound Recorder, WordPad, and System tools, such as Disk Cleanup, Disk defragmenter, Task Scheduler, Tablet PC, and many more in Accessories group.

2.8.1 System Tools

System Tools option is found under Accessories. It provides a set of tools for Computer System Management. It includes Disk Defragmenter, Disk Cleanup, Backup, Scheduling, etc.

Disk Defragmenter

Disk Defragmenter consolidates fragmented files and folders on your computer's hard disk, so that each file occupies a single, contiguous space on the volume. As a result, your system can gain access to your files and folders and save new ones more efficiently. By consolidating your files and folders, *Disk Defragmenter* also consolidates the volume's free space, making it less likely for new files to be fragmented.

➡ **To open Disk Defragmenter, do this:**

1. Click **Start** button, Choose **All Programs**, highlight **Accessories**, highlight **System Tools**, and then choose **Disk Defragmenter.** Disk Defragmenter window will open up as shown in Figure 2.43.
2. To start defragmentation, under **Current status**, select the disk you want to defragment.
3. Click **Defragment** disk.

Disk CleanUp

You can use Disk CleanUp to free up space on your hard disk by removing temporary Internet files, removing installed components and programs that you no longer use, and emptying the Recycle Bin.

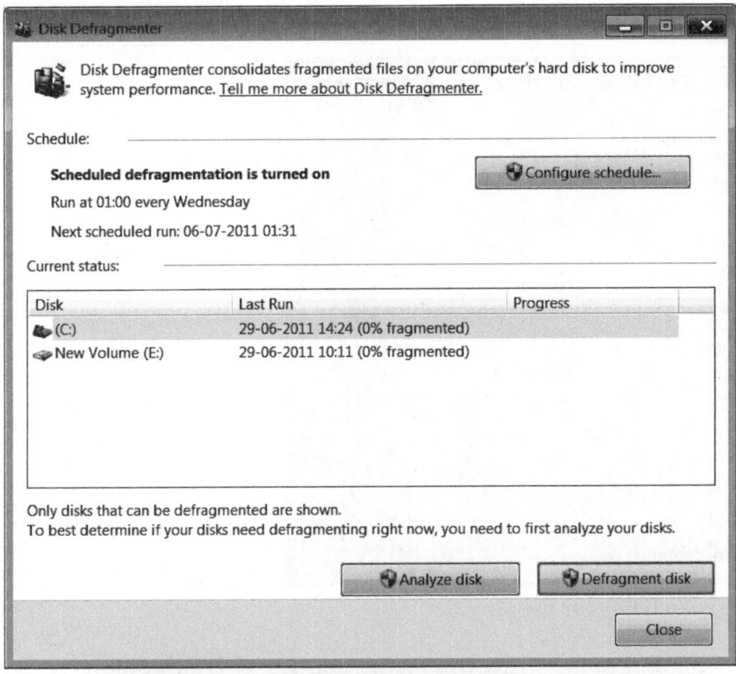

Figure 2.43 Disk Defragmenter window

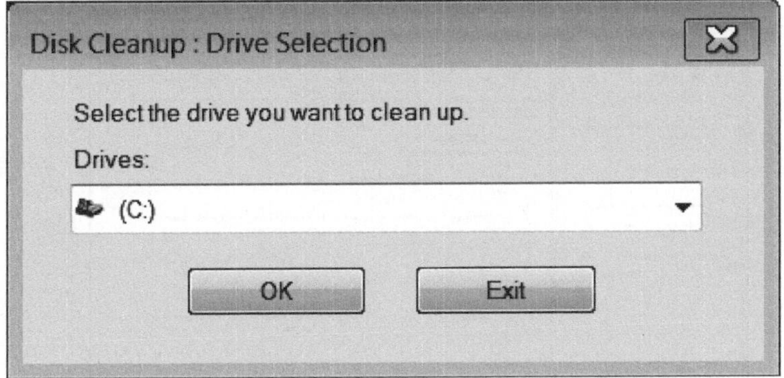

Figure 2.44 Disk Cleanup: Drive Selection dialog box

➡ **To open Disk Cleanup, do this:**

1. Click **Start** button, Choose **All Programs**, highlight **Accessories**, highlight **System Tools**, and then choose **Disk Cleanup**.
2. **Disk Cleanup: Drive Selection** dialog box appears as seen in Figure 2.44.
3. Choose the drive which you want to clean and then click OK.
4. The **Disk Cleanup** dialog box appears for the drive which you have selected (See Figure 2.45).

☞ *Disk Cleanup helps to free up space on your hard drive. Disk Cleanup searches your drive, and then shows you temporary files, cache files, and unnecessary program files that you can safely delete. You can direct Disk Cleanup to delete some or all of those files.*

5. Under **Files to delete:** list, click the check box for each file that you want to delete.
6. Then click OK button.

Task Scheduler

It is a tool that enables you to schedule tasks (such as Disk Defragmenter) to run regularly, at a time most convenient for

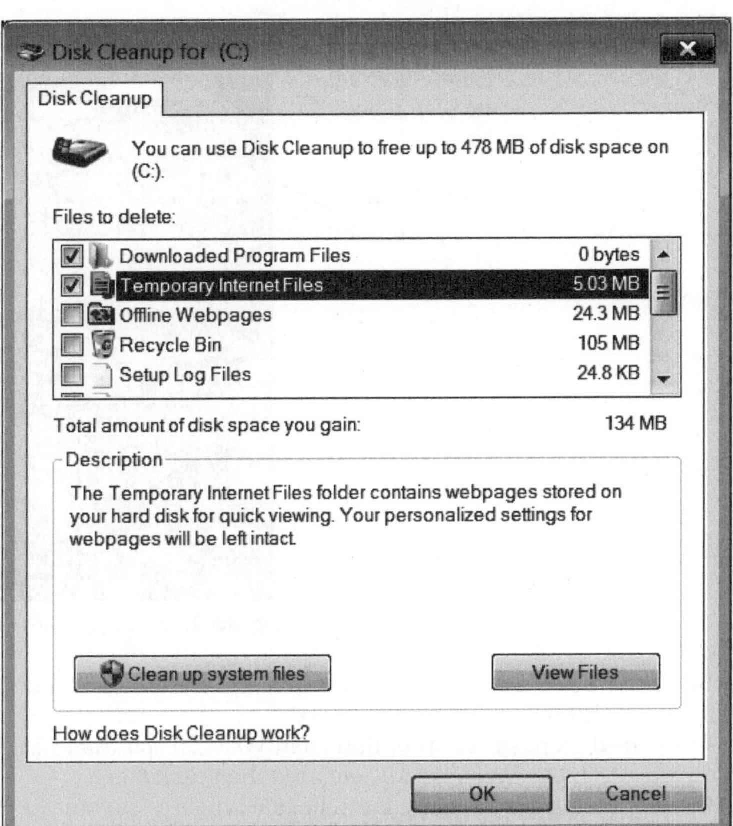

Figure 2.45 Disk Cleanup dialog box

you. The Task Scheduler starts each time you start Windows 7 and runs in the background.

➡ **To add scheduled task, do this:**

1. Click **Start** button, Choose **All Programs**, highlight **Accessories**, highlight **System Tools** and then choose **Task Scheduler**.
2. **Task Scheduler** window appears as seen in Figure 2.33.
3. In this Window, Click the **Action** menu and then click **Create Basic Task** (See Figure 2.46).

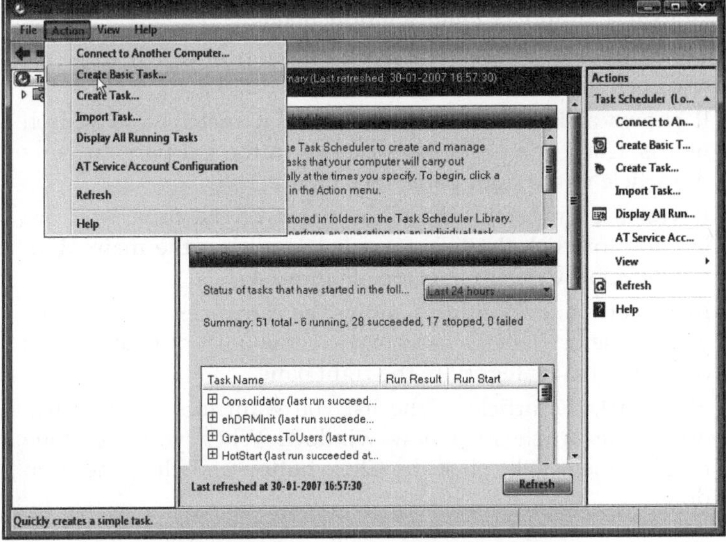

Figure 2.46 Task Scheduler window

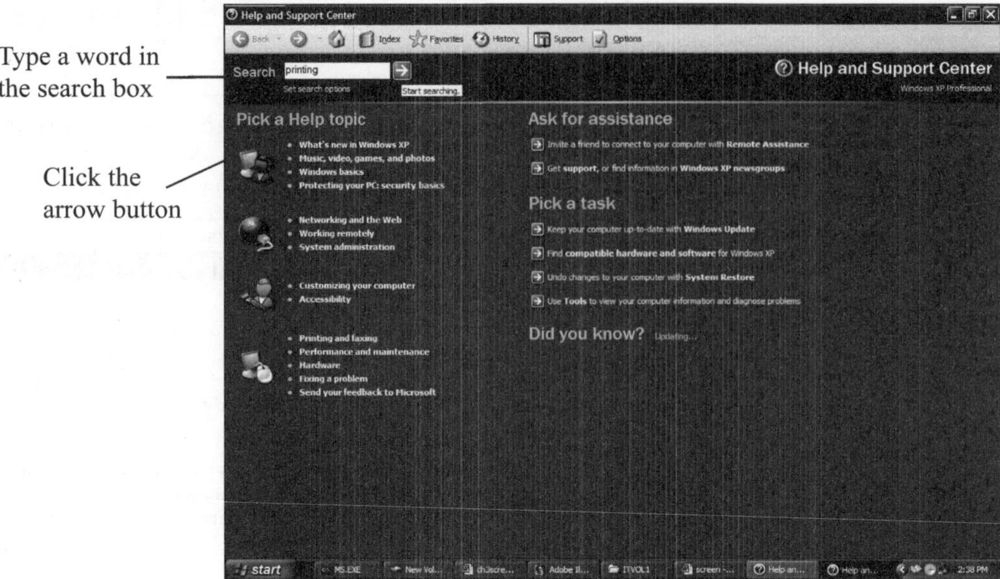

Figure 2.47 Type a Word in the Search box for help

4. In **Create Basic Task Wizard**, type a name for the task and give description, and then click **Next**.
5. In the next step, select an option from *When do you want the task to start*?, i.e., *Daily*, *Weekly*, etc., and then click **Next**.
6. In Next dialog box, specify the schedule which you want to use, and then click Next.
7. To schedule a program to start automatically, click **Start** a program, and then click **Next**.
8. Select a program from the list, or browse to the program you want to start, and then click **Next**.
9. Click **Finish**.

Using Help

If you want answer to a question about Windows 7 or other utility program for Windows, you can ask for help. Windows help will give information about what you have asked.

➡ **To get help, do this:**

1. Click **Start** button and then Choose **Help and Support**. The Help and Support Center window opens.
2. Type a word, phrase, or even a question in the **Search** box and click the **Search** button. (See Figure 2.47)
3. It shows a list of all help articles that match your search words. Click one of the result terms in the left pane to view the article in the right pane. (See Figure 2.48)
4. If you are uncertain about the name of the topic you are looking for click the link for a help topic on the main Help and Support Center page. (See Figure 2.49)
5. In the left pane, Windows shows the categories for the topic you can select. Click a category to show a list of help articles related to that category in the right pane.
6. Now click the article in the list you want to see. Windows opens the article in a new window. When you are done reading the article, click the Close button and close the window.

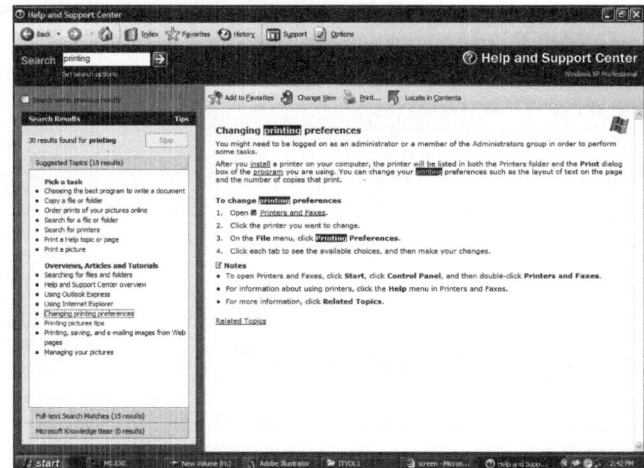

Figure 2.48 Selecting help article in the left pane

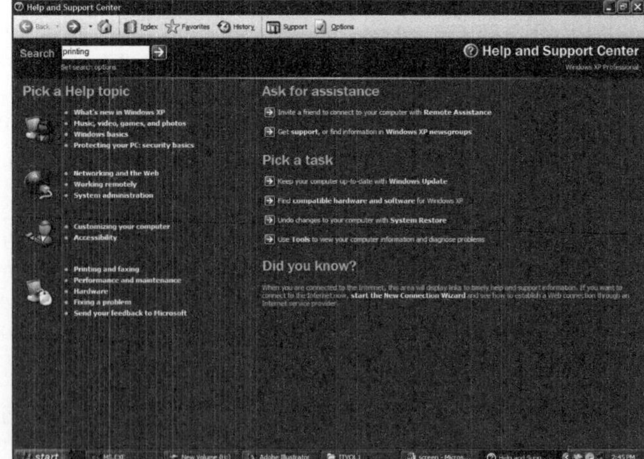

Figure 2.49 Selecting Help topic in the Help and Support Center

2.9 BASICS OF WINDOWS 7 (OS) SETUP

Installing Windows 7 on a blank hard drive is more difficult than upgrading from an existing version of Windows. It requires that you have a bootable CD-ROM. To begin, insert the CD-ROM into your CD drive and start your computer.
Before starting the installation we should make sure that the computer meets all the Hardware requirements for installing Windows 7.
The steps to install Windows 7 operating system are as follows:

1. Start your computer. Press F2 or delete at start up to enter the BIOS menu. Select First boot device as 'CD ROM' if you installing from DVD ROM. Second boot device as 'Hard Disk' so that the computer boots from Hard disk if OS is not in DVD ROM. Press F10 to save your settings and select yes to restart your computer.
2. Insert the installation disc for Windows 7 and start your computer. The computer will ask you to 'Press any key to boot from CD/DVD'. Press any key on your keyboard and it will start loading the operating system from the CD.
3. After loading windows 7 successfully, it opens an install window. Enter the Language time & currency format and keyboard or input method. Click 'Next'. The 'Install windows 7' screen will appear.
4. Click 'Install now'. Setup will start and you will see a message on the screen 'Set up is starting'
5. Now it will show the License agreement screen. Check the 'I accept the License terms' and click 'Next'. The 'Install windows' wizard will appear.
6. Select Custom (Advanced) option. The screen will prompt you to select the location to install windows. Click drive option (Advanced menu). Click on 'New', you are then asked to allot a size on the disk for installation. Enter the appropriate volume size and then click 'Apply' to create partitions for the installation, click 'Next'. Windows will start the installation. Now the installation status screen appears. You will have to wait for the following tasks to get complete.
   - Copying Windows
   - Expanding Windows files
   - Installing features
   - Installing updates
   - Completing Installation
   - The computer will restart several times during this process.
   - After successful installation of Windows 7 it will ask you to specify the 'computer name'. It will also ask you enter a 'User account' and 'Password'. Enter the password in the respective field and also the password hint, click 'Next'.
   - The setup key will open the 'Product Key' option. Enter the correct product key. Enter the 25-digit product identification number from the CD-ROM and click **Next**.
   - Now a window to set time on your computer will be displayed. Set the correct 'Time Zone', date and click 'Next' option.
   - The 'Computer network location' option will be displayed if your computer is already connected to a network. Select 'Network type' and click 'next'.
   - Windows will now finalize the setup and start to prepare your Windows 7 Desktop.

2.10 SUMMARY

This chapter, presents the concepts of GUI Based Operating System. It also explains basics of Linux and Windows operating systems. The User Interface, such as task bar, icons, start menu has also been discussed. It also discusses how to change System Settings like date and time, display properties, mouse properties and adding and removing printers, etc. File management and directory in Windows enable you to understand the basics operations such as copying, moving from one direction to another, renaming and deleting for of files and folder. You have also learnt a variety of different techniques to change the system tools such as disk cleanup, disk defragmenter and task scheduler. Finally, we have discusses how to install Windows 7 operating system.

MODEL QUESTIONS AND ANSWERS

1. Multiple Choice

1.1 A file deleted from disk drive A: in Windows goes to __________.

a. Recycle Bin b. My Computer
c. Windows Explorer d. Permanently deleted.

1.2 The term Operating System means __________

a. A set of programs which controls computer working
b. The way a computer operator works
c. Conversion of high-level language in to machine level language
d. The way a floppy disk drive operates

1.3 Which of the following is the first step in sizing a window?

a. Point to the title bar
b. Pull down the View menu to display the toolbar
c. Point to any corner or border
d. Pull down the View menu and change to large icons.

1.4 Which button appears immediately after a window has been maximized?

a. Close button b. Minimize button
c. Maximize button d. Restore button

1.5 __________ is the screen background and main area of window where you can open and manage files and programs.

a. Icons b. Desktop
c. Application window d. Screen Saver

1.6 An application can be opened through shortcut on desktop by

a. Double clicking on its shortcut
b. Right clicking and choosing "Open" option
c. Selecting the icon and pressing Enter key
d. All of the above

1.7 Which of the following statement is incorrect in context of shortcut icons.

a. Shortcuts can be created by dragging and dropping.
b. Shortcuts can be created using cut and paste methods.
c. Shortcuts can be created by using the Shortcut wizard.
d. None of the above

1.8 A new printer can be added by Devices and Printers option in

a. Control Panel b. File Manager

c. Dynamic Data Exchange d. None of these

1.9 GUI is used as an interface between

a. Hardware and software b. Man and machine

c. Software and user d. None of the above

1.10 Exchange of images or data from one application to another is done by using

a. Driver b. Control Panel

c. Clipboard d. None of these

2. State whether the following are True or False

2.1 When a folder is copied to another place, the subfolders in the folder also get copied.

2.2 When no object has been deleted, the desktop does not contain the Recycle Bin icon.

2.3 The contents of a Window can be scrolled by clicking the scroll bar.

2.4 Linux is a multiuser, multitasking operating system developed by Linus Torvalds in the year 1991.

2.5 Recycle bin does not allow you to easily recover deleted files and folders in Windows.

2.6 A folder can not contain files as well as sub folders.

2.7 Programs available in CD-ROMs are always 'virus' free.

2.8 Title bar at the top most line of a window bar.

2.9 Taskbar provides a common way to perform varied activities such as starting various programs, accessing commonly used folders, searching for files, folders and programs, etc.

2.10 By default, the taskbar displays only three buttons corresponding to Internet Explorer, Media Player, and Windows Explorer program.

Answers

1.	1.1	d	1.2	a	1.3	c	1.4	d	1.5	b
	1.6	d	1.7	d	1.8	a	1.9	c	1.10	c
2.	2.1	T	2.2	F	2.3	T	2.4	T	2.5	F
	2.6	F	2.7	F	2.8	T	2.9	F	2.10	T

CHAPTER 3

Understanding Word Processing

3.0 INTRODUCTION

Word processing is the most common application package to create, edit, and print documents using a computer. To perform word processing, you need a computer, a special program called a word processor, and a printer. A word processor enables you to create a document, store it electronically on a disk, display it on a screen, modify it by entering commands and characters from the keyboard, and print it on a printer.

The great advantage of word processing over using a typewriter is that you can make changes without retyping the entire document. If you make a typing mistake, you simply back up the cursor and correct your mistake. If you want to delete a paragraph, you simply remove it, without leaving a trace. It is equally easy to insert a word, sentence, or paragraph in the middle of a document. Word processor also makes it easy to move sections of text from one place to another within a document, or between documents. When you have made all the changes you want, you can send the file to a printer to get a hardcopy. You can also mail it electronically to the addressee.

3.1 OBJECTIVES

The reader will be able to understand the following:

- Word processing basics
- Using Word 2010 Interface
- Opening and Closing documents
- Text Creation and manipulation
- Formatting the Text
- Table Manipulation

3.2 WORD PROCESSING BASICS

Word processing package, such as Word 2010 helps to enter text and manipulate words and phrases. You can change typed letter, document and report easily and store them for future use. You can even print these documents as and when desired.

☞ *A word processor allows you to function more effectively and efficiently with minimum effort.*

Word 2010 is a Word Processor that operates under Windows Operating System. When you use a computer program to create, and edit text documents, you are using word processor. Word 2010 is one of the most sophisticated word processing programs available to day. With Word 2010, it is easier than ever to efficiently create a wide range of business and personal documents, from a simples letter to the most complex project report. Word 2010 includes many desktop features that you can use to enhance the appearance of documents so that they are easy to read.

3.2.1 Opening Word Processing Package (MS Word 2010)

➡ **To start Word 2010, do this:**

1. Click **Start** button, highlight All **Programs** and click **MS Office**. Select **MS Office Word 2010** (See Figure 3.1).

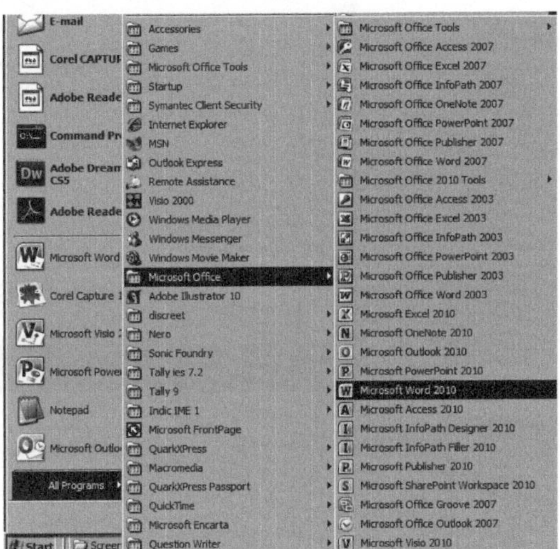

Figure 3.1 Starting MS Word 2010

3.2.2 Using Word 2010 Interface

User interfaces of MS Word 2010 is similar to MS Word 2007. MS Word 2010 has introduced several new features, such as improved WordArt, improved themes, background removal, and other image editing features. The new user interface that replaces menus, toolbars, and most of the task panes from previous versions of MS Word have been replaced by the File tab and Ribbon. It is designed to help you to be more productive. You can find the right features of various tasks more easily, discover new functionality and be more efficient. Figure 3.2 shows the elements of Word 2010 application window and an open Word 2010 document in detail.

3.2.3 File Tab

File tab is the colored tab which is located in the upper-left corner of MS Office 2010 programs and below the Quick Access Toolbar (See Figure 3.2). When you click the File tab, you can see the Backstage view. File Tab replaces the office button in Word 2007. It contains commands like New, Open, Save, Save As, Print, etc.

3.2.4 Quick Access Toolbar

This toolbar is located by default at the top of Word 2010 window. By default, this toolbar displays the Save, Undo and Repeat buttons.

3.2.5 Dialog Box Launcher

Dialog box launchers are small icons that appear in some groups. Clicking a Dialog Box Launcher opens a related dialog box or task pane, providing more options related to that group.

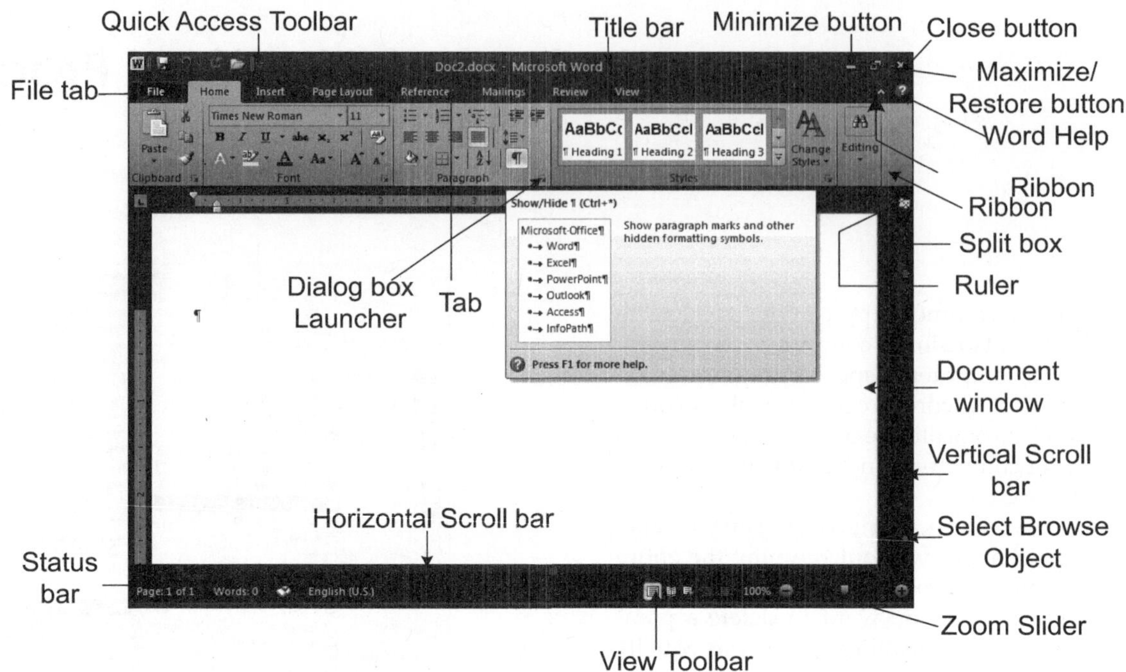

Figure 3.2 Elements of Word 2010 window

3.2.6 Terminology

Following terminology for Word 2010 is used in this book.

Select–Highlight or mark a section of text, menu name, command, dialog box option, or graphical object with the keyboard or with mouse actions.

Choose–Execute and complete a command. You may execute some commands when you select the command on the Ribbon tabs. Other commands are executed when you choose OK from a dialog box.

Active–Bring an application or document window to the foreground. When you are working with more than one application or more than one document within Word 2010, the active window is the window in which you are currently working.

3.2.7 Word 2010 Document Window

Title Bar

It is at the top of an open window and is called Title bar (See Figure 3.2).

Minimize button

An underscore(_) at the right of a title bar which stores an application programme at the bottom of the screen.

Maximize button

A box at the right of a title bar that fills available space with the document or application.

Close button

A box at the right of a title bar marked as (X) that closes the window or dialog box, when you click it with a mouse pointer.

Restore button

A double box at the right of a title bar that restores an application or document into a sizable window.

Help button

It appears at the right end of the Ribbon. When the mouse pointer is over any button for a few seconds (called hovering), it displays a ScreenTip with not only the button's name but also its function.

Status bar

It is present at the bottom of the window, and gives you information about the current document. You can turn off the display of an item of information by right-clicking the status bar and then on clicking that item.

View toolbar

At the right end of the status bar is the view toolbar. It provides tools for adjusting the view of document.

Mouse pointer

The on-screen arrow, I-beam, or drawing button indicates the current location affected by mouse actions.

Select Browse Object

The toolbar that enables you to browse through an active document by field, endnote, footnote, comment, section, page, edits, heading, graphic, or by table. Go To and Find functions are also part of this toolbar.

Ruler

A bar containing a scale that indicates *tabs, paragraph indents*, and margins in the paragraph where the insertion point (cursor) is located. The ruler can be used with the mouse to format paragraphs quickly.

Split box

Light gray bar present at the top of the vertical scroll bar, that you can drag down to split a window into two views of the same document.

ScreenTips

Screentips show the name of the command button shown in ribbon. Screentips appear as soon as you position the mouse pointer on the selected tabs command.

3.2.8 Ribbon Command

Ribbon is displayed just below the title bar. In Ribbon, Commands are organized in logical groups, which are collected together under tabs (See Figure 3.2). You can hide the Ribbon by double-clicking the active tab. Different types of Tabs are available in Word 2010.

- *Home Tab:* This button is related to working with document, such as *clipboard, font, paragraph, styles,* and *editing.*
- *Insert Tab:* This button is used to insert *tables, header* and *footer,* and *symbols.*
- *Page Layout Tab:* This button is related to page-formatting options. You can format your themes, set margins, insert page and section breaks, add line numbers, add background colors and water marks and adjust the entire document's indentation and spacing.
- *Reference Tab:* By using this button you can add *Tables of Contents, Footnotes, Bibliography, Captions, Index* and *Table of Authorities.*
- *Mailing Tab:* This button contains commands related to creating mass mailings. It contains *create, start mail merge, write & insert fields, preview results* and *finish.*
- *Review Tab:* This button is related to *proofing, language comments, tracking, changes, compare* and *protect.*
- *View Tab:* This button contain commands related to changing the view or the display of documents.

Scroll Bar

The scroll bar appears at the *left* for vertical scrolling and at the *bottom* for horizontal scrolling as seen in Figure 3.2.

In Word 2010, you can work simultaneously with more than one document.

Using Quick Access Toolbar

You can add buttons to the Quick Access Toolbar which expands to accommodate them. If you add many buttons, it might become difficult to view the text in the title bar or all the buttons might not be visible. To resolve this problem, you can move the Quick Access Toolbar below the Ribbon by clicking the Customize Quick Access Toolbar button and then clicking Show Below the Ribbon.

1. At the right end of the **Quick Access Toolbar**, click the **Customize Quick Access** Toolbar button.

   By default, the Save, Undo, and Repeat buttons appear on the Quick Access Toolbar (See Figure 3.2).

3.2.9 Using Quick Access Icons by Ribbon Command

If you click the Save icon in the Quick Access toolbar, Word 2010 saves your current file. If you are saving a new file, a dialog box pops up, asking you to choose a name for your file. If you click the Print icon, it immediately prints your entire file through the default printer.

The Redo icon reverses the last Undo command you choose. For example, if you delete a paragraph, it disappears. Then if you immediately click the Undo icon, the paragraph reappears. If you immediately click the Redo icon, the Redo command reverses the Undo command and deletes the paragraph once more.

The Undo icon is unique. It offers two ways to use it. First, you can click the Undo icon to undo the last action you chose. Second, you can click the downward-pointing arrow that appears to the right of the Undo icon to display a list of one or more of your previous actions as shown in Figure 3.3.

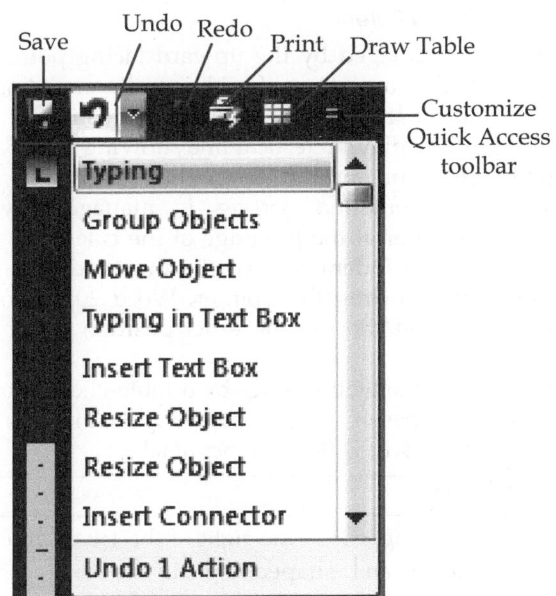

Figure 3.3 The Undo icon displays a list of actions

Rulers

The ruler helps you to control the *margins, paragraph indentation,* and *tab* settings for a document.

☞ *The horizontal ruler is always displayed at the top of the document window. The vertical ruler is displayed only in the Page Layout view or in Print Preview.*

Displaying or Hiding Rulers

Word 2010 gives you the flexibility to hide or display ruler according to your working needs.

➡ **To display the ruler, do this:**

1. On the **View** tab, in the **Show** group, select the **Ruler** check box (See Figure 3.4).
2. Horizontal and vertical rulers appear above and to the left of the page.

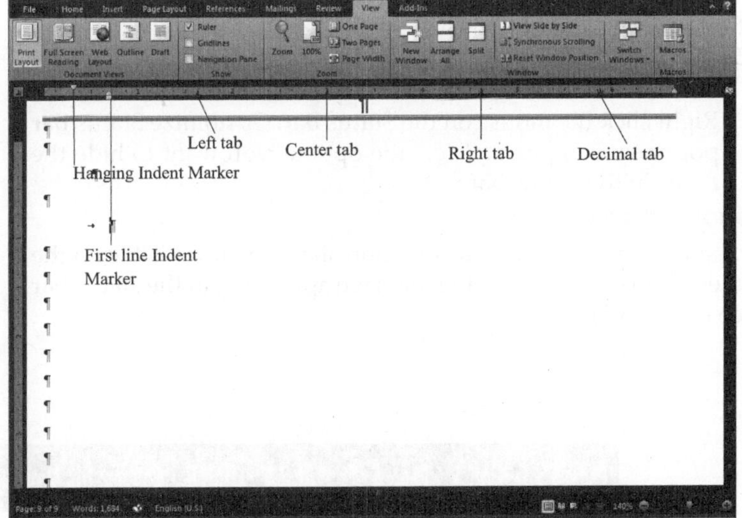

Figure 3.4 Word 2010 horizontal ruler including tabs marking

Reading the Horizontal Ruler

Margin settings are managed by the upward facing pointers at the bottom edge of the ruler. Dragging these pointers adjust the position of the right or left margin. However, if you drag these pointers, Word 2010 displays a vertical line showing the position of the margin in the document.

The paragraph indentation setting is managed by the downward-facing pointer at the top edge of the ruler. Dragging this pointer adjusts the indentation of the first line of a paragraph. However, if you drag the pointer, Word 2010 shows a vertical line so that you can see the exact position of the new indentation setting.

Note that you can adjust tab settings by double-clicking on the ruler. There are four types of tab with details given in Table 3.1.

Table 3.1 Different types of tab

Tab	Function
Left-aligned	Characters appear to the right of the tab as you type; indicated by an L-shaped angle in the box.
Centre-aligned	Characters are centred at the tab position; indicated by an angle with the vertical bar centred over the base line.
Right-aligned	Characters extend to the left of the tab as you type; indicated by a reverse L-shaped angle.
Decimal	The decimal point aligns with the tab position; indicated by the symbol for a centre-aligned tab with a decimal point to the right of the vertical member.

The Status Bar

The Status bar, seen at the bottom of Word 2010 Window shows information about the active document or the work you are processing.

Displaying Status Bar

The location of the insertion point is displayed on the status bar. By default, status bar tells you, which page the insertion point is on, but you can also display its location by section, line, and column and in inches from the top of the page. Simply right-click the status bar, and then click the option you want to display. After selecting the options, the screen appears as seen in Figure 3.5.

➡ **To hide the items on the status bar, do this:**

1. Right click the mouse on the Status Bar, Customize Status Bar pop menus appears. Select the options you want to hide the items in the Status bar.

Reading the Status Bar

The status bar shows the information about the text visible on the screen. Table 3.2 explains the message appearing in the status bar (See Figure 3.5).

Table 3.2 Message in the Status Bar

Message	Explanation
Page 6	You are in page 6 of the document.
Sec 1	In section 1 of the document.
Page 6 of 6	On page 6 of 6 pages in the document. This page number is based on the actual number of pages in the document, not on the printed page number. If you have started numbering pages from a number other than 1, this will not match the printed page number.
At 8.4"	A line of text that is vertical position from the top of the page.
Line 6	The six line of the text on this page.
Word count	Number of words in the document.
Col 1	Beginning of the line character position within the line of the text.
Over/Insert	Indicates with overtype mode is *on* or *off*.
View tabs	Different view of the document.
Zoom	Click the Zoom slider. If you move Zoom In (i.e.+ icon) moves to increases. If you move Zoom Out (i.e - icon) it moves to decrease.

3.2.10 Getting Help

You can use the Word Help system to get assistance on any Word topic or task. This system is a combination of tools and files that were stored on your computer when Word 2010 was installed. If your computer is connected to the Internet, you can also access resources from Office.com.

➡ **To get help, do this:**

1. Click the Word Help button located at the right end of the Ribbon. Or, press the **F1** key. The Word Help window opens displaying a list of general help topics as shown in Figure 3.6.
2. Click any topic to display the corresponding information (See Figure 3.6).
3. To find help on a specific topic, type a word or phrase related to the topic in the **Search** box, and then press the **Enter** key. For example, we have type the word, such as **SmartArt graphics** in the Search box (See Figure 3.7).
4. The Help window displays a list of topics, i.e. searched for *Alignment text*. Choose the selected list topic you want (See Figure 3.7).
5. The Help window displays step-by-step explanations.
6. Click the **Close** button to close the Help window in the upper-right corner of the window.

➡ **To resize or reposition the help, do this:**

1. To resize the Help Window, move the pointer over a corner of the Help window until you see the double-headed arrow and then drag the corner until the window is of the size that you want it to be.
2. To move the Help window, move the pointer to the title bar and drag the window as you want to keep it.

Figure 3.5 Word 2010 Status Bar elements

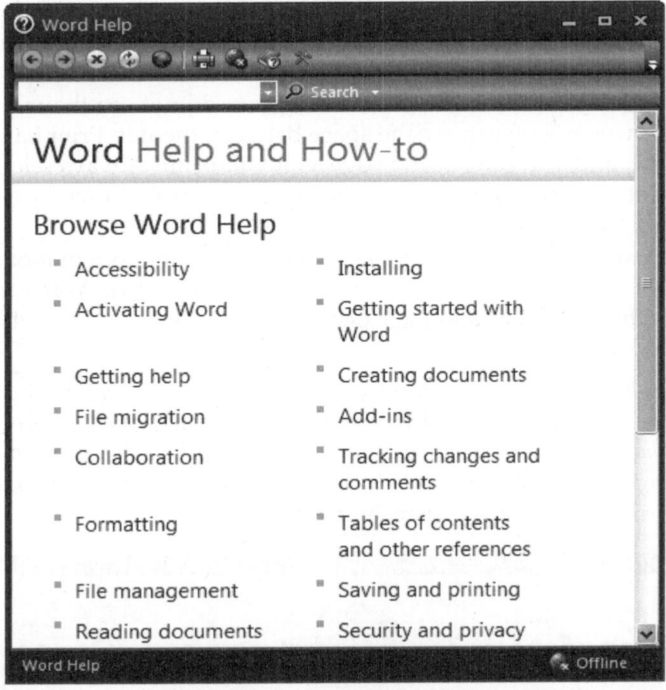

Figure 3.6 Word Help dialog box

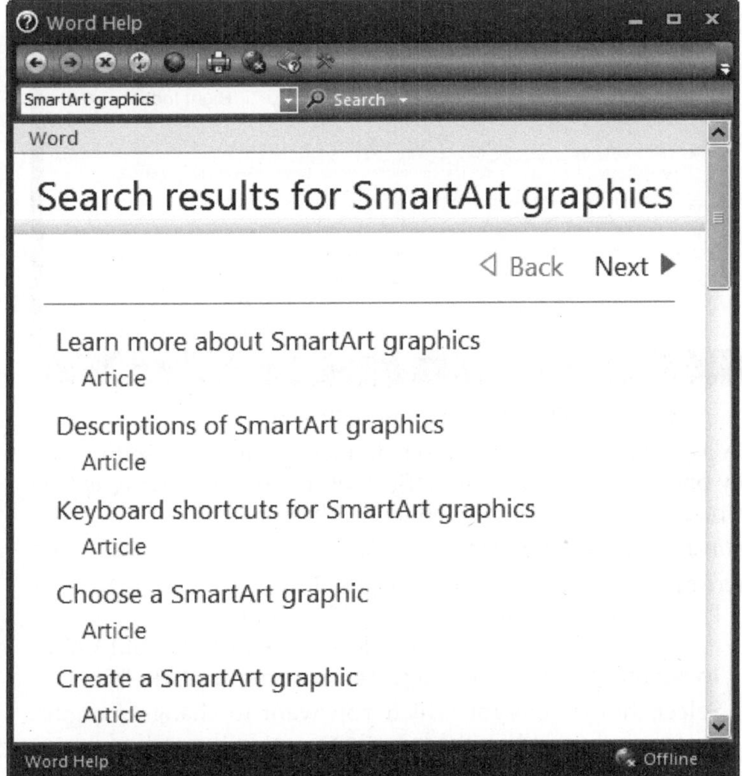

Figure 3.7 Type a word in the search box

3.3 OPENING AND CLOSING DOCUMENTS

3.3.1 Opening an Existing Documents

You can open Word document, can make modifications and save it with another name in different location.

➡ **To open an existing document, do this:**

1. Click the **File** tab, the Backstage view appears.
2. Click the **Open** tab. The **Open** dialog box appears as shown in Figure 3.8.

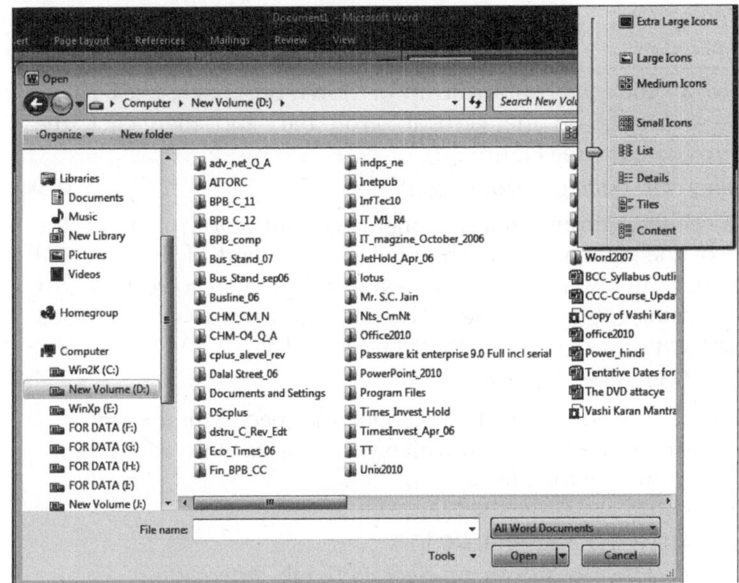

Figure 3.8 Open dialog box

3. In the Look in: drop-down list choose the location of the file you want to open.
4. Click the drop-down triangle views button to change the way the folder and file list is displayed in the Table 3.3 below.

Table 3.3 List Options of open dialog box

Button	Function
Thumbnails	It displays icons in Thumbnails. When you click a folder name, a thick highlighted border appear.
Tiles	It displays icons in medium size.
Icons	It displays icons in smaller size.
List	Displays a list of commands.
Details	Displays the details the size type, last modified, etc.
Properties	Displays the properties of the file.
Preview	Displays a preview of the file.

5. Select the document from the list, and then click the Open button.
6. The selected Word 2010 document is opened.

Moving around in a Document

Scroll through a document

You can scroll through a document by using the mouse or the keyboard. If you split the document window, you can see two different parts of a document.

Scrolling through a document using the mouse

To	Do this
Scroll up one line	Click the up scroll arrow
Scroll down one line	Click the down scroll arrow
Scroll up one screen	Click above the scroll box
Scroll down one screen	Click below the scroll box
Scroll to a specific page	Drag the scroll box
Scroll left	Click the left scroll arrow

(Contd...)

Scroll right	Click the right scroll arrow
Scroll left, beyond the margin, in normal view	Hold down Shift key and click the left scroll arrow

For a quick way to scroll up or down one page, click Select Browse Object on the vertical scroll bar, and then click the desired option (See Figure 3.2).

Typing and Editing a Document

You can start typing in a document without worrying about the end of the right margin. The words at the end of the line will automatically wrap text to the next line. You may correct the text by pressing Backspace key. The editing of documents is based on the windows principle, that is *select* and *do*.

3.3.2 Save and Save As

The first time you save a file, you need to specify three items:

1. The drive and folder in which you want to store your file.
2. The name of the file.
3. The format to save the file.

➡ **To save a document, do this:**

1. Click **File** tab and then select **Save** tab. *Alternatively*, choose the save button on the Quick Access toolbar.
2. When you save a document for the first time, Word 2010 displays the Save As... dialog box, so that you can type a name for the document (See Figure 3.9).
3. Click Save in: drop-down, to specify a drive and folder to save your file.
4. Click in the File name: text box and type a name of the file.
5. Click Save button.

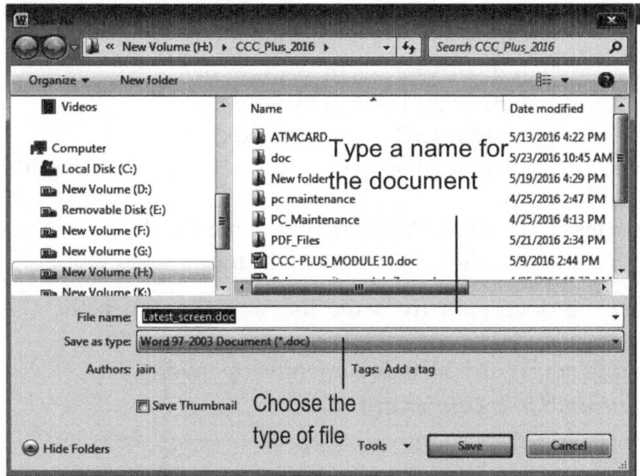

Figure 3.9 Save As dialog box

Naming a Document

In Windows, a filename can be from one to 255 characters along, followed by a period and upto three character filename extension. (In most cases, it is best to let Word supply the default extension for Word documents, which is **.docx**). You can use any characters except the following characters for naming the files:

* ? : [] + = \ / : / <>

You cannot use a period except to separate the filename from the extension.

3.3.3 Page Setup Options

Word 2010 default margins are 1 inch at the *top* and *bottom* each and 1 inch on the *left* and *right*. You can change the margins for the entire document or for different parts of the document (if you divide the document into sections).

Note that in Draft and Outline view, you do not see the margins. However, you can see the space between them in Print Layout view, and you can see the page as it will print. Always select the Print Layout view if you want to see *headers, footers, page numbers, footnotes*, etc.

You can also select one of the two types of page orientations namely, portrait (*vertical*) and landscape (*horizontal*). You can change the paper size and page orientation for a section or for the entire document.

☞ *Indents are added to margin settings. That is, if you specify a 1.0" left margin and a 1/2" left indent, your text will print 1 1/2 from the left margin. If you set a 1.0" right margin and indent the right edge of a paragraph 1.0", the text will stop 2.0" from the right edge of the page* (See Figure 3.10).

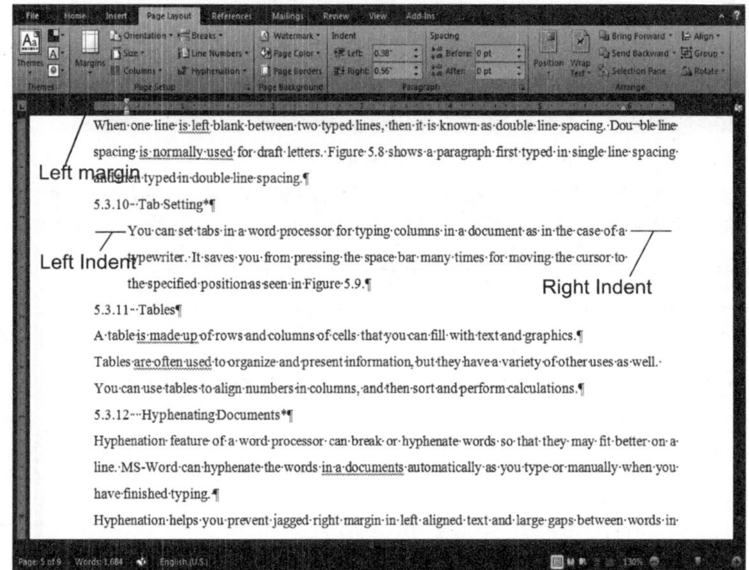

Figure 3.10 Page margins and indents

A *page* can have only one user-defined left margins setting and only one user-defined right margin setting, but each *paragraph* on the page can have different left and right indentation.

Setting Document Margins

There are two methods to set margins. These are:

- Page Setup command in the Page Layout tab.
- Adjust the margin using the rulers in the Print Layout View.

➡ **To set margins with the page setup command, do this:**

1. Select the sections for which you want to change margins. *Alternatively*, position the insertion point in the section whose margins you want to change.
2. Click **Page Layout** tab and click the right corner arrow of **Page setup**. The **Page Setup** dialog box appears. Click the **Margins** tab property sheet as seen in Figure 3.11 appears.
3. Margins Property sheet has the following options:

Option	Description
Top:	Select or type out the desired margin from the top of the page.

(Contd...)

Bottom:	Select or type out the desired margins from the bottom of the page.
Left:	Select or type out the desired margin from the left edge of the page.
Right:	Select or type out the desired margin from the right edge of the page.
Gutter:	Select or type out the gutter space as required. Gutter is the extra space added to the margins to leave the space for binding the documents.
Orientation	Select between Portrait (vertical) or Landscape (horizontal) page setting.

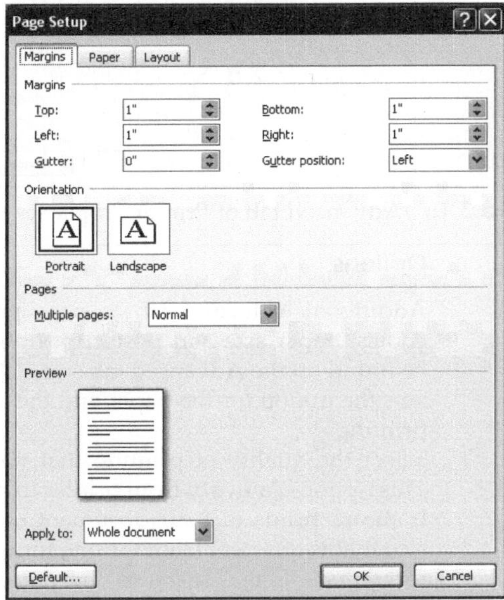

Figure 3.11 Page Setup dialog box

4. In the Pages area, select the Multiple pages: list.
   Mirror margins—This option adjusts left and right margins so that when you print on both sides of the page the inside and outside margins of the facing pages are of the same width.
   The Preview box displays the effect of the settings you select.
5. In the Apply to: choose the portion of the document from where you want to apply the new settings.
6. Click OK.

➡ **To set the margins using the ruler, do this:**

1. Switch to Print Layout view.
2. If the ruler is not displayed, click **View** tab. In the **Show** group, click the **Ruler** check box.
3. Point to the transition area on the ruler that is where *gray becomes white.*
4. The mouse pointer will become a two-headed arrow.
5. Drag the margin to the desired position with a mouse. The ruler's dimensions change as you drag (See Figure 3.12).

Paper Size

Page margins are usually set in according to paper size you use.

➡ **To select paper size, do this:**

1. Select the text, in the section you want to change.
2. In the **Page Setup** dialog box click **Paper** tab. The property sheet shown in Figure 3.13 appears.

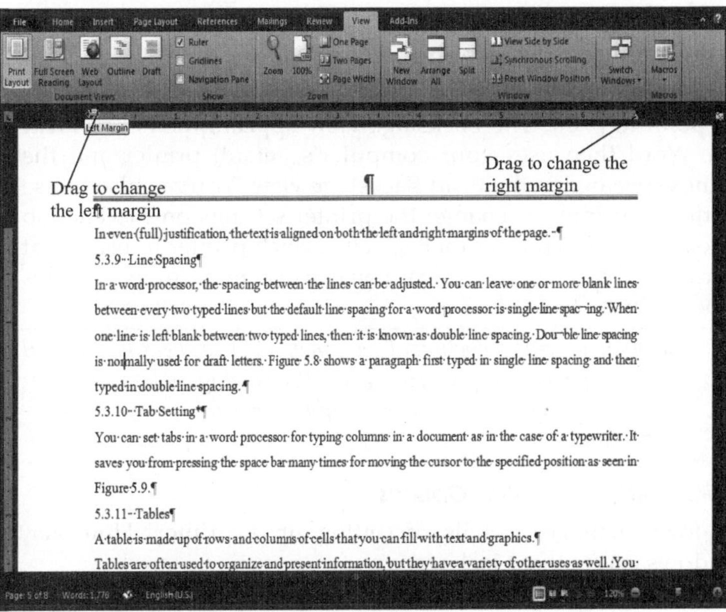

Figure 3.12 Drag ruler ends in print Layout to change the margins

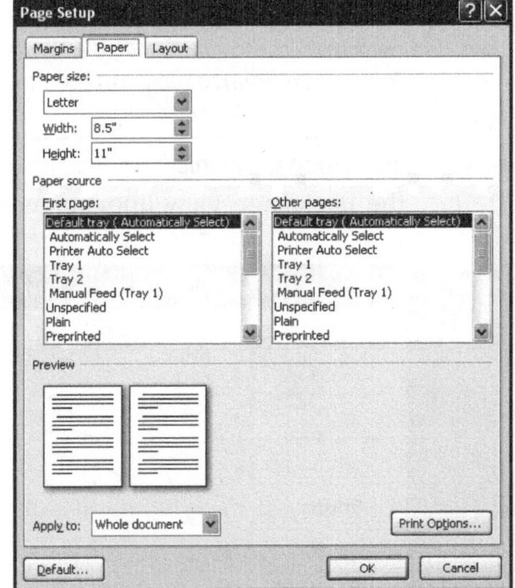

Figure 3.13 Paper size property sheet tab

3. The Page Setup dialog box has the following options:

Option	Function
Paper size:	The list in the form of drop-down offers different standard paper size. Select from the standard sizes or specify the width and height as the case may be. The commonly used paper size is A4 and legal.
Width:	Type or select the width of the paper you are using.
Height:	Type or select the height of the paper you are using.

5. In the Apply to: select the portion of the document you want to print on the selected paper size.
6. Click the Default... buttons if you want to save these settings as default settings, so that they can apply to all pages printed hereafter.

7. Click OK.

3.3.4 Printing of Documents

When you are ready to print a document, you can click the **File** tab, point to print. The Backstage view appears then click **Print** icon. Word then uses your computer's default printer and the settings specified in the **Print** Backstage view. You can also to use a different printer or change the printer settings on the File tab Backstage view. You can then specify which printer to use, what to print, and how many copies. You can also make other changes to the settings.

☞ *Before you print a document, you may want to check how it will look on paper by previewing it. Previewing is essential for multi-page documents but is helpful even for one-page documents also.*

Setting Printer Properties Options

Windows manages details of setting up a printer. However, Windows leaves three tasks for you:

- Selecting the printer you want to use in Word 2010.
- Installing the printers if not available in the list of Windows printers.
- Changing the printer setup for special printing needs.

☞ *Most of the printer options are set by Word 2010 depending upon the printer selected by you. All the same, many options are available to you so that you can customize the printing options as per your requirement.*

➡ **To set printer specific options, do this:**

1. Click the **File** tab, the Backstage view appears as shown in Figure 3.14.

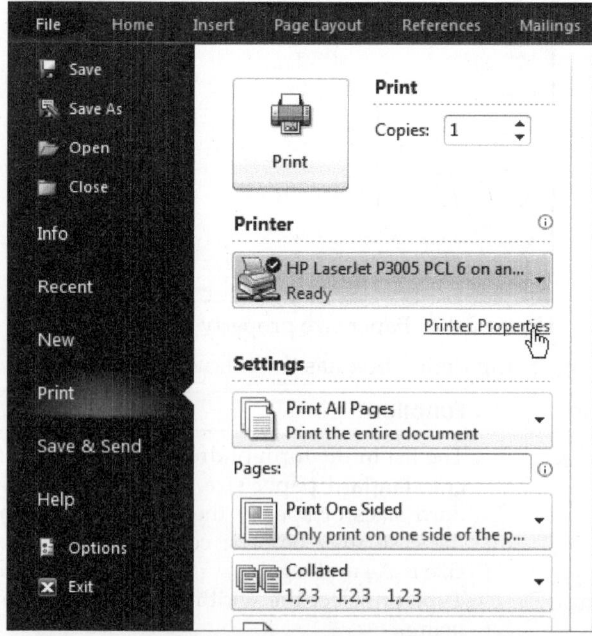

Figure 3.14 Selecting Printer Properties in the File tab

2. Under the **Printer** drop-down list select the printer.
3. Click the **Printer Properties** in the **File** Backstage view as shown in Figure 3.14.
4. The **Printer Properties** dialog box appears as shown in Figure 3.15.
5. The **Properties** dialog box generally has the following tabs.

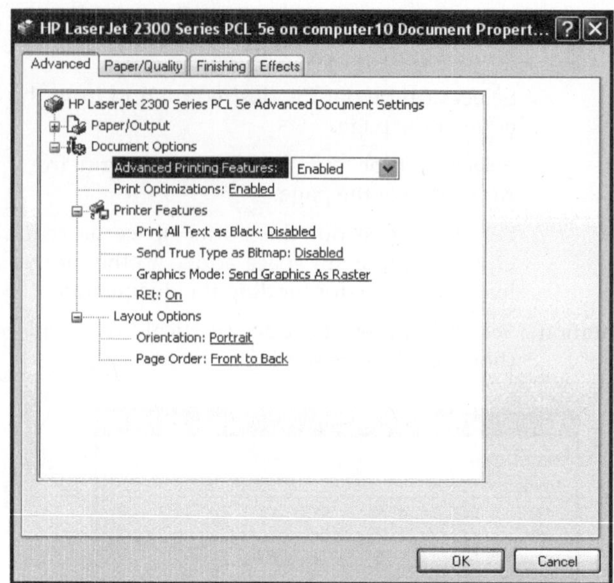

Figure 3.15 Advanced tab of Printer Properties

Tab	Options
Advanced	Additional features, such as page protection, copies, paper size and postscript options may be found on the Advanced tab.
Paper/ Quality	Sets the option for the paper and the quality of printing.
Finishing	Select the quality of printing that you desire. This options can vary from printer to printer.
Effects	It shows prints of your document on a paper size that is different from the one for which it is formatted. It also specifies the percentage of normal size.

6. Click the **Advanced** tab. The options are:

   In the page order section

   - If you choose Fr<u>o</u>nt to Back, it specifies the order in which the pages of your document will be printed. It starts printing from page 1 to end.
   - If you choose <u>B</u>ack to Front, it prints the document from end to first page.

7. Click the Paper/Quality tab as shown in Figure 3.16 the options are:

   In the paper options

   - Click use different paper to enable settings that allow you to select a different paper source and type settings for the first page, other pages and back cover in the print job.
   - <u>S</u>ource is: click the drop-down list and choose the desired option where the paper is located in the printer.
   - <u>T</u>ype is: select the kind of paper you want to use.

8. Click OK.
9. In the **Print** dialog box, again click OK.

Printing the Current Document

The simplest way to print is to open a document, click **File** tab, choose Print tab. The Backstage view appears choose **Print** icon. *Alternately*, click the Print button on the Quick Access toolbar. By default, Word 2010 prints one copy of all pages of the currently open document on the selected printer without printing hidden text.

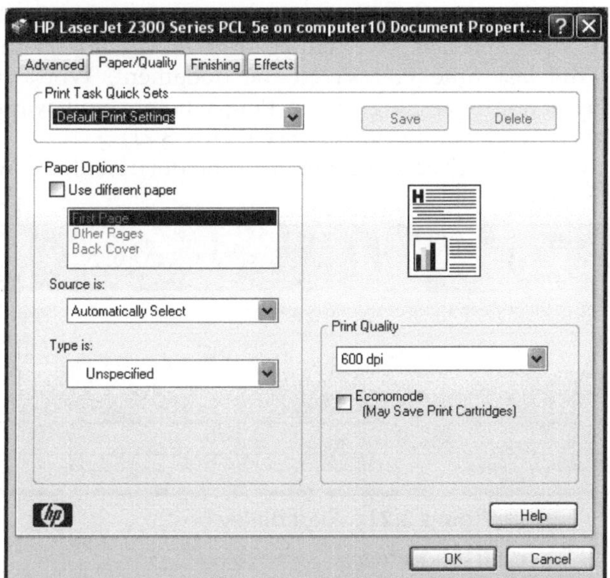

Figure 3.16 Properties options of Paper/Quality tab property sheet

➡ **To print a copy of the document, do this:**

1. Open the document you want to print.
2. Click the **File** tab and then choose **Print** command. The Print backstage view appears then click Print icon or press Ctrl+Shift+F12 keys together (See Figure 3.17).
3. The Print Backstage view closes and in the status bar displays the process of the print job (Figure 3.18).

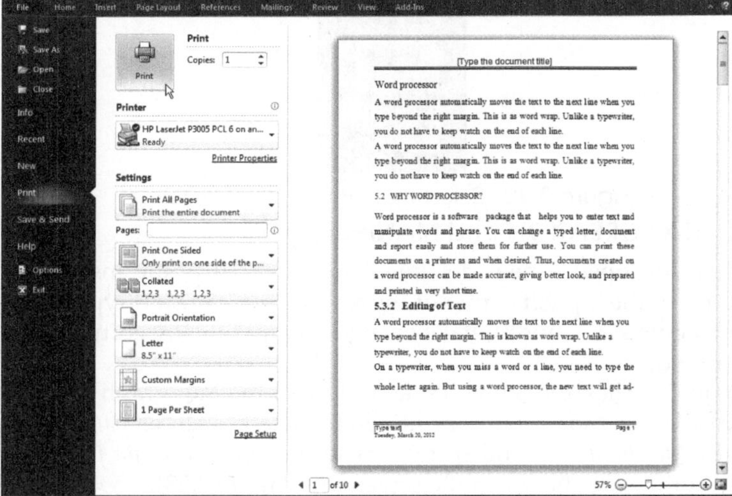

Figure 3.17 Print Backstage view

Page Range Options

- To print the entire document, click All button.
- To print just the page in your document currently containing the insertion point, click on the Current Page button.
- To print the selected text, first select it, then in the Print dialog box, use the Selection button in the Page Range area. This choice will be dimmed unless you have selected something in your document.
- To print a range of pages, say, pages **6-10** in a 50 page document, type the first page number and the last desired page number in the Pages: text box. Separate the numbers with hyphens (like **6-10**).

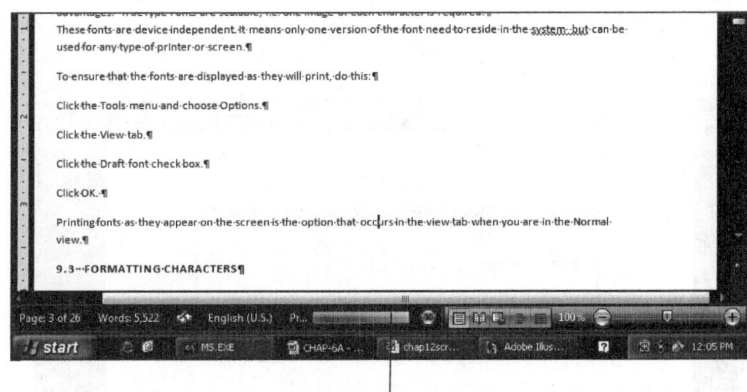

The process of print job in the status bar

Figure 3.18 Displaying the print process in the status bar

- You can also print pages in a certain section. To print the second section in your document, type **s2** in the Pages box. If you want to print from page 7 in the second section to page 10 in the third section, type **p7s2-p10s3** in the Pages box.
- The Print: drop-down list has the option which allows you to select the pages you want to print.

Option	Description
All pages	This is the default option and Word 2010 prints all pages in the range.
Odd pages	This option when selected prints the odd numbered pages in the range.
Even pages	This option when selected prints the even numbered pages in the range.

Odd and Even pages option is very useful when you want to do double-sided printing.

Copies: In the number of Copies: box, specify the number of copies of the document you want to print.

Collate: This option determines how multiple copies are printed. Say, you print five copies of a 10-page document without the Collate option, Word 2010 will first print all five copies of page 1 then all five copies of page 2 and so on. You will need to arrange them manually to make the sets. With the Collate option Word 2010 prints five sets, each one complete and in order.

➡ **To cancel printing, do this:**

1. Click the Start button and then click **Printers and Faxes**.
2. In the **Printers and Faxes** dialog box, open the printer that you are using by double-clicking the printer's icon (See Figure 3.19).
3. Select the document of which you want to cancel printing, and then choose **Document Name**, right click and choose Cancel Printing.

Previewing a Document

Previewing a document allows you to visualize the document in its printable format before actually executing the Print command. The preview of a document displays the document in a printable format and shows how the document will appear after taking a printout.

➡ **To preview the document, do this:**

1. Open the document whose print preview you want to view.

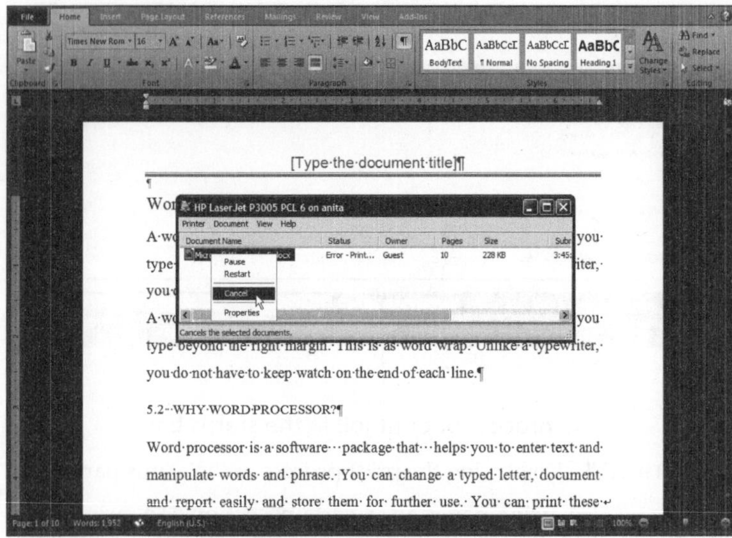

Figure 3.19 Printer folder open

2. Click the **File** tab and then choose **Print** option from the **File** tab. The **Print** options are visible in the Backstage view as shown in Figure 3.20.

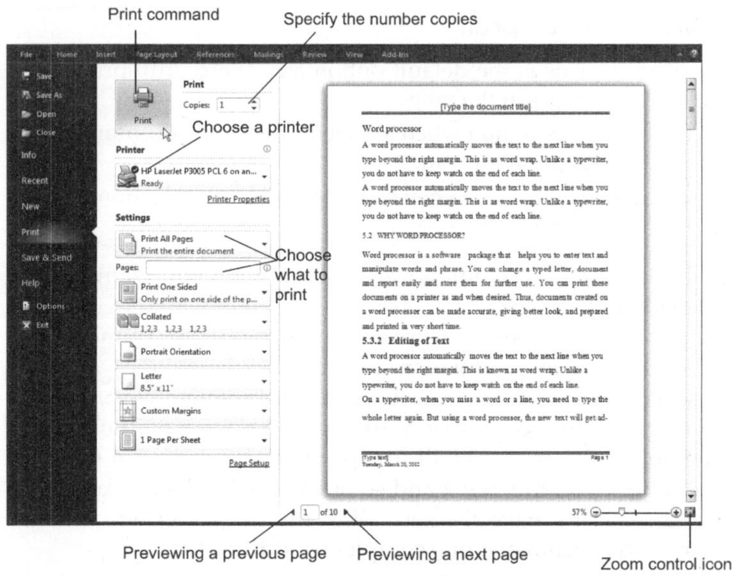

Figure 3.20 Print preview in the Backstage view

3. The Backstage view (See Figure 3.20) consists of three panes. The left pane contains several options, such as Save, Save As, Open, Close, Info, Recent, etc. In the middle pane, print options and its related printer settings are shown. In the right pane, the preview document is seen. In the bottom of the right pane, the Zoom control button is available. The + (plus) button is used to increase the document and the – (minus) button is used to decrease the preview document. The Next button goes to next page of document and the previous button to move to the previous page of document.

3.3.5 Closing, and Quitting Word 2010

After finishing a document, you should close the window to remove it from the screen and to free computer's main memory.

➡ **To close a document and exit Word 2010, do this:**

1. Click the **File** tab, and then choose **Close** tab.
2. The window closes if no changes have been made to the document since the last save. However, if you made changes since the last time you saved the document, Word 2010 displays an Alert dialog box, asking whether you want to save your work before closing (See Figure 3.21).
3. After you have saved the contents of the document, the window is closed.

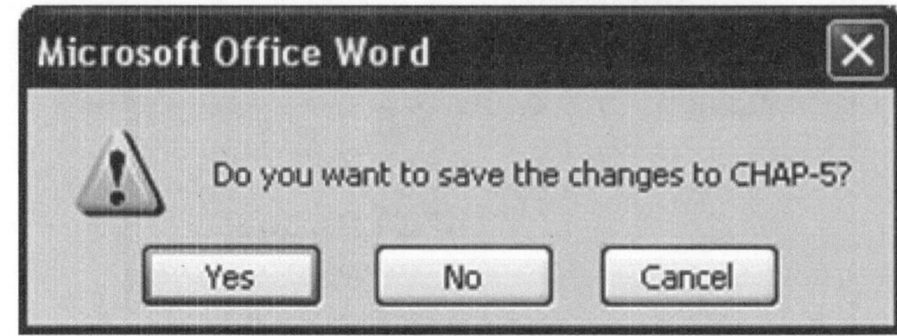

Figure 3.21 Alert dialog box

➡ **To quit Word 2010, do this:**

1. Click **File** tab, and then choose **Exit**. Word 2010 window closes, and the application is terminated (See Figure 3.22).

Figure 3.22 Selecting Exit from the File tab

3.4 TEXT CREATION and MANIPULATION

When you open a new document in Word 2010, the insertion point is at the top left corner of the screen. You can start typing in this document. You can make changes at any time by editing the document.

You can click the Show/Hide button on the Paragraph group to display or hide all non-printing characters, such as *paragraph marks*, *tab characters*, and *spaces*. These characters are *not printed*, even if they are shown on the screen (See Figure 3.23).

3.4.1 Creating a Blank Document

If you are creating a document, such as *memo*, *letter*, *report*, or *resume*, *Brochures*, *Calendars*, *Card*, etc., you can save time by using one of the wizards or templates that come with Word 2010.

You can also create a blank document which is based on the blank template of Word 2010. The blank template offers you the flexibility to create and edit documents according to your requirements.

➡ **To create a new document, do this:**

1. Click **File** tab, a Backstage view appears, click the **New** tab in the Backstage view as shown in Figure 3.24.
2. Select the **Blank document** option under **Available templates** as shown in Figure 3.24.
3. Click the **Create** button as seen in Figure 3.24. The new blank document is created as seen in Figure 3.25.

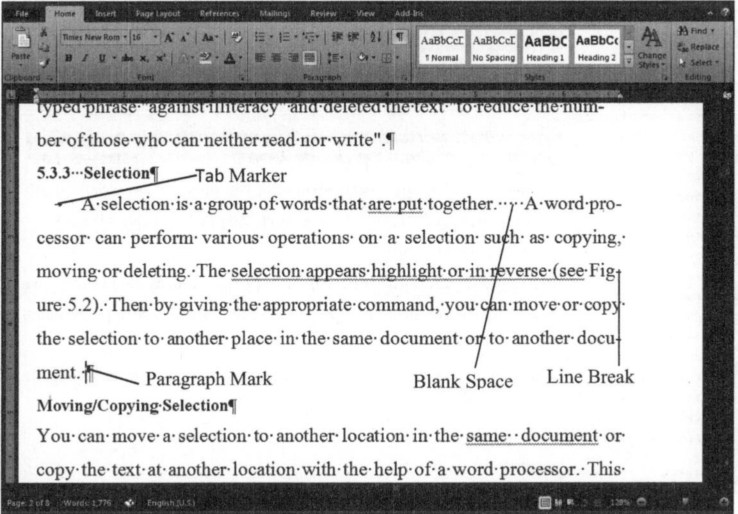

Figure 3.23 A screen displaying non-printing characters

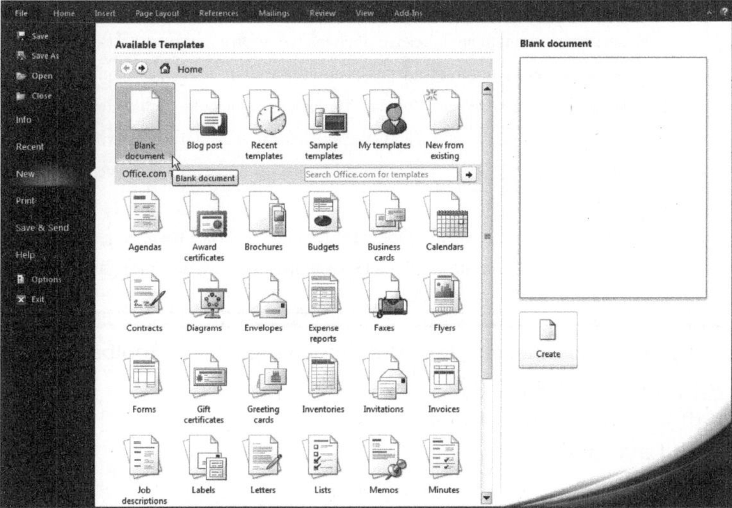

Figure 3.24 New tab Backstage view

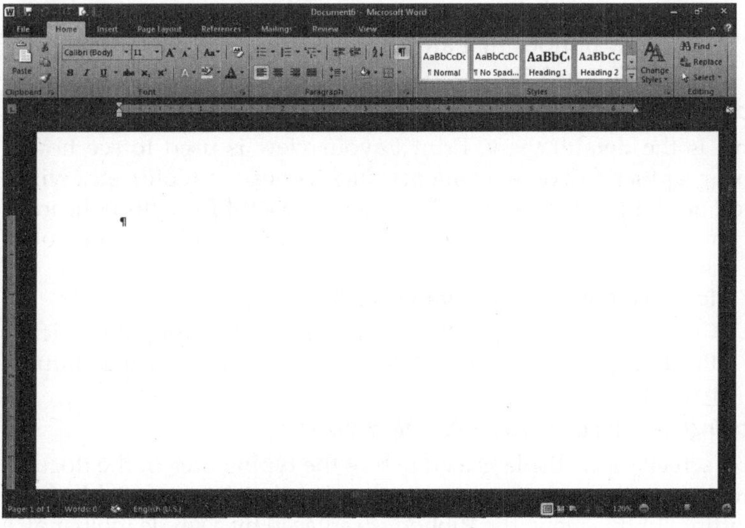

Figure 3.25 Word blank document

Starting a New Paragraph

In Word 2010, a paragraph is any amount of text or graphics followed by a paragraph mark. A paragraph ends whenever you press the Enter key. Even if you have not typed any text but press Enter key, Word 2010 inserts a paragraph mark (¶). In Word 2010, many types of formatting (for example, justification and line spacing) are applied to paragraphs as a whole.

➡ **To start a new paragraph, do this:**

1. Position the insertion point where you want to start the new paragraph, and press the Enter key.

When you press Enter key, Word 2010 inserts a paragraph mark and moves the insertion point to the first line of the new paragraph.

Starting a New Line

Word 2010 automatically wraps text to the next line when the typed text reaches the end of the right margin.

➡ **To start a new line within the same paragraph, do this:**

1. Position the insertion point where you want to start the new line, and then press Shift+Enter keys together.
2. Word inserts a line break character and moves the insertion point to the beginning of the next line.
3. To see the line breaks, click the Show/Hide command on the **paragraph** group of **Home** tab.

3.4.2 Editing Text

On a typewriter, when you miss a word or a line, you need to type the whole letter again. But using a Word 2010, you can insert new words, new sentences or paragraphs anywhere in the text typed earlier. The new text will get adjusted automatically. Similarly, you can delete any portion of the text and the remaining part of the matter will get adjusted automatically.

In Figure 3.26, you can see the highlighted text is newly inserted and rest of the text gets deleted.

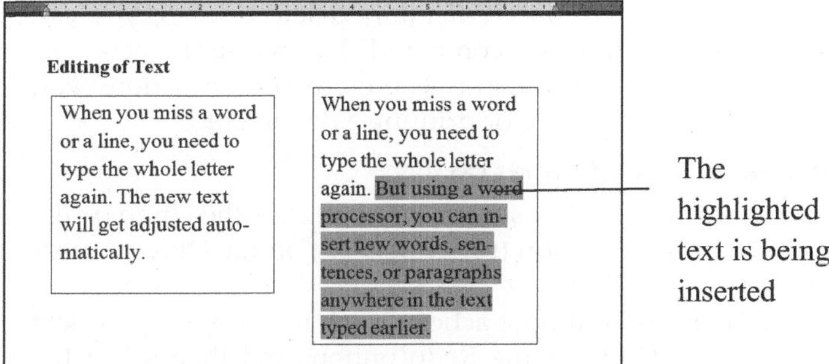
Editing of Text

When you miss a word or a line, you need to type the whole letter again. The new text will get adjusted automatically.

When you miss a word or a line, you need to type the whole letter again. But using a word processor, you can insert new words, sentences, or paragraphs anywhere in the text typed earlier.

The highlighted text is being inserted

Figure 3.26 Adding/deleting text

Inserting Text

If you notice that some text has been left out of the document, you can move the Insertion pointer to that position and type it in. This method is called *Inserting*.

Typing over the Existing Text

By default, Word moves the existing text to the right as you insert new characters. If you want the new text to replace the existing text, character by character, switch to *overtype* mode. Again clicking the *overtype* mode in the status bar will automatically replace the *insert* mode.

➡ **To type over the existing text, do this:**

1. Click the **File** tab and then choose **Options**.

2. The **Word Options** dialog box, click **Advanced** tab in the left pane and then under **Editing options**, select *use the Insert key to control overtype mode* check box.
3. Click OK.

Applying Corrections in the Typed Text

To correct simple typing mistakes, press Backspace or Del keys. To delete more characters, *first select the text you* want to delete and then press the Backspace or Del key. Table 3.4 lists different methods for deleting texts and graphics.

Table 3.4 Key Combinations for deleting Text or Graphics

To delete	Key combination
Selected text	Press Backspace or Del
Characters before the insertion point	Press Backspace key
Characters after the insertion point	Press Del key
A word before the insertion point	Ctrl+Backspace
A word after the insertion point	Ctrl+Del

➡ **To restore the deleted text, do this:**

1. On the Quick Access toolbar, click the Undo button. *Alternatively*, click the Ctrl+Z keys together.

➡ **To replace a selection with a new text, do this:**

1. Select the text you want to replace.
2. Type the new text.

The text you type replaces the entire selection.

Undoing Mistakes

If you make a mistake in Word 2010, you can apply "Undo" command. For example, if you accidentally delete a word, you can bring it back with the Undo command. To reverse the action of undo use the "Redo" command. There are certain actions you cannot undo, such as saving or printing a document.

➡ **To undo or redo changes do this:**

1. To undo or redo the most recent action, click the Undo (press Ctrl+Z) or Redo button (press Ctrl+Y) on the Quick Access toolbar.
2. To undo or redo multiple actions, click the down arrow next to either the Undo or the Redo button, and then select the actions you want to undo or redo (See Figure 3.27).

Select the Text with the Pop-up Toolbar

Word 2010 displays a pop-up toolbar. For example, select the text on which you want to apply formatting, such as *bold, font size,* etc., a pop-up toolbar appears to the upper right of the selected text as a faint image. The closer you move the mouse towards this pop-up toolbar, the darker and sharper the toolbar appears as seen in Figure 3.28.

Displaying Different Views of a Document

The type of work that you do will help you to determine the best screen view as per your needs. There are different views available in Word 2010. These are:

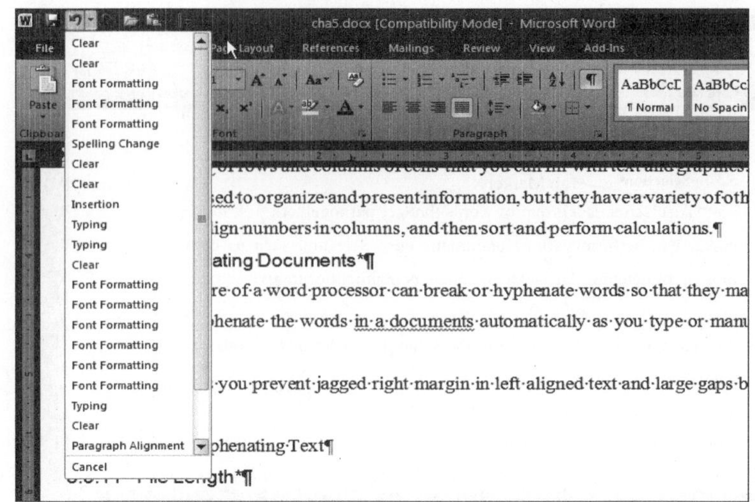

Figure 3.27 Selecting undo list

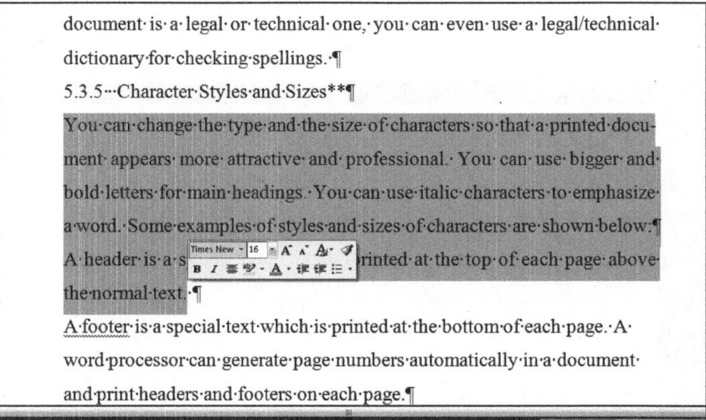

document is a legal or technical one, you can even use a legal/technical dictionary for checking spellings.¶
5.3.5 Character Styles and Sizes**¶
You can change the type and the size of characters so that a printed document appears more attractive and professional. You can use bigger and bold letters for main headings. You can use italic characters to emphasize a word. Some examples of styles and sizes of characters are shown below:¶
A header is a s[...]rinted at the top of each page above the normal text.¶
A footer is a special text which is printed at the bottom of each page. A word processor can generate page numbers automatically in a document and print headers and footers on each page.¶

Figure 3.28 Selecting text and displaying pop-up toolbar

- Print Layout View
- Full screen Reading View
- Web Layout View
- Outline View
- Draft View

There are two ways so that you can change the view. These are:

- Click the View tab, in the Document views group, and switch to any view you wish to see the document.
- Click view buttons that are found on the right side of the status (See Figure 3.29).

Editing text in Print Layout View

This is the default view. Print Layout view is used to see how text, graphics and other elements, such as header, footer, etc., will look on the printed output. This view is useful for editing headers and footers, for adjusting margins and for working with columns and drawing objects.

➡ **To work in Print Layout view, do this:**

1. Click the **View** tab, in the Document views group and click Print Layout command. Alternatively click from the status bar icons (Figure 3.29).

Editing text in Full Screen Reading View

Full screen view displays as much of the typing area of the document as will fit on the screen at a size that is comfortable for reading. In this view, the Ribbon is replaced by a single toolbar at the top of the screen. You can print the document, highlight text and write comments. You can also move from page to page and adjust the view.

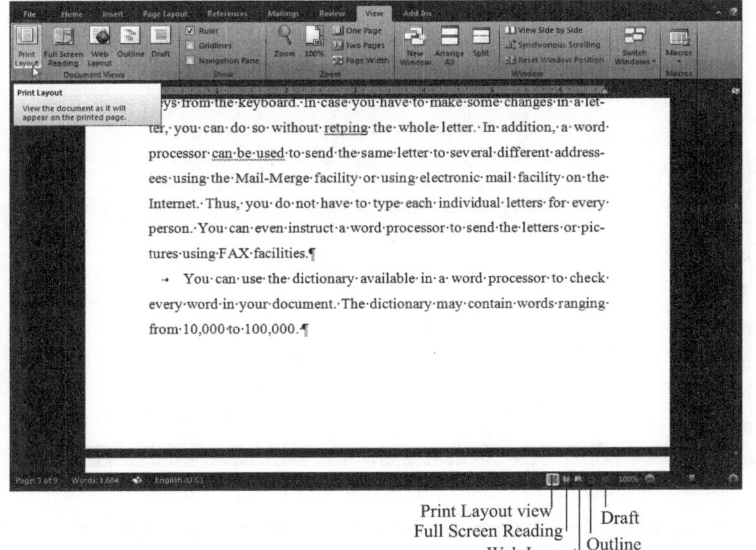

Figure 3.29 Editing a document in Print Layout view

➡ **To switch to full screen view, do this:**

1. Click the **View** tab, in the **Document Views** group and click Full Screen Reading command as in Figure 3.29. *Alternatively*, click Full Screen reading from the status bar icons.
2. In Full reading screen, click the View Options, a drop-down menu appears. You can make the text larger or smaller for reading by clicking Increase Text Size or Decrease Text Size. This will temporarily change as to fits text on a page. It does not affect the original document.
3. You can read one page at a time by clicking Show one page, or you can read two pages at a time by clicking Show Two pages.
4. While reading in full screen view, you can edit document by clicking Allow Typing.

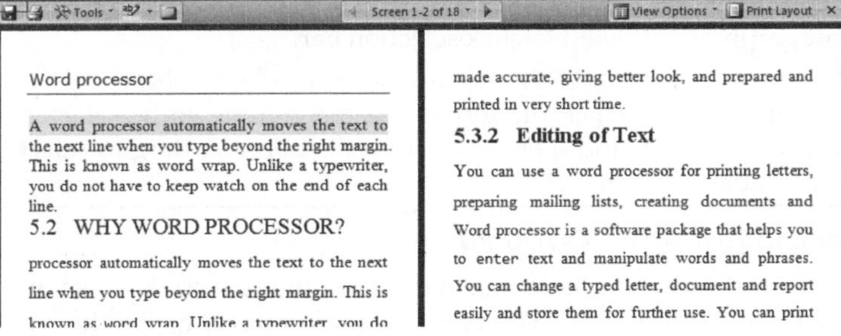

Figure 3.30 Full Screen View

5. To go to the *previous screen* or to the *next screen*, click jump to a screen at the top of the title bar in the full screen view (See Figure 3.30).
6. To exit Full Screen Reading view, click Esc button or click Print Layout button (See Figure 3.30).

Editing in Web Layout View

While creating a Web page in Word 2010, you should work in Web Layout view. In Web Layout view, you can see that background text is wrapped to fit the window. Graphics are positioned at proper places, so that the page will look just as it would look in a Web browser (See Figure 3.31).

➡ **To switch to Web Layout view, do this:**

1. Click the **View** tab, in the **Document views** group and click **Web Layout** view command as in Figure 3.31. *Alternatively*, click Web layout from the status bar icons.

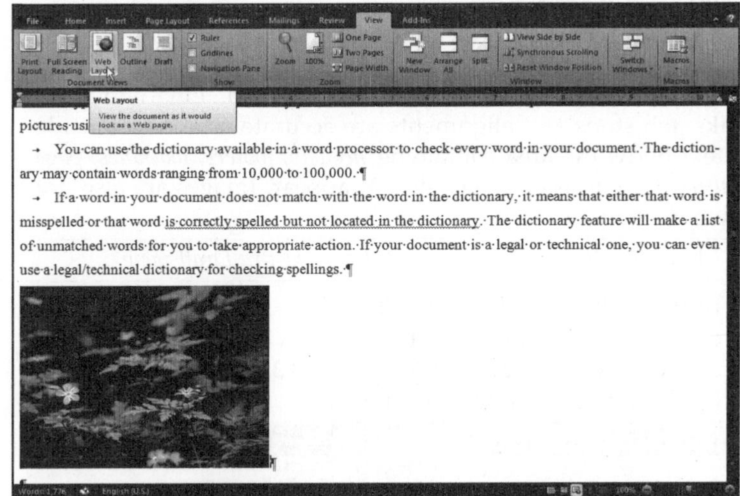

Figure 3.31 Document seen in Web layout view

Editing text in Outline View

In the Outline View, you can collapse a document to see only the main headings or expand it to see the entire document. In this view it is easy to scroll or move text to a longer distance or to change the hierarchy of topics (See Figure 3.32).

➡ **To switch to Outline View, do this:**

1. Click the **View** tab, in the **Document views** group and click **Outline** view command as in Figure 3.31. *Alternatively*, click Outline view from the status bar icons.

In the outline view, the outline toolbar appears as seen in Figure 3.32. Word 2010 indents the formatting headings and body text paragraphs to different levels. Note that (+) or (–) sign appears to the left of each heading.

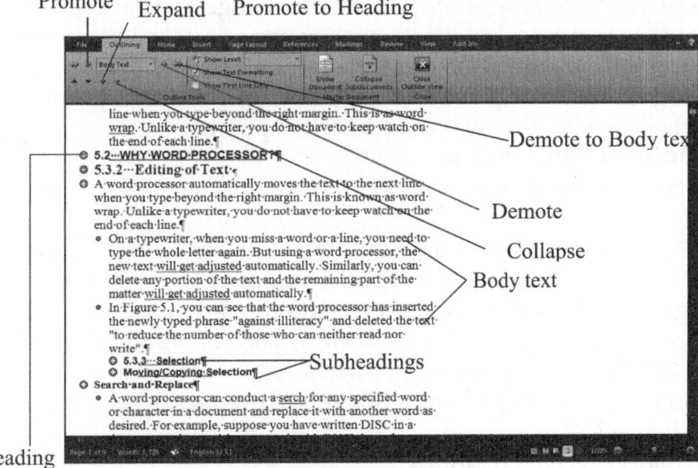

Figure 3.32 Document in Outline view

- A plus sign (+) indicates that sub-heading or paragraphs of the body text are associated with the heading.
- A minus sign (–) indicates that no headings or paragraphs are beneath the heading.

☞ *In the outline view you will also get the options of viewing headings at different levels or of viewing entire document, including the body text.*

Editing in Draft View

Draft view is the best view for most of your typing and editing as can be seen (Figure 3.33). In this view, you can see character and paragraph formatting as they will be printed. Line and page breaks, tab stops and alignments are accurate. The area outside the text body–the area containing *headers, footers, footnotes, page numbers, margin spacing*, etc., do not appear. Images are also not shown in Draft view.

☞ *Note that the cursor movement is very fast in Draft view.*

➡ **To switch to Draft view, do this:**

1. Click the **View** tab, in the **Document** views group and click **Draft** view command as in Figure 3.33. *Alternatively*, click Draft view from the status bar icons.

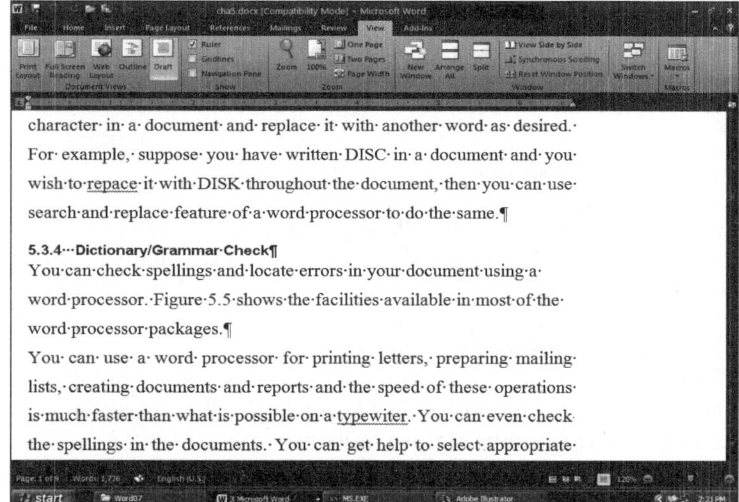

Figure 3.33 Document in Draft view

3.4.3 Text Selection

Before you can *move, format, delete*, or change text or a graphic picture, you must select the items. You can select the item using a mouse or keyboard. Note that the selected text or graphics are highlighted. To cancel the selection, click outside the selection, or use the arrow keys to move the insertion point.

➡ **To select text, do this:**

1. Position the insertion point from where you want to select text.
2. Now press the left mouse button and select the text by moving mouse pointer. *Alternatively*, you can also select text and graphics by positioning the insertion point at the beginning of the text or graphic you want to select, holding down the Shift key, and then clicking where you want the selection to end. The selected text highlighted appears as seen in Figure 3.34.

Selecting Text with a Mouse

You can select a piece of text, or a single character or an entire document. You can also combine mouse and keyboard selection techniques.

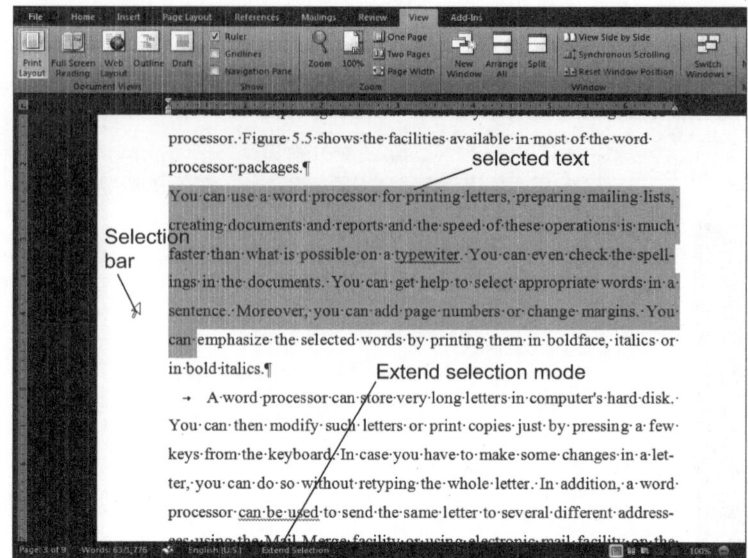

Figure 3.34 Using selection bar to select text

➡ **To select a small amount of text with the mouse, do this:**

1. Click and hold the mouse button at the beginning of the text you want to select.
2. Drag the pointer in any direction across the text you want to select.

☞ *If the pointer touches the edge of the window as you are dragging, the window scrolls in that direction if more text exists.*

You can select text using one of the methods given in Table 3.5.

Table 3.5 Method for Selecting Text

Text to select	Mouse Action
A word	Double-click the word.
A line	Click selection bar (blank margin to left of a line of text).
Multiple lines	Click selection bar and drag up or down till the end of lines.
A paragraph	Double-click selection bar.
Document	Press Ctrl key and click in selection bar.
Rectangular block or column (not within a table)	Click the top left of the column to be selected and then hold Alt key while you drag to select the text.

Selecting Text with a Keyboard

The method for selecting text is to hold down the Shift key as you move the insertion point. You can select text by using Shift key in combination with any move key. Some of these key combinations are listed in Table 3.6.

Table 3.6 Key Combination for Selecting Text

To Select	Press
A word	Shift+Ctrl + ← or → arrow key
To the beginning of a line	Shift+Home
To the end of a line	Shift+End
To the end of a paragraph	Ctrl+Shift+↓
To the beginning of a paragraph	Ctrl+Shift+↑

(Contd...)

To Select	Press
One line at a time	Shift+↑ or Shift+↓
To the beginning of a document	Shift+Ctrl+Home
To the end of a document	Shift+Ctrl+End

➡ **To select from the insertion point to a distant location, do this:**

1. Move the insertion point to the beginning of the text you want to select.
2. Press F8 (Extend Selection).

☞ *While you are in Extend Selection mode, the word appears on the status bar at the bottom of the screen.*

3. Press one of the keys listed in the Table 3.7. And finally press Esc key.

Table 3.7 Selecting Text from the Insertion Point

To Select	Press
Next or previous character	← or → arrow key
The end of a line	End key
The beginning of a line	Home key
The top of the previous screen	PgUp key
The bottom of the next screen	PgDn key
The beginning of a document	Ctrl+Home keys
The end of a document	Ctrl+End keys

3.4.4 Cut, Copy and Paste

"Copying" means to make a copy of the selected text or graphic and insert it in another location, leaving the original document unchanged.

➡ **To copy text from one location to another in the same document, do this:**

1. Select the text you want to copy.
2. Click **Copy** option from the **Clipboard** group. The selected text will be placed on the Clipboard which is an accessory in Word (see Figure 3.35).

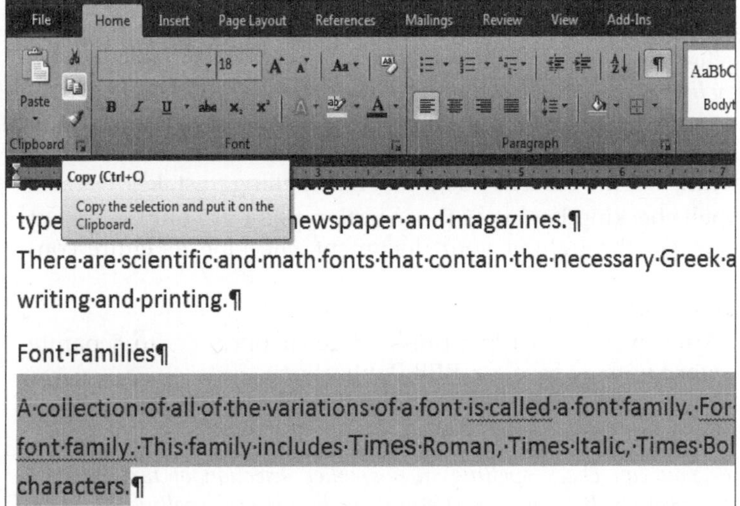

Figure 3.35 Select the text to be copied

3. Now position the insertion point at the location you want to place the text.
4. Click the **Paste** option from the **Clipboard** group as shown in Figure 3.36. The selected text will be pasted.

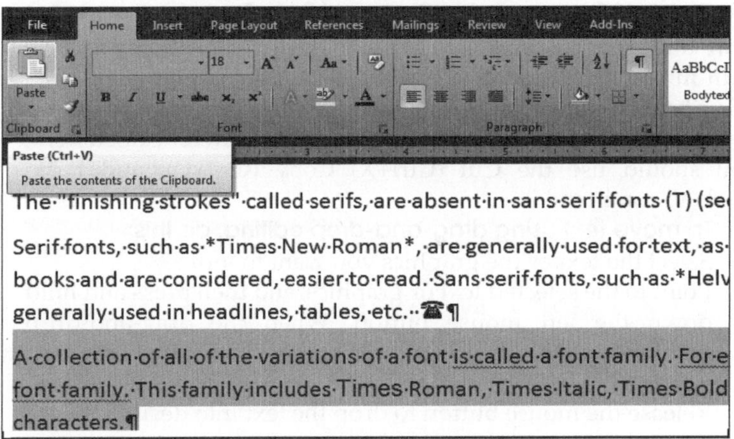

Figure 3.36 Selected text has been pasted

Moving Text

"*Moving*" means to remove (cut) the selected text or graphic from one location and insert it in another location in the same document in another document.

➡ **To move text from one location to another in the same document, do this:**

1. Select the text you want to move (See Figure 3.37).

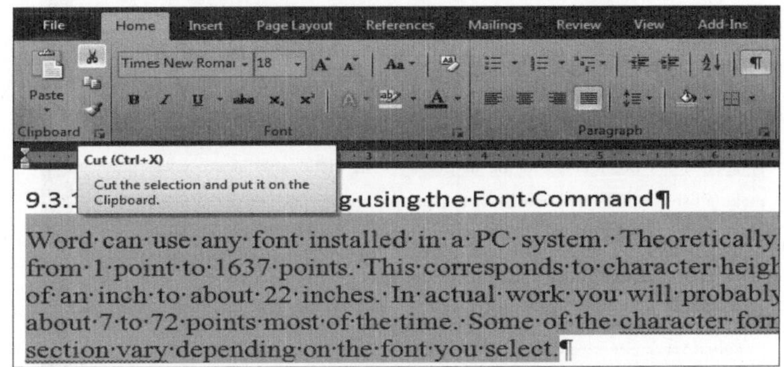

Figure 3.37 Highlight the text to move

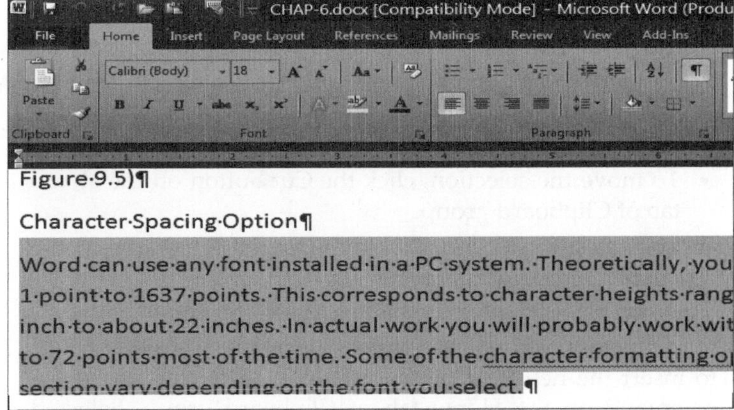

Figure 3.38 Highlighted text pasted in the new location

2. Click the **Cut** option from the **Clipboard** group. The selected text will disappear from the screen and will be placed on the Clipboard.
3. Now position the insertion point at the location you want to paste the text.

4. Click the **Paste** option from the **Clipboard** group. The selected text will be moved (See Figure 3.38).

Moving and Copying using Drag and Drop Technique

Drag-and-drop editing is an easy way to move or copy a selection with in a short distance of a document. You can *drag* and *drop* items between documents. However, to move or copy a selection to a longer distance in a document or to a different document, you should use the Cut (Ctrl+X) Copy (Ctrl+C), and Paste (Ctrl+V) commands.

➡ **To move text using drag-and-drop editing, do this:**

1. Select the text or the graphics you want to move.
2. Point to the selected text or graphics, and then press and hold down the left mouse button. When the drag-and-drop pointer appears as in Figure 3.39, drag the dotted insertion point to the new location.
3. Release the mouse button to drop the text into desired place.

➡ **To copy text/graphics using drag-and-drop editing, do this:**

1. Select the text or the graphics you want to copy.
2. Press and hold down Ctrl key, point to the selected text or the graphics, and then press and hold down the left mouse button while you drag the dotted insertion point to the new location.

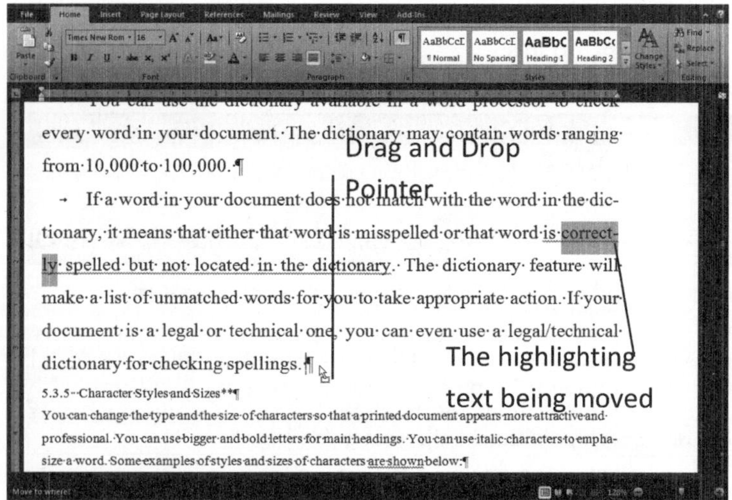

Figure 3.39 Drag and Drop mouse pointer

➡ **To move or copy the text/graphics using the toolbar, do this:**

1. Select the text or the graphics you want to move or copy.
2. Do one of the following:
   - To move the selection, click the Cut button on the Home tab of Clipboard group.
   - To copy the selection, click the Copy button on the Home tab of Clipboard group.

   Word places the selected text to the Clipboard.
3. Place the insertion point in the new location, where you want to insert the new text or the graphics. Now click the paste command on the Home tab of Clipboard group. Selected text/graphic will be pasted.

Using Keyboard Shortcuts for Moving and Copying

Word 2010 has many keyboard shortcuts, i.e., combination of keys for moving and copying text and graphics. Table 3.8 lists different methods for cutting, copying and moving text or graphics using the keyboard shortcuts.

Table 3.8 Keyboard Shortcuts for Moving and Copying Text or Graphics

Action	Key combination
Copy the selected text or the graphics to the Clipboard	Ctrl+C keys pressed together.
Move the selected text or the graphics to the Clipboard	Ctrl+X or Shift+Del keys pressed together.
Paste Clipboard contents into a document	Ctrl+V or Shift+Ins keys pressed together.
Move a paragraph up	Alt+Shift + ↑ arrow keys pressed together.
Move a paragraph down	Alt+Shift + ↓ arrow keys pressed together.

Deleting Text

To Delete characters to the right of insertion point press Del key but to delete characters to left of insertion point use Backspace key. However, when you have to delete number of lines, deleting one letter at a time becomes a lengthy process. It would be better if you select or highlight all the lines to be deleted as a block.

➡ **To delete text do this:**

1. Select the text to be deleted by pressing the left mouse button, and dragging to text, you want to select.
2. Now press Del key from the keyboard.

3.4.5 Using Spelling Checker

Spelling checker is a flexible and powerful tool that will automatically check spelling in a paragraph or in the entire document. It finds and corrects the spelling errors but does not consider the context of words. For example, it cannot check the improper usage of various words, namely *farm* in place of *form* or *no* in place of *know*.

The spelling checker compares each word in the document with the correct spelling stored in its electronic dictionary. If it does not find a word, then it asks you to verify the spelling of that word.

When automatic spell checking is on, Word 2010 uses a *red wavy line* to underline words it thinks are not spelled correctly, so that you can spot them on the screen. An icon of an open book with a red cross also appears at the right in the status bar to indicate that the current document has spelling mistakes.

Spell checking begins at the insertion point in your document and works throughout your document, checking its entire contents.

Writing Rules:

1. After ever word type, press spacebar once, i.e. to separate word with a space e.g. BPB Publications.
2. While using punctuation after a word, don't use space between the word and symbol. e.g. Oh!

☞ *You can check spelling in a smaller selection of text by first selecting that area of text and then checking the spelling.*

Checking a Document's Spelling Automatically

Spell checking and underlining occur as you type the text in Word 2010 document. However, automatic spell checking works only when this feature is enabled.

➡ **To switch on automatic spelling check, do this:**

1. Click the **File** tab on the ribbon. The backstage view appears select **Options**.
2. The **Word Options** dialog box appears. In the left side pane options, select **Proofing** as seen in Figure 3.40.

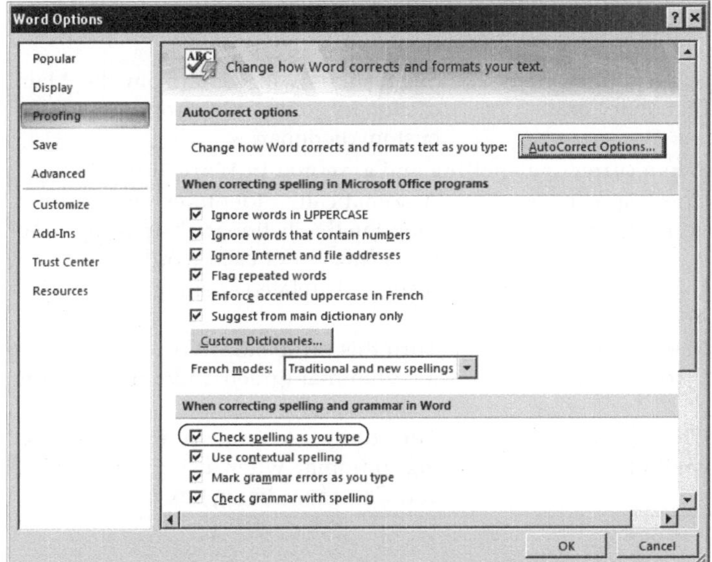

Figure 3.40 Word Options displaying Proofing Options

Icon indicating that the document has spelling mistakes

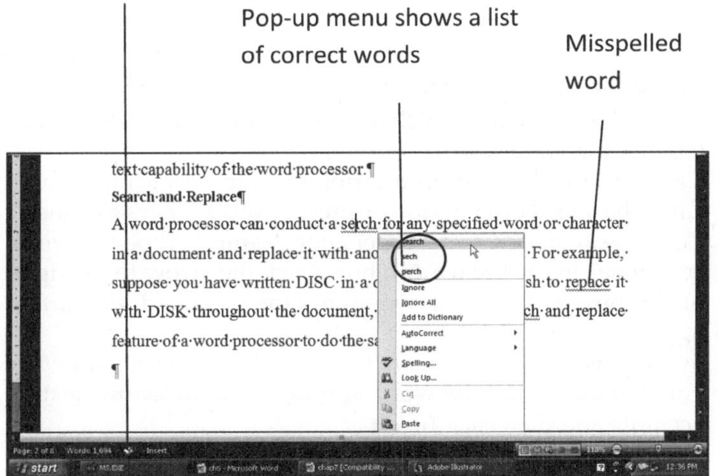

Figure 3.41 Popup Menu showing a list of suggested words

3. In Proofing page options, right side pane, under **When correcting spelling and grammar in Word**, select *Check spelling as you type* check box. Then click OK.

➡ **To check spelling of words with a wavy underline, do this:**

1. Right-click an underlined word. A popup menu appears (Figure 3.41). It displays a list of suggested words and additional options.
2. You have five choices for correcting the misspelled word. These are:
   - Select a word from the list shown in the pop-up menu.
   - Select Ignore to leave the word as it is.
   - Select Ignore All to ignore all occurrences of the word in your document.
   - Select Add to Dictionary to add the word to the selected dictionary displayed in the Custom Dictionary in the Spelling dialog box.
   - Select AutoCorrect and choose the correct spelling to automatically correct the misspelled word.

   To go to the next word, double-click the open book icon in the Status bar at the bottom of the screen to find the next underlined word in the document.
3. Repeat step 2 for each word of which you want to check spelling.

Spelling Command for Checking Spelling

➡ **To check spelling with spelling command, do this:**

1. Select the word or a document that you want to check for spelling. If you select nothing, Word 2010 checks the entire document.
2. Click the **Review** tab. Click **Spelling & Grammar** icon or press F7 key in the **Proofing** group. Word 2010 scrolls through your document and selects words that it does not recognize. The misspelled word is highlighted in the text and displayed in the **Not in Dictionary:** box (Figure 3.42).
3. Select the correct word from the Suggestions: list and then choose any one from the following list:
   - Click Ignore Once, to leave the word as it is.
   - Click Ignore All, to ignore all occurrences of the word in the document.
   - Click the Add to Dictionary, button to add this word to the Word 2010 dictionary. The selected word will be added to the dictionary.
   - Click the Change button to change the word.
   - Click Change All to change all occurrences of the misspelled word in the document.

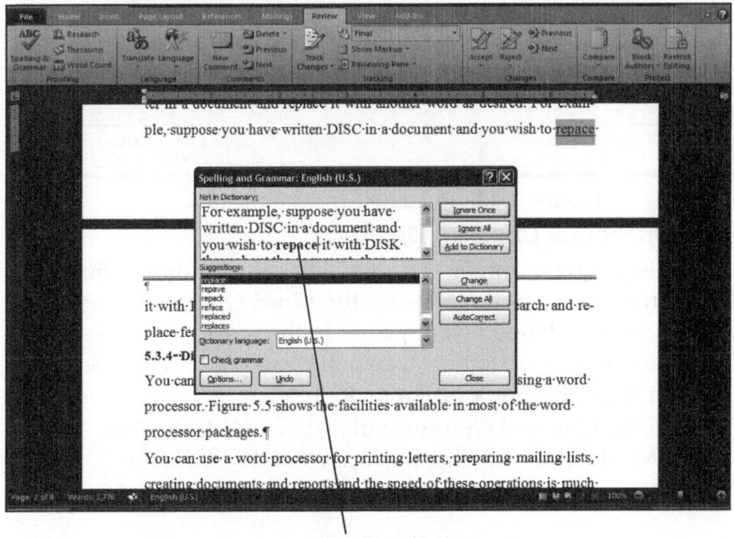

Figure 3.42 Spelling and Grammar dialog box

4. If none of the words in the **Suggestions:** list are correct, you can edit the word from within the **Not in Dictionary:** box.
5. After editing the word do one of the following:
   - Click the Change button to update the document window.
   - Click the Undo Edit button to undo the spelling change.
6. Word will now continue search the misspelled word. Click **Cancel** to stop the spell checking if so desired.
7. If you are checking a selected portion of a document, then after reaching the end of the selection, a dialog box asks whether you want to check the remaining portion of the document. Click Yes to check the remaining document or No to exit the spell checker.

➡ **To edit your document without closing the spelling and grammar dialog box, do this:**

1. Drag the Spelling and Grammar dialog box away from the area that you want to edit.
2. Click in the document or press Ctrl+Tab keys to activate the document window.
3. After editing the document, click the Resume button in the Spelling and Grammar dialog box or press Ctrl+Tab keys to resume checking spelling, from where you had stopped.

Double Words Correction

When Word spelling checker detects double words, (say the the) then the Not in Dictionary: box changes to the **Repeated Word:** box, (Figure 3.43) and the repeated word get highlighted in red.

To delete the repeated word, click the Delete button.

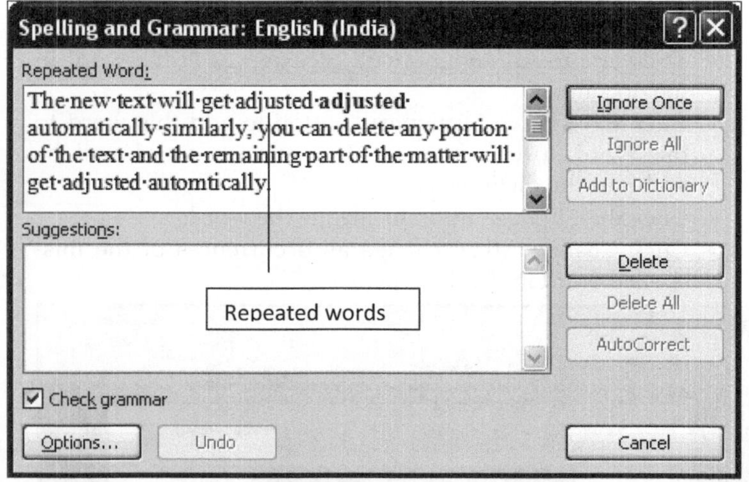

Figure 3.43 Repeated word indicated

Setting Options for Checking Spelling

The Spelling and Grammar dialog box has the Options... button. Clicking this button, will opens up the Word Options and Proofing page options dialog box appears. In this page, you can select different options to customize the spell checking operations.

➡ **To set spelling check options, do this:**

1. In the Spelling and Grammar dialog box click Options... button. Word Options dialog box appears. (Figure 3.40)
2. Various options of Proofing in Word option are as follows:

Option	Function
When correcting spelling in MS Office programs	
Ignore words in UPPERCASE	Ignores words in all uppercase letters namely proper nouns.
Ignore words that contain numbers	Ignores words that include numbers.
Ignore Internet and file addresses	Ignores Internet addresses and file names.
Flag repeated words	Ignores the repeated words in the document.
Suggest from main dictionary only	Suggestions will come from the Main dictionary only, not from any open custom dictionaries.
When correcting spelling and grammar in Word 2010	
Check spelling as you type	Automatically identifies words not found in the dictionary by placing a red wavy line under each word.
Use Contextual spelling	It suggests related spelling.
Mark Grammar Errors as you type	Turn this off to stop Word from checking grammar (green underlining words and phrases)
Check grammar with spelling	Turn this off to stop word from checking grammar when using the spelling and Grammar dialog box

3. Click OK.

3.4.6 Using Thesaurus

Thesaurus is a Word 2010 electronic database, that contains English words with similar meaning. It defines selected words and offers alternative terms. When you are not sure of a particular word's meaning, or you think you are using a particular word too often, or when you cannot come up with the right word, use thesaurus. The Thesaurus is one of a set of Research services provided by Word 2010.

➡ **To use the thesaurus, do this:**

1. Select the word for which you want to locate a synonym (similar meaning word).
2. Click the **Review** tab on the ribbon in the **Proofing** group. Click the **Thesaurus** button or press Shift+F7 keys together.
3. The **Research** task pane opens. For example, type the word *appropriate* in the **Search for:** box. Click the arrow to the right of the box. A listing of synonyms for the word *appropriate* appears. (Figure 3.44)
4. Synonyms for *appropriate* are now listed in the task pane.
5. For example, select the word **proper**. Click the arrow next to accurate and then click **Insert**.
6. The word *proper* replaces *appropriate* in the document.
7. Close the **Research** task pane.

3.5 FORMATTING THE TEXT DOCUMENT

Formatting is the process of specifying how a document should appear when printed. Formatting refers to the appearance and

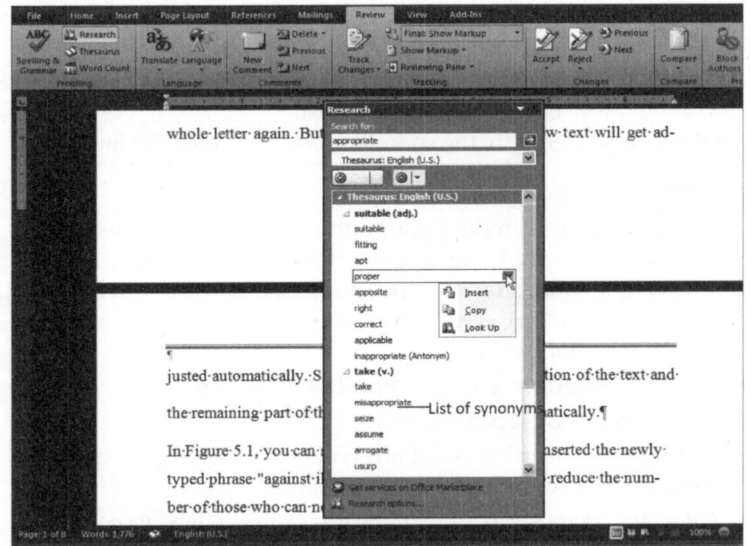

Figure 3.44 List of synonyms in Research dialog box

arrangement of the text in the document. You can apply formatting to a single character, a word, a line or an entire paragraph. The basic formatting involves changing the font and font size of text and alignment of text.

The Paragraph formatting involves controlling the appearance of text in a paragraph as a whole. The Paragraph formatting options are: *text alignment, paragraph indentation, line spacing, spacing before and after the paragraph,* and *border and shading*, etc.

3.5.1 Font and Size Selection

To modify character appearance, you can also use the commands in Ribbon or when you select the text, a mini toolbar appears.

➡ **To change the font using Ribbon, do this:**

1. Select the text of which you want to change the font. Click the down arrow to the right of the font list box (See Figure 3.45).

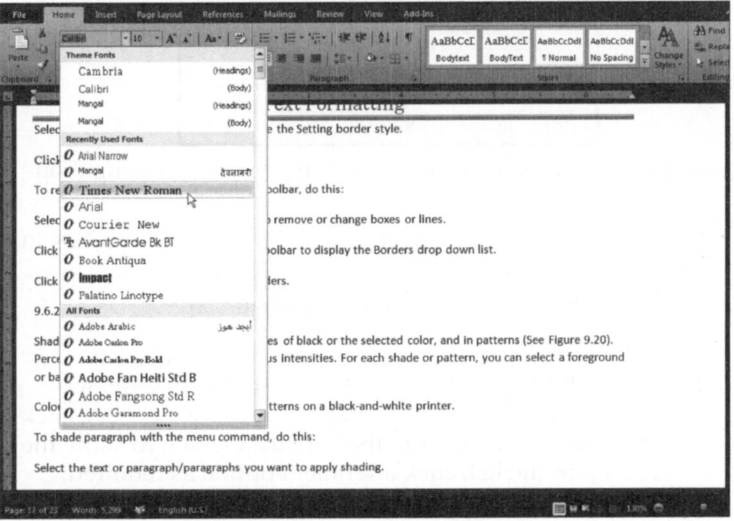

Figure 3.45 Font drop-down list

2. The drop-down list shows all the available fonts. Use the scroll arrow on the right of the drop-down list to scroll through the list. When you move the cursor over the font you can see the changes in the appearance of text.
3. To change the size, enter the desired font size in Font size list box and press (Enter). Or you can select from the mini toolbar (See Figure 3.46).

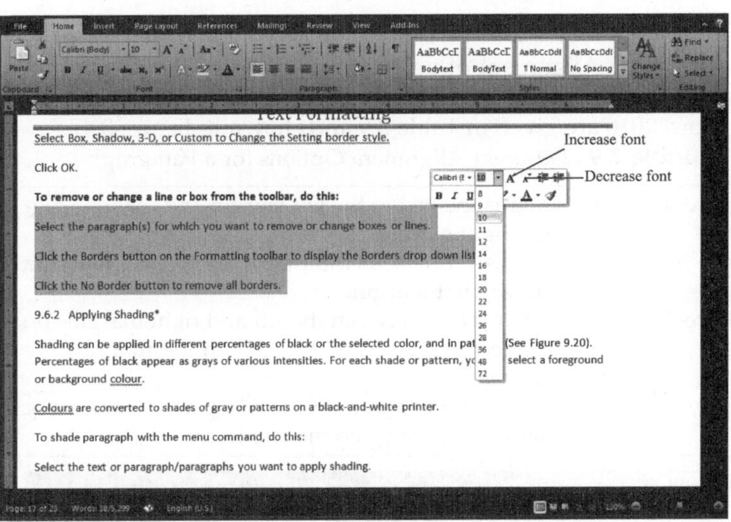

Figure 3.46 Font size drop-down list on the mini toolbar

4. To make a character *Regular, Bold, Italic* click the corresponding button on the mini toolbar (See Figure 3.46). These are toggle buttons clicking them once switches *on* the option and clicking them the second time switches *off* the option.

Applying Character Formatting using Keyboard

Most of the character formatting can also be applied using the keyboard shortcut as discussed in the following sections:

➡ **To format using shortcut keys, do this:**

1. Select the text you want to format and use the shortcut key combinations for the desired formatting effect.

Format	Shortcut
Bold	Ctrl + B
Italic	Ctrl + I
Single underline	Ctrl + U
Word underline	Ctrl + Shift + W
Double underline	Ctrl + Shift + D
SMALL CAPS	Ctrl + Shift + K
ALL CAPS	Ctrl + Shift + A
Hidden text	Ctrl + Shift + H
Superscript	Ctrl + Shift + =
Subscript	Ctrl + =
Copy formatting	Ctrl + Shift + C
Paste formatting	Ctrl + Shift + V
Remove formatting	Ctrl + Spacebar
Change case of letter	Shift + F3
Font	Ctrl + Shift + F. This command activates the Font dialog box. Type a new font name or use the arrow keys to highlight the desired font.
Symbol font	Ctrl + Shift + Q
Next larger point size available for selected fonts	Ctrl + Shift + >
Next smaller point size available for selected fonts	Ctrl + Shift + <
Up one point size	Ctrl +]
Down one point size	Ctrl + [

3.5.2 Alignment of Text

The attribute Alignment of a paragraph refers to the position of the main document text on the page. Different alignment options in Word 2010 are given in Table 3.9 and shown in Figure 3.47.

Table 3.9 Different Alignment Options for a Paragraph

Left Alignment	Aligns the text at the left margin and makes a zig-zag right margin.
Right Alignment	Aligns the text to the right margin and makes a zig-zag left margin.
Centre Alignment	Centres text between the left and right margins on the centre line. In this case both the margins are zig-zag.
Justify	Aligns the text at both the margins by increasing the spacing between the words.

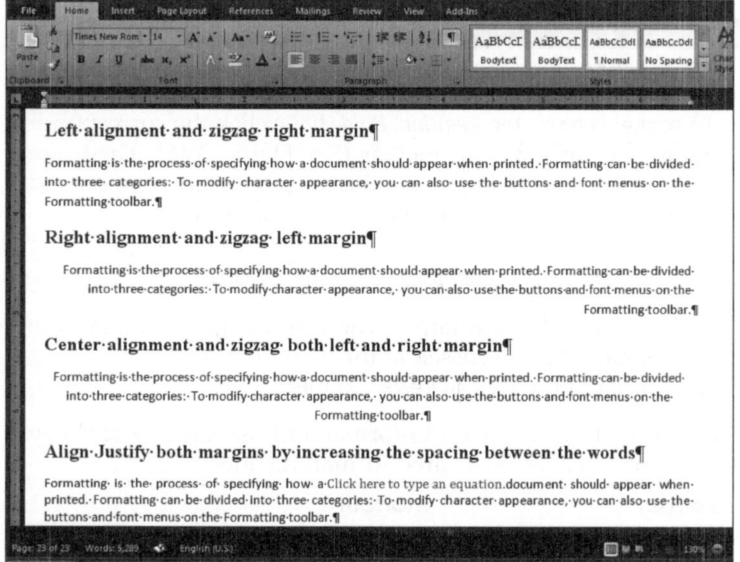

Figure 3.47 Paragraph alignment options

3.5.3 Paragraph Indenting

Indents are the white space added to the margins, and thus decreasing the text area for paragraphs. So, when you have a "right margin and you want to add a right indent of 1.0", your text will be printed 2.0" from the right edge of the paper.

☞ *The first line of each paragraph can be indented differently from other lines in the paragraph. The first line can be shorter than the others, creating a regular indent, or longer than the others creating a hanging indent.*

Once you change the indent, each new paragraph you start by pressing the Enter key will maintain the same indentation setting until you change it.

Line Spacing

Line spacing in a paragraph means the amount of space between the lines. Word 2010 offers the line spacing options as given in Table 3.10.

Table 3.10 Different Options of Line Spacing

Option	Description
Single spacing	No blank line space appears between the lines of text.
Double spacing	A blank line space appears between the lines of text.
1 1/2 spacing	Half the height of one line space of text appears between the lines of text.
Exact line height	Specify the space you want between the lines.

Space before and after Paragraphs

There is a spacing box in the Paragraph dialog box which lets you to define the amount of white space that Word 2010 must place before and after paragraphs. Space settings can be entered in *points* (pts), *inches* (in), *centimetres* (cm), or *lines* (li). Thus, 12 points would be entered as **12 pt**.

Formatting Paragraphs using Dialog Box Launcher

➡ **To format paragraphs, do this:**

1. Position the insertion point anywhere in the paragraph to be formatted or select multiple paragraphs.
2. Click the **Home** tab of **Paragraph** group. Click **Paragraph launcher** dialog box. The **Paragraph** dialog box as in Figure 3.48 appears.

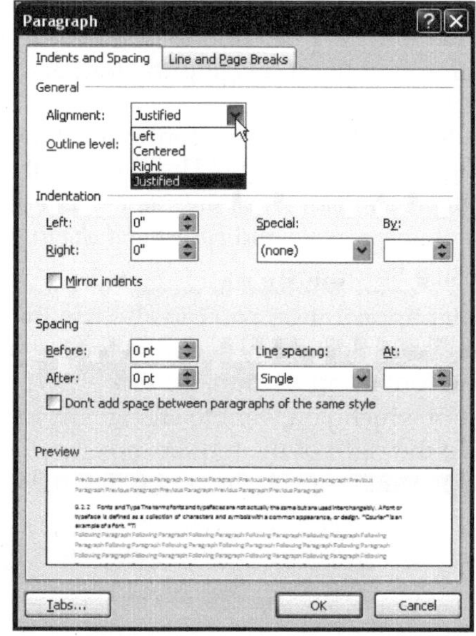

Figure 3.48 Paragraph dialog box with Indents and Spacing Property sheet

3. Click the **Indents and Spacing** tab, the property sheet as in Figure 3.48 appears.

   Various options in Indents and Spacing tab are:

   General Options:

   - The Alignment list box show the current alignment.
   - Change the current alignment, if need be. For this, click the down arrow next to the list box. Open it to show the list. From the list, click alignment option as required.

   Paragraph Indent Options:

   - The Indents and Spacing tab to displays line spacing/indentation options (See Figure 3.49).
   - The Left text box shows the current left indentation. Enter the new value for indentation or use the up and down arrow keys to change the indentation.
   - The Right text box displays the current right indentation. Enter the new value for indentation or use the up and down arrow keys to change the indentation.

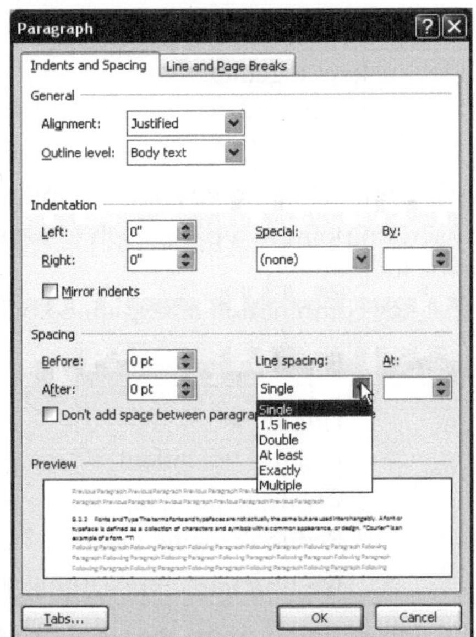

Figure 3.49 Indents and Spacing tab with line spacing options

- To apply the first line indent or the hanging indent use the Special: list box. Click the down arrow key of the Special: list box to display the options as given below:

Option	Effect
First line	This indents only the first line of the paragraph.
Hanging indent	This indents all except the first line of the paragraph.

Click the option as needed to select it.

- In the By: text box, enter the indention or use the up and down arrow to give the required indentation. The Preview box displays the effect of the selected indentation.

Line Spacing Options:

- Line spacing text box has the options for controlling the line spacing. Click the down arrow in the spacing box. The options are given below:

Option	Explanation
Single	Default value.
Double	Places a blank line between successive lines.
1.5 Lines	Leaves half the line space between the lines.
At Least	Indicates the minimum space between lines.
Exactly	Gives the exact space between lines.

Space Before/After Paragraphs Options:

- Type the space or select the space required in the Before: text box for adding space before the paragraph.
- Type the space or select the space required in the After: text box for adding space after the paragraph.

4. Click OK or press the Enter key to close the paragraph dialog box.

Hanging Indent

A hanging indent refers to a paragraph that has all lines except the first one indented. It is called a hanging indent, because the first line hangs out over the rest of the paragraph. They look something like this as shown below:

On the Insert tab, the galleries include items that
your document. You can use these galle
pages, and other document building blc
they also coordinate with your current
formatting of selected text in the docur
from the Quick Styles gallery on the Ho
the other controls on the Home tab.

Create a hanging indent by pressing the space key to create spaces, or even by tabbing across the page. Better way to create a hanging indent in Word, is to place the cursor anywhere in the paragraph. On the **Home** tab, click the dialogue launcher for the **Paragraph** group.

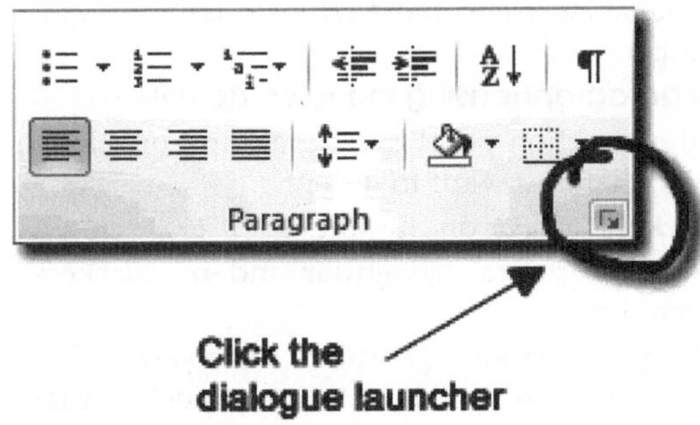

When the Paragraph window opens, go down to the Special selector and choose hanging. You can either keep the default setting for the size of the indent, or you can adjust it by typing a new number into the box or by clicking on the up and down arrows to the right as shown in Figure 3.50.

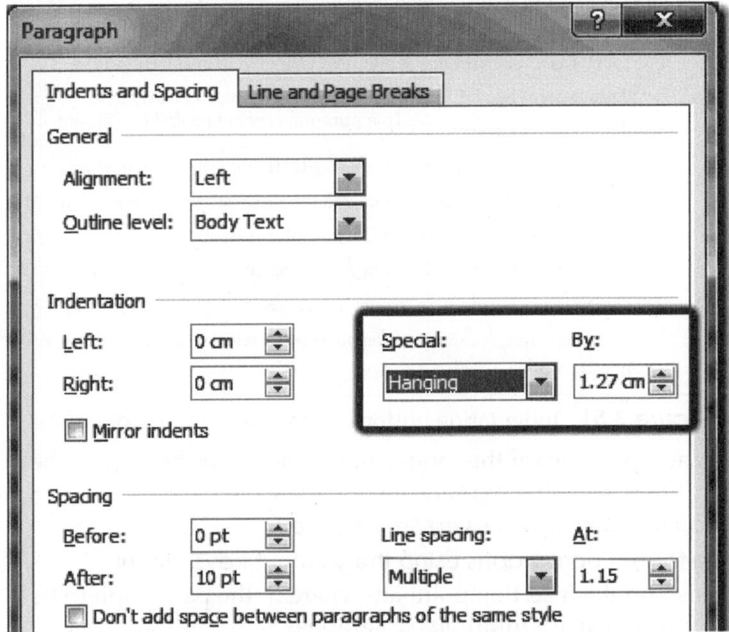

Figure 3.50 Selecting Special selector in paragraph dialog box

To adjust or remove a hanging indent that is already there, just repeat the steps above: click the Paragraph dialogue launcher and then change the Special selector or adjust the indent size.

☞ *The hanging indent is only applied to the current paragraph i.e. the paragraph in which the cursor is placed. All other paragraphs remains unaffected.*

Formatting Paragraphs using Ruler

➡ **To format paragraphs using ruler, do this:**

1. Position the insertion point anywhere in the paragraph you want to format or select multiple paragraphs to align.
2. Click the appropriate alignment button, e.g., *left, centre, right, justified* alignment on the **Home** tab of **paragraph** group.

➡ **To indent paragraphs using mouse, do this:**

1. Position the insertion point in the paragraph to be indented or select as many paragraphs, as you want to indent.
2. On the **Home** tab of **paragraph** group click the indentation button.
3. The *increase* Indent button moves the indent marker to the right by one tab stop and the *decrease* indent moves it back by one tab stop.

➡ **To indent paragraphs using the ruler, do this:**

1. Position the insertion point in a paragraph or select multiple paragraphs, that you want to indent.
2. Indent markers appear on the ruler.
3. Drag the appropriate triangular indent markers to the desired location.
4. As you drag the marker, the rulers scale shows the position of the indent mark in relation to its respective margin (See Figure 3.51).

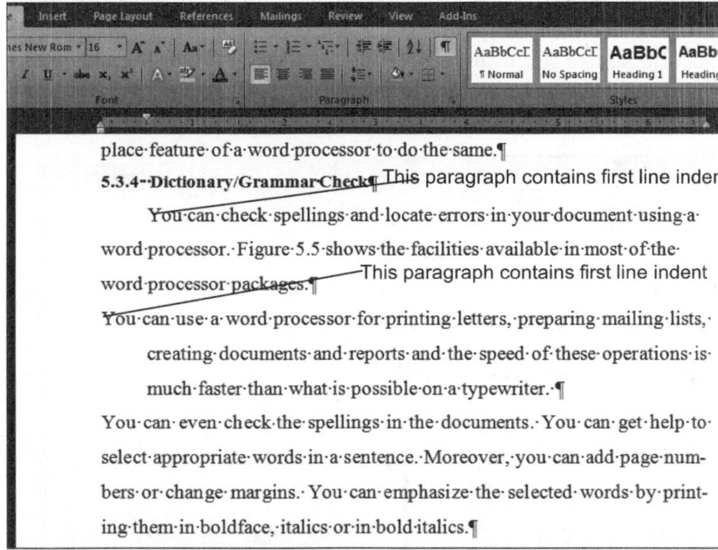

Figure 3.51 Indentation buttons on the paragraph group

5. When you release the mouse button after positioning it, the text in selected paragraphs moves accordingly.

Formatting Paragraphs using Shortcut Keys

➡ **To format paragraphs using the shortcut keys, do this:**

1. Position the insertion point anywhere in the paragraph to be aligned or select multiple paragraphs.
2. Use one of the keyboard shortcuts given below:

Alignment	**Key combinations**
Left	Ctrl+L keys together.
Right	Ctrl+R keys together.
Centre	Ctrl+E keys together.
Justify	Ctrl+J keys together.

➡ **To indent paragraphs using the keyboard shortcuts, do this:**

1. Position the insertion point in a paragraph or select multiple paragraphs to be indented.
2. Use the shortcut key combination as explained below:

Key combination	**Effect**
Ctrl+M	Left indent.
Ctrl+Shift+M	Remove left indent.
Ctrl+T	Create hanging indent.
Ctrl+Shift+T	Reduce hanging indent.
Ctrl+Q	Remove paragraphs formatting.

➡ **To change the line spacing using the keyboard shortcuts, do this:**

1. Position the insertion point in a paragraph or select the paragraphs for which you want to change the line spacing.
2. Use one of the keyboard shortcuts given below:

Key combination	**Effect**
Ctrl+1	Creates single spaced lines.
Ctrl+2	Creates double spaced lines.
Ctrl+5	Creates one and half spaced lines.
Ctrl+0(zero)	Add or remove one line space preceding a paragraph

➡ **To add a single line of space before a paragraph, do this:**

1. Position the insertion point in a paragraph or select the paragraph before which you want to add single line of space.
2. Press Ctrl+0 (zero) keys together.
3. To remove the single line of space added before the paragraph, add Ctrl+0 (zero) a second time.

Paragraphs and Sections within a document

By default, a document contains a single section. Section breaks divide the document into sections. The breaks appear as double-dotted lines. You will see section breaks in Normal view if all *non-printing* characters are displayed. You can use section break to change the formatting of pages in a document. You can also create a different header or footer for a section of your document.

➡ **To display non-printing characters, do this:**

1. Click **File** tab on the ribbon. The backstage view appears. Click Options.
2. Select the **Display** option in the left pane, under **Always show these formatting marks on the screen** and then click All in Formatting marks area.

➡ **To insert a section break, do this:**

1. Position the insertion point where you want the section break to occur.
2. In the **Page Layout** tab, choose **Page Setup** group, at the top right corner, click **Breaks** drop-down arrow. The list of options appear as shown in Figure 3.52.
3. Choose an option from the following:

Option	Description
Next page	This selection would start the new section on a *new* page.
Continuous	This selection would Insert a section break without starting it on a new page.
Even page	This selection would start a section on an even numbered page (i.e., left hand page).
Odd page	This selection would start a section on an *odd* numbered page (i.e., on the right hand page).

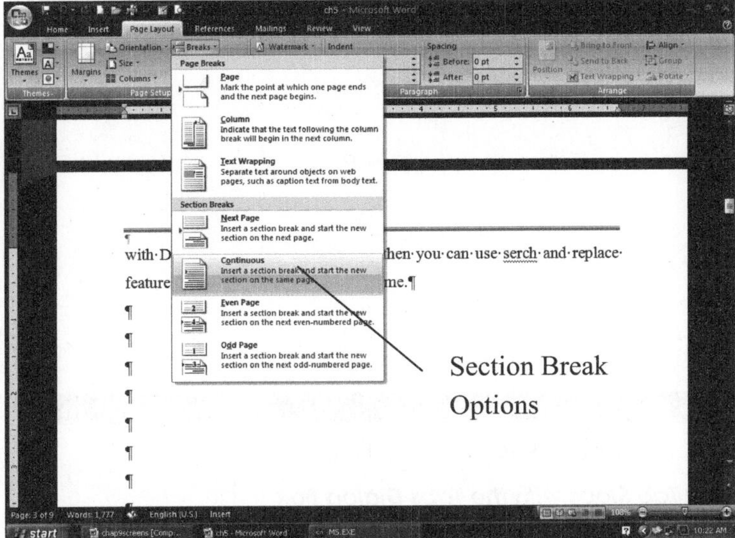

Figure 3.52 Section breaks group dialog box

A section insertion places a double-dotted, non-printing line containing the words *End of Section* at the insertion point on your screen (See Figure 3.53).

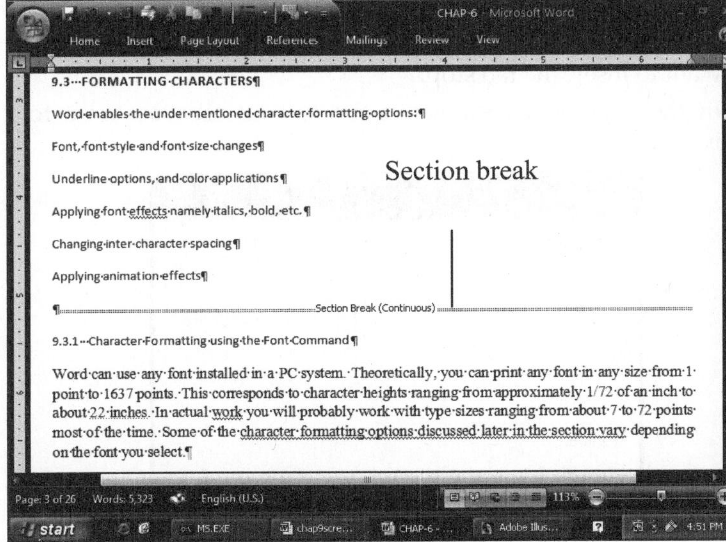

Figure 3.53 Selected section break

Section-formatting information is stored with section breaks. You can copy section information by copying and pasting section breaks, to the chapters where you wish to apply the new document formatting.

☞ *Section breaks differ from paragraph marks (¶), in that a section break controls the information below it, while a paragraph mark controls the information that precedes it.*

Click section break to select it. Selected section break appears as in Figure 3.53. Now use the Cut/Copy and Paste command to copy the section breaks.

Deleting Section Breaks

Select a section break and press the Backspace or Del key. Text after the removed section break will take on the characteristics of the preceding text. It may take a moment for Word 2010 to reformat and re-paginate the document.

Keeping Two Or More Paragraphs Together

Automatic page breaks may occur where it should not be, namely, just after paragraph headings or in the middle of a table. Word 2010 offers methods to keep such *paragraphs/lines* together. These are explained in the following paragraphs.

➡ **To keep lines together, do this:**

1. Select the lines you wish to keep together.
2. Click the **Page Layout** tab.
3. Click the **Paragraph Launcher** arrow at the right corner of **Paragraph group**. The **Paragraph** dialog box appears.
4. Click the **Line and Page Breaks** tab property sheet as in Figure 3.54 appears.
5. Enable the *Keep lines together* option by clicking the check box so that a check mark appears.
6. Click OK.

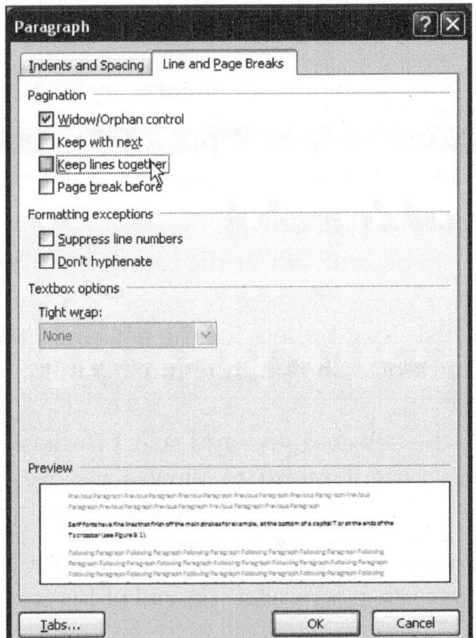

Figure 3.54 Line and Page breaks property sheet of paragraph dialog Box

➡ **To use keep with next option command, do this:**

1. Select the paragraphs you wish to keep together.
2. Click the **Home** tab. Click the **Paragraph Launcher** arrow present at the right corner of **Paragraph** group. The **Paragraph** dialog box appears.
3. In the Paragraph dialog box, click Line and Page breaks tab (See Figure 3.54). Enable Keep with next option by clicking the check box so that a check mark appears.
4. Click OK.

➡ **To remove special paragraph and line options, do this:**

1. Select the Paragraph(s)/Lines you wish to change.
2. Click the **Page Layout** tab and choose **Paragraph** group.

3. In Paragraph dialog box, click the Line and Page breaks tab as shown in Figure 3.54. Click the check boxes to remove the check marks.
4. Click the unwanted options from keep together option.
5. Click OK.

3.5.4 Bullets and Numbering

Word 2010 provides the ability to create bulleted, numbered and multilevel lists. A bulleted list is a list with a graphic character, a very small picture or a bullet at the beginning of each paragraph in the list. A numbered list is similar to bulleted list, except each paragraph is numbered or lettered. The style of each list type can be changed and different bullets can be used.

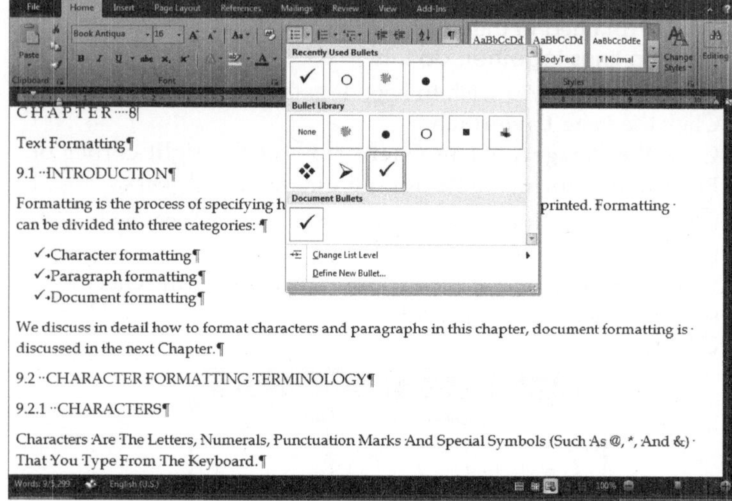

Figure 3.55 Bullets and numbering dialog box

➡ **To create a bulleted list, do this:**

1. Select the text to be bulleted or the location of the new list to be created.
2. To use the last style of bullets for the list, press the Bullets or Numbering button as shown in Figure 3.55. Press it again to end the list. Or

   Right-click in the selected text and select Bullets or Numbering from the shortcut menu to view a gallery of available styles.

☞ *The bullet or number appears at the beginning of a line of text when the Enter key is pressed at the end of the preceding line of text.*

Use of Tab and Tab Setting

Tabs are used for creating relatively simple lists of items. Each paragraph in a Word 2010 document can take several different tab settings. It offers four types of tab settings (See Figure 3.56). Each tab is meant to align text. Tabs are particularly useful for making columnar lists. The different tabs and their functions are as given below:

Tab	Function
Left Tab	Text typed at these tabs aligns against the left edge of the stop.
Centre Tab	A centre tab stop, centres your text around the tab stop.
Right Tab	Right tab stop, positions whatever you type to the left of the tab.
Decimal Tab	Decimal tab stops, align columns of numbers on the decimal point. This is mainly used for financial reports.

(Contd...)

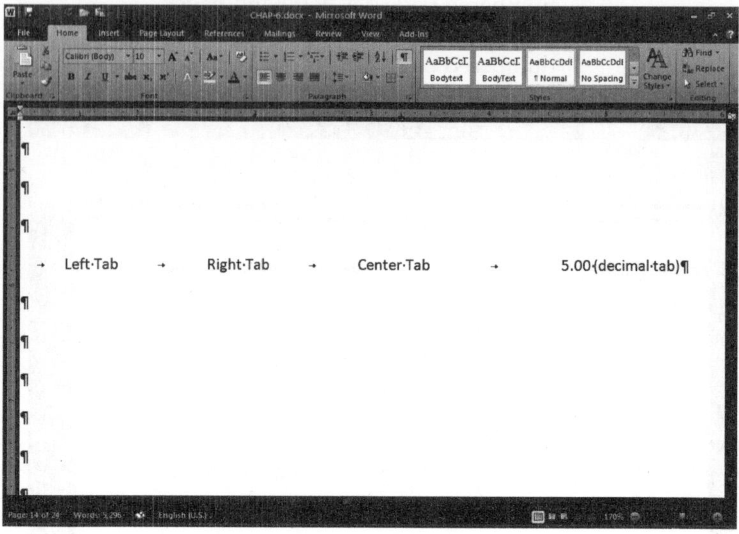

Figure 3.56 Tabs available in Word 2010

Setting Tab Stops with the Tabs Dialog Box

➡ **To set tabs using the tabs dialog box, do this:**

1. Position the insertion point in paragraph in which you want to insert tab.
2. Click the **Home** tab. Click **Paragraph Launcher** dialog box.
3. The **Paragraph** dialog box appears, click **Tabs...** button. **Tabs** dialog box appears as shown in Figure 3.57.
4. In the Tab stop position box, enter the position where you want to insert the tab stop.
5. In the alignment area, select the type of tab you want to insert.

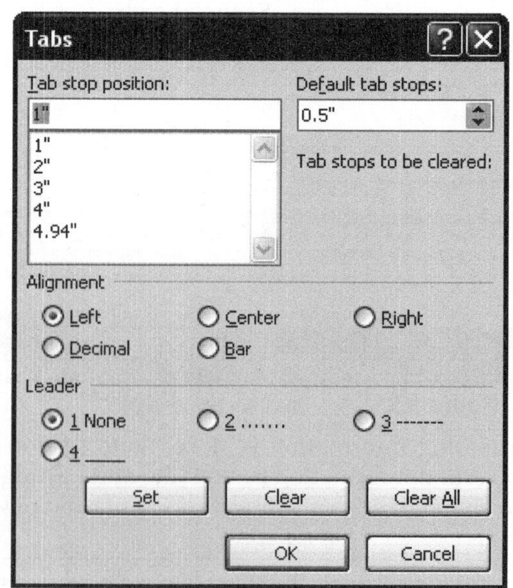

Figure 3.57 The Tabs dialog box

☞ *Measurements in the Tabs dialog box are in inches as default, unless you type another one (cm for centimeter, pt for point, or pi for pica). As an example, 5 cm would position the left tab stop five centimetres from the left margin.*

3.5.5 Using the Change Case Command

Word provides facilities to change to capital letters of any text by using the Change Cas*e* command.

➡ **To apply capitalization, do this:**

1. Select the text for which you want to change capitalization.
2. Click the **Home** tab of **Font** group. Click **Change Case** command (Figure 3.58).
3. The options offered by the Change case dialog box are as follows:

Option	Description
Sentence case	The first character of the first word is capitalized.
lower case	All the characters are in lowercase.
UPPER CASE	All the characters are in uppercase.
Capitalize Each Word	The first letter of each word is capitalized.
tOGGLE cASE	The first letter of each selected word is in lowercase, the rest are in uppercase.

4. The above options are applied in the text and shown in Figure 3.58.

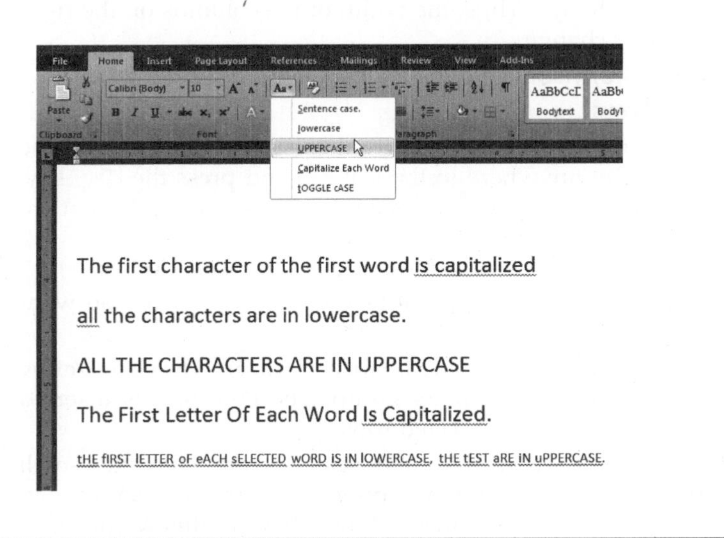

Figure 3.58 Changed case options

3.6 TABLE MANIPULATION

You should use tables to create documents, such as *forms*, *financial reports*, *catalogs* and *biodata*. Word tables consist of horizontal *rows* and vertical *columns*. You type in the areas called cells which is formed by the intersection of rows and columns. Cells can contain *text*, *numbers*, or *graphics*.

You can even control the size, shape, and appearance of the cells, and use border and shading features. You can insert and delete rows and columns in a table.

☞ *A new feature called the Table Wizard helps you to automate table creation.*

3.6.1 Draw Table

Word 2010 allows you to draw a table by selecting the Insert Table grid on the **insert** tab or Insert table... using the Table options in the Table groups.

➡ **To draw a table using the mouse, do this:**

1. Position the insertion point where you want to insert a table.
2. Click the **Insert** tab of **Tables** group. Click down arrow and choose the Insert table grid as shown in Figure 3.59 appears. Drag the mouse button to highlight the desired number of *rows* and *columns*.
3. The displayed grid represents the required number of rows and columns. Click the mouse button after getting the right number in the grid.

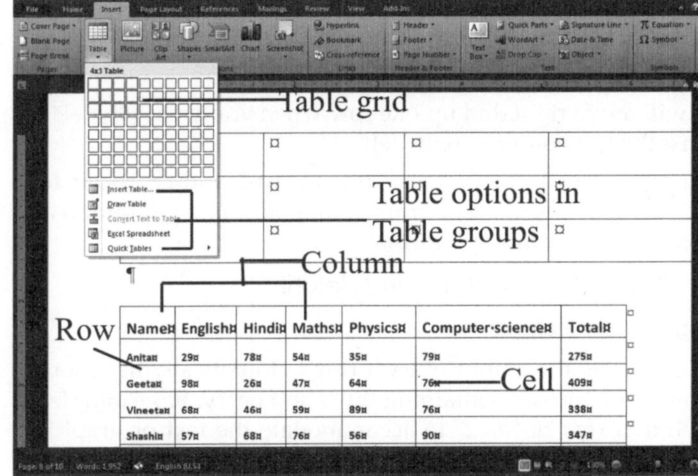

Figure 3.59 Table grid

4. Word inserts an empty table when you release the mouse button (See Figure 3.59).

➡ **To create a table using the table option, do this:**

1. Position the insertion point where you want to insert the table.
2. In **Insert** tab of **Tables** group, click the **Table** down arrow highlight **Insert Table...** options. The **Insert Table** dialog box as shown in Figure 3.60.

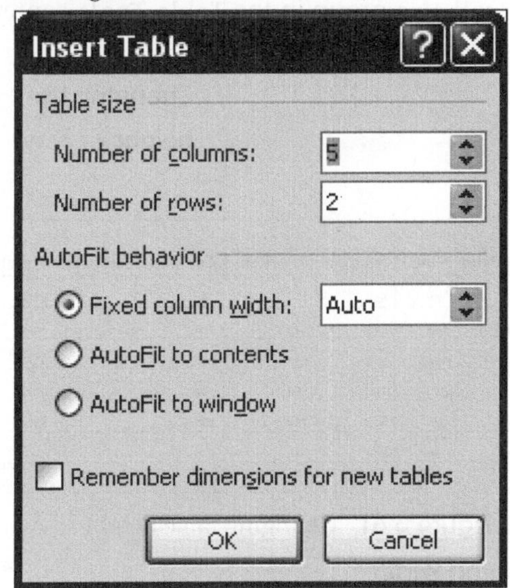

Figure 3.60 Insert Table dialog box

3. Enter the desired number of rows and columns as required in the table.
4. Click OK.

Entering and Editing Text in a Table

You can move, enter and edit text in a table just as you do with other types of text matter. Use mouse or arrow keys to position the insertion point, then type the text. The cell borders work as margins. Word 2010 automatically wraps text within the cell as you reach the right edge.

➡ **To move within a table using the mouse, do this:**

1. Position the pointer in the cell you want to move and click.

➡ **To move within a table using the keyboard, do this:**

1. The insertion point will move *left* and *down* to the next row when you press Tab key in the last column on the right side of a table.
2. It will move right and up one row when you press Shift+Tab past the last column on the left.

You can apply all of Word 2010 paragraph and character formats to the text in cells. Cells can contain multiple paragraphs as well as multiple paragraph formats.

3.6.2 Changing Cell Width and Height

Changing Row Heights

Word 2010 sets the height of each row automatically in order to accommodate the cell containing the tallest entry. For example, if one cell in a row needs 2" to accommodate the text or graphics, then all the cells in that particular row will be 2" high.

➡ **To adjust the height of a row, do this:**

1. Click anywhere in the row where you want to change its height.
2. Move the pointer to the vertical ruler at the left edge of the screen or to the top of the row. The pointer changes to an up-and-down arrow. Use it to drag the row to the desired height (See Figure 3.61).
3. Release the mouse button. Or

   Click **Table Row Height** scroll box, to change the height of row in the **cell size** group in the **Table Tools** contextual tab of **Layout** tab.

Changing the height of row

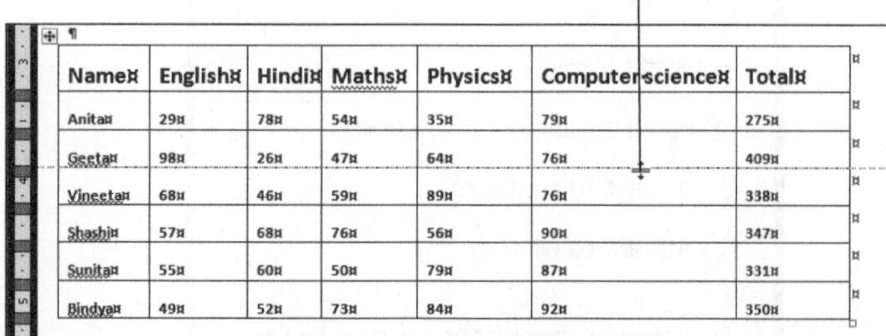

Name	English	Hindi	Maths	Physics	Computer-science	Total
Anita	29	78	54	35	79	275
Geeta	98	26	47	64	76	409
Vineeta	68	46	59	89	76	338
Shashi	57	68	76	56	90	347
Sunita	55	60	50	79	87	331
Bindya	49	52	73	84	92	350

Figure 3.61 Changing table height

Changing Column Width

➡ **To change the width of column, using mouse do this:**

1. Point to a column boundary.
2. The pointer will change shape to a double arrow (See Figure 3.62). Drag the column width marker. Watch the dotted line as well as the ruler settings, then release the mouse button when it reaches the desired width. Or

Changing Column Width

Name	English	Hindi	Maths	Physics	Computer-science	Total
Anita	29	78	54	35	79	275
Geeta	98	26	47	64	76	409
Vineeta	68	46	59	89	76	338
Shashi	57	68	76	56	90	347
Sunita	55	60	50	79	87	331
Bindya	49	52	73	84	92	350

Figure 3.62 Adjusting column width

Click **Table Column Width** scroll box, to change the Table Column Width in the **cell size** group.

- If you hold down the Shift key while dragging, the column to the right does not changes size while the table's overall width increases.
- If you hold down Ctrl key while dragging mouse, all columns to the right changes size, but the table's overall width will not change. Thus, the width of the columns on the right will only change.

3.6.3 Delete/Insertion of Row and Column

Inserting Rows

To add a new row at the end of an existing table, position the insertion point anywhere in the last cell and press the Tab key. Word 2010 inserts a new row using the styles of the cells that are immediately above it.

➡ **To insert a single row in the middle of a table, do this:**

1. Position the insertion point below the row where you want the new row to be inserted.
2. Click the **Layout** contextual tab, click **Insert Above or Below** in the **Rows & Columns** group. The new row is inserted below or above the selected row.

   Alternatively, right click and select Insert, click the small triangle, a sub menu option appears as shown in Figure 3.63. Select the Insert Rows Above or Below option.
3. To add multiple rows, either repeat the Insert Rows command by clicking right mouse button or select as many existing rows as you want to insert. Word 2010 inserts as many rows as you have selected.

Inserting Columns

➡ **To insert a single column in the middle of a table, do this:**

1. Select the column to the right of which you wish the *new* column to appear.
2. Click the **Layout** contextual tab, click **Insert Left** or **Right** in the **Rows & Columns** group. The new column is inserted left or right to the selected column.

   Alternatively, right click and select **Insert** option. Click the small triangle. A sub menu appears. Select the **Insert Columns to Left** or **Right** option from the sub menu list.

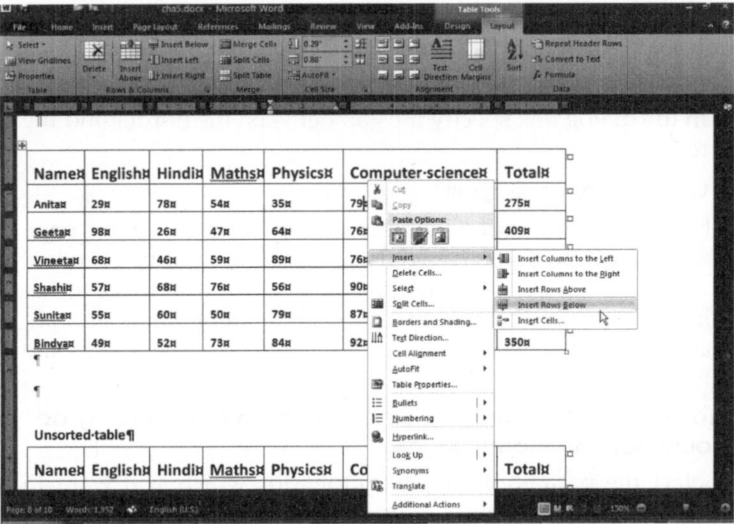

Figure 3.63 Inserting rows

3. Word 2010 will add a new column but it will not change the width of the earlier columns to accommodate this new inserted column. In order to make the enlarged table fit on your page, you will have to adjust *margins, column widths* or change *page orientation*.

☞ *New column retains the format of the column, adjacent to which it is inserted but borders will not change.*

To insert multiple columns, select as many existing columns as you want to insert new ones to the right of the desired location of the new columns. If you want to add three columns, select the three existing columns to the right of the desired insertion point, then click on the Insert columns to the Left button.

➡ **To insert a column at the right edge of a table, do this:**

1. Select an end-of-row marker (See Figure 3.64).
2. Right click and select Insert. A small triangle, a sub menu option appears. Select **Insert Columns to Right** option.

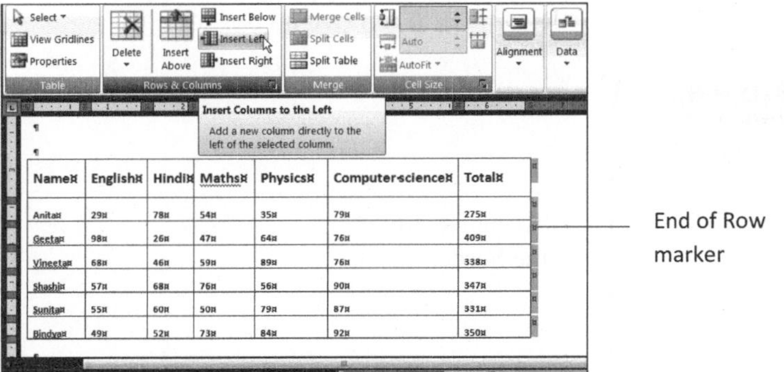

Figure 3.64 End of row marker

Deleting Rows

➡ **To delete a row or rows of cells, do this:**

1. Select the row(s) to be deleted.
2. Click the **Layout** contextual tab, click **Rows & Columns** group. Click down arrow and choose Delete Rows. This will delete the rows and their contents.
3. To delete the *contents* of cells only, leave the cells intact, select text or graphic and press the Del key.

Deleting Columns

➡ **To delete columns, do this:**

1. Select the column or columns to be deleted.
2. Click the **Layout** contextual tab. Click Table down arrow and choose Delete Columns.
3. Click OK.

3.6.4 Alignment of Text in Cell

You can align text in a table cell in nine different ways: Top Left (the default alignment), Top center, Top Right, Centre Left, Centre Right, Bottom Left, Bottom Centre, and Bottom Right as shown in Figure 3.65.

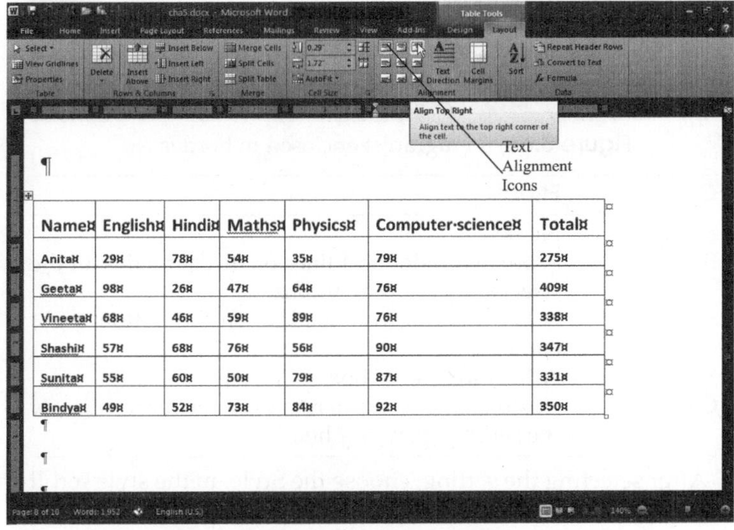

Figure 3.65 Alignment of text in cell

3.6.5 Border and Shading

A *border* may be a box around a paragraph (or paragraphs) from all sides. It could be a line that sets a paragraph off on one or more sides. A border can include *shading*, which fills a paragraph with a pattern. Boxes and lines can be solid black and shading can be gray or in colour.

If a group of paragraphs is formatted with a box around them and you press Enter key at the end of the last paragraph, your new paragraph falls within the box. However, if you want to create a new paragraph outside the border, then move the insertion point outside the border before you press Enter key.

Applying Borders

➡ **To apply borders to a paragraph, or group of paragraphs, do this:**

1. Position the insertion point anywhere in the paragraph to be enclosed in a border or select multiple paragraphs or select the text to be enclosed (See Figure 3.66).
2. In **Paragraph** group, click **Borders and Shading**. A drop-down menu appears. Choose the selected border you want to apply for paragraph as seen in Figure 3.66.
3. In **Paragraph** group, select **Borders and Shading...** option. The **Borders and Shading** dialog box appears as in Figure 3.67.
4. Choose from the options given below:

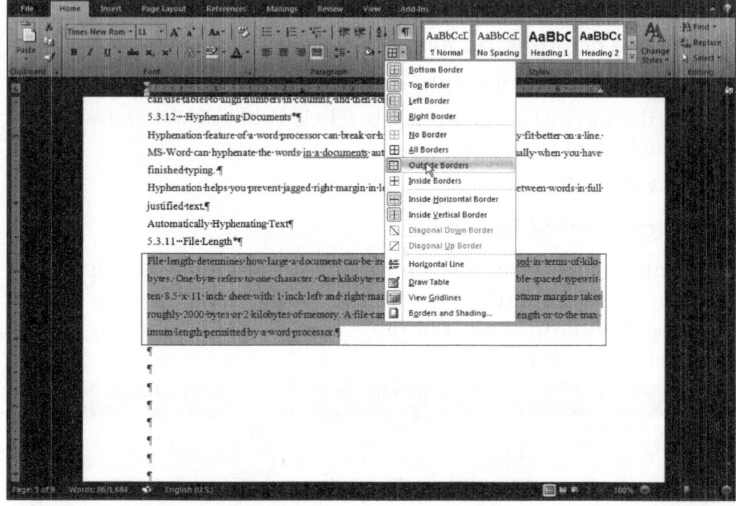

Figure 3.66 Paragraphs enclosed in border

Option	Effect
None	No box.
Box	A box with identical lines on all four sides, of the selected text or paragraphs.
Shadow	A box with a drop shadow on the bottom right corner.
3-D	A "Picture frame" box.
Custom	Custom design borders on one or more sides of the selected paragraph(s).

4. After selecting the setting, choose the Style: in the style scroll list. Style determines the type of line used for border.
5. In the Color: drop-down list, choose the colour you want the border to be in. If you choose Auto option, the default colour for text is used.
6. In the Width: drop-down list specify the width for the border.
7. The Preview box shows how the borders are applied to the selected text.
8. In Apply to: Choose width you want to apply border to a selected text or paragraph.
9. Click Options... to bring up dialog box as in Figure 3.67.

   In the dialog box specify the gap between the border and the text if need be.
10. Click OK or press Enter.

When paragraphs extend exactly to the margins of your page (as they always do if you do not indent the paragraphs), borders extend slightly outside the margins. If you want borders to fall within or exactly on the margins, you must indent the paragraph. To make borders fall on the margins, indent the paragraph by the width of the border.

➡ **To remove or change a box or line from the dialog box launcher command, do this:**

1. Select the paragraph or paragraphs for which you want to remove or change boxes or lines.
2. In **Paragraph** group, select **Borders and Shading...** click on option.
3. The **Border and Shading Options** dialog box appears as shown in Figure 3.68. Select the Borders tab. Click OK.
4. Select the None option in the Setting: group to remove all borders.
5. Select the line you want to change and choose a different option from the **Style:** box. You also can select a different line colour from the Color: list box.
6. Select Box, Shadow, 3-D, or Custom to Change the Setting border style.
7. Click OK.

➡ **To remove or change a line or box, do this:**

1. Select the paragraph(s) for which you want to remove or change boxes or lines.
2. Click the **Borders and Shading** option on the **Home** tab of **Paragraph** group. A list of options appears.
3. Select the No Border option to remove all borders.

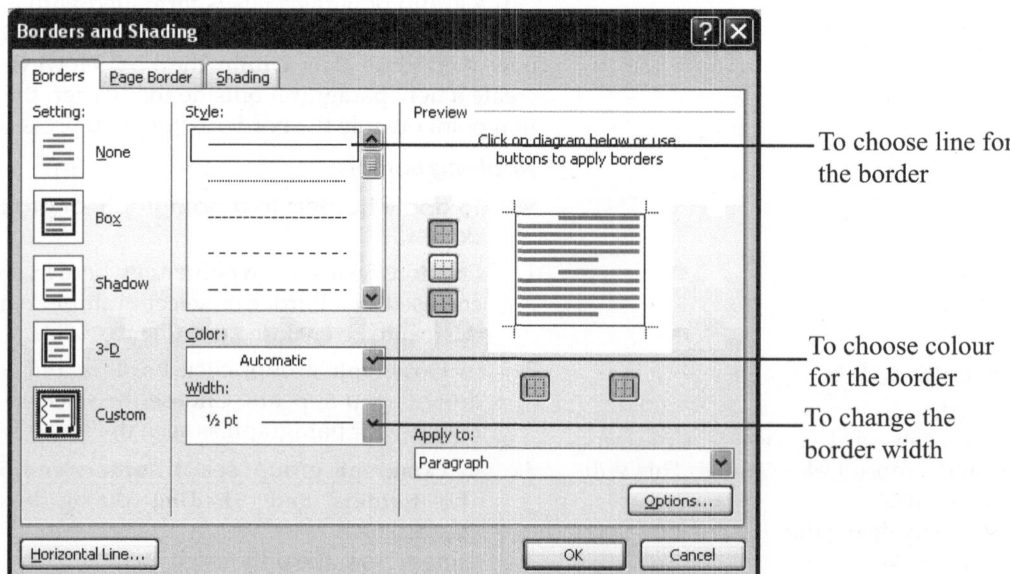

Figure 3.67 Border and Shading dialog box

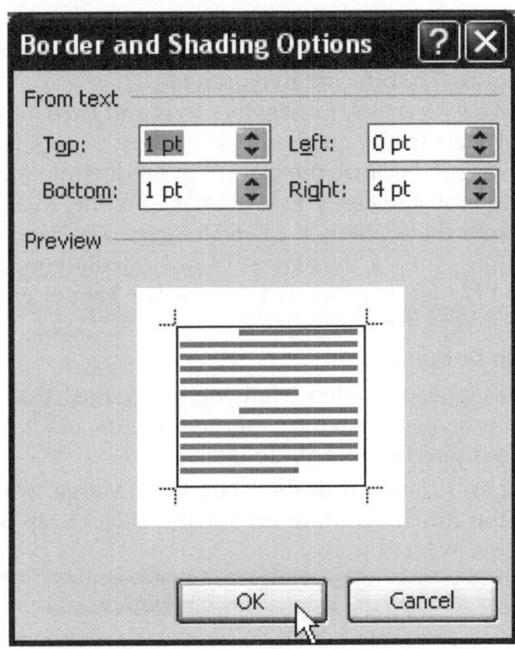

Figure 3.68 Border and Shading options

Applying Shading

Shading can be applied in different percentages of black or the selected colour, and in patterns (See Figure 3.69). Percentages of black appear as grays of various intensities. For each shade or pattern, you can select a foreground or background colour.

Colours are converted to shades of gray or patterns on a black-and-white printer.

➡ **To shade paragraph with the mouse, do this:**

1. Select the text or paragraph/paragraphs on which you want to apply shading.
2. In **Paragraph** group click **Border** down arrow and choose Borders and Shading.. . In the Borders and Shading dialog box click the **Shading** tab property sheet as seen in Figure 3.69 appears.

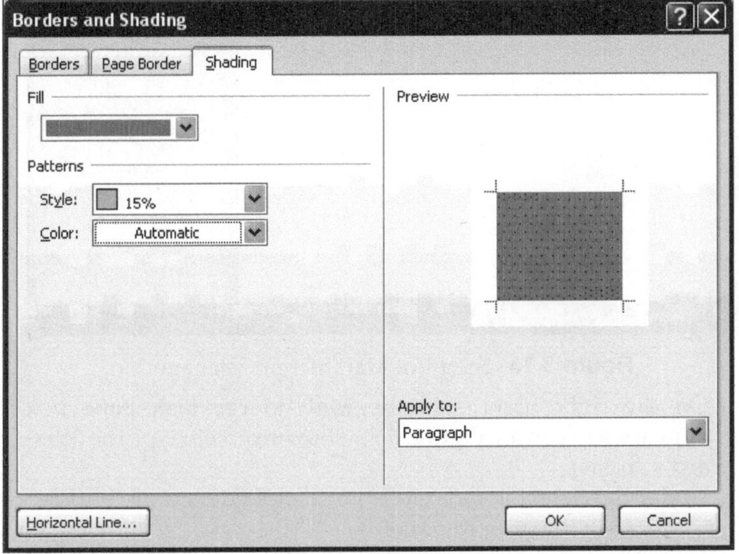

Figure 3.69 Shading tab of Borders and Shading dialog box

3. Fill: In this box click the fill colour you want for the shading or click None to remove shading colour.

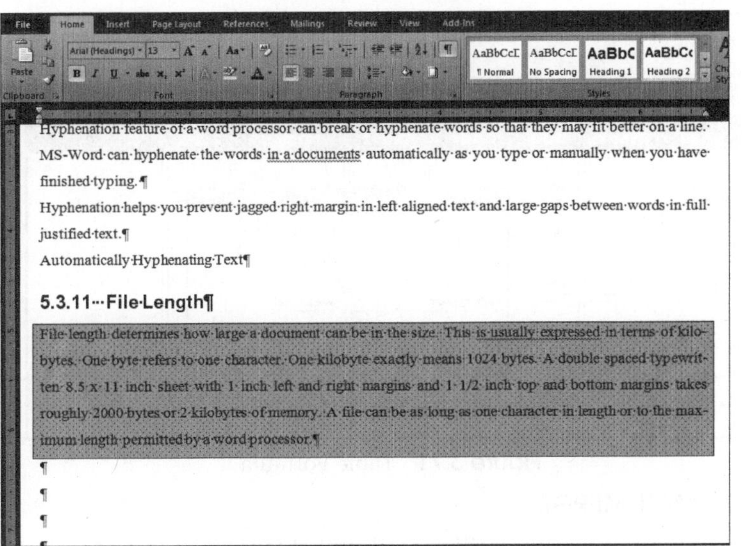

Hyphenation feature of a word processor can break or hyphenate words so that they may fit better on a line. MS-Word can hyphenate the words in a documents automatically as you type or manually when you have finished typing.

Hyphenation helps you prevent jagged right margin in left aligned text and large gaps between words in full justified text.

Automatically Hyphenating Text

5.3.11 File Length

File length determines how large a document can be in the size. This is usually expressed in terms of kilobytes. One byte refers to one character. One kilobyte exactly means 1024 bytes. A double spaced typewritten 8.5 x 11 inch sheet with 1 inch left and right margins and 1 1/2 inch top and bottom margins takes roughly 2000 bytes or 2 kilobytes of memory. A file can be as long as one character in length or to the maximum length permitted by a word processor.

Figure 3.70 Paragraph with shading effects

4. Style: In this drop-down list click the shading style you want to apply "over" this fill colour.
5. Color: In this drop-down list, click a colour for the line and dots in the selected shading pattern. The Color: box is not visible if you click colour in the style: box.
6. Select a colour from the Fill list to colour a percentage pattern or a pattern background. The effect of the selection option appear in the preview box.
7. Click OK.
8. The selected shading style option is applied in the paragraph as shown in Figure 3.70.

➡ **To remove shading using mouse, do this:**

1. Select the paragraph or paragraphs from which you want to remove shading.
2. In Borders and Shading dialog box, select the Shading tab.
3. Choose No fill from the Fill group and also clear Style from the patterns group.
4. Click OK.

Table Formula

When you want to perform calculations on numbers in Word 2010 table, you can create formula that uses a built-in mathematical function.

1. Position the insertion point in the cell in which you want to enter the formula.
2. Click **Layout** tab. Click **Data** group. Click **Formula**. The **Formula** dialog box appears.
3. In the **Formula:** box enter the formula or In the **Paste function:** drop down list select the function you want to use and specify the range of cells to be used for the calculation (See Figure 3.71). Or
   In the **Number format:** drop down list, select the number format.
4. Click OK.

☞ *You can define the range of the columns or row of table under the brackets in the formula. You can use ABOVE, LEFT, RIGHT to indicate the range of the cells in the formula, such as SUM (LEFT) or SUM (B2:E2).*

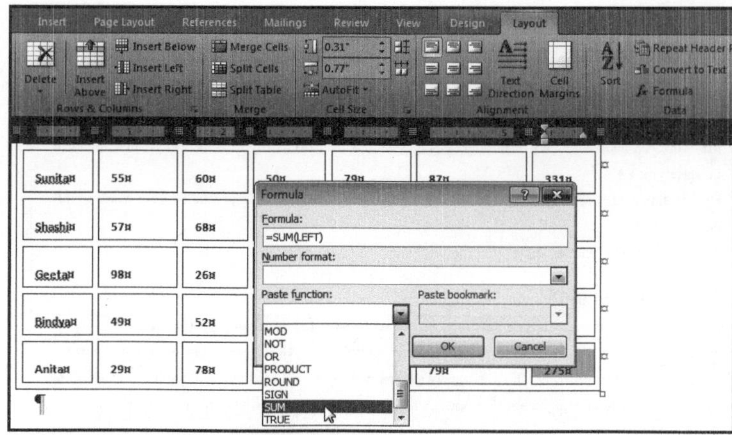

Figure 3.71 Table Formula

3.7 MAIL MERGE

Mail Merge is a mass-mailing facility that takes names, addresses and pertinent facts about the recipients and merges the information into the form of a letter. Mail Merge printing (merge printing in short) uses two files: a data file that contains a listing of data items (or fields) arranged in some specific order and a master file that contains the standard text as well as the data variables which are replaced with specific data items from the data file during the merge operation performed by Word 2010.

3.7.1 Creating a Mail Merge Letter

The best way to learn how to create and print a merged document is to consider a practical example. This is described in the following sections.

Creating a Document for Mail-Merge

For mail-merge, you need to do the following:

- Create a data source.
- Create main document.
- Insert fields into the main document.
- Check for design and data entry errors.
- Merge the data source document and the main document and finally, print merged documents.

Planning Data Source

Designing a data source document is one of the most important parts of mail merge feature. To begin with, you may want to create a data source document which has one field for the *name of your friend*; *one field for the address* and *one field each for the city and pincode*. It is always good if you read data into multiple fields. That is you should use two fields namely, *Last name* and *First name* for name field. Similarly, keep separate fields for *house number*, *colony*, *city* and *pin*. For example, if you want to deliver an invitation through a messenger, you may need to sort the addresses on the basis of *colony* field in the address, so that invitations belonging to one colony can be sent together through a messenger.

Starting Mail Merge

Word 2010 has a step-by-step Mail Merge Wizard that guides you through the steps for creating merged documents.

➡ **To use the mail merge helper, do this:**

1. First create a blank document.
2. Click the **Mailings** tab, choose **Start Mail Merge** group and click on the down pointing arrow, after that a list appears as seen in Figure 3.72 offering five options – *Letters, E-Mail Messages, Envelopes, Labels* and *Directory*.

   The first step in the mail merge process is to Create the Main document, because the type of main document governs the subsequent choices you can make in the Mail Merge Helper. Note that *Letters*, E-*Mail Messages, Envelopes, Labels*, and *Catalogues* are various types of documents you can produce using Mail Merge Wizard. Hence, the Helper offers you different choices of data source.

Creating Main Document

Word 2010 has a step-by-step Mail Merge Wizard that guides you through the steps for creating merged documents.

➡ **To create main document, do this:**

1. Click the **Mailings** tab in the **Start Mail Merge** group and click on the down pointing arrow and select **Step by Step Mail Merge Wizard...**.

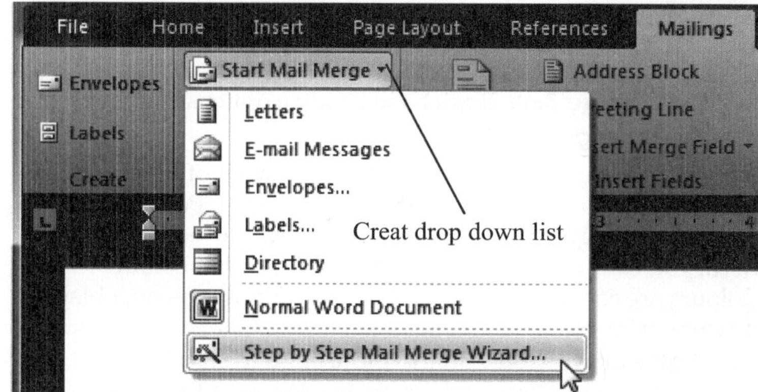

Figure 3.72 Select step-by-step Mail Merge Wizard

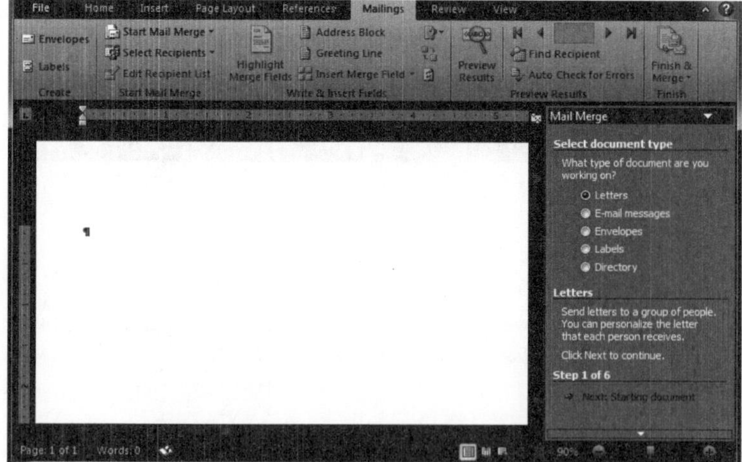

Figure 3.73 Step 1 of Mail Merge task pane

2. On the right hand side the Mail Merge task pane box appears as seen in Figure 3.73 showing Step 1 of the Wizard's six steps.
3. Under the **Select document type**, click Letters radio button.
4. Click **Next: Starting document**.
   - The wizard guides you through the rest of the mail process. The following are more details, listed in step-by-step order.

- There are three options under **select starting document**, click **use the current document** radio button, which specifies *how do you want to set up your letters*? (See Figure 3.74).

5. Click **Next: Select recipients.**
   - Under **Select recipients**, click **Type a new list** radio button (Figure 3.75).
   - Click **Create...** under Type a new list section.

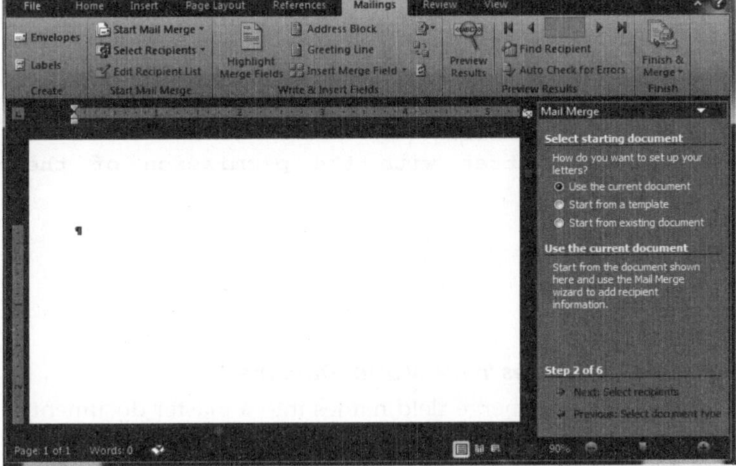

Figure 3.74 Step 2 of Mail Merge task pane

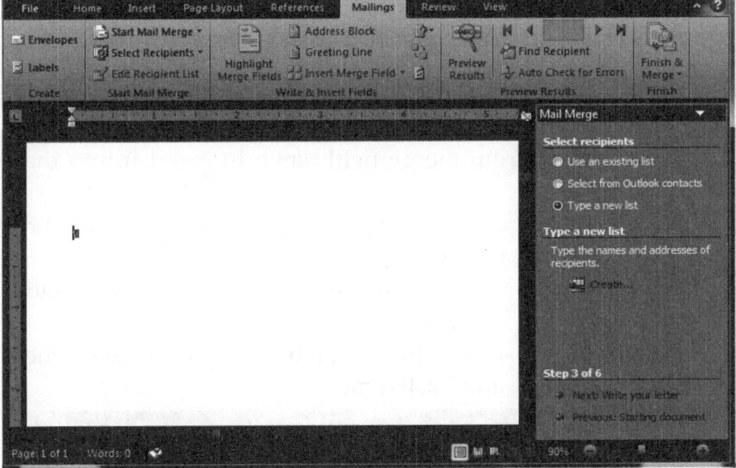

Figure 3.75 Step 3 of Mail Merge task pane

6. A **New Address List** dialog box appears as shown in Figure 3.76. Type the information you want to include for the data source.

Adding and Removing Field Names

As you may not require all the field names in the **New Address List** dialog box, so for each of the following field names, first select the field and then click the **Customize Columns...** button. The Customize Address list dialog box appears as shown in Figure 3.77.

7. Select the Field names order appears in the **Customize Address list** dialog box, If you don't want any field, select the field and then click delete button.
8. The Selected Field names are: *Title, First Name, Last Name, Address Line 1, City, Zip Code.*

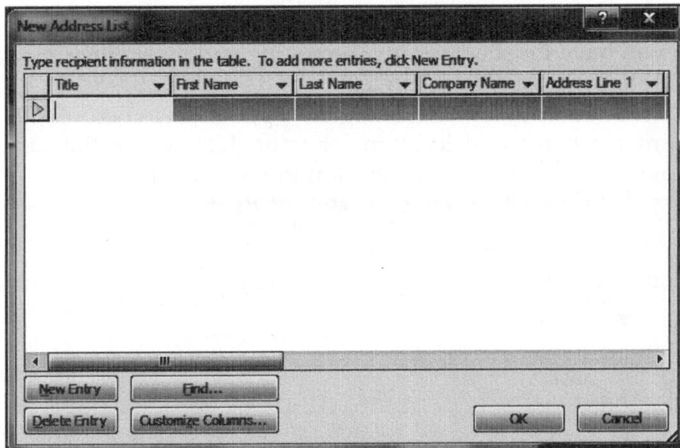

Figure 3.76 New Address List dialog box

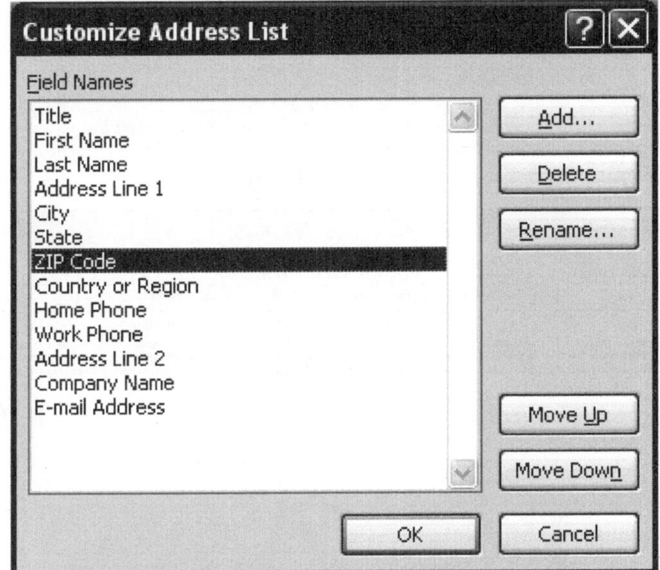

Figure 3.77 Customize Address list dialog box

9. Under Field names: type (use tab key to go next field)

```
Title: Mr.
First Name: Sanjay
Last Name: Sharma
Address Line 1: 120-A, Vikaspuri
City: New Delhi
Zip Code: 110 018
```

After completing the First entry, click New Entry to enter another data records as follows:

```
Title: Ms.
First Name: Uma
Last Name: Shankar
Address Line 1: A-3, Janakpuri
City: New Delhi
Zip Code: 110 049

Title: Ms.
First Name: Asha
Last Name: Arora
Address Line 1: B2/4, Model Town
City: New Delhi
Zip Code: 110 009
```

Saving Data Source

When you have finished adding, removing and arranging fields, click OK to save your data source.

10. The **Save Address List** dialog box appears as in Figure 3.78. Enter a name and location for your data source file, say, **Data.doc** and click **S**ave button to save the file.

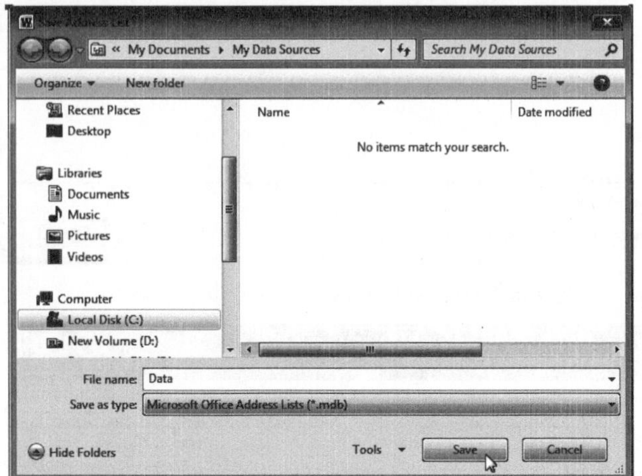

Figure 3.78 Save Address List dialog box

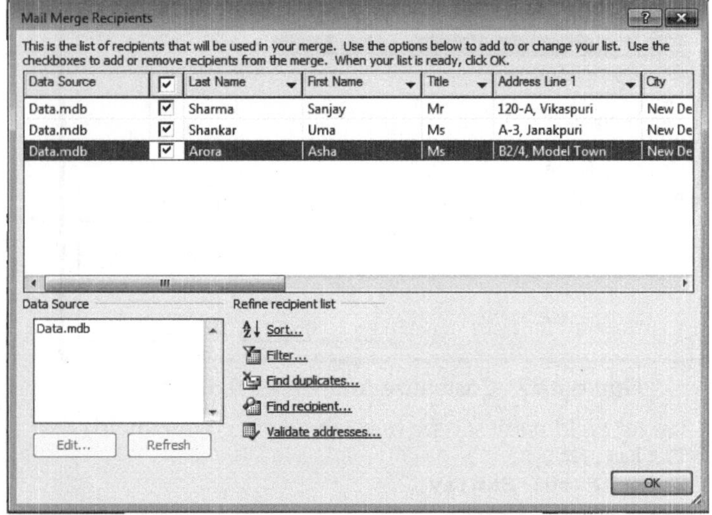

Figure 3.79 Mail Merge Recipients dialog box

11. The Mail Merge Recipients dialog box appears as in Figure 3.79. Select the recipients that will be used in your merge process.
12. Click OK.
13. Click **Next: Write your letter.**

Typing Letter

Now type the following letter.

Rohini
New Delhi-110 056
Ref.Rahul/Comm/20

Dated: 3rd May, 2016

To
<<Title>> <<First_Name>>
<<Last_Name>>
<<Address_Line_1>>
<<City>>-<<ZIP_Code>>

Dear <<Title>> <<Last_Name>>

I have to inform you that the meeting of the club committee will be held at the Club House, 36-N, Chanakyapuri, Vinay Marg on Tuesday 25th June, 2016 at 10.30 A.M. I hope you will make it convenient to attend the conference.

The agenda for the conference is as under:

1. **Confirmation of the minutes of the last meeting (enclosed).**
2. **Accounts and Internal Auditors Report for the months of Feb and March 2016 (enclosed).**
3. **Election of new members.**
4. **List of outstanding.**
5. **Any other matter with the permission of the Chairman.**

Yours faithfully,

P.K. Verma
(Secretary)

Inserting Fields Names in the Master Document

When you place the merge field names into a master document, you will see that Word 2010 encloses each *field name* in chevrons, i.e. the marks represented as << >>.

➡ **To insert a field, do this:**

1. In the **Mailing** tab, click **Insert Merge Field** in the **Write & Insert Fields** group. Click the down pointing arrow and choose the field names that you can insert in your master document appears. You can also select the field names from this list (See Figure 3.80).
2. Click the Title from merge field name to insert it into the document.
3. Press the Spacebar key to insert a blank space between the Title and the FirstName.
4. Click the Insert Merge Field button to insert the next field name and select FirstName.
5. Press the Spacebar key to insert a blank space between the fields FirstName and LastName.

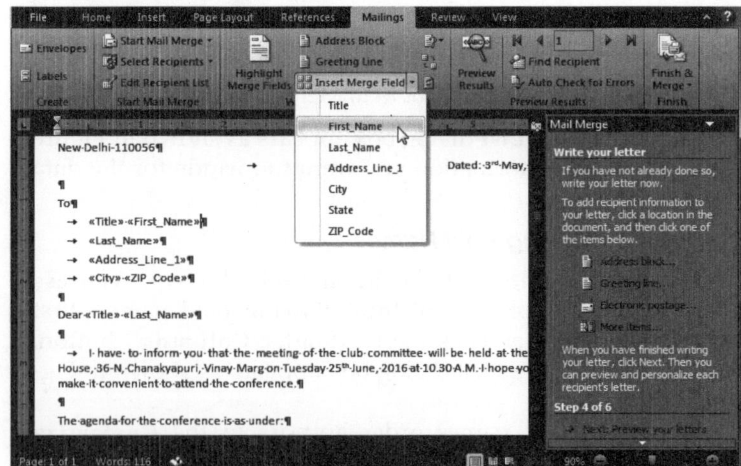

Figure 3.80 Step 4 of Mail Merge task pane

6. Click the Insert Merge Field button and select LastName.
7. Press the Enter key to move to the next line.

8. Place the cursor below the **<<Title>>**. Click the Insert Merge Field button. Select **<<Address1>>** and press the Enter key.
9. Again place the cursor below **<<Address1>>**. Click the Insert Merge Field button. Select **<<City>>** type a hyphen and select **<<Pin>>** from the merge field button and press Enter key.
10. Press the Enter key twice to leave a blank line.
11. Type *Dear* and press the Spacebar key.
12. Click the Insert Merge Field button and select **<<Title>>**.
13. Press the Spacebar to leave a space between the Title and the LastName.
14. Click the Insert Merge Field button and select **<<Last-Name>>**.
15. Type a comma, and then press the Enter key twice to leave a blank line.

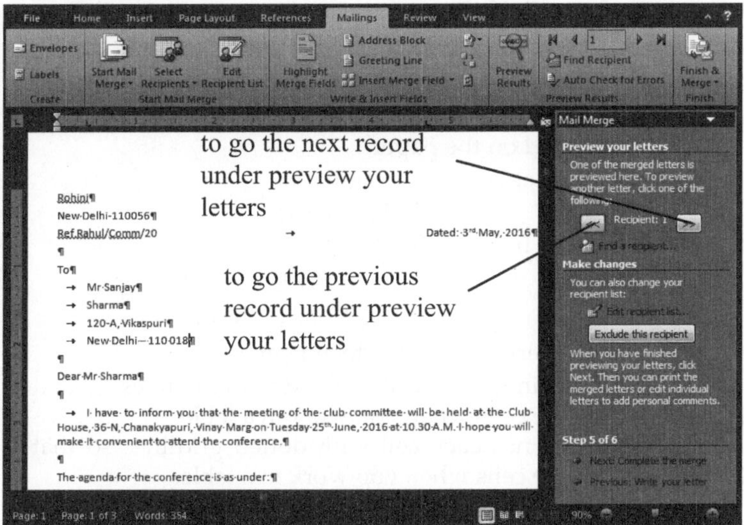

Figure 3.81 Step 5 of partially completed screen

16. After completing the above steps, your screen will be as shown in Figure 3.81.
17. Now type the remaining part of the letter.

Saving the Master Document

18. After you have completed the main document and inserted all of the merge fields, click Save As on the Office button.
19. Give the name of the document, and then Click Save button.
20. Click **Next: Preview your letters.**
21. In the Preview your letters, click arrow button, i.e., (<<) to show the first record, and to go the second record click (>>) arrow button (See Figure 3.82).
22. Click **Next: Complete the merge** (See Figure 3.82).
23. To personalize individual documents, you actually complete the merge, and then edit the information you want in the resulting merged document.
24. Click **Edit individual letters....** . under **Merge** section. The Merge to New Document dialog box appears as shown in Figure 3.83.
25. In the Merge records area, select the records you want to merge.

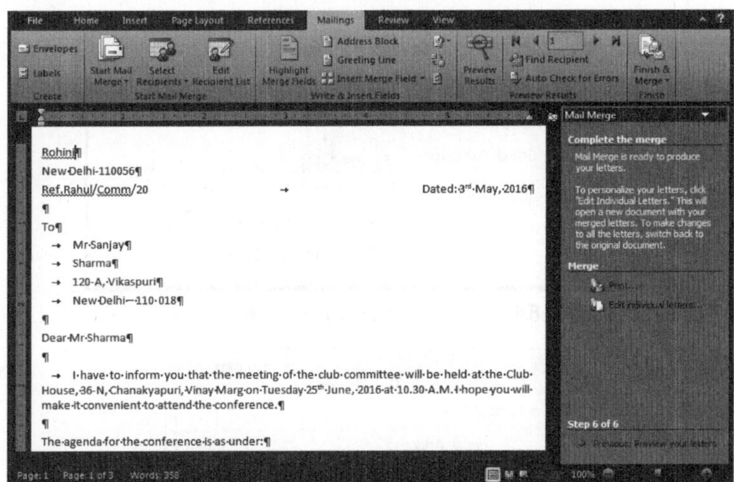

Figure 3.82 Step 6 of partially completed screen

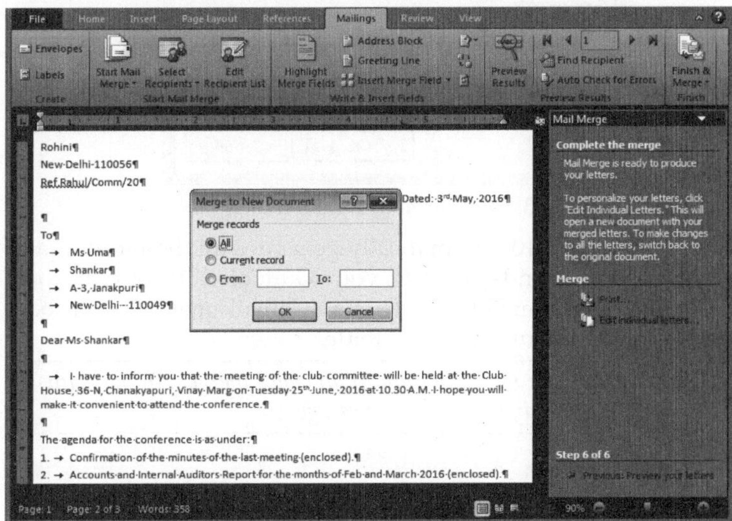

Figure 3.83 Merge to New Document dialog box

26. Click All radio button and then click OK.
Word 2010 creates and opens a new merged documents. Your main document also remains open. You can switch back to it if you want to make a change to all the documents and then save all the merged documents. Click Office button and Save the file.

Printing the Merged Letters

If you want to print the letters, make sure that the printer is switched on and is in ready to print. Then click **Finish & Merge** in **Finish** group. Click down pointing arrow and choose **Print Documents...** . The **Merge to Printer** dialog box appears. Select the records and click OK.

Merging for sending emails using outlook.

27. In the **Finish** group on the **Mailings** tab you will see a button called **Finish & Merge**. Click on it, and then click **Send E-mail Messages...** as shown in Figure 3.84)
28. Merge to E-mail dialog box appears as shown in Figure 3.85. You will be asked to give your message a **Subject line:** and then you can click on OK to send the messages.

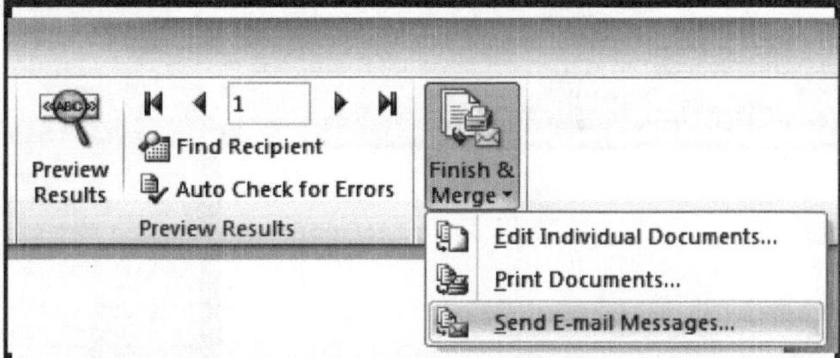

Figure 3.84 Selecting Send E-mail messages

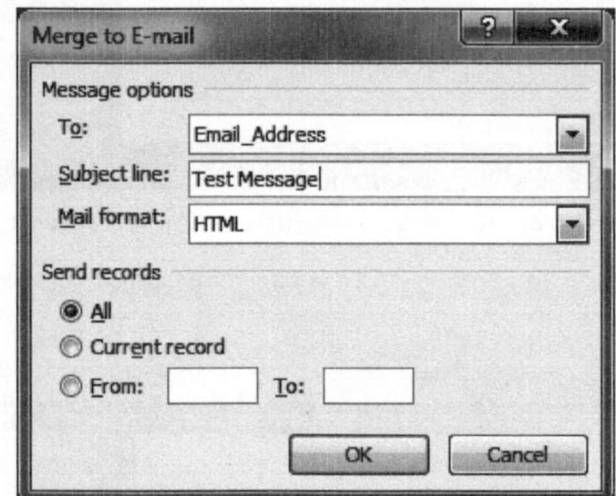

Figure 3.85 Merge to E-mail dialog box

29. Now Word 2010 automatically generates all the individual emails, and sends them to your Outlook 2010 outbox (or your default email client). Your email merges will be recorded in your sent items folder.

☞ *Attachments are not an option in an email merge. All data must be within the body of the email message.*

3.8 SUMMARY

This chapter presents the concepts of *Word Processing* using MS Word. This package is a program that helps you create documents easily and quickly compared to a typewriter. You can store documents in your computer and reuse them easily whenever you need them. It also discussed how to open and save and print documents with the help of MS Word. Text creation is also important in Word, such as how to create text and how to select text. It also allows you to change the appearance of text and organize the information in a document in a systematic manner. This chapter also discusses how to align the text, Indents paragraph and apply bullets and numbering. The appearance of the text can be changed by changing the font sizes, styles. Finally, how to create table, and changing cell height and width as well as border and shading have also been explained.

MODEL QUESTIONS AND ANSWERS

1. Multiple Choice

1.1 Word offers certain ways by which you can move around in a document
a. By scrolling b. By moving to a specific page
c. Both a and b above d. None of the above

1.2 Word automatically places a default left aligned tab stop at every
a. 0.2" b. 0.4"
c. 0.3" d. 0.5"

1.3 After a table has been created, which of the following operations can be performed?
a. Insert rows in a table b. Delete and insert columns
c. Split the table into two tables d. All of the above

1.4 When Word gets loaded, the opening screen displays a document named:
a. Document1 b. Document
c. Doc1 d. No document name is displayed

1.5 You specify the save details of your file in the
a. Save As... dialog box b. Save the File As... dialog box
c. File Save dialog box d. None of the above

1.6 The contents of the Clipboard remain the same until
a. You cut other text b. You shut down your computer
c. you copy other text d. All of the above

1.7 What is the term used for the word processing programs that show you directly on the PC screen the appearance of your final document as you might expect when the document is printed on the paper.
a. Search & Replace b. Pagination
c. Soft Copy d. WYSIWYG

1.8 Word text can be made Italic by
a. Ctrl+I b. Ctrl+B
c. Ctrl+U d. None of the above

1.9 When you insert a table in a document
a. Word outlines each cell with continuous lines so that you see the cells when you work in a table.
b. Word outlines each cell with dotted gridlines so that you see the cells when you work in a table.
c. No line is drawn.
d. None of the above

1.10 What Ribbon do you use to change margins?
a. Page Layout b. View
c. Insert d. Home

1.11 What can be shown on the status bar?
a. Name of document, insert button, spell check
b. Number of spellings errors, page number, document name
c. Size of Margins, word count, web layout
d. Number of pages in the document, word count, spelling/grammar check

1.12 Which Ribbon shows what fonts are available for use?
a. View b. Page Layout
c. Reference d. Home

1.13 What Ribbon do you need to be on to see the document views that are available?
a. Insert b. View
c. Page Layout d. Home

1.14 What page view can you use to see what it will look like when printed?
a. Outline view b. Draft view
c. Reading view d. Print view

1.15 What is NOT a new feature in Word 2010?

a. Ribbon b. Button
c. Charts d. Drop down menu

1.16 What is the name of the small toolbar at the top that can show the save disk?
a. My Documents b. Quick Access
c. Title bar d. Find Me

1.17 What is NOT on the insert Ribbon?
a. Shapes b. Clip Art
c. Page Numbers d. Thesaurus

2. State whether the following are True or False

2.1 Cutting means to cut the selection from the document and put in on the Clipboard.

2.2 Paragraph formatting is applied to the entire paragraph even if only part of the paragraph is included in a block.

2.3 Character formatting decides how a block of text appears.

2.4 You cannot undo certain operations like saving, printing, opening and creating documents.

2.5 Superscript character are lower than regular characters.

2.6 Insertion point shows where the typed text will appear.

2.7 Print Preview is a useful feature of Word which lets you preview and makes changes to pages before printing.

2.8 A word processor package may have the facility for checking the spelling of words in a document.

2.9 Using Insert menu you can insert various objects such as page numbers, headers and footers, picture etc.

2.10 Print button on the Quick Access toolbar will print the entire document using the default settings.

2.11 Using Review tab you can access to various utilities of word such as spell check, macros and mail merge etc.

2.12 Formula bar is available in MS Word 2010.

Answers

1.	1.1	c	1.2	d	1.3	c	1.4	a	1.5	a	1.6	d
	1.7	d	1.8	a	1.9	b	1.10	a	1.11	d	1.12	d
	1.13	b	1.14	d	1.15	d	1.16	b	1.17	d		
2.	2.1	T	2.2	T	2.3	T	2.4	T	2.5	F	2.6	T
	2.7	T	2.8	T	2.9	T	2.10	T	2.11	F	2.12	F

CHAPTER 4

Using Spreadsheet

4.0 INTRODUCTION

Spreadsheet applications (sometimes referred to simply as spreadsheets) are computer programs that let you to create and manipulate spreadsheets electronically. In a spreadsheet application, each value sits in a cell. You can define what type of data is in each cell and how different cells depend on one another. The relationships between cells are called formulas, and the names of the cells are called labels.

A table of values are arranged in rows and columns. Each value can have a predefined relationship to the other values. If you change one value, therefore, you may need to change other values as well, or they will change automatically.

Once you have defined the cells and the formulas for linking them together, you can enter your data. You can then modify selected values to see how all the other values change accordingly. This enables you to study various what-if scenarios.

Excel 2010 is a popular spreadsheet program, where you design worksheets by using this software package. Excel 2010 uses a workbook-style presentation which is made up of several worksheets, like pages in a notebook.

4.1 OBJECTIVES

The reader will be able to understand the following:

- Elements of spreadsheet
- Manipulation of cells in MS Excel
- Formulas and functions

4.2 ELEMENTS OF ELECTRONIC SPREADSHEET

When you are working with a spreadsheet package, such as MS Excel 2010 you have to know some spreadsheet terminologies. Some such terms are given in the following paragraphs.

Workbook

A workbook is a collection of many worksheets. In a single workbook, you can store information in an organized manner. By default, a workbook opens with three worksheets and it can contain a maximum of 255 worksheets.

Worksheet

A worksheet is a sheet which is made up of rows and columns. It is used for planning a project or financial documents of an organization. Worksheet refers to the actual document you create by using the spreadsheet program. A worksheet is always stored in a workbook.

☞ *Excel is a popular spreadsheet program, where you design worksheets by using this program.*

Chartsheet

Chartsheet is a separate sheet in a workbook that contain only graphs or charts. It is useful when you want to see a chart or tabular data separated from other type of data.

Row

A row is a horizontal block of cells that runs through the entire width of the worksheet. The rows are numbered from top to bottom along the left edge of the worksheet. The first row is numbered 1, the second 2, and so on. There can be a maximum of 1,048,576 rows and 16,384 columns in an Excel 2010 worksheet.

Column

A column is a vertical block of cells that runs through the entire worksheet. A worksheet contains 16,384 (A to XFD) columns. The first column is **A**, the second is **B** and so on until you reach **Z**. Then comes column **AA** through **XFD**. The last (or rightmost) column of the worksheet, **XFD** is the 16,384th column.

Cell

A cell is the intersection of a row and a column. For example, the uppermost cell is A1 (column A, row 1). Cell G9 is the intersection of column G, row 9. When you select a cell by clicking it with the mouse, or moving to it using the keyboard, it becomes an active cell.

Formula

Formulas are equations that perform calculations on values in your worksheet. It is an order of values, names, cell references, functions and operators in a cell that together give a new values. A formula always begins with = (equal) sign.

Function

Functions are the pre-defined formulas or programs that perform calculations in Excel on specific values, called arguments. Each function takes specific types of arguments such as numbers, references, text, or logical values.

Working with Spreadsheet

In Excel 2010, each workbook can contain many worksheets. These sheets may also contain *charts*, *macros*, etc. Sheets may contain different types of information but all the data or information is related to each other.

☞ *Generally, spreadsheet is a software tool and worksheet is a work file created with spreadsheet software. But sometimes, worksheet is also called a spreadsheet.*

Each worksheet contains 16,384 columns and 1,048,576 rows. The intersection of a row and a column forms a cell in which you can enter data or a formula. Column headings start at **A** and as they reach the letter **Z** column, headings restart with **AA**, **AB**, and so on till **XFD**. Row headings, down the left side of a sheet, go from **1** to **1,048,576**. It is equally easy for formulas to refer to information in another worksheet of the same workbook as it is in the same worksheet.

Terminologies used in MS Excel

The following terminologies should be kept in mind, while using MS Excel.

Select Highlight a cell or group of cells, dialog box option, or graphical object with the keyboard or mouse action.

Choose Execute and complete a command.

Active Bring an application or document window to the foreground.

Table 4.1 gives the details of the terminology for the mouse operations.

Table 4.1 Terminologies for Mouse Function

Action	**Function**
Position	Position the mouse pointer on an item.
Click	Point to an item and then quickly press and release the mouse left button.
Double click	Point to an item and quickly press and release the mouse left button two times.
Drag	Point to an item, press and hold the mouse left button as you move the mouse pointer to a new location, then release the mouse button.
Right click	Point to an item and click the right mouse button.

4.2.1 Opening of Spreadsheet (Excel 2010)

MS Excel 2010 needs *Windows 7* as an operating system to run on an IBM PC. However, Excel 2010 can also be run on *Windows XP* operating system, if *service pack 3* is installed on *Windows XP*.

➡ **To start Excel 2010 in Windows 7, do this:**

1. Click the **Start** button on the taskbar, highlight **All Programs**, click **MS Office** and then click **MS Excel 2010** (See Figure 4.1).

Figure 4.1 Starting Excel 2010 in Windows 7

➡ **To start Excel 2010 in Windows XP, do this:**

1. Click the **Start** button on the taskbar, highlight **All Programs**, click **MS Office** and then **MS Excel 2010** (See Figure 4.2).

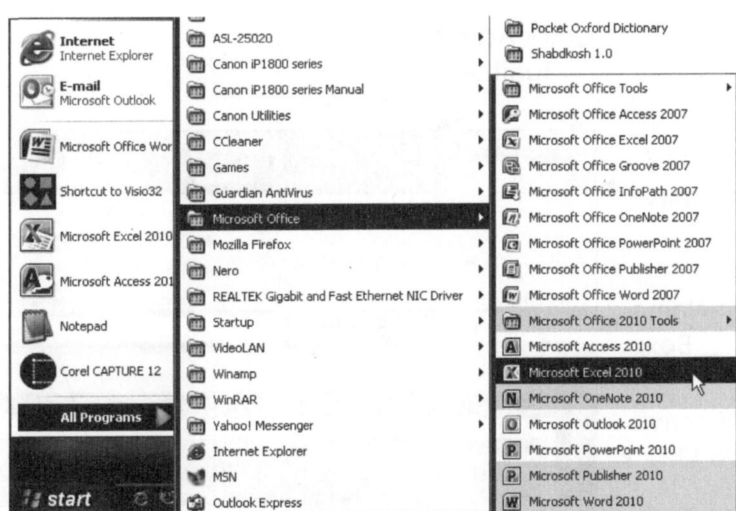

Figure 4.2 Starting Excel 2010 in Windows XP

Excel 2010 Interface

Excel 2010 includes the MS Office Fluent interface, which consists of a customizable visual system of tools and commands. Figure 4.3 shows the elements of Excel 2010 application window and an open Excel 2010 workbook in detail.

Title Bar

At the top of an Excel 2010 window, there is the title bar. The left edge of this bar has the Office button next to which the name of the open document is displayed. On the right edge of the title bar, the *Minimize*, *Restore/Maximize* and *Close* button are placed (See Figure 4.3).

Application Window

The window within which Excel 2010 runs.

Quick Access Toolbar

The Quick Access Toolbar is a customizable toolbar that contains a set of commands that are independent of the tab that is currently displayed. You can add buttons that represent commands to the Quick Access Toolbar. You can move the Quick Access Toolbar from one of the two possible locations. This toolbar is located by default at the top of Excel 2010 window. It provides tools that you use frequently, such as Save, Undo and Repeat buttons (See Figure 4.3). You can customize the Quick Access Toolbar by adding commands to it.

Workbook Window

A window within the Excel 2010 application window in which a worksheet, chart, or dialog box is shown.

File Tab

File tab is the coloured tab which is located in the upper-left corner of MS Office 2010 programs and below the Quick Access Toolbar (See Figure 4.3). When you click the File tab, you can see the Backstage view. File Tab replaces the Office button in Excel 2007. It contains commands like New, Open, Save, Save As, Print, etc.

Active Workbook

The Excel 2010 workbook window that accepts entries and commands.

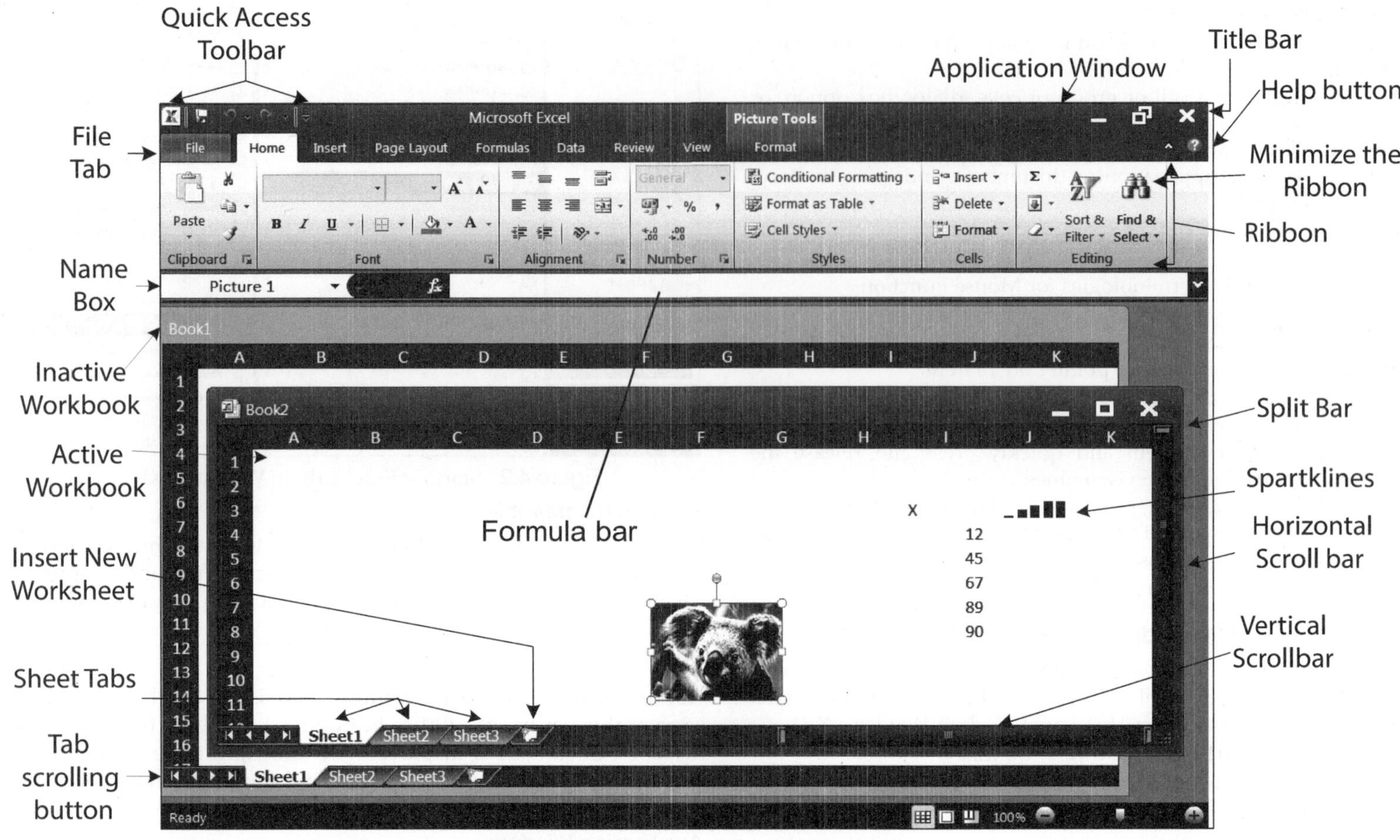

Figure 4.3 Elements of Excel 2010 window

Inactive Workbook

A window that contains Excel 2010 information. It is not affected by commands. Such a window has a gray title bar and is behind the active workbook window.

Ribbon

Ribbon is displayed just below the title bar (See Figure 4.3). In Ribbon, *Commands* are organized in logical *groups*, which are collected together under *tabs*. You can hide the Ribbon by double-clicking the active tab. Different types of Tabs described here under are available in the Ribbon of Excel 2010.

- *Home Tab:* When you open Excel 2010, Home Tab is active. It contains the buttons related to the worksheet contents, such as entering, editing, and formatting data. It is divided into seven groups, i.e., Clipboard, Font, Alignment, Number, Style, Cells and Editing.
- *Insert Tab:* Insert tab contains the button related to the items which you can insert in your worksheet. Groups of this tab are Tables, Illustrations (picture, clipart) Charts, Sparklines, Filter, Links, Text and Symbols.
- *Page Layout Tab:* It includes the buttons related to the appearance of the worksheet. This tab is divided into five groups, i.e., Themes, Page Setup, Scale to Fit, Sheet Options, and Arrange.
- *Formulas Tab:* It contains the button related to functions. Group of this tab are Function Library, Defined Names, Formula Auditing and Calculation.
- *Data Tab:* It contains the button related to data analysis. Get External Data, Connections, Sort & Filter, Data Tools, Outline and Analysis are the group of this tab.
- *Review Tab:* It contains the button related to security and accurate data. Proofing, Language Comments and Changes are the group of this Tab.
- *View Tab:* It contains the button related to the view of the worksheet, i.e., how you want to view the worksheet. Workbook view, Show/Hide, Zoom, Window are the group of this tab.
- *Developer Tab:* It contains the button related to create, run and edit macros. It also includes commands or buttons to import XML (eXtensible Markup Language) view of the worksheet, i.e., how you want to view the worksheet Code, Add-Ins Controls, XML and Modify are the groups of this tab.

Scroll Bar

The scroll bar appears at the *left* for vertical scrolling and at the *bottom right* for horizontal scrolling as seen in Figure 4.3.

- To scroll one cell at a time, click the scroll button with arrows at the corners of the scroll bars.
- To scroll more, drag the scroll button in the scroll bar.

Split Bar

The split bar is located at the top of the *vertical* scroll bar and to the right of the *horizontal* scroll bar (See Figure 4.3). Double click the split button on the vertical scroll bar. It splits the sheet horizontally.

Tab Scrolling Buttons

These are the arrow buttons to the left of the sheet tabs for scrolling the worksheet (See Figure 4.3).

- To scroll between sheet tabs, click an arrow for the direction you want to scroll.
- To scroll one sheet tab at a time in left or right direction, click the middle tab scrolling buttons.
- To scroll through a group of sheet tabs in left or right direction, click the tab scroll buttons at the left and right corner.
- To display a list of the sheets in the workbook right click a tab scrolling button to display the menu.

Sheet Tabs

A tab is near to the bottom of a work book window that displays the name of a sheet (See Figure 4.3). Click the sheet tab to move to the next sheet. To display the shortcut menu, right click the sheet tab. To scroll through the sheet tabs, use the tab scrolling button.

Name Box

The *name box* is at the left end of the formula bar (See Figure 4.3). It identifies the selected *cell, chart item* or *drawing object*.

Formula Bar

The *formula bar* displays the constant value or formula used in the active cell. The formula bar is also used for editing the cell contents (See Figure 4.3).

Shortcut Menus

Shortcut menus are meant to display frequently used commands related to the selected *item* or *object*.

ScreenTips

ScreenTips show the name of the command button shown in ribbon. ScreenTips are shown in small windows appearing as soon as you position the mouse pointer on the toolbar button. Enhanced ScreenTips are larger windows that display more descriptive text than a ScreenTip and can take a link to a Help topic.

Status Bar

Status bar appears at the bottom of the Excel 2010 window. It displays information regarding a selected command or an operation in progress. Note that the right side of the status bar shows zoom slider, different views tool, such as Normal, Page Layout and Page Break view.

Creating a New Workbook

➡ **To create a new workbook, do this:**

1. Click the **File** Tab as seen in Figure 4.4. Here, Select **New**. Under **Available Templates**, click **Blank Workbook** and then click **Create** button or *alternatively*, press Ctrl + N keys together.

☞ *You can create a blank workbook or create new workbook based on an existing workbook, the default workbook template, or any other template.*

4.2.2 Opening a Workbook

➡ **To Open a workbook, do this:**

1. Click the **File** Tab as seen in Figure 4.4. Here, choose **Open** or *alternatively*, press Ctrl + O keys together. The Open dialog box appears as shown in Figure 4.5.
2. In dialog box, choose the drive, folder name that contains the workbooks. After finding the required workbook, select it.

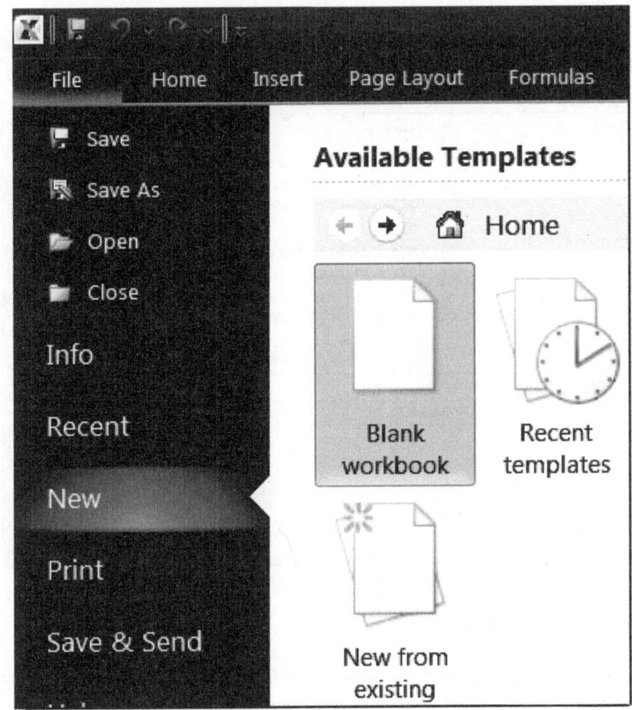

Figure 4.4 File Tab

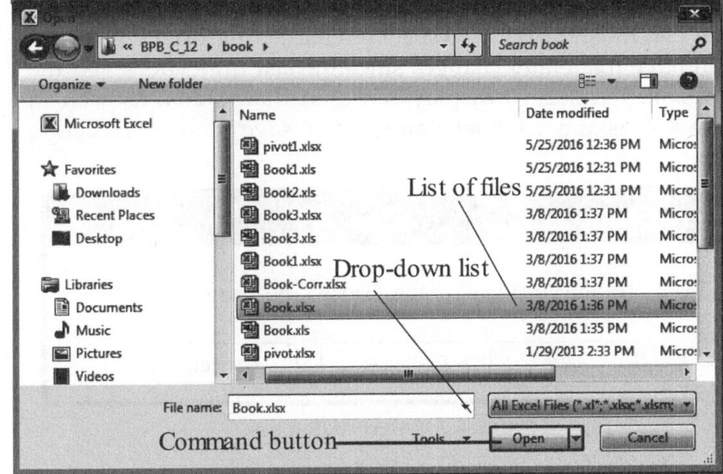

Figure 4.5 Open dialog box

3. Then click OK.

➡ **To Open more than one workbook simultaneously, do this:**

1. Repeat step 1. and 2. of opening a single workbook.
2. Click the name of one file and then hold down Ctrl key and click another file name and then press Enter key.

4.2.3 Saving a Workbook

Excel has two commands for saving workbooks. *Save* command is use to save an existing workbook; *Save As* command is use to save the workbook when you save it for the first time or save the workbook under a new name.

➡ **To save the workbook for the first time, do this:**

1. Click on the **File** Tab as seen in Figure 4.4. Here, choose **Save As**. The *Save As* dialog box appears as in Figure 4.6.
   You can also specify the location where you want to save the file in the Save in: box
2. In the File name: box give the name of the file.
3. In the Save as type: box give the type of file.

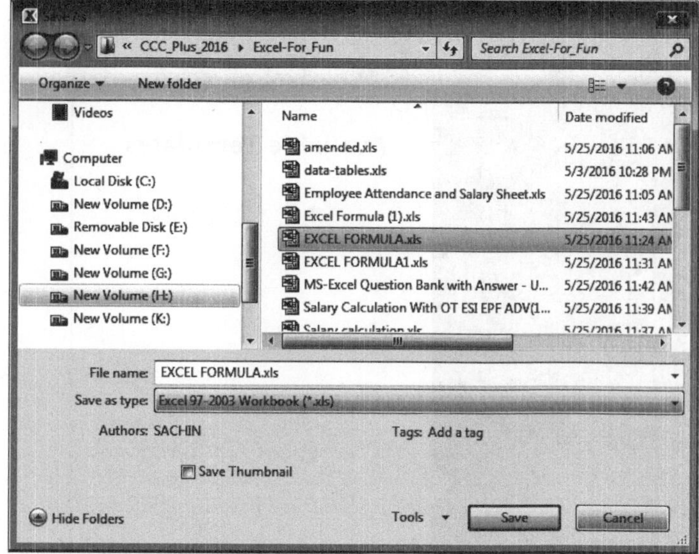

Figure 4.6 Save As dialog box

4. Click Save button.

☞ *Excel 2010 worksheet is saved with .xlsx extension indicating that it uses the XML-based file format.*

Closing a Workbook Window

When you finish using worksheet or chart, you close its window. If you have made any changes since the last time you saved the workbook, Excel 2010 displays an alert dialog box, as seen in Figure 4.7, asking whether you want to save your work before closing.

Figure 4.7 Alert dialog box

➡ **To close a file in a workbook, do this:**

1. Click on the **File** Tab as seen in Figure 4.4. Here, choose **Close**. The window closes provided no change has been made to the workbook since it was saved last.
2. If you have made changes to the workbook since the last save, the Alert dialog box appears. In the dialog box, choose *Don't Save* if you do not want to save a changed version of the file, or choose *Save* if you do want to save changes (See Figure 4.7). Type a new file name and choose **Save** button.

Quitting Excel 2010 Program

➡ **To quit Excel 2010, do this:**

1. Click on the **File** Tab and then choose **Exit**. *Alternatively*, click the Close button (x) in the top-right corner or press Alt+F4 or double-click the Control icon at the left of the title bar.
2. When all workbooks are closed, Excel 2010 window closes, and the application is terminated.

4.2.4 Printing a Spreadsheet

The simplest way to print any opened worksheet is to choose **Print** option from the Backstage view or *alternately*, click the **Print Preview and Print** button from the **Quick Access toolbar**. In Excel 2010, you can print entire or partial worksheets and workbooks, one at a time, or several at once. And if the data that you want to print is in a MS Excel table, you can also print just the Excel table by setting the print area.

☞ *You can also print a workbook to a file instead of to a printer. This is useful when you need to print the workbook on a different type of printer from the one that you originally used to print it.*

➡ **To print a spreadsheet, do this:**

1. Open the worksheet that you want to print.
2. Click the **File** tab and then choose **Print** command (See Figure 4.8). or *Alternatively*, press Ctrl+Shift+F12 keys together.
3. The Print Backstage view appears. Here, click **Print** icon.
4. The Print Backstage view closes and in the status bar displays the process of the print job.

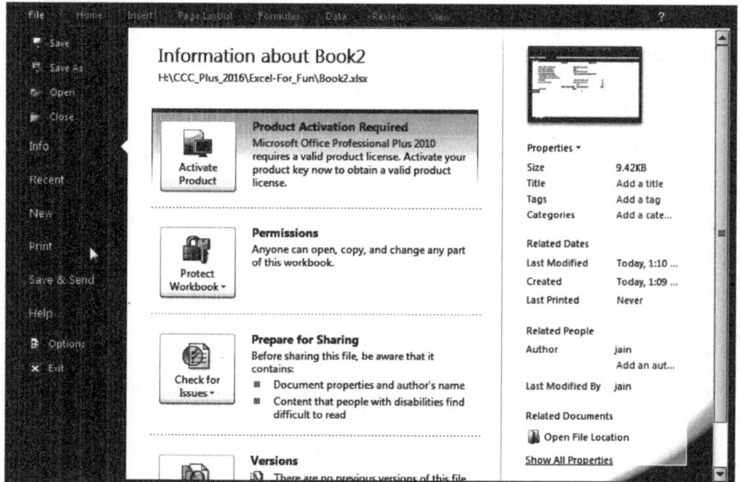

Figure 4.8 Print command in Backstage view

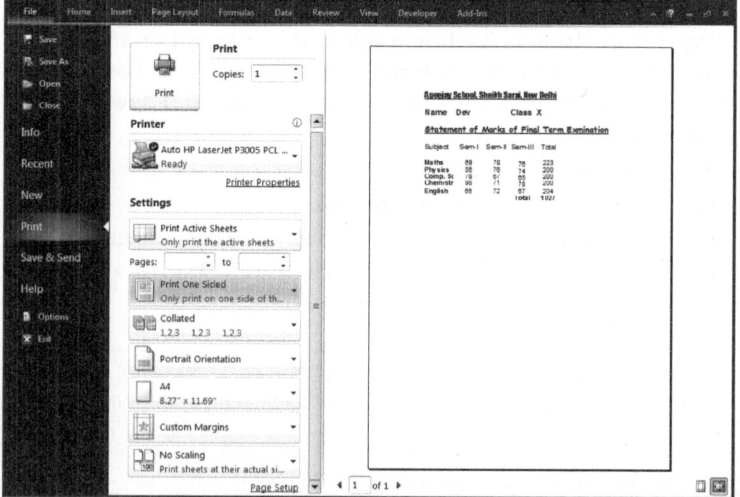

Figure 4.9 Print Options

Backstage Print Options shown in Figure 4.9, are described in Table 4.2 below.

Table 4.2 Backstage print options

Option	Function
Print Section:	
Copies	Specify the number of copies to be printed.
Printer Section:	This section shows selected printer from a drop-down list, print queue status, type, printer port being used, and whether the printer is busy or idle is also shown below the print selection. Select the desired printer from the Printer drop-down list.
Print to File	Select this option to create a disk file for the selected printer.
Settings:	This section shows the Page Setup options such as page orientation, paper size, and page margins. These options are described below:
Print what option:	
Print Active Sheets	Prints only selected worksheet.
Print Entire Workbook	Prints currently open workbook
Print Selection	Prints selected cells.
Ignore Print Area	Select this option if you want to ignore the print area you have selected.
Page(s) From:/To:	Select this option to print pages you wish to print.
Collate	Select this option to collate multiple copies.
Page Orientation	Allows you to change the page orientation, i.e., portrait (vertically) or landscape (horizontally).
Page Size	Allows you to select the paper size.
Margin	Allows you to set the margin of the pages.
Scaling	Allows you to adjust the size of the worksheet.

Printing Sections of a Worksheet or Multiple Worksheets

Suppose you have a year's worth of data accumulated in a given worksheet, but you want to print just one month's worksheet data, then you use this method.

➡ **To print a section of a worksheet, do this:**

1. Select the range of cells to print.
2. In the **Print Backstage** window, under **Setting** section, in the **Print what drop-down list**, select **Print Selection** to print the selected cells (See Figure 4.9). Excel 2010 ignores any Print Area that has been set and prints the selected range.

➡ **To print several worksheets with one command, do this:**

1. Select all the sheets (the worksheets must be within the same workbook) you want to print.
2. In the **Print Backstage** window, under **Setting** section, in the **Print what drop-down list**, select **Print Active Sheets.**

4.2.5 Addressing of Cells

A spreadsheet consists of rows and columns which combine to form cells. A cell is a box where you can enter data. Columns form the vertical lines of cells while rows form the horizontal lines of cells. Cell is an intersection of rows and columns. To describe the location or address of a cell, we have to write the names of the column and the row whose intersection has created this cell. Figure 4.10, the intersection of the Column C and the Row 3 is C3. Here C3 is called as a cell and C3 is its address.

Cells can have two types of data in a worksheet.

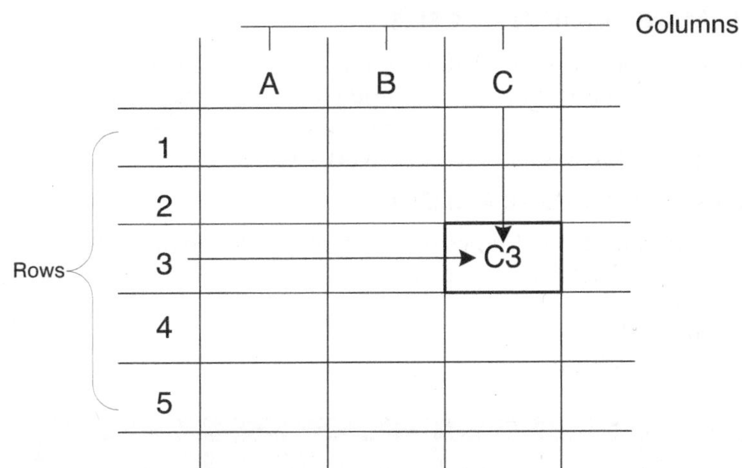

Figure 4.10 Addressing of cells

Constant value: A constant value is data that you type directly into a cell. It can be a number, a date, time, currency, percentage, fraction or text. Constant values do not change unless we edit them.

Formula: A formula is a sequence of values, cell references, names, functions or operators that produce a new value from the existing values. Formulas always start with the equal sign (=). A value that is produced as the result of the formula changes automatically when other values involved in the formula in the worksheet to change.

MS Excel helps you to perform calculations on numerical data. For example, you need to find the sum of some data or calculate through a complex set of formulas and Excel can quickly provide the answer. By using formulas, you can efficiently keep track of your business or personal finances.

To find the sum of numbers from cell address A1 to A10 the formula would be as follows:

= +Al+A2+A3+A4+A5+A6+A7+A8+A9+A10

A function is a shortcut for a formula. For example, to calculate the sum of numbers from cell address Al to A10, the function used would be as follows:

= Sum(A1:A10)

Colon (:) Symbol indicates a group of cell addresses. It is easier to write a function as compared to a formula.

Formulas using Cell Addresses

A formula can also contain cell addresses instead of values or numbers. In that case, the formula is applied on the contents of cell address included in it. Cell addresses could be included in a formula by typing or highlighting them. In a formula, the cell addresses can be used along with numbers, mathematical operators and functions. For example, if the contents of cell address B20 have to be added to that of cell address D13, then type the following formula:

= B20+D13

If a formula contains various operators then Excel performs calculations in a preset order, i.e., multiplication is done before addition. For example, in the formula 2*3+4, it will multiply 2 and 3 first. And then, 4 will be added to their product. So, the result will be 10 and not 14.

4.3 MANIPULATION OF CELLS

The power of Excel lies in storing, manipulating, and displaying data items. Before you can manipulate and display data, you must enter it correctly. This chapter discusses the types of data you can enter in a cell of the Excel worksheet.

Types of Data Entered in a Cell

There are four distinct types of data that can reside in a cell (See Figure 4.11). These types of data are:

a. Text
b. Numerals
c. Logical values
d. Error

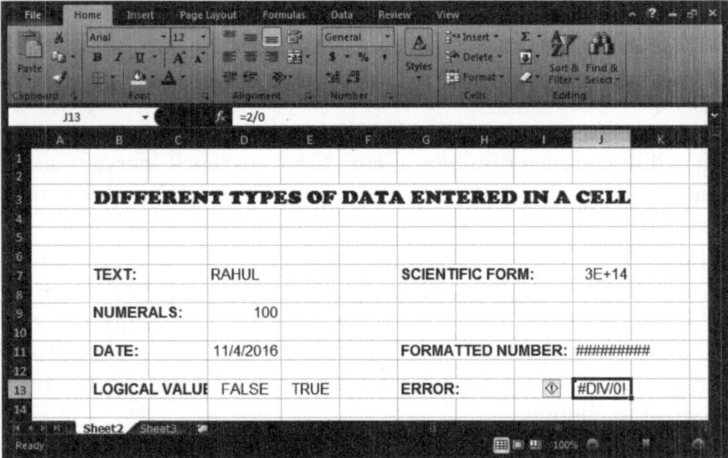

Figure 4.11 Different types of data entered in cells

Text

Text in a cell can include any combination of *letters*, *numbers* and *keyboard symbols*.

- A cell can contain up to 32,000 characters.
- If column width prevents a text string from fitting visually in a cell, the display extends over neighboring cells. However, if the neighboring cells are occupied, the display is truncated.

Numerals

Numerals contain all the decimal digits, such as 0 to 9 on which you can do *addition*, *subtraction*, *multiplication*, and other mathematical or statistical operations. Numeric calculations is the most common thing that is done with Excel 2010. Therefore, it is important to understand how Excel understands numerals.

- A number may be displayed by using *commas*, *scientific notation*, or one of many built-in numeric formats. The number's in Excel have two aspects *displaying format* and the *underlying value*. The *display format* is what you see in the cell and the *underlying value* is the calculated value (which you can see in the formula bar).
- *Date* and *time* are numbers, but with special formatting. If you try to enter 1-9 as a text string. Excel 2012 will interpret this as 9th January as a date and display it as 9-Jan.
- When an unformatted number does not fit in a cell, it is displayed in scientific notation (See Figure 4.11).
- When a formatted number does not fit in a cell, number signs like hash (####) are displayed.

Logical Values

You can enter the logical values namely, TRUE or FALSE into cells. Logical values are often used in writing conditional formulas. Also, there are many formulas that give the calculated result in terms of logical values. Thus, if you say 3 > 4, the result is FALSE because 3 is not greater than 4.

Error

An error value is a distinct type of data. For example, if a formula attempts to divide a number by zero, the result is the # DIV/0! Error value.

4.3.1 Entering Text, Numbers and Dates in a Worksheet

When you see the message *Ready* as shown in Figure 4.11 in the status bar then you can enter data items in a worksheet. Entering data in Excel 2010 worksheet actually consists of three steps:

1. Activate the cell in which you want to enter data.
2. Type the data you want to enter.
3. Finalize the data entry by pressing Enter key, Tab, or any one of the arrow keys.

Example 1

How do you enter data item in a cell?

Solution

1. Click on the desired cell where you want to enter data, just to make it active. The active cell appears with a dark border and its row and column headings appear to be raised to easily identify the cell address.
2. Type your data in the active cell. Two buttons appear in the formula bar: ***Enter*** button and ***Cancel*** button. The status bar shows *Enter* to indicate that you are in the process of entering data (See Figure 4.12).

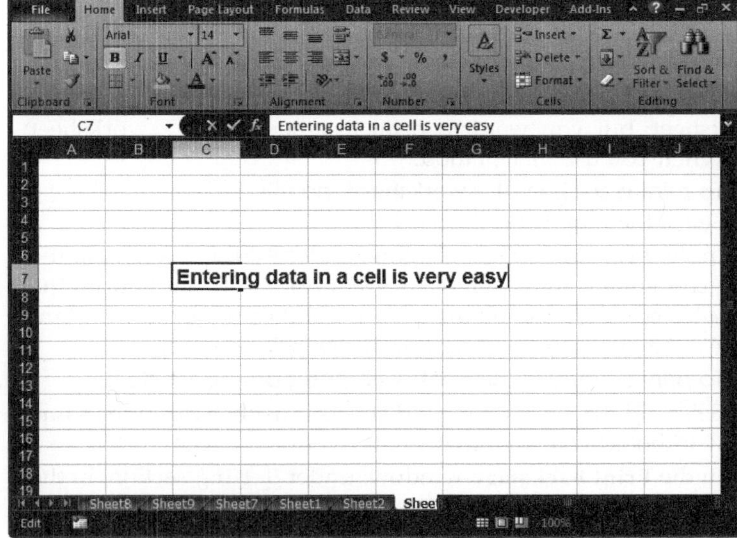

Figure 4.12 Entering data in a cell

3. Click the ***Enter*** button to indicate that you have completed the data typing. You can also press Enter key, Tab key or any one of the arrow keys to complete the data entry.
4. If you make a mistake before finalizing your data entry, press the Backspace key to delete the character to the left of the insertion point. To erase every thing that you have typed, click the cancel button or press Esc key.
5. Repeat the above steps to complete the data entry.

Excel provides you with the following two option to enter and edit data:

- You can enter data in the formula bar.
- You can also enter and edit data directly in the cell.

To enter and edit data directly in the cell you need to turn on the in-cell editing option, if not done already.

☞ *If the Edit directly in-cell feature is turned off, the entry you type appears in the cell but the cursor appears in the formula bar.*

➡ **To turn on in-cell editing option, do this:**

1. Click the **File** Tab and then click **Options. Excel Options** dialog box appears. In this dialog box, click on **Advanced** button on the left side. **Excel Options** dialog box appears with **Advanced** properties as seen in Figure 4.13.
2. Click on the check box i.e. Allow editing directly in cells under the **Editing options** group as seen in Figure 4.13. The option is *on* when a check mark appears.
3. Click OK to accept the settings you change.

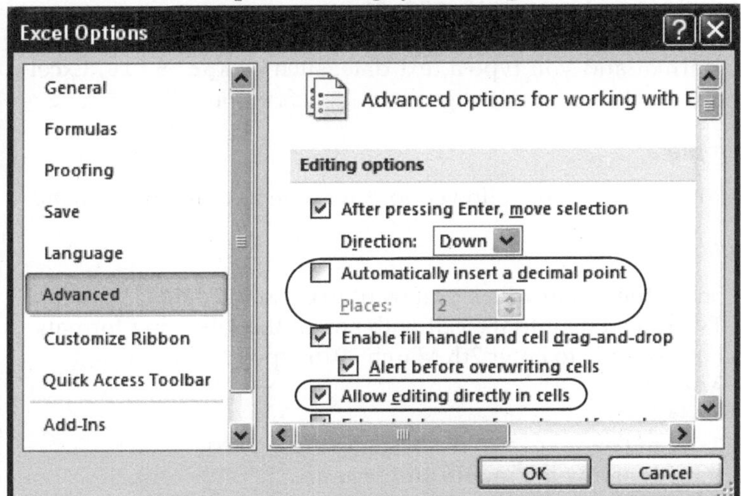

Figure 4.13 Excel Options with Advanced Properties

Entering Text

Text entries can include *alphabetical characters, numbers* and *symbols.*

➡ **To enter text in a cell, do this:**

1. Select the cell, type the text entry, and then enter the text by clicking the **Enter** button in the formula bar or by pressing Enter key.

- To enter numbers as text, type an apostrophe (') followed by the number—for example, '45,000. *Alternatively,* place an equal sign in front of the numbers and enclose the number in quotation marks. For example, to enter the number 45,000 as text, type ="45,000".
- Notice that in a cell with the General format, numbers entered as text will align on the left like text. When you enter a number as text, you can still use the number if it is needed in a numeric formula.

Example 2

How do you quickly format a range of numbers as text in your worksheet by using the Text numeric format?

Solution

1. Select the range of cells containing the numbers.
2. Select the **Text** option from the drop down list of the **Number** group from the **Home** Tab (See Figure 4.14). *Alternatively,* press Ctrl+1 keys or click on the **Home** tab and then in the **Number** group, click the **Dialog Box Launcher.** In this dialog box, click on the Number tab, and select the Text from the Category list: and click OK.

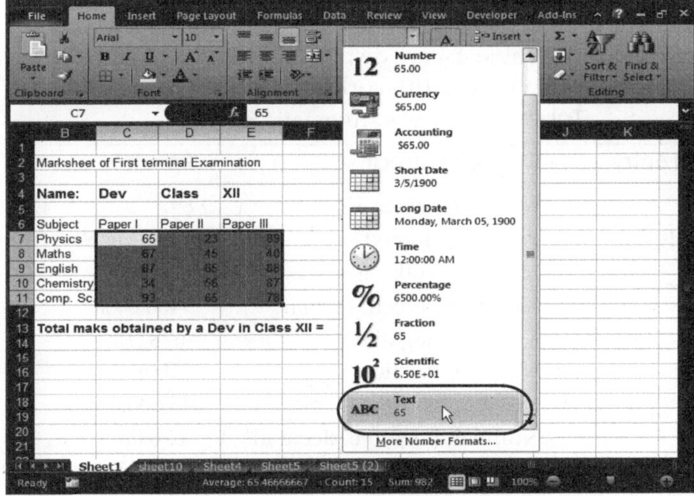

Figure 4.14 Drop-down list

Entering Numbers

Numbers are having constant values and contain the following characters given in Table 4.3.

Table 4.3 Special Characters for Numeric Entries

Character	Function
0 through 9	Any combination of numerals.
+	Indicates exponents when used in conjunction with E, such as 3E+3 means $3x10^3$.
–	Indicates negative number.
()	Indicates negative number.
, (comma)	Thousands marker.
/	Fraction indicator (when fraction is preceded by a space) or date separator.
$	Currency indicator.
%	Percentage indicator.
. (period)	Decimal indicator.
E	Exponent indicator.
e	Exponent indicator.
:	Time separator.
(single space)	Separators of compound fractions (e.g 4 1/2); and date time entries (e.g 1/2/94 5:00).

➡ **To enter a number, do this:**

1. Select the cell, type the number, and then press Enter key or click the Enter button in the Formula bar.
2. You can enter *integers,* such as 145; *decimal fractions,* such as 145.437; *integer fractions,* such as 1 1/2; or *scientific notation,* such as 1.45437E+2.

☞ *Entering a number as text enables the number display to exceed the cell's width. If you enter a number in the normal way and the cell is not wide enough to display it, the cell fills with # signs or in some cases may display the number in scientific notation.*

Excel 2010 stores the numbers typed into a cell as well as the format or appearance in which the numbers should be shown. When you enter a number into a cell, Excel tries to establish how the number should be formatted. For example, it accepts and displays the entries listed in Table 4.3 with the formats indicated. The entries of the Table 4.4 are displayed in Figure 4.15, as entry would appear in an Excel 2010 worksheet.

Table 4.4 Excel's Automatic Formats

Typed Entry	Chosen Format	Result
897	Number, General	897
7999 Mg Rd.	Text, left aligned	7999 Mg Rd
450.09	Number, dollar format	$450.09
54.6%	Number, percent format	5460.00%
(678)	Number, negative	-678
2 3/4	Number, fraction	2 3/4
45600	Number, comma format	45,600.00
-678	Number, negative, decimal	-678.00
1/5/16	Date, m/d/yyyy	01/05/2016
4/5	Date, m/d/yy (current year assumed)	05-Apr

Entries	Format of the entry	Result of entry
897	Number, General	897
7999 Mg Rd.	Text, left aligned	7999 Mg Rd.
450.09	Number. Currency format	$450.09
54.6	Number, percentage format	5460.00%
2 3/4	Number, fraction	2 3/4
45600	Number, comma format	45,600.00
-678	Number, negative, decimal	-678.00
(678)	Number, negative	-678
1/5/16	Date, m/d/yyyy	1/5/2016
4/5	Date, m/d/yy	5-Apr

Figure 4.15 Automatic formats done for data given in Table 4.4

☞ *Entering a number as text enables the number display to exceed the cell's width. If you enter a number in normal way and cell is not wide enough to display it, the cell gets fills with # signs or in some cases may display the number in scientific notation.*

➡ **To control fixed decimal option, do this:**

1. Click the **File** Tab and then click **Options**. Excel Options dialog box appears. In this dialog box, click on **Advanced** button on the left side. **Excel Options** dialog box appears with **Advanced** properties as seen in Figure 4.13.
2. Click the Automatically insert decimal point: check box under the **Editing options** group so that the check mark does not appear (See Figure 4.13).
3. Click OK.

☞ *Using fixed decimal representation feature of Excel 2010, you can automatically add decimals to every value entered in a worksheet.*

Entering Date and Time in a Worksheet

Excel 2010 automatically understands date and time typed in most of the common ways. When you type a *date* or *time*, Excel converts your entry to a serial number. The serial number represents the number of days from the beginning of the century until the date you type. Time is recorded as a decimal fraction of a 24-hour day.

If your entry is recognized as a valid date or time format, you see the date or time on-screen. Correctly entered dates appear in the formula bar with the format `mm/dd/yyyy`, regardless of how the cell is formatted. Here, **mm** for month, **dd** for day and **yyyy** is for year.

For example, if you type **2 March 16** in a cell formatted to show numbers with a comma and two decimal places (#,##0.00), you will see that date as **40,970.00**.

If Excel 2010 does not recognize the entry as a valid date or time format and you type a text date, such as **Apr 5 16**, Excel treats the entry as text. It aligns it to the left in the cell.

Example 3

Explain the step to be followed to enter date in different formats.

Solution

1. Select the cell in which you want to enter the date.
2. Type the date into the cell with any of the following formats. For example to enter 7th March 2016 type:
   3/7/16
   7-Mar-16
   7-Mar (The year from the system date is used)
   Mar-16 (Only the month and year are shown)
   3/7/16 0:00

You can also enter the dates as **3/7, 03/07/16, Mar-16,** or **March 7, 2016** (See Figure 4.16). In any of these date formats, you can use either /, -, or space to separate different elements.

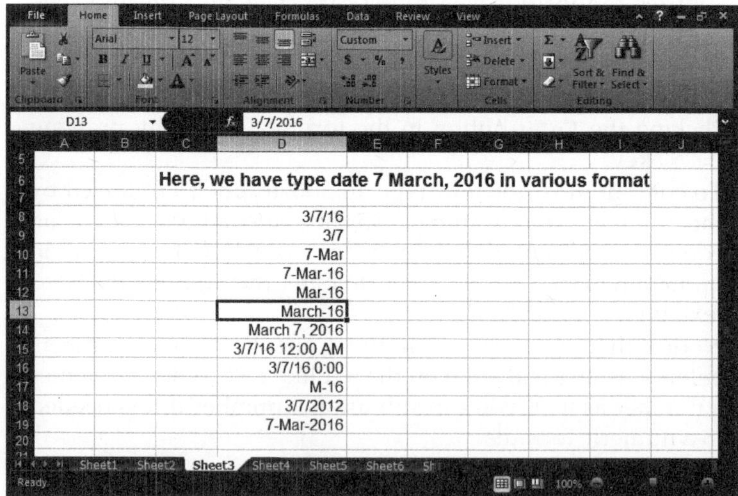

Figure 4.16 Various ways to enter date in a worksheet

Example 4

How do you enter time in an Excel 2010 worksheet?

Solution

1. Select the cell in which you want to enter the time.
2. Type the time in any of the following formats. For example to enter `1:32 PM`, type:

```
13:32
13:32:45
1:32 PM
1:32:45 PM
3/7/16 13:32
```

The first two examples are from a 24-hour clock. If you use a 12-hour clock, follow the time with a space and A, AM, P, or PM (in either upper or lowercase letters).

☞ *Leave a space before the AM or PM. Do not mix a 24-hour clock time with an AM or PM. As the last format shows, you can combine the date or time during entry.*

➡ **To enter the current date/time in a cell, do this:**

1. To enter the current date select the cell and press Ctrl+; keys together.
2. To enter the current time select the cell and press Ctrl+: keys together.

☞ *To format a date in the default date format, press* Ctrl+# *keys together. To format a time in the default time format, press* Ctrl+@ *keys together.*

4.3.2 Creating Text, Number and Data Series

Creating Text

To create text in a cell, position the cell-pointer at the desired cell address and then type the entry from the keyboard. For example, to enter text `Entering text` in cell address A1, do the following steps:

1. Move the mouse-pointer to cell address **A1** and click the left mouse-button just once. Instantly, the cell pointer changes like rectangle shape at cell address **A1** (See Figure 4.17).
2. Now type Entering text in a cell.
3. Then press the Enter key from the keyboard. Your workbook will look like as shown in Figure 4.17.
4. Text entries are normally used as row and column headings, for entering phone numbers, addresses, etc. All texts are left aligned. And a formula cannot be applied over text entries.

Each cell has a default width of 9-10 characters, i.e., each cell can hold up to 9-10 characters. In case, the entry of cell address is more than its default width, its display gets extended to the next cell. This does not mean that it has occupied the space of the next cell. It has just got displayed over it.

For example, entering text in a cell at cell address A1. You will observe that the type text gets extended to the next cell B1 (See Figure 4.17).

Although the label occupying two cell addresses (Al and B1) it is normally in cell address A1. To find out cell, in which the text is actually displayed, do this:

- Click the left mouse button over the cell address B1. You will see that the Formula bar does not display the text entry.
- Now, click the left mouse-button over the cell address A1. You will see that the Formula bar displays the text Entering text in a cell.

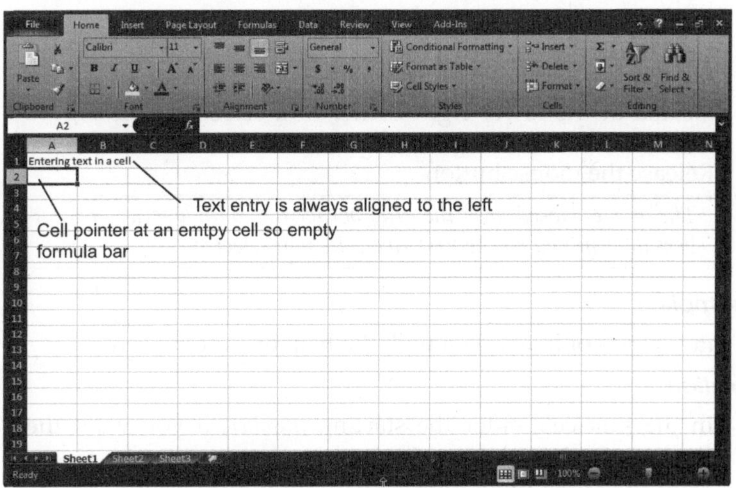

Figure 4.17 Creating text in a cell

Using Number and Date Series

Excel 2010 makes it very easy to enter a series of dates, number or text. For example, you can insert column heading like *Jan*, *Feb*, *Mar*, etc., or enter number at equal intervals, such as 2, 4, 6, 8, etc., very easily.
You can enter the above type of series in two ways:

1. Using the mouse to drag the fill handle.
2. Using a command that gives you the capability to create many types of series.

☞ *Dragging the fill handle to the right and down fills the series in increasing order; dragging the fill handle up or left fills the series in decreasing order.*

Creating a Linear Series

➡ **To create a linear series, do this:**

1. Enter the first two elements of data in the series in adjacent cells, namely 1 and 3 in cells D6 and E6 (See Figure 4.18). Excel uses these two data items to determine the amount of increment in each step and the starting number for the series.

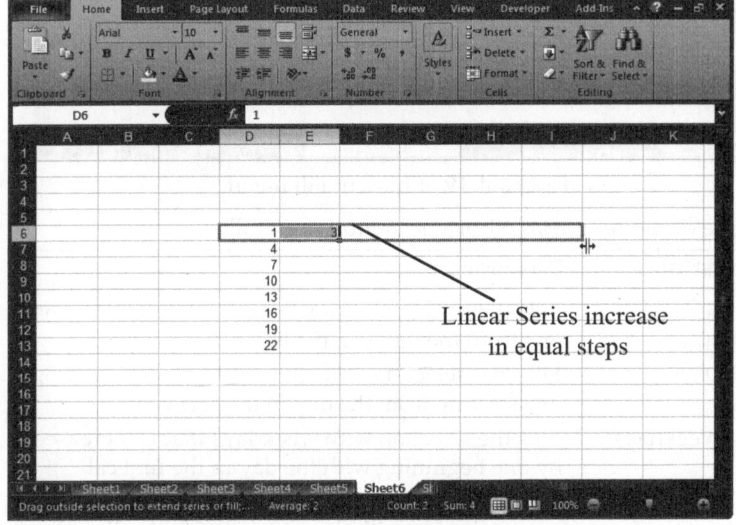

Figure 4.18 Creating a Linear series

2. Select these two cells and then drag the fill handle *down* or *right* to fill in increasing and drag the fill handle *up* or *left* to fill in decreasing order. The fill handle is the small square located at the lower right corner of a selection (See Figure 4.18).
3. Release the mouse button.

☞ *The area enclosed with the gray border fills with a series of numbers determined by the first two cells you selected.*

Example 5

Create a series of linear data with the help of AutoFill command.

Solution

1. In the first cell, enter the starting *number*, if you want the range to be filled with values that increment by one. If you want the range filled with values that increment differently, fill the first cell in the range with the initial value and the second cell in the range with the second value that increases or decreases as you want the series to increase or decrease.
2. Select the range of cells containing numbers used as starting values for the series. At the lower-right corner of the selection is the square fill handle.
3. Select the range to be filled by dragging the fill handle with the *right mouse button*. Release the right mouse button to display the shortcut fill menu as shown in Figure 4.19.

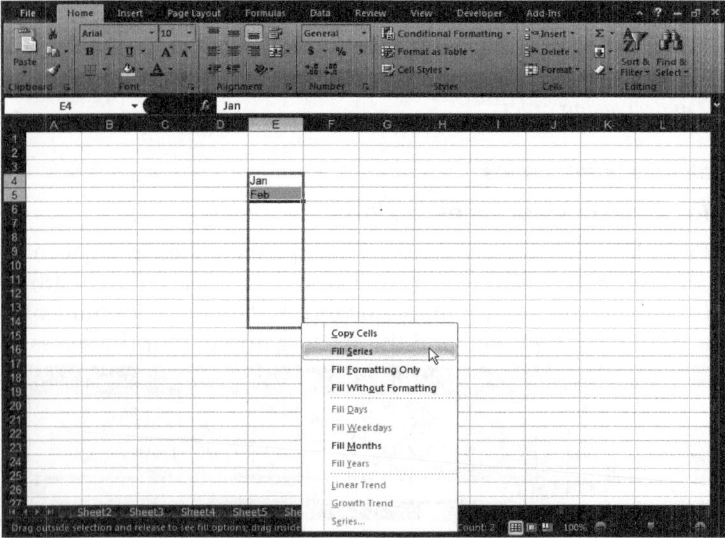

Figure 4.19 Shortcut Fill menu

Some of the options of shortcut menu are as follows:

Command	Description
Fill Series	Fills the selection with values that is increased by one from the value in the first cell.
Fill Days	Fills the selection with days that is increased by one starting from the day in the first cell.
Fill Weekdays	Fills the selection with weekdays that is increased by one beginning with the day in the first cell.
Fill Months	Fills the selection with months that is increased by one beginning with the year in the first cell.
Linear Trend	Fills the blank cells in the selection with linear regression (best fit) values. Starting values are not overwritten. This command is only available when more than one cell is filled with a starting value.
Growth Trend	Fills the blank cells in the selection with values calculated from growth (exponential) regression. Starting values are not over written. This command is only available when more than one cell is filled with a starting value.
Series	Displays the Series dialog box.

(Contd...)

4. Select the option as shown in the Table given above that you want.

Example 6

Create a number series with the help of Fill Series dialog box.

Solution

1. In the first cell, enter the *first number* or *date*.
2. Select the range of cells you want to be filled.
3. Click on **Home** Tab and then in **Editing** group, click on the **Fill** drop down list and then choose Series... to display the Series dialog box (See Figure 4.20).

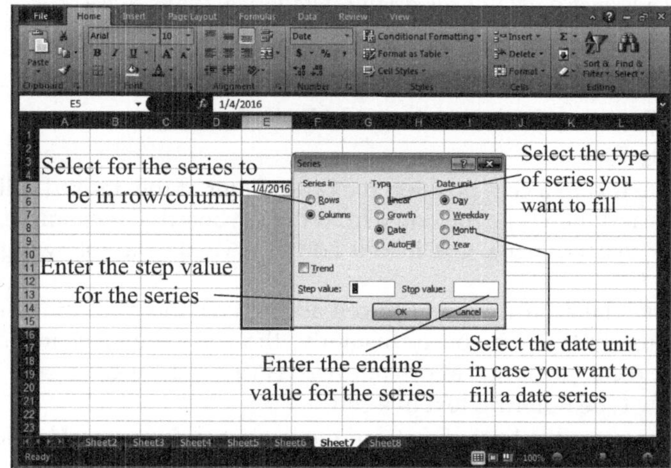

Figure 4.20 Series dialog box

4. Click the Rows or Columns option that matches the type of range you want to fill. This is automatically selected to match the orientation of the cells you choose.
5. Select the Trend check box if you want selected values to be replaced by values for a linear or exponential best-fit. This selection limits Step 6 to Linear or Growth options.
6. Select one of the following Type options:

Option	Description
Linear	Adds the Step Value to the preceding number in the series.
Growth	Multiplies the Step Value by the preceding number in the series.
Date	Enables the Date Unit group so that the increment applies to a Day, Weekday, Month, or Year.
AutoFill	Creates automatic series that may include text dates and labels.

7. Depending on the kind of series you want to create, use one of the following sets of steps.

➡ **To create a Linear or Growth, do this:**

1. In the Step value: box enter the step value. This number is the constant amount by which the series changes from cell to cell. The Step Value may be positive or negative.
2. In the Stop value: box enter a value at which you want to stop the fill. This is required only if you think that you highlighted too many cells when you selected the range to fill.
3. Click OK.

➡ **To create Date Series, do this:**

1. Click the Date unit area of the Series dialog box (See Figure 4.20).
   Select either Day, Weekday, Month or Year to designate the date increment. Note that *Weekday* gives you dates without *Saturdays and Sundays.*
2. To specify the increment amount, enter the Step value in the Step value box. If the starting value is `12/1/2016`, and you choose Month as the Date Unit and 2 as the Step Value, the second date in the series becomes `2/1/2016`.

☞ *When the series reaches either the end of the selected range or the Stop Value, Excel stops filling the cell. If you use a negative Step Value, the Stop value must be less than the starting value.*

3. To stop the series enter the Stop value in the Stop value: box (e.g. `12/1/2016`). The stop value indicates the last date in the series.
4. Click OK.

Creating Series of Text and Headings

Excel can extend series of headings which are not dates or numbers. For example, there may be a text headings that includes a number, such as *Trend, Quarter, Task,* etc. (See Figure 4.21).

The text series that Excel recognizes includes the text shown in Table 4.5.

Table 4.5 Text Series Recognized by Excel

Type	Example
Day	Tuesday, Wednesday, or Tue, Wed
Month	September, October, or Sep, Oct
Text	Project, Task
Text number	Task 1, Task 2, Paragraph 1.2, Paragraph 1.3
Quarterly	Quarter 1, Quarter 2, Qtr 2, Qtr 3, Q1, Q2

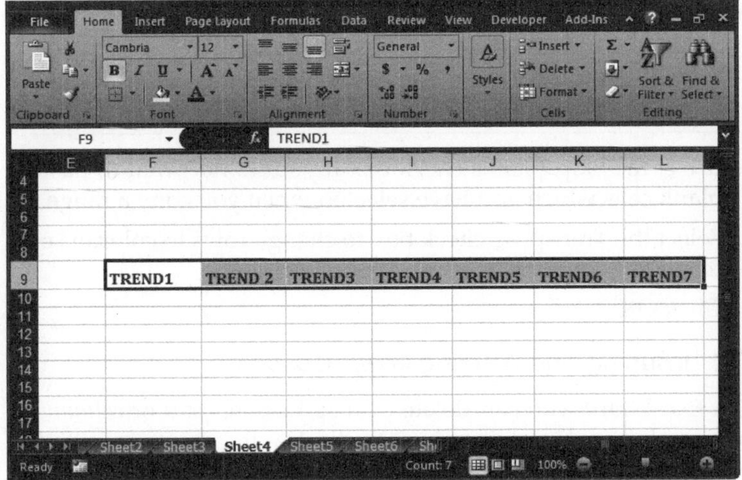

Figure 4.21 Headings that are not Dates or Numbers in a Series

The AutoFill feature in Excel recognizes key words, such as days of the *week, month* names, and *Quarterly* abbreviations. Excel extends a series to repeat correctly, namely, Qtr1 follows Qtr4 and then the series continues.

➡ **To type in a custom list for use with AutoFill, do this:**

1. Click the **File** Tab and then click **Options**. Excel Options dialog box appears. In this dialog box, Click on **Advanced** button on the left side. Excel Options dialog box appears with Advanced properties. In this dialog box, under the **General** group, click on the Edit Custom Lists... Custom Lists dialog box appears as seen in Figure 4.22.

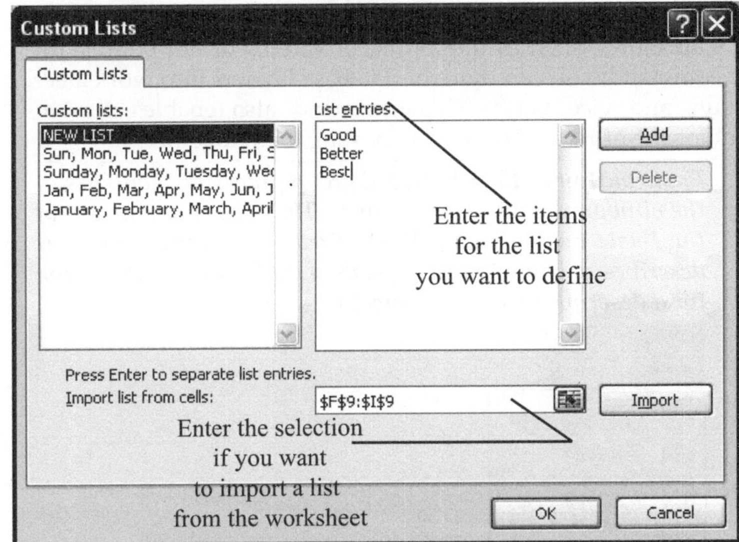

Figure 4.22 Custom Lists Dialog box

2. Select NEW LIST in the Custom lists: box.
3. Select the List entries: list box, and type each item you want in the list. Press (Enter) to separate items.
4. To add the list to the Custom lists: list box, click Add. Your list appears in the Custom lists: list box.
6. Click OK if you have no more lists to enter. If you have additional lists to enter, select NEW LIST from the Custom Lists list box, and then begin typing your list in the List entries: list box.

➡ **To add a list that is in a range of cells on the worksheet, do this:**

1. Select the cells that contain the list you want to create. Now follow the Step 1 as given above.
2. The selection range appears in the Import list from cells: box you can reselect the list by clicking the arrow on the right.
3. After the selection is final, click Import, and then click OK.

The list you create is stored in Excel file. The list can then be used in any other worksheet also.

4.3.3 Editing Worksheet Data

While editing a cell entry, you can edit the text either in the formula bar or in the cell itself.

Editing Cell Entry in the Formula Bar

➡ **To edit cell entry in the formula bar, do this:**

1. Select the cell containing the data you want to edit.
2. Move the insertion point into the text in the formula bar. Position the pointer in the text you want to edit, and then click. A flashing insertion point indicates where typing and editing take place.

3. Edit the cell entry or type new text.

Editing Directly in a Cell

➡ **To edit an entry directly in a cell, do this:**

1. Double-click the selected cell or press F2 key.
2. Press the arrow keys to move the I-beam that marks the insertion point to place where you want to edit.
3. Make the desired changes to the cell entry.
4. Press Enter key to change the text. Alternatively, press Esc key to leave the contents unchanged.

Using Paste Special Feature

Paste Special feature is very useful to copy and paste part of a cell's attributes, such as the format or value, but not both. With this command, you can reorient database layouts into worksheet layouts and vice versa. This command also enables you to combine the attributes of cells by pasting them together.

☞ ***Paste button of the Clipboard group places the contents of the clipboard where the cursor is. The drop-down arrow of the Paste button called Paste Preview (shown below). It describes various ways to paste data. Point to an option for a description, click to select it.***

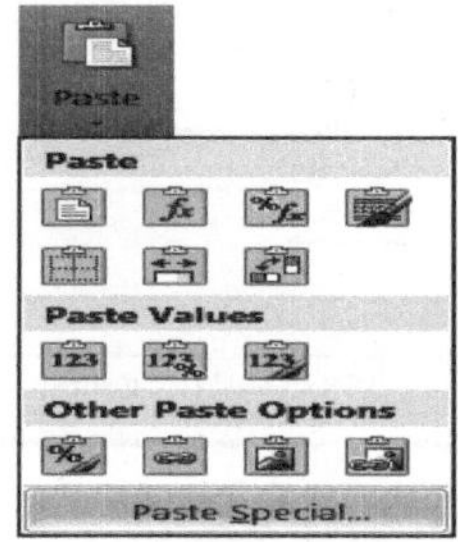

➡ **To use Paste Special Feature, do this:**

1. Select the cell or range of cells.
2. Click on the **Home** Tab and then click **Copy** button under the **Clipboard** group, or press Ctrl+C keys together.
3. Select the upper-left corner of the worksheet where you want to paste. When transporting (flipping) rows and columns, be sure to consider which cells are covered when the pasted area is rotated 90 degrees.
4. Click the arrow next to **Paste** button under the **Clipboard** group and then select Paste Special... to display Paste Special dialog box (See Figure 4.23).
5. Select the characteristics you want to be transferred as explained in the following Table 4.6.

Table 4.6 Characteristics of Paste special options

Option	Function
All	Paste all the original contents and characteristics.
Formulas	Paste only the formulas.
Values	Paste only the values and formula results.
Formats	Paste only the cell formats.
Comments	Paste only note contents.
Validation	Paste data validation rules.
All using Source theme	Paste all cell contents and formatting using the theme.
All except border	Paste everything except any borders applied to the selected range.
Column widths	Paste the width of one column to another.
Formulas and number formats	Paste formulas but not values with their number format.
Values and number formats	Paste only values with their number format.

(Contd...)

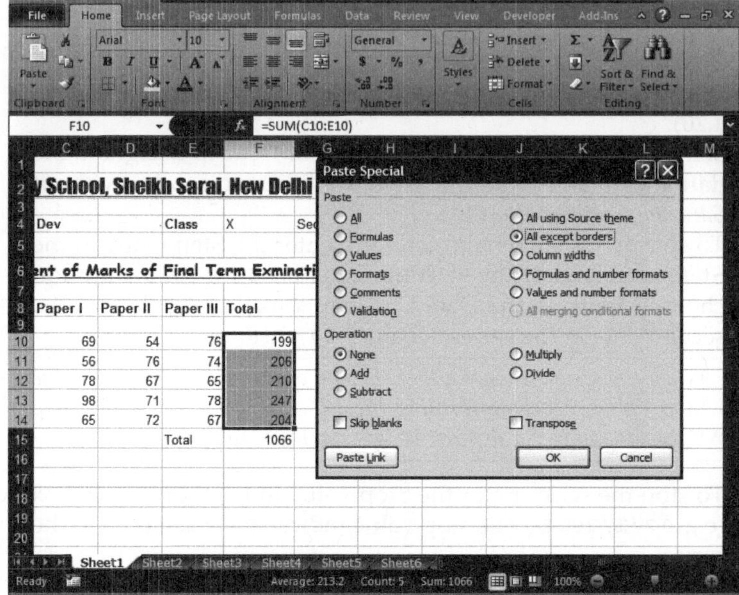

Figure 4.23 Paste Special dialog box

6. Select from the dialog box how you want to transferred characteristics or information combined with the cells being pastes into.

   Table 4.7 below gives the different options and their functions.

Table 4.7 Different options and their functions

Option	Function
None	Replaces the receiving cell.
Add	Adds to the receiving cell into which they are being pasted.
Subtract	Subtracts from the receiving cell into which they are being pasted.
Multiply	Multiplies by the receiving cell into which they are being pasted.
Divide	Divides into the receiving cell into which they are being pasted.

7. Select the Skip Blanks check box if you do not want to paste blank cells which you have selected when you copy a range.
8. Select the Transpose check box to change rows to columns or to change columns to rows.
9. Click OK.

4.3.4 Inserting and Deleting Rows, Columns

With Excel 2010, you can delete or insert entire *rows* or *columns*. You can also easily delete or insert cells, leaving the surrounding rows and columns unaffected. This technique enables you to add or remove cells without having to change entire rows or columns.

Inserting Cells, Rows, or Columns

Sometimes you may need to insert cells, rows, or columns to make room for new formulas or data. You can insert cells, rows, or columns as easily as you can delete them.

➡ **To insert cells, do this:**

1. Select a cell or range of cells where new cells are to be inserted. Or, select cells in the rows or columns where you want to insert new rows or columns.
2. Select Insert Cells... option from **Insert** drop down list of the **Cells** group of the **Home** Tab. *Alternatively*, press Ctrl + + (plus) keys or click the right mouse button and select Insert... . The Insert dialog box appears as in Figure 4.24.
3. To insert cells, select the direction you want selected cells to be inserted.

The various options to insert cells are summarized in Table below.

Option	Function
Shift cells right	Selected cells move right.
Shift cells down	Selected cells move down.
Entire row	Insert a row at each selected cell.
Entire column	Insert a column at each selected cell.

4. Click OK.

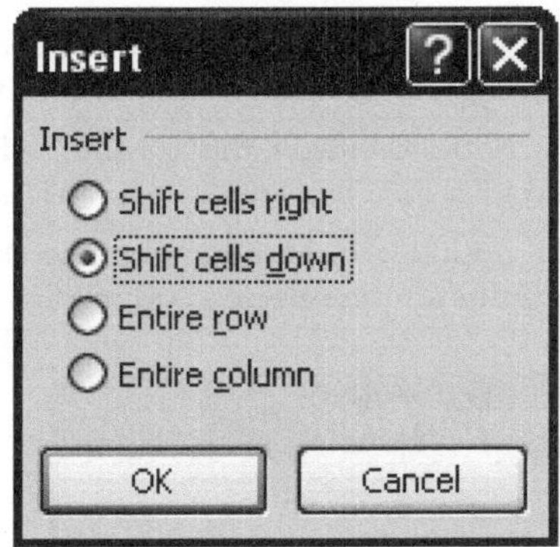

Figure 4.24 Insert dialog box

➡ **To insert *rows* or *columns*, do this:**

1. Select cells in the *rows* or *columns* where you want to insert **new** rows or columns.
2. Select Insert Sheet Rows from **Insert** drop-down list of the **Cells** group of the **Home** Tab to insert rows.
3. Select Insert Sheet Columns from **Insert** drop-down list of the **Cells** group of the **Home** Tab to insert columns.

Deleting Cells, Rows or Columns

The Delete command completely removes *cells*, *rows*, or *columns* from the worksheet. This is different from the **Clear** command in the **Editing** Group. The **Clear** command removes a cell's *contents*, *format*, or **comments**, but it leaves the cell intact.

➡ **To delete *cells*, *rows* or *columns*, do this:**

1. Select the cells or range of cells to be deleted, or select cells in the rows and columns to be deleted.
2. Click on the **Home** Tab and then click arrow next to **Delete** button under the **Cells** group and then select Delete Cells... as shown in Figure 4.25, or press Ctrl+- (minus) keys together, or click the right mouse button and select Delete... . The **Delete** dialog box appears (See Figure 4.26).

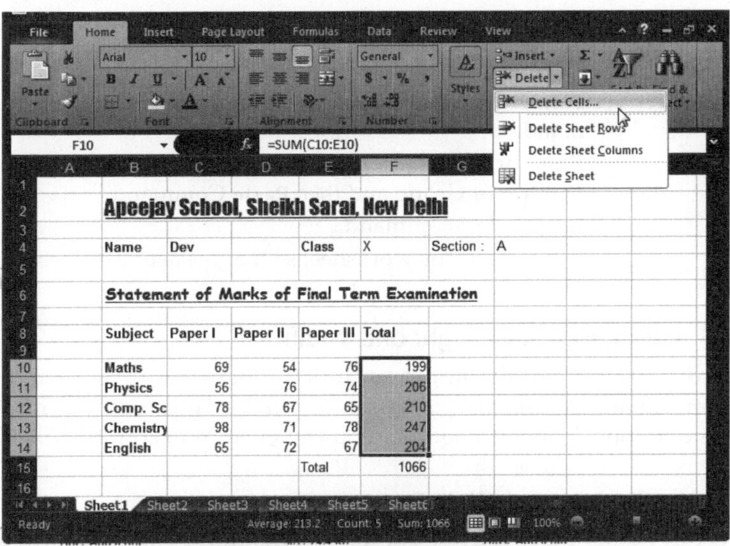

Figure 4.25 Selected group of cells

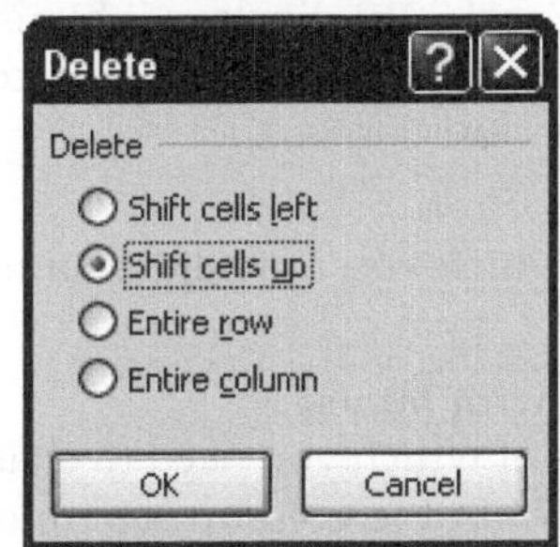

Figure 4.26 Delete dialog box

3. To delete cells, select the direction in which you want the remaining cells to move.
4. Click OK.

Option	Description
Shift cells left	Cells to right of the deleted cells move left.
Shift cells up	Cells below the deleted cells move up.
Entire row	Deletes entire row containing a selected cell.
Entire column	Deletes entire column containing a selected cell.

Clearing, Inserting or Deleting Cells in a Worksheet

After you have drafted and tested the worksheet, you may find that you need to reorganize or restructure the layout of the worksheet. When you restructure, you may need to insert or delete cells, rows or columns.

Shortcuts keys that are very helpful in reorganizing the worksheet layout are given in Table 4.8.

Table 4.8 Shortcut Keys for Changing the Worksheet Layout

key(s)	Action
Del	Clears selected formulas or contents; same as the **Home**, Tab, **Editing** Group and then Clear Contents.
Backspace	Clears the formulas bar; activates and clears the formula bar's contents.
Ctrl+C	Copies the selection so that it can be pasted; same as the **Home** Tab, **Clipboard** Group and then **Copy** Command.

(Contd...)

key(s)	Action
Ctrl+X	Cuts the selection so it can be pasted; same as the **Home** Tab, **Clipboard** Group and then **Cut** Command.
Ctrl+V	Paste at the selected cell; same as the **Home** Tab, **Clipboard** Group and then **Paste** Command.
Ctrl+Z	Undoes last command.
Ctrl+ Backspace	Repositions the worksheet so that the active cell is in view.

4.3.5 Changing Cell Height and Width

In order to improve the appearance of a worksheet or table in it, you can adjust *columns width* and *row height*. Thus, you can fit more data on a page. If need be, you can even hide confidential data.

How to adjust Column Width?

You can adjust the width of one or more columns to get better look in a worksheet. If a column is not wide enough to display a *number*, *date*, or *time*, Excel 2010 displays it by using # characters in the cell. Therefore, you may need to adjust columns width to show complete information.

Example 7

Describe the ways by which you can adjust columns width.

Solution

Adjust column width with mouse

1. Select the columns of which you need to change the width.
2. Move the pointer onto the column separator to the right of the column heading (See Figure 4.27). Pointer changes to a two-headed, horizontal arrow.
3. Drag the column left or right until the column is of the required width. Then release the mouse button. The Width box that appears as you drag the column, displaying the numeric value for the column width.

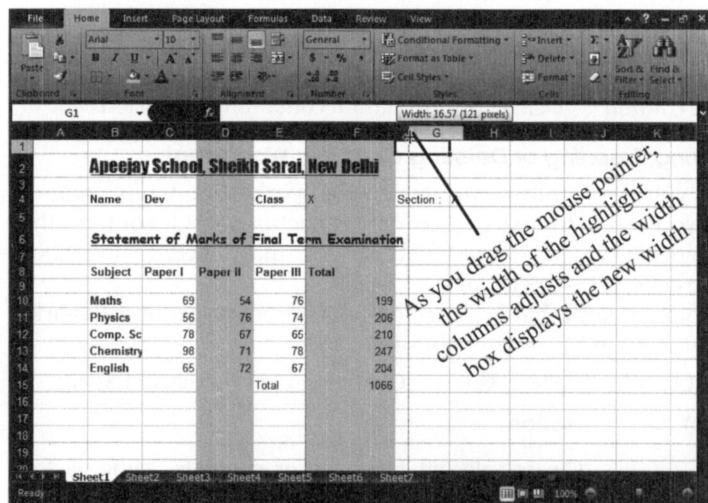

Figure 4.27 Changing Column Width with Mouse

Adjust column width using Ribbon

1. Select the columns of you want to change the width.
2. Under **Home** Tab, click **Cells** group and then click arrow next to **Format**. It pops up the menu (See Figure 4.28).
3. Use one of the following options to adjust column width (See Figure 4.28).

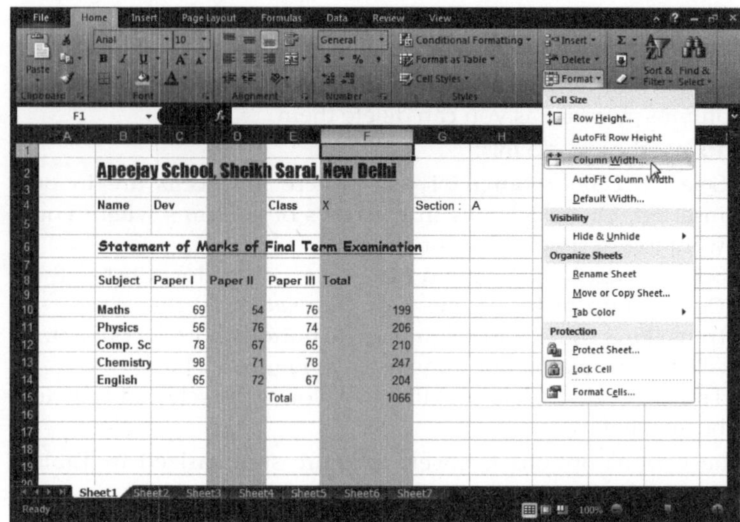

Figure 4.28 Format Column option

➡ **To copy a column width, do this:**

1. Select cells in the columns that you want to copy the column width.

Option	Description
Column Width...	The Column Width dialog box appears (See Figure 4.29). Type the width, and then click OK.
AutoFit Selection	This option adjusts the column width automatically.
Default Width...	This option would adjust to the default column width for all the selected columns.

Figure 4.29 Column Width dialog box

2. Click **Copy** button on **Clipboard** group of the **Home** Tab.
3. Select the cells where you want to apply this width.
4. Under the **Home** Tab, click the arrow next to the **Paste** button in the **Clipboard** group and then click **Keep Source Column Widths** button as shown in Figure 4.30 or choose Paste Special... . **Paste Special** dialog box appears .
5. In this dialog box, choose Column widths from Paste group.
6. Click OK.

How to adjust Row Height?

You can adjust row height in a worksheet to create enough space for *titles*, *subtotals*, *grand totals*, etc.

Example 8

How would you adjust row height?

(a) Using mouse
(b) Ribbon

Keep Source Column Widths button

Figure 4.30 Copy column width using Paste options

Solution (a)

1. Select the rows of which you want to adjust the height.
2. Move the mouse pointer to the line directly under the header of the row you want to change. The mouse pointer changes to a two headed vertical arrow (See Figure 4.31).
3. Drag the two-headed arrow pointer up or down until the row is of the required height. Then release the mouse button. The screen tip displays the numeric value for the row height.

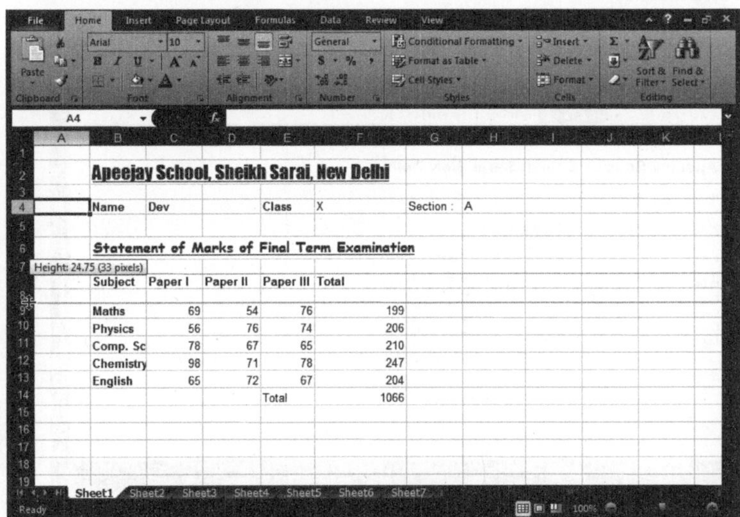

Figure 4.31 Changing row height with a mouse

Solution (b)

1. Select a cell in each row you want to change.
2. Under **Home** Tab, click **Cells** group and then click arrow next to **Format**. It pops up menu (See Figure 4.28).
3. Click one of the following options.

Option	Description
Row Height...	To display the Row Height dialog box. Here, type the row height and click OK (See Figure 4.32).
AutoFit Row Height	Excel 2010 adjusts rows height automatically.

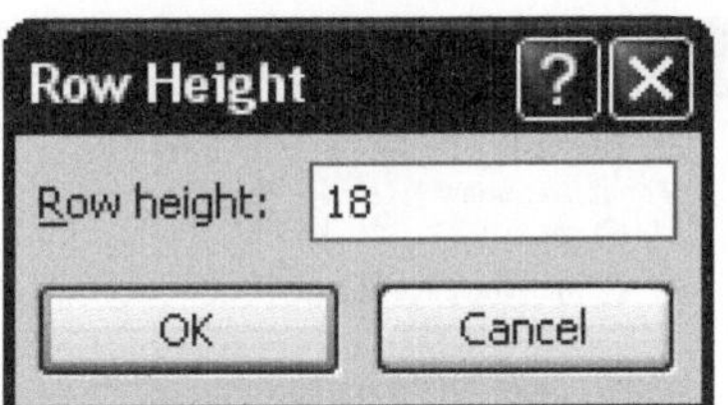

Figure 4.32 Row Height dialog box

4.4 FORMULAS AND FUNCTION

A formula in Excel is a mathematical equation that performs calculations based on constants, cell references or both. A formula always begins with = (equal) sign. For example, the formula =A1+A2 add the numbers contained in the cells A1 and A2 of the worksheet. Formulas include the use of operators which tell Excel what to do with the constants and cell references. For example, * (asterisk) represents the multiplication operator.

A function is built-in formula, which can save time when working with lot of numbers. While entering functions, the name of the function appears immediately after the = sign. The arguments to the function are contained in parentheses. Arguments are the constants or cell references that function uses to perform calculations. For example, instead of using the formula = A1+A2+A3+A4 to add up the numbers in the cell range, you can use the function =SUM(A1:A4).

4.4.1 Using Formulas

A formula is entered into a cell. It performs a calculation of some type and returns a result, which is displayed in the cell. Formulas in Excel always begin with an equal sign (=) and can include the following types of data items:

a. *Numeric* and text values (constants)
b. Arithmetic operator, comparison operators, text operators, functions, parentheses
c. Cell references, and names

☞ *By combining these components, you can calculate the result you want by using the information in the worksheet.*

Excel also gives you the option to display formulas on a worksheet, or the results of the formulas.

➡ **To control the display of formula result, do this:**

1. Click the **File** Tab and then click **Options**. Excel Options dialog box appears. In this dialog box, click on **Advanced** button on the left side. Excel Options dialog box appears with **Advanced** properties as seen in Figure 4.33.
2. Click on the Show formulas in cells instead of their calculated results check box so that it appears under the **Display options for this worksheet** group.
3. Click OK.

☞ *To switch between viewing formulas and the results of formulas, click Show Formulas button from the Formula Auditing group of Formulas Tab or alternatively, click* Ctrl + ` *keys pressed together* (See Figure 4.34).

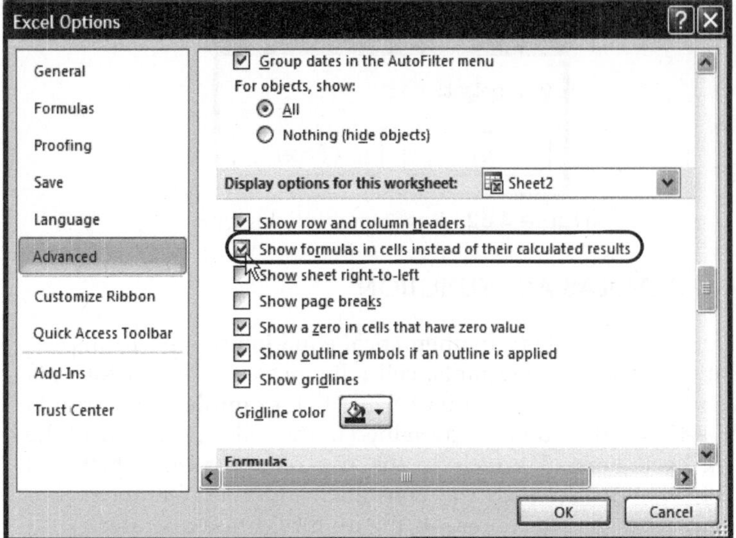

Figure 4.33 Excel Options with Advanced Properties

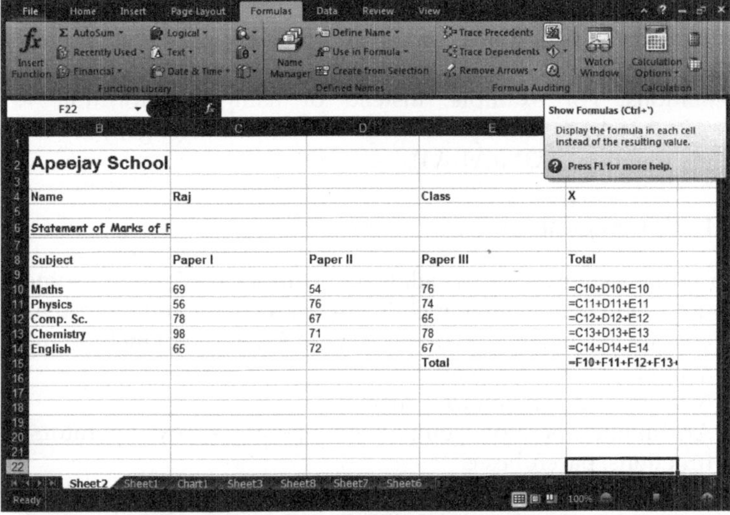

Figure 4.34 Formula displayed in cells

When you display formulas, Excel automatically doubles the width of all columns (See Figure 4.34). The column widths will return to their original settings when you return to displaying the formula results. Formulas automatically recalculate and produce current results after you update data used by the formulas.

☞ *Make sure that you start the formula with an equal sign (=). If you forget to put an equal sign, Excel 2010 does not interpret the entry as a formula. For example, if you enter B12*D15 (with no equal sign), the B12*D15 is actually entered into the cell as text.*

How to Enter Formulas?

To enter a formula, start a formula with an equal sign (=) and then construct the formula using *values*, *operators*, *cell references*, *functions*, and *names* to calculate the required result.

You can enter formulas either in the formula bar or in the cell. You can enter a formula using the formula bar by simply typing in it and pressing Enter. You can also enter a formula directly in the cell and bypass the formula bar.

☞ *Make sure you remember to start the formula with an equal sign (=). If you forget the equal sign, Excel 2010 does not interpret the entry as a formula. If you enter B12*D15 (no equal sign), then B12*D15 is actually entered into the cell as text.*

➡ **To enter a formula in the formula bar, do this:**

1. Select the cell in which you want to enter the formula.
2. Then click on the Formula bar and type an equal sign (=).
3. Type a *value*, *cell reference*, *function*, or *name*.
4. If the formula is complete, press Enter or click the Enter box (a check mark) in the formula bar. If the formula is incomplete, go to Step 5.
5. Type an operator. There are many types of operators. The most common operators are math symbols, such as + (plus) and – (minus).
6. Return to Step 3.

➡ **To enter a formula in a cell, do this:**

1. Double-click the cell or select the cell and press F2 key in which you want to enter the formula and type an equal sign (=) (See Figure 4.35).
2. Type a value, cell reference, function, or name.
3. If the formula is complete, press Enter key. If the formula is incomplete, go to Step 4.
4. Type an operator.
5. Return to Step 2.

Always separate terms in a formula with an operators or parentheses.

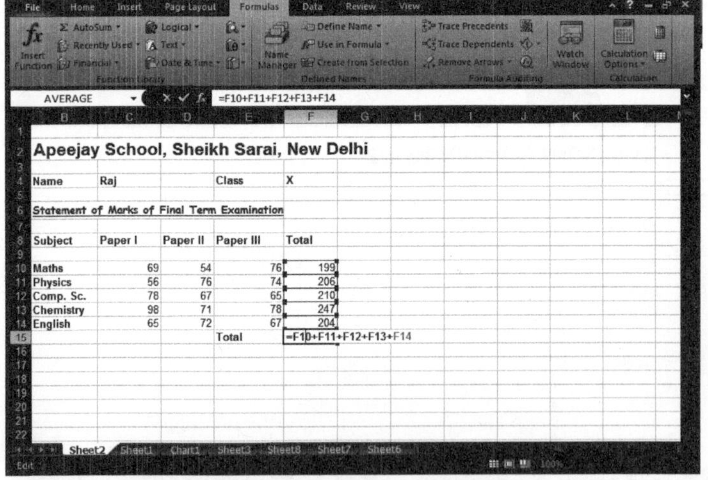

Figure 4.35 Entering a formula in Excel

Use the SUM function to Sum Several Ranges

To sum several ranges, simply refer to each of them, separated by a comma, using the SUM function.

➡ **To sum several ranges, do this:**

1. In cells A20:A26 enter prices from Re. 1 to Rs. 100.
2. Select cells B20:B26 and type the formula = A20*8% to calculate the tax amount.
3. Press Ctrl+Enter keys together.
4. In Cells C20:C26 type some discount values from -1 to -3.
5. In Cell C28, sum all three columns with the following functions (See Figure 4.36).
   =SUM(A20:A26, B20:B26,C20:C26) (Figure 4.36).
6. Press Enter key.

Moving or Copying Formula

When you move a formula from one cell to other, the cell references within the formula do not change. But when you copy a formula, then

- Absolute cell references do not change.

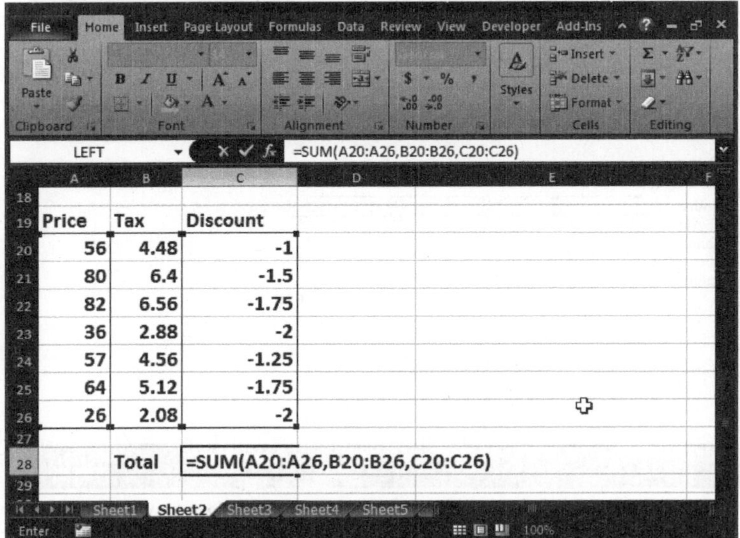

Figure 4.36 Entering Sum function to several ranges

- Relative cell references will change when you copy a formula.

➡ **To move or copy a formula, do this:**

1. Select the cell that contains the formula you want to move or copy.
2. Point to the border of the selection.
3. To move the cell, drag the selection to the upper-left cell of the paste area. Excel 2010 replaces any existing data in the pasted area.
4. To copy the cell, hold down Ctrl key as you drag the mouse.

☞ *You can also copy formulas into adjacent cells by using the fill handle. Select the cell that contains the formula and then drag the fill handle over the range you want to fill.*

Entering Cell References

Cell references allow you to use values from different parts of a worksheet and execute and enables you to do the desired calculation. You can use any cell or group of cells in a formula.

☞ *The reference of the active cell is displayed in the name box at the left end of the formula bar.*

Entering the Cell References by Pointing

The easiest method of entering cell references in a formula is by pointing to the cell you want to include in a formula. Although you can type an entire formula, you often can make a typing error or misread the row or column headings. Say for example, you may end up with D52 in a formula when it should be E52.

☞ *When you point to a cell to include it in a formula, you actually move the pointer to the cell you want in the formula. It is found out only when you select the correct cells.*

➡ **To enter a cell reference into a formula by pointing, do this:**

1. Select the cell for the formula.
2. Type an equal sign (=).
3. Point to the cell you want it in the formula and click, or press the arrow keys to move the dashed marquee to the cell you want in the formula. The address of the cell you point to appears at the cursor location in the formula bar.
4. Enter an operator, such as the + symbol.
5. Point to the next cell.
6. Repeat the steps from step 4 to continue the formula, or enter the formula by clicking the Enter box or pressing Enter key.

☞ *The cell reference in a formula changes after you copy the formula to a new location or after you fill a range with a formula. You would usually want formulas to use relative cell references, only.*

Using Cell References in Formulas

You refer to a cell's location with a *relative* reference or an *absolute* reference. Let us understand the difference in the two types of cell references.

Suppose that you are in your office, and you want someone to take a letter to the post office. Using a relative reference, you tell the person. "*Go out the front door; turn left cross the road and move two building then turn right and go to the second building.*" These directions are relative to your office location at the time you give the instructions. If you move to a different location, these directions are no longer valid.

To make sure that the letter gets to the mailbox no matter where you are then you give different set of directions. You must say something like this. "*Take this letter to the I.P. Estate post office.*" No matter where you are when you speak, the post office is at one absolute location: I.P ESTATE.

☞ *Thus, the difference between relative and absolute reference is that in absolute reference, the cell is fixed once for all. In the relative reference it depends on the location where your pointer is.*

Using Relative References

A relative cell reference in a formula, is based on the relative position of the cell that contains the formula and the cell the reference refers to. If the position of the cell that contains the formula changes, the reference is changed. If you copy or fill the formula across rows or down columns, the reference automatically adjusts.

Excel uses relative referencing for cell addresses when you enter a formula.

In Figure 4.37, the formula in cell F10 is =C10+D10+E10. All these references are relative. The formula, translated into English, would read as follows:

"In cell F10, add the number in the 10th column to the left (C10), second column to the left (D10) and the adjacent column on the left (E10)" in the same row.

Suppose you copy formula across Column G, the formulas adjust their cell references to their new positions. The copied formulas are as follows:

Cell Containing Formula	A1 Format
G10	= D10+E10+F10
G11	= D11+E11+F11
G12	= D12+E12+F12

You will notice that the formulas change to give the cell references with relative position from the cell that contains the formula.

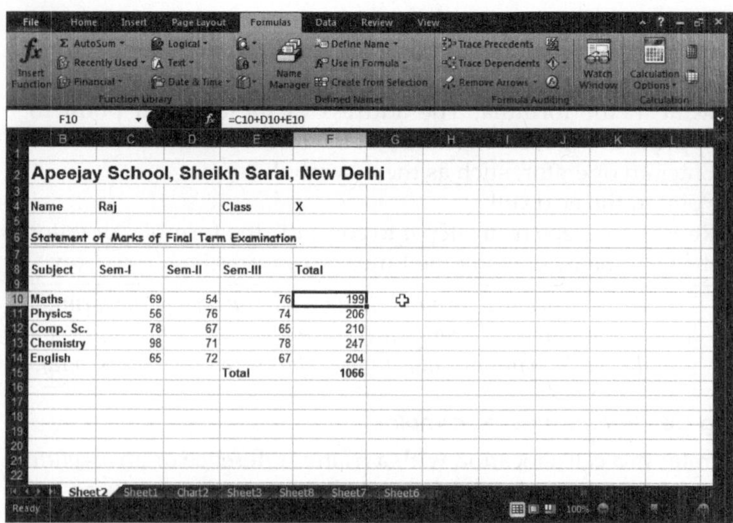

Figure 4.37 Formula entered with relative reference

Using Absolute References

You use absolute references only to keep the cell reference values from changing as and when you copy a formula to a new location in a worksheets.

➡ **To enter an absolute reference by using the F4 key, do this:**

1. Type an equal sign (=) and the cell reference you want to be absolute.
2. Press F4, the absolute reference key, until the correct combination of dollar signs appears.

☞ *Indicate absolute references by putting a dollar sign ($) in front of the column letter or row number that you want to freeze or both (See Figure 4.38).*

3. Type the next operator and continue to enter the formula, also.

You can use the F4 key when editing an existing formula.

Using Mixed References

In some cases, you may want either the row to stay fixed or the column to stay fixed when copying the cells from one place to other in a worksheet. In such cases, use a mixed reference. Such references contain both absolute and relative reference. For example, the reference $B5 prevents the column from changing, but the row changes relative to a new copied location. The dollar sign prevents the column from changing. In B$5, just the opposite occurs. The column adjusts to a new location but the row always stays fixed at 5 because the dollar sign prevents the row from changing.

☞ *Each time you press F4, Excel 2010 cycles through all combinations of relative and absolute references. Press F4 four times, for example, and you cycle from B22 through B22, B$22, $B22, and B22.*

You can create mixed references the same way as you can create absolute references. Type the dollar signs or specific row and column numbers without brackets or press F4 key. Each press of F4 cycles the cell reference to a new combination.

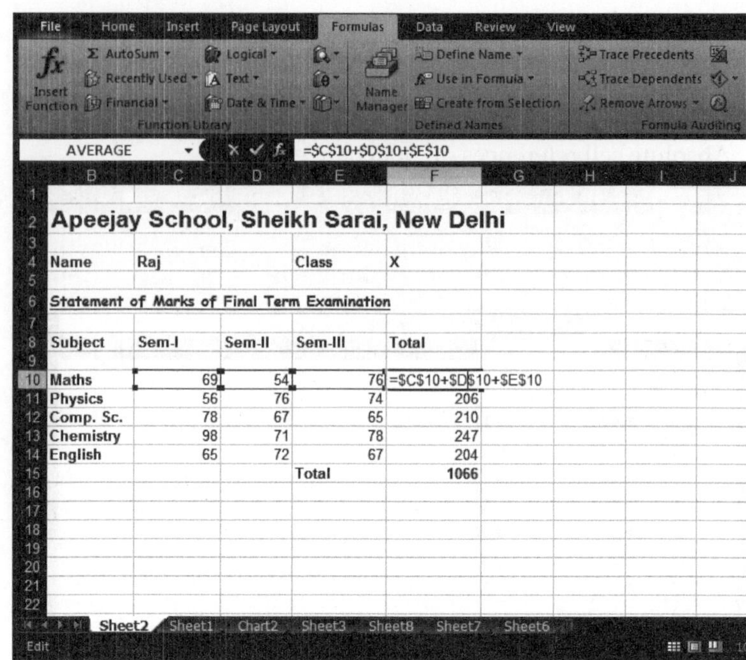

Figure 4.38 Formula with absolute reference

Referring to Other Sheets in a Workbook

You can also refer to other sheets in a workbook by including a sheet reference as well as a cell reference in a formula. For example, to refer to cell A1 on Sheet6, you would enter Sheet6!A1 in the formula.

You can use the mouse to enter a reference to a cell or range of cells on another worksheet in a workbook.

➡ **To refer to cell or range of cell in a different worksheet, do this:**

1. Start entering the formula in the cell where you want the result to appear.
2. Click the sheet tab for the worksheet you want to refer to.
3. Select the cell or range of cell that you want to refer to. The complete reference, including the sheet reference, appears in the formula bar (See Figure 4.39).
4. If the sheet name includes spaces, Excel surrounds the sheet reference with single quotation marks.
5. Finish the formula and press Enter key.

4.4.2 Using Operators in Formulas

Operators are used in formulas to execute operations on the values taken by formulas. Excel uses four types of operations. These are given below:

Operators	Signs
Arithmetic	+, –, *, /, %, ^
Text	&
Comparative	=, <, <=, >, >=, <>
Reference	Colon (:), comma(,), space ()

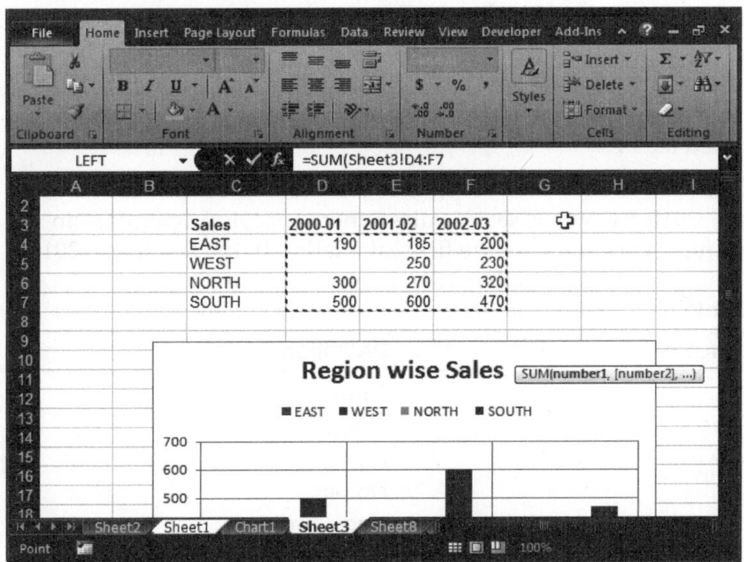

Figure 4.39 Referring a cell or range of cells in another worksheet

Arithmetic Operator

How to use each of the arithmetic operators in formulas are explained in the following example.

Example 9

Figure 4.40 shows the result of the use of arithmetic operator used in the following Table 4.9.

Table 4.9 Arithmetic Operator

Operator	Formula	Result	Type of Operation
+	=5+2	7	Addition of 5 with 2
–	=5–2	3	Subtraction of 2 from 5
–	–5	–5	Negation (negative of the number)
*	=5*2	10	Multiplication of 5 with 2
/	=5/2	2.5	Division of 5 by 2
%	5%	.05	Percentage
^	=5^2	25	Exponentiation (to the power of)

Text Concatenation Operator

The ampersand (&) operator, joins text within quotation marks or text contained in referenced cells. Joining text is known as *concatenation*, as explained in the following example.

Example 10

Figure 4.40 shows the result of the concatenation operator used in the following table.

Operator	Formula	Result	Type of Operation
&	=A12&""&C15	Ms.Gibbs	Text in A12 and C15 is joined

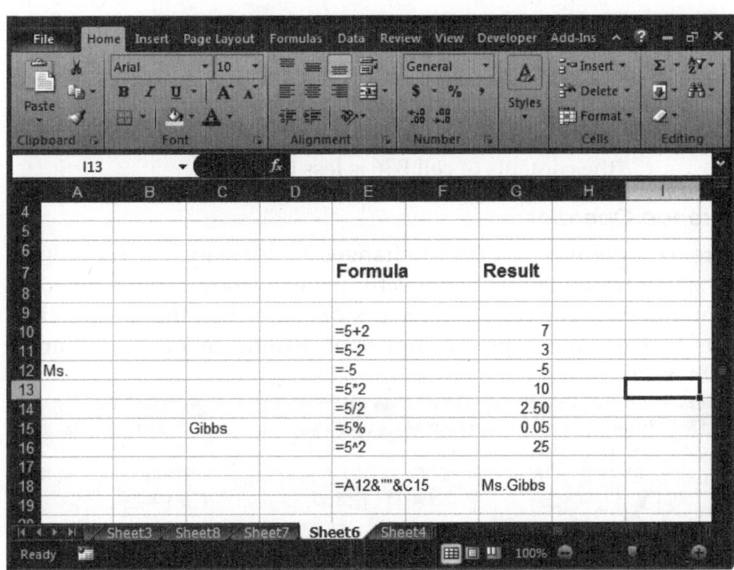

Figure 4.40 Arithmetic and text operators

Comparison Operators

To compare values, you can create formulas using comparison operators. These operators return a TRUE or FALSE result, depending on how the formula evaluate the condition. Subsequent Table formulates some Comparison operators and Figure 4.41 shows the use of such comparison operators.

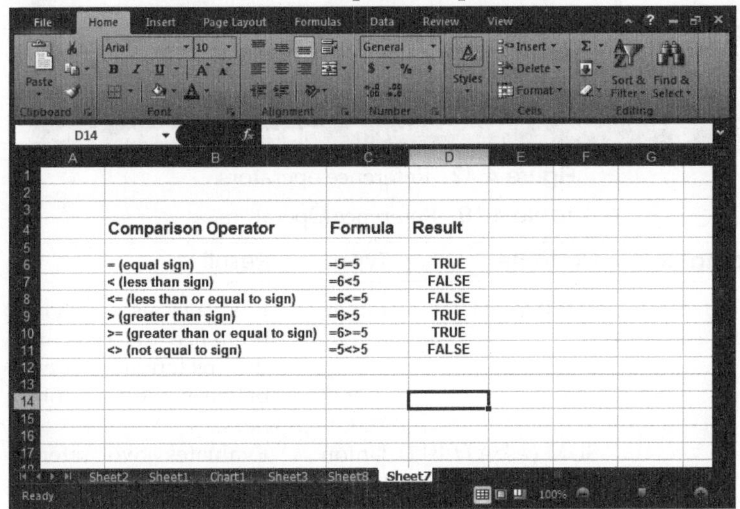

Figure 4.41 Comparison operators

Operator	Type
=	Equal to
<	Less than
<=	Less than or equal to
>	Greater than
>=	Greater than or equal to
<>	Not equal to

The following are examples of comparative operators in formulas:

Formula	Result
=A12<15	TRUE if the contents of cell A12 is less than 15; FALSE if the contents of cell A12 is 15 or more.
=B36>=15	TRUE if the contents of cell B36 is 15 or more; FALSE if the contents of cell B36 is less than 15.

Reference Operator

Reference operators make no changes to constants or cell contents as summarized in Table 4.10. Instead, they control how a formula groups the cells and ranges of cells when the formula is made to calculate. The examples of Reference operators are shown in Figure 4.42.

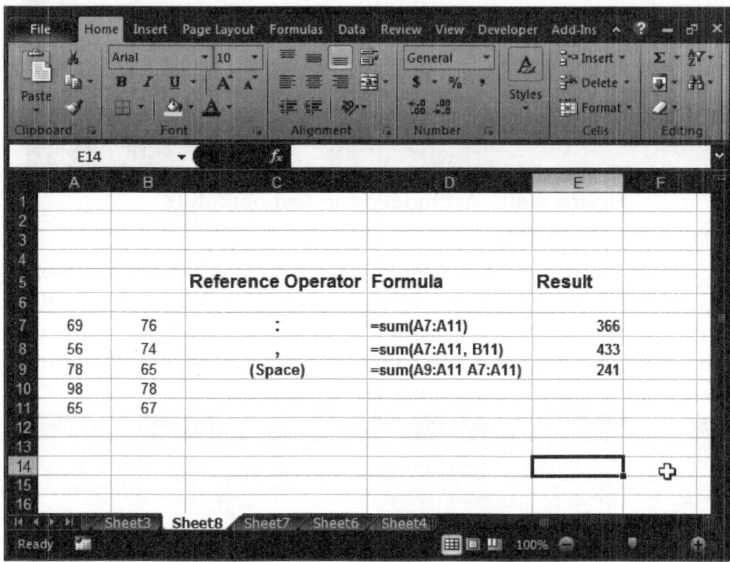

Figure 4.42 Reference operators

Table 4.10 Reference Operators

Operator	Example	Type	Result
:	SUM(A7:A11)	Range	Evaluates as a single reference the cells in the rectangular area between the two corners.
,	SUM (A7:A11,B11)	Union	Evaluates two references as a single reference.
space	SUM(A9:A11 A7:A11)	Intersect	Evaluates the cells common to both references (if no cells are common to both, then #NULL results).
space	=Yr99 Sales	Intersect	Cell contents at the intersect of the column named Yr99 and the row named Sales.

☞ *Reference operators enable you to combine absolute and relative references and named ranges. Reference operators are valuable for joining cells (union) or referring to a common area shared between different ranges (intersect).*

Range Operator

Use the range operator (:) to reduce your work in formulas. If you want a formula to refer to all cells in column B, type B:B. Similarly, the range that includes all cells in rows 5 through 12 is entered as 5:12.

Evaluation (Precedence) of Formulas

Excel 2010 follows a set of rules when applying operators in a formula. Working from the first calculation to the last, Excel 2010 evaluates operators in the order shown in Table 4.11.

Table 4.11 The Order in which Excel 2010 Evaluates Operators

Operator	Definition
()	Parentheses
:	Range
space	Intersect
,	Union
–	Negation
%	Percentage
^	Exponentiation
* and /	Multiplication and division
+ and –	Addition and subtraction
&	Text joining
=, <, and <= >, >=, and <>	Comparisons

If you want to change the order in which calculations are performed then enclose in parentheses the terms you want Excel 2010 to calculate first.

For example, you will notice the difference between the results of the following formulas:

Formula	Result
`=6+21/3`	`13`
`=(6+21)/3`	`9`

Entering Text, Date and Time in Formulas

You can use *text*, *dates*, and *times* in formulas by including the data in quotation marks. For example.

```
="The Total Budget is" &TOTAL_BUDGET
```

shows the Total Budget and the value in the cell named TOTAL_BUDGET.

If you want to perform date math on explicit dates, which are the dates that are not in cells, then:

```
="4/14/2016" – "4/14/2015"
```

or

```
="14April16" – "14April15"
```

These formulas produce the number of days between the two dates.

4.4.3 Functions

Functions are the predefined formulas that perform calculations on specific values, called arguments. Each function takes specific types of arguments, such as *numbers*, *references*, *text*, or *logical values*. You can enter the arguments, enclosing them in parentheses, i.e., ( ), after the function name. Functions use these arguments in the same way that algebraic equations use variables. For example, the SUM function adds values or range of values, and the PMT function calculates the loan payments based on an interest rate, the period of loan, and the principal amount of loan. Excel includes many functions that can be divided into the following categories:

4.4.4 Find the Right Function

Functions are basically a fast way to enter a complex formula. Excel 2010 has hundreds of functions you can use, and are grouped together into the following categories:

1. Math and trigonometry
2. Logical
3. Statistical
4. Date and time
5. Text
6. Financial
7. Database
8. Engineering
9. Information
10. Lookup and Reference
11. Add-ins and Automation
12. Cube
13. Compatibility

By using functions, you can save time and cuts down on typographical errors that are so easy to make when typing formulas.

4.4.5 Fixing Formula Errors

There are a number of error messages that may appear when you type a formula. Some are typing mistakes and some may be a result of a cell value. Other errors may appear in the formula result cell.

Following are a few common error messages.

- #DIV/0!: This type of error occurs when a number is divided by either an empty cell (a cell that contains no value) or one with a value of zero (0). Make sure all cells in the division have a nonzero value.
- #REF!: This type of error occurs when the formula includes an invalid cell reference.
- #N/A: This type of error occurs when the value is not available to a function or formula.
- #VALUE!: This type of error occurs when formula includes cells that contain different data types. This type of problem can be fixed by making minor changes to the formula.
- #NAME?: This type of error occurs when Excel does not recognize text in a formula because of a range name or function name misspelling.
- #NUM!: This type of error occurs when a formula or function contains invalid numeric values.
- #####: This type of error occurs when a column is not wide enough to display all of its content, or that a negative date or time is used in a cell.

Now you are familiar with the basic concepts of functions, function syntax and the different types of error which generate when you use incorrect function. Let us now move on how to add functions in a worksheet.

Basic Mathematical Functions

Excel 2010 includes many math and trigonometry functions. Mathematical functions are used to perform, wide variety of simple or complex calculations, such as totaling the value for a range of cells, rounding of a number.

SUM( )

Adds all the numbers in a range of cells (See Figure 4.43).

Syntax

`SUM(number1,number2,...)`

Round( )

`Round()` function rounds a number to a specified number of digits (See Figure 4.43).

	A	B	C	D	E	F	G	H
1	5	15		30	40	50		
2								
3				Mathematical Functions		Examples		Results
4				SUM() FUNCTION		=SUM(3, 2)		5
5						=SUM("3",2, TRUE)		6
6						=SUM(A8, A9, 2)		2
7						=SUM(B1:E1,15)		150
8	text			ROUND() FUNCTION		=ROUND(3.27, 1)		3.3
9	text1					=ROUND(-1.475, 0)		-1
10						=ROUND(31.5, -1)		30
11				ROUNDOWN() FUNCTION		=ROUNDDOWN(3.27, 1)		3.2
12						=ROUNDDOWN(-1.475, 0)		-1
13	Salary	Commission				=ROUNDDOWN(31.5, -1)		30
14	10000	1000		ROUNDUP() FUNCTION		=ROUNDUP(3.27, 1)		3.3
15	20000	1500				ROUNDUP(-1.475, 0)		-2
16	30000	2500				=ROUNDUP(31.5, -1)		40
17	40000	3000		ABS() FUNCTION		=ABS(-5)		5
18				SQRT() FUNCTION		=SQRT(ABS(-16))		4
19				TRUNC() FUNCTION		=TRUNC(-8.9)		-8
20						=TRUNC(8.9654, 2)		8.96
21				SUMIF() FUNCTION		=SUMIF(A14:A17,">12000",B14:B17)		7000

Figure 4.43 Mathematical functions and their results

Syntax

`ROUND(number,num_digits)`

Rounddown( )

`Rounddown()` function rounds a number down towards zero (See Figure 4.43).

Syntax

`ROUNDDOWN(number,num_digits)`

Roundup( )

`Roundup()` function rounds a number up away from 0 (zero) (See Figure 4.43).

Syntax

`ROUNDUP(number,num_digits)`

ABS( )

`ABS( )` function returns the absolute value of a number. The absolute value of a number is the number without any + or – sign.

Syntax

`ABS(num)`

Where **`num`** is the real number of which you want the absolute value.

SQRT( )

`SQRT( )` returns a positive square root of a number.

Syntax

`SQRT(num)`

TRUNC( )

`TRUNC( )` function truncates a number to an integer value by removing the fractional part of the number.

Syntax

`TRUNC(num,num_digits)`

Logical Functions

Logical functions are used when we want to check whether a given condition is true or false.

IF( )

`IF( )` function is used to determine whether a condition specified with in braces is true or false. It returns one value if a specified condition evaluates to TRUE and another value if it evaluates to FALSE (See Figure 4.44).

Syntax

`IF(logical_test,value_if_true,value_if_false)`

Where

`Logical_test` is a value or expression that can be evaluated to TRUE or FALSE. For example, A10 = 100 is a logical expression.

`Value_if_true` is the value that is returned if logical_test is TRUE. For example, if the value in cell A10 is equal to 100, the expression evaluates to TRUE.

`Value_if_false` is the value that is returned if logical_test is FALSE. For example, if the value in cell A10 is not equal to 100, the expression evaluates to FALSE.

☞ *In Excel 2010, up to 64 IF() functions can be nested to construct more elaborate tests.*

Example 11

On a Marksheet, cell A10 contains a formula to calculate the result. If the result of the formula in A10 is greater than 50, then the following function displays "Pass". Otherwise, the function displays "Fail" (See Figure 4.44).

`IF(A10>=50,"Pass","Fail")`

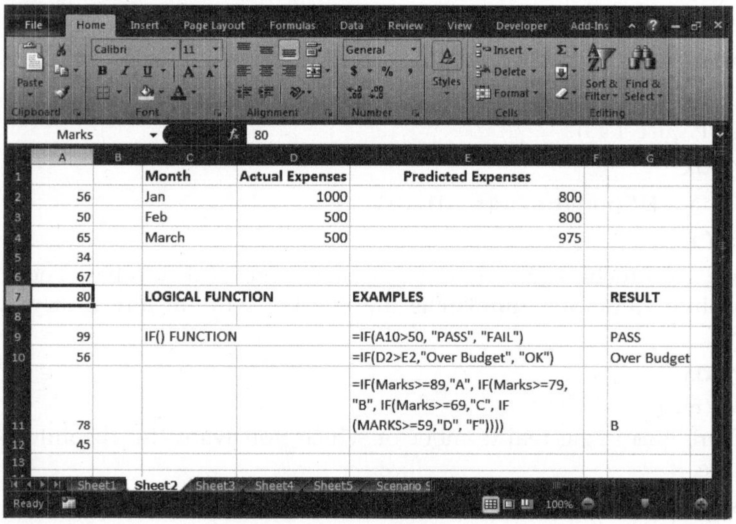

	A	B	C	D	E	F
1			Month	Actual Expenses	Predicted Expenses	
2	56		Jan	1000	800	
3	50		Feb	500	800	
4	65		March	500	975	
5	34					
6	67					
7	80		LOGICAL FUNCTION	EXAMPLES		RESULT
8						
9	99		IF() FUNCTION	=IF(A10>50, "PASS", "FAIL")		PASS
10	56			=IF(D2>E2,"Over Budget", "OK")		Over Budget
11	78			=IF(Marks>=89,"A", IF(Marks>=79, "B", IF(Marks>=69,"C", IF (MARKS>=59,"D", "F"))))		B
12	45					

Figure 4.44 Logical functions

Suppose an expense worksheet in D2:D4 contains the following data for "Actual Expenses" for January, February, and March: 1000, 500, 500. E2:E4 contains the following data for "Predicted Expenses" for the same periods: 800, 800, 975.

You can write a formula to check whether you are over budget for a particular month, generating text for a message with the following formulas:

```
IF(D2>E2,"Over Budget","OK") equals "Over Budget"
IF(D3>E3,"Over Budget","OK") equals "OK"
```

We can also use nested IF function:

```
IF(Marks>89,"A",IF(Marks>79,"B",
IF(Marks>69,"C",IF(Marks>59,"D","F"))))
```

In the above example, **`Marks`** in the name of the cell **`A7`** if the first logical_test (Marks>=89) is TRUE, "A" is returned (See Figure 4.44). If the first logical_test is FALSE, the second IF statement is evaluated, and so on.

☞ *When averaging cells, keep in mind the difference between empty cells and those containing the value zero, especially if you have cleared the Zero values check box from the Advanced properties of the Excel Options. Empty cells are not counted, but zero values are counted and evaluated.*

TRUE( )

`TRUE( )` returns the logical value TRUE and it takes no arguments.

Syntax

`TRUE( )`

FALSE( )

`FALSE( )` function is same as TRUE( ) but it returns the logical value FALSE.

Syntax

`FALSE( )`

Statistical Function

Statistical functions are used to perform statistical analysis on ranges of data. Excel 2010 includes simple as well as complex statistical functions, such as *average, min, max, standard deviation, slopes* etc (See Figure 4.45). Apart from this, it also includes a set of more accurate statistical and other functions. Certain existing functions have also been renamed to better describe what they do.

MAX( )

Max function returns the largest value in a set of values stored in a cells.

Syntax

`MAX(number1,number2,...)`

MIN( )

Min function returns the smallest number in a set of values.

Syntax

`MIN(number1,number2, ...)`

Average( )

The Average function returns the average (arithmetic mean) of the arguments which are passed in function as an argument (See Figure 4.45).

Syntax

`AVERAGE(number1,number2,...)`

Count( )

Count function counts the number of cells that contain numbers and numbers within the list of arguments. Use COUNT to get the number of entries in a number field in a range or array of numbers (See Figure 4.45).

Syntax

`COUNT(value1,value2,...)`

Date and Time Function

With date and time functions, you can analyze and work with date and time values in formulas (See Figure 4.46). For example, if you need to use the current date in a formula, you can use the TODAY ( ) function, which returns the current date.

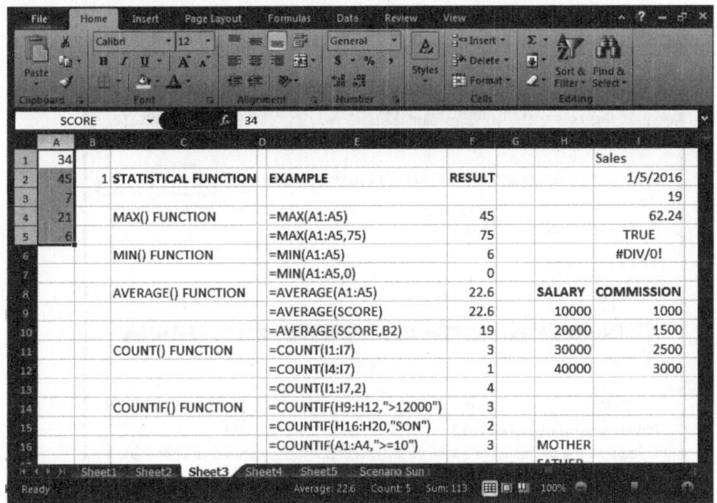

	A	B	C	D	F	H	I
1	34						Sales
2	45	1	STATISTICAL FUNCTION	EXAMPLE	RESULT		1/5/2016
3	7						19
4	21		MAX() FUNCTION	=MAX(A1:A5)	45		62.24
5	6			=MAX(A1:A5,75)	75		TRUE
6			MIN() FUNCTION	=MIN(A1:A5)	6		#DIV/0!
7				=MIN(A1:A5,0)	0		
8			AVERAGE() FUNCTION	=AVERAGE(A1:A5)	22.6	SALARY	COMMISSION
9				=AVERAGE(SCORE)	22.6	10000	1000
10				=AVERAGE(SCORE,B2)	19	20000	1500
11			COUNT() FUNCTION	=COUNT(I1:I7)	3	30000	2500
12				=COUNT(I4:I7)	1	40000	3000
13				=COUNT(I1:I7,2)	4		
14			COUNTIF() FUNCTION	=COUNTIF(H9:H12,">12000")	3		
15				=COUNTIF(H16:H20,"SON")	2		
16				=COUNTIF(A1:A4,">=10")	3	MOTHER	

Figure 4.45 Statistical functions

Today ( )

It returns the current date of the system (See Figure 4.46).

Syntax

`TODAY( )`

Now()

Returns the current date and time (See Figure 4.46).

Syntax

`NOW( )`

Day()

It returns the day of a date passed as an argument. The day is given as an integer ranging from 1 to 31 (See Figure 4.46).

Syntax

`DAY(serial_number)`

Where `serial_number` is the date of the day you are trying to find. Dates may be entered as text strings within quotation marks.

Example 12

`DAY("4-Jan")` equals `4`

`DAY("16-Apr-2016")` equals `15`

`DAY("4/15/2016")` equals `15`

`DAY("2016/10/10")` equals `10`

Month()

It returns the month of a date which is passed as argument. The month is given as an integer, ranging from 1 (January) to 12 (December) (See Figure 4.46).

Syntax

`MONTH(serial_number)`

Where `serial_number` is the date of the month you are trying to find.

Example 13

`MONTH("6-Sept")` equals `9`

`MONTH("2016/04/01")` equals `4`

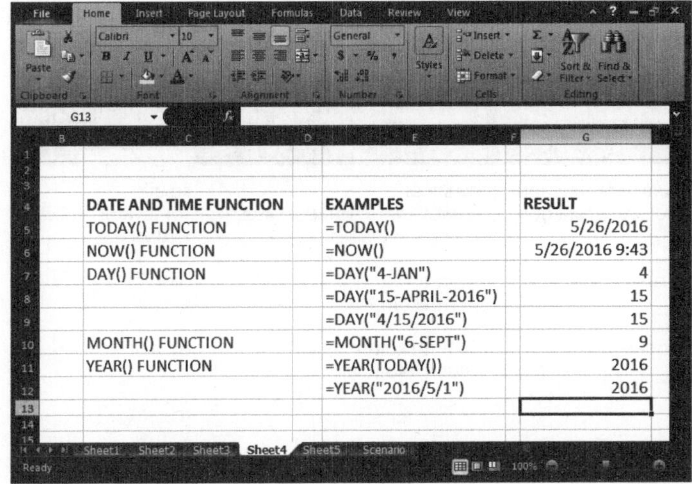

	C	D	G
4	DATE AND TIME FUNCTION	EXAMPLES	RESULT
5	TODAY() FUNCTION	=TODAY()	5/26/2016
6	NOW() FUNCTION	=NOW()	5/26/2016 9:43
7	DAY() FUNCTION	=DAY("4-JAN")	4
8		=DAY("15-APRIL-2016")	15
9		=DAY("4/15/2016")	15
10	MONTH() FUNCTION	=MONTH("6-SEPT")	9
11	YEAR() FUNCTION	=YEAR(TODAY())	2016
12		=YEAR("2016/5/1")	2016

Figure 4.46 Date and Time functions

Year()

Returns the year corresponding year to a date (See Figure 4.46).

Syntax

`YEAR(serial_number)`

Where `serial_number` is the date of the year you want to find.

Text Function

With text functions, you can use text strings in formulas. You can also change the case of the string, find out the length of a text string or you can join two strings, etc (See Figure 4.47).

Concatenate( )

Joins two or more text strings into one text string (See Figure 4.47).

Syntax

`CONCATENATE (text1,text2,...)`

Where `text1, text2,...` are 2 to 255 text items to be joined into a single text item.

The `"&"` operator can also be used to join text items.

Example 14

`CONCATENATE("Total"," Value")` equals `"Total Value"`.

If you use '&' operator to join strings then

`"Total"&" "&"Value"`

LEFT( )

LEFT returns the first character or characters in a text string, based on the number of characters specified as arguments (See Figure 4.47).

Syntax

`LEFT(text,num_chars)`

Where `text` is the text string.

`num_chars` specifies the number of characters to be extracted. By default, it is assumed to be 1.

Example 15

`LEFT("PROJECT",4)` equals `"PROJ"` (See Figure 4.47)

If A1 contains "SUBJECT", then:

`LEFT(A1)` equals `"S"`

Because S is the left most character and by default it will be left most character value.

RIGHT( )

It is same as LEFT but it returns the last character or characters in a text string, based on the number of characters specified as a arguments (See Figure 4.47).

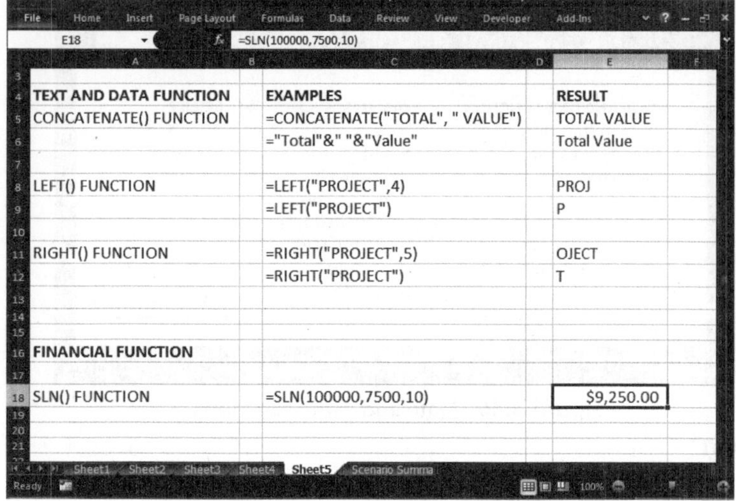

TEXT AND DATA FUNCTION	EXAMPLES	RESULT
CONCATENATE() FUNCTION	=CONCATENATE("TOTAL", " VALUE")	TOTAL VALUE
	="Total"&" "&"Value"	Total Value
LEFT() FUNCTION	=LEFT("PROJECT",4)	PROJ
	=LEFT("PROJECT")	P
RIGHT() FUNCTION	=RIGHT("PROJECT",5)	OJECT
	=RIGHT("PROJECT")	T
FINANCIAL FUNCTION		
SLN() FUNCTION	=SLN(100000,7500,10)	$9,250.00

Figure 4.47 Text and Financial functions

Syntax

`RIGHT(text,num_chars)`

Where `text` is the text string.

`num_chars` specifies the number of characters to be extracted.

Example 16

`RIGHT("PROJECT",5)` equals `"OJECT"` (See Figure 4.47)

`RIGHT("PROJECT")` equals `"T"`

Financial Function

Financial functions perform common business calculations For example, determination of the payment for a loan.

SLN( )

Returns the straight-line depreciation of an asset for one period (See Figure 4.47).

Syntax

`SLN(cost,Last_value,life)`

Where `Cost` is the initial cost of the asset.

`Last_value` is the value at the end of the depreciation.

`Life` is the number of year in which the asset is being depreciated (the useful life of the asset).

Example 17

Suppose you purchased a Car for `1,00,000` that has a useful life of 10 years and a salvage value of `7,500`. The depreciation allowance for each year is:

`SLN(100000, 7500, 10)` equals `9,250` (See Figure 4.47)

PMT( )

Suppose you want to buy a car and you want to calculate your monthly installment you can use the `PMT()` function built in Excel 2010.

Example 18

1. Activate a cell.
2. Under the **Formulas** tab, click on the **Insert Function**. *Alternatively,* click on the **Insert Function** button on the center of the formula bar, i.e., *fx* or press Shift+F3 keys together. It will display the Insert Function Dialog box as seen in Figure 4.48.

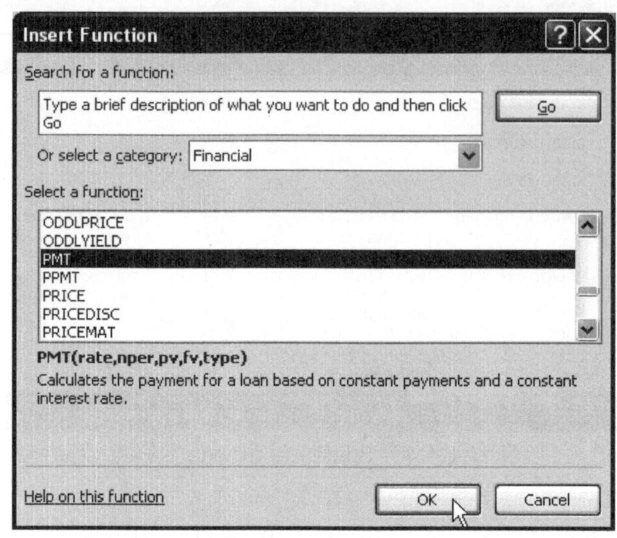

Figure 4.48 Insert Function dialog box

3. Select a Financial category from the select a category: drop-down list.
4. Click on PMT Function from the Select a function: list box.
5. Click OK. It will display a Function Arguments dialog box as seen in Figure 4.49.

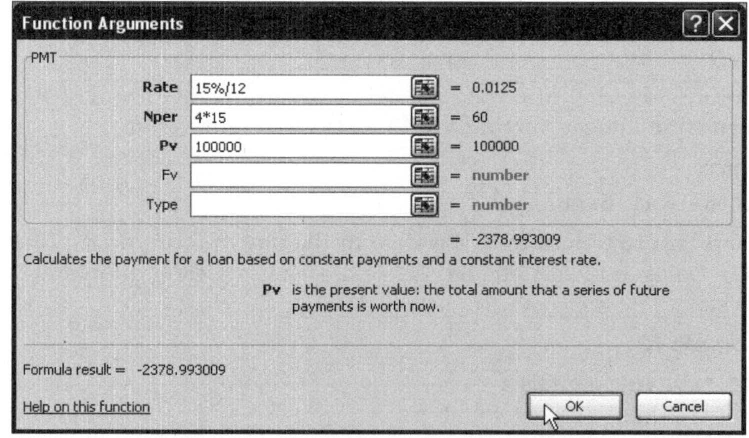

Figure 4.49 Function Arguments dialog box

The arguments required by the function are as follows:

Argument	Description
Rate	Is the *interest rate* for the loan.
Nper	Is the total number of payments for the loan.
Pv	Is the present value, or the total amount that a series of future payments is worth now; also known as the principal amount which is 100000 in our case.

(Contd...)

Fv	Is the future value, or a cash balance you want to attain after the last payment is made. If Fv is omitted, it is assumed to be 0 (zero), that is, the future value of a loan is 0.
Type	Is the number 0 (zero) or 1 and indicated when payments are due.

Set type equal to	If payments are due
0 or omitted	At the end of the period
1	At the beginning of the period

Example 19

The following Figure 4.50 shown a simple Excel for Salary Calculation.

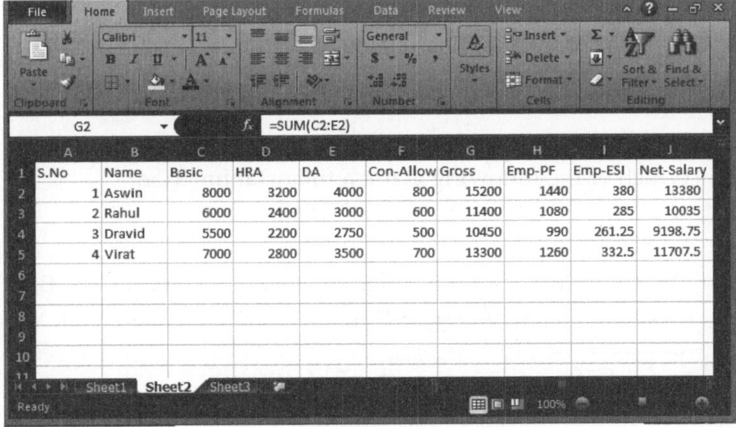

G2 =SUM(C2:E2)

S.No	Name	Basic	HRA	DA	Con-Allow	Gross	Emp-PF	Emp-ESI	Net-Salary
1	Aswin	8000	3200	4000	800	15200	1440	380	13380
2	Rahul	6000	2400	3000	600	11400	1080	285	10035
3	Dravid	5500	2200	2750	500	10450	990	261.25	9198.75
4	Virat	7000	2800	3500	700	13300	1260	332.5	11707.5

Figure 4.50 Salary Calculation

HRA = House Rent Allowance 40% = Basic * 40%
DA = Dearness Allowance 50% = Basic * 50%
Gross = Total of HRA + DA = Basic + HRA + DA
PF = Provident Fund (Employee PF contribution) = Basic + DA = 0.12%
ESI = Employ Salary Insurance = Basic * .0475%
Net Salary = Gross - PF - ESI

4.4.6 Using Formulas with Multiple Cell References

In Excel one can use multiple pieces of data for each calculations. You will need to be able to reference multiple cells at the same time

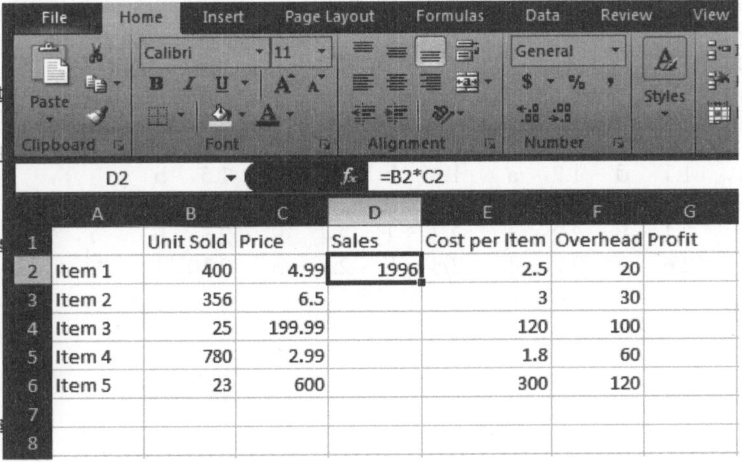

D2 =B2*C2

	Unit Sold	Price	Sales	Cost per Item	Overhead	Profit
Item 1	400	4.99	1996	2.5	20	
Item 2	356	6.5		3	30	
Item 3	25	199.99		120	100	
Item 4	780	2.99		1.8	60	
Item 5	23	600		300	120	

Figure 4.51 Data entered in the worksheet

The following table of data: (See Figure 4.51)

In order to calculate profit for item, sales need to be calculated and then the cost of the items need to be subtracted from the sales.

To do this, first calculate the sales. Enter =B2*C2 in cell D2: (See Figure 4.52)

D2 =B2*C2

	Unit Sold	Price	Sales	Cost per Item	Overhead	Profit
Item 1	400	4.99	1996	2.5	20	
Item 2	356	6.5	2314	3	30	
Item 3	25	199.99	4999.75	120	100	
Item 4	780	2.99	2332.2	1.8	60	
Item 5	23	600	13800	300	120	

Ready Average: 5088.39 Count: 5 Sum: 25441.95 100%

Figure 4.52 Entering formula in the cell D2

This calculation is easy to type because it only deals with two cells. However, if you need to create a formula based on many different fields, it can be very tedious to track down the correct cell reference. To make entering formulas easier, you can simply click the cells you need to use to automatically insert them.

Instead of entering the same formula as rest of the data you entered the above (units sold × price) (i.e. same formula), simply click and drag the cells as shown below: (See Figure 4.53).

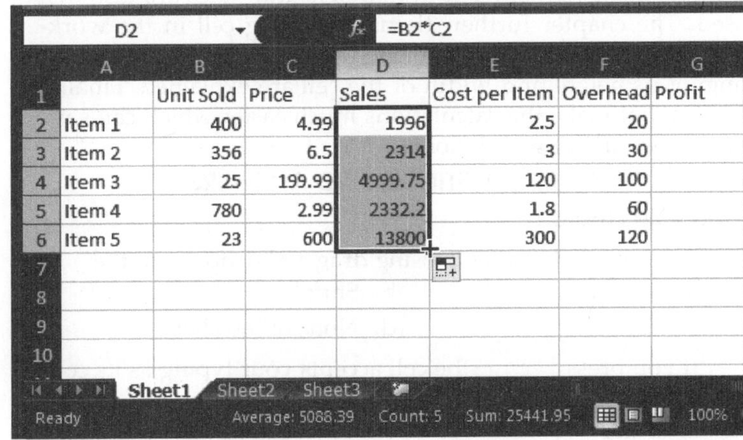

D2 =B2*C2

	Unit Sold	Price	Sales	Cost per Item	Overhead	Profit
Item 1	400	4.99	1996	2.5	20	
Item 2	356	6.5	2314	3	30	
Item 3	25	199.99	4999.75	120	100	
Item 4	780	2.99	2332.2	1.8	60	
Item 5	23	600	13800	300	120	

Ready Average: 5088.39 Count: 5 Sum: 25441.95 100%

Figure 4.53 Drag the cells

Once all the sales values have been calculated, we can now calculate the profit. Profit is calculated by subtracting the expenses from the sales.

*Sales - (Unit sold * cost per item + Overhead) = profit*

In our example, this translates into the following formula. Note the color coding for each cell: (See Figure 4.54)

Once the correct formula has been entered in the cells in the Profit column, the worksheet is complete. For the rest of the data you need not to enter the same formula, simply click and drag the cells as shown in Figure 4.55.

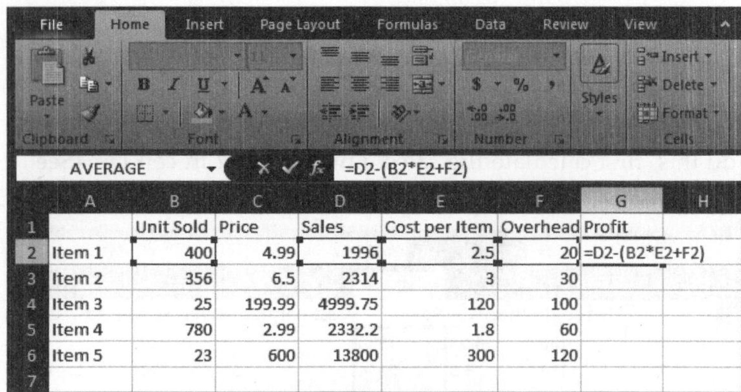

	A	B	C	D	E	F	G
1		Unit Sold	Price	Sales	Cost per Item	Overhead	Profit
2	Item 1	400	4.99	1996	2.5	20	=D2-(B2*E2+F2)
3	Item 2	356	6.5	2314	3	30	
4	Item 3	25	199.99	4999.75	120	100	
5	Item 4	780	2.99	2332.2	1.8	60	
6	Item 5	23	600	13800	300	120	

Figure 4.54 Entering formula in the Cell G2

G2 =D2-(B2*E2+F2)

	A	B	C	D	E	F	G
1		Unit Sold	Price	Sales	Cost per Item	Overhead	Profit
2	Item 1	400	4.99	1996	2.5	20	976
3	Item 2	356	6.5	2314	3	30	1216
4	Item 3	25	199.99	4999.75	120	100	1899.75
5	Item 4	780	2.99	2332.2	1.8	60	868.2
6	Item 5	23	600	13800	300	120	6780

Figure 4.55 Drag the cells

4.5 SUMMARY

This chapter presents concepts of a very popular *Spreadsheet Package* namely, MS Excel. It is one of the most versatile spreadsheet program. First, we discussed elements of an electronic spreadsheet. We also discussed how to create, edit, save and print documents. Entering text, numbers and dates are also discussed. The chapter further discusses editing cell in the worksheet data. Inserting and deleting rows and columns and changing its height and width of the cell are explained. Finally, formulas that make the calculations much easier which can save time when working with lot of numbers.

MODEL QUESTIONS AND ANSWERS

1. Multiple Choice

1.1 To copy a cell contents using drag and drop, press the
a. End key b. Shift key
c. Esc key d. None of the above

1.2 If you press _______ the cell accepts your typing as its contents
a. Enter b. Ctrl + Enter
c. Tab d. Insert

1.3 The autofill feature
a. Automatically adds a range of cell values
b. Extends a sequential series of data
c. Applies a border around selected cells
d. None of the above

1.4 "Qtr 1, Qtr 2, Qtr 3" is an example of a
a. Formula b. Function
c. Series d. Syntax

1.5 You can edit existing Excel data by pressing the
a. Fl key b. F2 key
c. F3 key d. F4 key

1.6 In Excel the intersection of a row and column is called
a. Square b. Cell
c. Cubicle d. Worksheet

1.7 In MS Excel to select a column the easiest method is to
a. Double click any cell in the column
b. Drag from the top cell in the column to the last cell in the column
c. Click the column heading
d. None of these

1.8 Extension of Excel file is
a. .TMT b. .XXL
c. .xlsx d. None of the above

1.9 Which of the following is not a financial function?
a. FV() b. NPV()
c. SUM() d. PMT()

1.10 The cell reference for a range of cells that starts in cell B1 and goes over to column G and down to row 10 is __________.
a. G1-G10 b. B1.G10
c. B1;G10 d. B1:G10

2. State whether the following are True or False

2.1 Cells are named by their positions either by rows or columns.
2.2 Last column of the worksheet window is IV.
2.3 Sheet tab is displayed when you split a sheet.
2.4 If the Bold and Underline buttons appear lighter than before, it means they are currently in use.
2.5 To create a new worksheet, select worksheet from the file menu.
2.6 Standard width of a column is 18.43.
2.7 To open a file quickly from the open dialog box, double click the file's icon.
2.8 You can simultaneously select an entire row and an entire column.
2.9 You cannot move the active cell within a selected range.
2.10 Using the undo command you can undo multiple actions.

Answers

1.	1.1	d	1.2	a	1.3	b	1.4	c	1.5	b
	1.6	b	1.7	c	1.8	c	1.9	c	1.10	d
2.	2.1	F	2.2	T	2.3	T	2.4	F	2.5	F
	2.6	F	2.7	T	2.8	F	2.9	F	2.10	T

CHAPTER 5

Introduction to Internet, WWW and Web Browsers

5.0 INTRODUCTION

Communication is one of the most popular use of the Internet. The Internet is making it easier for people to communicate with one another using computers. The most popular way of communication on the Internet is the electronic mail (e-mail). With e-mail topping the list of all the technologies used. Some of the types of communication technologies used also to include e-mail discussion groups, Usenet news, chat groups, etc. These are unique to networked computer environments and have come into wide popularity because of the Internet. Other technologies, including video and audio conferencing and Internet telephony, are also available on the Internet. They require more multimedia capabilities of computer systems. They are more taxing of network resources than the others. They also are adaptations of other technologies to the Internet.

The Internet provides a capability so powerful that it can be used for almost any purpose that depends on information. It is accessible by every individual who connects to one of its constituent networks. It supports human communication via electronic mail (e-mail), chat rooms, newsgroups, and audio and video transmission. It allows people to work collaboratively at many different locations. It supports access to digital information by many applications, including the World Wide Web (WWW). The Internet has proved to be a spawning ground for a large and growing number of "e-businesses" that carry out most of their sales and services over the Internet. Many experts believe that the Internet will dramatically transform business as well as society.

5.1 OBJECTIVES

The reader will be able to understand the following:

- Basics of computer networks
- Concept of Internet
- Web Browsing Software
- Search Engines
- Understanding URL
- Surfing the Web

5.2 BASIC OF COMPUTER NETWORKS

A network is a group of computers connected in some fashion in order to share resources. A group of computers in a network would provide greater storage capacity and processing power than that by stand-alone independent machine. In addition to computers, a network also consists of peripheral devices with carrier and data communication devices used for the purpose of exchanging data and information.

By using computer networks, the cost of data transfer can be made economical because computers can send data at a *very fast speed*. Thus, computers enable us to reduce both cost and time in transferring data or information. In a network, computers of different make can be connected together and users can work together in a group. Software packages have been developed for group working in Database Management System (DBMS) as well as in graphical artworks. Also, data from different departments located at distant places can be transferred to and stored on a central computer. This data can then be accessed by the computers located in different departments. The data at the central computer is updated and accessed by all users. This method would prevent any bottlenecks in the smooth functioning of the organization because all the users will get the latest information (for example, inventory) stored in the central computer.

5.2.1 Advantages of Network

The following are the advantages of computer networking:

1. **Resource sharing:** The aim of resource sharing is to make all programs, data and peripherals available to authorized users on the network irrespective of the physical location of the resources.
2. **Reliability:** This advantage is provided by having an alternative source of supply. For example, files can be replicated on two or three machines, so if one of them is unavailable (due to hardware failure), the other copies can be used. In addition, the presence of multiple Central Processing Units (CPUs) means that if one goes down, the others may be able to take over its work. This is of utmost importance for military, banking, air traffic control, etc., which need to continue operating in case of hardware problems.
3. **Financial benefits:** Small computers (PCs) have better price-to-performance ratio compared to large ones. A mainframe computer may be ten times faster than a PC, but it may cost about a hundred times more. As a result, most organizations prefer to maintain a computer network consisting of a set of personal computers rather than a centralized large computer.
4. **Better communication medium:** In an organization with a number of branches at far-off places, networking of computers facilitates cheap and easy mode of communication. It is possible to transfer any information to any other destination immediately. Whenever a user updates a file, it is visible to the other users logged on to the network.
5. **Access to remote database:** By getting access to the remote database, it is possible to get rid of unnecessary trouble and wastage of precious time, especially in works such as airplane and railway reservations, booking hotels, etc. From a remote place in any part of the world, one can book an air ticket from one city to another, accommodation in hotels and get instant confirmation also.

5.2.2 Types of Networks

There are many types of computer networks that are described as follows:

5.2.3 Local Area Network (LAN)

Local Area Network (LAN) is a group of computers located in the same room, on the same floor, or in the same building that are connected to form a single computer network. LANs allow users to share storage devices, printers, applications, data, and other network resources. They are limited to a specific geographical area, usually less than one kilometer in diameter.

Figure 5.1 illustrates the basic physical characteristics, information transfer and shared device concepts underlying LAN operation. The line printer and magnetic tape storage are "shared" resources, since any user attached to the network can access these devices through PCs acting as the resource manager, or server, as it is commonly called in LAN terminology. In some networks, the users can directly exchange data or files from Mainframe or mini computers.

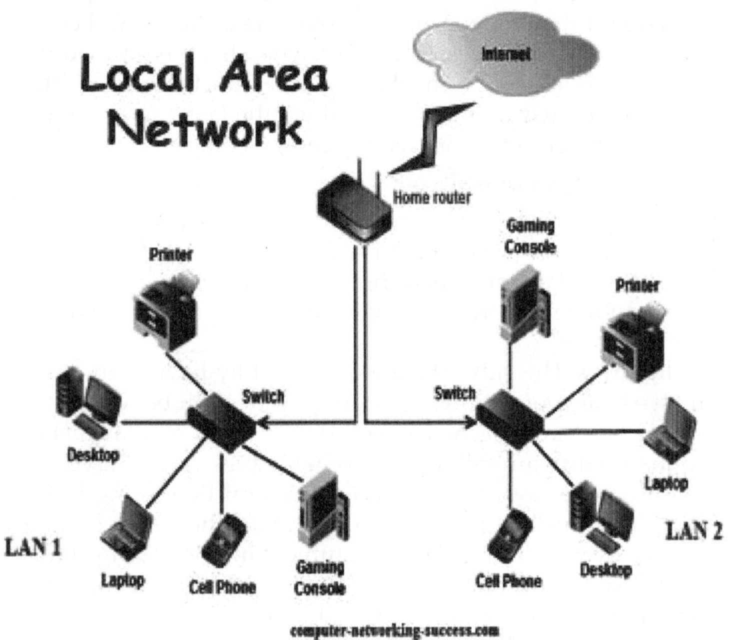

Figure 5.1 Typical LAN system in an organization

Advantages of LANs

(a) Local area networks allow sharing of expensive resources such as coloured laser printers and high capacity, high-speed mass storage devices among a number of users.

(b) Local area networks allow for high-speed exchange of essential information between key people in an organization. If properly managed, this sharing will promote greater efficiency and productivity and will lead to more sophisticated applications, such as electronic mail and company's Web site.

(c) Local area network provides the catalyst to increase the range of potential applications for PCs where an application package can be used by users.

(d) LANs contribute to increased productivity. A LAN installation should be studied closely in the context of its proposed contribution to the long-range interests of the organization.

In the case of a business, a LAN should be a visible contributor to increased profitability.

Disadvantages of LANs

(a) The financial cost of local area networking is still high. If one plans to use a network to share a laser printer, the user might find it cheaper to purchase another laser printer than to purchase networking hardware and software.

(b) Local area networking software requires memory space in each of the computers used on the network.

(c) Local area networking adds another level of complexity to the computer operation. Users may have difficulty in learning the network commands. The installation and management of a LAN requires more technical and administrative skills than installing and managing several computers that are not networked.

(d) Some control on the part of the user is lost. You may have to share a printer with other users. You may face a situation like, for example, the entire network suddenly locking up because one user has made a mistake.

(e) Some type of security system must be implemented if it is important to protect confidential data.

(f) Many current application programs will not run in a network environment. The program may require too much memory or have other technical constraints.

Characteristics of LANs

Local area networks are a specialized form of communication systems, however, there are three primary characteristics of LANs that distinguish them from wide area networks such as Telnet, Tymnet, CompuServe and the Public-Switched Telephone Network (PSTN). These are:

(a) LANs work in a restricted geographical area.

(b) LANs operate at relatively high speed when compared to the typical wide area networks currently in use.

(c) LANs are private networks, not subject to tariffs or other regulatory controls.

5.2.4 Wide Area Network (WAN)

WAN (Wide Area Network) is a digital communication system which interconnects different sites, computer installations and user terminals. It may also enable LANs to communicate with each other. This type of network may be developed to operate nationwide or worldwide. The transmission media used in WANs are normally public systems, such as telephone lines, microwave link and satellite links.

☞ *WAN is used to interconnect LANs which may be at opposite sides of a country or located around the earth's globe.*

Wide area networks WANs combine the continuous error detection and correction techniques included in synchronous communications with robust network problem determination and data routing to form powerful *backbones* that ensure high-quality, reliable service for end users. These networks allow multiple users to access a variety of host computers simultaneously through the same physical medium, while separating each user's session so that no user is aware of another on the network. Wide area networks also operate at speeds much higher than the 19,200-bps limit of normal voice-grade telephone lines.

Figure 5.2 shows a wide area network that a large company might use to connect regional computers. In this example, different centres, such as manufacturing, distribution and accounting are all connected to national headquarters and therefore to each other for communication purposes. Most WANs are complex and serve many users and many functions as compared to LANs.

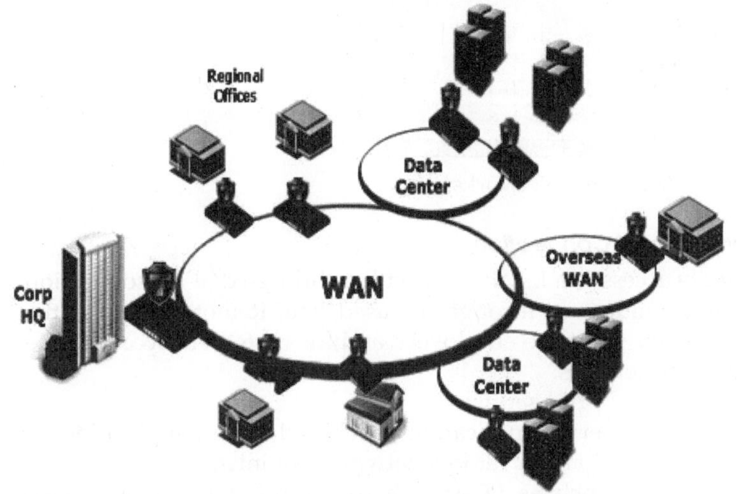

Figure 5.2 A wide area network connected to regional computers

WANs are typically created using specially conditioned telephone lines, microwave communications or satellite data transmission.

Some of the functions that can be performed on WANs are as follows:

Remote Data and Job Entry

It is possible to enter data for sales and transactions at the point-of-sale terminals using WANs. It is also possible to centralize this data in a computer for processing or reporting purposes. For example, Supermarkets in advanced countries connected through WANs can send all sales data from their remote sale centres and the central purchase and distribution centre can monitor all the sale figures on a day to day basis. The central distribution center can thereafter act to supply the grocery items needed in different supermarket branches based on the data collected from these branches. This helps the control of all the branches and timely supply of all the items to different branches.

Similarly, Remote Job Entry at colleges and universities enables faculty and students to write and execute their own programs on a central computer. For example, if all Indian Institute of Technology (IITs) are connected through WANs then the research projects can be implemented easily because a program developed at one of the IITs can be used on-line by students of other IITs and duplication of efforts can be avoided. This not only brings efficiency but also economy of efforts.

Centralizing Information

It is often convenient for a business to centralize regional/national information. For example, auto-part dealers can be helped in locating rare-auto parts using a centralized computer file of inventory items. WANs enable such dealers to query centralized databases.

Facilitating Communications

Corporations in advanced countries often use WANs to facilitate employee communications, to save on long-distance phone calls and letter writing, to cut costs on the preparation of written documents, and to overcome the time lags involved in overseas communications. Computer conferencing, in which users communicate with each other through their computer systems is another possible function of WANs.

Two particularly important types of WANs are:

(a) Hierarchical Networks
(b) Distributed Data-processing Networks

Hierarchical Networks Many WANs configure computers in a hierarchy and are therefore called *hierarchical networks*. The basic idea is that local minicomputers and microcomputers cluster around regional mini and Mainframe computers. This creates a reporting arrangement similar to the hierarchical relationships of an organizational chart. The most powerful computer of a hierarchical network is usually a large Mainframe computer. Often, a front-end processor is used on this Mainframe site to handle input/output, data communications, and computer security tasks of the system, enabling the back-end processor to perform the required data-processing jobs.

Distributed Data-processing Networks Distributed data-processing networks place computers or terminals at local or regional sites, thereby providing computer power (e.g. access to Mainframe computer resources) to these locations. A distributed data-processing system enables the sharing of many hardware and significant software resources among several users who may be located far away from each other.

Using WAN and Network Services

Many *wide area network services* are emerging these days due to the increasing demand of corporate business houses and public and private sectors.

Users are demanding Wide area network accesses that offer support for transmission of data, video, imaging, fax and voice. The primary driving forces of increased capacity and sophistication for wide area network services are:

(a) Host to terminal connection
(b) LAN to LAN connection
(c) Remote LAN connection

Host to Terminal Connection A terminal is an I/O (Input/Output) device, consisting of a keyboard and a monitor and the host is a back-end processing computer. Hosts and terminals may be located in different locations. Hosts can be connected to different terminals through local area network connections or through remote dial-up connections. User's commands are typically entered through a terminal. This information is transmitted to a host computer (generally Mainframe computer) over an Ethernet or Token Ring local area network connection. The mainframe computer processes the input and sends the output over the network to the terminal monitor. Thus, application runs in the host and the terminal does user interfacing function.

Terminals can be of two types:

(a) *Local Terminals*: It is directly connected to the host via a serial or LAN connection.
(b) *Remote Terminals*: It is connected to the host via a phone line with a modem at both the ends.

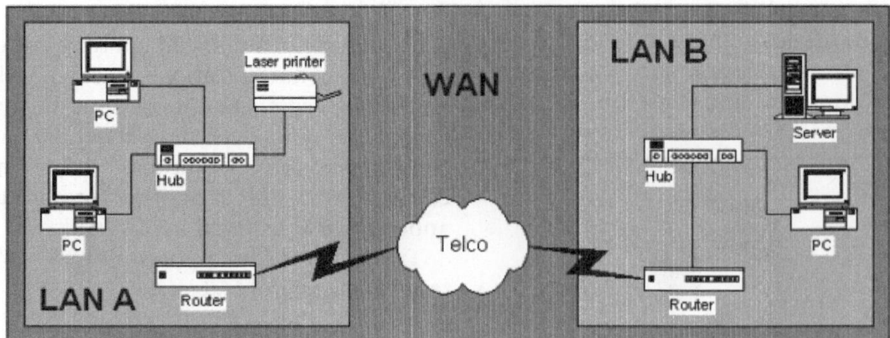

Figure 5.3 LAN to LAN connection via Wide Area Networks

LAN to LAN Connection Wide area networking may be used for communicating with devices that reside beyond one's local LAN. For the communication to take place, the two LANs must be in the same WAN. Routers can be used to connect LANs that employ similar protocols. Figure 5.3 shows the interconnection between two Ethernet LANs.

When two dissimilar LANs are to be connected, *tunnels* and *gateways* are made use of.

Tunnels are simple constructs that can be used to pass data packets through an otherwise incompatible network region. Data packets are encapsulated with a framing that is recognized by the network that transports it. The original framing and formatting of the data is retained inside the encapsulation.

A gateway is a device that is capable of interconnecting networks with dissimilar routing protocols.

☞ *A communication link that joins two or more LANs into a WAN is known as WAN link.*

WAN links can be grouped into the following three main categories:

(a) Circuit-switched services
(b) Leased lines
(c) Packet-switched services

Circuit-switched Services A temporary switched circuit established through the telecommunications system for the duration of the communication session. When the connection is terminated, the carrier's switches are freed up for other uses. Examples are modems and dial-up Integrated Services Digital Network (ISDN) connections.

Leased Lines These are dedicated connections that establish a permanent switched circuit that is always ready to carry network traffic.

An example of a leased line is a T1 line or fractional T1 line.

☞ *Leased lines are very expensive because they are dedicated to the customer even when they are not in use.*

Packet-switched Services

These are dedicated or dial-up connections to a public packet-switching network, such as X.25, a public frame-relay network, or even a Virtual Private Network (VPN). Intermediary switches send data packets along the best route possible by using the logical address of the destination node, which is contained in the packet header.

Remote LAN Connection

Remote access to a LAN can be either through dial-up connection using a modem or through a leased line. Remote access to the office LAN gives the employees and/or customers access to the following services:

(a) File and print services
(b) Client/Server applications, such as database applications
(c) Applications for remote network administration

Programs, such as PCAnywhere control the network-access remotely. However, since remote connection is mainly made using a slow modem, network-access control is often slow and jerky. But it provides high security, saves on hardware and licensing costs, and is simple to implement on a network.

Remote LAN connection allows users to access file, print and other services of the company from remote locations.

Advantages of WAN

- Messages can be sent very quickly to anyone else on the network.
- Share informtion/files over a larger area.
- Shared by all the computers on the network without having to buy a different peripheral for each computer such as printer or phone lines to the Internet.
- Large network cover

Disadvantages of WAN

- WAN is a very big and complex network
- It is slow in speed.
- Need a good firewall to restrict outsiders from entering and disrupting the network.
- WAN is not very much secured means not reliable.
- It is very expensive because we have to pay every time for transferring data.
- Very much dependency on the third party because it is public network.

Characteristics of WAN

- It connects devices the are separated by a wide geographical area than a LAN.
- Lower bandwidth compared to LANs.
- Typically interconnect multiple LANs
- Usually data communication equipment, is managed externally to organisations using the WAN.
- It use serial connection.

5.3 INTERNET

The Internet has been in a state of continuous evolution since the late 1960s. Some simplified descriptions of the Internet, are "a large computer network" or "network of networks", "an instantaneous and global messaging system". However, the Internet has become much more than this. It has grown into an important infrastructure supporting widespread, multi-disciplinary community. This community now consists of students, scientists and researchers, large corporations, non-profit organizations, government agencies, and individual consumers.

5.3.1 Concept of Internet

Internet is an interconnection between several computers of different types belonging to various networks across the world. It is a network of networks. Millions of people use the Internet to search and share information and ideas, etc. It has grown into an important infrastructure supporting a widespread, multi-disciplinary community. This community now consists of students, scientists and researchers, large corporations, non-profit organizations, government agencies, and individual consumers.

The Internet is an immensely complex combination of thousands of technologies and dozens of services used by millions of people around the world each day. Figure 5.4 shows a Web of computers which is laid around the globe. The Internet links thousands of computer networks. Every network and every computer in these networks exchange information according to certain rules called protocols. These different computers and networks are united with the common thread of two protocols, i.e., Internet Protocol (IP) and Transmission Control Protocol (TCP).

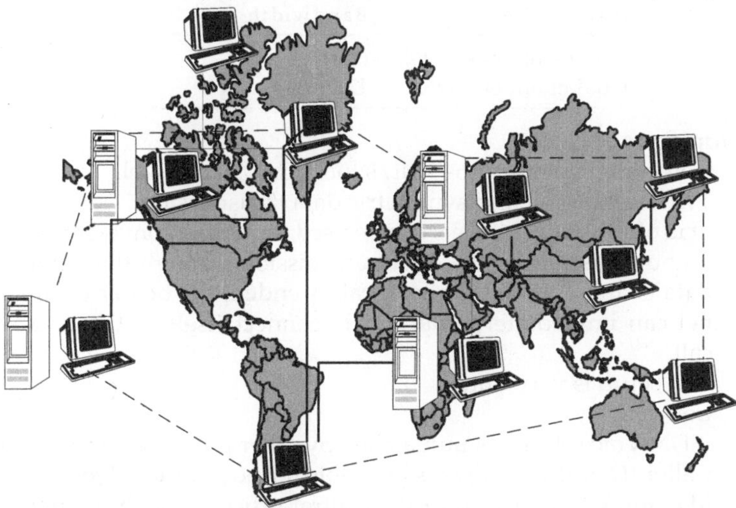

Figure 5.4 Internet as the network of computers connected with one another all over the world

5.3.2 Applications of Internet

With the help of Internet you can:

- Exchange messages using e-mail (Electronic mail).
- Transfer files as well as software.
- Browse through information on any topic on web.
- Communicate in real time (chat) with others connected to the Internet.
- Search databases of government, individuals and organizations.
- Read news available from leading news groups.
- Send or receive animation and picture files from distant places.
- Set up a site with information about your company's products and services.

Various Applications of the Internet

Internet applications are now widely available and continues to increase along with advances in information technology. Internet applications are then used in various fields such as academic, military, medical, media, and various other industrial sectors. Of the many existing Internet applications, the widely known and used, among others are: Word Wide Web (www), Electronic mail, mailing lists (mailing lists), newsgroup, Internet Relay Chat (IRC), File Transfer Protocol (FTP), Telnet, Gopher, and Ping.

5.3.3 Connecting to the Internet

To activate Internet services an Internet connection from a Internet Service Provider is required. To have a connection one needs to contact the Internet Service Providers. There are several Internet Service Providers (ISP) in each locality. There are some nominal charges that you need to pay to the ISP for the installation of the connection and for the rent (either monthly or annually). Depending on the requirement you can choose any one of the available options. If you need a high speed dedicated network then you can opt for a high bandwidth broadband or leased line connection.

If you need to have connection on a single PC then you choose a low bandwidth or dialup connection . For small services at your hand you can even have mobile phones connected to your Internet. There are many ways to get connected to the Internet.

You can get Internet connection in any of the following ways:-

1. **Through dial-up connection:** User is supposed to get connected to the internet after dialing up the number used for connection. This is useful if your network is either confined to small group of computers or for a single PC.
2. **Through leased lines:** In this a dedicated line is laid specifically for connection. Typically, leased lines are used by businesses to connect geographically distant offices. Unlike normal dial-up connections, a leased line is always active. For example, a T-1 channel is a type of leased line that provides a maximum transmission speed of 1.544 Mbps.
3. **Though broadband:** In this you can get a broadband connection which provides a high bandwidth for the internet connection. This also provides high-speed internet, also commonly called broadband internet, is internet access of at least 200 Kilobits per second (Kbps).

Now a days even wireless connections are available. For this you need to have a Wi Fi card attached to your computer which can be useful if you do not have proper place to lay down the wires.

To connect to the Internet you need a PC (personal computer) with requisite software including a browser, a telephone connection or a leased line, and a modem, which allows the PC to communicate with other computers.

Methods of Connecting to the Internet

There are a lot of different ways of connecting to the Internet today.

Dial-up Connections

There are many different ways to connect to the Internet. One of the most common ways is via a dial-up connection. With a dial-up connection, the Internet user can connect to the Internet via his telephone line and an Internet service provider.

Table 5.1 Five Categories of Dial-up Internet Connectivity

Bandwidth	Common Reference	Comments
14.4 Kbps	"fourteen-four"	The slowest analog dial-up connection in common use.
28.8 Kbps	"twenty-eight-eight"	The previous industry standard; now the second most common type of analog Internet connection.
33.6 Kbps	"thirty-three-six"	The most common type of analog Internet connection (27% of all connections)
56.6 Kbps	"fifty-six-K"	The fastest analog dial-up connection available; actually never faster than 53.3 Kbps
Integrated Services Digital Network	ISDN	A digital (not analog) dial-up connection type that is also available as a direct connection.
Digital Subscriber Line	DSL [in the forms of ADSL (the most common), HDSL, IDSL, SDSL, and VHDSL]	A digital connection that operates over common copper phone lines. DSL is the fastest dial-up connection type available. Few metropolitan cities in India currently offer DSL; very small installed base (25,000)

Dial-up connection is also known as Level Two connection. This provides connection to Internet through a dial-up terminal connection. The computer, which provides Internet access is known as 'Host' and the computer that receives the access, is known as 'Client'. The client computer uses modem to access a "host" and acts as if it is a terminal which is directly connected to that host. 56K modem access is now widely available and supported by most ISPs. It allows user to surf the Web at 56 Kbps with graphics. So this type of connection is also known as "Remote Modem Access" connection. And the host to which the client gets connected is actually connected to the Internet by a full time connection.

Dial-up Types and Bandwidth

A dial-up connection is categorized by the bandwidth it provides and whether it is analog or digital. Dial-up connectivity has evolved substantially in only a few years. Six categories of dial-up connectivity are available, as seen in Table 5.1 (top to bottom, slowest to fastest).

Your ISP or online service must support the type of modem you are using. If your ISP has installed 33.6 Kbps modems and you are using a 56.6 Kbps modem, your connection speed will only be 33.6 Kbps (because modems are bandwidth backward compatible).

ISDN Connections

ISDN stands for "Integrated Services Digital Network". ISDN is a data transfer technology, created in 1984, that can transfer data significantly faster than a dial-up modem. ISDN enables wide-bandwidth digital transmission over the public telephone network, which means more data can be sent at one time. It support transfer rates of 64K or 128K of data per second. While these speeds are faster than what you can get with a dial-up modem. The newer DSL technology can support even faster transfer rates and is less costly to set up and maintain.

The characteristics of ISDN are as follow:

- Both your PC and your ISP must employ special digital ISDN modems.
- A digital ISDN phone line from a local telephone provider is required.
- ISDN is unique among dial-up connectivity types because it is available in both dial-up and direct connection types.
- ISDN connections are defined in terms of channels; two channels can be combined to form a single data path. Thus, a "dual-channel" ISDN connection has a bandwidth of 128 Kpbs (2 x 64 Kbps), as shown in Table 5.2.

Table 5.2 ISDN Types and Speeds

ISDN Type	Bandwidth
Single-channel ISDN	64 Kbps
Dual-channel ISDN	128 Kbps

Advantages of ISDN

1. Constant data rate at 64 kbit/s for each DS0 channel.
2. Two way broadband symmetric data transmission.
3. One of the data channels can be used for phone conversation without disturbing the data transmission through the other data channel. When a phone call is ended, the bearer channel can immediately dial and re-connect itself to the data call.
4. Call setup is very quick.
5. Low latency.
6. ISDN Voice clarity is unmatched by other phone services.
7. Caller ID is almost always available for no additional fee.
8. Maximum distance from the central office is much greater than it is for DSL.
9. When using ISDN-BRI, there is the possibility of using the low-bandwidth 16 kbit/s "D" channel for packet data.

Disadvantages of ISDN

1. ISDN offerings are dwindling in the marketplace due to the widespread use of faster and cheaper alternatives.
2. ISDN routers, terminal adapters ("modems"), and telephones are more expensive than ordinary Plain Old Telephone Service (POTS) equipment, like dial-up modems.
3. ISDN provisioning can be complicated due to the great number of options available.
4. ISDN users must dial in to a provider that offers ISDN Internet service, which means that the call could be disconnected.
5. ISDN is billed as a phone line, to which is added the bill for Internet ISDN access.
6. "Always on" data connections are not available in all locations.

7. Some telephone companies charge unusual fees for ISDN, including call setup fees, per minute fees, and higher rates than normal for other services.

Broadband Connections

A high speed Internet connection is termed as a Broadband connection. A channel may be broadband if it sends a signal without modulation on a carrier. The signal covers the whole range of frequency that medium can carry. It services at a high-speed internet transmission (usually 256 Kpbs) a permanent connection.

A customer's basically use land line phone for getting this service. He can use his telephone for a normal telephone call even while he is browsing Internet. There is no separate telephone charges for the connection to the Internet. The access to the Internet will be around 8 times faster than a normal dial up access. The advantage are

(i) Low (ii) High (iii) No setup time (iv) Always On

Dial-up uses regular phone lines to connect, whereas broadband uses a variety of other means. There are different types of Broadband service. These are as follows:

Digital Subscriber Line

It is a high speed Internet Service, which allows Internet and telephone service to work over the same phone line as it is used to transmit digital data over telephone line. It is widely used in home and in small businesses as it works over a limited physical distance. DSL service can be delivered with wired telephone service on the same telephone line, as it uses high frequency bands of data. On customer side, a DSL filter which is present on each non-DSL outlet blocks high-frequency interference, thus enabling simultaneous use of the voice and DSL services.

Cable Broadband

Cable is another broadband connection option, where the cable operator provides the internet connection. It requires a special modem which is connected to the cable TV box. Majority of the cable companies provide packages which have telephone and TV channels as well as a broadband internet connection.

Leased Lines

A leased line is a telephone line that is directly form the telephone and sometimes is referred to as direct connections to the Internet. T-carrier Level (T1) line, enables data transmissions at speeds of 1.544 Mbps. A T-1 line actually consists of 24 individual channels, each of which supports 64 Kbps. Each 64 Kbps channel can be configured to carry voice or data traffic. Another type of leased line, Tcarrier Level 3 (T3) line, has a speed of about 43 Mbps. A T-3 line actually consists of 672 individual channels each of which supports 64 Kbps.

Satellite Broadband

Satellite is the ultimate option for people living in remote areas and who can not receive any other form of broadband internet. It requires the installation of a special satellite dish. There are mainly two types of connections: one-way connections and two-way connections. In the one-way connection, you will be able to receive data, but for sending data, you will need a dial-up modem through a telephone line or IDSN line. In the two-way connection, data is both sent and received through the satellite dish, though it is more expensive. Satellite transmission may be affected by weather conditions. The cost of installing and running satellite broadband can be quite expensive as compared with other types of broadband.

Getting Started with the Internet

➡ **To connect to the Internet, do this:**

1. Click on the **Start** button and then choose **Connect to** and then Select the connection, i.e., **MTNL1** (in our case) as shown in Figure 5.5.

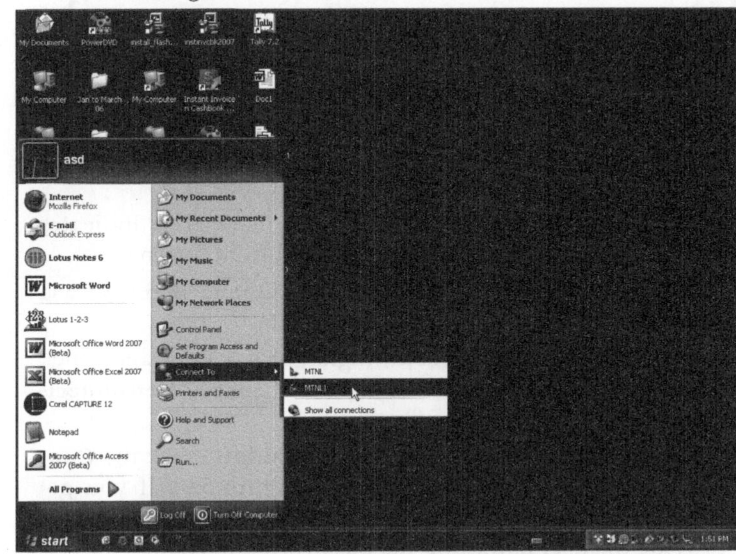

Figure 5.5 Connect to the Internet

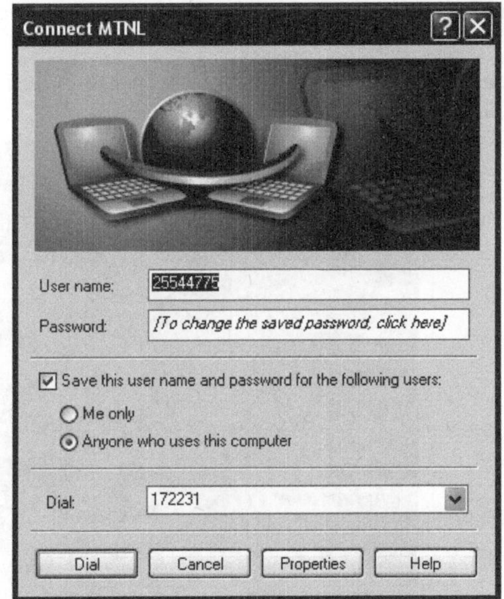

Figure 5.6 Connect MTNL Dialog box

2. A Connect MTNL dialog box appears as shown in Figure 5.6. In this dialog box, click **Dial** button. When you click on this button another dialog box appears as shown in Figure 5.7. This dialog box indicates that computer is dialing and trying to connect to the service provider.
3. Immediately Connecting to MTNL dialog box appears with message **Verifying user name and password**. After a few seconds computer is connected to the Internet.

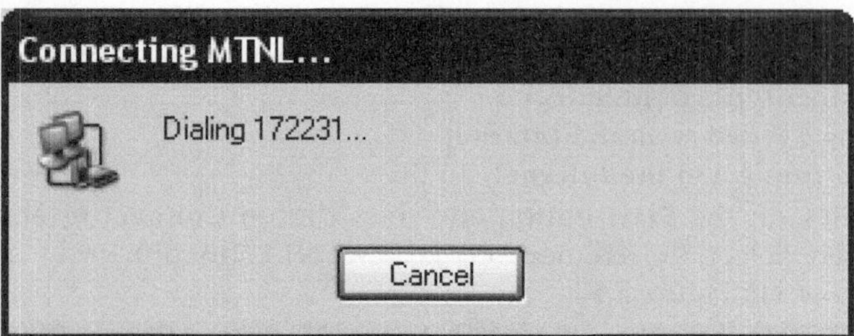

Figure 5.7 Dialing the number to connect to the Internet

➡ **To disconnect the Internet, do this:**

1. In the Right side of the task bar, double click the computers. A dialog box appears. In this dialog box, click **Disconnect** button to disconnect the Internet Connection.
2. You will see computers with cross (x) mark. This indicates that you have successfully disconnected from Internet.

➡ **To connect Internet using mobile broadband (here we use Reliance Broadband), do this:**

1. Click **Start** button on taskbar, highlight **All Programs**, click **Accessories** and then click **Reliance Netconnect-Broadband+** (See Figure 5.8).
2. In Reliance Netconnect-Broadband+ window, click the **Connect** to connect to the Internet (See Figure 5.9). If you get connected with Internet for the first time, you have to provide the user name and the password and change the settings according to your need.

➡ **To disconnect a mobile broadband Internet connection, do this:**

1. In Reliance Netconnect-Broadband+ window, click **Disconnect** (See Figure 5.10).

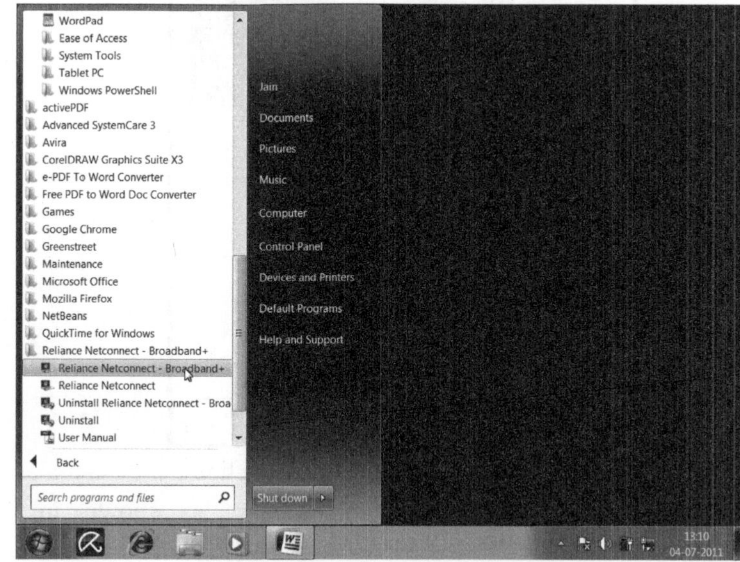

Figure 5.8 Connecting Internet

5.3.4 Troubleshooting

Any one of the following issues can cause problems when you try to communicate with a server on the Internet:

- The server is not functioning properly or has been temporarily disconnect from the Internet.
- Your Internet browser is not configured correctly.

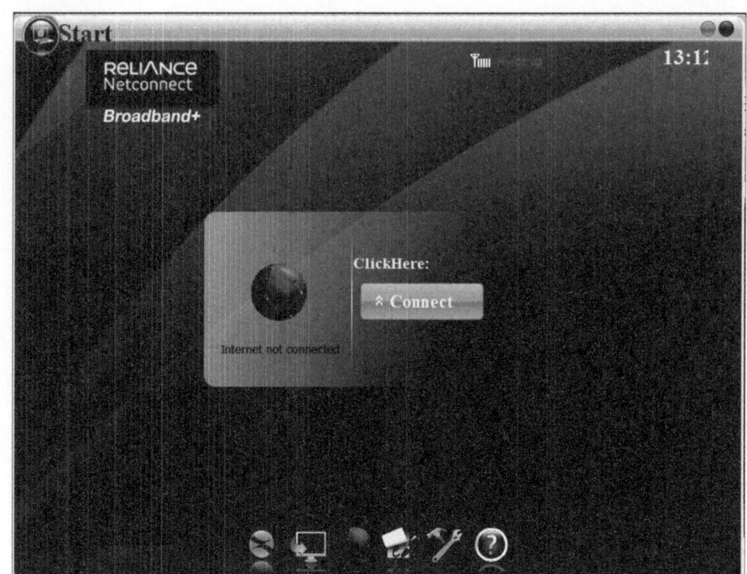

Figure 5.9 Connecting Internet using Reliance Netconnect-Broadband+

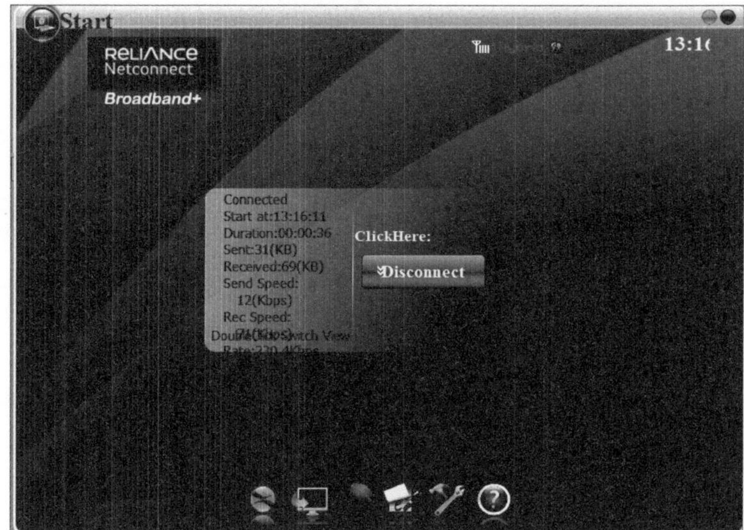

Figure 5.10 Disconnecting Internet

- The TCP/IP configuration for your dial-up connection to your ISP is incorrect.
- Your ISP's Domain Name Service (DNS) server is not working correctly.

Step 1: Configuring Internet Settings

1. This steps involves configuration of Internet settings to detect your Internet connection.

   IP Address
   Subnet Mask
   Default Gateway
   DNS Servers

   After getting the above details from your ISP, you need to view the current IP details on your PC by do the following:

   Go to **Start** menu and then choose **Run...** command. In the **Run** dialog box type cmd then press Enter key.

   Type IPCONFIG/ALL in the command prompt window. You will see the details of the router is used as shown in Figure 5.11.

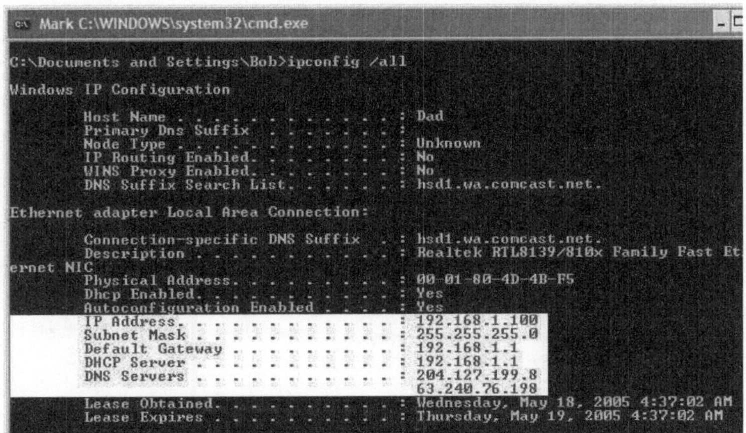

Figure 5.11 Showing the IP config command in the command prompt window

IP Address: If you have a router, common examples would be:
192.168.0.x, 192.168.1.x

Subnet Mask: Make sure you have the correct subnet mask. Most commonly this would be 255.255.255.0

Default Gateway: Make sure you have the correct Default Gateway IP address.

If the IP address that is displayed for your dial-up connection to your ISP does not match the IP address that your ISP gives you, change the IP address that is displayed so that it matches the address that your ISP has given you.

To connect ISP all details of connection at router, then router LAN gives Internet access to our computers.

DNS Servers: Make sure you have the correct DNS Servers. Sometimes this is the IP address of your router, so it would be the same as the Gateway IP.

2. Checking whether the Internet Protocol Suite (other known as TCP/IP) is configured correctly by performing a Ping test. Use the ping command to cause your modem to send test information.

   Go to **Start** menu and then choose **Run...** command. In the **Run** dialog box type ping, i.e., (router's address).
   e.g. ping 192.168.1.1
   If you get a reply, then your connection to the router is working.
3. You can also use the Windows Network Diagnostics tool together information about your Internet/Network connection.

   If you connect to a local network by using a network adapter and, at the same time, connect to your ISP by using a modem, configure your dial-up connection so that any routing conflicts are resolved in favour of your dial-up connection to your ISP. Follow these steps:
   - In **Control** Panel, double-click **Network Connections**.
   - Right-click your **Internet connection**, click **Properties**, and then click the **Networking** tab.
   - Click the **Internet Protocol** adapter, click **Properties**, and then click **Advanced**.
   - Click to select the **Use default gateway on remote network** check box, and then click OK.
   - Click OK.

Step 2: Make sure that your browser configuration is correct

Make sure that your Internet browser is correctly configured to connect to the Internet through the dial-up connection to your ISP, and make sure that your Internet browser is not configured to connect through a proxy server.

To verify these settings, start Internet Explorer, and then click Internet Options on the Tools menu click the connections tab, and then choose LAN settings. **Uncheck the Automatically detect settings** and **use a proxy server for your LAN** options to uncheck. Click OK and then click the apply button.

5.4 WORLD WIDE WEB (WWW)

The World Wide Web, or simply "the Web" is a global information system that is the fastest-growing area of the Internet. In other words World Wide Web is a series of servers that are interconnected through hypertext. *Hypertext* is a method of presenting information in which certain text are highlighted, that, when selected, displays more information on that particular topic (See Figure 5.12).

The Web, like all Internet services, is based on the interaction and transfer of data between special server computers (Web servers) and your PC (using Web browser software such as Internet Explorer from Microsoft).

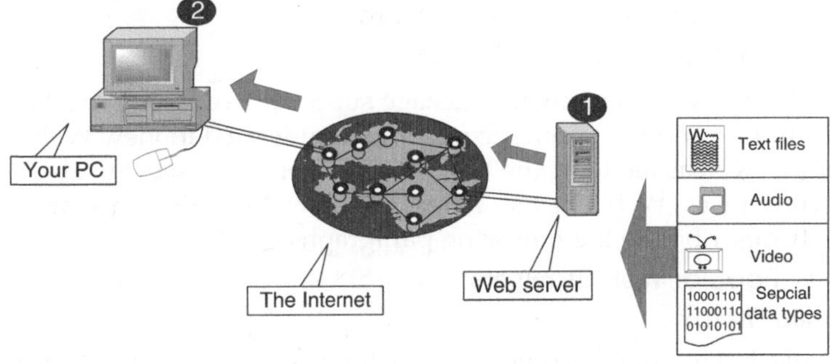

Figure 5.12 Some data types available on the Web

☞ *Different browsers may format and display the same file differently, depending on the capabilities of the hardware and the default layout options for the browser itself.*

How it Works?

1. The World Wide Web is the fastest growing and most innovative part of the Internet. When you browse the Web, you view multimedia pages composed of text, graphics, sound and video. The Web used hyptertext links that allow you to jump from one place to another on the Web. The language that allows you to use hypertext links and to view Web pages is called Hypertext Markup Language, more commonly knows as HTML.
2. The Web works on client/server model in which client software–known as Web browser–runs on a local computer. The server software runs on a Web host. To use the Web, you first make an Internet connection, and then launch your Web browser.
3. In a Web browser, you type the Uniform Resource Locator (URL) for a location you want to visit or click on a link that will send you to the desired location. The names for Web locations are URLs. Your Web browser sends the URL

request using HTTP (Hyper text Transfer Protocol), which defines the way the Web browser and the Web server communicate with one another.

4. URLs contain several parts. The first part–the http://–details which Internet protocol to use. The second part– the part that usually has a www in it–Sometimes tells what kind of Internet resource is being contacted. The third part –such as satishibm.com, can vary in length and identifies the Web server to be contacted. The final part identifies a specific directory on the server and a home page, document or other Internet object.
5. The request is sent to the Internet. Internet routers examine the request to determine which server to send the request to. The information just to the right of the http://in the URL tells the Internet on which Web server the requested information can be found. Routers send the request to that Web server.
6. The Web server receives the request using the HTTP protocol. It is told which specific document is being requested.
7. When the server find the requested home page, document, or object, it sends that home page, document, or object back to the Web browser client. The information is then displayed on the computer screen in the Web browser.

5.5 WEB BROWSING SOFTWARE

A Web browser is a software package supplied free by Microsoft Corporation and many other companies that is used to view Web pages as well as navigate the World Wide Web. Browsers are also referred to as Web clients. Three popular Web browsers are briefly described in the following paragraphs.

5.5.1 Popular Web Browsers

Mozilla Firefox

Mozilla Firefox has become popular because it is fast, full featured Web browser and makes browsing very efficient. Firefox includes pop-up blocking, tab-browsing, integrated Google searching, simplified privacy controls. It lets you cover tracks more effectively. A streamlined browser window that shows you more of the page than any other browser and has a number of additional features that work with you to help you get the most out of your time online. This browser is also available free of cost.

Safari

Safari is a very popular web browser among Apple computers. Safari is also the native browser on the iPhone and iPod touch. Safari is available for Windows, but has not reached a very high level of Windows users.

Microsoft Internet Explorer

This browser was made by Microsoft Corporation and bundled together into Windows operating system. The latest operating system, Windows comes with Microsoft's latest web browser named Internet Explorer 8. If you purchase a genuine copy of Windows you will get Internet Explorer 8 for free otherwise it is free for downloading from Microsoft's Web site (http://www.microsoft.com/ie/).

Google Chrome

Google built Google Chrome just for speed for any type of user to browse the Web. It has become popular due to its fast loading speed. Google Chrome designed with minimal-istic user interface. It is built with fast browsing engine.

➡ **To open Internet Explorer, do this:**

1. Click on the **Start** button.
2. Type Internet in the **Search box.**
3. Select **Internet Explorer** from the list of results (See Figure 5.13).

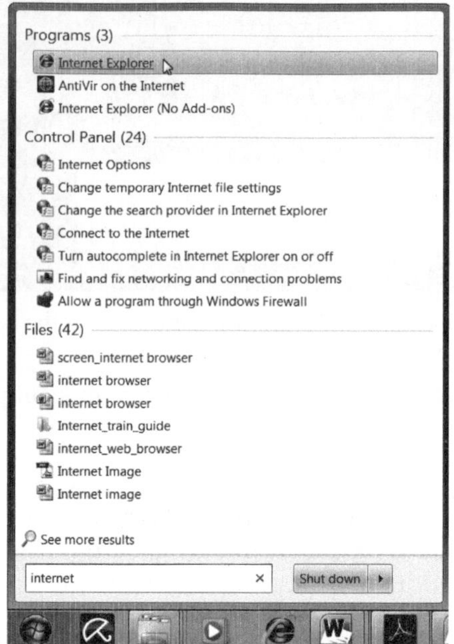

Figure 5.13 Selecting Internet Explorer from the start menu

4. Finally, press **Enter** key.

The part of Internet Explorer are explained below:

Title Bar—On the left the title bar displays the name of the Web page currently open and on the right side the maximize/minimize, restore and close buttons (See Figure 5.14).

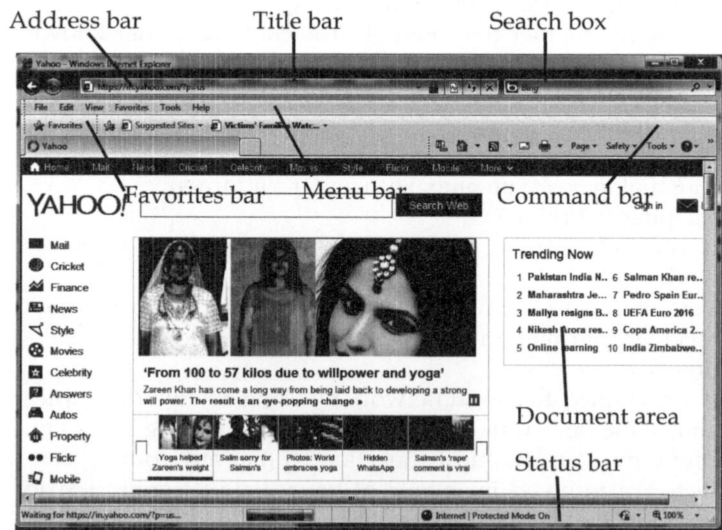

Figure 5.14 Different components marked as seen on Internet Explorer Window

Address bar—It displays the address of the page you are currently viewing. You can also use the Address bar for navigation. Type the address of a page you want to go to in the Address bar and press Enter key. Address Bar contains the following buttons:

- ***Back:*** Displays a page in the list of previously viewed pages.
- ***Forward:*** Displays a page in the list next to viewed pages.
- ***Stop:*** Stops downloading the current page.

Figure 5.15 Status bar

- *Refresh:* Displays the latest version of the Web page is displayed.

Search box—It is located in the upper-right corner next to the Address bar. To search any topic, type in the search box and then press Enter or click on the button.

Menu bar—This is located just below the Address bar and has the pull-down menu.

Command bar—The Command bar is located at the upper-right side of the Internet Explorer window and offers easy access to setting in Internet Explorer.

Favorites bar—The Favorites bar replaces the Links toolbar that appeared in previous versions of Internet Explorer. It provides one-click access to your favorite Web sites, as well as feeds and Web Slices.

Explorer animation—It is indicated when Internet Explorer is waiting to receive information from a computer on the Internet. The flag icon shimmers incase Internet Explorer is waiting.

Status bar—It gives you information about what Internet Explorer is currently doing.

Document area—It displays the Web page you are currently viewing.

The Status Bar

The *Status bar* provides information about the current state of the browser. The Status bar is organized into sections, with each section providing a different type of information (See Figure 5.15).

These sections are as follows:

1. On the left side of the Status bar is the current progress status. While you download a Web page, an icon and text in this area explains what the browser is currently doing. After the page has arrived, this area shows the address for any link you point to, and to the right of the progress status text is the Progress bar, which is active only while Internet Explorer downloads information. The bar fills up, as the data for the current page gets downloaded.
2. Middle section of the status bar is the security zones area. This area displays an icon and name for the security zone that the current Web page is in.
3. On the right side of the Status bar is an indicator showing the status of *InPrivate Filtering* and the *Zoom level.*

The Explorer Bar

An *Explorer bar* is a separate window pane. It is displayed on the left side of the Internet Explorer window that displays a specific kind of information. Internet Explorer has four different Explorer bars namely *Search, Favorites, History,* and *Channels,* such as *Adobe PDF, Research & Groove Folder Synchronization* (See Figure 5.16).

➡ **To display an Explorer bar do this:**

1. Click on the **Tools** button of the Command bar (See Figure 5.16).
2. Choose **Explorer Bars.**
3. Then click on the desired Explorer Bar.

➡ **To close an Explorer Bar, do this:**

1. click on the **Tools** button, choose **Explorer Bars** and then uncheck the desired explorer which you want to close or click the **X** (the close button) in the Explorer bar's upper right corner.

Figure 5.16 Explorer bar

Using Full Screen View

Internet Explorer provides a special view called full screen view. In full screen view, only the Status bar is normally visible. While working in full-screen mode, you can move the mouse pointer to the top of the screen to display the address bar, search box, tabs row, and Command bar. If you click in the search box or address bar, these interface elements remain visible while you type. As soon as you move the mouse pointer away or click in the page itself, they slide away again. In full-screen mode, Internet Explorer is maximized, even if it was previously not maximized. The Windows Taskbar is not visible in full screen view. However, You can still display the Taskbar by pressing the Windows logo key.

To switch from full screen view back to Internet Explorer's normal window, press F11 key.

➡ **To switch to full screen view, do this:**

1. Click on the **Tools** button of the Command bar.
2. Then click on **Full Screen**. *Alternatively* press **F11** key. (See Figure 5.17).
3. The screen displayed in Full Screen view.

Using Tabs and Tab Groups

Internet Explorer 8 (IE8) is a tabbed browser which allows you to keep multiple pages open in the same application window and switch between them quickly. It also adds the convenience of tab grouping. When you open a new tab by clicking a link in the current tab, Internet Explorer displays the original tab and the newcomer in the same color, showing you at a glance that the two tabs hold related content. Any additional tabs generate from pages in the current tab group also acquire the same color as shown in the Figure 5.18.

☞ *To open a new, blank browser tab, press Ctrl + T keys together or click **New Tab** button just to the right of the current tabs.*

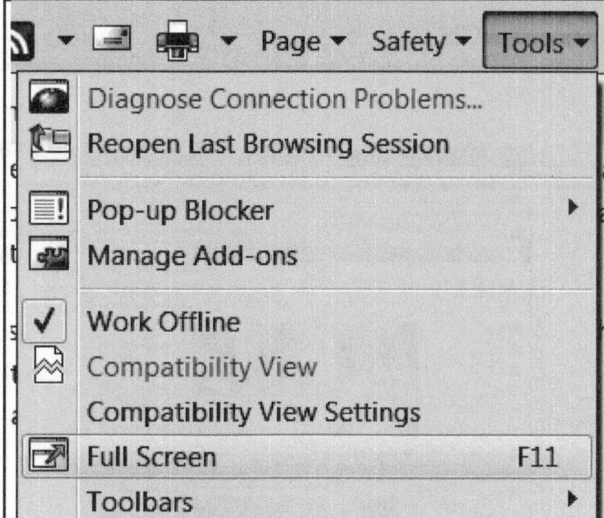

Figure 5.17 Selecting Full Screen

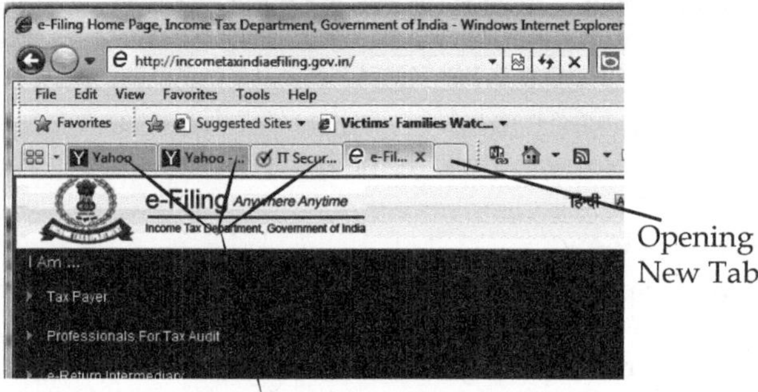

Related tabs (tabs that orginate from the same Web page) in Tabs groups

Figure 5.18 Tabs and Tab Groups

Quick Tabs

Quick Tabs window displays thumbnails of all tabs open in the current browser window as seen in Figure 5.19. Click once to thumbnail to switch to a tab, or click the × in the tab's upper right corner to close that tab.

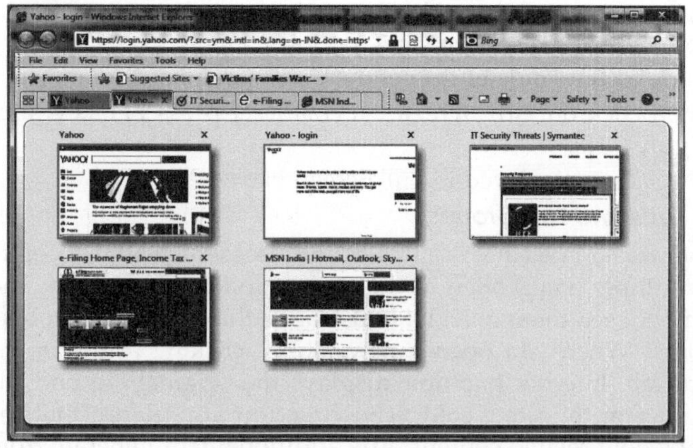

Figure 5.19 Quick Tabs

☞ *To see a visual display of all open tabs in the current browser window, click the **Quick Tabs** icon or press* Ctrl + Q *keys together.*

Configuring Web Browser

While using Internet Explorer you can customize the way the browser looks. displays information and operates.

➡ **To configure the Web browser do the following:**

1. Click the **Tools** menu and choose **Internet Options**. The **Internet Options** dialog box appears as shown in Figure 5.20.

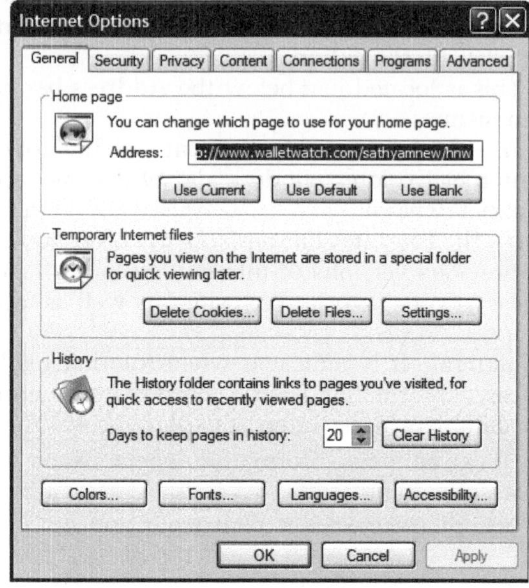

Figure 5.20 Internet Options dialog box

2. Home page is the first Web page that will be displayed when you open your browser. To set a Home page type the address of the page which you want to make home page in the Home page **Address:** Text box.
3. To use Internet Explorer, Web pages are saved along with graphics and other files included on a page. These files are stored in a subfolder called **Browsing history** in the main Windows folder. Click the **Delete Files**... button, to clear the disk space free.

Adjust the Temporary Internet Files and History Settings

4. Internet Explorer deletes temporary files when the folder exceeds a maximum size. To adjust the maximum, click the **Settings** button on the **General** tab to open the **Settings** dialog box. Click the up and down arrow spinner button where you want the set maximum to be. Click OK to confirm and return to the **Internet Options** dialog box. (See Figure 5.21).
5. History folder contains links to recently viewed web pages. You can specify the number of days to keep pages in history. You can also delete history by clicking on **Delete** browsing history on exit check box.

Change the Default Font

6. You can make many Web pages more readable by choosing different fonts for the text display. Click the **Fonts** button on the **General** tab to open the **Fonts** dialog box. To change default font, select a font for Web pages and a font for the text. Click OK to save the changes (See Figure 5.22).
7. After you have finished changing the settings in the **Internet Options** dialog box, click OK to save your settings and close the dialog box. The next time you start your browser, all your new settings will be active.

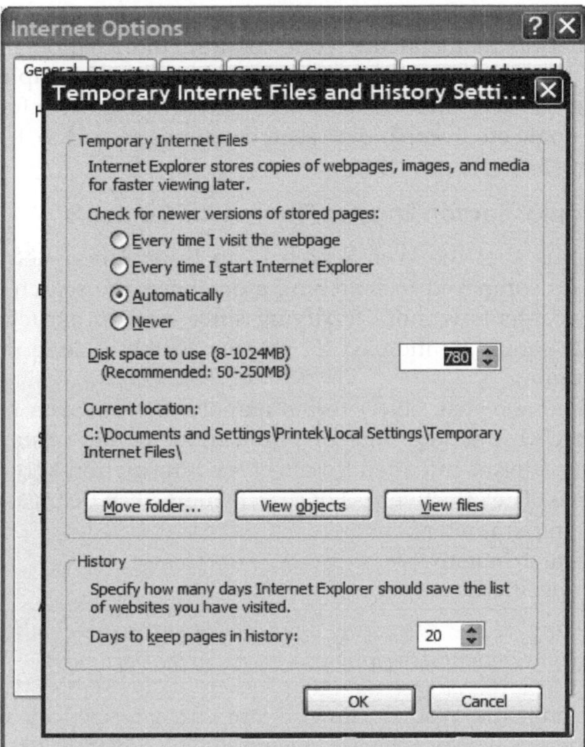

Figure 5.21 History Settings dialog box

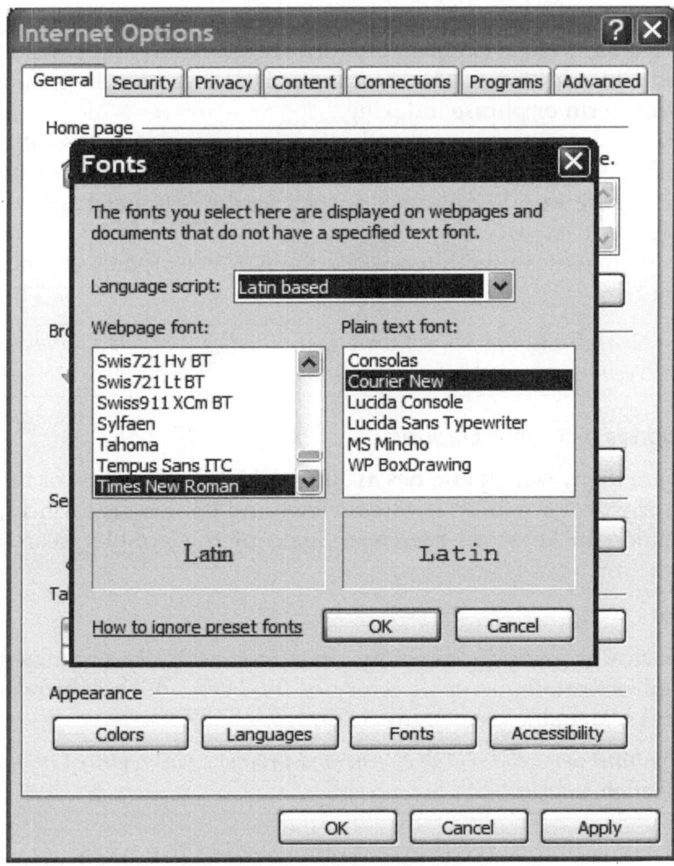

Figure 5.22 Fonts dialog box

Returning to Sites through History

To return to a site you visited in a previous session, or to a site that is many steps back from your current location, you will need to use Internet Explorer's History feature. Internet Explorer hides the History list as a tab within the Favorites Center.

☞ *You can sort the History list in a variety of ways. More important, you can search through it.*

➡ **To open History Explorer Bar, do this:**

1. Click on the **Tools** button of the **Command** bar.
2. Choose **Explorer Bars**.
3. Then click on the **History**. (See Figure 5.23)

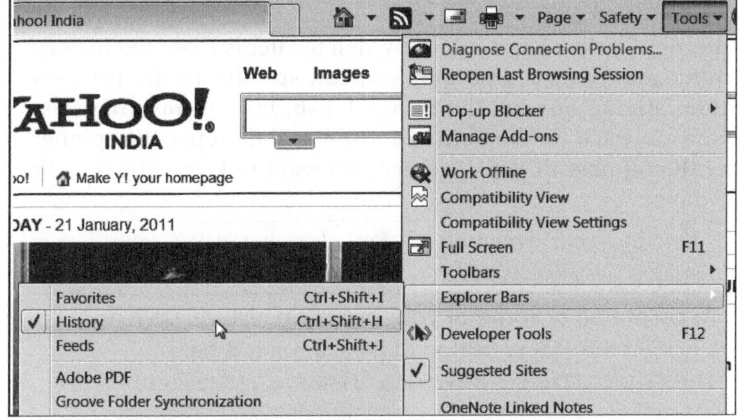

Figure 5.23 The History Explorer bar

A pane on the left side of the Internet Explorer window shows a list of pages you have visited, that are sorted by date and then by site. You can sort the History list in various ways as shown in Figure 5.24.

Figure 5.24 Selecting View by Site

More important, History list includes a search command to help you search important page or site you have surf in recent days (See Figure 5.24).

Delete Browsing History When you browse the Web, Internet Explorer stores information about the Web sites you visit, as well as information about that Web sites frequently ask by you to provide (such as your name and address). Internet Explorer stores the following types of information:

1. Temporary Internet files
2. Cookies
3. A history of the Web sites you've visited
4. Information that you've entered into Web sites or the Address bar
5. Saved Web passwords

Internet Explorer automatically deletes items from the history list after a period of time that you can specify. In the **Internet Options dialog box**, on the **General Tab**, in the **Browsing History** group, click on the **Setting button** and then use the spinner to set the number of days' history you want to keep. The default is 20 days.

☞ *Deleting your browsing History does not delete your list of favorites or subscribed feeds.*

➡ **To delete all or some of your browsing history, do this:**

1. Click on the **Safety** button of the **Command** bar.
2. Then choose **Delete Browsing History...** . (See Figure 5.25)

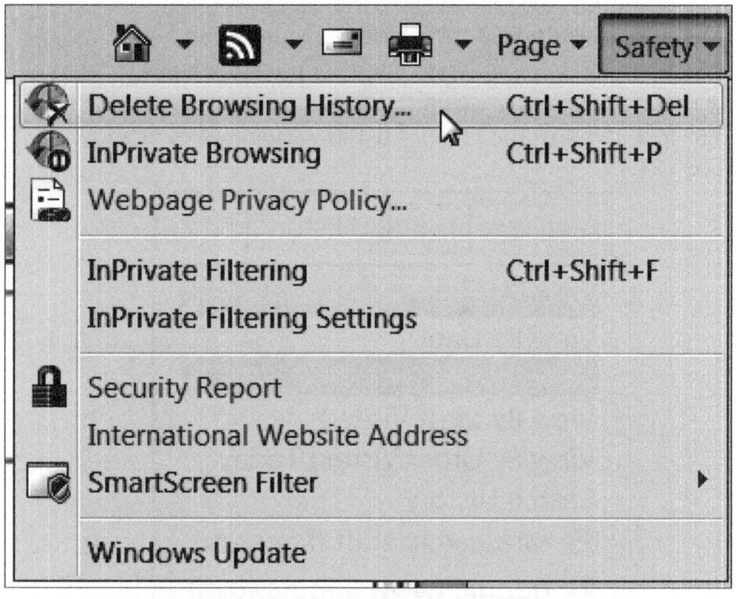

Figure 5.25 Delete Browsing history

3. Select the check box next to each category of information you want to delete.
4. Select the **Preserve Favorites website data** check box if you do not want to delete the cookies and files associated with websites in your Favorites list.
5. Then click **Delete**.

5.6 SEARCH ENGINES

A Web search engine is used to search for information on the Internet. The search results are generally presented in a list and are often called *hits*. The information may consist of Web pages, images, and other types of files.

A search engine is a program which looks through its database for information that matches your request. Information in the database are about websites and their contents. Examples of search engines are, Alta Vista, Yahoo, Hot Java Excite, Infoseek, HotBot, Google etc. Some Indian search engines are Jadoo, Khoj, I love India, 123 India etc.

5.6.1 Popular Search Engines/Search for Contents

We can think that the Web Search is an Information Retrieval Problem. As compared to searching a database, the search for a document contents is more terrifying since it is not structured. Documents should be indexed for making search easier and less time consuming.

Each document has object terms namely, the author's name, document URL and the date of publication. It may also have non-objective terms intended to reflect the information known as *content terms*. The effectiveness of search engine can be measured by two main parameters:

- Indexing exhaustivity
- Term specificity

☞ ***Indexing*** *is the processing of a document representation by assigning content descriptions or terms to the document.*

In Indexing, the Web documents are characterized by recall (ratio of the number of relevant documents retrieved to the total number of documents retrieved). This function can be performed either manually or automatically. But many of Web sites render manual indexing quite impractical.

Automatic indexing includes single term indexing, statistical methods, as well as information theoretical and probabilistic methods. In addition to this, automatic indexing uses linguistic and multi-term or phrase indexing.

Since the Internet is a vast collection of information, it is difficult to find specific information you actually need. Therefore, the search feature in a Web browser, such as the Internet Explorer provides an easy access to a special facility called *search engine*. Search engines scan the Internet for the words or topics you are looking for.

☞ *A* ***Search Engine*** *is a software that searches through a database of Web pages for specific information.*

Categories of Search Engines

There are many search engines available on the Web. Most of the search engines provide Web site reviews and homepage services, in addition to keyword searches. Some of the popular search engines are:

Yahoo!

It is basically a search directory. It is hierarchically organized with subject catalogue or directory of the Web which is browsable and searchable (See Figure 5.26).

☞ ***Yahoo!*** *is a good search engine and provides you required information quickly.*

Links to various services are accomplished in two ways:

a. By user's submissions.
b. Through robots that retrieve new links from known pages.

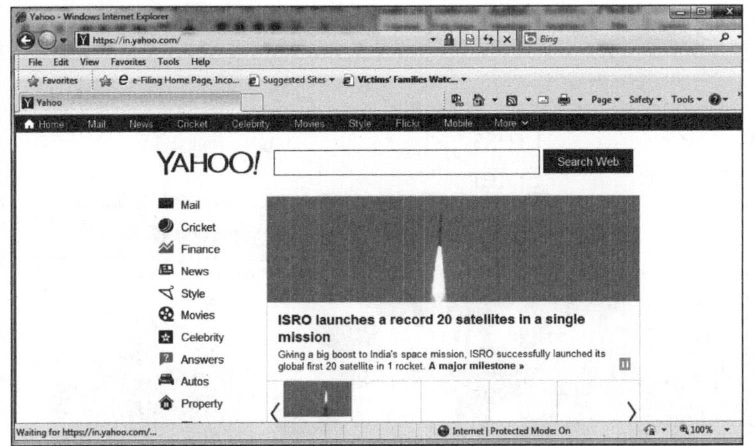

Figure 5.26 A view of Yahoo! Web site

Yahoo! Indexes Web pages, Usenet and e-mail addresses. This search engine has 14 categories listed on its home page. Each of these categories is divided into several subcategories. A search box is provided for user search in all these options.

You can search Yahoo! in two modes:

a. Yahoo! Search page
b. Yahoo! Search options

Yahoo! Search page uses operators, such as (+) inclusive and (-) exclusive, etc. Yahoo! Search options are meant to get switches for fine-tunning your search. These switches use relevancy ranking in obtaining the query output. The query output is a list of documents and related Yahoo! categories, along with the first few lines of the document.

If the search request fails in Yahoo!, it is automatically routed to AltaVista for more search. Yahoo! offers a lot of extra services like free e-mail accounts, region-specific sites, searches to locate people, site reviews, and a customisable news page.

Bing

Bing is a search engine from Microsoft that was launched on May 28, 2009. It is designed to return search results in a format that organizes answers to address your needs. When you search on Bing, in addition to providing relevant search results, the search engine also shows a list of related searches on the left-hand side of the search engine results page (SERP). You can also access a quick link to see recent search history.

Bing launched with several features that are unique in the search market. For example, when you mouse-over a Bing result a small pop-up provides additional information for that result, including a contact e-mail address if available.

Opera

Open PLC European Research Alliance (OPERA) is a web browser developed by Opera Software. The latest version is available for Microsoft Windows, OS X, and Linux operating system. Opera siblings are Opera Mobile, Opera Mini and Opera Coast – work on devices running Android, iOS, Windows Phone, Symbian, Maemo, Bada, BlackBerry and Windows Mobile operating systems, while Opera Mini runs on Java ME-capable devices.

It is the first browser with tabs, RSS support, and built-in BitTorrent client and tab thumbnails. It allows for duplication of tabs, Goto URL feature for web address that is not hyperlinked, fitting to window size, rewinding, crash recovery, page zoom, instant back, tab closing etc.

MSN

Acronym for the Microsoft Network. The network includes web-based programs and services offered by Microsoft Corporation. MSN offers a range of services including news, search engines, user-driven forums, instant messaging, e-mail, and services to connect to the internet. Microsoft Windows users are able to synchronize their computer system with online services offered as a method of centrally organizing and managing tasks.

In 1996, MSN 2.0 offered a version of Internet Explorer for Web access titled MSN Program Viewer. In addition to dial-up, MSN also partnered with Verizon and other carriers to offer DSL connections. Later, the MSN brand was retained for Internet access and the general portal, while Web-based services such as e-mail and messaging migrated to the Windows Live platform.

Ask.com

Ask.com (originally known as Ask Jeeves) is a question answering-focused e-business and web search engine founded in 1996 by Garrett Gruener and David Warthen in Berkeley, California. The Ask browser toolbar is an extension that can appear as an extra bar added to the browser's window. It was often unintentionally installed during the installation of partner software, including Oracle Java, i.e., taking advantage of a user's lack of technical experience.

Google

Google is an interesting search engine having many unique features. For example, you want search company information. It is useful for company searches because of the unusual way it ranks Web sites. Type `http://www.google.com` in the Address bar and press Enter to go to the Google homepage. When you are there, type the company name in the search box and click the Google Search button. Google is so good at finding the best matching Web sites in a search, it offers a feature to automatically look for the best possible match and load it. To use this feature, type a company's name in the search box and click the I'm Feeling Lucky button. It gives the related company information.

Searching Information on Google Web Site

1. Open www.google.com Web site.
2. Type one or more search terms into the search box that best describe the information you want (See Figure 5.27).

Figure 5.27 Google Search

3. Then Press Enter key or click on **Google Search** button.
4. Google produces a list of web pages related to your search terms.

☞ *A search engine continuously sends out the so-called spiders, which start on a homepage of a server and pursues all links step-by-step.*

Basics of Google Search

1. Choosing the right search terms is the key to finding the information you need. It is advisable to use multiple search terms. Choose your search terms carefully because Google looks for the search terms you select.
2. Google searches are not case sensitive. All letters, regardless of how you type them, will be understood as if written in lower case.
3. By default, Google only returns pages that include all of your search terms. There is no need to include "and" between the terms. Keep in mind that the order in which the terms are typed will affect the search results. To restrict a search further, just include more terms.
4. Google ignores common words and characters, such as "where" and "how", as well as certain single digits and single letters, because they tend to slow down your search without improving the results.
5. When you want results that include an exact phrase, simply put quotation marks around such search terms. For example "Mother Teresa".
6. If your search term has more than one meaning, you can focus your search by putting a minus sign ("-") in front of the words related to the meaning you want to avoid.

5.6.2 Accessing Web Browser

Internet Explorer makes it easier to get the most from the World Wide Web, whether you are searching for new information or browsing your favourite Web sites.

➡ **To access Web browser do this:**

1. Click the **Start** button highlight **Programs** and then select the **Internet Explorer** or any other popular browser's name.
2. The starting page is called the browser's home page, and it can be set to any page on the Internet.

Enter a Web Page Address

If you know the address of a specific Web page, you can type the address into the Web browser and the program will display the page. Internet Explorer's Address bar list the Web page addresses you have entered most recently. By pulling down the list you can see these recent addresses and select one to return to that site.

➡ **To type a Web page Address, do this:**

1. Click in the address bar.
2. Type the address of the Web page. For example, we have type http://gmail.com (See Figure 5.28).
3. Click the **Go** button or press **Enter**. The Web page appears (Figure 5.29).

☞ *Most Web addresses begin with http://. You can leave off these characters when you type your address, Internet Explorer adds them automatically.*

➡ **To redisplay a Web page, do this:**

1. Click drop-down arrow in the address bar.
2. A list of the addresses you have typed appears (See Figure 5.30). Select the desired site address you want display. That Web page appears.

Figure 5.28 Type the address in the address bar

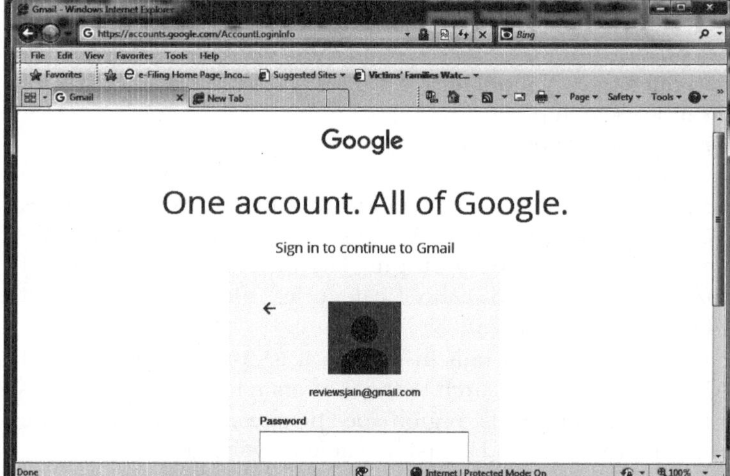

Figure 5.29 Gmail Web page appears

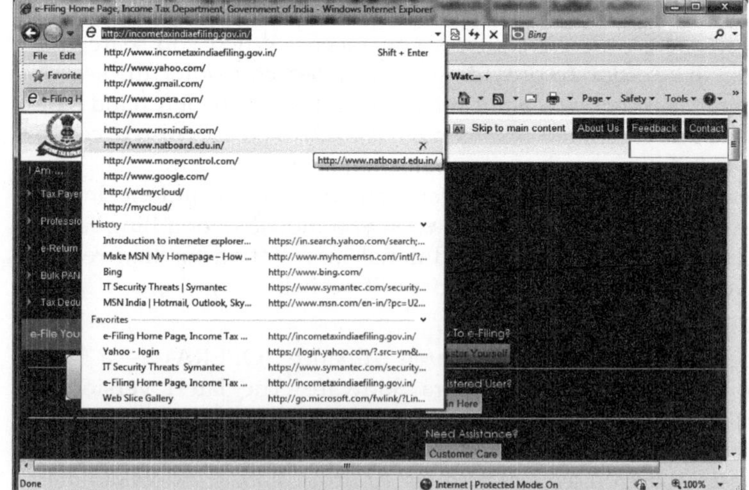

Figure 5.30 List of previous Web page addresses

Open a Web Page in a Tab

You can make it easier to work with multiple Web pages simultaneously by opening each page in its own tab. When you use a Web browser normally, each page appears in the main part of the browser window, which is usually called the content area. A tab is like a second content area and it appears *behind* the first one, with only a small tab visible. Click the tab and you see the second content area and its loaded Web page. You can open as many pages as you want in their own tabs.

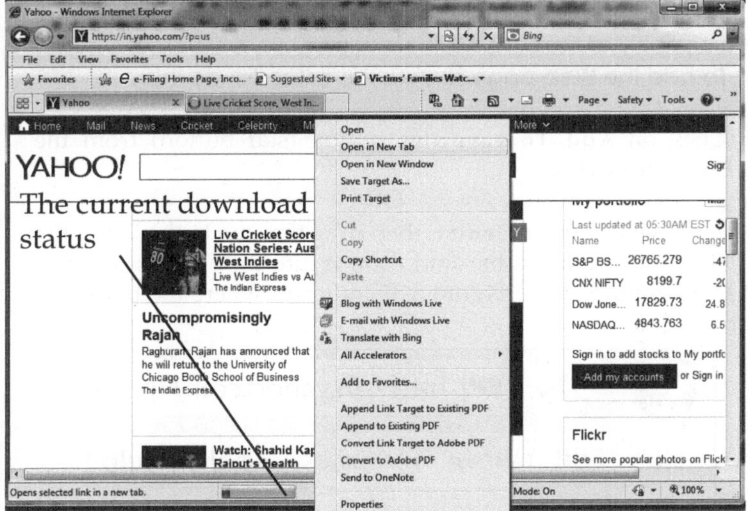

Figure 5.31 Open in New Tab

1. Right-click the link you want to open.
2. Click **Open in New Tab** (See Figure 5.31).
3. A new tab appears with the page title (See Figure 5.32).
4. Click the tab to display the page.

You can also open a page in a tab by holding Ctrl while clicking the link. If you press Ctrl + Shift while clicking a link, the tab displays automatically. If you type an address, press Alt + Enter to open the page in new tab.

➡ **To Navigate Tabs, do this:**

1. Click the **Tab Left** button or the **Tab Right** button to display the tab you want (See Figure 5.33).

☞ *You see the Tab Left and Tab Right buttons only if Internet Explorer does not have enough room to display all the tabs.*

2. Click the tab. The Web page loaded in the tab appears.

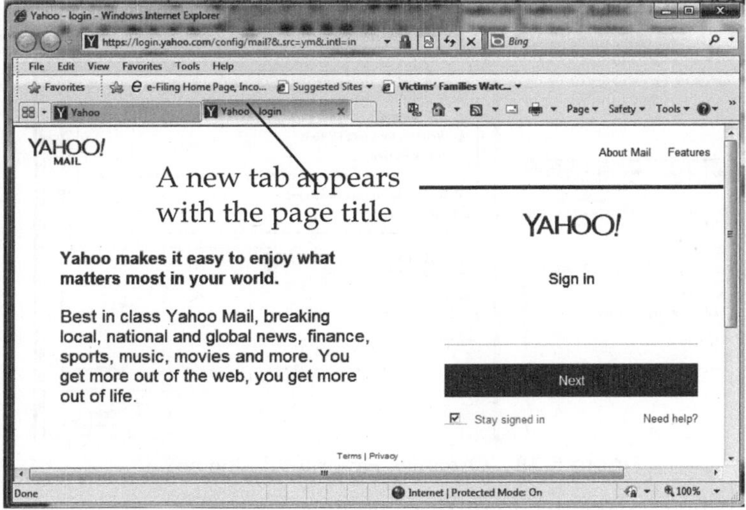

Figure 5.32 A new tab with the page title

Figure 5.33 Navigate tabs through Tab left and Tab right arrow

Navigate Web Pages

After you have visited several pages, you can return to a page you visited earlier. Instead of you retype the address or look for the link, Internet Explorer gives you some easier methods.

When you navigate Web pages, you can go back to page you have visited in the current browser. After you have done that, you can reverse and go forward through the pages again.

Go Back One page

1. Click the **Back** button. The previous page you visited appears.

Go Back Several Pages

1. Click the **Recent Pages**. A list of the sites you have visited appears.
2. The current site appears with a *check mark* beside it (Figure 5.34).

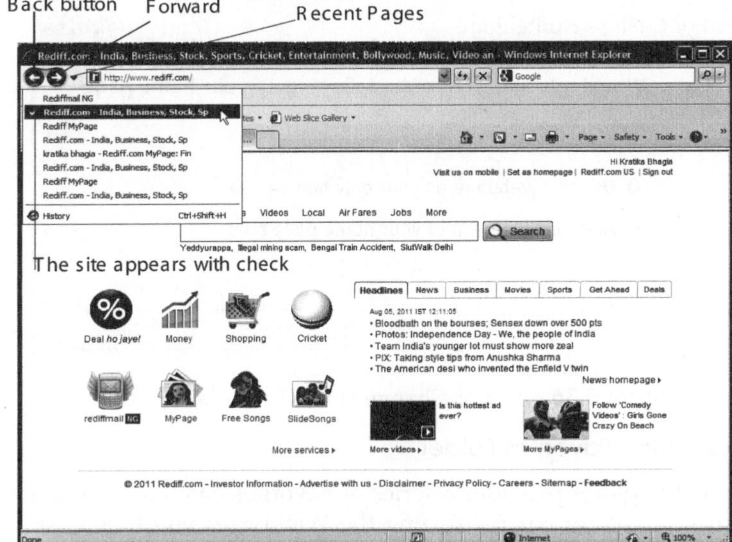

Figure 5.34 Recent pages list

3. Items listed below the current site are ones you visited prior to the current site.
4. When you position the mouse over a previous site, Internet Explorer displays the **Go Back** arrow.

5. Click the page you want to display. The page appears.

Go Forward One Page

1. Click the **Forward** button. The next page visited appears.

☞ *If you are at the last page of selected link the Forward button is not active.*

Setting the Home Page

While browsing, it is easy to get puzzled wandering around the Web. Therefore, you should designate one page or multiple pages as your home page. Home page is the first page which appears after opening a Web browser. It is also known as by different name like 'front page' 'start page' or 'Web page'.

➡ **To set the home page, do this:**

1. Open a site which you want to set as your home page.
2. Click on the arrow next to Home button of the command bar as shown in Figure 5.35.
3. Then choose Add or Change Home Page as shown in Figure 5.33.
4. The **Add or Change Home Page** dialog box appears as shown in Figure 5.36.
5. In this dialog box, select an option according to your need.
6. Then click **Yes** button.

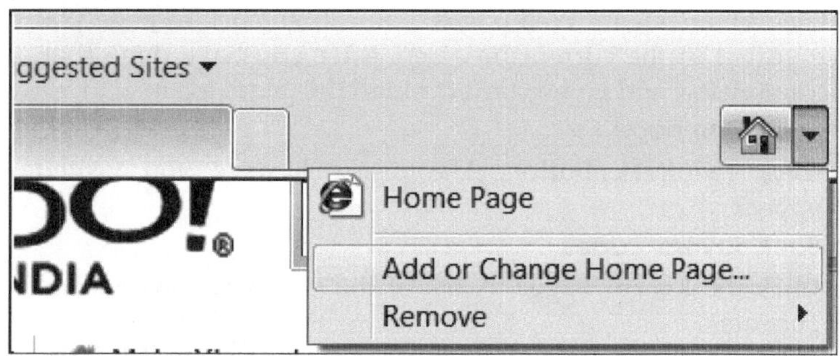

Figure 5.35 Selecting home in the command bar

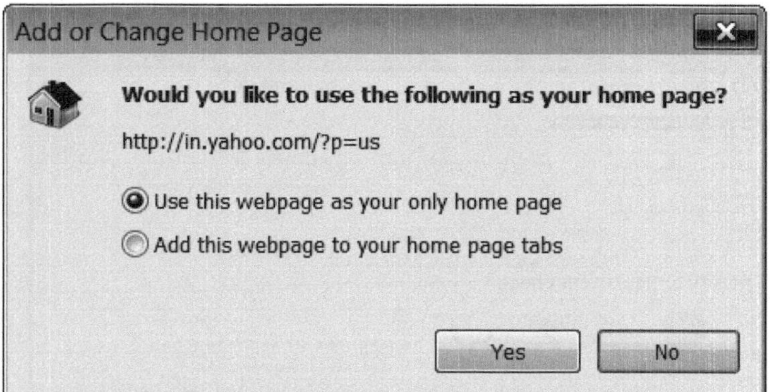

Figure 5.36 Add or Change Home Page dialog box

5.6.3 Using Favorites Folder

Internet Explorer provides a series of Favorites commands and a Favorite Explorer bar for surfing the Web pages you like most. Using Favorites commands, you can create a list of favorite pages and organize them into folders. Then, to go to a favourite page, you simply select the page you want from the Favorites menu.

To display your saved favorites in the Favorites Center, click on the **Favorites icon** from the Favorites bar.

Adding an Item to Favorites

Internet Explorer makes it easy to add the currently displayed webpage or an entire group of tabs to your Favorites. The Add To Favorites command allows you to create a favorite-page listing for the page you are currently viewing.

➡ **To add the Web page to your Favorites list, do this:**

1. Click Command bar.
2. Click on **Add To Favorites** button (star button) from the **Favorites Center**.

OR

3. Open the **Favorites Center**, then drag the icon to the left of the URL in the address bar and drop it into the Favorites bar. A Move button in the Figure 5.37 indicates where the page will be added.

Figure 5.37 Favorites center

☞ *If the Favorites bar is not displayed just to the left of your browser tabs, press* Ctrl + Shift + I *or* Alt + C *key together to open the Favorites Center.*

Organize Favorites

This command permits you to view, organize, and return to your favorite pages. The Organize Favorites dialog box's buttons are used to add subfolders to your Favorites tree, move items between folders, rename folders and shortcuts, and delete folders.

➡ **To open Organize Favorites dialog box, do this:**

1. In the Favorites Center, click the down arrow next to **Add to Favorites**.

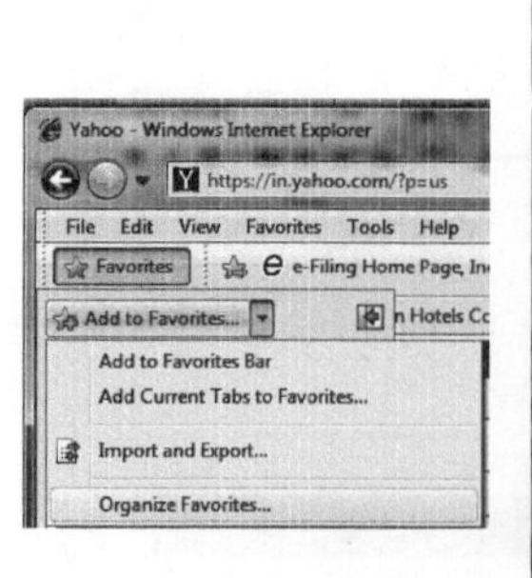

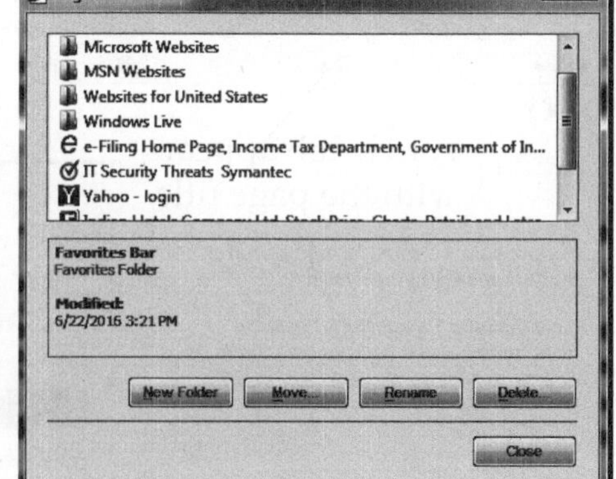

Figure 5.38 Organize Favorites dialog box

3. Choose **Organize Favorites...** option.

4. It will display **Organize Favorites** dialog box as shown in Figure 5.38.
5. The dialog box's button provide a quick way to create new folders, rename items, and organize things as you like.

5.6.4 Downloading Web Pages

Uploading is the transmission of a file from one computer system to another, usually larger computer system. From a network user's point-of-view, to upload a file is to send it to another computer that is set up to receive it. People who share images with others on Bulletin Board Services (BBS) upload files to the BBS.

Transmission in the other direction is downloading -- from one, usually larger computer to another, usually smaller computer. From an Internet user's point-of-view, downloading is receiving a file from another computer.

The FTP is the Internet facility for downloading and uploading files. (If you are uploading a file to another site, you must usually have permission in advance to access the site and the directory where the file is to be placed).

When you send or receive an attached file with an e-mail note, this is just an attachment, not a download or an upload. However, in practice, many people use "upload" to mean "send" and "download" to mean receive.

In short, from the ordinary workstation or small computer user's point-of-view, to upload is to send a file and to download is to receive a file.

The Web is one of the most popular components parts of the Internet. The Web is made up of hypertext documents stored on many servers around the world.

☞ ***Hypertext documents*** *contain links you can click on to move to another section of the page, to different documents, or to another type of Internet resource, such as electronic mail (e-mail) or newsgroups.*

Web pages include text, graphics, animation, sound, and sometimes movies also. The rich content, along with the ability to jump from one page to other page using links, has contributed to the explosive growth of the Web.

For example, you have found a file that you want to save. As a example, let us imagine you are researching an art course paper and want to save an entire page.

➡ **To download a web page, do this:**

1. Click the **File** menu and choose **Save Web page** dialog box appears as shown in Figure 5.39.
2. Notice that there is a default value in the **File name:** text box. Either accept this name or change it to something appropriate.
3. Choose the Location you want to save the file in the **Save in:** list box.
4. Then click **Save** button to save the file.

5.6.5 Printing Web Pages

As you browse, you may come across pages containing information that you want to keep as hard copy. Internet Explorer (IE) 8.0 provides many print options. These are:

- Printing all documents linked to the current page
- Printing a list of links contained on the current page
- Printing selected portions of a page that has been constructed using frames. This option is available only if the current page has frames.

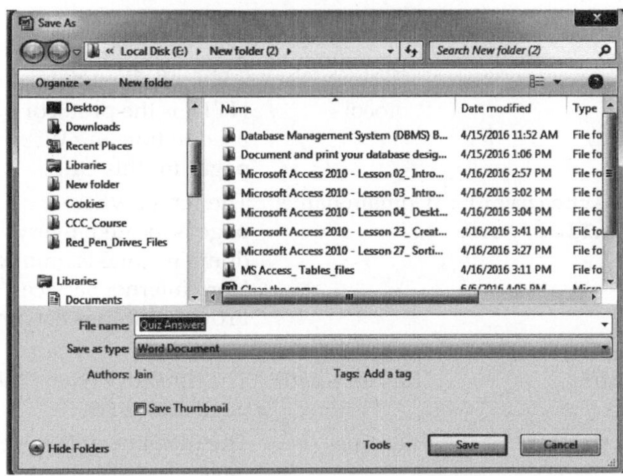

Figure 5.39 Save Web page dialog box

➡ **To print a Web page using the Print dialog box, do this:**

1. Click on the **File** menu and choose **Print**. Or
2. Click on the arrow next to **Print** button on the Command bar.
3. Then choose **Print Option**.
4. A Print dialog box appears as seen in Figure 5.40. In this dialog box, select the printer, pages, and number of copies you want.

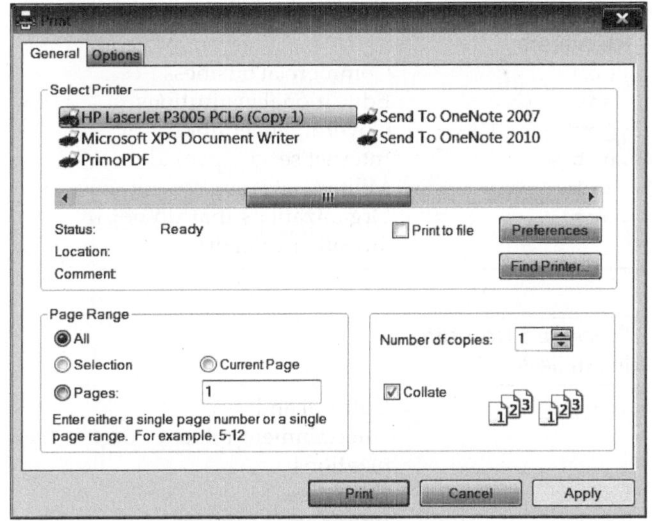

Figure 5.40 Print Dialog box

5.7 UNDERSTANDING URL

Every page on the Web has a unique address, called a *Uniform Resource Locator* (URL). The URL contains the following information.

- The Internet name of the site containing the resource (document data).
- The type of service the resource is served by (HTTP, FTP etc).
- The Internet port number of the service. (If this is omitted, the browser assumes a commonly accepted default value).
- The location of the resource in the directory structure of the server.

Table 5.3 shows the components that make up a URL. The URL used as the example in the Table 5.3 is

`http://www.entertainment.satyam-online.com/contents/horoscope.asp`

Table 5.3 Components that make up a

Example	Explanation	Description
`http://`	Protocol	HTTP is the protocol used to transmit Web pages for this URL.
`www.entertainment. satyamonline .com`	Domain name	The server where the page is located. Every domain name is unique. Here Internet Service Provider (ISP) is Satyam online.
`contents/`	Directory path	The directory where the page is located.
`horoscope.asp`	Filename	The filename of the Web page.

Domain Names

Most organizations use domain names that are easy to remember. Each domain name ends with an identifier that tells you what type of Web site it is. Table 5.4 shows the identifiers commonly used today, and identifiers proposed for use in the future.

Table 5.4 Current and Proposed Domain Name Identifiers

Current Domain Identifiers	
`.com`	Commercial business
`.edu`	Educational institutions
`.gov`	Government entities
`.net`	Internet service providers
`.mil`	Military sites
`.org`	Organizations that do not fit any other category

Proposed Domain Identifiers	
`.arts`	Cultural and entertainment-related organizations
`.firm`	Businesses
`.info`	Information services
`.nom`	Web sites of individuals
`.rec`	Recreation-related organizations
`.store`	Stores and shops
`.web`	World Wide Web-related organizations

☞ *To know the full URL of a Web page is not always necessary to locate the page. If you know the domain name, you can start at the home page of the site and click links until you find the Web page you want.*

5.8 SURFING THE WEB

You must have heard people talking about surfing or browsing the Internet. Someone is surfing the Web means he/she is checking out sites on the Internet. The Internet contains a graphical, easy to use system that offers vast amount of information. This system is called the *World Wide Web* (WWW) or Web. It contains of a huge collection of pages containing information, images, sounds and video clips stored in PC around the world. Each page on WWW is called a *Web page*. The site which stores Web pages is called a *Web site*. Various universities, government agencies, etc., have their own websites which contain several webpages of information about the services provided by them. The first page of website is called the *home page*. The Web lets you move around different Web pages and Web sites and gather information with a single click of mouse.

Elements of the Web

Web Browser

A Web browser is a software application program that resides on your PC can display text, images, and multimedia data found on different Web pages. It allows you to specify a Web page, navigate using links, and "bookmark" your favorite Web pages. The commonly used Web browsers are Internet Explorer, Netscape Navigator and Mozilla Firefox.

Web Page

World Wide Web (WWW) information is presented on Web pages, which you download to your computer using a Web browser, such as Internet Explorer. Each Web page can combine text with images, sound, music, and video.

Web Site

A Web site is a collection of Web pages associated with a particular person, business, government, school and organization. Web sites are stored on a Web server, a special computer that makes Web pages available for people to browse.

Web Address

Every Web page has its own Web address that uniquely identifies the page. This address is sometimes called a URL. If you know the address of a page, you can type the address into your Web browser to view the page.

Links

A link (also called hyperlink) is a kind of "cross-reference" to another Web page. Each link is a bit of text or an image that, when you click it, loads the other page into your Web browser automatically.

Select a Link

Almost all Web pages include links to other pages that contain information related to something in the current page and you can use these links to navigate to other Web pages. When you select a link, your Web browser loads the other page.

1. Position the mouse over the link (i.e., the mouse pointer changes to hand symbol) (See Figure 5.41).
2. Click the text or image (See Figure 5.41).
3. The status bar shows the current download status.
4. The linked Web page appears. The Web page title and address change after the linked page is loaded.
5. The status bar shows *Done* when the page is completely loaded (See Figure 5.42).

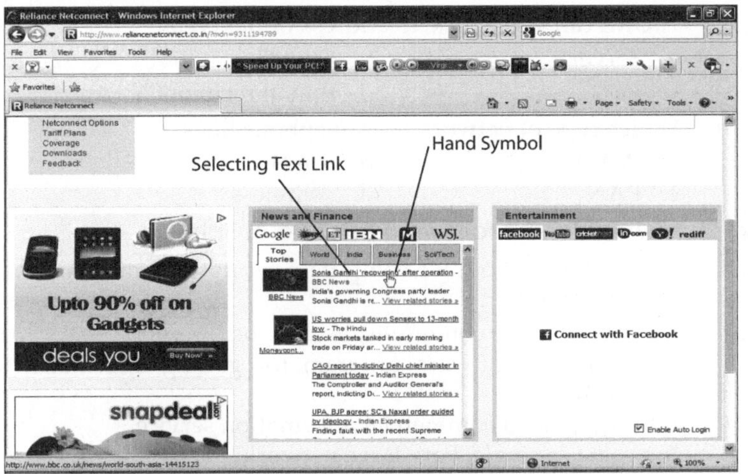

Figure 5.41 Selecting the text link

Figure 5.42 The linked Web page gets loaded and the status bar showing the Done message

☞ *The address shown in the status bar when you point at a link may be different from the one shown when the page is downloading.*

5.8.1 Using E-Governance Website

E-government describes the use of technologies to facilitate the operation of government and the disbursement of government information and services.

E-government, short for electronic government, deals heavily with Internet and non internet applications to aid in governments.

Examples of E-government

E-government should enable anyone visiting a Web site to communicate and interact with city employees via the Internet with Graphical User Interfaces (GUI), Instant Messaging (IM), audio/video presentations, and in any way more sophisticated than a simple e-mail letter to the address provided at the site and "the use of technology to enhance the access and delivery of government services to benefit citizens, business partners and employees".

- The use of Information and communication technologies, and particularly the Internet, as a tool to achieve better government.
- The use of information and communication technologies in all facets of the operations of a government organization.
- The continuous optimization of service delivery, constituency participation and governance by transforming internal and external relationships through technology, the Internet and new media.

A study of some of the important Government Web sites reveals that most of the Government Web sites are providing basic information about the concerned department/entity. Some of these Web sites are also being updated at regular interval. However, many of them are still far from contributing in a true sense, to the concept of e-governance. Although the effort is very much visible, the realization seems to be missing that to have a truly citizen friendly and effective Web site and to thrive in the internet-centric world full of competition, governments will have to offer its citizens, a flawless service with real functional advantages.

During the study, some good examples of effective application of e-governance in the Indian context came into light. The prominent ones are being mentioned below:

- The Web site of the Government of Delhi (http://delhigovt.nic.in) comprises a section called Licences and Certificates which provides, at the click of the mouse, for all the information needs and queries regarding the various public services of the Delhi Government, ranging from obtaining a driving license to getting a marriage-registration certificate made. Along with details on the service, all relevant Application Forms have also been provided online for downloading.
- The Web site of Income Tax Department, Delhi (http://incometaxdelhi.nic.in) gives exhaustive information about the Income Tax procedures in an interesting and easy-to-understand manner. Therefore, one can download the application form to fill the annual tax return. Another online searching facility provides details of Tax Accessing Officer specific to a locality.

Web sites are a powerful channel to facilitate e-governance. It would take a lot of commitment and planned efforts on the part of the governments to make the concept work and bear fruit.

5.9 SUMMARY

This chapter explained Introduction to Internet, WWW and Web Browsers. Chapters starts with the basic concepts of computer networks namely, LAN and WAN. Next, we discussed concept of Internet such as Internet application, connecting to the Internet and Troubleshooting in detail. It also explains using Popular Web browser such as Internet Explorer, Mozilla Firefox etc. How to configure web browsers is also discussed. Search Engines such as Yahoo, and Google, etc., are also discussed. It also explain how to access Web browser. Using Favorites folder you can create a list of favorite pages and organize them into folders. It also explain printing a Web page to store the information that you want to keep as hard copy has also been explained. Finally, we discussed about surfing the web and using e-governance website.

MODEL QUESTIONS AND ANSWERS

1. Multiple Choice

1.1 The World Wide Web integrates which of the following:

a. E-mail, Telnet, Usenet b. Sound and movies files

c. A and B   d. All Internet communication tools

1.2 The speed of your net access is defined in terms of

a. RAM   b. Kbps
c. MHz   d. Megabytes

1.3 Which of the following is not a method of accessing the Web?

a. ISDN   b. MODEM
c. DSL   d. CPU

1.4 What do you call a computer on a network that requests files from another computer?

a. A client   b. A host
c. A router   d. A Web server

1.5 WANs operate at the speed of less than 1 Mbps while LANs operate between

a. 1 and 4 Mbps   b. 2 and 6 Mbps
c. 4 and 10 Mpbs   d. 1 and 10 Mbps

1.6 Web pages are uniquely identified using

a. IP address   b. Domain
c. URL   d. File name

1.7 Printek India has five workstations and two printers. This is most likely a

a. LAN   b. MAN
c. WAN   d. None of the above

1.8 The World Wide Web is composed of

a. 1 page   b. Only 100 Web pages
c. Only 500 Web pages   d. Millions of Web pages

1.9 A URL can specify the IP address of the Web ________.

a. Server   b. Client
c. Page   d. E-mail recipient

1.10 Which type of network uses telephone lines

a. WAN   b. LAN
c. PAN   d. Wireless

2. State whether the following are True or False

2.1 Network is a group of computers set up to communicate with one another.

2.2 E-mail is used to communicate over the Internet.

2.3 Browser is a software program for getting information from WWW.

2.4 Internet is not a commercial information service.

2.5 Internet is a single, very large network.

2.6 A set of rules for exchanging information on Internet is known as protocol.

2.7 E-mail can be used to send broadcast messages, but only within your own company.

2.8 E-mail is short for electric mail.

2.9 FTP is a means of transferring fun pages from one computer to another.

2.10 Download means to copy a file from your computer to another.

Answers

1.	1.1	c	1.2	b	1.3	d	1.4	a	1.5	d
	1.6	c	1.7	a	1.8	d	1.9	a	1.10	a
2.	2.1	T	2.2	T	2.3	T	2.4	F	2.5	F
	2.6	T	2.7	F	2.8	F	2.9	F	2.10	F

CHAPTER 6

Communication and Collaboration

6.0 INTRODUCTION

Communication is an essential aspect of business life. Everyday, business persons have to communicate with people at different levels of the organization. Where as collaboration is a joint effort of multiple individuals or work groups to accomplish a task or project. Within an organization, collaboration typically involves the ability of two or more people to view and contribute to documents or other content over a network.

Effective communication is always a two-way process and without effective communication, true collaboration is impossible. The two go hand in hand. With an Internet connection, you can communicate and collaborate with your friends, team members and business partners across the world.

The Internet offers one of the most exciting and effective ways to teach students how to both communicate and collaborate by connecting teams of students with other classrooms around the world. The creation of "telecommunities" can unite students and teach them to work cooperatively. Collaborative learning becomes even more significant when the students who are working together are from different nations with varied cultures, histories, and socio-political beliefs.

6.1 OBJECTIVES

The reader will be able to understand the following:

- Basics of E-mail
- E-mail Addressing
- Using E-mail with Opening, Creating and Forwarding
- Advance E-mail Features
- Instant Messaging and Collaboration

6.2 BASICS OF E-Mail

E-mail is a method of sending messages, voice, video and graphics over digital communication link, such as the Internet any where in the world at very cost-effective rate. Technically, e-mail is a type of client/server application that provides a routed, stored message service between any two e-mail accounts. Because all modern computers can be connected to the Internet, users can send e-mail over the Internet to any location that has telephone or wireless digital service.

☞ *The backbone of an electronic mail system is a communication network that connects remote terminals to a central system or a local area network that interconnects personal computers. Users can send mail to a single recipient or they can broadcast it to any number of selected users on the system.*

6.2.1 What is an Electronic Mail (E-mail)

E-mail is the electronic equivalent of sending a letter through the mail. The primary component of the electronic mail system is a "post office," an area on the shared hard disk that is reserved for mail. This post office serves as the central message holder and has both "in" and "out" baskets for each user (See Figure 6.1). To send a message, a link is established between the sender's "out" basket and the addressee's "in" basket.

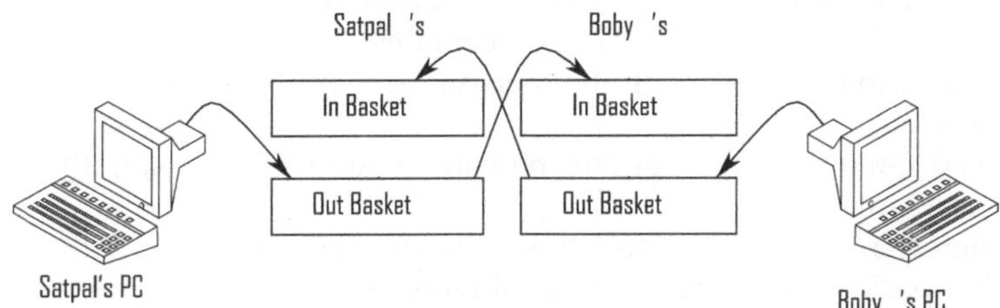

Figure 6.1 Sending mail

The method for receiving mail depends on the sophistication of the system. When multitasking personal computers and workstations are used, mail can be delivered to users while they are working on something else. Otherwise, users have to interrogate their mailboxes (diskspace) in a central system, or file server.

☞ *Electronic mail programs often come with local area network software or as add-on options. Or, they may be independent programs designed to work with a particular network environment.*

How does E-Mail Work?

The person you communicate with could be any other user on the Internet, some one using the same computer system as you, or someone on a computer system thousands of miles away. The e-mail is transmitted between computer system, which exchange messages or pass them onto other sites according to certain Internet protocols or rules for exchanging e-mail. You do not need to be concerned with many of the details, that is the computer's job. But you should know a little bit about the way e-mail works. Sending e-mail is similar to sending something by a postal service.

Steps for sending a mail through posted service are:

- Write the letter or make up the package.
- Put an address on it.
- Put on the proper postage or pay the charge to send it.
- Drop it in the post box so it can be sent on its way and eventually delivered.

You do not have to worry about the methods that are used to deliver it or what route it takes. You prepare what you want to send, address it, and hand it to the postal office.

The steps for sending an e-mail are:

1. Start an e-mail program.
2. Give the address of where to send the e-mail.
3. Compose a message using that e-mail program.
4. Give a command to send the message.

You have probably noticed that we have left out the part about adding postage and paying charges. Individual users do not pay a per message fee for e-mail in many organizations, such as schools, companies – that have Internet access.

You use an e-mail program to *address*, *compose*, and *send* the message. E-mail programs are called mail user agents, because they act on the user's behalf. User agent lets you prepare and send messages and also work with the mail you have received. E-mail program acts as a go-between with you and computer systems, and the computer systems handle the details of delivering and receiving mail. Once again, you do not have anything to do with how mail is delivered.

Messages are sent from one site to another on the Internet in this way. When you compose your message it is all in one piece, but when it is sent out to the Interent, it is divided into several pieces called *packets*. The number of packets depends on the size of the message. Each of the packets contains, among other things:

- The e-mail address of the person who sent the mail, the sender.
- The e-mail address of the person to receive the mail, the recipient.
- Between 1 and 1500 characters of the message.

The packets are sent to the destination, passing through several Internet sites. Thousands of networks and millions of computers make up the Internet, and packets are passed from system to system. Each site accepts the packets addressed to it, but passes on the messages destined for another address. The packets can travel or arrive at their destination in any order and they do not all have to take the same path. When you communicate with a remote site, you may think you have direct connection, but that is usually not the case. At the destination the packets are collected and put in order, so the e-mail appears to be in the same form it was sent. If there are errors in the packets or if some are lost, the destination sends a request back to the source, asking for the message to be resent. All of this takes place according to Simple Mail Transfer Protocol (SMTP) the protocol the Internet uses to transport message between computer systems. SMTP uses Transmission Control Protocol (TCP) which provides a reliable means of communication.

When you read your e-mail, once again you use a program (a mail user agent) that helps you work with the messages you have been waiting for you. On many systems you are told if you have e-mail when you log in, access the system you use to contact the Internet, or start your system. The e-mail message can arrive at any time. They are added to a file that is part of a directory that holds all the e-mail for the system. The packets making up an e-mail message arrive at the system, they are assembled, and then added to the file for each user. That file is often called a *system mailbox*. It holds all the messages on the system addressed to you and only you can read your mail. If for some reason your mailbox gets scrambled, corrupted, or is changed so you can not read your mail, allocated for the directory that holds e-mail. Usually there is enough space to hold a lot of messages, but it is important that you delete old e-mail messages and messages you have read so there is space to hold everybody's e-mail.

Advantages and Disadvantages of E-Mail

Advantages

E-mail has a number of advantages over some other forms of communication. It is quick, convenient, and non-intrusive.

- **Easy to Use:** You can communicate quickly with anyone on the Internet. E-mail usually reaches its destination in a matter of minutes or seconds. An e-mail service helps manage our contacts, allows us to send mails quickly, helps maintain our mailing history and provides sufficient storage space. An email can be sent from any terminal (computer) in the world with Internet access.
- **Environment Friendly:** Mails sent by postal service make use of paper. Thus, electronic mail prevents a large number of trees from getting axed. Using the electronic mailing service also saves the fuel that is consumed in the process of transporting letters.
- **Speed:** An e-mail can be delivered instantly and almost anywhere across the globe. No other mailing service matches the e-mail in terms of speed. You can send a message/mail simultaneously to multiple users; thus, e-mail service saves a lot of time.
- **Informal and Conversational:** Generally, the language used in emails is simple. It makes the process of communication informal. The process of sending and receiving emails does not require much time. Therefore, it can be used as a tool for conversing, just like chatting.
- **Data Storage:** The e-mail service providers with enough space for storage of data. Also, the process of sorting and arranging mails, as per the subject or other criteria (date, sender, etc.), is made easier for users.
- **Provision of Attachments:** The feature of attachment allows users to send huge chunks of data in a single mail.
- **Easier for Reference:** When a person has to reply to an email, he/she can use the provision of attaching previously sent/received mails. Such mails can be used for the purpose of reference in the communication process. It helps the recipient understand what he/she is reading.
- **Reliable and Secure:** Constant efforts are taken to improve the security needed for using an electronic mailing service. Today, electronic mailing service is considered as one of the most secure ways of communicating online.
- **Use of Graphics:** Users can send colorful greeting cards and interesting pictures through emails. This provision adds great value to the email service.
- **Advantages of Technological Development:** Development in computer technology has enabled users to send emails not only from their desktop computers, but also smartphones and other such devices. Thus, a user can send and receive emails even while he/she is travelling.

Disadvantages

The email service, although has many benefits to offer, it also has certain limitations. Disadvantages of the email service are listed below.

- **Spam:** Emails when used to send unsolicited messages and unwanted advertisements create nuisance and are termed as spam. The activity of checking and deleting unwanted mails may consume a lot of user's time. Therefore, it has become necessary to block or filter unwanted emails through spam filters. Email spoofing is another practice which is commonly used for spamming. The act of spoofing involves deceiving a recipient by altering email headers or addresses from which a mail is sent.
- **Hacking:** The act of breaking into computer security is termed as hacking. In this form of security breach, e-mails are intercepted by hackers.

- **Not Suited for Business:** Many a time, business documents go unnoticed amidst large number of mails which get accumulated in the inbox. Thus, urgent transactions and especially those which require signatures cannot be easily managed through emails.
- **Viruses:** Viruses are computer programs which have the potential to harm computer systems. Viruses are known to copy themselves and further infect the computer system. Recipients are required to scan their mails because, viruses can be transmitted through them.
- **Crowded Inbox:** The email inbox tends to get crowded with mails after a certain period of time. Thus, it becomes difficult for users to manage huge chunks of emails.
- **Misinterpretation:** One has to be careful while posting content through an email. If typed in a hurry, the matter can be misinterpreted by readers.
- **Checking the Inbox Regularly:** In order to stay updated, one has to check his/her email account regularly. If a person, due to his/her busy daily routine, does not check the inbox, he/she can miss out on some of the important and urgent messages.

Every new technology which enters the social world has its share of advantages and limitations. Different people interpret and utilize technology in different ways. In order to make the most of the available technology, users should try to understand both, the positive and negative aspects of the tools they use.

Structure of E-Mail Message

An e-mail message is made up of binary data, usually in the American Standard Code for Information Interchange (ASCII) text format. ASCII is a standard that enables any computer, regardless of its system or hardware, to read the text. ASCII code describes the characters you see on your computer screen.

Figure 6.2 shows the similarity of an e-mail message with the postal mail message. In the To line, you type in the e-mail address of the person to whom you are sending a message. The address must be typed according to a set of very strict rules. If you type a single letter or the syntax is wrong, your message will not get to the intended recipient. Your e-mail address will appear on the From line. Using this address, the recipient of your message will be able to respond to you.

On the subject line, you may type in the subject of your message or a very brief summary. At the bottom of the message is a "signature" area that can contain personalized information about you. Some mail programs will automatically append this signature to the bottom of every message you send. Signature areas are not required and are used at the discretion of the person who creates the e-mail message. Signature portion should not exceed five lines.

There are five sections of an e-mail message:

- E-mail address
- Header
- Body
- Signature (optional)
- Attachment(s) (optional)

Figure 6.3 shows the major sections of an e-mail message. Note that signatures and attachments are optional. Many messages do not show them, and some e-mail applications do not support them.

6.2.2 E-Mail Addressing

An e-mail address is composed of two separate parts.

- The domain name of the mail server computer on which you have an e-mail account.
- Your personal identity or account name (user name) on that mail server.

```
Mr. Ram Singh
18, Gandhi Lane
Ramesh Nagar,
New Delhi - 110051

United Diamonds
180, Main Street,
Connaught Place
New Delhi - 110051

June 2, 2016

Subject:Interview for Programmers

Dear Mr. Singh
      You will be pleased to know that the
company has selected you for the post of Senior
programmer. Please send your confirmation of
the acceptance of our offer.

                  Yours Truly
                  (S. Jain)
                    M.D.
```

(a)

```
   To: bpb@vsnl.com

   From: "Sales@bpbonline.com

   Subject:    Interview for Programmers

Date: Thu, 2 Jun 2016 11.47:10+0530

   Dear Mr.Singh,
      You will be pleased to know that the company
has selected you for the post of Senior program-
mer. Please send your confirmation of the accep-
tance of our offer.

            Yours Truly
            (S. Jain)
              M.D.
```

(b)

Figure 6.2 (a) Postal mail format (b) e-mail format

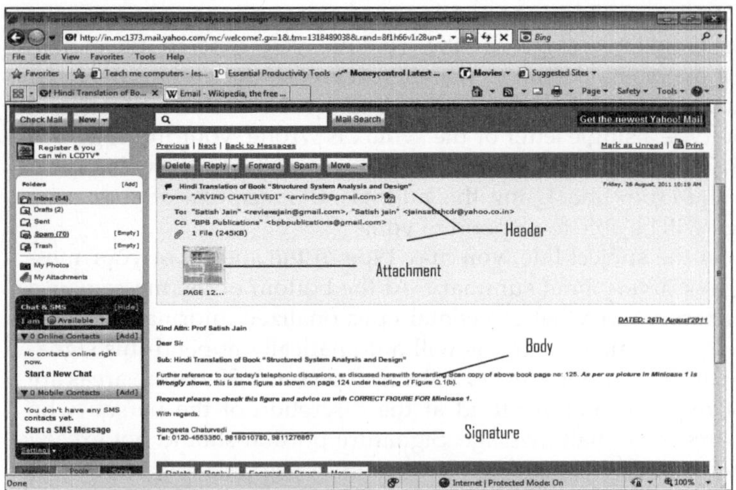

Figure 6.3 Major sections of an e-mail message

For example, 100 people have e-mail accounts with the same Internet Service Provider (ISP) or organizations. All 100 users will share the same domain name (say **hotmail.com**), but each person will possess a unique user name, such as "rakesh" or "aparna." The user name and domain name are separated by an @ ("at") symbol. Together, they form a complete e-mail address.

The components of a typical e-mail address are shown in Figure 6.4. Users with multiple e-mail accounts – perhaps with different ISPs or organizations – will have a different e-mail address for each account.

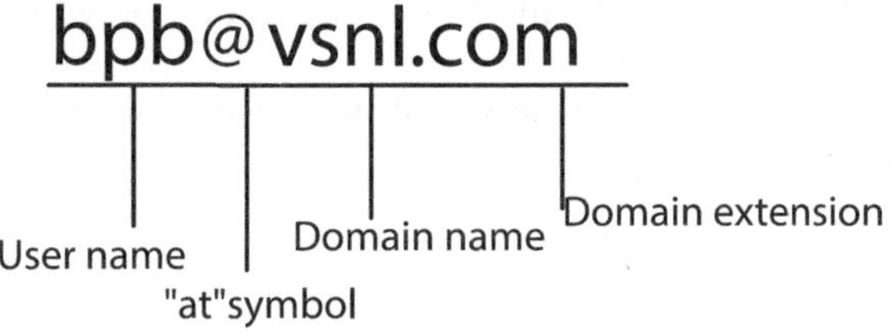

Figure 6.4 Syntax for E-mail address

Header

The header of e-mail message is the upper-most section. It displays information regarding the status of the messages. A header records message information and provides it to the recipient(s) of the message. Headers are present in both outgoing (sent) and incoming (received) messages.

The principal header fields related to message transported are listed in Table 6.1. These are mandatory to be used by all the people using e-mail facilities on the Internet.

Table 6.1 Header Fields in an E-mail

Name	Function
To:	E-mail address/addresses of primary recipient (s).
Cc:	E-mail address/addresses of secondary recipient (s) to whom copy needs to be sent.
Bcc:	E-mail address/addresses of secondary recipient (s) to whom copy needs to be sent but the primary recipient should not know about the dispatch of mail to these addressees.
From:	The originator or the creater of the e-mail.
Sender:	E-mail address of the actual sender.
Received:	Line added by each transfer agent along the route containing the agent's identity, the date and time the message was received.
Return Path:	May be used to identify the path back of the sender.

(Contd...)

☞ *Note that there are no spaces in the above address; e-mail software and server computers will not accept spaces in an address. Messages will not reach their destination if spaces are included.*

In addition to the header fields given in Table 6.2, there are additional headers which are not mandatory but may be used if required.

Table 6.2 Additional Header Fields in a E-mail

Name	Function
Date:	Date and time the message was sent.
Reply-to:	E-mail address to which replies should be sent.
In-Reply-to:	Message-identification number of the message to which this is a reply.
Message-ID:	A unique number identifying the message and may be used to refer to the message.
References:	Other relevant message identification numbers.
Keywords:	Keywords selected by the user.
Subject:	A summary of the message for the one-line display.

The header shows information, such as:

- Time and date of a message,
- Subject of a message (as typed by the sender),
- Whether carbon copies were sent,
- Whether files are attached to the message, and
- The e-mail address of the sender.

Body

The body of e-mail message is the primary focus because it contains the actual message. Although there is no limit to the size (number of characters) of an e-mail message, but many ISPs do limit the size of an e-mail message.

Attachments

E-mail has become all the more attractive to businesses because now it allows users to attach a file to any e-mail message. Any file format – such as *word processing documents, spreadsheets, images*, or *video* files – can be attached to an e-mail message. E-mail allows complex data as attachments but not in the body.

☞ *E-mail messages cannot contain viruses, but they can still be sent through attachments. Therefore, you should scan all e-mail attachments with a virus detection and eradication software program, such as McAfee VirusScan or Norton Anti Virus before opening, or forwarding them.*

Most e-mail applications alert you if an incoming message contains an attachment. Such e-mail applications show an icon within the body of the messages to represent an attached file. The icon indicates the type of file that is attached and allows the recipient to double-click the icon to automatically launch the attachment on their computer.

Signature

The signature for an e-mail message is the personal information which automatically appears at the bottom of the outgoing message. Use of a signature is optional. You can provide any signature information you wish.

☞ *The purpose of a signature (also called a signature block, signature file) is to provide a message recipient with personal contact information.*

Information in a signature block may include the following:

- Full name
- Job title/position
- Organization name and division
- Phone and fax numbers
- Physical (snail mail) address
- E-mail address
- Web site address Uniform Resource Locator (URL)

☞ *A signature allows information in this part to be included with each outgoing message in an automated and time-saving manner for the message sender.*

Under Blind Carbon Copy (Bcc) option, the recipient of your mail does not know the other recipients of the same mail.

By utilizing the signature feature of the e-mail software, you can avoid typing information for each outgoing message. Figure 6.5 shows a typical e-mail signature.

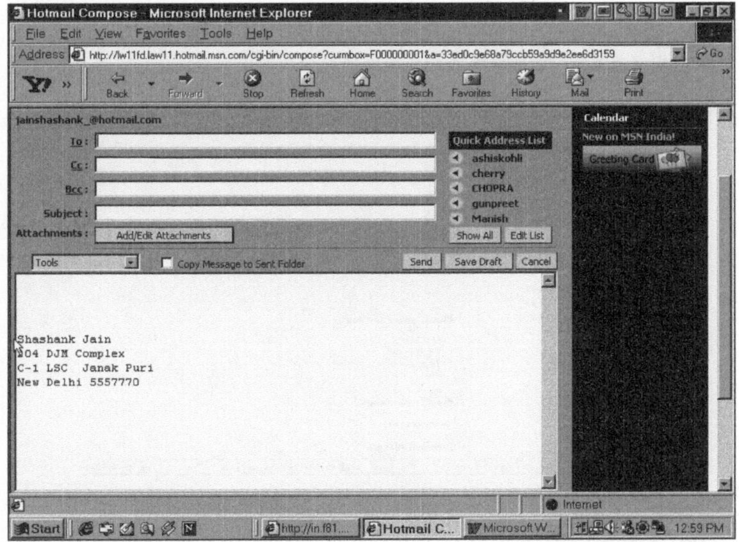

Figure 6.5 Signature block on an e-mail message

Carbon copy (Cc)

This feature lets you send a copy, i.e., carbon copy of the mail to another recipient. In this case the main recipient is informed about the other people who receive the same message (See Figure 6.6).

Blind Carbon Copy (Bcc)

In this option the recipient of the first e-mail copy does not come to know the name of the other recipients, who receive the carbon copies of the same message.

Bounced Mail

Bounced mail is an e-mail message that has failed to reach its destination and therefore such e-mail messages are returned to the sender. The message "bounces" back to its sender from the mail server after the server fails to locate the message recipient address (or the recipient's Internet Service Provider).

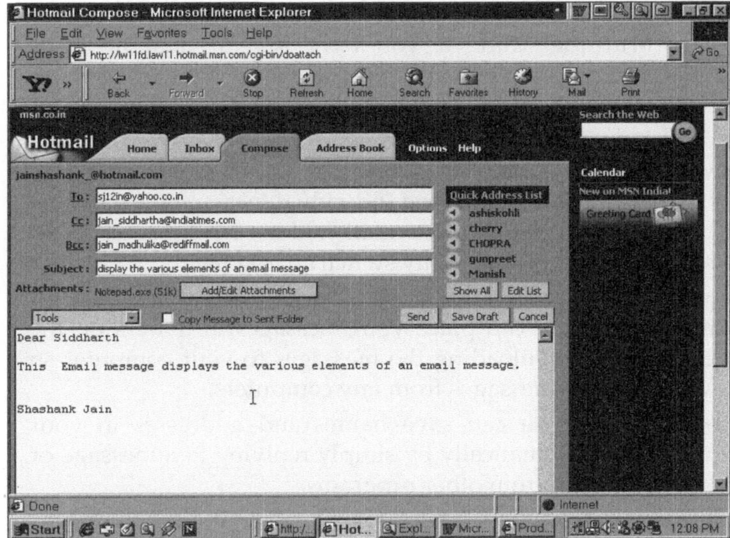

Figure 6.6 E-mail message with the carbon copy and Bcc, and attachments

Bounced mail messages typically feature a text clip near the top of the message and/or in the subject field, such as "Returned Mail" or "Mail Undeliverable". A bounced message alerts you that your e-mail has gone undelivered and that you must again send the message with correct address in order to ensure that your message reaches its recipient.

Configuring E-mail Client

When an e-mail software is run, the user may ask for a summary of his e-mail. The mailbox may contain a number of messages. In a simple e-mail message system, the choice of fields displayed is built into the program which may be one of the following types.

Sl. No.	Flags	Size in bytes	Sender	Address	Subject

In the above format, the first field is the message number. The second field is the Flags, which can contain various words, such as the **new message**, etc. The third field gives how long the message is and the next field indicates the sender and its address. The final column indicates the subject of the e-mail message. Once the messages are listed by the e-mail package, the user can process his e-mail box and can lay priority to the different messages received from various senders. E-mail has come a long way from the earlier days when it was just file transfer to very sophisticated software, such as Lotus Notes and Microsoft Outlook Express. The user agents make it possible to manage a large volume of e-mail.

☞ *The RFC 822 gives the format of the e-mail messages and multimedia extensions.*

Outlook 2010

Outlook 2010 is the Microsoft's e-mail program that is included with Windows and with Internet Explorer 8.0 onwards. Outlook 2010 puts the world of online communication on your computer's desktop. If you want to exchange e-mail with colleagues and friends or join newsgroups to trade ideas and information, then you have to use the different tools of Outlook 2010. You can perform the following functions with the help of Outlook 2010.

Manage Multiple Mail If you have several mail or news accounts, you can use them all from one window with the help of Outlook 2010. You can also create multiple users, or identities, for the same computer.

Browse Messages quickly Using the message list, you can view a list of messages and read individual messages at the same time. The Folders list contains mail folders, news servers, and newsgroups, and you can easily switch among them.

Keep Mail on a Server If your ISP uses an IMAP mail server for incoming mail, you can place your messages in folders on the server without downloading the messages to your computer so that you can view messages from any computers.

Address Book You can save names and addresses in your Address Book automatically by simply replying to a message or by importing them from other programs.

Send and Receive Secure Messages You can digitally sign and encrypt messages by using digital IDs. So that you can send and receive secure messages.

Download Newsgroup Messages for Offline Reading You can also use Outlook 2010 to use your online time efficiently by downloading messages or entire newsgroups, so that you can read newsgroup messages for offline reading.

Web based E-Mail

Each e-mail service – whether it is an online service, commercial e-mail service, has its own way to handle mail. Most of the E-mail services use the Internet as their gateway (describe the path how messages are passed from one service to another service). Internet connects the computers around the world so that people could share information with each other. When we send the message from e-mail service to someone's system, the message will travel across the Internet to reach its destination. We have given only the addressing of the message properly so that the Internet knows where to deliver the message. Here is some Web based free E-mail account, such as HotMail and rediffmail.com, that offer Web based e-mail access.

6.3 USING E-MAIL

E-mail or electronic mail can be sent over the Internet to anybody who has an e-mail address. To use e-mail, you need both an e-mail address and a program to handle it. To create a free e-mail account by Internet or Outlook Express.

6.3.1 Opening E-Mail Account/Client

Before you actually settle down to send a mail, you will first need to create an e-mail account. There are various sites in the Internet by which you can create free e-mail account. Some of the sites are given below:

(a) www.yahoo.com

(b) www.rediffmail.com

(c) www.msn.com

(d) www.hotmail.com

Here, you create an e-mail account with the Gmail.com.

➡ **To open an e-mail account, do this:**

1. Log on to site **www.gmail.com**. Type the www.gmail.com in the address bar as shown in Figure 6.7.
2. Click the Create an account button in the Gmail from Google window as shown in Figure 6.7.

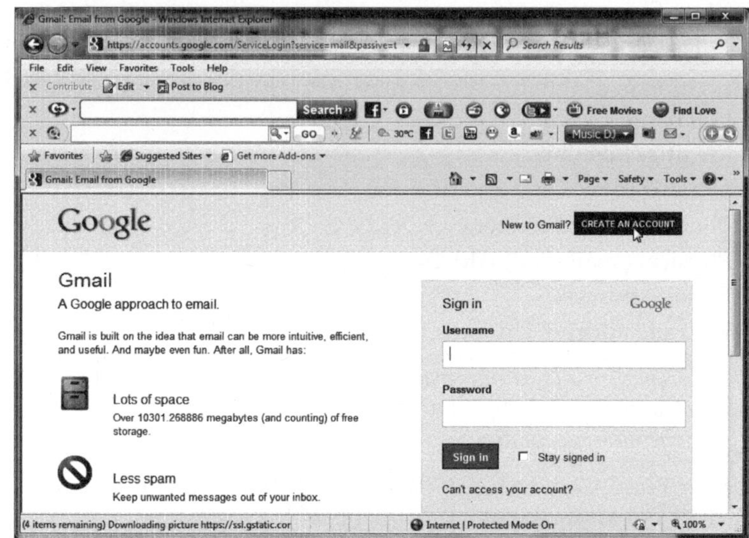

Figure 6.7 Gmail Google Window

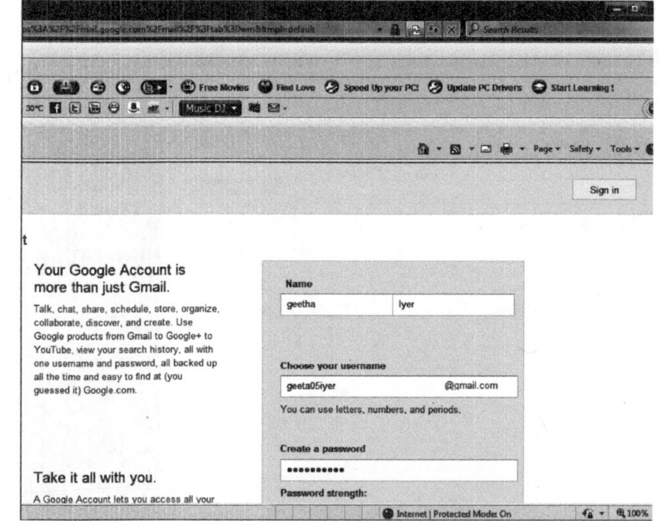

Figure 6.8 Type the information in the Google account text box

3. The Gmail Accounts window appears as shown in Figure 6.7.
4. Type the first and last name in the Name box as shown in Figure 6.8.
5. Type a desired login id which you want to create in the Choose your username text box.
6. Type the password in the Create a password text box (See Figure 6.8).
7. Again, type the password in the Confirm your password textbox as shown in Figure 6.9.
8. Type the Date of Birth in the Birthday text box as shown in Figure 6.9.
9. Select the Type of Gender in the Gender drop-down list (See Figure 6.10).

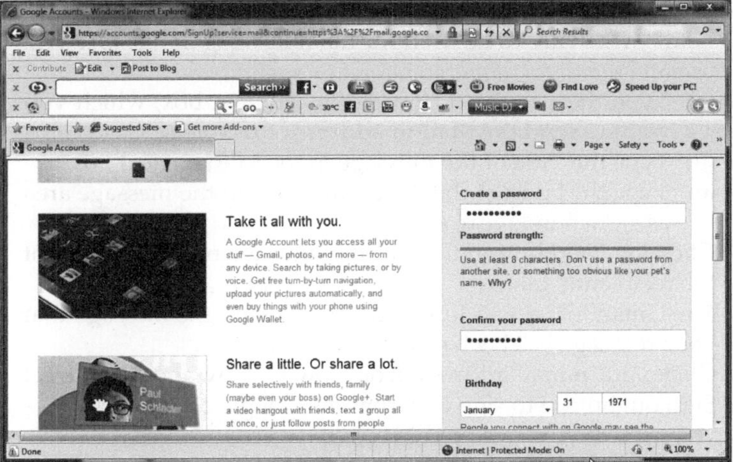

Figure 6.9 Type the password in confirm your password textbox

10. Type the mobile number in the Mobile phone text box (See Figure 6.10).
11. Type an e-mail address in the Your current e-mail address text box to keeping your account secure.
12. Type the character you see in the picture in the text box below Type the two pieces of text: box (See Figure 6.11).
13. Select the place in the Location drop-down list.
14. Click the Next Step to continue to next page.

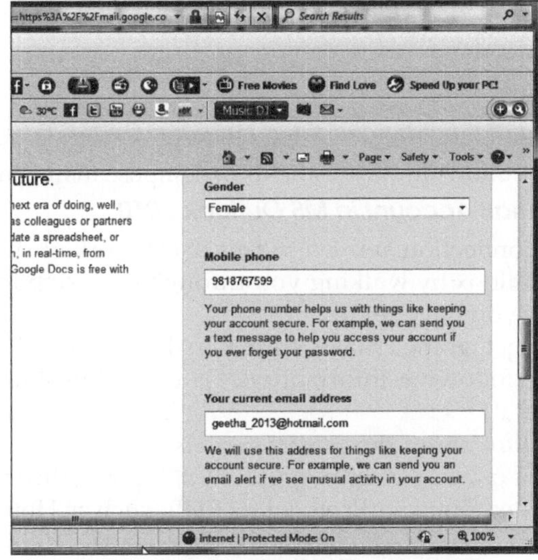

Figure 6.10 Type Mobile number in the Mobile Phone textbox

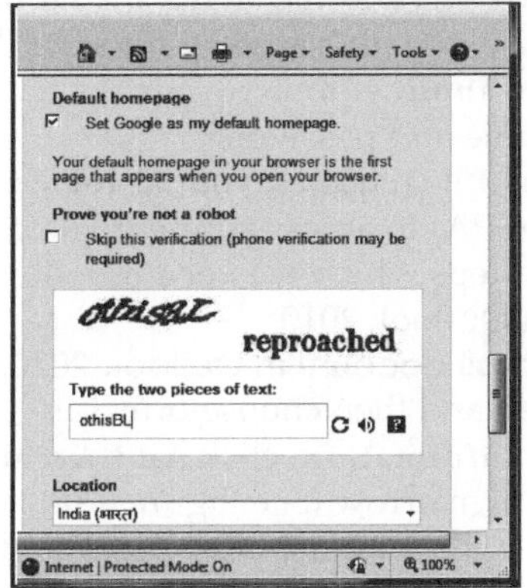

Figure 6.11 Character

15. The verify your account page appears as shown in Figure 6.12.
16. Select the desired option from verify your account page i.e., how should we send your codes? by Text message (SMS) or Voice call. For instance, if you select the Text message (SMS), you will receive a verification code form the Google to your mobile number, then you have entered in the Verify your account page.

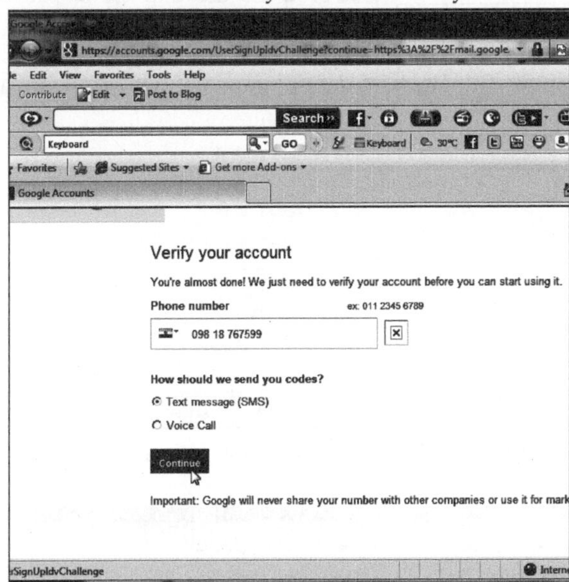

Figure 6.12 Google Accounts shows Verify your account

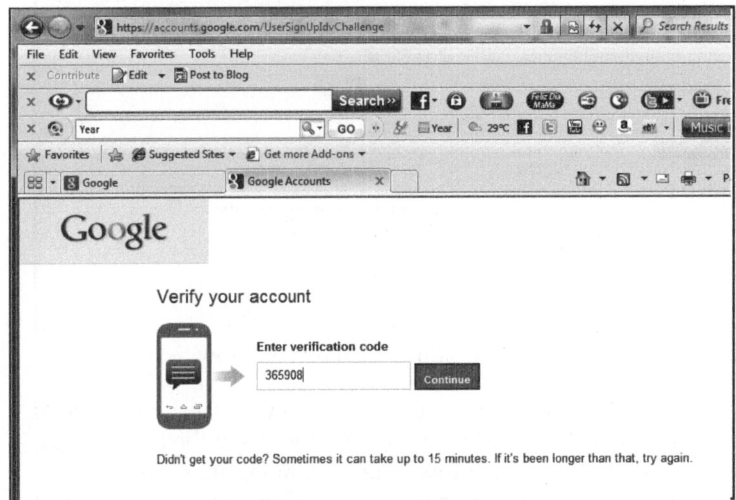

Figure 6.13 Mobile verification

17. Click Continue button (See Figure 6.12).
18. Type the code that you have received in your mobile number in the Enter verification code text box in the Verify your account page (See Figure 6.13).
19. Click Continue button.
20. The Google Welcome! page shows, which you have created a new e-mail address. Click Continue to Gmail button which is ready to use (See Figure 6.14). The Gmail inbox shows the e-mail messages that you have entered. You can click the e-mail to view the message (See Figure 6.15).

Figure 6.14 Google Welcome page screen

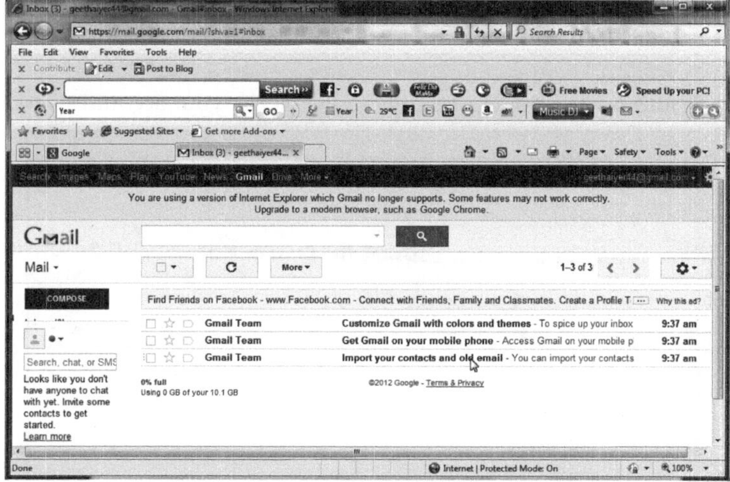

Figure 6.15 Gmail mail box window

21. Click the e-mail that you have received from the Gmail Team, as shown in Figure 6.15. You will see the e-mail message on the Gmail window as shown in Figure 6.15.
22. To write an e-mail message click the Compose mail button at the left side of the Gmail window. The Compose Mail window appears as shown in Figure 6.16.

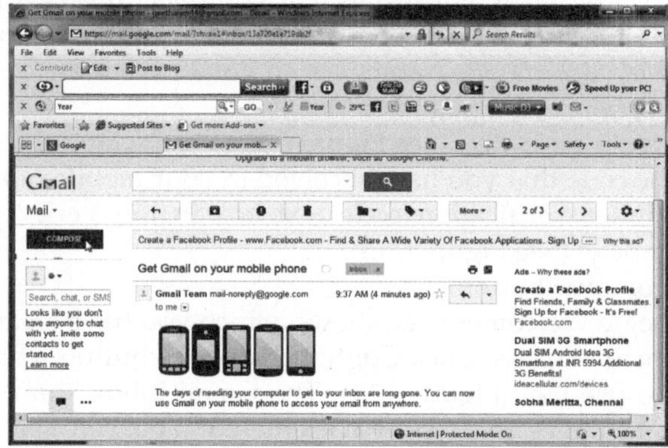

Figure 6.16 Selecting Compose mail

23. In the Compose Message window, you will see various fields, which are to be used for the following things (See Figure 6.17).
    (a) Type the e-mail address in the **To:** text box, which you want to send the Mail-id address of recipient.
    (b) Type the Title of the message in the **Subject:** text box.
    (c) Type the body of the e-mail message in the message area as shown in Figure 6.17.
24. Click the Send button to send the message on the address of the recipient's Inbox.
    The Gmail inbox window appears showing the message that your message has been sent.
25. Click your e-mail address drop-down arrow and then select Sign out button to sign out from the Google account.

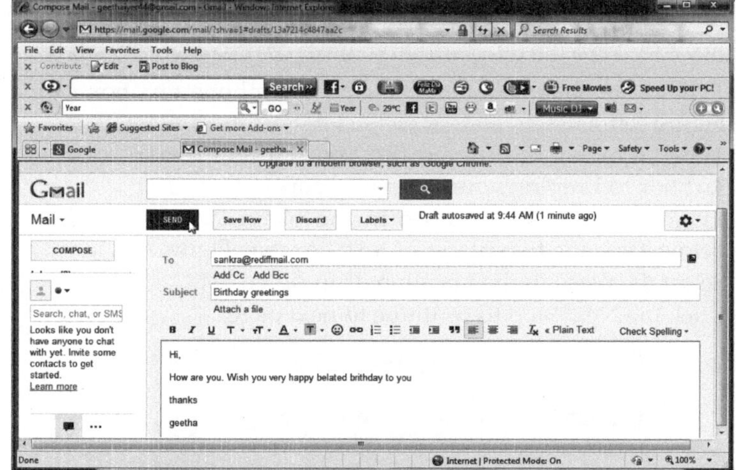

Figure 6.17 Showing various fields of compose mail window

Adding an E-mail Account in MS Outlook 2010

The Internet Connection Wizard makes short work of setting up your online mailbox by walking you through each step for every e-mail account you have set up.

Before you get going, make sure you know e-mail address along with the following information. [You may need to contact your ISP, to get it.

First, information about the e-mail servers:

(a) The type of e-mail server you use: POP3 (post office protocol 3), Hyptertext Transfer Protocol (HTTP) (such as Hotmail), or IMAP

(b) The name of the incoming e-mail server

For POP3 and IMAP servers, the name of the outgoing e-mail server (generally Simple Mail Transfer Protocol (SMTP).

Second, information about your account:

(a) Your account name and password.

(b) Find out if your ISP requires you to use Secure Password Authentication (SPA) to access your e-mail account.

Let us look at the steps which we need to follow for setting up an e-mail account in Outlook 2010.

➡ **To set up an e-mail account in Outlook 2010, do this:**

1. Click the **File** Tab and then choose **Info** Tab.
2. Under **Account Information**, click **Add Account** or **Account Settings** drop-down arrow (See Figure 6.18).
3. The **Account Settings** dialog box appears as shown in Figure 6.19. In this dialog box, click the **New...** button. It will display **Add New Account** dialog box as shown in Figure 6.20.

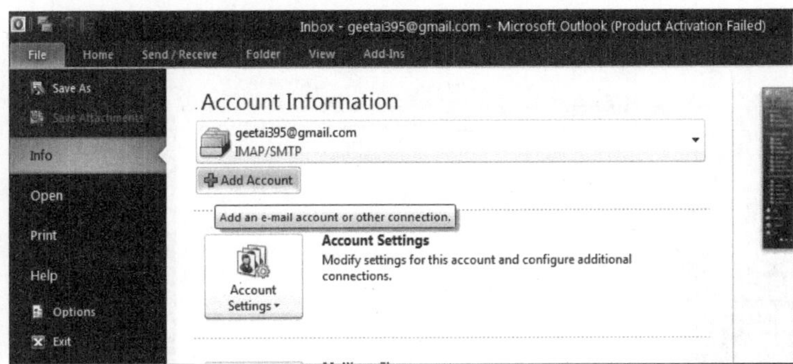

Figure 6.18 Setting E-mail Account

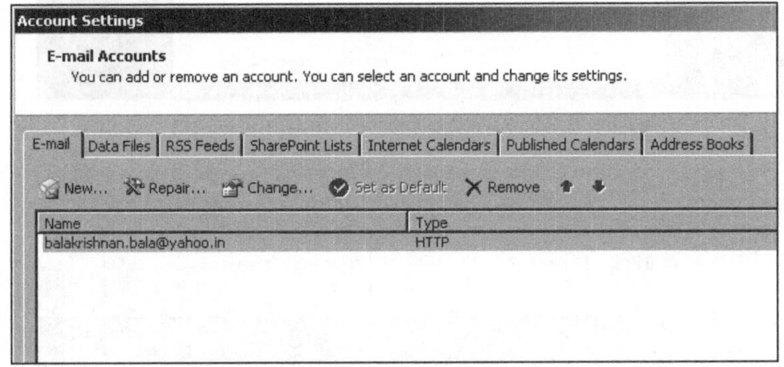

Figure 6.19 Account Settings dialog box

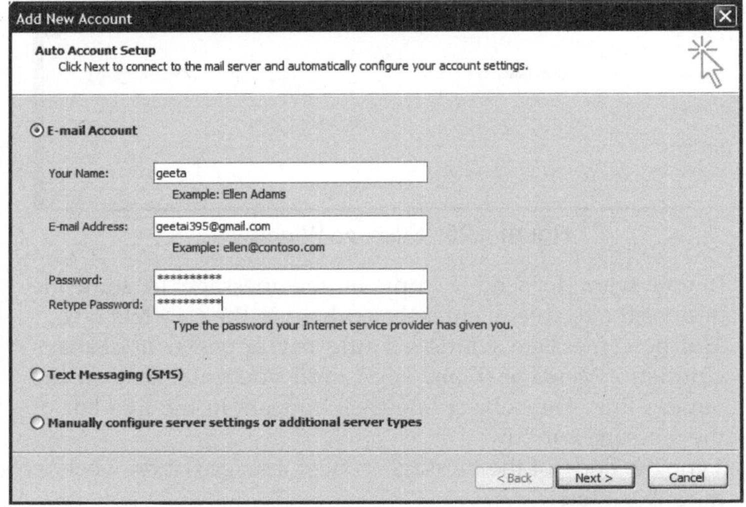

Figure 6.20 Add New Account dialog box

4. In this dialog box, type the name in the **Your Name:** text box and type e-mail address in the **E-mail Address:** text box. After that Type password in the **Password:** text box and in the **Retype Password:** text box confirm the password. Then click **Next >** button.
5. Another dialog box appears to the choose the service (See Figure 6.21). In this dialog box, click the **Internet E-mail** radio button and then click **Next >** button.
6. As soon as you click the **Next>** button, it will display another dialog box showing the progress indicator as your account is being configured. It may take several minutes (See Figure 6.22).
7. After the account is successfully added, you can add more accounts by clicking **Add another account...** button.

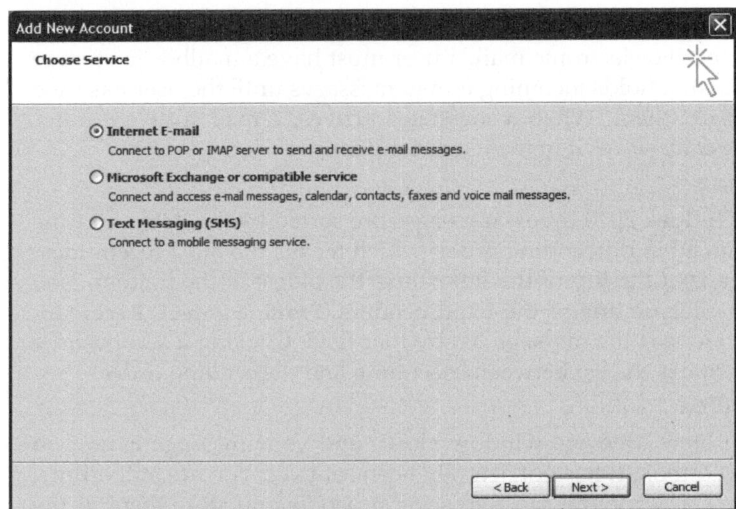

Figure 6.21 Add New Account to Choose Service

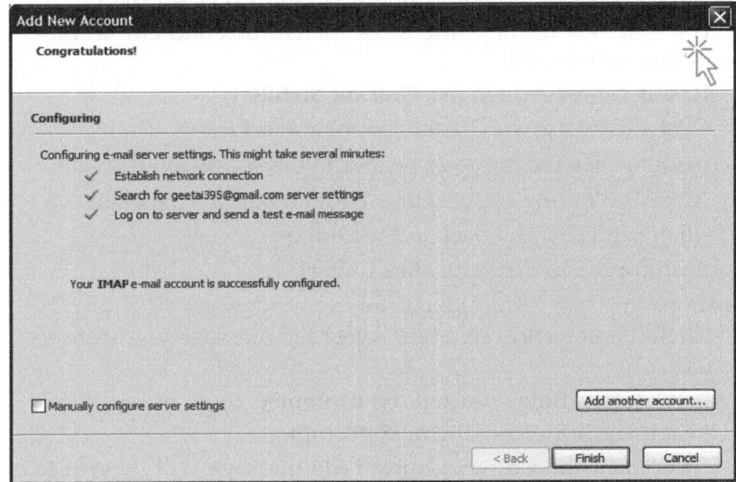

Figure 6.22 Add New Account showing configuring e-mail server settings

8. To exit the **Add New Account** dialog box, click **Finish** button to configure your e-mail account ready to use as seen in Figure 6.23.

☞ *If Outlook 2010 fails to set up the e-mail account automatically, there is one more thing you can try, if you get this message: An encrypted connection to your server is not available. Click Next to attempt using an unencrypted connection.*

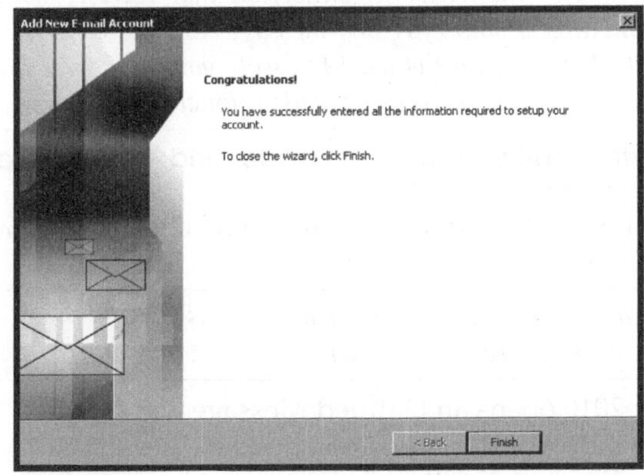

Figure 6.23 Add New E-mail Account dialog box

6.3.2 Mailbox: Inbox and Outbox

To receive electronic mail, a user must have a mailbox, a storage area, that holds incoming e-mail messages until the user has time to read them. When a messages arrives, e-mail software automatically stores it in the user's mailbox.

Inbox

In Outlook 2010 Inbox, messages are sorted by the date and time received in descending order, which means the most recent message is at the top of the Inbox and the oldest at the bottom. You can click on any of the Field headers (**From, Subject, Received,** etc.) to sort the message list by that field. Clicking a second time alternates the list between ascending and descending order.

Outbox

The New Message window closes and your message is now in the Outbox. It has not actually been sent yet. You are still offline. You can write messages to several people and store them in the Outbox. When you are ready, you can send them all at once. This uses only a few seconds of online time and saves on the phone bill. You can look at the contents of the Outbox and edit a message before you send it.

➡ **To edit a message in the Outbox do this:**

1. Click Outbox in the Folders pane to select it.
2. Double-click the message header in the Message List pane.
3. An Edit window appears and you can edit the message.
4. Click Send to put it back in the Outbox.
5. If prompted to Connect, click Cancel.

Sending a message from the Outbox

6. Click the **Send/Receive** tab. Select the message you want to edit.

   If you are offline, you will be prompted to go online. Click **Yes**, then **Connect** at the next prompt.
7. After click the **Connect** button the message will be sent to the recipient address.
8. Edit the message and then click the **Send** button.

6.3.3 Creating and Sending a New E-mail

One of the most common task for Outlook users is sending and receiving e-mail. The mail message window, like other item windows in Outlook 2010, features the new Ribbon in place of menus and toolbars.

☞ *To send and receive e-mail, you need to be connected to a mail server. You can think of the mail server as the post office. It is the computer with the network connection that receives your messages and directs your outgoing messages to other computers on a network. The computer is used to create your messages and read the messages you have received. This is known as the mail client.*

➡ **To create a new e-mail message and type the e-mail address, do this:**

1. In the **Home** Tab, under the **New** group, click **New E-mail** as shown in Figure 6.24.

☞ *Shortcut key to open New mail message is* Ctrl + N *or* Ctrl + Shift + M *keys pressed together.*

2. Outlook 2010 opens an Untitled Message window.
3. In this window, enter the recipient addresses in the **To...** text box (See Figure 6.25). If you want to enter multiple recipient addresses, you can separate it by a semicolon and one space.

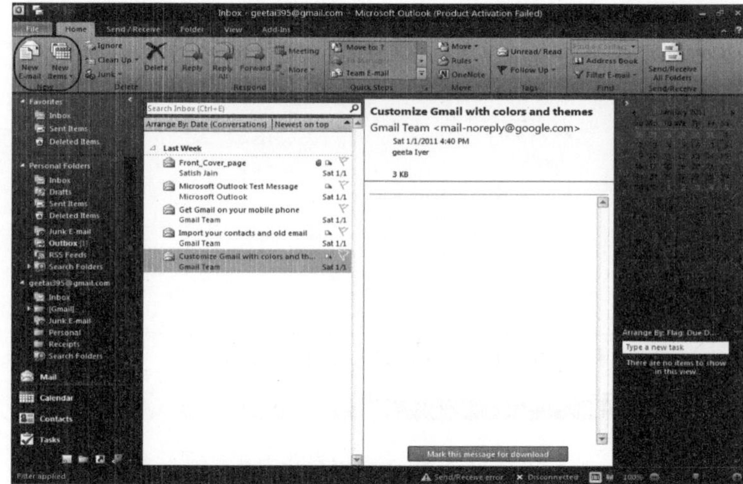

Figure 6.24 Creating new e-mail message

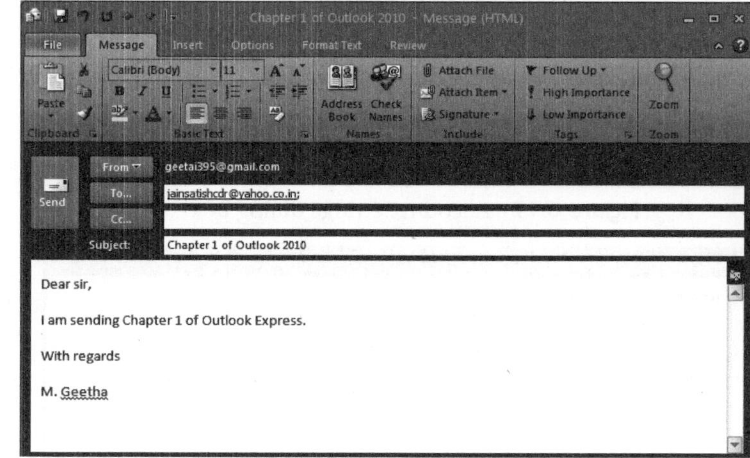

Figure 6.25 Message Window

4. If you want to send a copy of the message to someone besides the recipient, enter the address in the **Cc...** text box.
5. The new message window's title bar appears. It displays Untitled - Message (Plain Text) until you enter text on the Subject line. The subject line then appears in the title bar of the message window.
6. Type the body of the message in the message window below the subject line.
7. Then click **Send** icon to send the message.

6.3.4 Replying to an E-mail Message

Replying to an e-mail is like answering a letter – it acknowledges your receipt of the message and allows you to respond.

☞ *The Shortcut key to Reply a message is* Ctrl + R *keys pressed together.*

➡ **To reply to an e-mail message, do this:**

1. In the **Home** Tab, under the **Respond** group, click **Reply** or **Reply All** icon as shown in Figure 6.26.
2. Outlook displays a message window with the recipient's e-mail address and subject line already typed in along with a copy of the original message (See Figure 6.27).
3. To add a recipient, click in the **To, Cc** or **Bcc** box. Compose the message and then click the **Send** icon.

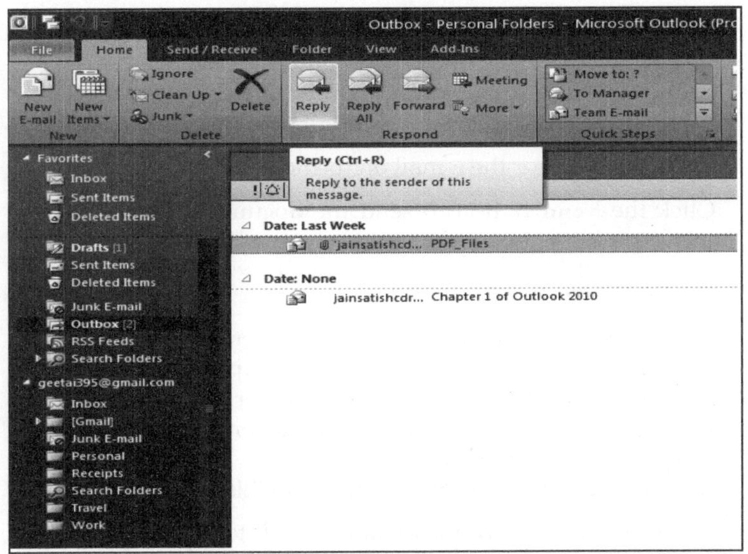

Figure 6.26 Select Reply button in the Respond group

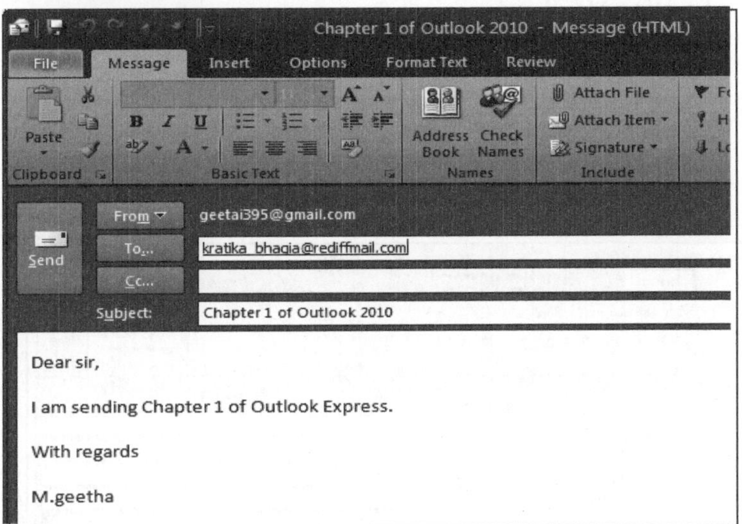

Figure 6.27 Message window with the recipient's e-mail address

6.3.5 Forwarding an E-mail Message

Sometimes you may receive a message, but rather than reply to it, you want to send it (forward it) to someone else. Forwarding a message essentially copies a message and sends it to someone else whom the original sender may not even know.

☞ *The Shortcut key to forward a message is* Ctrl + F *keys pressed together.*

➡ **To forward an e-mail message, do this:**

1. In the **Home** Tab, under the **Respond** group, click **Forward** icon or double-click the message that you want to forward.
2. A message window appears that contains your chosen message.
3. Click in the **To:** text box and type an e-mail address.
4. Click in the message window and type any additional text you want to send along with the forwarded message.
5. Click the **Send** button.

☞ *You can forward only one message at a time. If you want to forward two or more messages, select the first message, hold* Ctrl *key and then select each additional message. Each message will be forwarded as attachments in a new message.*

6.3.6 Sorting and Searching E-mails

Sorting E-mail

Outlook 2010 lets you sort by single column or multiple columns. For example, if you select the column heading that is the exclamation mark (!) icon (located below the folder banner), all your important messages will be listed at the top of the Message list. Or if you click the From button, the messages will be sorted in alphabetical order by first name of the person who sent you the message. To sort by more than one column, select the column headings in reverse order.

In addition, to sorting your e-mail using the column headings, you can sort e-mail using the Sort dialog box.

➡ **To sort e-mail using the Sort command, do this:**

1. Click the **View** tab on the Ribbon. In the **Arrangement** group click the **More** drop-down arrow as shown in Figure 6.28. Select **View Settings...**.

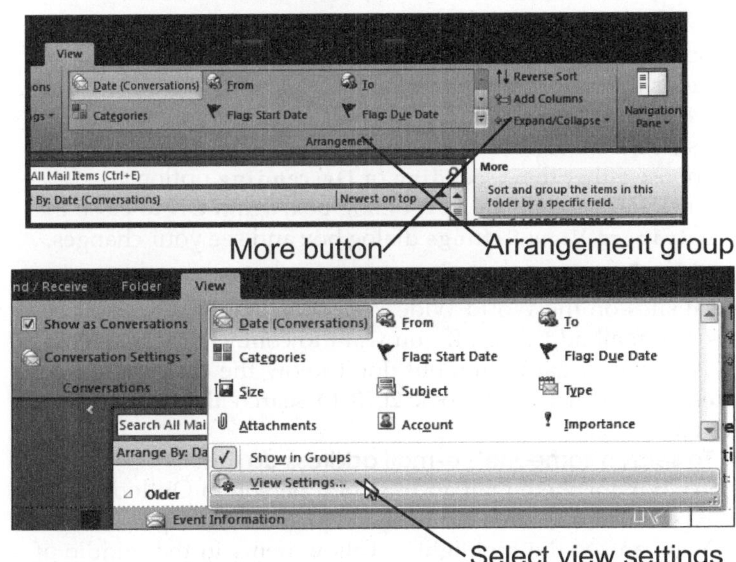

Figure 6.28 Selecting View Settings in the Arrangement group

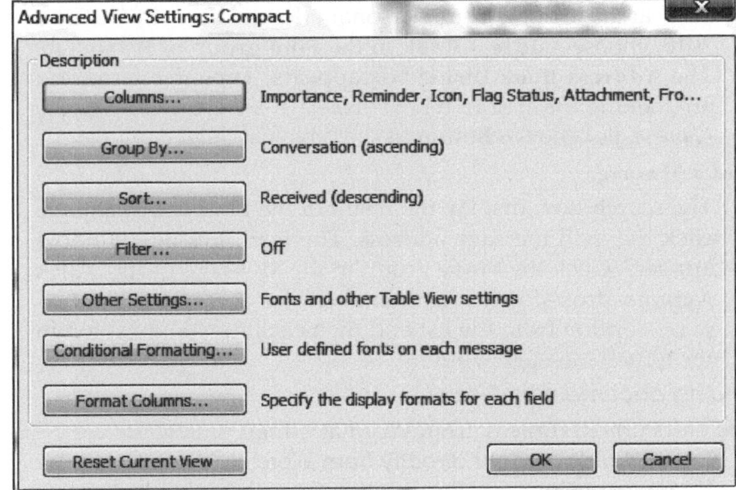

Figure 6.29 Advanced View Settings dialog box

2. The **Advanced View Settings** dialog box appears as shown in Figure 6.29.
3. In the **Advanced View Settings** dialog box, click the **Sort...** button. The **Sort** dialog box appears as shown in Figure 6.30.

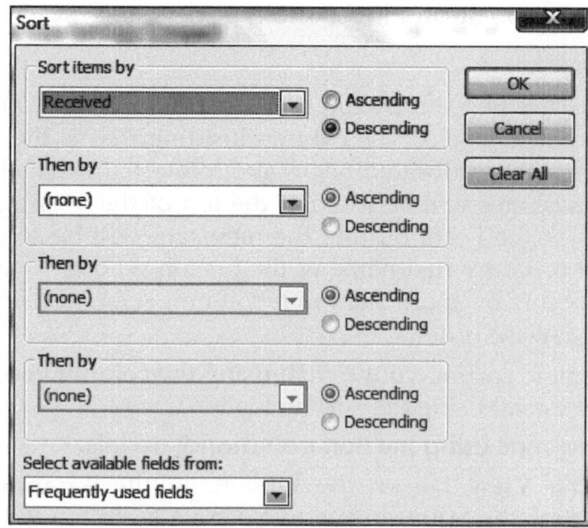

Figure 6.30 Sort dialog box

4. In the **Select available fields from:** drop-down list at the bottom of the dialog box, select the field set containing the fields that you want to use for sorting.
5. In the **Sort Items by** drop-down list, select an item from the list, such as **Subject, Received, Sent** and **Size** and then choose either the **Ascending** or **Descending** option.
6. Click OK to close the **Sort** dialog box, again OK to close the **Advanced View Settings** dialog box and see your changes.

Searching E-mail

Several sites on the World Wide Web (WWW) offer huge directories of e-mail addresses. If you want to contact a person, company, or other organization but don't know the contact's e-mail address, you can use Outlook 2010 to search through each of these directories.

➡ **To search someone's e-mail address do this:**

1. To look for the e-mail address of a person in Outlook 2010, type word to search for in the **Search** box and press **Enter.** You can see the highlighted yellow items in the middle of the window.

Search Address Book

2. To search through your personal address book in Outlook 2010, choose **Address Book** in the **Find** group of **Home** tab. The **Address Book** dialog box appears. Type the name you are looking for in Search box – *Name, E-mail Address, Display Name.* Click the **Go** button to start the search.

Send a Message

3. The search item display the result of the Find items. Double click the mail message address. The mail message window appears. Click the **Move** group in the **Message** group. Click **Actions** drop-down arrow and choose **Resend this Message...** option from the list and then click the **Send** button in the e-mail message window.

Sending document by E-mail

Send a document directly from Word as e-mail.

➡ **To send a document directly from Word as e-mail, do this:**

1. If you are using MS Word, select **File** tab highlight **Save & Send**. The **Save & Send** options appears, then click **Send as Attachment** to send the document as the body of the message.
2. The mail Message window appears.
3. Type the e-mail name of the recipient in the **To:** line or select the e-mail name from your **Address Book.**
3. Leave the **Cc:** box blank. This is used if you want to send a copy of the message to someone.
4. Type a subject for the e-mail on the Subject line.
5. Click the **Send** button to send the document as an attachment.

Sending Softcopy as Attachment

Any file that is stored on computer can be sent through e-mail. Before the file can be opened by the recipient, it must be downloaded–transferred from the mail server to the recipient's computer. The amount of time take depends on the Internet connection speed and the file's size.

➡ **To send a softcopy as attachment, do this:**

1. You send any type of file by attaching it to e-mail messages you are sending out.

Starting MS Word

2. In Word, open or create the file that you want to send as attachment.
3. Click the **File** tab highlight **Save & Send.** A sub options appears. Select **Send Using Email** and then choose **Send as Attachment.**
4. The Outlook Message window appears as shown in Figure 6.31.

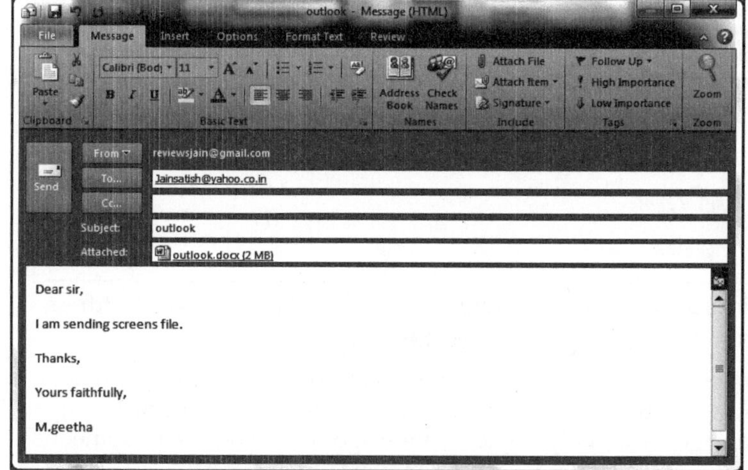

Figure 6.31 Word Attached the file in the outlook message window

5. Select the From address in **From:** drop-down list.
6. Type the e-mail name of the recipient in the **To:** line or select the e-mail name from your Address Book.
7. Leave the **Cc:** box blank. This is used if you want to send a copy of the message to someone.
8. Type a subject for the e-mail on the Subject line.

Attach a File

9. Word attached the file in the **Attached:** list box as shown in Figure 6.31.
10. Click the **Send** button to deliver the message and its **attached file.** The file is uploaded to mail server, so the time it takes to send the message depends on the speed of Internet connection and the size of the file.

Opening and Saving Attachments

Attachments are files that can be included with an e-mail message. Messages that have attachments are identified by a paper clip icon in the message list. Depending on the format of the message that you receive, attachments appear in one of two locations in the message.

- If the message format is Hypertext Markup Language (HTML) or plain text, attachments will appear in the attachment box under the Subject line.
- If the message format is the less-common Rich Text Format (RTF), attachments will appear in the body of the message. Even though the file appears in the message body, it actually remains a separate attachment.

➡ **To open/save a mail containing an attachment, do this:**

1. Select any e-mail message in the Inbox folder containing an attachment of a Portable Document Format (PDF) document. After selecting the e-mail message, read the message boy in the Reading pane.
2. In the Reading pane, you can see a pdf document attached along with the e-mail message.
3. The following commands are listed in the context menu, which is displayed when you right click a pdf document:
   - **Preview:** It enables a preview of the attached file in the reading pane.
   - **Open:** It opens the attached document.
   - **Quick Print:** It sends the currently selected attachment to the default printer for printing.
   - **Save As:** It Opens the Save Attachment dialog box, where you can specify the appropriate location and file name to save the attached item.
   - **Save All Attachments:** It saves all the attachments included with an e-mail message on your computer system.
   - **Remove Attachment:** It removes the currently selected attachment from an e-mail message.
   - **Copy:** It copies the currently selected attachment. You can place the copy of the attachment at a desired location on your system using the Paste command.
   - **Select All:** Selects all the attachments included in an e-mail message.
4. Select the **Save As** option from the context menu to save the pdf document.
5. The **Save Attachment** dialog box appears.
6. Click the Save button to save the file.

Deleting E-mail Messages

To delete an e-mail message from the message window or from the Inbox do the following options:

1. Click the e-mail in the Inbox folder you want to delete.
2. On the Home tab in the Delete group, click Delete icon.
3. Your message is deleted and send to the Deleted Items folder.

6.4 DOCUMENT COLLABORATION

Document collaboration enables organizations to share project-specific information across departments without time and space constraints. By logging into just one common virtual platform employees can instantly collaborate with one another. Routine work and time critical functions can be managed and reviewed. Business persons can communicate with employees, share documents, schedule work and effectively monitor performance . Employees can gain timely clarifications from company experts and information can be shared globally.

☞ *Document collaboration refers to share data in a consistent manner, so it can be retrieved, reviewed, approved and audited by authorized individuals.*

Your success in using document collaboration depends on selecting tools that provide a secure way to upload, find, and review documents and then involving others in the review process.

Let us take a look at some of the risks associated with sending documents over e-mail compared to more secure methods.

Document Review Risks

The risk associated with document collaboration can improve the business processes. Here some examples of how we get started.

1. **Guidelines**–We work with organizations to develop a set of guidelines for reviewing the documents so each contributor understands what is expected of them during the review process. What may be obvious to you, especially if you are more proficient with Web technologies, may be more challenging for other individuals.
2. **Ownership**–Each document must have a Document Owner. Thus, person is responsible for driving the document through the review cycle and ensuring that it is approved on time.
3. **Security**–Sharing documents by e-mail creates different security risks, especially for confidential documents.
4. **Progress Reports**–While we all enjoy the convenience of e-mail, there is no way to tell if others have started reviewing the document or if they have even opened it.
5. **Scheduling**–One of the limitations of e-mail is that while you can remind others to complete the document review by a specific date, they may ignore this or simply do not see it in e-mail.
6. **Workflow**–The true measure of success with Document Collaboration lies in improvements to the current processes, reduction in costs, and satisfied clients. You do not want a scenario where highly-paid team members spend hours in cutting and pasting between documents.

6.5 INSTANT MESSAGING AND COLLABORATION

Instant Messaging (IM) is a form of real-time direct text-based communication between two or more people using personal computers or other devices, along with shared clients. The user's text is conveyed over a network, such as the Internet. More advanced instant messaging software clients also allow enhanced modes of communication, such as live voice or video calling.

Instant messaging allows effective and efficient communication, allowing immediate receipt of acknowledgment or reply. In many cases, instant messaging includes added features which can make it even more popular. For example, users may see each other via Webcams, or talk directly for free over the Internet using a microphone and headphones or loudspeakers. Many client programs allow file transfers, although they are usually limited in the permissible file-size.

Many instant messaging services offer video calling features, Voice Over Internet Protocol (VoIP) and Web conferencing services. Web conferencing services can integrate both video calling and instant messaging abilities.

☞ *Some instant messaging companies are also offering desktop sharing, IP radio, and IPTV to the voice and video features.*

6.5.1 Using Instant Messaging

Instant Messaging (IM) is a form of electronic communication enabling ad hoc collaboration through sending and receiving messages across a network connection. Some of the popular and widely used instant messenger programs available today. Steps given below will make you to understand exactly what happens with an instant-messaging service:

1. You go to download page i.e http://www.google.com/talk/ or http://www.skype.com and get a free software client for your computer.
2. You install the software and open the client.
3. The client tries to connect to the server. It uses a proprietary protocol for communication.
4. Once the client is connected to the server, you can enter your name and password to log in to the server. If this is your first time on, you can sign up for an account and immediately begin using it. When server verifies your name and password, you are logged in.
5. The client sends connection information (IP address and number of the port assigned to the client) to server of the computer you are using. It also provides user with names of everyone in your contacts list.
6. The server creates a temporary file that has the connection information for you and the list of your contacts. It then checks to see if any of the users in your contact list are currently logged in.
7. If the server finds any of your contacts logged in, it sends a message back to the client on your computer with the connection information for that user. The server also sends your connection information to the people in your contact list that are signed on.
8. When your client gets the connection information for a person in your contact list, it changes the status of that person to "online." You click on the name of a person in your contact list who is online, and a window opens in which you can enter text into. You enter a message and click "send" or hit return to communicate with that person.
9. Because your client has the IP address and port number for computer of the person that you sent the message to, your message is sent directly to the client on that person's computer. In other words, the server is not involved at this point. All communication is directly take place between the two clients.
10. The other person gets your instant message and responds. The window that each of you sees on your respective computers expands to include a scrolling dialog of the conversation. Each person's instant messages appears in this window on both computers.
11. When conversation is complete, you close the message window. Eventually, you go offline and exit. When this happens, your client sends a message to the server to terminate the session. The server sends a message to the client of each person on your contact list who is currently online to indicate that you have logged off. Finally, the server deletes the temporary file that contains the connection information for your client.

Some of the popular Instant Messenger are Yahoo Messanger, MSN Messenger, Rediff Bol, Google Talk and Skype.

Using the Skype Instant Messengers

Skype is one of the well known Instant Messengers. It allows the users to explore the facilities of instant messaging provided by it. Apart from instant messaging, the other feature of Skype are file transfer, video conferencing, etc. Skype also provides the users with short message service. It is Niklas Zennstrom and Janus Friis who have created the Skype software program.

You have to download a Skype program, install it, register as a Skype user, and make use of the Skype applications.

Once installed, the program itself has the feel and look of any chat program. You can add contacts, block them, see if they are online, and communicate with them.

6.5.2 Instant Messaging Providers

The first instant messaging service was introduced in 1996 by an Israeli based ICQ. ICQ is an instant messaging computer program, owned by Time Warner's AOL subsidiary. ICQ was first developed by the Israeli company Mirabilis. The first version of the program was released in November 1996. After that it was later acquired by America Online. The major Instant Messaging Providers are AOL's Instant Messenger (AIM), ICQ, Yahoo! Messenger, Rediff Bol, Google Talk, Jabber and Microsoft's incarnations: Microsoft Network or MSN Messenger, Windows Messenger and Windows Live Messenger.

Instant messaging providers may also provide services like video phoning, file sharing, PC-to-PC voice calling and PC-to-regular-phone calling. Instant messaging has promoted IP telephony because the IM software makes it easy to switch from "text chat" to "voice chat," provided the user has a headset or microphone and speakers. The instant message providers give the option to the users to set up a buddy list. You also have to add the user names of the people you want to message with to your "buddy list" which is also called friend list or contact list. When they log on to the Internet with their Instant message software, and provided they have not configured themselves as "invisible," you are instantly alerted. When they log off, you are also notified. Each system has its own method for blocking incoming and outgoing messages.

Many of us e-mail instead of writing letters or even calling people on the phone. People around the world send out billions of e-mail messages every day. One should remember that sometimes even e-mail is not that fast enough. You might not know if a person you want to e-mail is online at that moment. Also, if you are e-mailing back and forth with someone, you usually have to click through a few steps. This is why instant messaging (IM) has become so popular. Most of the Instant Messaging Providers give you the following facilities:

- Instant messages - Send notes back and forth with a friend who is online.
- Chat - Create a chat room with friends or co-workers.

- Web links - Share links to your favorite Web sites.
- Video - Send and view videos, and chat face to face with friends.
- Images - Look at an image stored on your friend's computer.
- Sounds - Play sounds for your friends.
- Files - Share files by sending them directly to your friends.
- Talk - Use the Internet instead of a phone to actually talk with friends.
- Streaming content - Real-time or near-real-time stock quotes and news.
- Mobile capabilities - Send instant messages from your cell phone.

6.5.3 Netiquette

Netiquettes are the rules for correct behaviour on the Internet. Netiquettes distinct the Internet from traditional forms of communications, such as telephone conversion, face-to-face meetings, paper based letters. It helps you to avoid misunderstanding that may arise during communication accomplished via any Internet services especially e-mail, chat and mailing lists, etc.

Nature of Poor Netiquette

Poor Netiquette have following parts:

- Poor grammar and spelling errors
- Junk mails
- Harsh language

Rules for Internet Etiquettes

- Be concise, Use appropriate language
- No Spam and Include a subject line

Characteristics of Good Netiquette

Communications that do not waste the users' time are considered as good netiquette.

6.6 SUMMARY

This chapter presents details of Communication and Collaboration. The introduction of the chapter begins with Communication. It is the process by which a message or information is exchanged from a sender to a receiver. Electronic mail is a method of exchanging messages, designed primarily for human use. It is important means of communication. The chapter also discusses sending and receiving mail. The recipient can save the address for future reference in an address book; reply to the original message, forward the message to a third party. Using Outlook Express, Inbox folder is used to store all incoming mails. Outbox is a folder to store all outgoing mails which are also discussed.

MODEL QUESTIONS AND ANSWERS

1. Multiple Choice

1.1 SMTP is a simple
a. TCP protocol b. IP Protocol
c. TCP/IP protocol d. None of the above

1.2 A simple protocol used for fetching e-mail from a mailbox is
a. POP3 c. IMAP
b. POP2 d. None of the above

1.3 A popular application of computer networking is the World Wide Web of newsgroup called
a. News c. Netnews
b. Gateways d. Both (a) and (b)

1.4 E-mail address is made up of
a. Single part c. Three parts
b. Two parts d. None of the above

1.5 The program supplied by VSNL when you ask for Internet connection for the e-mail access is
a. ISP c. Pine
b. HotDog d. None of the above

1.6 SMTP stands for
a. Server Mail Transfer Protocol
b. Simple Mail Transfer Protocol
c. Small Mail Transmission Protocol
d. Short Mail Transmission Protocol

1.7 The steps for sending an e-mail are:
a. Start an e-mail program
b. Give the address of where to send
c. Compose a message to send the message
d. All of the above

1.8 Messenger Mailbox is present in
a. Internet Explorer c. Both a and b
b. Netscape Communicator d. None of the above

1.9 The convenient place to store contact information for quick retrieval is
a. Message box c. Address book
b. Address box d. None of the above

1.10 Which one of the following statements is not correct for Digital signature?
a. It is a mechanism for authentication
b. It is the scanned image of one's signature
c. It is created by encrypting information
d. It cannot be duplicated

2. State whether the following are True or False

2.1 To specify multiple recipients of carbon copy of same mail message, Cc: field is used.
2.2 In SMTP, the message can be of any length.
2.3 A protocol used for fetching e-mail from a mailbox is POP1.
2.4 All incoming e-mail messages are to be stored in the Outbox folder.
2.5 The e-mail component of Internet Explorer is called "Outlook Express"
2.6 When sending an e-mail, the subject line describes the contents of the message.
2.7 Recipient's log-in name must form a part of his e-mail address.
2.8 Unsolicited e-mail advertising is known as spam.
2.9 E-mail is limited to text based messages.
2.10 The two parts of e-mail address is separated by @ symbol.

Answers

1.	1.1	a	1.2	a	1.3	c	1.4	b	1.5	c
	1.6	b	1.7	d	1.8	b	1.9	c	1.10	b
2.	2.1	T	2.2	F	2.3	F	2.4	F	2.5	T
	2.6	T	2.7	F	2.8	T	2.9	F	2.10	T

CHAPTER 7

Making Small Presentations

7.0 INTRODUCTION

PowerPoint 2010 is a presentation program developed for the Windows and Mac OS computer operating systems. Being widely used by business people, educators, and trainers, it is among the most prevalent forms of persuasion technology. According to its vendor, MS Corporation, some 30 million presentations are made with PowerPoint every day.

In MS PowerPoint, as in most other presentation software, text, graphics, movies, and other objects are positioned on individual pages or "slides". The "slide" is a reference to the slide projector, a device which has become somewhat obsolete due to the use of PowerPoint and other presentation software. Slides can be printed, or displayed on-screen and navigated through at the command of the presenter. Transitions between slides can be animated in a variety of ways, as can the emergence of elements on a slide itself. The overall design of a presentation can be controlled with a master slide. The overall structure, extending to the text on each slide, can be edited using an outliner. Presentations can be saved and run in many types of file formats.

7.1 OBJECTIVES

The reader will be able to understand the following:

- Basics of PowerPoint
- Creating a Presentation
- Preparation of Slides , such as Inserting Tables in MS Excel Worksheet, Adding Clip Arts etc.
- Presentation of Slides
- Slide Show

7.2 BASICS OF POWERPOINT

PowerPoint is the largest selling presentation graphics software package by MS Corporation of USA and since its introduction in 1987, PowerPoint has set new standards for the working of presentation graphics.

PowerPoint 2010 helps you bringing *ideas* and *information* that you want to convey to your audience with no difficulty. With PowerPoint 2010, you can:

- Quickly create *paper for Overhead Projector (OHP), 35mm slide,* or *on-screen* presentations.
- Supplement your presentations with *speaker's notes.*
- Use material you have created in other application packages, such as Word 2010 and Excel 2010.

7.2.1 Using PowerPoint

Presentations

You can make presentation in the form of *slides, handouts* or *speaker's notes.*

Slides

Slides are individual "*pages*" of a presentation. It may contain *text, graphs, clipart,* etc. You can even print slides for overhead projector transparencies.

Handouts

Handouts consist of printed versions of your slides – either two, three, or six slides per page.

7.2.2 Opening PowerPoint 2010 for Presentation

➡ **To start PowerPoint 2010, do this:**

1. Click the **Start** button on the Taskbar.
2. Highlight **All Programs** menu item and click **MS Office** and choose **MS Office PowerPoint 2010** (Figure 7.1).

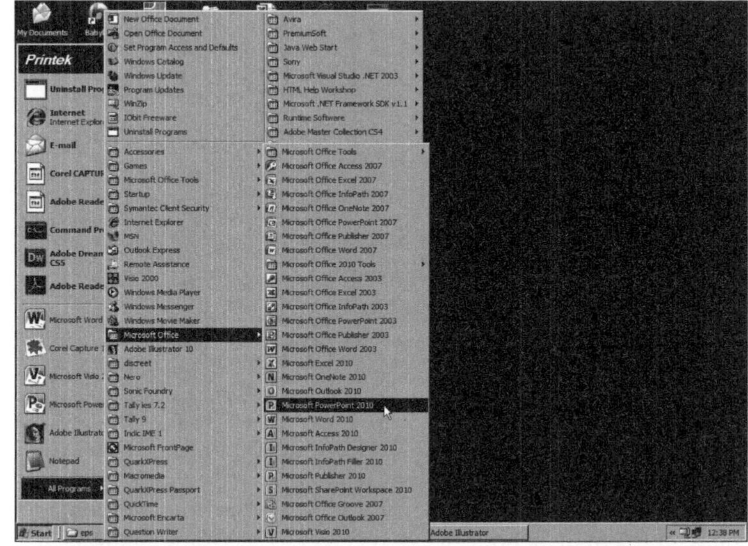

Figure 7.1 Starting PowerPoint with the Start Button

When you first start PowerPoint 2010, it displays a blank presentation with a single slide showing. The layout is simple, with a title at the top and a subtitle below (See Figure 7.2).

Understanding the Screen Elements

You will notice a close resemblance of the PowerPoint 2010 opening screen with the opening screens of Word 2007 and Excel 2007. The main elements of the PowerPoint window are as shown in Figure 7.2.

Title bar: The *Title bar* is at the top of the screen (See Figure 7.2). It shows the title PowerPoint and the name of presentation. If you have not yet saved any presentation then it displays the default name for the presentation which is *Presentation1.*

Ribbon: Ribbon is displayed just below the title bar. In Ribbon, Commands are organized in logical groups, which are collected together under tabs (Figure 7.2).

Quick Access Toolbar: This toolbar is located by default at the top of PowerPoint 2010 window. By default, this toolbar displays the Save, Undo and Repeat buttons.

Minimize button: Shrinks the application window to a bar on the taskbar, you can click its button on the taskbar to reopen it.

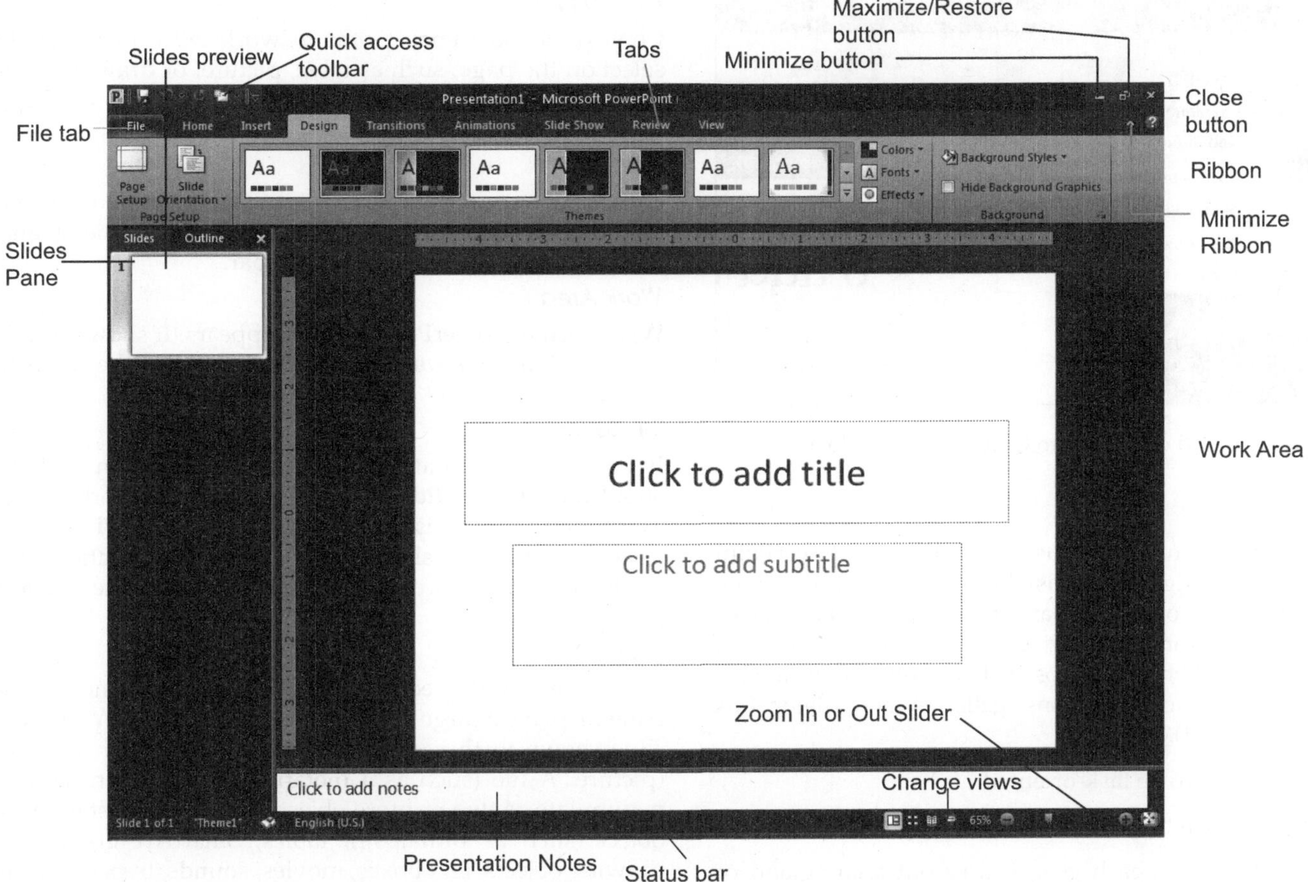

Figure 7.2 A blank presentation displayed by PowerPoint

Restore button: A double box at the right of a title bar that restores an application or document into a sizable window.

Close button: A box at the right of a title bar (X) that closes the window or dialog box.

Work area: Where active PowerPoint slide(s) appear. Figure 7.2 shows it in Normal view, but other views are available that make the work area appear differently.

Status bar: It gives the information about the presentation and provides shortcuts for changing the view and the zoom.

Exploring PowerPoint 2010 Interface

There is a new look for PowerPoint 2010. There is also a new user interface that replaces menus, toolbars, and most of the task panes from previous versions of PowerPoint. The new user interface is designed to help you to be more productive in PowerPoint; more easily find the right features for various tasks and also be more efficient.

The PowerPoint 2010 interface consists of various components, which are as follows:

Minimize/Maximize/Restore and Close buttons

The Minimize, Maximize and Close buttons are located on the top right corner of the MS PowerPoint window. The Minimize button is used to minimize the MS PowerPoint window over the Task bar whereas the Maximize button is helps to restore or maximize the MS PowerPoint window. The Close button is used to close the document (See Figure 7.2).

File Tab

File tab is the colored tab which is located in the upper-left corner of MS Office 2010 programs and below the Quick Access Toolbar. When you click the File tab, you can see the Backstage view. File tab replaces the office button in PowerPoint 2010. It contains commands like New, Open, Save, Save As, Print, etc.

Quick Access Toolbar

The Quick Access Toolbar is a customizable toolbar that contains a set of commands that are independent of the tab that is currently displayed. You can add buttons that represent commands to the Quick Access Toolbar. You can move the Quick Access Toolbar from one of the two possible locations. This toolbar is located by default at the top of PowerPoint 2010 window. It provides tools that you use frequently, such as Save, Undo and Repeat buttons (See Figure 7.2). You can customize the Quick Access Toolbar by adding commands to it.

➡ **To add command to Quick Access Toolbar, do this:**

1. Right click the appropriate command that you want to add to the Quick Access Toolbar (See Figure 7.3).
2. Then click **Add to Quick Access Toolbar** from the context menu as shown in Figure 7.3.

Dialog Box Launchers

The dialog box launchers are small icons that appear in some groups on the Ribbon. Clicking a Dialog Box Launcher opens a related dialog box or task pane, providing more options related to that group.

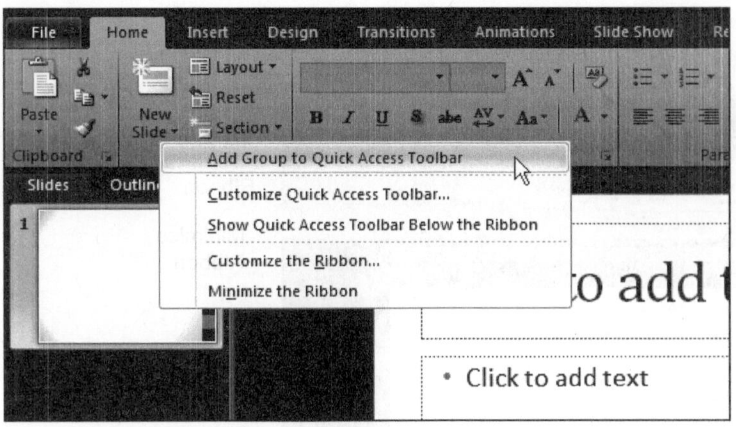

Figure 7.3 Add command to Quick Access toolbar

Ribbon

The primary replacement for menus and toolbars in PowerPoint 2010 is the Ribbon. Designed for easy browsing, the Ribbon consists of tabs that are organized around specific scenarios or objects. The controls on each tab are further organized into several groups. The Ribbon can host richer content than menus and toolbars can, including buttons, galleries, and dialog box contents (See Figure 7.4).

1. Tabs are designed to be task-oriented.
2. Groups within each tab break a task into subtasks.
3. Command buttons in each group carry out a command or display a menu of commands.

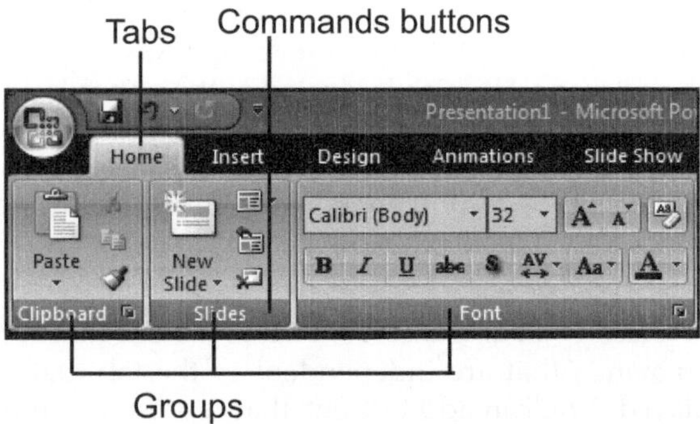

Figure 7.4

Contextual Tools

Contextual tools enable you to work with an object that you select on the page, such as table, picture, or drawing. When you click the object, the pertinent set of contextual tabs appear in colour next to the standard tabs (See Figure 7.5).

Scroll Bar

The Scroll bar appears at the right side of the PowerPoint. You can also scroll between different slides by using the up and down arrow buttons present in the scroll bar.

Work Area

Where active PowerPoint slide(s) appears. It shows it in Normal view, but other views are available that make the work area different.

Status Bar

It gives the information about the presentation and provides about the current slide, such as slide number and theme name. The slide number displays the currently selected slide with the total number of the slides present in the presentations; whereas, the theme name represents the name of the theme applied to the presentation.

Slides Pane

In the upper-right section of the PowerPoint window, the Slide pane displays a large view of the current slide. With the current slide shown in this view, you can add text and insert pictures (picture: A file (such as a metafile) that you can ungroup and manipulate as two or more objects, or a file that stays as a single object (such as bitmaps).), tables, SmartArt graphics, charts, drawing objects, text boxes, movies, sounds, hyperlinks, and animations.

Notes Pane

In the Notes pane below the Slide pane, you can type notes that apply to the current slide. Later, you can print your notes and refer to them when you give your presentation. You can also print notes to hand out to your audience or include the notes in a presentation that you send to the audience or post on a Web page.

Zoom Control

You can use Zoom controls to get a larger or smaller view of your presentation by drag the Zoom slider right to left. You can click the Zoom In (+ plus) button to get a larger view of the presentation and the Out (- minus) button to get a smaller view of the presentation.

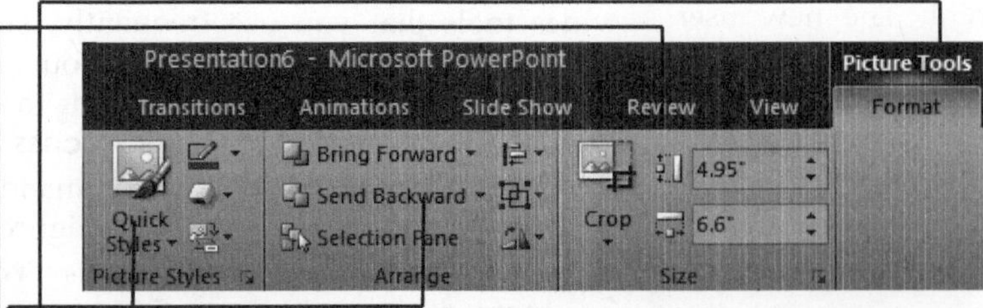

1. Select an object in your presentation.
2. The name of the applicable contextual tools appears in an accent color, and the contextual tabs appear next to the standard set of tabs.
3. The contextual tabs provide controls for working with the selected item.
4. A standard tab available on the Ribbon.

Figure 7.5 Contextual Tools

Exploring the Tabs

Ribbon in PowerPoint 2010 is a group of tabs. This tab consists of two types, command tabs and contextual tabs. A command tab is a collection of commands of a specific category. Commands in a command tab are placed into different group. Each command set representing a subcategory of commands. Contextual tabs appear on the Ribbon when you add or select some object, such as image, a table, or a chart on a PowerPoint slide. An example of a contextual tab is the Format tab Some of the tabs are discuss in the following sections.

Home Tab: When you click it, this tab is active. Buttons related to working with document contents are organized in this tab. It has six groups: Clipboard, Slides, Font, Paragraph, Drawing and Editing. Only the button representing commands that can be performed on the currently selected document element are active (See Figure 7.6).

The groups for the Home Tab are:

(a) ***Clipboard:*** This contains the Cut, Copy, and Paste commands.

(b) ***Slides:*** This section allows you to insert new slides (clicking on the 'New Slide' button allows you to select the slide type you wish), as well as adjust the layout of your individual slides, reset slides to default, and delete slides.

(c) ***Font:*** Select the font here. Adjust the font type and size. Make it bold, italic, or underline. Change the colour or highlighting. Using the tab, you can also change case of selected text to uppercase or lowercase.

(d) ***Paragraph:*** Bullets or numbered lists. It also changes the alignment of text and change the spacing between lines.

(e) ***Drawing:*** Insert shapes. Arrange objects on a given slide. It also applies fill colour in the selected shape and add effect to the shapes.

(f) ***Editing:*** Find, edit, select, and replace text.

Insert Tab: Click this button for related items you can insert. These are organizing on this tab. It has seven groups: *Tables, Images, Illustrations, links, Text, Symbols* and *Media* (See Figure 7.7).

When you need to insert anything into your slide show, this is where you come to do it. The groups available to you are:

(a) ***Tables:*** Insert tables into the slide. These can be pre-made, or you can make them as you like.

(b) ***Images:*** It allows you to insert pictures from a file as well as from the Clip Art in a slide. You can also create photo album and apply visual effects to pictures. Screenshot which allows you take screenshot of all currently opened windows on the computer.

(c) ***Illustrations:*** It allows you to insert pre-defined shapes, Smart Arts and charts in the presentation.

(d) ***Links:*** Add a hyperlink, to take you out of your slideshow to a Web resource. Add an action to cause something to happen in the slide show if you point to an object with the mouse.

(e) ***Text:*** It is not just about typing text into a slide: Insert text boxes, which allow you to play with the location and orientation of words. Insert headers and footers. Turn your text into "***Word Art***". Insert date, times, slide numbers and other embedded objects.

(f) ***Symbols:*** It allows you to insert and edit equations and insert symbols in the presentation.

(g) ***Media:*** Insert video and sound into your slide, to create a truly vibrant presentation.

Design tab: Click this tab which will show buttons that are related to items. You can give design to your slides. They are organized on this tab. It has three groups: *Page Setup, Themes, Background* (See Figure 7.8).

Adjust the look of individual slides with the contents of the design tab. Change just one slide, or apply your changes to the whole presentation:

(a) ***Page Setup:*** Adjust margins, page size, and orientation (portrait or landscape).

(b) ***Themes:*** PowerPoint 2007 comes with 20 built-in themes (combinations of color, layout, and font). You can browse the Web for more themes, or create your own custom ones.

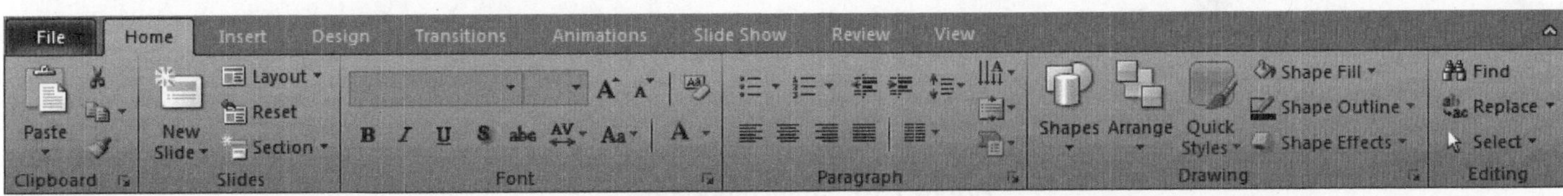

Figure 7.6 Home tab

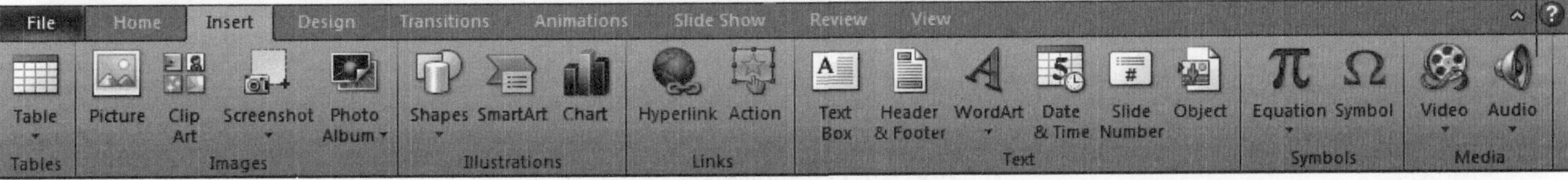

Figure 7.7 Insert

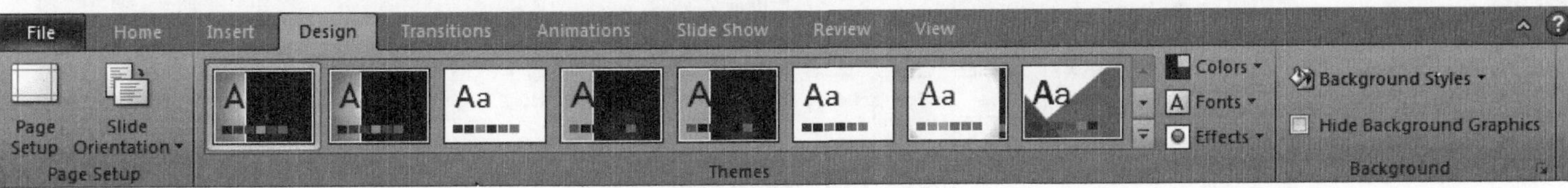

Figure 7.8 Design tab

(c) ***Background:*** It adjust the background look of your slides by changing the color, or adding special images like watermarks.

Transitions: The transitions tab let you preview the presentation after applying effects, add transitions to a slide, and set the timing for the slide show of the presentation. It has three groups: *Preview, Transition to this slide, timing* (See Figure 7.9).

(a) ***Preview:*** It helps to view the slide after the transition effect is applied.

(b) ***Transition to this slide:*** It allows you to apply transition to a slide and set the effect option specific to a transition.

(c) ***Timing:*** It allows you to add transition sound and set the time to move to the next slide.

Animations tab: Click this tab which will show buttons that are related to items. You can give animations to your slides. For example, you can animate individual objects on the slide. They are organized on this tab. It has three groups: *Preview, Animation, Advance Animation* and *Timing* (See Figure 7.10).

(a) ***Preview:*** To preview the animation applied in the slide, include transition effect and animation applied on objects and text.

(b) ***Animation:*** It allows you to apply animation to a slide and the effect based on the animation type.

(c) ***Advanced Animation:*** It allows you to apply advanced features to the applied animation and apply trigger effect.

(d) ***Timings:*** To set the duration of the slides and delay between the slides. You can reorder the animation.

Slide Show: Click this tab which will show buttons that are related to items. In this tab, you can view; take up the full computer screen, like an actual presentation. For example, you can see how your graphics animated effects will look during the presentation. It has three groups: *Start slide show, Set Up* and *Monitors* (See Figure 7.11).

(a) ***Start Slide Show:*** Run it from the beginning or from a selected slide. Or, create a second slide show using only those slides in the presentation you want to use.

(b) ***Set Up:*** Record narration for your slide show. Practice your timing as you speak while the show's slides transition automatically.

(c) ***Monitors:*** It allows you to select a screen resolution or a presenter view.

Review tab: Click this tab which will show buttons that are related to items. In this tab, you can view and add comments to your presentation and you might prefer to check spelling all at once when you finish your document. It has three groups: *Proofing, Language, Comments* and *Compare* (See Figure 7.12).

(a) ***Proofing:*** Check the spelling, open research task pane to references for more information; find synonyms so you do not use the same word repeatedly, check the grammar etc.

(b) ***Language:*** It allows you to translate the text in other language.

(c) ***Comments:*** Add or edit comments about a given slide, or about a specific bit of content on a slide. Helpful when planning narration.

(d) ***Compare:*** To compare different presentations, accept or reject the changes, and show the review pane.

Figure 7.9 Transitions

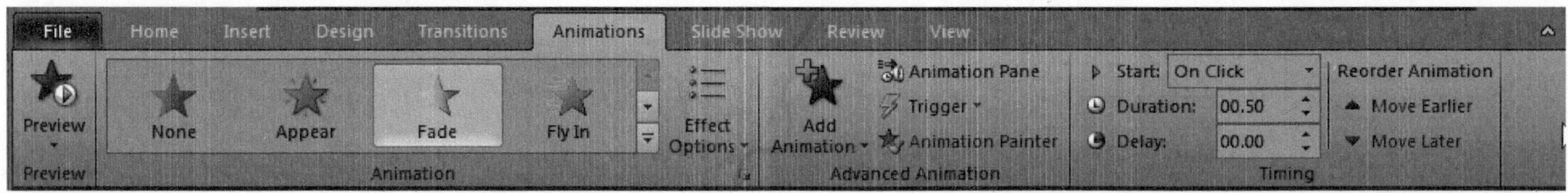

Figure 7.10 Animations tab

Figure 7.11 Slide Show

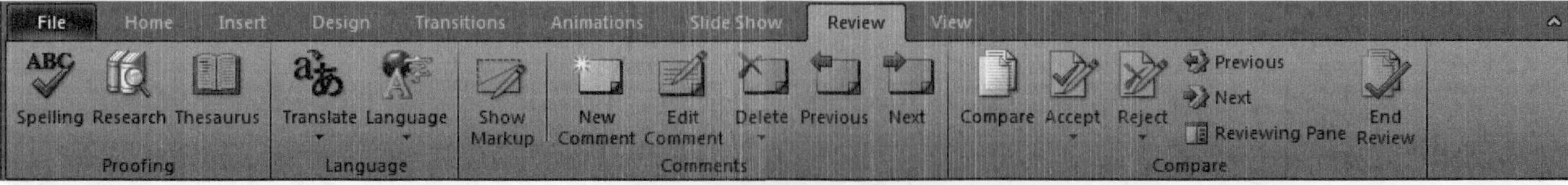

Figure 7.12 Review tab

Figure 7.13 View tab

View tab: Click this tab which will show buttons that are related to changing the view during presentation. It has six groups: *Presentation views, Master Views, Show/Hide, Zoom, Color/Grayscale, Window* and *Macros* (See Figure 7.13).

(a) ***Presentation View:*** Choose from normal, slide sorter, notes view, handout view, and other options, either for on screen viewing, or printouts.

(b) ***Master Views:*** To view the presentation in slide master view, handout master view and notes master view.

(c) ***Show/Hide:*** It display, gridlines, rulers and other tools to help you place objects into the slides exactly where you want them.

(d) ***Zoom:*** Zoom In or Out to change the size of the slide window.

(e) ***Color/Grayscale:*** View the presentation in color, grayscale or even black and white.

(f) ***Window:*** Arrange the windows in which you are working to help you be more productive.

(g) ***Macros:*** Create and use custom macros to do complex tasks with just a click or two.

Opening an Existing Presentation

PowerPoint 2010 opens files in any of the several format, such as (.pptx, .pptm, .potx, .ppt, .pot, etc.)

➡ **To open an existing presentation, do this:**

1. Open the **File** tab on the Ribbon. The Backstage view appears. Alternatively, press Ctrl+O (See Figure 7.14).

Figure 7.14 Selecting Open option from the File tab

2. Click the **Open** option from the Backstage view (See Figure 7.15).
3. The **Open** dialog box appears as shown in Figure 7.15.
4. Choose the files and folders in the **Look in:** drop-down list.
5. Select the name of the file you want to open from the list.
4. Click Open button to open the presentation.

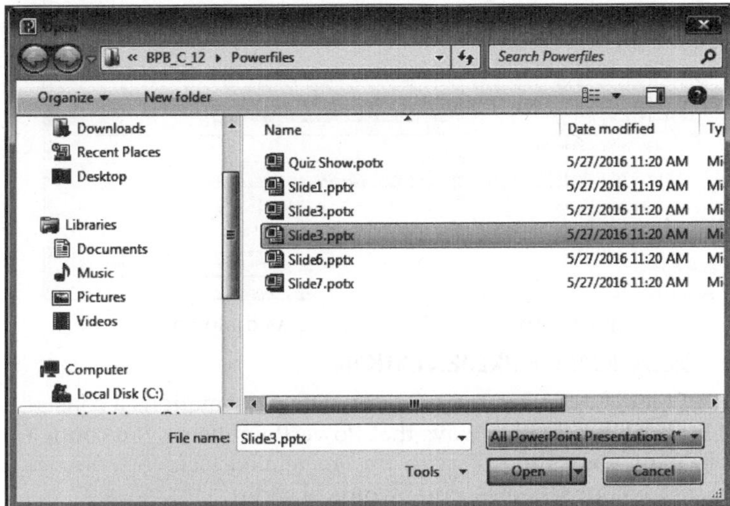

Figure 7.15 PowerPoint's Open dialog box

7.2.3 Saving the Presentation

When working on a presentation, it is very important that you save it at regular intervals so that in case there is system failure you do not loose much of your work.

PowerPoint has two commands to save your file – Save and Save As command.

- The Save command is used to save the presentation.
- The Save As command is used when you want to save an existing presentation under a new name or you are saving your presentation for the first time.

➡ **To save a presentation, do this:**

1. Click the **File** tab and on the Ribbon. The Backstage view will appear. Select the **Save** option from the **File** tab. Or click the **Save** button on the Quick Access toolbar or from the keyboard press Ctrl+S.
2. If you have already saved the file then PowerPoint updates the earlier saved file. If you have not saved the file before, the **Save As** dialog box as in Figure 7.16 appears.
3. In the **Save As** list box specify the location where you want to save the file in the **Save in:** drop-down list. (Choose PowerPoint Template). It adds the template to your list of available templates.
4. Type the desired file name which you want to save the presentation in the **File Name:** list box.
5. Click **Save** button.

➡ **To save a presentation using Save As command, do this:**

1. Click the **File** tab and choose **Save As...** . The **Save As** dialog box in Figure 7.16 appears. Now follow Step 1 through 5 in the save procedure.

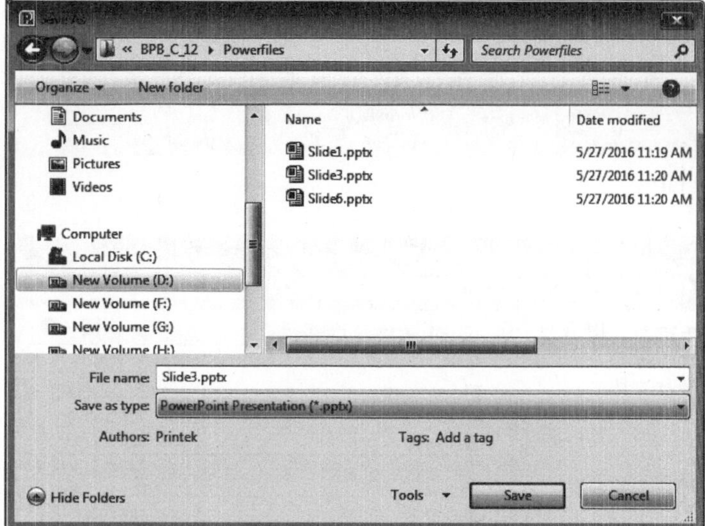

Figure 7.16 PowerPoint's Save As dialog box

7.3 CREATION OF PRESENTATION

PowerPoint is designed to give your slide presentations a consistent look. There are four ways that PowerPoint helps you control the look of your slides – with design related elements, Visual elements, colour schemes, and layouts of slides.

7.3.1 Creating a Presentation using an Installed Template

A template is a file that contains many types of documents, including resumes, cover letters, business plans, business cards, etc. MS provided templates and presentations that come pre-installed with PowerPoint. These templates offer various layouts, visual elements, and other design-related elements to create presentations.

➡ **To create a presentation by using an installed template, do this:**

1. Click the **File** tab. The Backstage view appears as shown in Figure 7.17.

Figure 7.17 Select Sample templates under the available templates themes

2. Select the **New** option from the Backstage view. It displays the list of all available templates appears in the middle pane as shown in Figure 7.17.
3. Under the **Available Templates and Themes** category, select the **Sample templates** option.
4. In the Sample templates, you can see a different types of templates, with all formatting, such as background, themes colors, font, etc., (See Figure 7.18).

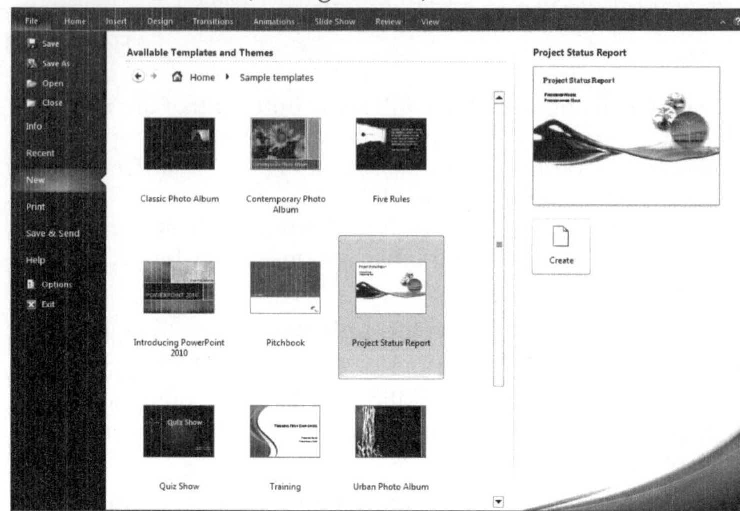

Figure 7.18 Select desired template from the sample templates

5. Select the desired template you want to apply. For example, we have selected, **Project Status Report** (See Figure 7.18).
6. In the **preview** box, you see a sample presentation for which the template is designed.
7. Click **Create** button.
8. You can see the selected template as default presentation title name (See Figure 7.19).

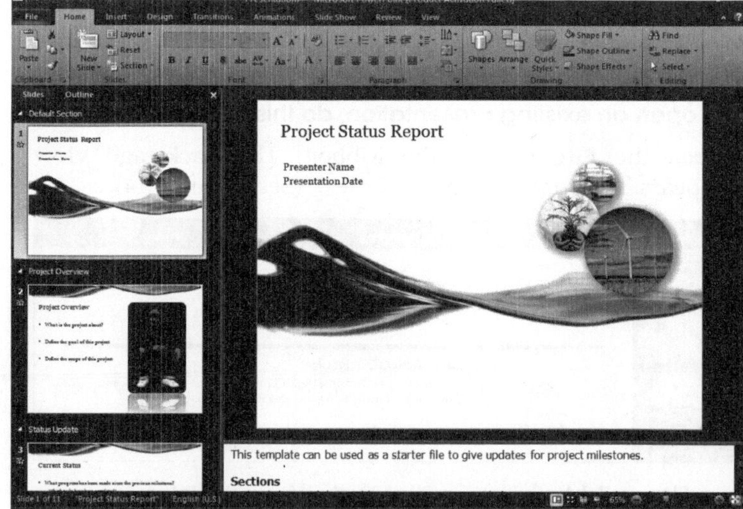

Figure 7.19 PowerPoint opens the selected template

7.3.2 Creating a Blank Presentation

When you start PowerPoint 2010, the program displays a blank title slide by default. You can begin to add text and pictures on that slide choose a different slide layout, apply a design, etc.

If you want to create a PowerPoint presentation on your own, you can use the blank template in PowerPoint 2010. The blank template offers only the basic visual elements of a presentation, such as placeholder to add a title to a slide.

➡ **To create a presentation by using the blank template, do this:**

1. Click the **File** tab. The Backstage view appears, displaying various options as shown in Figure 7.20.

Figure 7.20 File Backstage view

2. Select the **New** option from the Backstage view.
3. The list of all available templates appears in the middle pane.
4. Under the **Available Templates and Themes** category, select the **Blank presentation** option.
5. Click the **Create** button.
6. The new presentation is created with the name Presentation2 as shown in Figure 7.21.

You can see that a blank presentation contains a single slide with text boxes (placeholders) to enter a title and a subtitle. You can also apply different styles and background to it.

Creating a New Template based on an Existing Presentation

You can create a template in almost the same way as you create a presentation. If you have a template that already has most of the features you want, you will save time by creating a new presentation based on that existing template.

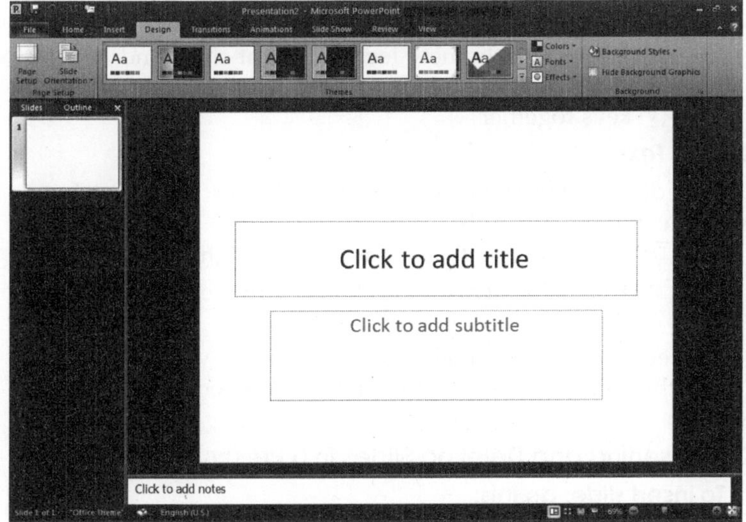

Figure 7.21 Blank presentation with the default name presentation2

1. Click the **File** tab on the ribbon. The Backstage view appears. A list of options appears as seen in 7.20.
2. Click the **New** option from the list.
3. Under **Available Template and Themes** click **New from existing** icon (See Figure 7.17).
4. The **New from Existing Presentation** dialog box appears as shown in Figure 7.22.
5. Select the template that is similar to the one that you want to create.
6. Then click **Create New**. Make the changes you want to apply, such as themes colours, fonts and other formats.
7. Click the **Save As** button to save the template.
8. The **Save As** dialog box appears. Give the new name to template file in the **File name:** drop-down list.
9. Select the PowerPoint template in the **Save as type:** drop-down list, and then click **Save** button (See Figure 7.16).

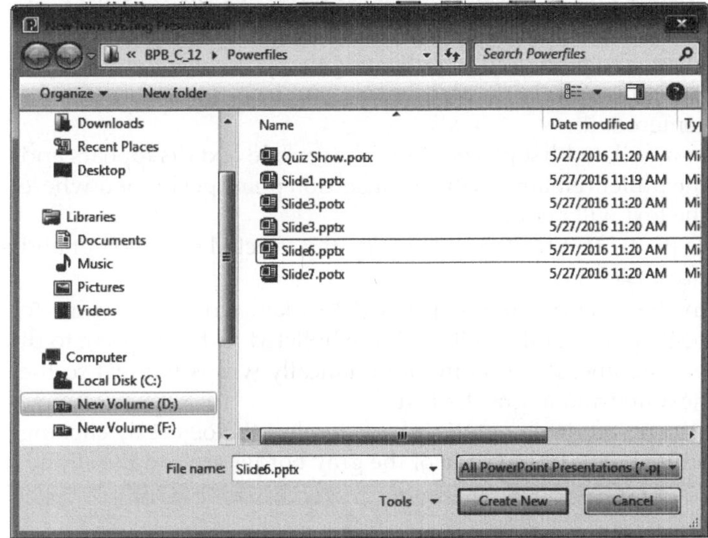

Figure 7.22 New from existing presentation

7.3.3 Entering and Editing Text

PowerPoint slide always contains text of some kind, even if it is just a title. Entering and editing text in PowerPoint is similar to entering and editing text in Word or Excel.

Entering Text to Slides

You can enter text in a presentation in two ways:

- Inserting a new slide with text place holder.
- Inserting text in an existing slide.

Adding Text in a Placeholder

PowerPoint 2010 comes with predefined layouts you want to use, or you can add a blank slide and create a custom layout. Many of these layouts contain text placeholders for title, body and bulleted list.

➡ **To insert a new slide with text, do this:**

1. Click the **Home** tab. In the **Slides** group click New slide down pointing arrow. A list of layout slides appears as shown in Figure 7.23.
2. Click anywhere within a placeholder to select it. This border indicates that the current placeholder is selected (See Figure 7.24).

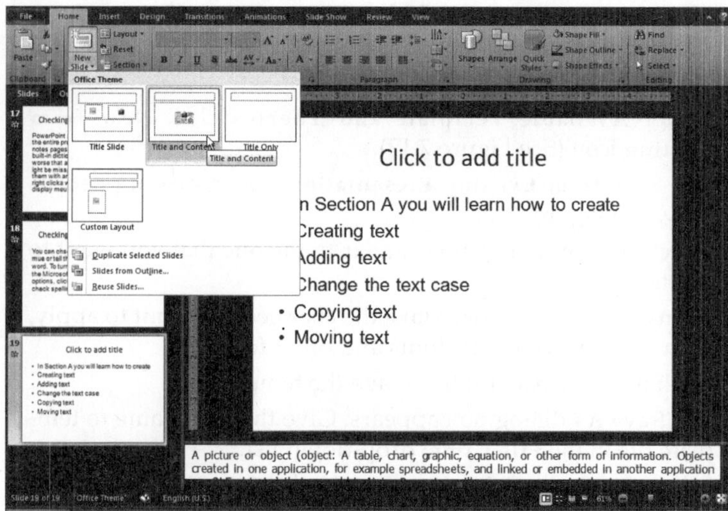

Figure 7.23 Selecting slide layout with title and contents

3. The sample text disappears and an insertion point appears inside the placeholder, indicating that you can enter text.
4. In a title or subtitle placeholder, the insertion point may be centered.
5. In a bulleted-list placeholder, the sample text disappears and the bullet remains, with the insertion point positioned where the text will begin.
6. Type the text for the slide inside the selected placeholder and press Enter key.
7. In the case of bullets, press Enter key when you want to begin a new bulleted item. If the bulleted text is too long to fit on one line, PowerPoint automatically wraps the text to the next line and aligns the text.
8. When you finish entering text, deselect the object by clicking a blank area of the slide of the gray border around the slide.

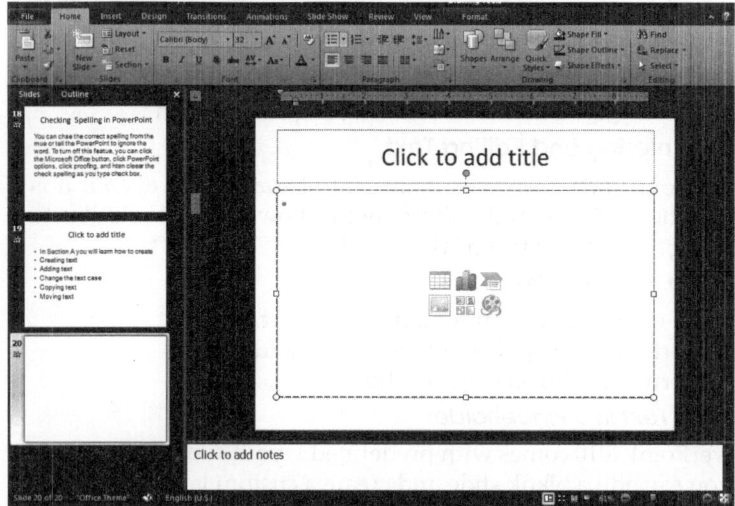

Figure 7.24 The Slide Layout with Placeholder

Editing Text on a Slide

You can make changes to the text in any text object simply by clicking the object. An insertion point appears, indicating that the text is ready for editing. Then you can start making changes to the text. Before you can change existing text, you have to select it by using the following techniques:

- Select an individual word by double-clicking it. The word and the space following it are selected.
- *Alternatively*, position the insertion point at the beginning of the text you want to select, hold down the Shift key, and either press an arrow key to select characters one at a time or click the end of the text you want to select.
- Select an entire slide title by clicking its slide icon on the Outline tab.
- Select all the text in a placeholder by clicking inside the placeholder and then clicking select and then **Select All** in the **Editing** group on the **Home** tab.

Copying Text

You can copy text that appears in one place to another place. Copying of text occurs with the assistance of the Windows Clipboard. The *Clipboard* is an area of your computer's memory that is used for holding data. As long as the data is on the Clipboard, you can place it anywhere in any Windows software application. The data stays on the Clipboard until you replace it with new data, or until you exit Windows.

➡ **To copy text using ribbon command, do this:**

1. Select the text you want to copy.
2. In the **Home** tab, click copy icon on the **Clipboard** group or (press Ctrl+C keys together).
3. Move to the place in your presentation where you want to insert this text.
4. Click Paste down pointing arrow and choose Paste command on the **Clipboard** group (or press Ctrl+V keys together.

Moving Text

The move operation is similar to the copy operation except that text is moved, i.e., it is deleted from the original location and copied to a new place.

➡ **To move the text using Ribbon command, do this:**

1. Click the text to put the text box in edit mode.
2. Select the text you want to move.

☞ *Using Cut and Paste is the way to move text around between slides. Just select and cut the text, move to the appropriate slide, and paste it where you want it.*

3. Right-click and choose Cut from the shortcut menu or click the Cut button on the **Home** tab (or press Ctrl+X keys together). Move to the new location, right-click, and choose Paste or click the **Paste** button on the **Home** tab (or press Ctrl+V keys together) .

Deleting Text

You can delete characters, words, or all the text in a text box. Using one of these methods:

- The Delete key erases the character to the right of the cursor.
- The Backspace key erases the character to the left of the cursor.

If you delete text accidentally, you can undo your action by clicking the Undo button on the Quick Access toolbar. (You can also press Ctrl+Z keys together).

7.3.4 Inserting and Deleting Slides in a Presentation

➡ **To insert slide, do this:**

1. In the slide view, display the slide after which you want to insert the slide.
2. In the **Home** tab click **New Slide** drop-down arrow and then choose New slide with layout. The **New** slide is inserted.

Deleting Slides

➡ **To delete slide, do this:**

1. In the Slides pane select the slide you want to delete.
2. Press Delete key. The selected slide gets deleted.

7.4 PREPARATION OF SLIDES

7.4.1 Inserting Word Table or an Excel Worksheet

To add some tabulated data, you can do with many ways such as inserting table from word file or can choose layout options of Powerpoint. You can insert data from Excel worksheet as well. You can also create a table in your presentation without using Word 2010.

➡ **To create a new slide with table, do this:**

1. Click the **Insert** tab. Click **New Slide** down pointing arrow in the **Slides** group. A list of slides appears.
2. Click the **Title and Content** Slide. A new slide appears as shown in Figure 7.25.

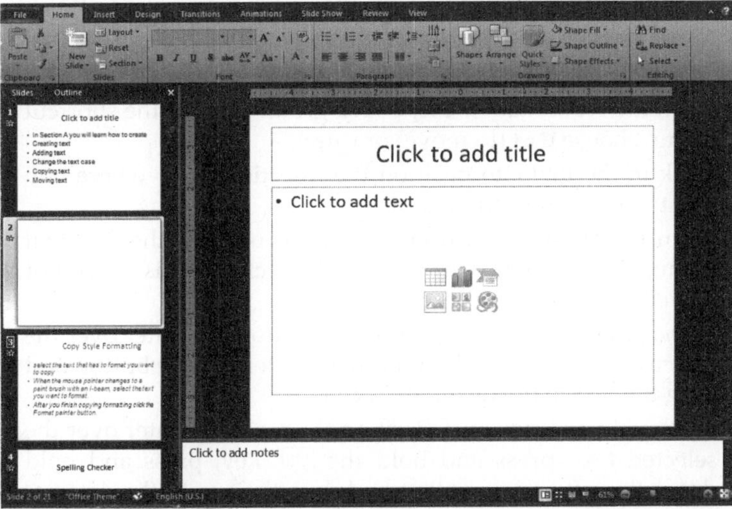

Figure 7.25 A new slide with table placeholder

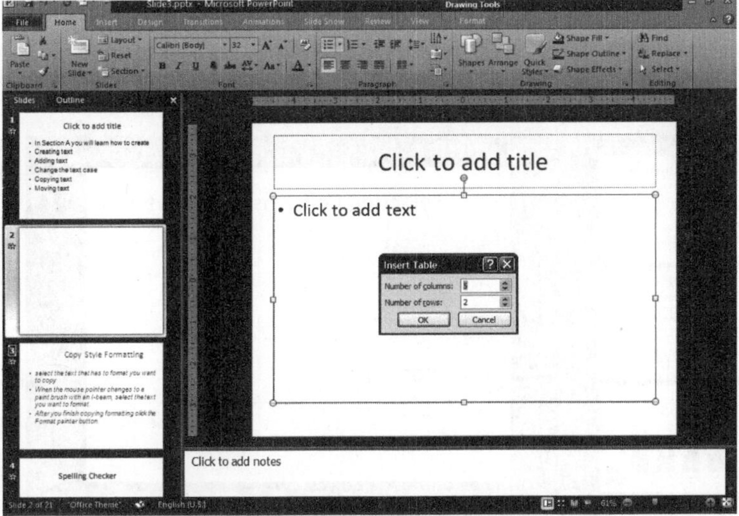

Figure 7.26 Insert Table dialog box

3. Click the **insert table** place holder. **Insert Table** dialog box appears as shown in Figure 7.26.
4. In the **Insert Table** dialog box, enter the number of *columns* and the number of *rows* you want to insert in the table. You can type the number of rows and the number of columns or click the up or down arrow on the right of the edit boxes to specify these numbers.
5. After you specify the number of rows and columns, click OK to create the table.
6. A table appears on the slide as shown in Figure 7.27.

Entering Text in a Table

When you create a new table, an empty table appears within a gray frame on the slide as seen in Figure 7.27. When you insert a table, the insertion point flashes in the first cell in the upper left corner of the table. The text you type appears at the insertion point. After entering the text in the table and to exit the editing mode, click anywhere outside the table.

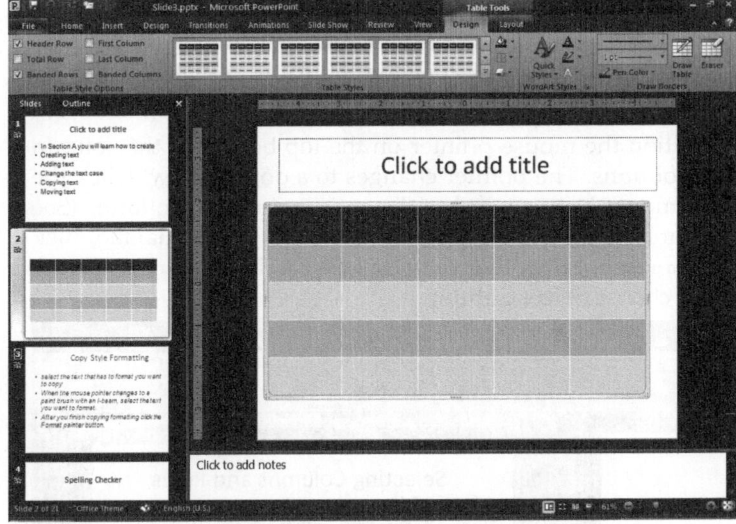

Figure 7.27 Slide with a Table

Editing a Table

Once you have created a table and entered text or numbers, you can modify its structure by *adding, deleting, moving* and *copying* cells, columns and rows. You can also change the width of columns, height of rows and merge or split cells to accommodate typed text in the cells.

Selecting Cells, Columns and Rows

➡ **To select cells, do this:**

1. For selecting a single cell, position the mouse pointer near the left inside edge of the cell. Once the pointer changes to a right arrow, click the cell.
2. To select adjacent cells in the same column, click any where in the first cell and drag the mouse pointer down the column.
3. To select adjacent cells in the same row, click anywhere in the first cell, and drag the mouse pointer across the row.
4. To select multiple cells click the first cell, press and hold down the Shift key, and click the other cell. Both the cells and any cell in between these two cells are selected.

➡ **To select a row of cells, do this:**

1. Position the mouse pointer near the left ledge of the table. Once the pointer changes to a right arrow, click the row as seen in Figure 7.28. *Alternatively,* in **Table Tools** contextual tab, click **Layout** tab. In **Table** group, click Select down pointing arrow and choose Select Row.

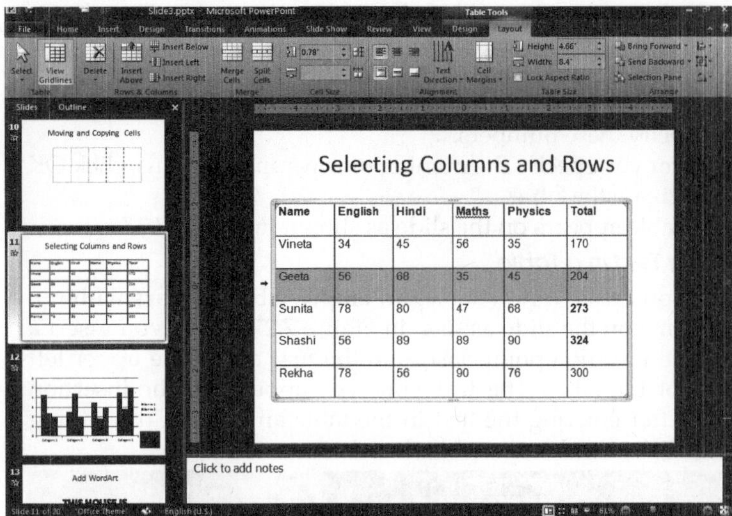

Name	English	Hindi	Maths	Physics	Total
Vineta	34	45	56	35	170
Geeta	56	68	35	45	204
Sunita	78	80	47	68	273
Shashi	56	89	89	90	324
Rekha	78	56	90	76	300

Figure 7.28 Selecting the entire row in a table

➡ **To select column or columns of cells, do this:**

1. Position the mouse pointer on the top border of the column or columns. The pointer changes to a down arrow. Click the left mouse button to select the entire column or columns (See Figure 7.29). *Alternatively*, in **Table Tools** contextual tab, click **Layout** tab. In **Table** group, click Select down pointing arrow and choose Select Column.

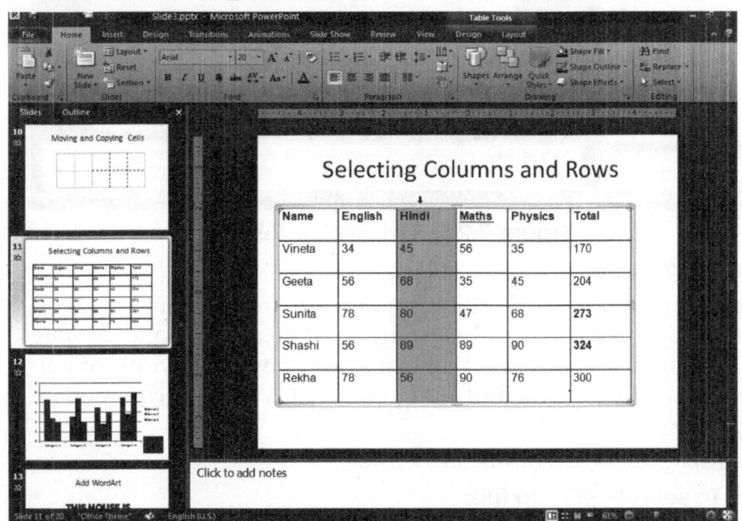

Name	English	Hindi	Maths	Physics	Total
Vineta	34	45	56	35	170
Geeta	56	68	35	45	204
Sunita	78	80	47	68	273
Shashi	56	89	89	90	324
Rekha	78	56	90	76	300

Figure 7.29 Selecting a Column

Adding Columns and Rows

➡ **To insert a column, do this:**

1. Click anywhere in the column next to where you want the new column to appear.
2. In **Table Tools** contextual tab, click **Layout** tab. In **Rows & Columns** group choose **Insert Columns to the Left** or **Right**. A column is inserted to the left or right of the selected column. Or

   Right click the mouse, choose Insert, a sub menu appears, choose Insert Columns to the Left or Right.

➡ **To insert a row, do this:**

1. Click anywhere in the row next to where you want the new row to appear.
2. In **Table Tools** contextual tab, click **Layout** tab. In **Rows & Columns** group choose **Insert Rows to the Above** or **Below**. A row is inserted to the above or below of the selected row. Or

   Right click the mouse, choose Insert Rows Above or Insert Rows Below. A row is inserted above or below of the selected row.

Deleting Columns and Rows

➡ **To delete columns/rows, do this:**

1. Select the columns/rows you want to delete.
2. In **Table Tools** contextual tab, click **Layout** tab. In **Rows & Columns** group choose Delete Columns or Rows. Or right click the mouse, choose Delete Rows or Columns.

Copying and Moving Cells

Once you select the contents of a cell, you can *copy* or *move* these to another location using drag and drop. *Alternatively*, use the Cut, Copy and Paste commands from the **Home** tab or from the shortcut menu that appears when you select a cell and click the right mouse button.

➡ **To move or copy cell contents using *drag* and *drop*, do this:**

1. Select the text you want to move or copy.
2. From the **Home** tab of **Clipboard** group or from the shortcut menu, choose **Cut** (to move) or **Copy**.
3. Click in the table, to position the insertion point where you want to insert the cut or copied text.
4. From the **Home** tab **Clipboard** group or from the Shortcut menu, choose **Paste**. Cut or copied selected text is moved or copied at the insertion point.
5. *To move the selected text* – Position the mouse pointer over the selected text, press and hold down the left mouse button and drag the text to the destination cell.
6. *To copy the selected text* – Position the mouse pointer over the selected text, press and hold the Ctrl key, press and hold down the left mouse button and drag the text to the destination cell.

   A *plus* sign appears next to the pointer to indicate that you are copying instead of moving (See Figure 7.30).

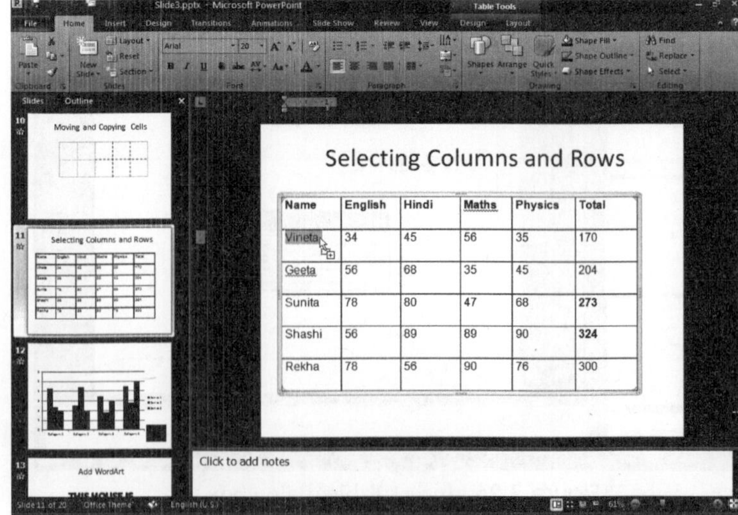

Name	English	Hindi	Maths	Physics	Total
Vineta	34	45	56	35	170
Geeta	56	68	35	45	204
Sunita	78	80	47	68	273
Shashi	56	89	89	90	324
Rekha	78	56	90	76	300

Figure 7.30 Copying a cell with contents

Changing Column Width and Rows Height

You can change the size of *rows* of a table by adjusting the height of the rows. Similarly, you can also change the size of the *columns* by adjusting the width of the columns.

Changing Column Width

➡ **To change the width of a column in a table, do this:**

1. Position the pointer anywhere on the column's right border until the pointer changes to a double line and arrow (See Figure 7.31).

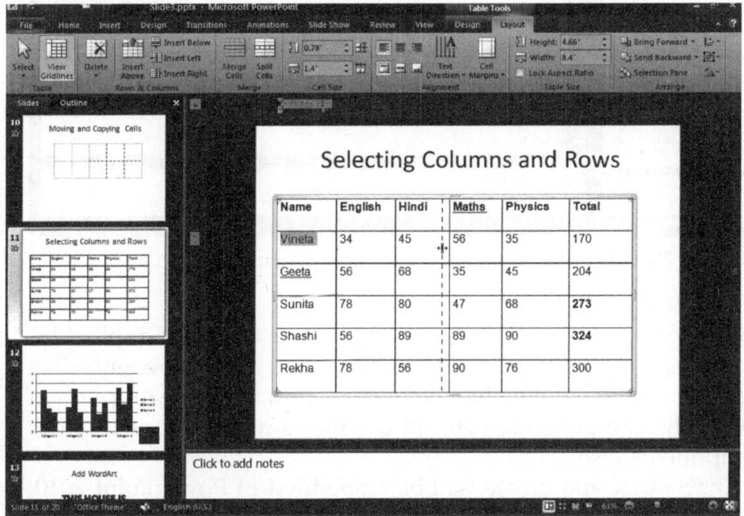

Figure 7.31 Changing column width

2. Drag the column border to the left or right to decrease or increase the column width. A dashed line indicates the target column width.
3. Release the mouse button. The column width is changed to the new size you specified by dragging.
4. In **Table Tools** contextual tab, click **Layout** tab. In the **Cell Size** group, click the **Table Column Width** up and down arrow, to set the width of the selected cells.

Changing Row Height

➡ **To change the height of a row in a table, do this:**

1. Position the pointer anywhere on the row's right border until the pointer changes to a double line and arrow.

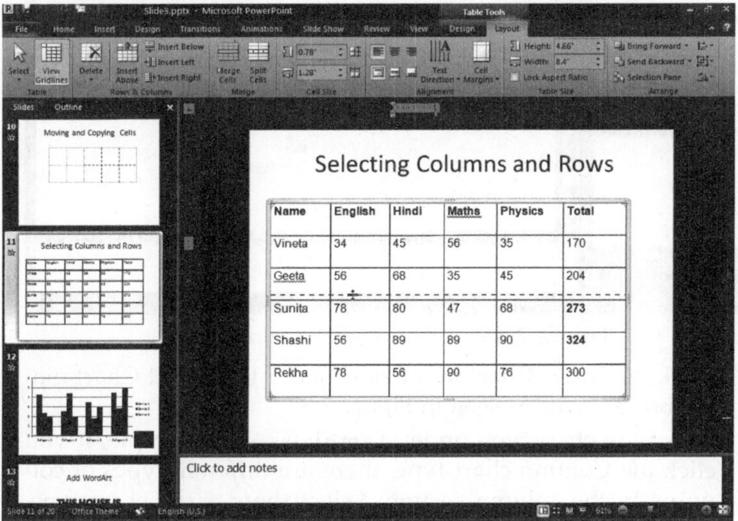

Figure 7.32 Changing row height

2. Drag the row border up or down to decrease or increase the row height. A dashed line indicates the target row height (See Figure 7.32).
3. Release the mouse button. The row height is changed to the new size you specified by dragging.
4. In **Table Tools** contextual tab, click **Layout** tab. In the **Cell Size** group, click the **Row height up** and **down** arrow, to set the height of the selected cells.

Merging and Splitting Cells

To create one cell that spans two or more cells, you can merge adjacent cells. In Figure 7.33, merging cells allows you to enter a column heading in one large cell that occupies the same width as several smaller cells below.

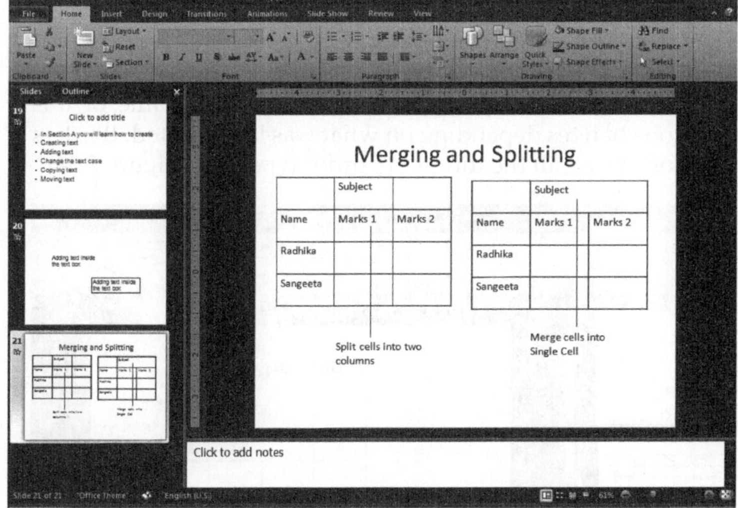

Figure 7.33 Merging in cell in first row and split it in two cells in row 2

➡ **To merge two or more cells, do this:**

1. Select the cells you want to merge.
2. Click the **Table Tools** contextual tab, click the **Layout** tab. Click **Merge** cells in the **Merge** group.

   Or right click the mouse and choose Merge Cells.

➡ **To split a cell, do this:**

1. Select the cell that you want to split. You can only split one cell at a time.
2. Click the **Table Tools** contextual tab, click the **Layout** tab. Click **Split** cells in the **Merge** group.
3. The cell is split into two cells of equal width, with any text appearing in the cell on the left. Or right click the mouse and choose Split Cells... .

☞ *After splitting a cell, you might want to adjust the cell width to make it look right in your current cell structure and layout.*

Adding Borders and Fills

PowerPoint establishes default borders around cells and the table itself, on the current presentation template. You can change borders separating cells, columns and rows or around the entire table.

Changing Table Borders

You may specify a variety of ways for border formatting in a table. You can choose:

1. The border format (*Top border, bottom border, Left border, Right border, All border*, etc.)
2. The border style (solid line, dashed line, dotted line, etc.)
3. The border width (1/4 point to 6 points)
4. The border colour.

➡ **To select the table cells that you want to add or change the table border, do this:**

1. Select the entire table, or the cells, columns, or rows around which you want to specify the border.
2. Under **Table Tools**, on the **Design** tab, click **Border** down arrow in the **Table Styles** group. The actual name of this button changes depending on what was last selected. Borders option shows all the different border types (See Figure 7.34).

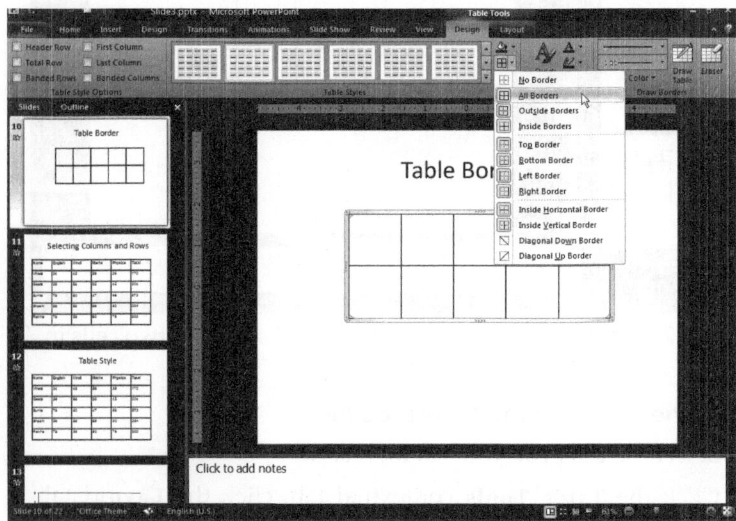

Figure 7.34 Borders palette

3. Click the border you want. The selected portion of the table changes to reflect the new border type.
4. If you want to change the border line style, click Draw borders down arrow, and choose Pen Style. Pen Style palette drop-down menu appears as in Figure 7.35.
5. Click the border style you want. The mouse pointer changes to pen style. Click the table row or column line. You can see the selected portion of your table changes to the new border style.
6. If you want to change the border width or border colour, repeat steps 2 to 4 with the border width and border colour button. After making a change, click the Border button if necessary to redraw the table with the new formatting.
7. If you want to delete borders between table cells, click Eraser, or press and hold Shift key while the pointer is a pencil, and then click the borders that you want to delete.

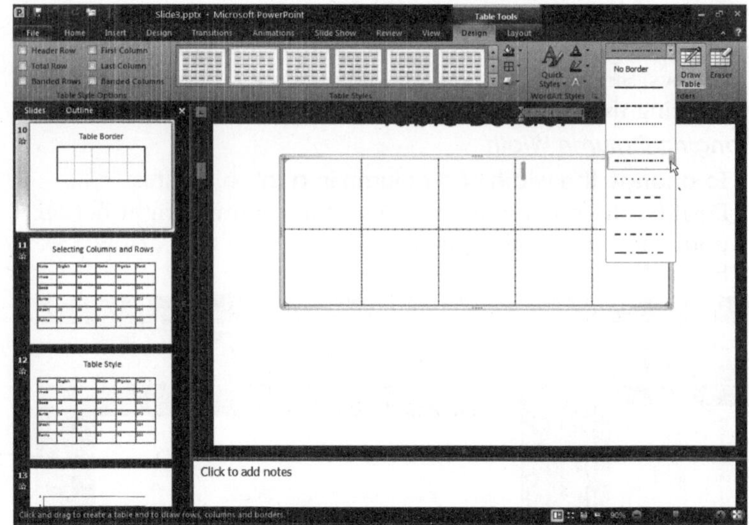

Figure 7.35 Borders Style drop down list appears

Creating a Chart Slide

PowerPoint creates or modifies a chart using MS-Graph. MS-Graph is a graphing program shared by all components like *Word, Excel, PowerPoint*. So if you know how to create graphics in one of the components, you can use the same technique in other components also.

Charts that you create will be embedded in PowerPoint 2010, and the chart data is stored in an Excel 2010 worksheet that is incorporated in the PowerPoint file.

➡ **To create a chart slide, do this:**

1. Click the **New slide** in the **Slides** group. It display, the slides after which you want to add the chart slide. Or click the **Insert** tab, on the **Illustrations** group, click the **Chart** icon.
2. The new slide appears. In the center of the slide contains *table, chart, Media clips, SmartArt*, etc., as seen in Figure 7.36.

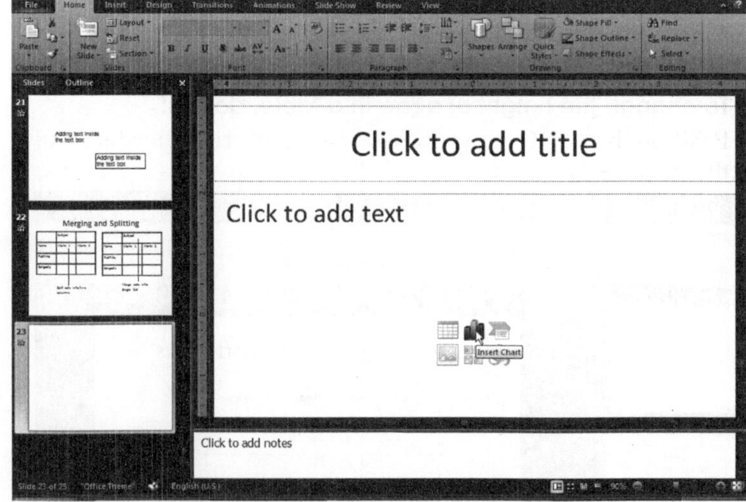

Figure 7.36 A new slide contains chart

3. Click the Insert Chart in the new slide. The Insert Chart dialog box appears as seen in Figure 7.37.
4. Select the chart type under **Templates**. For example, if you click the Column chart type, there are different types of columns in the column section. Select the desired chart type. Click OK.

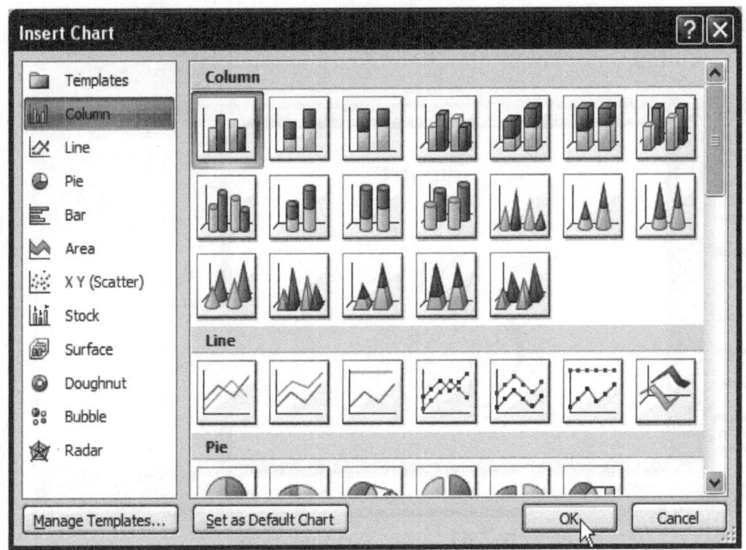

Figure 7.37 Insert Chart dialog box

5. A sample chart appears in the Excel worksheet and the data sheet window containing the sample data for the chart overlays as seen in Figure 7.38.
6. In Excel to replace the sample data, click a cell on the worksheet, and then type the data that you want. When you enter data in Excel you can see the PowerPoint the data as well chart also simultaneously appearing in the PowerPoint (Figure 7.39).
7. In Excel, click the Office Button and then click **Save As**.

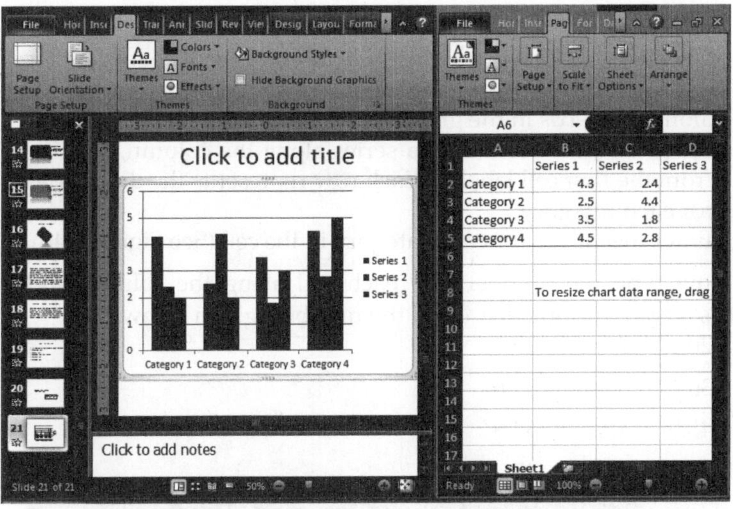

Figure 7.38 Sample Data graphically displayed

8. In the **Save As** dialog box in the **save in:** list, select the folder or drive that you want to save the worksheet.
9. In the **File name:** box, type a new name for the file.
10. Click **Save**.
11. In Excel, Click the Office button and then click Close.

Entering Data in the Datasheet

Entering data in the Datasheet consists of two steps. These are:

- Entering the labels in the left most column and top most row.
- Entering the data to be graphed in the remaining cells.

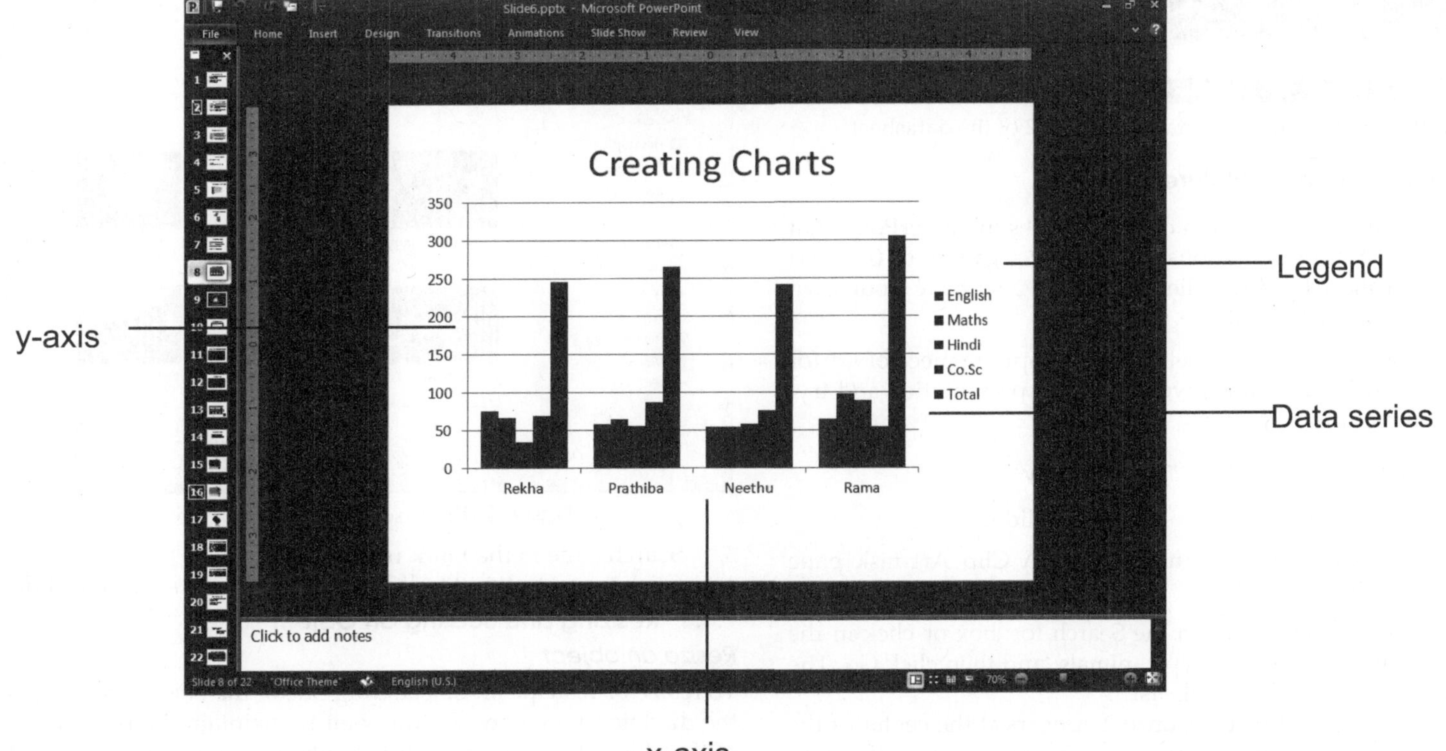

Figure 7.39 A Sample Chart appearing in PowerPoint

➡ To enter data in a datasheet, do this:

1. Click the top cell in column A and enter the category labels across the top row. (The categories along the rows appear along the *x-axis* in the graph).
2. Enter the name of the data series along the column, starting from the first cell labeled. Each row represents the data series for each category.
3. Enter the values for each category in the cell (See Figure 7.40).

Now type the numbers for each cell along the column and press (Enter). For practice, enter the numbers given below.

20.4	27.4	29.4
30.6	38.6	31.6
45.9	46.9	43.9
32.1	31.6	45

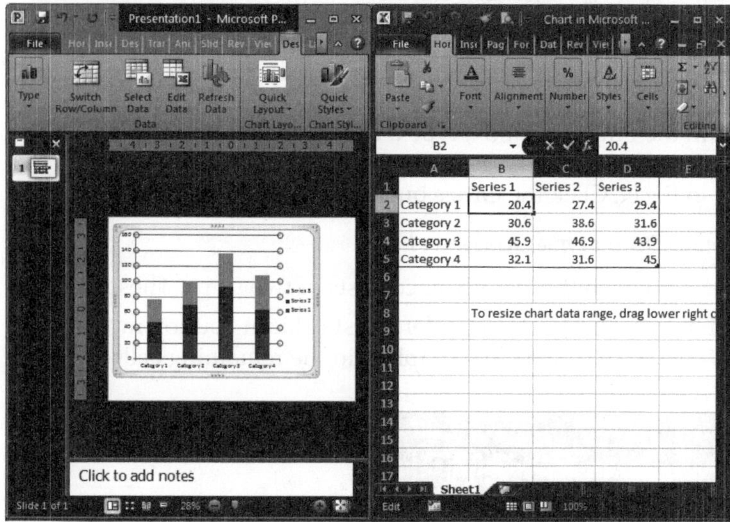

Figure 7.40 Entering Data in the cell B2 of the datasheet

7.4.2 Adding Clip Art Pictures

Clip Art gallery is a collection of graphic files in PowerPoint that you can insert in presentations. It has built a gallery of Clip Art images into the Clip Art gallery. But you also have your own collection of artwork available.

PowerPoint can help you select an appropriate piece of art for your slides by looking at keywords in your presentation and trying to find pictures to match.

Inserting a picture from the Clip Art Gallery

1. Select the slide that contain a Clip Art slide.
2. Click the Clip Art icon in the slide. A Clip Art task pane appears (Figure 7.41).
3. Select the current entry in the Search for: box or click in the box if there is no entry, type animals, and then click Go. The task pane displays animals list.
4. Click the selected picture, once it appears at the center of the slide or select the picture, it appears a small arrow at the right of the side of the picture. Click the arrow and then Insert (See Figure 7.41).
5. When you are finished using the Clip Gallery, click the Close button on the Clip Gallery title bar.

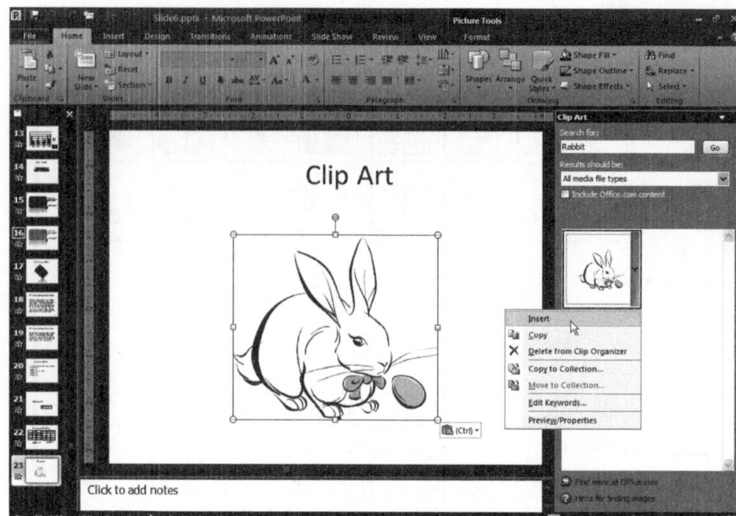

Figure 7.41 Clip Art task pane

7.4.3 Inserting Other Objects

You may want to add a particular graphic to a presentation but not maintain it in the Clip Gallery. You can insert picture from another application.

➡ To insert a picture from a file, do this:

1. Click where you want to insert the picture.
2. On the **Insert** tab, in the **Images** group, click **Picture**.
3. The **Insert Picture** dialog box appears as shown in Figure 7.42.

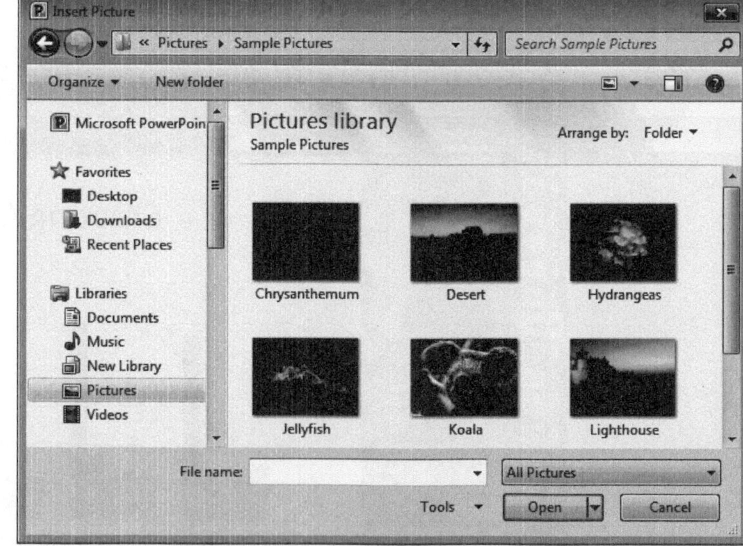

Figure 7.42 Insert Picture dialog box

3. Search a file in the **Look in:** drop-down list.
4. Click **Insert** button to place the graphic on the current slide.

7.4.4 Resizing and Scaling an Object

Resize an object

To resize or reshape an object, drag one of the object's handles in the direction you want. If you want to maintain the proportions of the object, hold down Shift key while drag a corner handle. If you want the object to grow out from its current center, hold down (Ctrl) while you drag a corner handle.

➡ To resize an object, do this:

1. Select the object you want to resize.

2. Drag a size handle until the object gets desired shape and size as you want (See Figure 7.43). Or

Scaling an object

Rather than drag objects into position, you can set object placements and sizing on the size and position tabs of the Format Picture.

➡ **To scale an object, do this:**

1. Select the object you want to scale.
2. Click the **Picture Tools** contextual **Format** tab in the **Size** group.
4. Enter the percentage you want change in the **Height:** and **Width:** boxes. *Alternatively*, click the **Size and Position** dialog box launcher dialog box.
5. The **Format Picture** dialog box appears as shown in Figure 7.44.

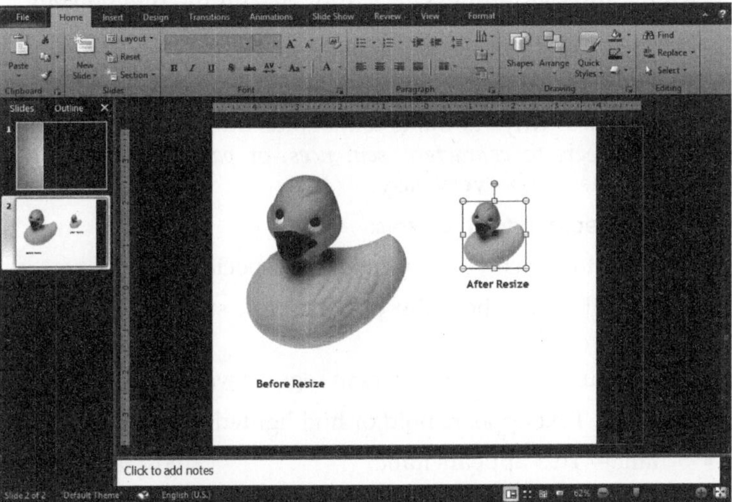

Figure 7.43 Object has to be resized

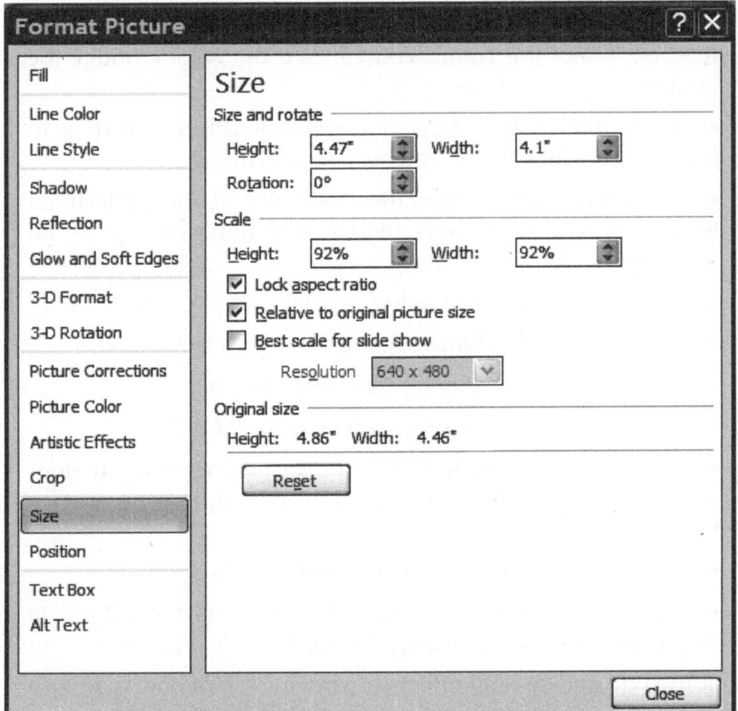

Figure 7.44 Format Picture dialog box

6. Click the Size tab, under the Scale, enter the percentage you want change in the **Height:** and **Width:** box.

☞ *To maintain the ratio between the object's height and width whenever to resize it, select the Lock aspect ratio check box on the size tab.*

7.5 PROVIDING AESTHETICS

PowerPoint is designed to give your slide presentations a consistent look. There are four ways that PowerPoint helps you control the look of your slides – with design templates, masters, colour schemes, and layouts of slides.

7.5.1 Enhancing Text Presentation

Enhancing the text presentation makes your presentation in a more presentable manner by formatting features, such as bold, italic, underline, alignment of text, font size, font style, colours, etc.

Aligning Text in a Slide

Alignment is the way text is placed between the margins of a page or a text box on a slide. The alignment choices are summarized in Table 7.1.

Table 7.1 Aligning Text in a Slide

Alignment	Effect
Left Align	The left margin of each line is at the same place on the left, while the right edge of each line ends wherever appropriate (called a *ragged right edge*).
Right Align	The right margin of each line is at the same place on the right. The left edge of each line falls in a different place, depending on the contents of the line (called a *ragged left edge*).
Center	Each line is centered. The left and right edges of each line will differ, depending upon the number and size of characters in the line.
Justified	Each line starts at the left margin and ends at the right margin. There are no ragged edges.

➡ **To align the text, do this:**

1. Select the text, then click the Left, Center, or Right alignment button on the Formatting toolbar. *Alternatively*, click the **Paragraph Launcher** dialog box and select the desired option in the alignment section.

Changing Fonts

Fonts are also called *typefaces* in computer programs. There are groups of characters that share the same style or look.

Fonts are divided into two groups.

- On the basis of the way, characters are spaced – *monospaced* or *proportionately* spaced (See Figure 7.45). In *monospaced* font, all the characters have the same width. In *proportionately* spaced font the widths are different, i.e., w has more width than i.
- On the basis of the finishing strokes. That is Serif and Sans serif. In Sans Serif the finishing strokes are not there (See Figure 7.45). In Serif fonts the finishing strokes are there.

While choosing fonts for your presentation, keep in mind the following points:

- Using too many fonts on the same slide looks unprofessional. It is advisable to use one font for the headline and another for the rest of the text or a third font for bulleted items. But do not use too many fonts.

- Fancy fonts, do not work well on slides, especially for headlines.
- Sans - Serif fonts tend to have a more authoritative and bold look.
- Proportional fonts work extremely well in body text.

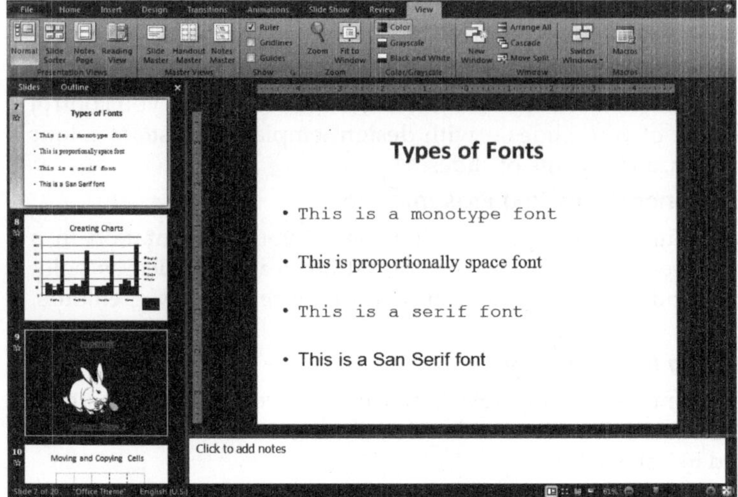

Figure 7.45 Display of various kind of fonts

➡ To change the font of any text in a slide, do this:

1. Select the text you want to change.
2. Click the **Home** tab and choose **Font** group. Or select the text, a mini toolbar appears. Select the font themes appears choose the desired font you want to apply. Or
3. Click the right mouse button and choose Font... from shortcut menu. The Font dialog box appears as in Figure 7.46. Click the Font drop-down list and select the required font. *Alternatively*, click the down arrow to the right of the Font box on the Ribbon command. A drop-down list of available fonts appears.

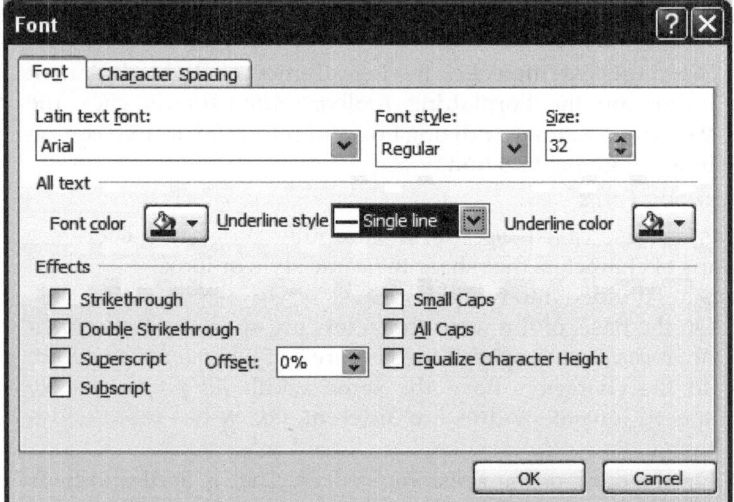

Figure 7.46 Selecting font using dialog box

☞ *Right type and size of font creates good impression on your audience.*

4. Click the font you want to use. The selected text changes to the selected font.

Changing the Text Size

Font size is measured in *points*, which is a height measurement, each point is 1/72 of an inch.

➡ To change the size of text, do this:

1. Select the text you want to change.
2. Click the **Home** tab and choose **Font** group. Or select the text. A mini toolbar appears. Choose the desired font size you want to apply. Or click the right mouse button and choose Font... . In the Font dialog box that appears, click the size drop-down list and choose the desired size or type the size. *Alternatively*, click the arrow to the right of the Font Size box on the Ribbon command to see the list of available sizes.
3. Select the new size. Or
4. Click the Increase and decrease font size on the Ribbon command.

Adding Special Effects to Text

One of the easiest ways to make text stands out is to add special formatting effects to *characters, sentences*, or *paragraphs*. PowerPoint makes these tasks very easy.

➡ To add special effect, do this:

1. Select text to which you want to apply special effect.
2. In the Font dialog box, the options Font style: box has the following:
   - Regular—The text appears in regular way.
   - Bold—Text appears bold or highlighted.
   - Italic—Text appears italic.
   - Bold Italic—Text appears bold and italic.

   The All text has this option:

   - Font color— Specifies the colour of the selected text. In the box, select the color. You can see the colour under the bucket.
   - Underline style— Specifies whether selected text is in underlined. Click None to remove underlining.
   - Underline color— Specifies the color of the underlined text. This option remains unavailable until you apply an underline style.

   The Effect Areas has following options:

   - Strikethrough—Draws a line through selected text.
   - Superscript—Text appears raised like x^2y
   - Subscript—Text appears lowered like H_20
   - Small caps—Selected text appears reduce size. It does not affect on numbers, punctuation, non-alphabetic characters.
   - All caps—It converts lowercase to capitals.
   - Equalize Character Height—It reformats text effects to apply an even character height to text.

The font style and special effects of above explanation as shown in Figure 7.47.

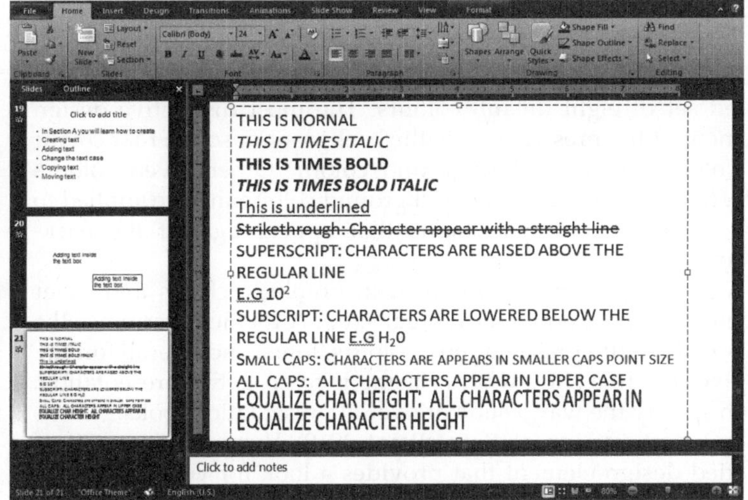

Figure 7.47 The font style effect

Changing Text Colour

➡ **To change the text colour, do this:**

1. Select the text you want to change.
2. In the **Home** tab, click the **Font** group. Click the font colour by pointing arrow. The font colors theme palette appears.
3. Move the mouse pointer over the colour, you can see the effect changes in the text. Choose the desired colour you want to apply to the text.

Applying Character Formatting using the Keyboard

Most of the character formatting can also be applied using the keyboard shortcut as discussed in the following sections.

➡ **To format using shortcut keys, do this:**

1. Select the text you want to format and use the shortcut key combinations for the desired formatting effects.

Format	Shortcut
Bold	Ctrl+B
Italic	Ctrl+I
Underline	Ctrl+U
Superscript	Ctrl+Shift++
Subscript	Ctrl+=
Copy formatting	Ctrl+Shift+C
Paste formatting	Ctrl+Shift+V
Remove formatting	Ctrl+Spacebar
Change case of letters	Shift+F3
Change the font	Ctrl+Shift+F
Change the font size	Ctrl+Shift+P
Increase the font size	Ctrl+Shift+>
Decrease the font size	Ctrl+Shift+<

Bullets and Numbering

PowerPoint 2010 provides the ability to create bulleted, numbered lists. A bulleted list is a list with a graphic character, very small picture or bullet at the beginning of each paragraph in the list. You might also consider using SmartArt for many bulleted or numbered lists. The style of each list type can be changed and different bullets can be used.

➡ **To create a bulleted list, do this:**

1. Select the text you want to add bullet.
2. Click the down arrow of the bullets command icon, in the Paragraph group.

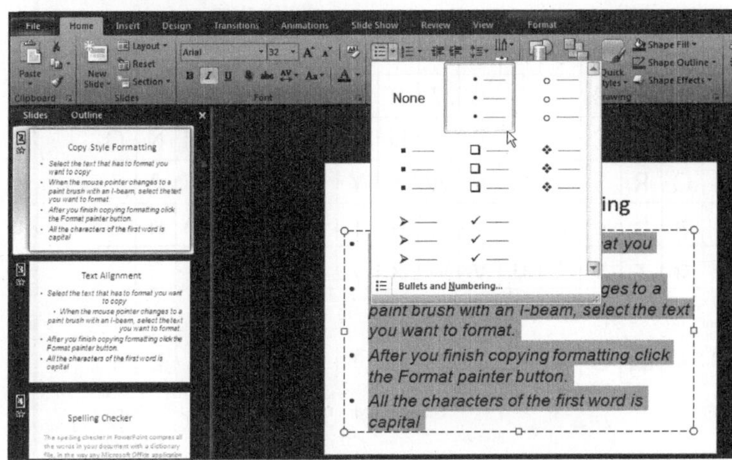

Figure 7.48 Selecting Bullets in the paragraph group

3. A drop-down list shows with the pre-defined bullet list.
4. Select the desired bullet type from the drop-down list. For example, we have selected the circled bulleted List (See Figure 7.48).
5. The selected bullet type is applied to the text as seen in Figure 7.49.

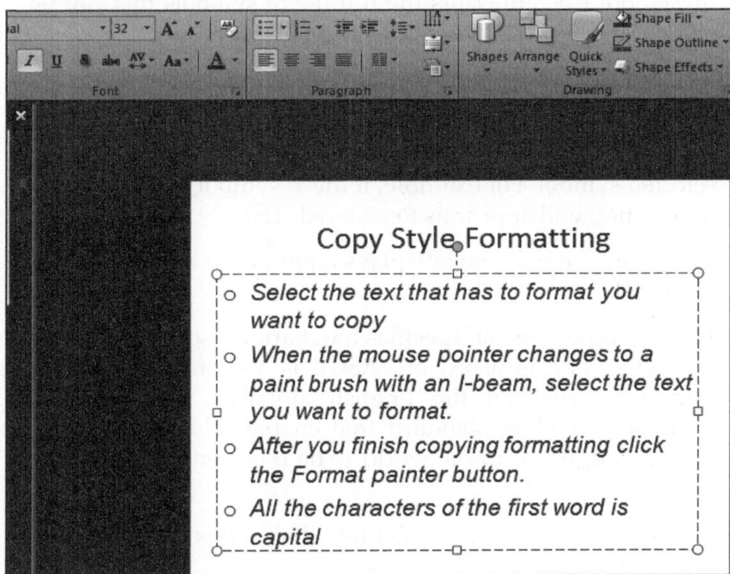

Figure 7.49 Bullet applied in selected paragraph

Adding Symbols

PowerPoint provides a full range of special symbol characters like the copyright or trademarks, registration symbol, etc.

➡ **To add symbol, do this:**

1. Click the **Insert** tab. In the **Symbols** group, click Symbol icon. The **Symbol** dialog box appears as shown in Figure 7.50.
2. By default, the **Font:** box is set to Symbol. Click the down arrow to see the choices for fonts, each of which provides a different set of symbols.
3. Select the font with the symbols you want to use. Select the symbols to insert by clicking it once. Or click the Insert button to insert the symbol.

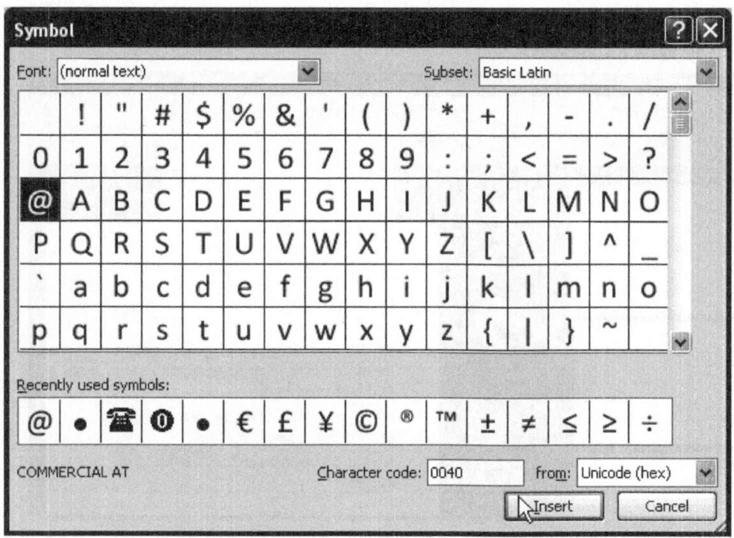

Figure 7.50 Symbol dialog Box

4. In the **Subset:** name box, specify a subset of special characters for the selected font, if available. A font subset can include an extended list of language characters, such as Greek or Russian (Cryillic), or a category of characters, such as Currency Symbols.
5. In Symbol list represents the full list of symbols that can be inserted from the selected Font and Subset.
6. In **Recently used symbols:** box, lists the most frequently used symbols that have been inserted.
7. **Description:** Provides a meaningful description of the selected symbol. For example, if the ® symbol is selected, the description will appear as Registered sign.
8. **Character code:** list box displays a unique code representing a symbol.
9. **From:** drop-down list, specifies the character set on which the character code is based on. ASCII is a character-encoding standard based on the English alphabet. Unicode is a character-encoding standard that enables almost all of the written languages in the world to be represented by using a single character set.
10. Click Close to leave the Symbol dialog box and return to your slide.

Removing Bullets and Numbering

➡ **To remove bullets and numbering, do this:**

1. Select the text or placeholders you want to remove bullets and number form.
2. In the **Paragraph** group of **Home** tab, choose the bulleted down pointing arrow, a bullet palette list appears, choose None. Or
   You can press Backspace to remove bullet or numbering from an item in a list. PowerPoint automatically adjusts the number sequence of a numbered list.
3. If you want to reorganize the elements of the list after removing bullets and numbering, use the promote and demote bullet on the Quick Access toolbar.

7.5.2 Working with Themes Color and Line Style

In earlier version colour and line styles, contains a colour scheme that provides the various parts of a presentation with a coordinated set of eight default colours. The most distinctive design element of the presentation is the background, so the first colour in colour scheme is background colour. Other seven colours effectively complement the background colour and are applied to text, charts, and other objects that appear against the background.

A layout determines where text, graphics, charts and other elements appear on an individual slide. A theme determines the look of an entire presentations' colours, fonts, and overall format. A layout is to a slide what a theme is to an entire presentation. Both specify the way a slide or overall presentation looks.

In Latest version of PowerPoint 2010, Themes refer a set of unified design element that provides a look for your document by using *colors*, *fonts* and *graphics*. You can use predefined themes that come with PowerPoint, or you can define your own.

➡ **To select a New slide and apply themes effect, do this:**

1. Click the **Home** tab, in the **slides** group. Click the **New Slide** down pointing arrow. PowerPoint opens a layout list from which you can select (See Figure 7.51).

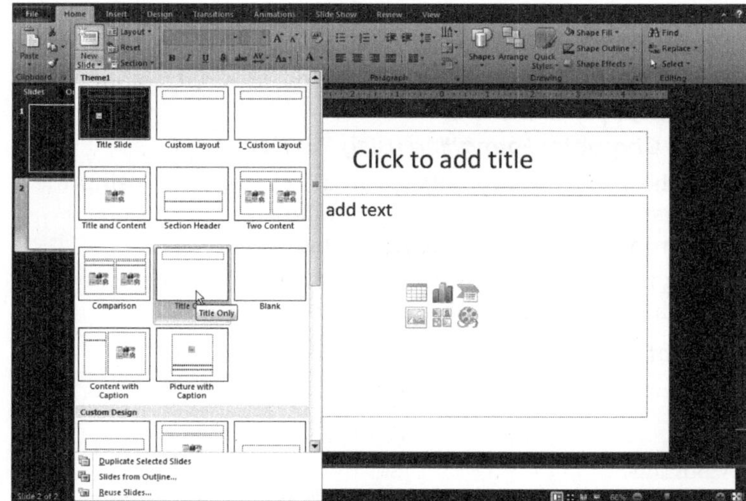

Figure 7.51 Selecting a New Slide from Home tab

2. When you click to select a layout, PowerPoint inserts a new slide at that location in your presentation with that layout.
3. Click the **Design** tab, in the **Themes** group. In the Themes group click the **More** button at the lower right corner. A list of themes appears as seen in Figure 7.52.
4. Select a desired style you want to apply your presentation.
5. If you want to modify the theme, select from the *Font*, *Colors*, and *Effect* buttons to the right of the Themes group.
6. After you have modified a theme to your liking, click down arrow next to the Ribbon's themes and select Save Current Theme.
7. The **Save Current Theme** dialog box appears as seen in Figure 7.53.
8. In the **Save in:** drop-down list contains a default folder (Document Themes).
9. Give the name in the **File name:** in the drop-down list.
10. Click the **Save** button.
11. After giving a name to the theme, PowerPoint makes that theme available in the Themes list.

Figure 7.52 Selecting a Themes from Design tab

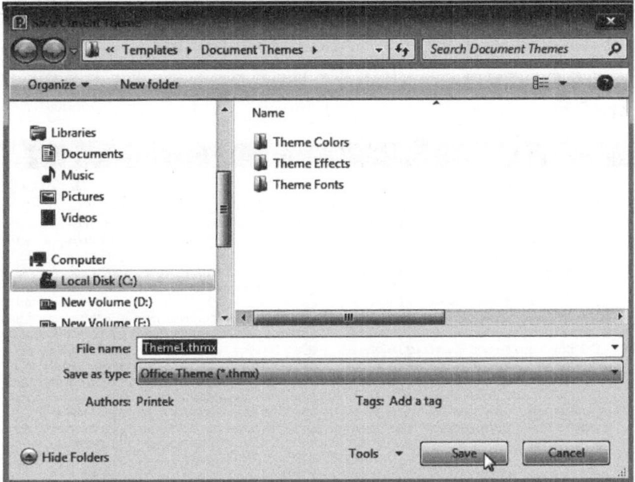

Figure 7.53 Save Current Theme dialog box

Change the Color, Style and Weight of a Line

You can change the look of a line shape by changing its colour, line style, or weight.

- Add a Quick Style to a line
- Change the color of a line
- Make a line dashed
- Change the weight of a line

Add a Quick Style to a line

Quick Styles for lines include theme colours from the document theme, shadow, line styles and three-dimensional perspectives.

1. Select the line that you want to change.

   If you want to change multiple lines, select first line, and then press and hold Ctrl key while you select other lines.
2. Under **Drawing Tools** on the **Format** tab, in the **Shape Styles** group, click the Quick style that you want.
3. To see more Quick Styles, click the **More** button (See Figure 7.54).

Change the Color of a Line

1. Select the line that you want to change.
2. Under the **Drawing Tools**, on the **Format** tab, in the **Shape Styles** group, click the arrow next to **Shape Outline**, and then click the colour that you want (See Figure 7.55).

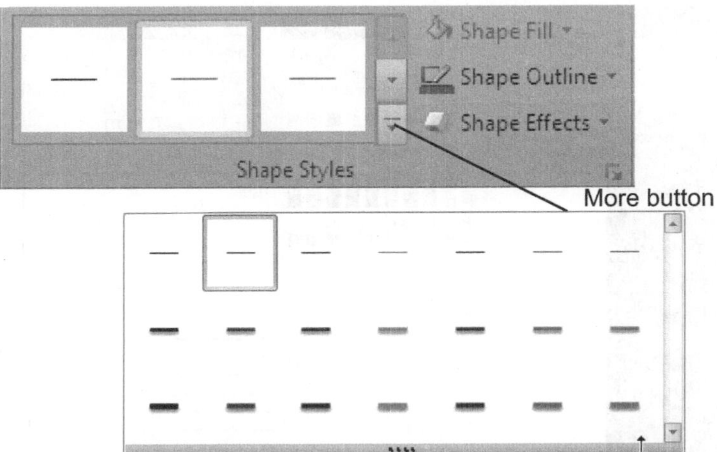

Figure 7.54 Select the line style from the More button

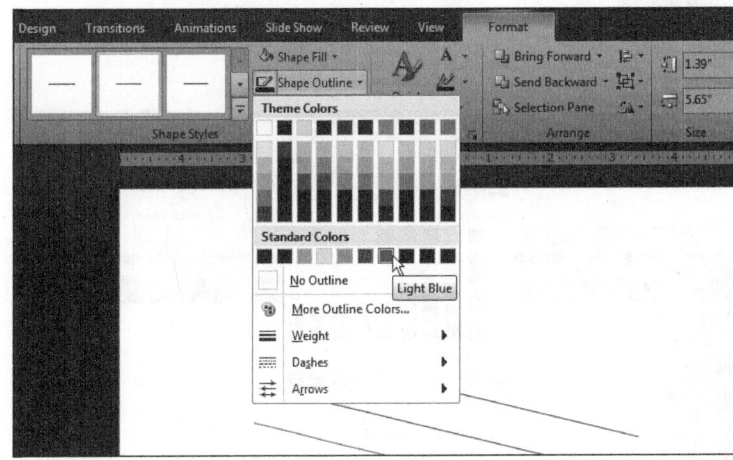

Figure 7.55 Select the color of a line from the Shape Outline drop-down list

3. To change to a colour that is not in the theme colours, click **More Outline Colors**, and then either click the colour that you want on the **Standard tab**, or mix your own colour on the **Custom tab**. Custom colours and colours on the Standard tab are not updated if you later change the document theme.

Make a Line Dashed

You can change *thickness, style* and *color*. To format a line first select it by clicking it. For selecting multiple lines press and hold the Shift key while you click the lines. The selected lines appear dimmed and dashed.

1. Select the line that you want to change.
2. Under **Drawing Tools**, on the **Format** tab, in the **Shape Styles** group, click the arrow next to **Shape Outline**.
3. Point to **Dashes**, and then click the line style that you want (See Figure 7.56).
4. To create a custom style, click **More Lines**, and then choose the options that you want.

Change the weight of a line

1. Select the line that you want to change.
   If you want to change multiple lines, select the first line, and then press and hold Ctrl while you select the other lines.
2. Under **Drawing Tools**, on the **Format** tab, in the **Shape Styles** group, click the arrow next to **Shape Outline**.
3. Point to **Weight**, and then click the line weight that you want (See Figure 7.57).

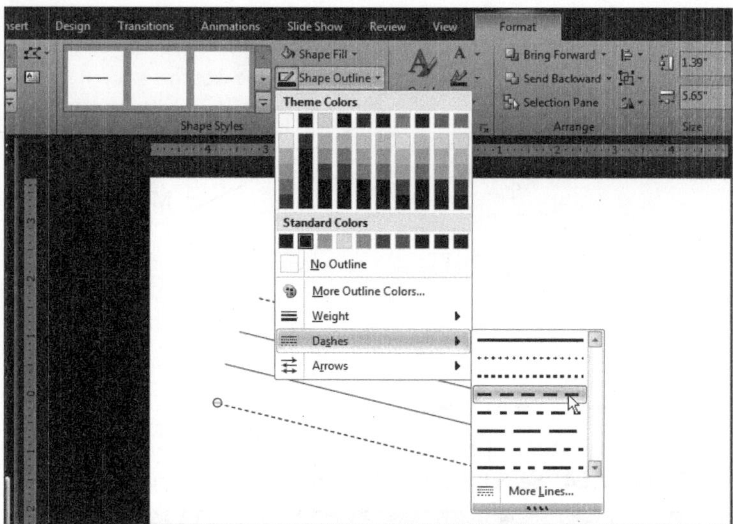

Figure 7.56 Select the line Dashes from the Shape Outline drop-down list

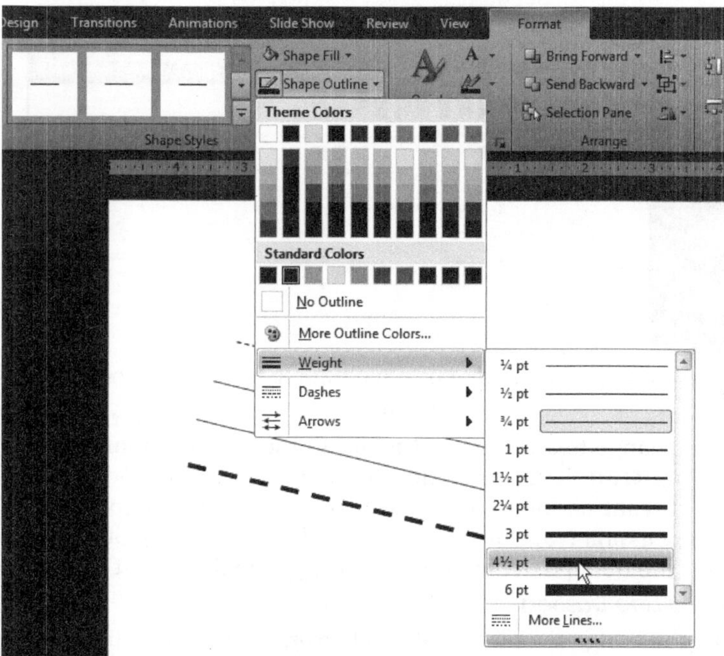

Figure 7.57 Select the line weight from the Shape Outline drop-down list

4. To create a custom style, click **More Lines**, and then choose the options that you want.

7.5.3 Adding Movie or (Video) and Sound

You insert a music, sound, or video clip on a slide where you want it to play during a slide show. You can choose either to have the sound or video start automatically when you move to the slide, or to have the sound or video start only when you click its icon during a slide show.

One of the exciting new features in PowerPoint 2010 is that you now have the ability to edit and style the video clips you add to your slides. You can insert video files from your computer, download them from the Web, or insert video clips from MS Office Clip Art. This enables you to add life to your slides and share compelling stories in a way that is sure to hold your audience's attention.

PowerPoint supports videos in various formats, such as Audio Video Interchange (.avi), Motion Pictures Group (.mpg) and Movie (.mov).

➡ **To insert a video from a Clip Art video, do this:**

1. Insert the new slide or display the slide that will contain **Media Clip Art**.
2. Click the **Insert** tab.
3. Click **Video** button under the **Media** Group. A drop-down list appears as seen in Figure 7.58.

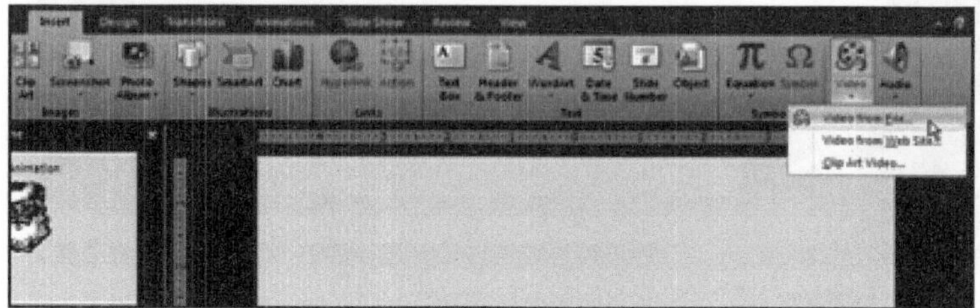

Figure 7.58 Selecting Video from file from the Insert tab

4. Select the Video from File option from the list.
5. The **Insert Video** dialog box appears as seen in Figure 7.59.

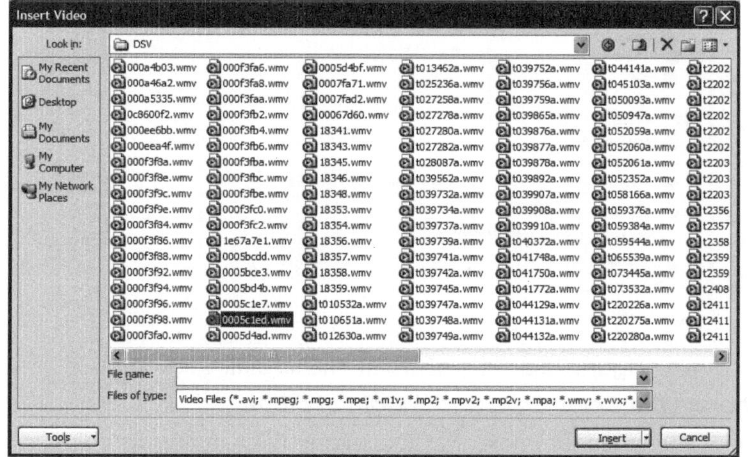

Figure 7.59 Insert video dialog box

6. Browse the location where the video is saved on your computer.
7. Select the desired video file. Then click **Insert** button.
8. The desired video is inserted in the slide as seen in Figure 7.60.
9. Drag the sizing handles of the image to set the size of your video, and then drag it to the location you want.
10. Play the video by clicking the Play button.

Adding Sound file

In PowerPoint 2010, you can easily add sound effects, voiceovers and music to individual slides. You can add a soundtrack and narration to the presentation as well. Sound effects, such as music and voice recordings, can add another level of professionalism to slide presentations. Music is an effective way to introduce or end a presentation and it gives your audience something to listen to as they enter and leave the presentation room. You could play a movie theme song as background music for several slides, or play a voice recording that contains advertising slogans to insert on a single slide, for example.

Figure 7.60 The video file is inserted in the presentation

There are many sound file formats. Two common types are wave files (with the .wav filename extension) and Musical Instrument Digital Interface (MIDI) files (with the .mid, .midi, or .rmi filename extension).

➡ **To insert a sound, into the slide, do this:**

1. Select the slide in which you want to insert the desired sound.
2. Click the **Insert** tab.
3. Click the **Audio** button under the **Media** group as seen in Figure 7.61.

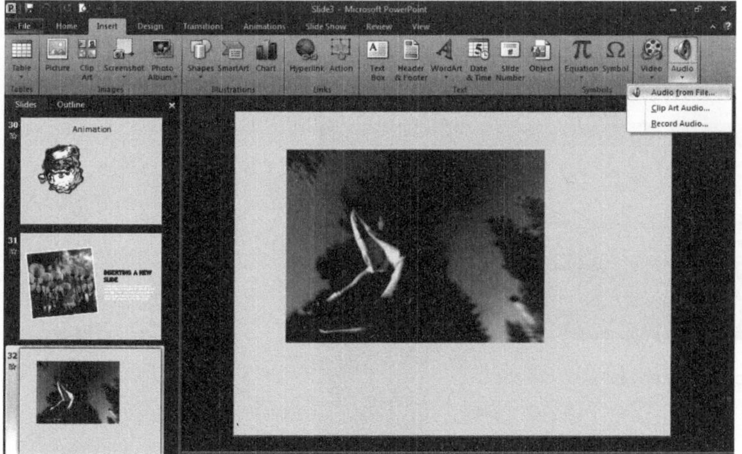

Figure 7.61 Selecting Audio from file from the insert tab

4. A drop-down list appears.
5. Select the **Audio from file** option from the drop-down list as seen in Figure 7.61.
6. The **Insert Audio** dialog box appears as seen in Figure 7.62.
7. Browse the location where the sound clip is saved on your computer. For example, we have selected the Sample Music folder as seen in Figure 7.62.
8. Select the desired sound clip and then click OK button.
9. The audio file is inserted in the slide as seen in Figure 7.63.

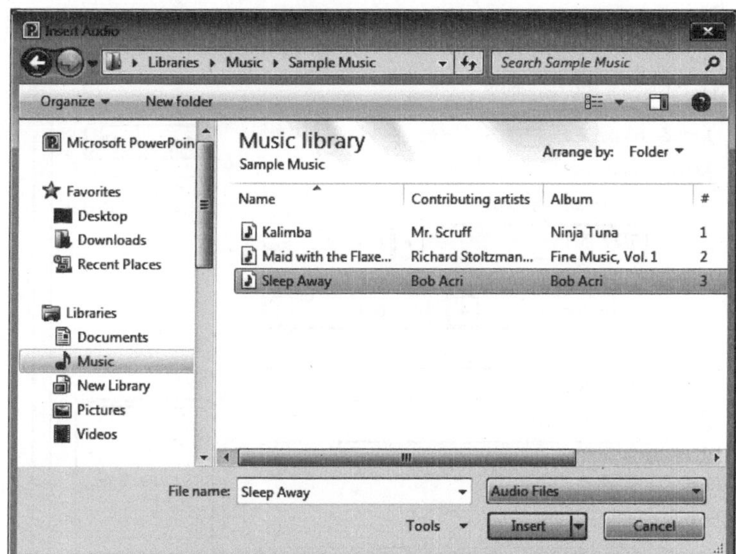

Figure 7.62 Insert Sound dialog box

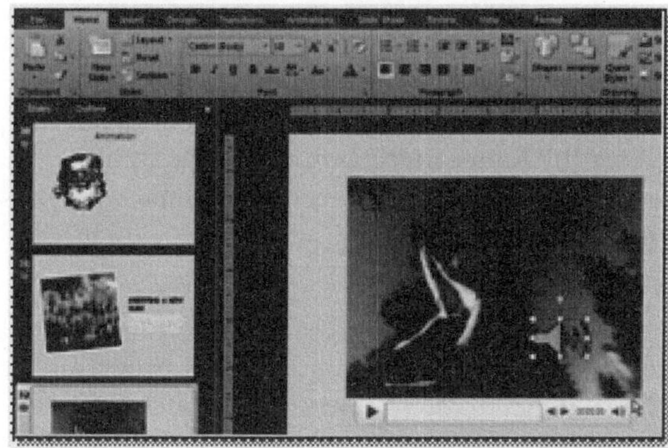

Figure 7.63 The audio file is inserted in the presentation

7.5.4 Adding Headers and Footers

You can add *headers, footers* and *page numbers* to each of the slide or the Note Pages.

➡ **To insert header and footer to the slide, do this:**

1. In the **Insert** tab, click **Header & Footer** in the **Text** group. Or In the **Print** Backstage view click **Edit Header & Footer** link option.
2. The **Header and Footer** dialog box appears. Now click the **Notes and Handouts** tab property sheet as in Figure 7.64.

The Notes tab property sheet of Header and Footer dialog box offers the following options.

Date and time – If you select this option, the date and time appear in the upper-right corner of the page.

- Update automatically – select this option to print the actual date and time when printouts are made. Use the list box to select the format you would like the date and time to appear in.
- Fixed – Choose this option if you want to specify the specific date to be printed in text box.

Header – The header appears on the top left corner of the page. Enter the text for the header in the box below the option.

Page Number – The page numbers are shown as numerals only and appear in the lower-right corner of the page. Numbering is automatic increased once this option is on.

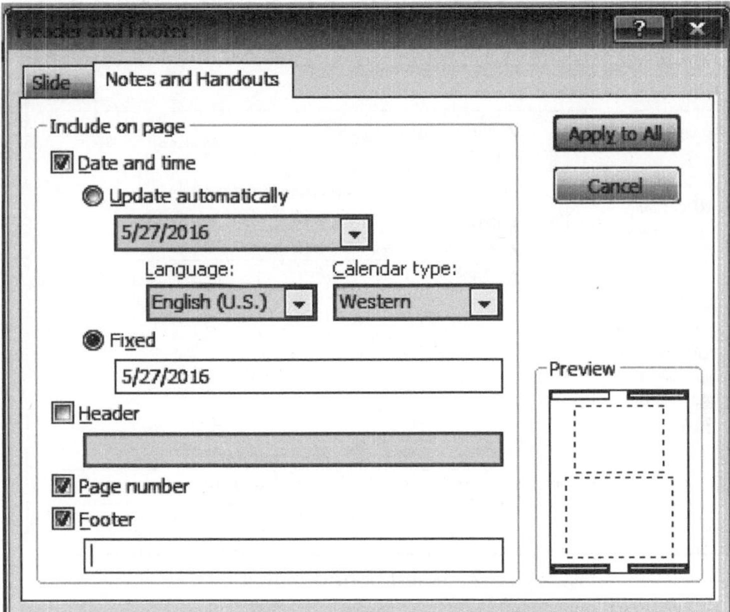

Figure 7.64 Header and Footer dialog box with Notes and Handouts Tab

Footer – The footer appears in the lower-left corner of the page. Enter the text for the footer in the box below the option.

3. Click Apply to All to use the selected settings.

7.6 PRESENTATION OF SLIDES

7.6.1 Viewing a Presentation

PowerPoint offers five ways (*views*) to look at your presentation. Each view enables you to work on a different aspect of the presentation. The changes made in one view are also reflected in all other views.

To understand the function of views, consider that you are looking at a house. Now assume you are standing in front of a house. You see one view. Now you move to one of the sides and you see a different view of the same house. PowerPoint views also allow you to see a presentation in various ways.

The buttons located at the lower left corner of the PowerPoint window just above the status bar as shown in Figure 7.65 help you to switch to different views.

In the following section, you will conceptually learn about the view.

Normal View

Normal view is the main editing view, where you write and design your presentation. The view has four working areas:

- Outline tab
- Slides tab
- Slide pane
- Notes pane

These panes let you work on all aspects of your presentation in one place. You can adjust the size of different panes by dragging the pane borders.

- **Outline tab:** Use the Outline tab to organize and develop the contents of your presentation. You can type all of the text of your presentation and rearrange bullet points, paragraphs and slides. The Outline tab shows your slide text in outline form.
- **Slides tab:** This is a great place to view the slides in your presentation as thumbnail-sized images while you edit. The thumbnails make it easy for you to navigate through your presentation and to see the effect of any design changes. You can also easily rearrange, add or delete slides.

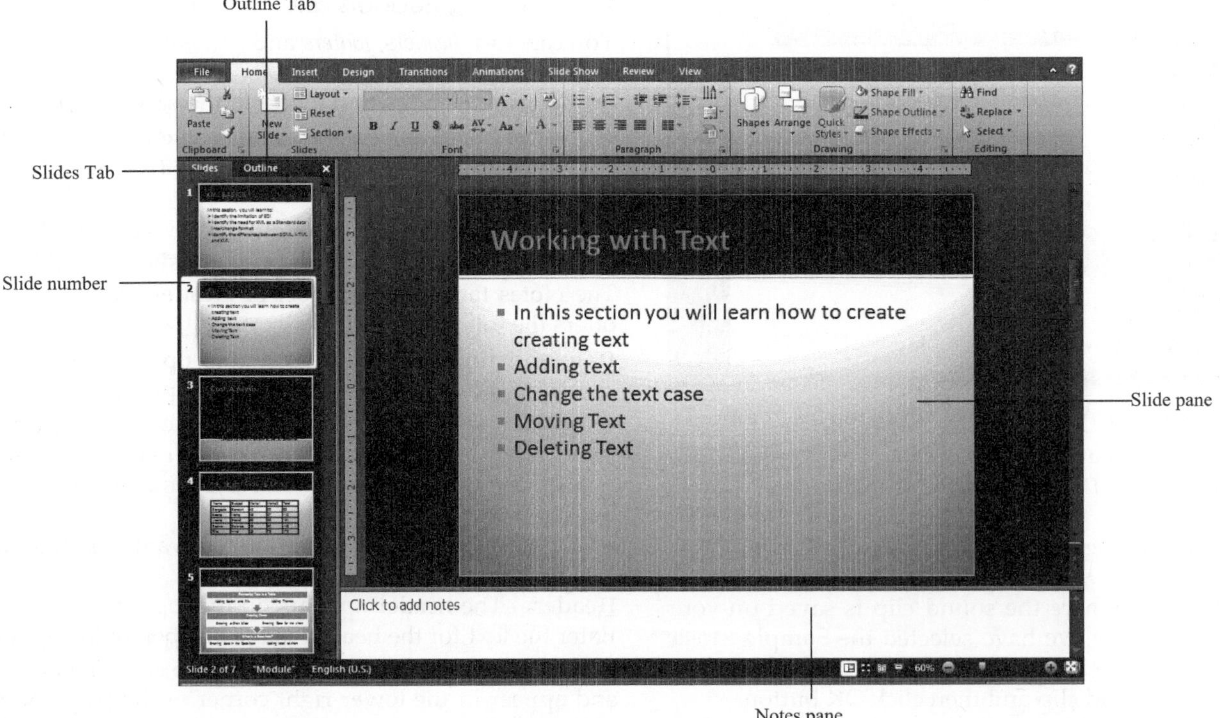

Figure 7.65 Normal View

- **Slide pane***:* In the slide pane, you can see how your text looks on each slide. You can add SmartArt graphics, movies and sounds, create hyperlink and add animations to individual slides.
- **Notes pane:** The Notes pane lets you add speaker notes or information you want to share with the audience. If you want to have graphic in your notes, you must add the notes in Notes page view.

  These pane are also shown when you save a presentation as a Web page. The only difference is that the outline pane displays a table of contents so that you can navigate through the complete presentation.

Slide Sorter View

The slide sorter view is a view of your slides in thumbnail form (See Figure 7.66). Working in this view is like laying out the pages of your presentation or report on the table so that you can see them all at once. In this view, you can see the design consistency and the flow of your presentation. If need be, you can easily reorder the slides, copy or delete the slides.

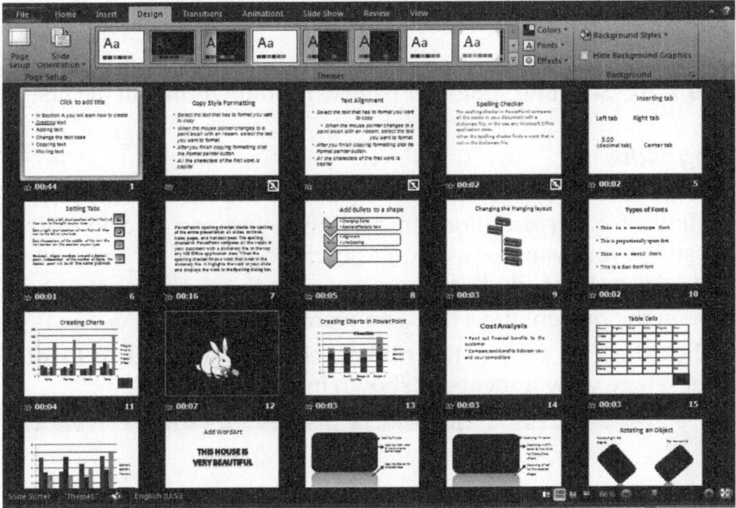

Figure 7.66 PowerPoint's Slide Sorter View

Notes Page View

This view helps you to prepare the speaker notes used while making the presentation to your audience. Notes pages view produces a smaller version of the slide on the top part of a page and leaves the lower part free for notes or keypoints (See Figure 7.67).

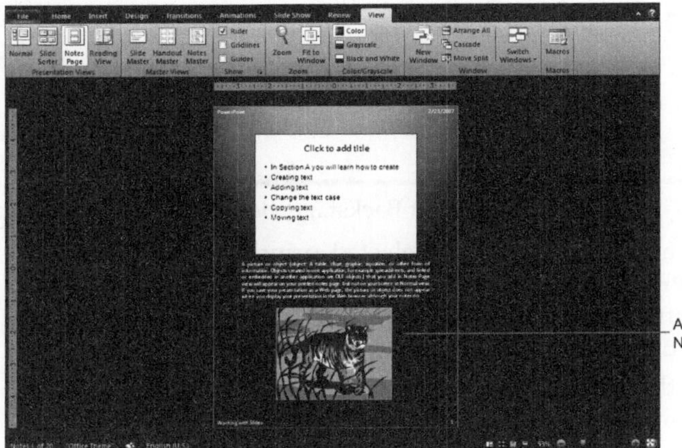

Figure 7.67 PowerPoint's Notes Pages View

Slide Show View

This view of PowerPoint shows the progress of the presentation form slide to slide just like a real slide show. In this view, all *menus, toolbars, rulers, status bar, scrollbars,* and the Windows *taskbar* are removed from the screen (See Figure 7.68).

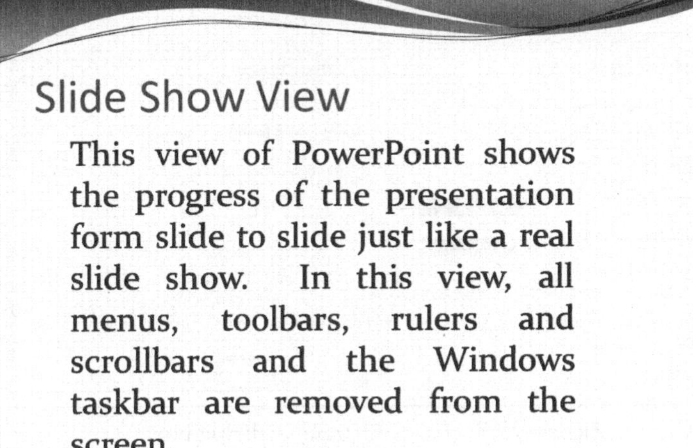

Figure 7.68 Slide Show View

7.6.2 Choosing a Set Up for Presentation

With the options in the Set up dialog box, you can choose the type of show to run and how the show should proceed.

Starting the Slide Show

When you view a slide show, you have following options:

1. Click **Slide Show** tab in the **Start Slide Show group**, choose Slide Show from beginning or press Shift+F5 keys together.
2. In the Slide show, you go to next slide, press N or click the Backspace key to go to the previous slide.

➡ **To set a slide show option, do this:**

1. Click **Slide Show** tab in the **Set Up** group, choose Set Up Show icon. The Set Up Show dialog box appears as shown in Figure 7.69.
2. To Show all slides in your presentation, Click All in the Show slides section.
3. To show a specific group of slides from your presentation, enter a starting and ending slide in From: and To: edit boxes.
4. To start a custom slide presentation that derives from another presentation, click Custom Show: drop-down list and then click the presentation that you want to view as a custom show.

Giving Special Show

PowerPoint offers three special slide show types. These are available on the Set Up Show dialog box (See Figure 7.69).

1. *Click Presented by a Speaker (full screen)*: Is the traditional, full-screen slide show.
2. *Click Browsed by an Individual (window)*: Runs the slide show in a standard window.
3. *Click Browsed at a Kiosk (full screen)*: It displays a full screen as a self running show which restarts after 5 minutes.

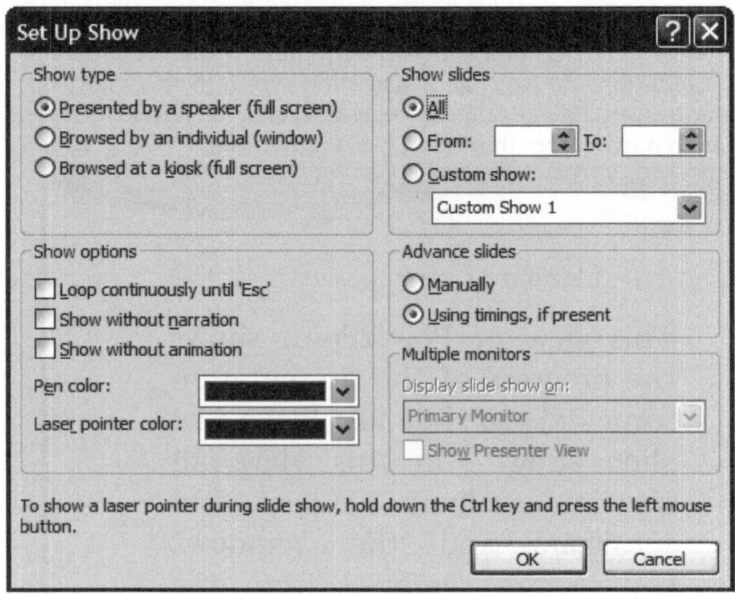

Figure 7.69 The Set Up Show dialog box

7.6.3 Printing Slides and Handouts

Handout lets you include two, three, or six small images of the slides in your presentation. You can select the format when you print them.

Handouts can be created in the following two ways:

- Print the Handouts using the standard PowerPoint format, i.e., two, three or six slide on a page format.
- The Handout format can be customized to your requirement using the handout master.

If you make Handouts, PowerPoint shrinks the slides you have created and fits them on a page, according to the option you choose in the print Backstage view. To use standard Handout formats, you only have to select the number of slides you want to print on a page when you take the printouts for Handouts.

☞ *The header, footers, page numbers and the date on each handout will be printed if you have selected any of these items on your Notes Pages. The same is automatically applied to your Handouts.*

In case you want to have different headers, footers, page numbers or dates on your Handouts as compared to the Notes Pages then you are required to change these in the Headers and Footer dialog box.

☞ *The golden rule in presentations is "Say more than you show and handout more than you say". Therefore the material that you hand out (either before or after your presentation) should be more than just pictures of your slides.*

Printing Handouts

You can print your entire presentation – slides, outline, notes and audience handouts. You can also print specific slides, handouts, notes pages, or outline pages.

➡ **To print handouts, do this:**

1. Open the presentation you want to print.
2. Click the **File** tab, the Backstage view appears.
3. To click one or multiple slides per page in handout format, under **Handouts**, click the number of slides you want per page, and whether you want them to appear in order vertically or horizontally (See Figure 7.70).
4. After applying the desired option, click OK.

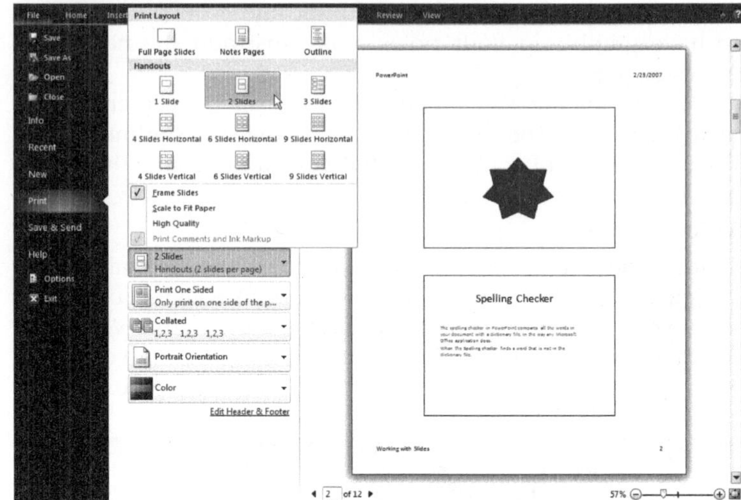

Figure 7.70 Selecting slides per page in handout format in the File tab

Printing Slides

In PowerPoint 2010, you can either print all the slides or the current slide of a presentation. In addition, you can decide how many slides you want to print on a single page.

➡ **To print a slides, do this:**

1. Open the presentation that you want to print.
2. Click the **File** tab on the ribbon, click **Print** tab. The **Print** Backstage view appears as shown in Figure 7.71.

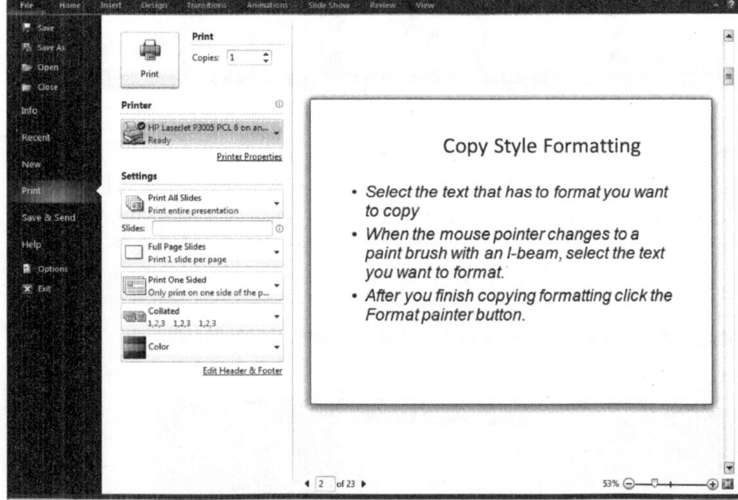

Figure 7.71 Print Backstage view

3. The name of the currently selected printer is shown at the under **Printer** drop-down arrow. To print the presentation on a different printer, select the desired printer from the **Printer** drop-down list.
4. Specify the number of copies you want to print, for each slide in the **Copies:** spinner box.
5. The **Setting** drop-down list has the option which allows you to select the pages you want to print.

Option	Description
Print All Slides	Choose Print All Slides option to print the entire presentation at one time.
Current slide	Choose the Current slide option to print the slide shown on the monitor.
Custom Range	Choose to print the selected slides, and enter the corresponding slide numbers in the **Slides:** edit box, e.g., to print slide 3 and 6 through 8, enter 3,6-8 in the Slides edit box.
Custom Show	Prints a certain custom show which has been set up. Each custom shows appears on the list.
Print Hidden Slides	If slides are hidden (do not display during a slide show), they can be printed by checking the *Print Hidden Slides* check box.

6. **Collate:** Specify if you want to arrange while printing multiple copies. When you choose collate option, each set is printed completely from first page to the last page. Then the next set is printed.
7. Click the Color button, and select the colour setting for the printouts:
   - **Color**–This is default. When you use this settings with a black-and-white printer, it results in slides with grayscale or black backgrounds.
   - **Grayscale**–To print in grayscale, select the grayscale check box.
   - **Pure black & white option**–converts all colours in the presentation to either black or white. Prefer this option if you need to print on a printer that cannot print gray shades.

7.7 SLIDE SHOW

7.7.1 Running a Slide Show

When you develop a slide show in Slide Sorter view, you can get a preview of transition effects for all slides. But to see the transitions full-screen and to see animated or bulleted text slides, you must select the presentation as a slide show.

Assigning Slide Transitions

Slides transitions are the animation-like effects that occur in the slide show view, when you move from one slide to the next. You can control the speed of each slide transition effect, and you can also add sound.

➡ **To assign the transitions, do this:**

1. Select the slide(s) you want to add a transition effect.
2. Click the **Transitions** tab. In the **Transition to This slide** group, click down arrow and then select the effect that will be applied during the slide show. For example here we select *Flash* under **subtle** (See Figure 7.72).
3. If you Apply to all slides, click **Apply To All** in the **Timings** group.
4. Select the Sound option to give sound transitions to your slide show from the **Sound:** drop-down list in the **Timings** group.
5. The Advance section has two options for transition:
   - On mouse click check box – if you want the transition to take place on clicking the mouse.
   - Automatically after – in this case the transition takes place automatically after the time you specify in the *seconds* box.

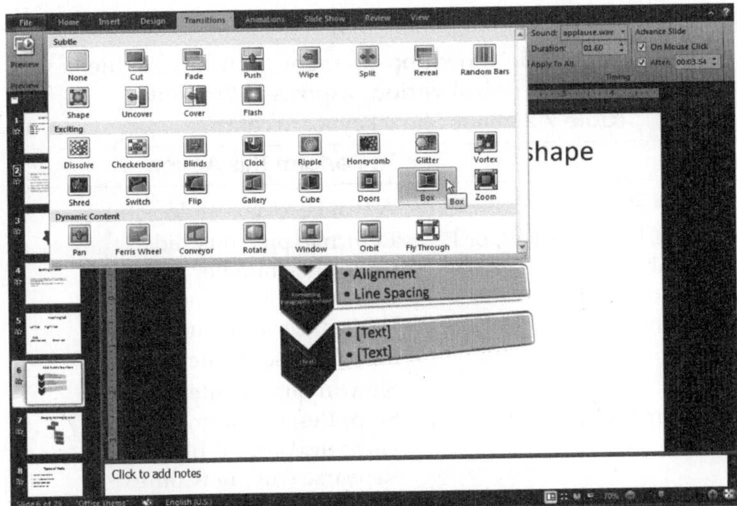

Figure 7.72 Selecting Transition effect to Slide

6. After apply all options, you can see the effect in the Slide show. Click the **Slide Show** tab, in the **Start Slide Show** group, click **From Beginning** icon. Click the next button (i.e. →) to go to the next slide.
7. Click preview command to preview the current transitions effect in the **Preview** group

Controlling the Slide Show with a Mouse

During a slide Show, you can use the pop-up menu button. A pop-up menu appears as shown in Figure 7.73. As mentioned earlier, the button appears in the lower left corner of the current slide as soon as you move the mouse pointer. You can then click the button to display slide show pop-up menu.

The Next and Previous commands on the pop-up menu let you move forward or backward through the slides in your slide show.

To move to a specific slide, click Go to Slide and then choose slide from the menu 7(See Figure 7.73).

To stop a slide show at any time during a presentation, simply choose End Show from the pop-up menu.

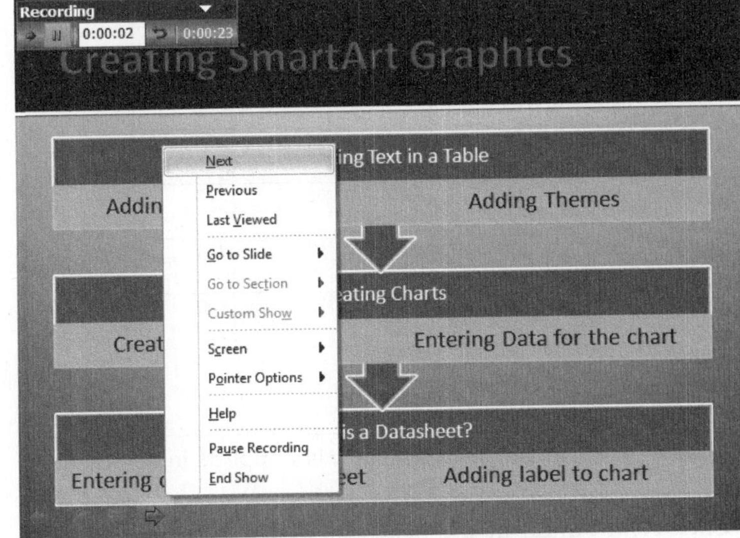

Figure 7.73 Pop-up menu during Slide show

Controlling the Slide Show with a Keyboard

In addition to the slide show pop-up menu, you can use the keys listed in Table 7.2 to control various aspects of the show.

Table 7.2 Slide Show keyboard controls

Press This	To Perform This Action
Spacebar, →, ↓, PgDn, N	Advance to next slide.
Backspace, ←, ↑, PgUp, or P	Return to previous slide
Slide number + Enter	Go to slide number
B or period	Blacks/Unblacks the screen
W or comma	Whites/Unwhite the screen
Ctrl+A	Show mouse pointer as arrow
Ctrl+P	Show mouse pointer as pen
S or + (numeric keypad)	Stop/Restart automatic show
H	Go to next slide if hidden.
T	Rehearse – use new time
O	Rehearse – use original time
Esc, Ctrl+break or (-)	End Show

7.7.2 Transitions and Slide Timings

If you do not want to move through a slide show manually, there are two ways you can set the length of time a slide appears on the screen. One way is to set a time manually for each slide, and then run the slide show and view the timings you set. The other way is to use rehearsal feature, where you can record timings automatically as you rehearse. You can also adjust the timings you have already set and then rehearse the new ones.

7.7.3 Automating a Slide Show

1. On the **Slide Show** tab, in the **Set Up** group, click **Rehearse Timings** to start the show in rehearsal mode.
2. It starts a full-screen slide show in which you can rehearse your presentation.
3. The Rehearsal dialog box appears in the slide show as seen in Figure 7.74. It starts slide timings in the first slide.

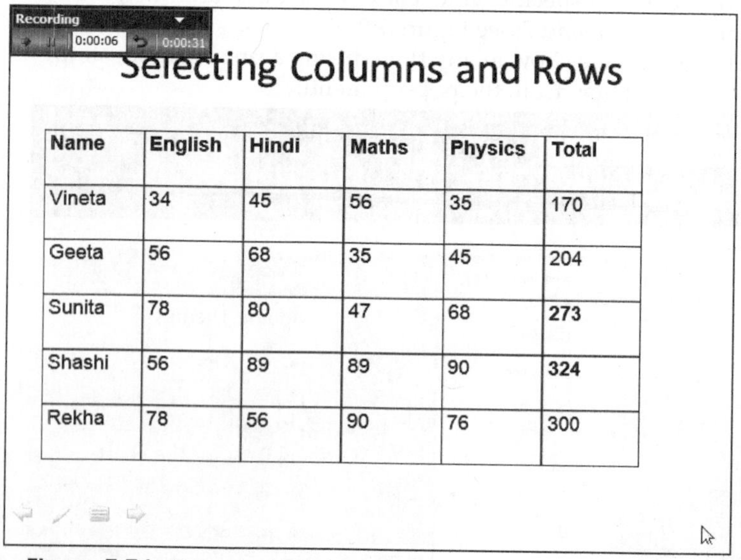

Recording

0:00:06 0:00:31

Selecting Columns and Rows

Name	English	Hindi	Maths	Physics	Total
Vineta	34	45	56	35	170
Geeta	56	68	35	45	204
Sunita	78	80	47	68	273
Shashi	56	89	89	90	324
Rekha	78	56	90	76	300

Figure 7.74 Rehearsal Timings dialog box appears in the slide show

4. Click Next button in the Rehearsal dialog box, and fix the time in the second slide.
5. When you reach the end of the slide show, the PowerPoint dialog appears. It asks *The Total time for the slide show was 0:00:42. Do you want to keep the new slide timings to use when you view the slid show?* Yes or No. Click Yes to accept the timings or No to try again.
6. The amount of time you spend on each slide is recorded and you can save those timings to run the show automatically in the future.

7.8 SUMMARY

This chapter presents details of making presentation in MS PowerPoint. This package, i.e, MS PowerPoint has innovative ways of working with presentation graphics. It is used for presenting information in a simple and effective manner. First, we discussed how to open and save a presentation. Later, we discussed how to create a template. Formatting features namely, aligning text, changing fonts, text size, adding bullets and numbering and special effects to text are also described. Adding Clip Art is used to add graphic objects to a slide. Modifying objects, such as resizing and scaling an objects are discussed. It also describes different views on a presentation, such as normal, slide, outline and slide sorter view. Each view lets your work on a different aspect of the presentation. It includes preset animation, which is the effect used to display text object during a slide show. Finally, a slide display time on the screen can be set during a slide show automatically using the Rehearse timings feature.

MODEL QUESTIONS AND ANSWERS

A. Multiple Choice

1.1 Which of the following views is not the PowerPoint views?

a. Slide Sorter view b. Slide view
c. Outline view d. Page view

1.2 The Save As dialog box can be used

a. For saving the file for the first time
b. To save file by some alternative name
c. To save file in a format other then Word
d. All of the above

1.3 Which of the following can be used to create presentation from scratch?

a. Autocontent wizard b. Design templates
c. Sample presentation d. Blank presentation

1.4 An electronic page in a presentation is called

a. Slide b. E-slide
c. E-page d. Page

1.5 Which of the following shortcuts is used to insert a New Slide in PowerPoint?

a. Ctrl+M b. Ctrl+N
c. Ctrl+O d. None of the above

1.6 Which extension is given to PowerPoint document by default?

a. `.EXT` b. `.COM`
c. `.PPTX` d. None of the above

1.7 Which of the following tab has the Background styles?

a. Design tab b. View tab
c. Insert tab d. Slide Show tab

1.8 Which of the following is true with reference to Clip Art?

   a. PowerPoint displays available pictures in the Clip Art Gallery
   b. You can use a toolbar button or a placeholder to insert Clip Art
   c. You can recolour clip art.
   d. All of the above

1.9 In which view notes pane appears
   a. Normal view b. Outline view
   c. Both (a) and (b) d. None of the above

1.10 In Handout master footer area appears at
   a. Top of the page b. Bottom of the page
   c. Center of the page d. None of the above

B. State whether the following are True or False

2.1 You can view a presentation using one out of ten views provided by PowerPoint.
2.2 The Slide Sorter View button automatically sorts the slides alphabetically.
2.3 Outline view, Slide view, and Slide Show are just different ways of viewing the same set of slides.
2.4 Speaker's Notes are pages with a copy of a slide on top and space below it for taking notes.
2.5 You can shut down PowerPoint 2000 by using the close button.
2.6 The first time you save a presentation you must name it.
2.7 A text box can be placed anywhere on the slide.
2.8 Bullets and numbering appear in the standard toolbar.
2.9 The crop tool allows you to alter an object by hiding or cutting portions of it.
2.10 Animation effects appears in the Standard toolbar.

Answers

I.	1.1	d	1.2	d	1.3	a	1.4	a	1.5	a
	1.6	c	1.7	a	1.8	d	1.9	c	1.10	b
2.	2.1	F	2.2	T	2.3	T	2.4	T	2.5	T
	2.6	T	2.7	T	2.8	F	2.9	T	2.10	F

CHAPTER 8

Financial Literacy for Banking Scheme and Applications

8.0 INTRODUCTION

Digital financial services, expands the delivery of basic financial services to the people through new technologies like the Internet, mobile phones and transfer of money through new digital channels. These channels have significantly drive down the costs for customers and service providers, thus opening the doors to provide 24 hours' service for 365 days. (Figure 8.1)

Figure 8.1 Digital Financial Service

8.1 OBJECTIVES

In this chapter you will be able to understand the application of digital financial services in India.

- Why Savings are needed?
- Drawbacks of keeping cash at home
- Why Bank is needed?
- Banking products
- Banking Service Derlivery Channels - I and II
- Various Schemes
- Bank on Mobile
- Insurance

8.2 WHY SAVINGS ARE NEEDED?

We need to save money for future needs, emergencies and for large expenses.

8.2.1 Emergencies

Saving must be top most priority for everyone, which allows you to easily meet any unexpected emergencies, such as:

- The emergency fund not only provides you with the money to pay for expenses, but gives you a "peace of mind".
- To meet unexpected expenses like Illness, accident, death of earning members, fire, flood, etc.
- Job layoff and sudden loss of income.
- It allows you to avoid borrowing money from others.

8.2.2 Future Needs

We save, because we cannot predict the future. With savings, in the future you can buy what you cannot buy today. There are few reasons why we need saving (See Figure 8.2):

- To buy something which we cannot afford from our regular income.
- To meet needs at old age when not able to earn.
- The costs for education is rising every year, and to provide better educational facilities to your family member.
- Starting of new business, purchasing own house.
- To meet regular expenses for life after retirement.
- In future, when the income is less and expenses are more.

Figure 8.2 Savings

8.2.3 Large Expense

Large expenses sometimes surprise us by popping up at the most inappropriate times.

Large expense includes:

- Plan for higher education of family members in India or abroad.
- Plan for marriage.
- Buying home.
- Starting of new business

8.3 DRAWBACKS OF KEEPING CASH AT HOME

Money can either get stolen by anybody if it is kept at home. In this section we will discuss few drawbacks of keeping cash at home.

8.3.1 Unsafe

Money kept at home can be stolen or lost. It can also be lost due to calamities (such as fire). While in the bank money is safer.

8.3.2 Loss of Growth Opportunity

Loss of Interest Income. By keeping your money in bank, you can earn extra income as an interest from the bank.

8.3.3 No Credit Eligibility

Deposits in Bank creates Credit Eligibility.

- You are not eligible to get a credit card/loan as no credit history is available to your bank.
- Bank can also give loans for future needs.

8.4 WHY BANK IS NEEDED?

A bank is a financial institution, which acts as an intermediary in transactions, and offer services like safekeeping and lending of money. It can be considered as an establishment, which is authorized by government to accept – Cash Deposits, pay interest and to provide following financial services which people requires.

Bank is majora needed to (Figure 8.3):

1. Safety of money
2. Inculcate habit of saving
3. Earn interest
4. Remittances using Cheque/Demand Draft
5. Loans-Home/Business/Vehicle
6. Avoid risk of chit funds, sahukars
7. Online banking
8. Bank lockers
9. Credit/Debit cards

Figure 8.3 Why bank is needed

8.4.1 Secure Money, Earn cash, Get loan

- Saving money in a bank account, offers you the opportunity to earn interest on deposits.
- Rates of interest of savings account also depends on how much you saved, i.e., more money you keep in the bank for longer duration, the higher the interest will be.
- Once you established good relationship with bank, you can apply for loans (vehicle, house, education or business loans) as deposited in bank creates credit eligibility.
- If you do not want carry cash with you because of safety issues, you can carry debit card or credit card provided by bank.
- Your money is secure as money can be stolen/lost otherwise.

8.4.2 Inculcate Habit of Saving

Person, whether doing a job, business, student, kids or housewives must have the habit of saving money, which can be used for future needs.

8.4.3 Remittances using Cheque /Demand Draft

Banks acts as a medium for the transfer of money (both domestic and foreign) from one place to another and from person to person safely, speedily and efficiently.

8.4.4 Avoid Risk of Chit Funds and Sahukars

Chit funds

Chit implies a transaction under which a person goes into an agreement with a predefined number of persons. Each one of them will subscribe to a certain amount of money by method for periodical instalments over a definite period of time.

Such subscriber shall, in his turn, as dictated by a lot or by auction or by tender or in such other way as might be determined in the chit agreement, be entitled to the prize sum.

Chit fund frauds have become a major issue and many people have been cheated in the past. The fund manager may disappear with the corpus amount. A member could default in an instalment payment or disappear after winning the first bid. The discount rate might be rigged and a desperate member might end up paying a higher discount. Due to this, it is not advisable to invest in chit funds.

Sahukars

They are Moneylenders,!who offers loans!at high!rates of interest and normally people go there when bank refuses to give them the loan.

Unfair Practices of Sahukars

Sahukars deceive in many ways such as:

- They manipulate the amount given to debtors (like, they may enter large amount than they actually lent.
- They give no receipt for repayments and sometimes they deny such repayments.
- They charge very high rate of interest.

☞ *Facts: The rate of interest on Bank loans is very low as compared to money lenders. So, if a money lender mentions 3% per month interest rate, it means 36% per year whereas a Bank might only give maximum interest rate of 12% per year for long term deposits.*

8.4.5 Documents needed for Opening a Bank Account

Presenting a copy of any one of the following documents can open a standard account:

- Idendity card or ID Card with person's picture issued by Central/State Ministry, Statutory/Regulatory Authorities, Public Sector Undertakings, Scheduled Commercial Banks, and Public Financial Institutions; Or
- A letter issued by a Gazetted officer, with a duly attested photograph of the person.

Know Your Customer (KYC)

It is a process by which banks acquire data about the identity and address of the clients. This procedure guarantees that banks' administrations are not abused. The KYC strategy is to be finished by the banks while opening accounts and also occasionally update the same from time to time.

☞ *Fresh KYC Documents to be submitted on attaining majority, i.e. 18 years in case of minor accounts.*

Photo ID Proof, Address Proof

Documents which are used for identity proof and are official valid are: (See Figure 8.4)

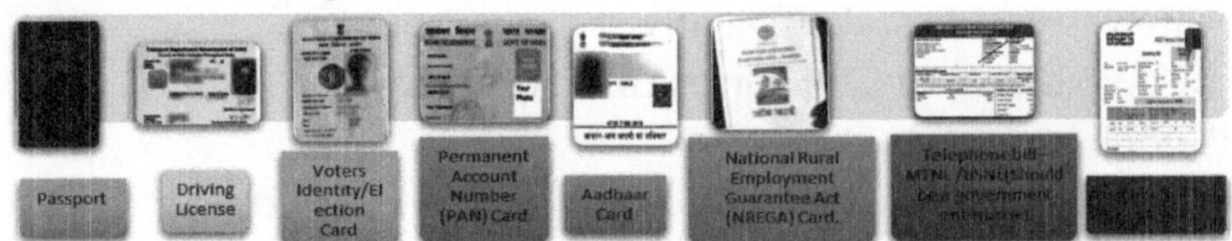

Figure 8.4 Eight Valid Documents for Identity Proof

- Passport
- Driving License
- Voter ID Card
- PAN Card
- Aadhar Card
- National Rural Employment Guarantee Card
- Electricity Bill
- Telephone Bill

You need to submit any one of these documents as proof of identity. If these documents also contain your address details, then it would be accepted as "proof of address". If the document submitted by you for evidence of identity does not include address details, then you will have to submit another officially valid document, which provides address details. These documents must contain the address details, then it would be also accepted as the proof of address.

Indian Currency

It is the official currency of the Republic of India, issued by Reserve Bank of India (RBI) and guaranteed by the Central government (See Figure 8.5).

Figure 8.5 Indian Currency and Symbol of Rupees

☞ **Do you Know?**

Two Rupees and above Note is signed by the Governer or RBI, while One Rupee Note is signed by the Finance Secretary, Ministry of Finance and the Coin is issued by the Government of India Mint.

8.5 BANKING PRODUCTS

Banks not only give a safe place to keep your money and valuable jewellery in lockers. However, they additionally offer accounts and products that permit you to pay your bills and, in the meantime, earn interest and help your money to grow and also offers the following types of Accounts and Deposits.

8.5.1 Types of Accounts and Deposit

Accounts: (See Figure 8.6)

a. **Saving Accounts:** It is meant for saving purposes. The benefit of having savings account is that Banks pay interest on the money present in the account.

Features:

- Flexibility in deposits and withdrawal of funds from the account.
- Passbook, Cheque Book, Automated Teller Machine (ATM), Debit Card are issued to customers.
- Interest is earned on the amount deposited.

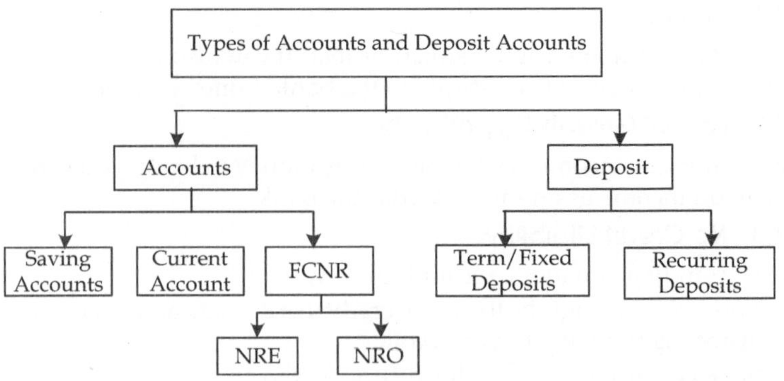

Figure 8.6 Types of Accounts and Deposits Accounts

b. **Current Account:** It is mainly used by business persons, firms, companies, public enterprises, etc.

Features:

- Current accounts are opened in the names of firm/company.
- No limits for number of transactions.
- No interest is paid by Banks on these accounts.

c. **NRO/NRE/FCNR Accounts**

i. **Foreign Currency Non-Resident Account (FCNR):** Account is opened by the NRIs in designated currencies, such as US Dollar (USD), Great Britain Pound (GBP), Euro (EUR), Japanese Yen (JPY), Canadian Dollar (CAD) and Australian Dollar (AUD), etc.

ii. **Non-Resident Ordinary Accounts (NRO):** Resident outside India can open this account. When a resident becomes a non-resident, his domestic rupee account gets converted to the NRO account, and he cannot take his money out of India.

c. **Non-Resident (External) Rupee Account NR(E)RA:** It is a Rupee account, and the NRI (Non-Resident Indian) can remit money to India from the abroad and can also take money out of India.

Deposits (See Figure 8.6):

a. **Term/Fixed deposits:** In this a particular amount of money is deposited in a bank for a given period of time mainly from 7 days to 10 years.

Features:

- Term deposits are for fixed tenure from 7 days to 10 years.
- Banks pay higher interest rates on Term deposits.
- Interest can be withdrawn at monthly/quarterly intervals or cumulated.

b. **Recurring deposits:** It is used to save a certain amount of money regularly for a particular period and earn a higher interest rate on recurring deposits.

Features:

- Periodic deposit of money for a fixed period.
- Interest paid on Recurring deposit accounts is higher than saving A/c.
- Withdrawal is permitted on maturity or pre-mature closure of account.

c. **Small Accounts**

- 'Small Account' can be opened by submitting recent photograph and putting signature or thumb impression in the presence of the Bank official.
- Valid for 12 Months.

- Balance in accounts at any point of time should not exceed Rs.50,000/-

d. **Basic Savings Bank Deposit Account**
- There is no requirement of minimum balance.
- Facility of Debit card.
- Any individual above the age of 10 years can open Basic Savings Bank Deposit (BSBD) Account.

***Interest Rate may vary from bank to bank and time to time.**

8.5.2 Types of Loan and Overdrafts

Banks provide loans for purchase of home, car household goods, business, education, etc. Loans are also provided for economic activities like agriculture, business, industry and service sector. Loans are not provided for unlawful activities like gambling. The rate of interest on bank loans is very low as compared to money lenders.

- **Home Loan:** This type of Loan is taken by people for a variety of home-related purposes, such as construction, renovation, extension of home or buying of property. Home loans comprise of an adjustable or fixed interest rate and payment terms.
- **Personal Loan:** This includes loan for paying debt, marriage expenses or vacation expenditure, and is given to individuals after accessing their credentials based on their profession or business.
- **Education Loan:** Provided to students who want to pursue higher education / vocational studies in India for Rs. 10 Lakhs or abroad for 20 Lakhs or more.

☞ Do you Know?
Students can also register on GOI Vidya Laxmi Portal for Educational Loan application and tracking.

- **Business Loan:** This type of loan is provided to either existing businesses or those getting into new business, on the basis of individual's credentials. For existing businesses, loan is provided in the following ways:
  - **Term loans:** Amount provided for a fixed tenure at the applicable interest rate, like 3 years for short term loan and 10-15 years for long term loans. You pay part of interest and part of loan in equal installments to bank every month.
  - **Bank overdraft limits:** Ability to withdraw more money than what is deposited.
  - **Bill Discounting:** Short-term borrowing used to improve a company's working capital and cash flow against bills/invoices raised by the company.
  - **Letter of credit for international business:** Bank guaranteeing a buyer's payment to a seller for a specified period against letter of credit.
  - **Hypothecation:** The established practice of a borrower pledging an asset as!collateral!for a loan, while bank retains the ownership of the assets till the amount is paid back.
- **Vehicle Loan:** This is provided to you for the purchase of old/new vehicle. The interest rates may vary from bank to bank and repayment process involves monthly EMIs (Equated Monthly Instalments) and early repayment options.
- **Loan against PPF (Public Provident Fund) /insurance policy/bonds/shares/**
Gold/Vehicle Loan are kept as a security by the bank to provide loan.
  - **Gold Loan:** Gold loan is given on providing gold as security to a bank.

Overdrafts

It is a kind of Loan!arrangement!under which bank!extends the credit up to a maximum!amount!(overdraft limit) against a!current!account. Consider an example, suppose you have Current Account, and its balance is Rs.10,000/-, Suddenly you need Rs.15000/- but you may be allowed to overdraw from your account under some terms and conditions as agreed by you and the bank on the basis of your eligibility.

8.5.3 Filling up of Cheques, Demand Draft

How to Fill Cheques?

In order to fill a cheque, person needs to mention the date, name of the person/ company (Payee), amount to be paid in words and in Figures as shown in Figure 8.7.

To fill the cheque do the following:

- Put your sign above your name to approve the transaction.
- Do not sign on the MICR (Magnetic Ink Character Recognition) Band.
- Do not forget to put the date.
- Do not overwrite/mark cut on the cheque.
- Keep the records of your cheques, by notifying it on a front page. Figure 8.8 shows the overwrite/cutting on the Cheque.

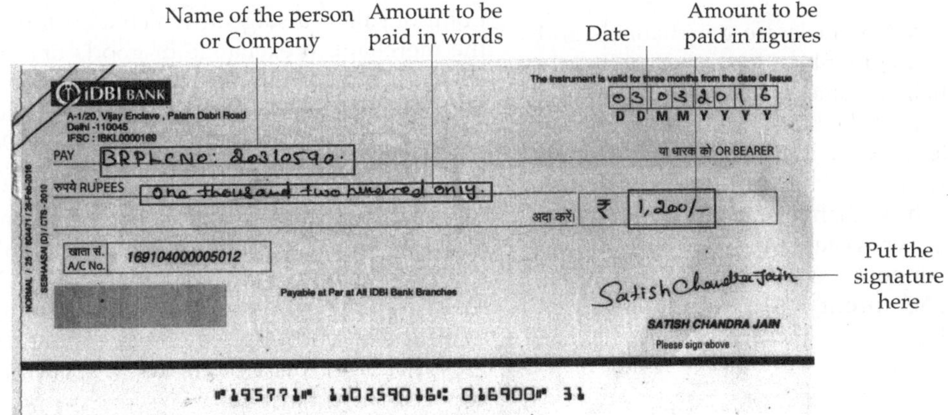

Figure 8.7 Cheque and its various fields

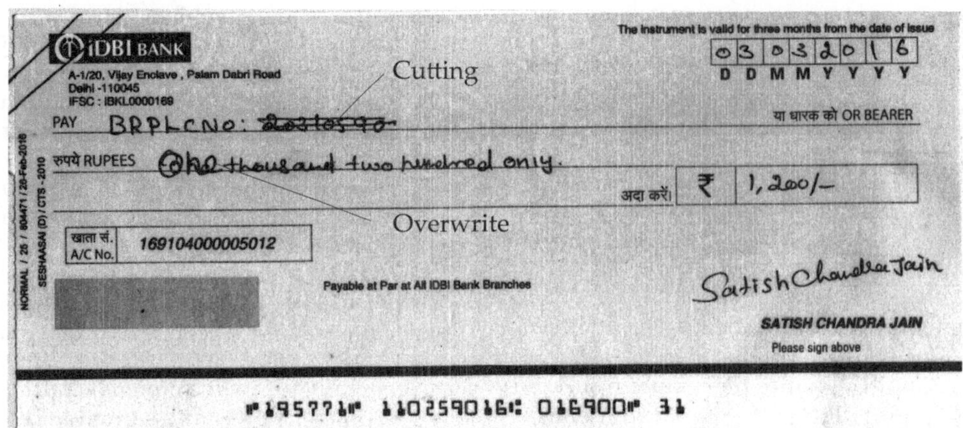

Figure 8.8 Overwrite/Cutting on the Cheque

How to fill Demand Draft (DD)?

Suppose you want to make a demand draft of Rs. 50,000/-. Bank will give you a form, you have to fill it, which contains the details like, amount or if you are giving a cheque you have to write cheque number on it, in whose favor the DD (Demand Draft) is to be made, your bank account number, the place (branch of bank) where your DD (Demand Draft) has to be issued and your signature, etc. Fill up the form, hand over the cash/cheque and the form to the designated bank employee. He will give you a receipt for it. Bank will take some commission/charges to make the draft for you and will deduct that money from your account. Figure 8.9 shows a sample Demand Draft.

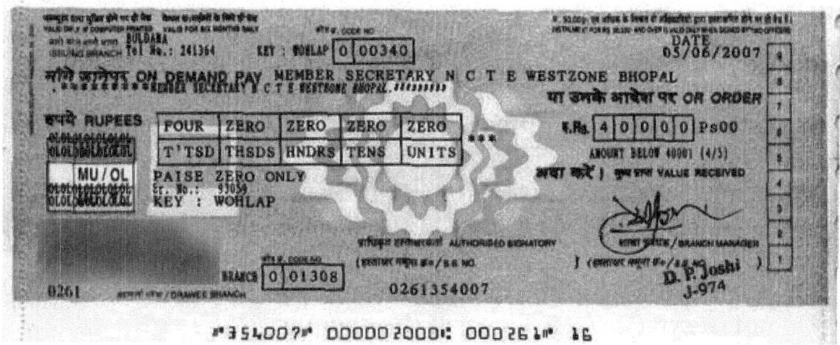

Figure 8.9 Sample Demand Draft

8.6 BANKING SERVICE DELIVERY CHANNEL–I

In the Banking Sector, Delivery Channels are the channels and methods which are used for providing banking services directly to the customers. By using this, customers can perform banking transactions through ATM, contact the bank's call centre for any inquiry, access the digital Interactive Voice Response (IVR), perform transactions through Internet Banking, and on smartphones through mobile banking, etc. These channels have enabled banks to reach a wide consumer-base across geographies.

Delivery channels ensure the smooth flow of regular transactions and provide banks with higher profit with lower operational expenses and transaction cost.

8.6.1 Bank Branch, ATM

Bank branch: It is a retail location where a bank offers a wide range of face-to-face and automated services to its customers. A bank has its branches at various location across the city or state so that customer can go there and avail its services.

ATM: (Automatic Transaction Machine or Automatic Teller Machine) enables the customers of a bank to perform financial transactions (cash withdrawal/deposit) without going to the bank.

In this machine, customer is identified by inserting a debit/-credit card, which is provided with a magnetic stripe or a plastic smart card having a!chip which contains information like some unique card number, expiration date (Card Verification Value - CVV). Customer need to insert a Personal Identification Number (PIN), for authentication purpose before using an ATM. Using an ATM, customers can withdraw cash, check balances and deposit money. One can use ATM service 24 hours per day throughout the year.

8.6.2 Bank Mitra with Micro-ATM

Bank Mitra: Bank Mitra are those individuals, who act as an agent of bank at those places where it is not possible to open a branch of bank. They provide all kind of assistance required in opening an account.

Micro-ATMs: Biometric authentication system enabled hand-held device. To make ATMs viable at rural/semi-urban centers, low cost Micro-ATMs are deployed at each Bank Mitra location, thus enables a person to instantly Deposit-Withdraw cash, Fund transfer and Balance enquiry. This devices work on a mobile phone connection.

Point of Sale

Point of sale is a stage at which a customer makes a payment to the merchant in exchange of goods or service. In this, the merchant prepares an!invoice!for the customer, calculate the amount owed by the customer and after that provide options to customer for making payment (either by Credit or Debit card).

8.7 BANKING SERVICE DELIVERY CHANNEL-II

In today's regulated and competitive market, banks need to stand with the customer expectations. Bank needs to offer a non-stop interactivity with customer, for building up loyalty with them. To achieve this, banks need to increase their business agility by anticipating customer needs and offer an engaging user experience. In this section we will learn about various banking services offered by bank.

8.7.1 Internet Banking

Internet banking is an electronic system which enables the customers to conduct transactions on bank's Website and perform activities, such as maintaining his account, transferring money, paying bills, etc. It is safe, secure but only thing required is that the customer must have the Internet connection, computer or mobile.

To access Internet banking:

- Open the bank secure website.
- Login to the Internet banking facility by using the Customer ID and other Password as shown in Figure 8.10.

Figure 8.10 Login Form

After successful authentication you will enter the customer area of the online banking (see Figure 8.11).

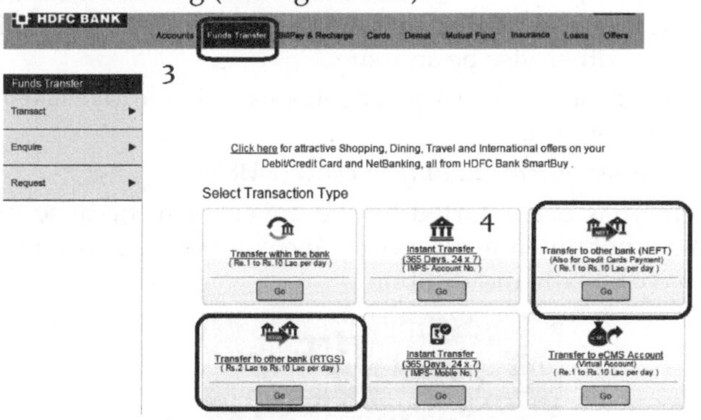

Figure 8.11 Customer Area

Features:

By using Internet banking, user can:

- View account balances, statement history, recent transactions and can transfer the fund!between the customer's linked accounts.
- Pay credit card bills.
- View the records of paid cheques, order and cheque books.
- Pay income tax, online tax remittance and other tax.
- Apply online for loan and top up for existing loan.
- Invest in mutual funds, buy insurance.
- Pay utility bills (Electricity, telephone, gas, mobile).
- Get the Demand Draft in favour of anybody.

Note: Donot/Don't give password to anybody else, under any circumstances.

8.7.2 National Electronic Fund Transfer (NEFT), Real Time Gross Settlement (RTGS)

National Electronic Funds Transfer, is the most prominent inter-bank electronic funds transfer systems of India, which provides a facility to bank customers to transfer the funds easily and securely on a one-to-one basis, which saves the time and is done via electronic messages. It is a "net" transfer facility, executed in hourly batches Figure 8.12 show the working of NEFT.

Real time gross settlement (RTGS), inter-bank transfer systems, which transfers money, from one bank to another on a "real time" and on "gross" basis. RTGS systems is used for high-value transactions which require an immediate clearing and is used to transfer of Rs.2 Lakhs and above.

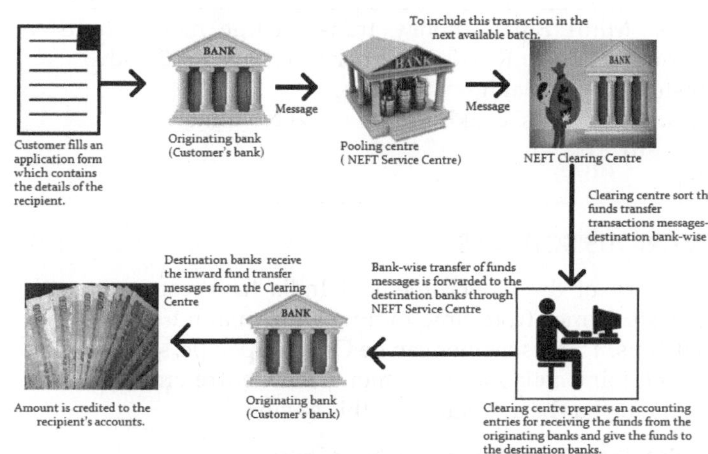

Figure 8.12 Process of NEFT

How this works?

In this example consider customer as a person who transfers the money and the recipient as a person who will get the money.

1. Customer fills an application form, in which the details (name, bank, bank branch name, IFSC code, type of account, account number and the amount to be deposited) of the recipient is filled.
2. After filling all the details, the Customer authorizes his/her bank branch to debit his account and pay the specified amount to the recipient.
3. Next, the originating bank (Customer's bank) branch prepares a message for the pooling center, called as NEFT Service Centre.
4. NEFT Service Centre, then forwards the received message to the NEFT Clearing Centre, operated by National Clearing Cell, Reserve Bank of India, Mumbai, for including this transaction in the next available batch.
5. NEFT Clearing Centre, then sort the funds transfer transactions messages; destination bank-wise and prepares an accounting entries for receiving the funds from the originating banks (to debit the amount from customer's account) and give the funds to the destination banks (to credit the amount in Recipient's accounts).
6. After that, bank-wise transfer of funds message is forwarded to the destination banks (originating bank or Customer's bank) through NEFT Service Centre.
7. Finally, the destination banks (originating bank or Customer's bank) receive the inward fund transfer messages from the Clearing Center and then pass the credited amount to the recipient's accounts. See Figure 8.12 for its working.

Note: Once the payment is processed, it is final and is irrevocable.

Table 8.1 Difference between NEFT and RTGS

Factors	NEFT	RTGS
Full form	National Electronic Fund Transfer	Real Time Gross Settlement
Speed	Slow	Fast
Time to credit the amount	Transactions are completed in batches at specific times.	Transaction is completed on a one-to-one basis

(Contd...)

Used for Minimum amount to be transfer*	Small money transfer Rs. 10,000/- to Rs. 2 lakh	Large money transfer above Rs. 2 lakh
Maximum amount to be transfer*	Rs. 2 lakh	No limit

8.8 VARIOUS SCHEMES

The ministry of the Government of India have come up with numerous schemes from time to time with an aim to support its poor citizens. These schemes can be Central specific, state specific or may be joint collaboration among the Centre and the state. Some scheme has been detailed in this section.

8.8.1 Pradhan Mantri Jan-Dhan Yojana

Pradhan Mantri Jan Dhan Yojana (PMJDY) is a nationwide scheme launched by Hon'ble Prime Minister on August 28, 2014. In this scheme financial inclusion of every **individual who does not have a bank account** is to be achieved in rural and urban areas.

The scheme will ensure financial access to everyone who was not able to get benefits of many other finance related government schemes.

These financial services include Banking/ Savings & Deposit Accounts, Remittance, Credit, Insurance, Pension which will be made available to all the citizens in easy and affordable mode.

1. Under the Jan Dhan Yojna anyone who is an Indian citizen and above the age of 10 years and does not have a bank account, can open the account with zero balance.
2. Account can be opened in any bank branch or Business Correspondent (Bank Mitra) outlet, specially designed for the purpose of opening the accounts under this scheme.
3. The scheme also provides facility of accidental insurance cover up to rupees one lac without any charge for the account holder.
4. The account holders under the jan dhan yojana will be given a RuPay debit card which can be used at all ATMs for cash withdrawal and at most of the retail outlets for making transaction for purchases.

Special Benefits under PMJDY Scheme

- Interest on deposit
- Ru-Pay debit card provides in-built Accidental insurance cover of Rs. 1 lakh.
- No minimum balance required.
- Overdraft facility up to Rs. 5000/-
- Life insurance cover of Rs. 30,000/-
- Easy transfer of money across India.
- Access to pension, insurance products.

8.8.2 Social Security Schemes

According to the Article 22 given in Universal Declaration of Human Rights, social security states: "*Everyone, as a member of society, has the right to social security and is entitled to realization, through national effort and international co-operation and in accordance with the organization and resources of each State, of the!economic, social and cultural rights!indispensable for his!dignity!and the free development of his personality.*"

In simple terms, it means that a society in which a person lives should help him or her to develop, make the most of all the features provided to them which may be of culture, work, social welfare.

Social security refers to the following terms:

- **Social insurance**, in this people receive benefits in recognition of their contributions to an insurance program. These plans include retirement pensions, disability insurance etc.
- **Services**, which are provided by government for social security provision. It includes facilities such as medical care, financial support during unemployment.
- **Basic security**, which is an insurance programs where eligibility may otherwise be an issue.

Some of the social security schemes have been discussed in the following sections.

Pradhan Mantra Suraksha Bima Yojna (PMSBY)

This scheme has been started by the government because poor people were not given insurance by the companies and they are not covered or death and disability.

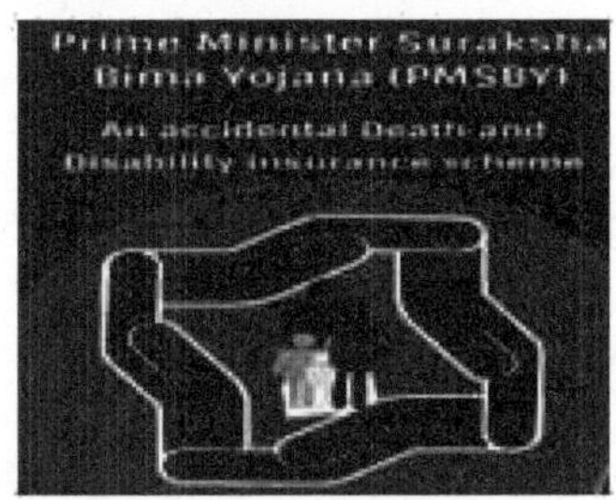

Pradhan Mantri Suraksha Bima Yojana is available to people between 18 and 70 years of age with bank accounts. It has an annual premium of Rs.12 excluding service tax, which is about 14% of the premium. The amount will be automatically debited from the account. In case of accidental death or full disability, the payment given to the nominee will be Rs.2 lakhs and in case of partial disability, payment of Rs.1 lakh, will be given. This scheme will be linked to the bank accounts opened under the Pradhan Mantri Jan Dhan Yojana scheme. Most of these account had zero balance initially. The scheme is valid for a year and it can be renewed every year.

Eligibility: Any person of the age group 18 to 70, with a savings bank account and with an Aadhaar Card can join this scheme.

To avail this service:

- Person will have to fill a simple form, mentioning the name of the nominee and Aadhaar Card number, and submit this form each year before 1st June to continue the scheme.
- By doing this, the account can be easily activated.
- Entire premium due will get auto-debited from the bank account.

Who will implement the PMSBY: All the government-sponsored insurance companies will offer this scheme. Other insurance companies have to sign-up with banks to offer this service.

Pradhan Mantri Jeevan Jyoti Bima Yojna (PMJJBY)

Pradhan Mantri Jeevan Jyoti Bima Yojana is available to people between 18 and 50 years of age with bank accounts. It has an annual premium of Rs.330/- excluding service tax, which is above 14% of the premium. The amount will be automatically debited from the account. In case of death due to any cause, the payment to the nominee will be Rs.2 lakhs.

This scheme will be linked to the bank accounts opened under the Pradhan Mantri Jan Dhan Yojana scheme. Most of these account had zero balance initially.

Eligibility: This scheme is available to the people of age group between 18 and 50 years and has a bank accounts from which the amount will get automatically debited.

Premium: Rs.330/- per annum per member, which will be deducted from the account holder's savings bank automatically.

Atal Pension Yojna (APY)

Atal Pension Yojana!is a government-backed pension scheme launched in India to target the unorganised sector. This scheme was formally launched by Prime Minister Narendra Modi.

In this scheme, for every contribution made to the pension fund, The Central Government would also co-contribute 50% of the total contribution, whichever is lower, to each eligible subscriber account, for a period of 5 years.

The minimum and maximum age to join this scheme is 18 years to 40 years, respectively.

Aadhaar is the primary, necessary document required for the identification. The subscribers are required to opt for a monthly pension from Rs. 1000/- to Rs. 5000/- and they have to pay a stipulated monthly contribution regularly, which is deducted automatically from the bank account.

Pradhan Mantri Mudra Yojna (PMMY)

Micro Units Development and Refinance Agency Ltd. (MUDRA), a new institution which is set up by Government of India for providing funds to the non-corporate, non-farm sector, shopkeepers, fruits/ vegetable vendors, truck operators, food-service units, repair shops, machine operators, below Rs.10 Lakh.

In this scheme, MUDRA has created three products as a stage of growth, which covers a loan amounts:

- **Shishu:** Covering loans up to Rs. 50,000/-
- **Kishore:** Covering loans above Rs. 50,000/- and up to Rs. 5 Lakhs.
- **Tarun:** Covering loans above Rs. 5,00,000/- and up to Rs 10 Lakh.

Bank branches gives loans facility under Mudra scheme as per customer requirements and the loans given under this scheme are collateral free loans.

Mudra Loans could be either availed for Vehicle loan (two wheelers, four wheeler), Business Instalment Loan (for working capital requirement) and Business Loans Group Loans (working capital loan).

8.8.3 National Pension Scheme (NPS)

It is a defined-contribution pension system, which is operated by Government of India. This scheme offers a range of investment options to employees which enables them to make their own decisions regarding where to invest their pension fund, to permit the withdrawal amount prior to retirement and reduces the total pension liabilities of the Government of India.

This scheme consists of two tiers

- **In tier 1:** Basic retirement pension account is available to all citizens and person cannot withdrawal its funds before retirement.
- **In tier-2:** Prospective payment system (PPS) account is there, which permits some withdrawal of pension amount prior to retirement.

The pension scheme is administered by the Pension Fund Regulatory and Development Authority (PFRDA), on the behalf of government.

Eligibility: All the citizens of India between the ages of 18 and 60 can avail this scheme.

8.8.4 Public Provident Fund (PPF) Scheme

It is a savings-cum-tax-saving instrument, which mobilizes small savings by offering an investment with reasonable returns and provides income tax benefits. It is established by centre government.

Individuals who are residents of India are eligible to open their account under the Public Provident Fund. Person need to deposit a minimum of Rs 500/- for opening and maintain the account and can deposit maximum amount to Rs 1.5 lakh. The current interest rate for PPF is **8.1% per annum**. Original duration is of 15 years, which can be extended for 5 years.

Pension: A plan for setting aside money to be spent after retirement On the maturity of PPF, person can:

- Either Completely withdraw all the money.
- Extend the PPF account with no contribution (does not pay any money) for 15 years.
- Extend the PPF account with contribution, in which person can put money in PPF account after extension.

8.9 BANK ON YOUR MOBILE

Bank on mobile means you can access bank from anywhere, anytime from your mobile and it has become simple to see your account, transfer funds, pay bills. It provides a convenient way to get connected with the bank.

8.9.1 Mobile Banking

It is a service provided by a bank, due to which customers can conduct transactions remotely by using a mobile device. By using this, you can access your account on your mobile. (See figure 8.13)

8.9.2 Mobile Wallet

It is a payment services which are operated under financial regulation and performed via a!mobile device. Consumer can pay for a wide range of services and digital or hard goods. It can be considered as a digital versions of traditional wallets, which holds digital information about credit and debit cards for making payments, store coupons and loyalty programs.

Figure 8.13 Mobile Banking

Working of Mobile Wallet

A customer can utilize all its stored information by opening an app on their phone, entering a PIN, password and then selecting the information they need to access. The app then does the transactions required and utilizes information transfer technology such as Near-Field Communications!(NFC) to interact with a mobile wallet ready payment terminals.

	Check List for Students	Tick the Appropriate	
1.	Have you ever visited a Bank Branch/Bank Mitra?	YES	NO
2.	Do you have a Bank Account?	YES	NO
3.	Have you ever used an ATM?	YES	NO
4.	Do you have a Debit Card?	YES	NO
5.	Have you received PIN?	YES	NO
6.	Do you have a Life Insurance?	YES	NO
7.	Do you have a insurance for your vehicle?	YES	NO
8.	Have you ever taken any loan?	YES	NO

8.10 INSURANCE

An agreement in which a person makes regular payments to a company and the company promises to pay money, up to the insured amount if the person is injured or dies, or to pay money equal to the value of something (such as a house or car) if it is damaged, lost, or stolen.

8.10.1 Necessity of Insurance

As insurance protects the interest of people or party from loss and the Insurer buys for the loses of insured.

Insurance is necessary as it:

- Provide financial safety and security to family members in case of untimely death.
- Provides medical support for managing risk in health by providing money in case of medical emergency.

8.10.2 Life Insurance and Non- Life Insurance

Life Insurance

Life insurance is a kind of contract among an insurance policy holder and an insurer, where the insurer promises to pay a sum of money in exchange for a premium, upon the death of an insured person. (See Figure 8.14)

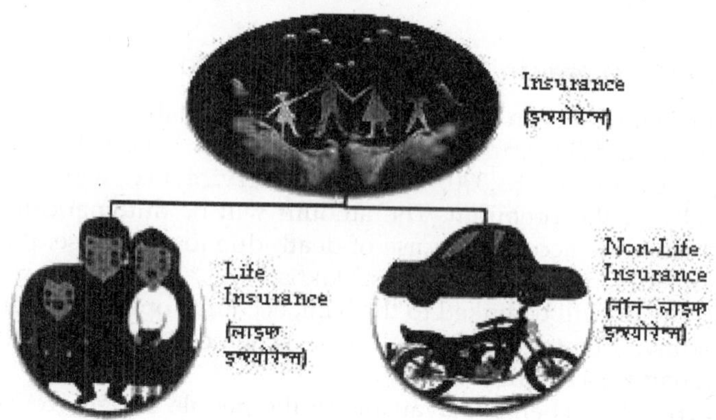

Figure 8.14 Types of Insurance

In this, a policy holder pays a premium, either on a regular basis or as one lump sum amount.

According to Bunion "*A contract of life insurance is that in which one party agrees to pay a given sum on the happening of a particular event contingent upon the duration of human life, in consideration of the immediate payment of a smaller sum or certain equivalent periodical payments by another.*"

Goal of life insurance is to provide financial security. The main risks that are covered by life insurance are:

1. Premature death
2. Income during retirement
3. Illness

Non-Life Insurance

It is basically an insurance policy that protects you against losses and damages other than those covered by life insurance. For more comprehensive coverage, it is vital for you to know about the risks covered to ensure that you and your family are protected from unforeseen losses.

The coverage period for most general insurance policies and plans is usually one year, whereby premiums are normally paid on a one-time basis.

The risks that are covered by general insurance are:

1. Property loss, for example, stolen car or burnt house
2. Liability arising from damage caused by yourself to a third party
3. Accidental death or injury

8.11 SUMMARY

This Chapter is based on application of Digital Financial services. The Chapter begins with the introduction of financial services and its objectives. It also discusses why savings are needed in various situations i.e. emergencies, future needs and in large expenses. It also discusses various drawbacks of keeping cash at home. The Chapter also emphasises on why bank is needed for securing money, earn interest and to get loans. The later part of Chapter describes the banking products, which included types of accounts and deposit, types of loan and overdrafts. It also helps to understand how to fill up a cheque and make demand drafts accurately. The Chapter focuses on the documents required for opening an account and also helps to understand the aspects of

KYC and helps to understand the various channels of banking service deliveries i.e. Internet banking, ATM, NEFT, RTGS. It also discusses the necessity of different kinds of insurances.

At the end of the Chapter you will be able to learn the various schemes implemented by the government to empower the individuals i.e. PMSBY, PMJJBY, APY, PMMY, PPF scheme and NPS. Finally, we discuss how to use your banking on mobile with the help of mobile banking and mobile wallets.

MODEL QUESTIONS AND ANSWERS

A. Multiple Choice

1.1 We should keep our savings with banks because
a. It is safe
b. Earns interest
c. Can be withdrawn anytime
d. All of above

1.2 ATM password to be shared only with
a. Spouse b. Obedient son
c. Obedient daughter d. None of above

1.3 KYC means
a. Know your customer
b. Know your character
c. Both (a) and (b)
d. None of above

1.4 Loans from money lenders involves:
a. High rate of interest
b. No proper accounting
c. No transparency
d. All of above

1.5 Life insurance means
a. Insurance of human
b. Insurance of life of Cattle
c. Insurance of Machines
d. Insurance of house

1.6 Non-life Insurance relates to insurance against
a. Fire b. Theft
c. Burglary d. All of above

1.7 Bank provides loans for
a. Home b. Car
c. Education d. All of above

1.8 Two Rupee note is signed by:
a. Finance Secretary b. Governor of RBI
c. Government of India Mint d. Ministry of Finance

1.9 The safest place for keeping money
a. A pit dug in the ground b. An iron box
c. Bank d. Money lender

1.10 Gold and silver ornaments should be kept in bank lockers as:
a. It is safe b. No risk of theft
c. Both (a) & (b) d. None of above

1.11 POS is:
a. Point of Sale b. Position of Sale
c. Point of Saling d. Position of Saling

1.12 Banks pays interest on
a. Deposits b. Loans
c. Withdrawal d. Transaction

1.13 Bank charges interest on
a. Deposits b. Loans
c. Withdrawal d. Transaction

1.14 Internet banking refers to
a. Operation of account through internet
b. Opening of account through ATM
c. Opening bank through Internet
d. All of the above

1.15 In Recurring Deposits,
a. A fixed sum is deposited every month
b. Period of deposit is not of fixed tenure
c. Interest is paid at lower rate
d. No interest is paid

1.16 ATM can be used for
a. Cash withdrawal b. Account enquiry
c. Statement of account d. All of above

1.17 What is RuPay Debit Card?
a. Domestic debit card
b. Introduced by National Payments Corporation of India
c. Accepted at all ATMs & PoS machines
d. All above

1.18 Aadhaar is
a. 12 digit number card
b. Identity proof issued by UIDAI
c. A saving account
d. Both (a) and (b)

1.19 PAN means
a. A kind of utensil b. Primary Account Number
c. Permanent Account Number d. Position Account Number

1.20 Currency notes are issued by
a. RBI b. NABARD
c. Public sector banks d. Central Government

1.21 Coins are issued by
a. Government of India b. NABARD
c. Public sector banks d. State Bank of India

1.22 Education Loans
a. Cover tuition fee & expenses
b. Are repayable after completion of course
c. Granted for studies in India & abroad
d. All of above

1.23 Who can open bank account
a. Indian citizen b. Non Resident Indian
c. Illiterate d. All of above

1.24 What is meant by Aadhaar seeding?
a. Linking of Aadhaar with Bank account
b. Issue of Aadhaar card
c. Transfer of Aadhaar
d. 12- digit number card

1.25 What are the benefits attached to PMJDY?
a. Accident insurance cover of Rs.1 lac
b. Life insurance cover of Rs.30,000/-
c. Overdraft facility up to Rs.5,000/-
d. All of above

1.26 Who can open an account under PMJDY?
a. Minor above the age of 10 years
b. Only lady of the house

c. Only head of the family
d. All of above

1.27 Who is Bank Mitra?
a. Banking Correspondents engaged by Banks
b. Valuable customer of Bank
c. Security guard in a branch
d. Bank accountant

1.28 What is Atal Pension Yojana (APY)?
a. Provides social security to the unorganized sector
b. Encourages workers not to save money for their retirement
c. Fixed pension is paid on attaining age of 60 years
d. Provide social security to organized sector

1.29 What is Pradhan Mantri Suraksha Bima Yojana (PMSBY)?
a. Accidental insurance cover
b. Life insurance cover
c. Overdraft up to Rs.5,000/-
d. Overdraft of Rs. 5000/-

1.30 What is Pradhan Mantri Jivan Jyoti Bima Yojana (PMJJBY)?
a. Covers life insurance up to Rs.2 lac
b. Accident insurance cover
c. Life Insurance up to 1 lac
d. Accidental Insurance up to l lac

1.31 Which type of deposits earns higher interest rate?
a. Current account b. Savings Account
c. Fixed Deposits d. Recurring deposit

1.32 Under PMSBY, accidental death claim is available for:
a. Rs.1 lac b. Rs.2 lac
c. Rs.3 lac d. Rs.4 lac

1.33 Can illiterate person be issued Debit card?
a. No
b. Yes
c. Only with joint account
d. Only for head of family

1.34 NEFT stands for
a. National Electric Fund Transfer
b. National Electronic Fund Transfer
c. National Electrical Fund Transfer
d. National Electronic Fund Transferring

1.35 RTFG stands for
a. Real Time Gross Settlement
b. Ready Time Gross Settlement
c. Ready Time Grocery Settlement
d. Real Time Grocery Settle

B. State whether the following are True or False

2.1 Digital financial services, does not expands the delivery of basic financial services to the people through new technologies like Internet.
2.2 Saving must be at the top of priority for everyone.
2.3 It is unsafe to keep cash at home.
2.4 Banks acts as a medium for the transfer of money.
2.5 Saving account is an account, which share a wealth of privileges and tailor-made solutions with your family.
2.6 Bank Mitra are branch of bank, who act as an agent to transfer the money.
2.7 Internet banking is used to pay utility bills.
2.8 Pradhan Mantri Suraksha Bima Yojna (PMSBY),is an accidental death and a disability insurance scheme.
2.9 MUDRA is Micro Units Development and Refinance Agency Ltd.
2.10 Kishore covers a loans above Rs 5000 and up to Rs 5 Lakh.

Answers

Multiple Choice

1.1	d	1.2	d	1.3	a	1.4	d	1.5	a
1.6	d	1.7	d	1.8	b	1.9	c	1.10	c
1.11	a	1.12	a	1.13	b	1.14	d	1.15	a
1.16	d	1.17	d	1.18	d	1.19	c	1.20	a
1.21	a	1.22	d	1.23	d	1.24	a	1.25	d
1.26	a	1.27	a	1.28	a	1.29	a	1.30	a
1.31	c	1.32	b	1.33	b	1.34	b	1.35	a

True or False

2.1	F	2.2	T	2.3	T	2.4	F	2.5	F
2.6	F	2.7	T	2.8	T	2.9	T	2.10	F

Absolute cell address A cell address or range name in a formula that always refers to the same cell or range of cells. To make a cell address absolute, prefix the row and column with a dollar sign ($); for example, AX2.

Abstraction The act of representing the essential features of something without including much detail.

Accent colors Colours that are applied to secondary features on a slide. Accent colours are also used on graphs.

Access time The time interval between the instant at which data is called from a storage device and the instant delivery begins.

Account A form of access to a computer or network for a specific user name and password usually with a home directory, an E-mail in box, and a set of access privileges.

Accounts Continuing financial relationship between a bank and a customer, in which deposits and debts are held and processed within a framework of established rules and procedures.

Action buttons Pre-drawn button icons that can be placed on a PowerPoint slide and associated with an animation effect.

Active area The part of the current worksheet into which you have entered data or have formatted cells. The active area starts at cell A1 and ends at the lowest and rightmost filled or formatted cell.

Alignment The placement of text along the left margin, right margin, or both margins.

Alphanumeric Pertaining to a character set that contains letters, digits, and usually other special characters, such as the comma, dollar sign, plus sign, etc.

ALU (Arithmetic Logic Unit) It is one of the components of the Central Processing Unit (CPU) of the computer which performs all mathematical and logical operations.

Anchored range A range of cells in which one corner is fixed. You can adjust the other corner with the pointer-movement keys. To anchor a range, press the period key (.).

Animate To create the illusion of movement during an electronic slide show by controlling how text is displayed.

Animate To add a special visual or sound effect to text or an object. For example – you can have your text bullet points fly in from the left, one word at a time, or hear the sound of applause when a picture is uncovered. You can animate any number of objects on a slide, and you can even animate elements of a chart.

Animation A set of images, pictures, or drawings displayed in sequence to imply movement. Computer animation files can be inserted in programs, such as PowerPoint and run by the speaker or viewer.

Annotate To draw or write a comment. In a PowerPoint slide show, annotation refers to using the electronic pen to write or draw.

Anywhere Banking Customer can deposit/ withdraw cash at any branch other than the branch in which he holds the account. Anywhere banking frees the customer from geographical boundaries and limitations and gives the flexibility to the customer to use his account across the board.

Applet A small application unable to run by itself. When you purchase PowerPoint or another application, it may come with additional applets. For example, PowerPoint comes with applets for manipulating fonts (WordArt), drawing graphs (MS Graph), and creating graphics (MS Draw).

Application program Software designed for a specific purpose, such as pay calculation, processing of examination results, stores accounting and inventory control, etc.

Applications Specific uses for a program. With Word, for example, you can create letters, mailing lists, proposals, resume, timetables, etc.

Architecture The overall design, construction, organization and interconnecting of the various components of a computer system. It refers particularly to the processor hardware and the size and ordering sequence of its bytes.

Archive Backup storage. Usually a secondary storage medium, such as magnetic tape or a mass storage device that operates on semi-direct access and sequential principles.

Ascending order Database records or other worksheet data can be sorted in either ascending or descending order. Ascending sorts labels in alphabetical order and values from lowest to highest.

ASCII File It is a document file in the universally recognized text *format* called ASCII (American Standard Code for Information Interchange). An ASCII file contains characters, spaces, punctuation, carriage return, and sometimes tabs and an end-of-file marker, but it contains no formatting information, like bold or italic character.

Attribute Features of an object that you can manipulate using the PowerPoint tools and commands, including line, fill, shadow, embossing, colour, and shape. Both graphic and text objects have attributes.

Audio response An output medium that produces verbal responses from the computer system.

AutoClipArt A feature that scans a PowerPoint presentation; by matching keywords with the presentation content. AutoClipArt suggests clip art images that might be appropriate to add to the slides.

AutoContent Wizard A tool that guides you through the steps of a proposed presentation and includes suggested content.

AutoLayout The slide layouts that are available when you add a new slide to a presentation. AutoLayouts contain ready-made placeholders fo titles, text, and objects, such as clip art, graphs and charts. You can change layouts whenever you want using the Layout button on the status bar.

AutoLayout object area The bordered areas, in addition to the title placeholder, that appear when your create a new slide. There are many kinds of object placeholders: placeholders for text, graphs, tables, organizational charts and clip art. Just click to add text in a placeholder, or double-click to add the specified object.

Automated Office A general term that refers to the merger of computers, office, electronic devices and telecommunications technology in an office environment.

Automatic Transaction Machine (Automatic Transaction Machine or Automatic Teller Machine) enables the customers of a bank to perform financial transactions (cash withdrawal / deposit) without going to the bank.

AutoShape A menu on the PowerPoint Drawing toolbar that contains a variety of common shapes (also called AutoShapes) which can be drawn automatically by clicking and dragging the cursor across a slide.

Background colour The underlying colour of a PowerPoint slide. If you are painting on a white canvas, for example, your background colour is white. You can paint any other colour on top of it, but the underlying colour remains white; everywhere you do not add paint, the white shows. The background colour on a slide works the same way.

Background item An object you can add to the Slide Master so that it will appear on all slides in a presentation that follow the Slide Master. PowerPoint considers any object on the Slide Master – other than the master title and master text – to be a background item. Background items typically include the date, the time, the page or slide number and the name of the presentation.

Backup Alternate facilities of programs, data files, hardware equipments, etc., that are used in case the original one is destroyed, lost, or fails to operate.

Backup File A duplicate of another file, which you create for safekeeping. A special kind of backup file, .bak, is automatically created by Word when you save the file you have been editing. You can not edit a .bak file.

Bank A bank is a financial institution, which acts as an intermediary in transactions, and offer services like safekeeping and lending of money.

Bank Branch It is a retail location where a bank offers a wide range of face-to-face and automated services to its customers. A bank has its branches at various locations across the city or state so that customer can go there and avail its services.

Bank Credit Includes Term Loans, Cash Credit, Overdrafts, Bills purchased & discounted, Bank Guarantees, Letters of Guarantee, Letters of credit.

Bank Debits The sum of the value of all cheques and other instruments charged against the deposited funds of a bank's customer.

Bank Draft An instrument issued by one branch of a bank on another branch of the bank containing an order to pay a certain sum on demand to the person named on the draft. It is used to transfer funds and to settle outstanding balances between banks, or to provide a customer with funds payable at a bank in a different location. Bank drafts are valid for certain period, generally, for 6 months, as indicated over face of draft.

Bank Mitra Bank Mitra are those individuals, who act as an agent of bank at those places where it is not possible to open a branch of bank. They provide all kind of assistance required in opening an account.

Bank on Mobile Bank on Mobile means you can access bank from anywhere, anytime from your mobile and it has become simple to see your account, transfer funds, pay bills. It provides a convenient way to get connected with the bank.

Banker's Cheque A cheque issued by a branch of a bank against consideration received. Banker's cheque are valid for a certain period as indicated on the face of the cheque.

Bar code A coding structure in which characters are represented by means of a series of parallel bars.

Bar graph A graph that shows numeric data as a series of vertical or horizontal bars of different height evenly spaced along the x-axis or y-axis respectively. Each bar reflects the value of a single worksheet cell. The bar graph has labels that identify what each bar represents.

Base The total number of digits (symbols) available to represent numbers in a positional number system.

BIOS (Basic Input Output System) Bios is responsible for handling the details of input/output operations including the task of relating a program's logical records to a peripheral device physical records.

Bit Acronym for binary digit which stands for one binary piece of information. This can be either 0 or 1.

BLOB Binary Large Object. Essentially, a long bit of string used for complex data.

Block A portion of text ranging in length from one word to several pages. During editing, you mark blocks in order to move, copy, or delete text.

Block A group of related items (records, characters, etc.) handled as a unit during input and output. A section of program coding treated as a unit.

Block move An operation in which data is moved to a different location. Block moves are typically used in re-organizing documents with a word processor, or editor in a high level language.

Blocking factor The number of logical records in a physical record.

Bounced Cheque A cheque, which a bank returns unpaid because there is not enough available balance in the account or for other reasons.

Buffer Either a device or a storage area where data are temporarily stored.

Bug An error in a computer program.

Byte A fixed number of adjacent bits that represent a particular character or symbol. Normally a byte consists of eight bits.

CAD (Computer Aided Design) Use of computers to automate design operations.

CAI (Computer Aided Instruction) A general term that refers to teaching with the help of a computer. Also called CAE (Computer Aided Education).

CAM (Computer Aided Use of computers to automate manufacturing operations.

Canceled Cheque A cheque that has been not paid and cancelled by the drawer û Account holder.

Canned Programs Programs prepared by an outside supplier and provided to the user in a machine readable form.

Card Holder Cardholder is a person who owns a debit or credit card issued by a credit card company, financial institution or bank.

Card Issuer A bank, financial institution, credit union, or agency that issues a credit card to public or its members is called a card issuer.

Cartridge A device used to contain a pre-recorded program.

Cash-in The exchange of cash for electronic value (e-money).

Cash-out The exchange of electronic value (e-money) for cash.

Cash Deposits A!cash deposit!is!money!placed in a financial institution for protective custody.

Cell The intersection of a column and a row in an Excel worksheet. The cell is the basic unit of a worksheet.

Cell address A cell's location in the grid of worksheet/column/row intersections. The cell address consists of the worksheet letter, a colon, and the column letter plus the row number.

Cell pointer The highlighted rectangle in the worksheet displays area that marks the current cell. You can move the cell pointer with arrow keys and a number of other keys on the keyboard.

Chain printer A printer in which the characters are embossed on a chain or a band. The chain is in the form of a loop which rotates at a high-speed and print heads are activated to print specified characters.

Character A single digit, letter, punctuation mark, space, or other symbol which the computer can read or write.

Character attribute An enhancement which you can add to a font, such as bold, italic or underline.

Character printer A printer with a print mechanism that prints one character at a time.

Character string Any group of contiguous characters (letters, numbers, punctuation marks, special symbols, etc.) enclosed in quotation marks and used in formulas and macros.

Chart A pictorial representation of data. A chart is also sometimes referred to as a graph.

Cheque Cheque is an important negotiable instrument, which can be transferred by mere hand delivery.

Cheque for Collection An instrument drawn on another Bank or Branch tendered by a customer of a Bank or by his representative, at the branch or in the drop box provided for the purpose for collecting the amount of the cheque.

Chip A thin wafer of silicon on which integrated electronic components are deposited.

Chit Funds Chit implies a transaction under which a person goes into an agreement with a predefined number of persons.

Clip Art A collection of images you can use in your documents. Clip is often distributed on CD-ROM in large collections (thousands of Clip Art pieces) organized into categories. Various Clip Art formats are sold, and the most popular are Computer Graphics Metafile (CGM), Windows (WMF), Bitmap (BMP), and Graphics Interchange Format (GIF) format files. PowerPoint comes with a set a Clip Art contained in the Clip Gallery 3.0.

Color palette A display consisting of various colour blocks; you can select a colour fill to add to an object or slide from a color palette.

Color scheme A set of eight coordinated colours you can use in a presentation.

Column selector A horizontal bar at the top of a column that you click to select an entire column in the query design grid or the filter design grid.

COM (Computer Output Microfilm) An output device that records computer output on microfilm.

Comma format A global or a local format that adds commas to numbers larger than 999 and places negative values in parentheses.

Command An instruction transmitted to your computer when you press specified keys.

Comment While viewing a PowerPoint presentation, notes objects called comments can be added directly to slides and are contained in comment boxes.

Compile To convert or translate a program written in a high-level language to an absolute or machine language form.

Computer An electronic equipment designed to automatically accept and store input data, manipulate them, and produce output results under the direction of a detailed step-by-step stored program or instructions.

Computer graphics The area of computer science which is concerned with the generation, manipulation and display of pictures with the aid of a computer.

Computer network A distributed data processing system in which multiple computers are linked together for the purpose of data communication and resource sharing.

Computer system The various components (input and output devices, storage, CPU) of a computer integrated together to perform the steps called for in the program being executed.

CONFIG.SYS A special text file that controls certain aspects of operating-system behavior in MS-DOS and OS/2. Commands in the CONFIG.SYS file enable or disable system features, set limits on resources (for example, the maximum number of open files), and extend the operating system by loading device drivers that control hardware specific to an individual computer system.

Connector A category of AutoShape object used to connect two or more objects. Connectors typically have arrowheads at one or both ends to indicate flow or direction.

Console The part of a computer system that enables human operators to communicate with the computer.

Constant A value, written into a program instruction, that does not change during the execution of program.

Constraint keys Modifier keys that let you restrict an aspect of an object as you draw it. When you draw shapes, you can hold down the Shift key as well as Ctrl to control the way an object is to be drawn. In this way, you an draw an object from its center, or you can draw regular shapes, such as circles and squares, or you can draw lines at precise angles.

Container document The document on the receiving end of a linked object which comes from the source document. A PowerPoint presentation that includes linked objects is a container document.

Control commands Commands issued to the computer when you press a key (or keys) while holding down the Ctrl key.

Control handle A square that appears to indicate a vertex of a freeform shape or a polygon. You can edit freeform shapes and polygons by adding, deleting, and moving their control handles.

Control Key Ctrl A key, often represented by the caret symbol (^), used with other keys to command the computer to perform specific functions.

Control panel A tool in Windows operating system which allows you to install software and change different settings fo Windows, such as Date, Time, Keyboard, Mouse, Password, Display, Sound Settings, etc.

Control Unit Part of the central processor which directs the sequence of operations, interprets the coded instruction, and checks the execution of program instructions.

CPU (Central Processing Unit) Control unit and arithmetic logic unit of a computer system are jointly known as the CPU. All calculations and comparisons are made inside the CPU and the CPU is also responsible for activating and controlling the operations of the other units of a computer system.

Criteria range The criteria range contains selection criteria that tells Excel which records in the input range to search for during a database query. The criteria range must contain exact copies of the field names from the input range.

Crop To trim vertical or horizontal edges of a picture by using the cropping tool on the Picture toolbar. After you crop a picture, you can always uncrop it. Photos are often cropped to focus attention on a particular portion of the photo.

CRT (Cathode Ray Tube) An electronic tube with a TV like screen upon which information may be displayed.

Cryptographic checksum A one-way function applied to a file to produce a unique "fingerprint" of the file for later reference. Checksum systems are a primary means of detecting filesystem tampering on UNIX.

Cryptography A system of secret communications to improve the security of confidential computerized files.

Current Account Current account is mainly for business persons, firms, companies, public enterprises, etc.

Cursor Usually a small rectangle or line of light on the screen, marking your place in the text. Cursor shapes differ with different operating systems.

Custom Animation A feature in PowerPoint that allows you to set special effects and the sequence of slides in an on-screen presentation.

Custom Shows A feature in PowerPoint that allows you to save different subsets of slides in a presentation to create different versions of the show from the same set of slides.

Customers A customer (sometimes known as a client, buyer, or purchaser) is the recipient of a Good or a service, or a product, or an idea, obtained from a seller, vendor, or supplier via a financial transaction or exchange for money or some other valuable consideration.

Cyberspace A term, popularised by author William Gibson, for the shared imaginary reality of computer networks. Some people use cyberspace as a synonym for the Internet. Others hold out for the more complete physical-seeming consensual reality of Gibson's novels.

Cylinder In a disk pack, a set of corresponding tracks in all the surfaces is called a cylinder. All tracks of a cylinder are accessible by a single movement of the access mechanism.

Daisy wheel printer A letter-quality printer that uses a printing head with the appearance of daisy and/or a wheel. Each petal of the daisy wheel has a character embossed on it.

DASD Acronym for Direct-Access Storage Device. It is the online secondary storage which is always available to a processor.

Data Information stored or processed by the computer.

Data A collection of facts in raw form that become information after proper organization or processing.

Data file A group of related pieces of information called records, stored together on a disk. A record belongs to a mailing list, for example, might contain all the information about a single addressee. One field within that record might contain name, street address, city, etc.

Data label Values or words that appear next to above, or below the data points on a graph.

Data range The range of cells containing the data records to be sorted or graphed.

Database A collection of data files integrated and organized into a single comprehensive file system, which is arranged to minimize duplication of data and to provide convenient access to information within that system to satisfy a wide variety of user needs.

Database administrator Responsible for defining, updating, and controlling access to a database.

Database Management System A general-purpose software package used as a tool for building individual database systems. The software used for the management, maintenance, and retrieval of the data stored in a data base.

Database server A system that receives requests from client applications over a network and responds by returning requested data (the answer set). Each database server is made up of a computer, an operating system, and database server software.

Database system A combination of software and hardware for performing some task or group of tasks that involve in handling a large amount of information.

Database table A collection of related data items arranged in rows and columns in a worksheet. An Excel database table consists of fields and records; fields are arranged in columns and records in rows.

Datasheet Data from a table displayed in a row-and-column format.

Date number Excel's internal method of keeping track of dates. Excel starts its calendar at January 1, 1900. It assigns the number 1 to that date, 2 to January 2, 1900, and so on.

Debit Card A plastic card issued by a Bank for cash withdrawal from a/c(s) through ATMs and payments at point of sale for purchases made. Debit Card denotes immediate debit to the customer's account.

Debugging Process of finding and correcting program errors (bugs).

Default A pre-set value or condition in a program, which you can change or allow to stand.

Default print settings The print settings unless you change the different settings.

Delivery Channel A method of providing products or services. Examples of delivery channels include traditional banking outlets such as bank branches, ATMs, or branchless banking channels, such as mobile banking and agent banking.

Demand Draft A demand draft is a negotiable instrument similar to a bill of exchange.

Demote To indent a line of text more that the previous line, indicating a lower level of importance.

Deposits Funds placed into an account at a depository institution to increase the credit balance of the account.

Design Visual elements of a slide. When changing presentation templates in PowerPoint, the Apply Design command is used. A template contains various design elements for slides, such as graphic objects and a colour scheme.

Design template A template whose format and colour scheme you apply to a presentation. A large selection of professionally designed templates come with PowerPoint, and you can also use any presentation as a template.

Desktop Publishing Packages (DTP) Software that combines text and graphics manipulating capabilities to allow users to format charts and pictures with text and headlines.

Desktop Publishing System A system that combines a computer and suitable peripherals with software that can produce attractive page layouts complete with pictures and text printed in a variety of typefaces.

Digital Digital usually refers to something using digits, particularly binary digits.

Digital Financial Services Digital financial services (DFS) can expand the delivery of basic financial services to the poor through new technologies like mobile phones, electronic money and new channels such as retail agents.

Digitizer An input device used to convert graphic and pictorial data into binary, numeric inputs for a digital computer.

Direct access Pertaining to storage devices where the access time is effectively independent of the location of the data.

Directory An on screen list of the file names on your disk.

Disk A flat, circular plate coated with a magnetic material on which data can be stored by magnetization of portions of the flat surface.

Dividend The return of part of the policy's premium for a policy issued on a participating basis by either a mutual or stock insurer. A portion of the surplus paid to the stockholders of a corporation.

Docked toolbar A toolbar that is attached to one edge of the program window. You can dock a toolbar below the program title bar or to the left, right, or bottom edge of the program window. When you drag a toolbar to the edge of the program window, the toolbar outline snaps into place along the length of program window edge.

Documentation Documentation of a software system involves collecting, organizing, storing, and maintaining a complete historical record of programs and other documents used or prepared during different phases of a system.

DOS An operating system which contains the disk-oriented commands and uses disk devices for permanent storage.

Downtime The period during which a computer is malfunctioning or not operating correctly due to machine failures.

Draft A written, signed and dated order from one Branch of a Bank to another , to pay a sum of money to a specific party.

Drag-and-drop To perform a move operation by selecting and dragging icon from one location to another location and then releasing the mouse button.

Drawee The person or entity on whom a draft/bill is drawn by the drawer.

Drawer The party who draws or issues the draft/bill. In a Letter of Credit it is the Beneficiary. The person who makes or draws a bill of exchange or cheque is called drawer.

Drum printer A line printer that uses a solid, rotating, cylindrical drum on which the characters to be printed are embossed.

Dumb terminal A terminal that has no local processing capability.

Dump A process whereby the contents of all or a part of primary storage are copied onto some secondary storage device or displayed on a printer or screen.

DVD DVDs have much more storage capacity as compared to CDs. These are of three types: DVD-ROM, DVD-R and DVD-RW.

Edit To change a cell entry. You modify a cell entry by pressing the Edit (F2) key, which displays the current entry in the second line of the control panel so that you can make changes to it. Press Enter to complete an edited entry.

Electronic Clearing Service (ECS) Electronic Clearing Facility: An inter bank arrangement where by a customer can give instructions to his bank where he holds a current or savings account to pay the monthly installments of payments due on loans/credit cards held with another bank.

Electronic funds transfer (EFT) Any transfer of funds initiated through an electronic terminal, telephone, computer, or magnetic tape for the purpose of ordering, instructing, or authorizing a financial institution to debit or credit a consumer's bank or e-money account.

Electronic mail A general term to describe the transmission of messages by the use of computing systems and telecommunications facilities.

Electronic slide show A pre-defined list of slides displayed sequentially on-screen or using a LCD projector.

Electronic spreadsheet An application package usually available with microcomputers that displays the equivalent of a worksheet made up of rows and columns. It may be used for computation or display of information in a tabular form.

Electrostatic printer A high-speed printer that uses charged pins to form character matrices on paper.

Electrothermal printer A high-speed printer that uses heated elements to create characters as matrices of small dots on heat-sensitive paper.

Emergencies An emergency is a situation that poses an immediate risk to health, life, property, or environment.

Emulator A program that permits one computer to execute the machine-language instructions.

End user Any individual who uses the information generated by a computer based system.

EPROM (Erasable Programmable Read Only Memory) A semi-conductor memory which allows the eraser of the information stored in it by exposure to ultraviolet light. Later, new information can be stored in it.

Ergonomics Science that focuses on how machines and other things should be designed and arranged so that people can interact with them in a comfortable and efficient way.

Error message A statement that appears on your screen when your computer is unable to continue processing. The message tells you what the problem is and how to solve it.

Expand A function in Outline view of PowerPoint that allows you to open up all the lines of an outline to display all the detail points.

Explode To separate and lift out one or more slices of a pie chart for emphasis.

Extended ASCII Extended ASCII provides added capability by allowing for 128 additional characters, such as accented letters, graphics characters, and special symbols.

Extended memory Main memory beyond 1 Mb in PC systems based on the Intel microprocessors. Extended memory is not typically available to MS-DOS programs. But Windows 9X makes use of this memory for better performance of the packages.

Extensibility A feature that allows the extension of existing code. This allows the creation of new objects from the existing ones.

Facebook It is a place where people can express their views and discuss things in an open way, as they can and do in may other places.

Facsimile (FAX) Transmission of pictures, texts, maps, graphs, etc., over transmission lines, phone lines, and other carriers between geographically separated points. An image is scanned at a transmitting point and duplicated at a receiving point.

Field Categories in a database record. For example, in a phone book record, the fields would be name, address, and phone number. In an Excel database table, fields are labeled as columns.

Fifth generation computers These computers will be introduced shortly. They will use a large number of processors working concurrently and independently. Simpler programming languages and knowledge based system implementations are expected in this generation.

File A collection of related records.

File Management System (FMS) A software package that allows users to define data items, place these items into specified records, combine these records into designated files, and then manipulate and retrieve stored data in various ways to achieve user's goals.

Fills color PowerPoint uses to fill objects with colours that contrast with both the background colour as well as the lines and text colour to make round out your colour scheme. You can change a fill colour any time which you want.

Financial Services Financial services are the economic services provided by the finance industry, which encompasses a broad range of businesses that manage money, including credit unions, banks, credit-card companies, insurance companies, accountancy companies, consumer-finance companies, stock brokerages, investment funds and some government-sponsored enterprises.

Firmware A sequence of instruction (software) that is substituted for hardware and stored in Read Only Memory (ROM). Another example of Firmware is PROM, i.e., programmable read only memory.

First-in, First-out (FIFO) A technique for processing jobs on a first-come, first-served basis.

Fixed Deposit A deposit of funds in a bank under an agreement stipulating that the funds must be kept on deposit for a stated period of time at a predefined interest rate.

Flash Memory It is electrically erasable and programmable permanent type memory. Its entire contents can be erased in one operation. Flash memory modules upto 4 GB capacity are available. The modules are available as flash cards and flash drives. Flash drives can replace hard disk drives in some applications. They are static and faster and hence costlier.

Floating-point numbers Signed numbers held in a fraction-exponent format. For example, 3216 would be represented as 0.3216×10^4 in floating-point notation.

Floppy disk See *disk.*

Font The typeface, type size, and type attributes of text or numbers.

Font size The size of a font is actually the height of a character, which is measured in points. A 72-point font has characters that are roughly one inch high.

Footer Text or graphics that appears at the bottom of page.

Format The way you arrange text on your screen, using commands for setting margins, centering text, etc.

Formula A mathematical expression that performs calculations on values in the worksheet. Formulas can contain numbers and arithmetic operators, as well as cell addresses, range names, and functions.

FORTRAN (FORmula TRANslation) A high-level, mathematically oriented programming language used for scientific and engineering applications.

Four-arrow pointer The pointer used to move paragraphs around on slides and in outlines.

Fourth-Generation Language (4GL) A language that specifies results of operations rather than procedures to achieve these results.

Fourth generation computers Computers built between 1975 and till date. They use large scale integrated circuits, semiconductor memories and powerful high-level languages and operating systems.

Frame Using a drawn object, such as a square as a border around another object on a slide.

Free rotate A PowerPoint function that allows you to turn an object in any direction, for example 360 degrees.

Freeform A drawing style and drawing object type that provides no preset definition to the object. Freeform drawing is similar to drawing on paper with a pencil and no ruler or guides to direct the line.

Front-end processor A CPU designed specifically to handle the communications between processing task. Its main purpose is to off-load communications processing task from the host computer, so that the host computer can be dedicated for applications and data processing jobs.

General purpose computer A computer capable of performing a variety of business and scientific applications.

General purpose programming A programming language intended to solve a number of different types of problems.

General software package A software package, such as payroll and word processing, developed for users.

Gradient A subtle shading from lighter to darker in a background of one or two colours giving the effect of a light source form the selected direction.

Graph A visual way to present data. A graph can often illustrate trends and projections more clearly and effectively than worksheet numbers.

Graph file A file in which you store a graph for use. The graph file can then be printed or edited by other software programs.

Graph window A part of the worksheet display that shows the current graph. You establish a graph window by moving the cell pointer to the column at which you want to start the Window.

Graphic Graphic images come in all shapes and sizes. Typical graphics include Clip Art images, drawings, photographs, scanned images, signature files, etc.

Graphic display terminal A visual display terminal which has a screen to display a graph or drawing as well as alphanumeric information.

Graphic format The protocol used to save a graphic file, such as GIF or EPS.

Group A multiple selection that you treat as a single object by using the Group command on the Draw menu. Nested groups are multiple groups of objects, in a drawing, for example, Clip Art often is built with nested groups.

Handouts Printed output of PowerPoint presentation containing miniature versions of two, three or six slides. Audience handouts are intended to be distributed to presentation viewers to help them follow a presentation.

Hard copy Printed or filmed output from a computer device in human readable form.

Hardware The physical components of a computer system, such as electronic, magnetic, and mechanical devices.

Header Text or graphics that appears at the top of every page.

Hidden object Slide or element on slide that does not temporarily appear on-screen and is not included in printed output of a PowerPoint presentation.

Hidden slide A slide that does not automatically display during a slide show. You decide which slide or slides you want to be "hidden" and whether you want them to appear during your show. That way you can tailor a show to fit several different audiences.

High-level language A programming language whose structure is application oriented and is independent of the structure of the computer.

High-Low-Close-Open (HLCO) graph A graph that plots up to four data points as a series of vertical lines. HLCO graphs are typically used to track the performance of a stock equity over time. They plot the high, low, closing, and opening prices of the stock. They are also called stock market graphs.

Highlight Emphasize, a character, word, or block of text by making it either brighter or dimmer than the surrounding text.

Host computer Main control computer in a network of distributed processors and terminals.

Hyphen Help A Word feature that finds places where hyphenation would improve the appearance of your text.

I/O (Input/Output) Pertaining to the techniques, media, and devices used for man-machine interaction.

Indexed file A file that includes an index directory to facilitate random access.

Indexed sequential access method A method whereby records are organized in a sequential order and can be referenced directly through an index based on some key or characteristic.

Indian Currency It is the official currency of the Republic of India, issued by Reserve Bank of India (RBI) and guaranteed by the Central government.

Information Result of data manipulation or processing which can be used to help people in making decisions.

Information hiding The principle which states that the state and implementation of an object or module should be private to that object or module and only accessible via its public interface (same as encapsulation).

Information Technology (IT) IT encompasses any combination of equipment (hardware) that facilitates the acquisition, creation, modification, retrieval, storage and transmission of information using electronic media. Thus, IT includes both computing and communications technology. Various aspects of IT are hardware, software, connectivity, telecommunications, science and human-computer interface.

Input Data entered into a data processing system.

Input/Output Input refers to any information coming into the computer. Output refers to processed information going out of a computer.

Input device A device used to enter information into a computer or other data processing devices; for example keyboard.

Insertion point A linking vertical line that appears on-screen at a location where you can enter data. The insertion point is sometimes called a cursor. Characters that you type appear to the left of the insertion point.

Insurance An agreement in which a person makes regular payments to a company and the company promises to pay money up to the insured amount if the person is injured or dies, or to pay money equal to the value of something (such as a house or car) if it is damaged, lost, or stolen.

Intelligent terminal A terminal having local processing capability. It has a built-in CPU and can perform specific functions, such as editing data, controlling other terminals, etc.

Interactive A PowerPoint or other multimedia presentation is interactive when the viewer is able to make selections as to how the presentation runs or what is displayed, in effect interacting with the presentation itself.

Interest Interest is the periodic amount credited/debited to a deposit/loan account by a Bank based on accepted agreed terms and conditions by the depositor and the Bank/the loan and the Bank. Interest is calculated at a specified percentage of the principal amount.

Internet assistant A programmed series of steps a PowerPoint user can invoke to create a folder of presentation files to be moved to an Internet server.

Internet banking Internet banking is an electronic system which enables the customers to conduct transactions on bank's Website and perform activities, such as maintaining his account, transferring money, paying bills etc.

Interpreter A language processor that translates a statement of a high-level language and immediately executes it before translating the next source language statement. It is the most common language processor for BASIC.

ISAM (Index Sequential Access Method) Relating to a file design technique whereby records organized in a sequential order can be accessed directly through an index (directory) based on some key or characteristic. Permits both sequential and random access of records.

Justification The alignment of text within given margins. The left margin is justified as you enter your text. Word Wrap justifies the right margin by adding small spaces between words.

K (Kilo) Used to represent 2^{10} = 1024 in computers only.

Key-to-disk A device used to enter data onto a disk device.

Key-to-tape A device used to enter data onto a magnetic tape.

Kiosk A booth or display area where an on-screen computer presentation may be set up for use by those visiting the area. An example of a kiosk would be an information counter in a shopping small or booth at a trade show.

Label Any cell that begins with a letter or a label-prefix character is a label.

Label prefix Indicates that a cell entry is a label, as opposed to a value. Label prefixes include the apostrophe (') for left-aligned labels, the quotation mark ('') for right-aligned labels, the caret (^) for centered labels, the back slash (\) for repeating labels, and the vertical bar (|) for printer setup strings and non-printing rows.

LAN (Local Area Network) A digital communication system capable of interconnecting a large number of computers, terminals and other peripheral devices within a limited geographical area, typically within 1 km.

Landscape mode One of two printing modes available on most printers (the other is portrait mode). In landscape mode, printed lines run parallel to the paper's direction of travel through the printer. The orientation of a print page of output with the longer side of the page running across the top of the document.

Landscape orientation A printer mode that causes text and graphs to be printed sideways on the page, across the long dimension.

Layering In PowerPoint, the process of placing objects one on top of another on your slide to give the appearance of a stack of objects. Objects can be brought forward to appear to be placed at the top of the stack, or sent back to any of the layers behind the first object.

Layout In PowerPoint, layouts (also called Auto Layouts) are applied to each slide in a presentation displaying various of placeholders used for entering slide content. Placeholders include title, bulleted lists, Clip Art, charts, organization charts, and multimedia clips.

Legend Legends explain the patterns, symbols, and colours used to identify the A through F data ranges on a graph. The legends and patterns, symbols, and colours appear beneath the graph.

Life Insurance An insurance policy that allows an individual's relatives to receive a preset sum of money upon the end of the insured person's life.

Light pen A pen shaped device that is used as an input device to computers by writing or sketching on the screen of a cathode ray tube.

Line graph A graph that represents worksheet values as a continuous line, a sequence of symbols, or both. Line graphs are generally used to show one or more values changing over time. The x-axis defines a specific period of time; the y-axis is a numbered scale.

Line printer A printer that prints one line at a time.

Linux Linux is an operating system kernal that behaves and performs similar to the famous UNIX operating system from AT & T Bells Labs. It has all the features of a modern operating system: true multitasking, threads, virtual memory, shared libraries, demand loading, shared, copy-on-write executables, proper memory management, loadable device driver modules, video frame buffering, and TCP/IP networking.

LISP (LISt Processing) A high-level programming language suitable for handling logical operations and non-numeric applications. It is used in the areas of pattern recognition, artificial intelligence and simulation of games.

Loans A loan is a debt provided by an entity (organization or individual) to another entity at an interest rate, and evidenced by a promissory note, which specifies, among other things, the principal amount of money borrowed, the interest rate the lender is charging, and date of repayment.

Local storage Storage areas, called registers, used by the CPU to interpret instructions and perform arithmetic and logical operations.

Logical operator Used in formulas to test for equality, inequality, and other conditions. The relational operators are : <, < =, >, > =, =, < >. The logical operators are #NOT#, #OR#, and #AND#. A logical formula evaluates either TRUE (1) or FALSE (0).

Long label A label that is longer than the column width of the cell.

Looping A type of programming structure which performs the process of iteration in which instructions are executed over and over again.

Looping macro A set of macro instructions that executes repeatedly. The macro commands {BRANCH} and {FOR} can create a loop in a macro.

Low-level languages Programming languages that normally translate from one source instruction to one object instruction. These languages are machine dependent.

Luminosity The brightness or dullness of a colour; one of three parameters used to specify a colour (the others are hue and saturation). It represents the brightness of a colour on a scale from black to white.

Machine language A low-level language that is directly understandable by the computer system. Each model of a computer has a unique machine language.

Macro A set of instructions for automating Excel's task. Macros include key strokes, macro commands, values, and labels. They can duplicate simple keyboard operations but can also be self-contained applications. Any Excel's task you can perform can be automated with a macro.

Macro command A special Excel's command that has meaning only within a macro. A macro command tells Excel to perform a built-in programming function. Each macro command consists of a keyword and its arguments (if any), enclosed in braces.

Macro library A file that contains Excel macros. When a macro library is in memory, you can run the macros in the library from any active file.

Magnetic-Ink Character Recognition (MICR) An input device that can read cards and paper documents printed with a special magnetic ink.

Magnetic bubble memory An electronic secondary storage device constituted of solid-state electronic chips. It uses the properties of certain materials, under applied magnetic fields, to represent binary 1s and 0s.

Magnetic storage Storage devices, such as disks, drums, tapes, cores, etc., that utilize the magnetic properties of materials to store data.

Magnetic tape A secondary storage device that uses a long plastic strip coated with a magnetic material as a recording medium.

Magneto-optical Drives An erasable or semi-erasable storage disc, similar to a CD-ROM disc and of very high capacity, in which a laser beam is used to heat the recording surface to point at which tiny region on the surface can be magnetically aligned to store bits of data. MO drives come in two formats: 3.5-inch, with capacities to 230MB: and 5.25-inch, which can now write 2.6 GB cartridge. Because of their excellent performance (20- to 50-ms access times and a 2-MBps transfer rate) and nearly indestructible media, MO drives are ideal for storing large amounts of frequently used data near-line.

Master A special slide or page on which you define formatting for all slides or pages in PowerPoint presentation. Each presentation has a master for each key component – slides, title slides, speaker's notes, and audience handouts. If you have pictures, text, or special formatting you want to appear on every slide, title slide, notes page, or audience handout, add it to the corresponding master.

Master text The slide text on the slide master. The master text determines the format of text on all slides – such as the font, color, size, line spacing, and alignment – as well as the shape of a text placeholder and its placement on a slide. The look of text you have added with the Text Box tool is not governed by the master text.

Master title The formatted placeholder for slide titles on the Slide Master. It is here that you set the font, color, size, and alignment of slide titles as well as the title's attributes, the shape of the title text box, and its placement on the slide.

Memory A device or medium that can accept data, hold them, and deliver them on demand at a later time.

Menu A list of options from which a program user can select any one in order to perform a desired action, such as choosing a command or applying a particular format to part of a document.

Menu pointer A pointer which is used to select a menu item and display its description. To select a menu command, use the pointer-movement keys to move the pointer and then press Enter key, or type the first letter of the command.

Metting Minder A PowerPoint feature used to coordinate the running presentation conference and take meeting minutes.

MICR Code A unique 9-digit code assigned to each Bank branch by Reserve Bank of India to facilitate sorting in clearing of instruments using the Magnetic Ink Character Recognition Technology.

Micro-ATMs Biometric authentication system enabled hand-held device.

Mixed cell address A cell address in which part of the address is relative as well as absolute. A dollar sign ($) precedes the part of the address that is absolute. When a mixed cell address is used in a formula and the formula is copied, the relative part of the address adjusts to the new location while the absolute part stays at the same place.

Mobile Banking Service provided by a bank, due to which customers can conduct transactions remotely by using a mobile device. By using this, you can access your account on your mobile.

Mobile Financial Services (MFS) The use of a mobile phone to access financial services and execute financial transactions. This includes both transactional and non-transactional services, such as viewing financial information on a user's mobile phone.

Mobile Wallet It is a payment service, which are operated under financial regulation and performed via a mobile device.

Money Transfer A payments transaction that moves money from one person or business to another. Money transfers allow individuals or businesses to make payments from one account to another (in order to pay a bill, pay taxes, or purchase a good or service). Money transfers also allow government to distribute money to households (in the form of tax rebates or welfare vouchers). Money transfers facilitate payments, which are one of the four basic financial services in the full suite of financial services.

National Electronic Funds Transfer (NEFT) National Electronic Funds Transfer is the most prominent inter-bank electronic funds transfer systems of India, which provides a facility to bank customers to transfer the funds easily and securely on a one-to-one basis, which saves the time and is done via electronic messages. It is a "net" transfer facility, executed in hourly batches.

Network interface card A chip-based circuit board used to connect the PC to a network or server. The card is activated by loading software on the PC.

Nibble 4 bits, half a byte.

Node An end point of a branch in a network, or a common junction of two or more network branches.

Non-impact printer A non-impact printer is a printer that prints without banging a ribbon onto paper, such as a thermal, inkjet and laser printer.

Non-volatile storage A storage medium that retains its contents even in the absence of power.

Non Performing Assets (NPA) When due payments in credit facilities remain overdue above a specified period, then such credit facilities are classified as NPA.

Notes Master A PowerPoint feature that controls the components and formatting features of all notes pages.

Nudge To move a drawing object on a slide by a very small, preset increment.

Object A single component of your drawing. You can draw objects with the text and drawing tools using Drawing and AutoShape toolbars. Objects can be rectangles, squares, circles, ovals, rectangles with rounded corners, diamonds, trapezoids, stars, freeforms, arcs, graphs, etc.

Object A single element for your slide. An object can be text, an imported graphic, a shape, a picture, and so on.

Octal number system A number system with a base of 8. The octal digits range from 0 to 7. It is commonly used as a shortcut notation for groups of three binary digits.

Off-line A device which is not directly connected to the CPU.

On-line A device or system directly connected to the CPU.

Online Banking A service that allows the account holder to access their account information and conduct a set of pre defined banking transactions, such as bill payment, fund transfer using the Internet facility. However, a customer needs to have Customer ID and a unique Net Banking Password in order to undertake this facility.

Operating system An integrated set of programs used to manage various resources and overall operations of a computer system.

Optical bar-code reader An input device that can interpret combinations of marks (bars) representing data.

Optical Character Reader (OCR) An input device which can read characters directly from an ordinary piece of paper by using a scanning mechanism. These characters are written in special type fonts.

Optical Mark Reader (OMR) An input device that can interpret pencil marks on paper media.

OR search You can conduct an OR search on a database when you want to find records that can match at least one criterion in the given criteria range.

Organization chart A chart object that can be placed in a PowerPoint presentation representing the hierarchical structure of an organization, such as a Corporation.

Orientation For printer paper, indicates whether the document is to be printed normally (for example, in Portrait mode) or sideways (in Landscape mode).

Outline Titles and main text from your slides. Pictures and other visuals do not appear in an outline. Other text that you have added using the Text tool and embedded text and graphics will not show up either, since they are not part of the main text.

Outline levels Different indentations at which paragraphs appear in an outline. Titles are always at the left and text is indented one to five levels to the right of a title.

Outline Master A master page where you can add headers, footers, etc., which appears when you print the outline.

Output Finished result of processing by a system.

Output range The range into which Excel copies extracted records.

Output unit The unit of a computer system that supplies information and results of computation to the outside world.

Overdrafts It is a kind of Loan arrangement under which bank extends the credit up to a maximum amount (overdraft limit) against a current account.

Overlapping objects Elements on a slide which appear to be stacked so that one is "behind" the other.

Pack and Go Wizard A wizard used to prepare a PowerPoint file for presentation at a remote location.

Page Break A place in text where one page ends and another begins. You can direct Word to place a page break between two blocks of text so that they will print on separate pages.

Palette A collection of tools. For example, in PowerPoint, there is a color palette that displays the colours available to use in creating a graphic.

Parity bit An extra bit added to a string of bits that enables the computer to detect internal errors in the transmission of binary data.

Parse To break something down into its component parts.

Pascal A high-level programming language named after Blaise Pascal that facilitates the use of structured programming techniques.

Passbook Book issued by a bank or financial institutions to record deposits, withdrawals, and interest earned in a savings account.

Password A code by which a user gains access to a computer system. It is used for security purposes.

PC Card PC cards offer large data storage and I/O capability, networking, modem and other functions with lower power consumption and fast data access speed in a compact size measuring the length and width of a credit card.

Pen While showing a PowerPoint on-screen presentation, you can draw on the slides themselves with an electronic pen. Pen colours can be determined while setting up the presentation.

Pension A plan for setting aside money to be spent after retirement.

Peripherals devices Since the input and the output devices are on the periphery (edge) of the main processing unit, they are sometimes referred to as peripheral devices.

Personal computer A small and inexpensive computer (usually a microcomputer) used by individuals for applications, such as entertainment, home management, and hobbies.

Picosecond One trillionth of a second or 10^{-6} second.

Pie chart A graph in the form of a circle divided into slices, where each slice stands for a value in the range. Pie charts show what proportion of the total each graphed value represents; if one value is twice as large as another, it gets a slice that is twice as large.

PIN Number Personal Identification Number (PIN) is randomly generated code for use of ATM Card at the time of withdrawal of money from ATM Machine and also at the time of making payment on PoS.

Pixel A picture element. It is used to represent one point in a raster scan display device.

Placeholder On a PowerPoint slide, an area that can accept text, graphics or objects (such as charts).

Plotter An output device that converts computer output into a graphic, hardcopy form.

Point-of-sale device An I/O device capable of immediately updating sales and inventory records at a central CPU and producing a printed sales transaction receipt.

Point of sale Point of sale is a stage at which a customer makes a payment to the merchant in exchange of goods or service.

Pointing Moving the cell pointer or highlight to a cell; menu choice; file, graph, or range name; or help screen choice.

Portrait mode A printer orientation in which the printer prints across the short dimension of the page, from top to bottom.

PowerPoint Animation Player An add-on program that works with a Web browser to play animated PowerPoint presentations on the Internet.

PowerPoint object Any shape you draw in PowerPoint or any graphic or picture you change from its original format to the PowerPoint format – for example, an AutoShape you draw or Clip Art you ungroup.

PowerPoint Viewer An application that comes with PowerPoint that's designed to support in preparing electronic slide shows.

Pradhan Mantri Jan-Dhan Yojana Pradhan Mantri Jan-Dhan Yojana (PMJDY) is National Mission for Financial Inclusion to ensure access to financial services, namely, Banking/ Savings & Deposit Accounts, Remittance, Credit, Insurance, Pension in an affordable manner.

Premium The price of insurance protection for a specified risk for a specified period of time.

Presentation A group of related slides you can create using PowerPoint.

Presentation conference The ability to have several people at different locations to view a PowerPoint presentation, over a network or the Internet.

Presentation graphics program A software application that helps you structure, design, and present information, such as graphs or bulleted lists to an audience so that it is visually appealing.

Primary key When you sort a database, you select a primary key to make index and sort the database.

Primary memory A section of the CPU that holds program instructions, input data, intermediate results, and the output information produced during processing. Also known as primary storage, internal storage and main memory.

Print range A range used to take print outs. A print range can be a cell, a single range, or a list of ranges.

Printer An output device used to produce hard copy of computer output that is readable by human beings.

Printer control code Code used in printer setup strings. Printer control codes vary from one printer to another.

Processor A unit of a computer system that interprets instructions and executes them.

Program A set of sequenced instructions used to direct and control the operations of the computer in order to solve a problem or to perform a particular task.

Programmer One who designs, writes, tests, and maintains computer programs.

Programming language A language used to express algorithms in computer understandable form.

PROM Similar to read only memory with the exception that these chips can be re-programmed by using special external equipments.

Promote To indent a line of text less than the previous line, indicating a greater level of importance.

Prompt One or more symbols used by the computer to indicate it is ready for data input from a user. The DOS prompt is the disk drive designator and a right arrow, such a C:\ >.

Protect You protect a worksheet, file, or range to avoid accidentally erasing or changing cell contents and settings accidentally.

Provident Fund (PF) Provident funds are a particular form of retirement savings. They may be mandatory and are defined contribution schemes that pay out the contributions made and interest accumulated as a lump sum on retirement or other predetermined circumstances.

Publisher The source document that creates an object you place in a PowerPoint presentation. Whenever a publisher is changed, the object in your presentation will be updated.

Query To query a database is literally to ask questions to it. When you query a database, you search for specific database records by establishing selection criteria.

Radix Same as base.

Random Access Memory (RAM) Semiconductor-based memory that can be read and written by the microprocessor or other hardware devices. The storage locations can be accessed in any order. The term RAM is generally understood to refer to volatile memory, which can be written as well as read.

Range A cell or a group of contiguous cells in the worksheet file.

Range name The name you give to a single cell or to a range of cells.

RD Recurring Deposits is used to save a certain amount of money regularly for a particular period and earn a higher interest rate on open recurring deposits.

Real-time systems Pertains to online computer processing systems which receive and process data quickly enough to produce output to control, direct, or affect the outcome of an ongoing activity or process.

Recalculation Formulas that contain references to changed cells are automatically recalculated if the default recalculation setting is Automatic.

Record In a database, a record is contained in a single row and a field in a column.

Record length A measure of the size of a record usually specified in units, such as characters.

Relative cell address A cell address in a formula that changes when you copy the formula to a different part of the worksheet file.

Repeating label Used to draw lines in the worksheet.

Resident program A program that remains in the memory while other programs are executed.

ROM (Read Only Memory) Special memory chips containing instructions which can be read only, therefore preventing accidental destruction of the instructions. ROM is used to store firmware.

RTGS Real Time Gross Settlement interbank transfer systems, which transfers money, from one bank to another on a "real time" and on "gross" basis. RTGS systems are used for high-value transactions, which require an immediate clearing and are used to transfer of Rs.2 Lakhs and above.

Run-time The time required to complete a single, continuous, execution of an object program.

Run-time error Program errors encountered while executing programs in a computer.

RuPay Debit Card Rupay Debit Card is an indigenous domestic debit card introduced by National Payment Corporation of India (NPCI). This card is accepted at all ATMs (for cash withdrawal) and at most of the PoS machines (for making cashless payment for purchases) in the country.

Sahukars They are Moneylenders, who offer loans at high rates of interest and normally people go there when bank refuses to give them the loan.

Saving Accounts Saving accounts is meant for saving purposes. The benefit of having savings account is Banks pay interest on the money in the account.

Scroll Move the screen view (or "window") up, down, to the right or to the left. You can scroll one line, one column, or one whole screen at a time.

Second generation computers Computers built during the period 1955-64 which used transistors in CPU, magnetic core main memories, and high-level languages like FORTRAN and COBOL for programming.

Secondary key You select a secondary key when you need to specify the sort order of records whose primary keys are the same.

Secondary storage Devices like hard disk to store data permanently.

Security A process to protect data from unauthorized user, and also save data and information from tampering, or destruction.

Seek time In a disk system, the time required for a read/write head to move to the track where the record to be read or written is stored. Maximum seek time equals the time taken for the head to move from the outermost track to the innermost track.

Segment The fragments of a physical record that are arranged in a hierarchical fashion.

Segmentation A method of providing virtual memory. A multidimensional linear address space implementation differentiates it from paging.

Select To define a section of text so that you can take action on it, such as copying, moving or formatting.

Semantic-Level Model A data model concerned with the interpretation and meaning of stored data.

Semiconductor storage A storage device whose elements are formed as solid-state electronic components on an integrated circuit chip.

Sequential File Organization A file organization technique in which records are organized in order of the value of selected field.

Sequential processing A technique in which a number of similar items or transactions to be processed are grouped together and processed in a designated sequence.

Serial access A storage device or medium where the access time is dependent upon the location of the data. Magnetic tape is a typical serial access medium.

Serial adder An adder in which the bits of the operands are added one after another.

Server An object which performs operations according to the client's requests but may not act upon other objects. It may only send messages to other objects as a result of a request from them unless it is also a client of other servers.

Setup string A series of characters that controls printer settings such as font size, line spacing, or other printer characteristics.

Shadow color Color which is used to add a shadow to an object. This colour often presents a darker shade of the background colour.

Shape The form of an object. A rectangle is a shape, and so is a circle, a triangle, and a trapezoid. Shape is also an attribute – you can change an object's shape without redrawing the object.

Shortcut key The keystroke combination that can be used to quickly execute commands (rather than opening a menu and choosing a command).

Simulation To represent and analyze properties or behaviour of a physical or hypothetical system by the behavior of a system model.

Single inheritance The situation in which a derived class has only one base class.

Sizing handle A square handle that appears at each corner and along the sides of the rectangle that surrounds a selected object. You can drag a handle to resize an object.

Slide The term for the working desktop area in Slide view of PowerPoint, as well as for each page of output of a PowerPoint presentation.

Slide icon A small icon that appears next to each slide title in Outline view. PowerPoint adds icon to show you where each slide begins. A slide icon will tell you if there are any graphics on the slide as well.

Slide master Slide that holds the formatted placeholders for the titles, main text, and any background items you want to appear on all slides in a presentation. If you make a change to the slide master, the change affects all slides in your presentation based on the master.

Slide show A term used for a PowerPoint presentation.

Slide Sorter A view in PowerPoint that shows miniatures of all slides in a presentation.

Slide transition A special effect used to introduce a slide during an electronic slide show.

Soft copy Computer output which is displayed on the screen.

Software A set of computer programs, procedures, and associated documentation related to the effective operation of a computer system.

Sort The process of arranging data into a desired sequence.

Sort key Specifies a field on which sorting process is done.

Source document A document on which data that are to be recorded in machine-readable code originates, that is, the original hand-written or typewritten document or a time card.

Source program/Code A program written in high-level language, such as C language, COBOL, BASIC, etc.

Speaker notes Notes that present speech.

Special character A graphic character that is neither a letter, a digit, nor a space character; for example, the dollar sign, comma, period, etc.

Special purpose computer A computer that is meant for doing only a particular type of job.

Special purpose programming A programming language designed to handle one specific type of problem or application.

Speech recognition The ability to input data directly into a computer system by speaking to it.

Speech synthesis Computer output in the form of spoken word. No cassette tapes are involved, rather a small LSI microchip is used which has the capability of reproducing the human voice via a small loudspeaker amplifier. Presently multimedia is using this concept.

Spooling A technique that has been successfully used on a number of computer systems to reduce the speed mismatch between slow speed I/O devices and fast CPU.

Spreadsheet A structure used for numeric or financial calculations. Spreadsheets contain columns and rows that intersect to form a pattern of boxes, called cells, each of which can hold a value.

SQL SQL is the abbreviated form of structured query language. A relational data-access language created by IBM. Most database server engines use SQL, as a standard way of accessing data from client applications.

Stack A memory in which the information stored last is on top and is retrieved first. Also known as LIFO (Last-In-First-Out) storage.

Stacked bar graph A bar graph in which related bars are placed on top of each other (stacked) rather than placed side by side. The height of the stack of bars usually represents a total.

Stacking Placing objects on top of one another.

Statement All transactions in a bank account for a period of time. Statements are usually given once a month.

Stop Payment When you ask a bank not to pay a cheque or payment you have written or authorized. Stop payments are generally placed on lost or stolen cheques or on cheques related to disputed purchases. Banks usually levy charges for registering stop payment instructions.

Storage See *memory*.

Stored program computer A computer where the program is used to solve a problem and necessary data are stored in its memory.

String concatenation operator The ampersand (&) is the only string operator used in Excel function and formulas. It combines two strings in a formula. (Combining two strings is called concatenation).

Structure The framework of a worksheet, as opposed to the data the worksheet manipulates. Worksheet structure includes titles, labels, and formatting specifications that control the worksheet's appearance.

Submenu A list of additional commands available when you select a main menu command. Many menu commands bring up a submenu. Some submenu commands, in turn, bring up additional submenus.

Subroutine A set of macro instructions that perform a specific task.

Syntax The set of rules of a programming language that define the pattern or structure of the word order and punctuation of an instruction. It is analogous to the rules of grammar in languages like English.

Syntax errors Errors in computer programs that typically involve incorrect punctuation, incorrect word sequence, undefined terms, or misuse of terms. These errors are automatically detected and pointed out by language processors.

Template A blueprint that MS applications, such as Word and PowerPoint use to create documents and slides respectively. The template includes the formatting options, colour, and graphics necessary to create a particular look.

Term/Fixed Deposits Term/Fixed deposits are a particular amount of money deposited in a bank for a given period from 7 days to 10 Years.

Terminal An input/output device which allows a user to communicate directly with a computer system.

Text tool A tool on the Drawing toolbar, used to add text anywhere on a slide.

Textured background A background design that emulates a texture, such as wood or marble.

Thermal printer A printing device that utilizes paper that is sensitive to heat.

Third generation computer Computers built between 1964 and 1975 that used integrated circuits in CPU, high-speed magnetic core main memories, powerful high level languages and saw the advent of time sharing operating system.

Throughput The total amount of useful processing carried out by a computer system within a given time period. It is a measure of efficiency of a computer system.

Timing The amount of time a slide stays on the screen during a slide show.

Title Titles always remain in view as you scroll through the worksheet.

Title master The slide that holds the formatted placeholders for a title and subtitle for your presentation. If you make a change to the title master, the change affects all slides in your presentation that are based on the title master.

Title placeholder The title box that appears when you create a new slide. Click in the title placeholder and type to make your slide title.

Transaction Action in a bank account. Could be a deposit, withdrawal, debit card payment, service charge or interest payment.

Transaction file A file in which the current data are stored for subsequent processing usually in combination with a master file.

Transparency A clear film printed with images and text and used with an overhead projector to display a presentation.

Ungrouping Act of disassociating objects which have been grouped together to function as a single object.

UNIX A popular operating system for 32 and 16-bit mini and micro computers that was designed by Bell Telephone Laboratories, USA.

Utilities Programs to perform some frequently required processes in the operation of a computer system-e.g., sorting, merging, transferring data files from one device to another.

Validation The process of making sure that the forms and documents from a particular transaction are correct.

Video Display Unit (VDU) An I/O device that consists of a television-like screen for displaying outputs and a keyboard for entering inputs.

Virtual memory The technique of using disk space to make programs believe that the system contains more RAM than is actually available. This can be implemented by using pure segmentation, pure paging, or a combination of both. Same as virtual storage.

VLSI (Very Large Scale Integration) An electronic circuit with about 10,000 transistors fabricated in a single silicon chip.

Voice recognition unit An input device used with voice recognition systems that converts spoken words into binary data suitable for input to the system.

Voiceband data A communication system that handles moderate volumes of data, typically from 300 to 9600 bauds. Phone lines that we use to talk to other people is an example.

Volatile storage A storage medium that loses its contents in the event of power failure or when the power is switched off.

Web camera A simple Web camera consists of a digital camera attached to the computer through USB or parallel port.

What-if scenario A calculation that uses variables in formulas to determine potential outcomes of different hypothetical situations.

Wide Area Network (WAN) A digital communication system which interconnects different sites, computer installations and user terminals, and may also enable LANs to communicate with each other. This type of network may be developed to operate nationwide or worldwide and the transmission medium used are normally public systems such as telephone lines, microwave and satellite links.

Word processing The use of computers to create, view, edit, format, store, retrieve, and print text materials for human communication.

WordArt A feature which allows you to create text enhancement effects.

Workbook An Excel file that contains one or more worksheets.

Workstation A desktop computer in a local area network for services provided by the network. It usually has its own processing capability.

World Wide Web Also called the Web, WWW, and W3 an interlinked collection of hypertext documents (Web pages) residing on Web servers and other documents, menus, and databases, available via URLs.

XY graph A graph that displays cell values as points. XY graphs use both a scaled x-axis and a scaled y-axis, so each point on the graph has an X value and a Y value. XY graphs are used to show how two different types of data are correlated. They are also known as scatter charts.

SOLVED SAMPLE PAPER – 1

Basic Computer Course

Total Time : 90 Minutes *Total Marks: 100*

PART – ONE

(Answer all questions; each question carries one mark)

1. Multiple choice

1.1 The connection between the computers and peripherals is called a
a. Port c. Bus
b. I/O device d. None of the above

1.2 Add, Subtract, Divide, Multiply and Logic operations are performed by
a. Registers c. ALU
b. Control unit d. None of these

1.3 Which of the following can be used as a primary memory?
a. Cartridge tape c. Optical disk
b. Hard disk d. None of these

1.4 Which one of the following is not an output device?
a. Printer c. Keyboard
b. Monitor d. None of the above

1.5 Find the odd one out:
a. Norton c. eScan
b. McAFee d. None of the above

1.6 An operating system is
a. Integrated software c. Application software
b. CD-ROM software d. System software

1.7 1 MB is equal to
a. The amount of RAM in every computer
b. 1 billion bytes
c. 1024 KB
d. 1 thousand bytes

1.8 The resolution of a printer is measured in
a. Megabits c. Dots per inch (DPI)
b. Hz d. Inches (diagonal)

1.9 The utility used to increase the speed of programs is called
a. Disk Fragmenter c. Disk Formatter
b. Disk Cleanup d. None of the above

1.10 Which of the following charts is not likely to be included in an analysis of presentation graphics package?
a. Bar c. Temperature
b. Pie d. Line

1.11 The printers that produce the output by pressing a print element and an inked ribbon against the face of a continuous paper form is called
a. Impact printer c. Non-impact printer
b. Scanning printers d. None of the above

1.12 Voice band:
a. Allows the user to download the messages
b. It is used for standard telephone communication
c. It is to connect minicomputers and centralized computers
d. Gives a high-speed communication channel

1.13 A virtual private network creates a ________ through the networks.
a. Tunnel c. Connection
b. BRI d. SSH session

1.14 Baud rate is
a. The difference between the lowest and the highest frequency transmitted
b. Transmission capacity
c. Transmission speed of channel
d. None of the above

1.15 Which one is an example of e-mail address?
a. http://vianet.com/index.htm
b. D:\\Email\Standard
c. joesmart@billme.com
d. Chaminade.org/teachers/mailaddresses

1.16 To insert picture from file into a Word Document, which of the following method is used?
a. Picture command in Home tab
b. Picture command in Transitions tab
c. Picture command in Design tab
d. Picture command in Insert tab

1.17 Which of the following is not a tool for analyzing spreadsheet data?
a. What-if analysis c. Goal seeking
b. Mail merge d. Sorting

1.18 A computer port is used to:
a. Communicate with other computer peripherals
b. Download files from the web
c. Communicate with all hard drives
d. Connect computers together

1.19 Which file extensions indicate only graphics files?
a. BMP and DOC c. TXT and STK
b. JPEG and TXT d. BMP and GIF

1.20 The multiplication arithmetic operator is represented by which of the following symbols?
a. ^ c. /
b. * d. x

1.21 Which of the following is not an example of an Application Software?
a. MS Word c. Operating system
b. Screen saver program d. Antivirus program

1.22 Hard disk is coated in both side above
a. Magnetic metallic oxide c. Carbon layer
b. Optical metallic oxide d. All of the above

1.23 Which statement is valid about computer program?
a. It is understood by a computer
b. It is understood by programmer
c. It is understood user
d. Both (b) and (c)

1.24 CD-ROM stands for
a. Compactable read only memory
b. Compact Data Read only memory
c. Compactable disk Read only memory
d. Compact disk Read only memory

1.25 Software in computer
a. Enhances the capabilities of the hardware machine
b. Increases the speed of central processing unit
c. Both (a) and (b)
d. None of the above

1.26 Which of the following devices can be used to directly image printed text?
a. OCR
b. OMR
c. MICR
d. All of the above

1.27 In the last generation computers, the instructions are executed
a. Parallel only
b. Sequential only
c. Both sequentially and parallel
d. All of the above

1.28 The first network developed:
a. ARPANET
b. NSFnet
c. Vnet
d. Inet

1.29 What is meant by a dedicated computer?
a. Which is used by one person only
b. Which is assigned one and only one task
c. Which uses one kind of software
d. Which is meant for application software

1.30 A computer program that converts an entire program into machine language is called a/an
a. Interpreter
b. Simulator
c. Compiler
d. Commander

1.31 _________ memory has the shortest access time?
a. Cache
b. RAM
c. ROM
d. Magnetic core

1.32 A computer consists of
a. A central processing unit
b. A memory
c. Input and output unit
d. All of the above

1.33 An application program that helps the user to change any number and immediately should result of that change is
a. Desktop publishing program
b. Database
c. Spreadsheet
d. All of the above

1.34 The instructions for starting the computer are stored in
a. Random access memory
b. CD-ROM
c. Read only memory chip
d. All of the above

1.35 Pressing F8 key twice, selects
a. A word
b. A sentence
c. A paragraph
d. Entire document

1.36 How can you disable extended selection mode?
a. Press F8 again to disable
b. Press Del to disable
c. Press Esc to disable
d. Press Enter to disable

1.37 What is the shortcut key you can press to create a copyright symbol?
a. Alt + Ctrl + C
b. Alt + C
c. Ctrl + C
d. Ctrl + Shift + C

1.38 What is the smallest and largest font size available in Font size drop-down list in the Home tab?
a. 8 and 72
b. 8 and 64
c. 12 and 72
d. None of the above

1.39 Which of the following is graphics solutions for word processors?
a. Clip Art
b. WordArt
c. Drop Cap
d. All of the above

1.40 The keystrokes Ctrl + I is used to
a. Increase font size
b. Insert a line break
c. Indicate the text should be bold
d. Applies italic format to selected text

1.41 Digital financial services, expands the delivery of basic financial services to the people through new technologies like
a. Internet
b. Mobile phones
c. Transfer of money through new digital channels
d. All of the above

1.42 Methods of saving include putting money aside in
a. deposit account
b. pension account
c. investment fund
d. All of the above

1.43 Saving allows you to easily meet any unexpected emergencies, such as:
a. Future requirements, like children education, starting of new business
b. Sudden illness, hospitalization, Natural calamity, Job layoff and sudden loss of income
c. It allows you to avoid borrowing money from others
d. All of the above

1.44 Why do we need saving
a. Education
b. Life after retirement
c. When the income is less and expenses are more
d. All of the above

1.45 What helps in Life after retirement?
a. Expenses
b. Burglary
c. Lottary
d. Savings

1.46 ________expenses sometimes surprise us by popping up at the most inappropriate times.
a. Short
b. Fixed
c. Frequent
d. Large

1.47 Large expense includes
a. Plan for higher education of family members in India or abroad
b. Plan for marriage
c. Buying home and Starting of new business
d. All of the these

1.48 By keeping your saved money at bank, you can
a. Earn extra income as an interest from the bank
b. Loss of growth opportunity
c. Double the money
d. None of these

1.49 A bank is a ________ institution.
a. Financial
b. Commercial
c. Joint
d. Sole

1.50 Who helps to Secure money, earn interest and get loans
a. Bank
b. Government
c. Home
d. None of these

PART – TWO

2. Select TRUE or FALSE in statements

2.1 A kilobyte is approximately 1,000 bytes.
2.2 The binary language consists of two digits 0 and 1.
2.3 When you connect to the internet your computer is communicating with a server at your ISP.
2.4 The most common type of memory that the computer uses to process data is ROM.
2.5 A Web browser is a special device that is installed in your computer that allows it to communicate with other devices on the network.
2.6 Being computer fluent means that you should be able to build a computer yourself.
2.7 The CPU and memory are located on a special circuit board in the system unit called the motherboard.
2.8 Hard disk drives and CD drives are examples of storage devices.
2.9 The devices you use to enter data into a computer system are known as input devices.
2.10 Main memory is a software component.
2.11 A computer's CD-ROM drive can read data disks, but it cannot play audio CDs.
2.12 The first successful GUI appeared on the Macintosh computer in 1984.
2.13 Motherboard is the main circuit board in the computer where memory, CPU and other components are plugged in.
2.14 Cache memory makes memory transfer rates higher and thus raises the speed of the processor.
2.15 The laser printer uses a technology called thermal process.
2.16 You can protect scenario so other users cannot change or modify it.
2.17 Without a mouse one cannot work with MS Windows.
2.18 Normal view by default shows 100% Word document screen.
2.19 The mouse was created by Ralph H. Baer.
2.20 Right click press and release the right mouse button once, typically to open a dialog box.
2.21 In Excel, the standard width of a column is 18.43.
2.22 The Request for comments (RFCs) core topics are Internet and the TCP/IP protocol suites.
2.23 If the text entered in a cell does not fit, Excel will display ##### to indicate that the text is too long.
2.24 A mouse is a pointing device.
2.25 A printer is an example of an input device.
2.26 MS office word is an application program.
2.27 When you download files you send files from your computer to the Internet.
2.28 Using Internet banking, one can access to one's accounts at anytime and from any location via the World Wide Web.
2.29 You can add dates to worksheets, but spreadsheets cannot use dates in calculations.
2.30 In a spreadsheet, ordinary text is called a "label".
2.31 Presentation programs creates notes for each slide, which are visible only to the presenter.
2.32 A storage device is a hardware component that writes data to and reads data from a storage medium.
2.33 In a binary representation, we use digits 1 and 2.
2.34 ROM, which stands for read-only memory and is also known as firmware, cannot be written on or erased by the computer user.
2.35 High-end laser printers offer resolutions as high as 300 dpi.
2.36 One of the operating system's functions is to manage the way information is stored on and retrieved from disks.
2.37 e-commerce consists primarily of the distributing, buying, selling, marketing, and servicing of products or services over electronic systems such as the Internet.
2.38 In order to create columnar data in Word you need to Set tabs or use the Table menu.
2.39 Shortcut menu cannot create a link to that program.
2.40 Interest Rate may vary from bank to bank and time to time.
2.41 Saving is income spent.
2.42 Saving involves reducing expenditures, such as recurring costs.
2.43 In economics more broadly, Saving refers to any income not used for immediate consumption.
2.44 In personal finance, saving specifies high-risk preservation of money.
2.45 In a deposit account, versus investment, wherein risk is low
2.46 Saving must be top most priority for everyone, which allows you to easily meet any unexpected emergencies.
2.47 The emergency fund not only provides you with the money to pay for these expenses, but gives you a ?peace of mind?
2.48 We save, because we can predict the future.
2.49 It is safe to keep cash at home, as you can protect when it gets stolen or destroyed in the event of fire.
2.50 Saving money in a bank account, offers you the opportunity to earn interest on deposits.

Answers

1.	1.1	a	1.2	c	1.3	d	1.4	c	1.5	d
	1.6	d	1.7	c	1.8	c	1.9	a	1.10	d
	1.11	a	1.12	d	1.13	a	1.14	c	1.15	c
	1.16	d	1.17	b	1.18	a	1.19	d	1.20	b
	1.21	c	1.22	a	1.23	d	1.24	d	1.25	a
	1.26	a	1.27	c	1.28	a	1.29	b	1.30	c
	1.31	a	1.32	d	1.33	c	1.34	c	1.35	b
	1.36	a	1.37	a	1.38	a	1.39	a	1.40	d
	1.41	a	1.42	a	1.43	d	1.44	d	1.45	d
	1.46	d	1.47	d	1.48	a	1.49	a	1.50	a
2.	2.1	T	2.2	T	2.3	T	2.4	F	2.5	F
	2.6	F	2.7	T	2.8	T	2.9	T	2.10	F
	2.11	F	2.12	T	2.13	T	2.14	T	2.15	F
	2.16	T	2.17	F	2.18	T	2.19	F	2.20	F
	2.21	T	2.22	F	2.23	T	2.24	T	2.25	F
	2.26	T	2.27	F	2.28	T	2.29	F	2.30	T
	2.31	F	2.32	T	2.33	F	2.34	T	2.35	F
	2.36	T	2.37	T	2.38	T	2.39	F	2.40	T
	2.41	F	2.42	T	2.43	T	2.44	F	2.45	F
	2.46	T	2.47	T	2.48	F	2.49	F	2.50	T

SOLVED SAMPLE PAPER – 2

Basic Computer Course

Total Time : 90 Minutes *Total Marks: 100*

PART – ONE

(Answer all questions; each question carries one mark)

1. Multiple choice

1.1 What do you call a computer on a network that request files from another computer?
a. A client c. A router
b. A host d. A Web server

1.2 ALU is:
a. Arithmetic Logic Unit c. Application Logic Unit
b. Array Logic Unit d. None of the above

1.3 Which of the following option in File pull down menu is used to close a MS Word 2010 document?
a. Quit c. Exit
b. Close d. New

1.4 WAN stands for:
a. Wap Area Network c. Wide Array Net
b. Wide Area Network d. Wireless Area Network

1.5 E-mail component of Internet Explorer, is called as:
a. Messenger Mailbox c. Outlook Express
b. Message box d. Gmail

1.6 Central processing unit, consists of:
a. Input unit, output unit and processing unit
b. Control unit, primary and secondary storage
c. Control unit, arithmetic-logic unit and primary storage
d. Input unit, processing unit and storage

1.7 A printer's image quality is usually measured in:
a. Characters per second c. Dots per inch
b. Pages per minute d. Pixels

1.8 What do folders let you do?
a. Organize the files on a disk
b. Ensures that the computer starts properly
c. Names your files
d. Creates a file allocation table

1.9 Some keyboards have a small joystick built into them, between the g and h keys. This type of device is called (an):
a. TrackStick c. Tracking device
b. Alternative pointing d. Integrated pointing device

1.10 In MS Word you can force a page break:
a. By positioning your cursor at an appropriate place and pressing the F1 key.
b. By using the Insert/Section Break.
c. By positioning your cursor at a appropriate place and pressing Ctrl+Enter.
d. By changing the font size of your document.

1.11 Embedded software is used in:
a. Online Railway Information System c. E-learning software
b. Mobile Phones d. Multimedia Movies

1.12 In a spreadsheet, a statement that performs a calculation is called (an):
a. Formula c. Argument
b. Reference d. Parameter

1.13 The slide must be designed in such a way that it ________
a. Attract the eyes of your audience
b. Coordinate with your company logo and color scheme
c. make the information easy to read
d. make the slides interesting and even exciting

1.14 Which of the accompanying storage device can be carried?
a. Hard disk c. Diskette
b. System cabinet d. Main memory

1.15 The number system that is the basis for computer operation as:
a. Hexadecimal System c. ASCII
b. Octal System d. Binary System

1.16 CPU reads the information from secondary memory:
a. First information is transferred to main memory and from there, the CPU reads
b. Directly
c. Through registers
d. None of the above

1.17 __________ involves the use of electronic platforms for conducting a company's business.
a. E-commerce c. E-procurement
b. E-business d. E-marketing

1.18 Find the odd one out
a. Control Unit c. Registers
b. Arithmetic Logic Unit d. Printer

1.19 Which of the following is not an Impact Printer?
a. Daisy-Wheel c. Chain Printer
b. Dot-Matrix Printer d. Laser

1.20 ROM means:
a. Read once memory c. Read on Memory
b. Read only memory d. Read other memory

1.21 The output quality of a monitor depends on:
a. Pixels
b. Resolution
c. Width
d. Height

1.22 CAD stands for:
a. Computer aided design

b. Computer algorithm design
c. Computer application in design
d. All of the above

1.23 To produce high quality graphics (hard copy) in colour, you would want to use a/(an):
a. RGB monitor c. Inkjet printer
b. Plotter d. Laser printer

1.24 Which of the following produces the best quality graphics reproduction?
a. Laser printer c. Plotter
b. Ink jet printer d. Dot matrix printer

1.25 Which of the following Memories allows simultaneous read and write operations?
a. ROM c. EPROM
b. RAM d. None of the above

1.26 An input/output device at which data enters or leaves a computer system is:
a. Keyboard c. Printer
b. Terminal d. Plotter

1.27 Each model of a computer has a unique
a. Assembly of a computer c. High level language
b. Machine language d. All of the above

1.28 Which term is used to describe RAM?
a. Dynamic RAM (DRAM) c. Video RAM (VRAM)
b. Static RAM (SRAM) d. All of the above

1.29 What is the meaning of 'Hibernate' in Windows XP/7?
a. Restart the computer in safe mode.
b. Shutdown the computer terminating all the running applications.
c. Restart the computer in normal mode
d. Shutdown the computer without closing the running applications.

1.30 Which shortcut key inserts a new slide in current presentation?
a. Ctrl+N c. Ctrl+S
b. Ctrl+M d. All of above

1.31 What happens if you select, first and second slide and then click on New Slide button on Home tab?
a. A new slide is inserted as first slide in the presentation.
b. A new slide is inserted as a second slide in the presentation.
c. A new slide is inserted as a third slide in the presentation
d. None of above

1.32 Which of the following method can insert a new slide in current presentation?
a. Right click on the Slide panel and choose New Slide
b. From Insert tab choose New Slide
c. Click on New Slide button on slides group
d. All of above

1.33 Which of the following is not a part of Slide Design?
a. Design Template c. Animation Scheme
b. Color Scheme d. Slide Layout

1.34 What is the best way to create another copy of a slide?
a. Click the slide then press Ctrl+A and paste in new slide.
b. From Home tab of New Slide drop-down list choose Duplicate Slide.
c. Redo everything on a new slide that you had done on previous slide.
d. None of above.

1.35 Which of the following methods can not be used to enter data in a cell?
a. Pressing an arrow key c. Pressing the Esc key
b. Pressing the tab key d. Clicking the enter button to the formula bar

1.36 To copy formatting from one area in a worksheet and apply it to another area you would use:
a. The Home tab > Copy Format and Home tab > Paste Format commands form the Insert tab.
b. The Copy and Apply Formatting dialog box, located under the Insert tab > Copy and Apply menu.
c. There is no way to copy and apply formatting in Excel you have to do it manually.
d. Number & values formatting in the Paste drop-down list on the Clipboard group.

1.37 In a worksheet, you can select:
a. The entire worksheet c. Columns
b. Rows d. All of the above

1.38 Which area in an excel window allows entering values and formulas:
a. Home tab c. Formula bar
b. Insert tab d. Data tab

1.39 Which of the following is the oldest Spreadsheet Package?
a. VisiCalc c. Excel
b. Lotus 1-2-3 d. StarCalc

1.40 To insert page number in a document. Which of the following lets you insert page number?
a. Page number from Insert tab of Header & Footer group
b. Page Layout from Page Setup group
c. References tab of Footnote group
d. Both (a) & (c)

1.41 =ROUND (12.5,1) displays ________ in a cell.
a. 2 c. 2.2
b. 2.1 d. 2.3

1.42 The costs for education is rising every year, and to provide better educational facilities to your family member you need
a. Savings c. Lottary
b. Expenditures d. Burglary

1.43 When the income is less and expenses are more, a person need to__________.
a. Spend c. Gamble
b. Save d. Lend

1.44 A client program which is used to access the Internet services and its available resources through the World Wide Web is:
a. ISP c. Web server
b. Web browser d. Client

1.45 By keeping your saved money at home, it is
a. Loss of growth opportunity c. Increase in money
b. Gain of growth opportunity d. Investment

1.46 What is No credit eligibility?
a. Not eligible to get a credit card
b. No credit history is available to your bank
c. Bank will not let you to borrow money
d. All of the above

1.47 Why bank is needed?
a. acts as an intermediary in transactions
b. safekeeping and lending of money
c. Cash Deposits
d. All of the above

1.48 ________ acts as an intermediary in transactions, and offer services like safekeeping and lending of money.
a. Company c. Bank
b. Institute d. Government

1.49 Bank can be considered as an establishment, which is authorized by _______ to accept Cash Deposits and to provide all financial services across the world.
a. Bank c. Organisation
b. Government d. NGO

1.50 The Bank provides services
a. Saving & Current Account c. Loans-Home/Business/Vehicle
b. Credit Cards d. All of the above

2. Select TRUE or FALSE in Statements

2.1 To be computer literate, you must be able to write computer programs.

2.2 The primary function of I/O peripherals is to facilitate computer-to-computer data transmission.

2.3 A Chit Fund member could default in an instalment payment or disappear after winning the first bid.

2.4 The File tab has buttons for the most common tasks you perform in PowerPoint, such as saving, printing, or exiting a presentation.

2.5 Port is an access channel for computers to exchange information.

2.6 Parallel port can transfer 8 bits of data at a time.

2.7 ICMP protocol is used to report error message.

2.8 The default file extension for all Word documents is .docx.

2.9 Motherboard is a large multilayered printed circuit board inside a computer that contains CPU, BIOS ROM chip and CMOS setup information.

2.10 A1 is an example of an absolute cell reference.

2.11 A presentation usually includes a single slide.

2.12 The errors that can be pointed out by the computer is called syntax errors.

2.13 An e-mail address only contains the username.

2.14 Actions buttons can be inserted in the slide, by Action button command of Insert tab of links group.

2.15 The background of any Word document is always white in color.

2.16 In PowerPoint, when you use Save as Web Page, the presentation is turned into an animated gif image.

2.17 To add a chart to a slide, click Chart button to get a blank datasheet.

2.18 Absolute cell referencing always refers to the same cell in spreadsheet.

2.19 Inkjet printer is an impact printer.

2.20 POP3 protocol is used by outlook express to fetch mails from the mail server.

2.21 WANs operate at the speed of less than 1 mbps while LANs operate between 4 and 10 mbps.

2.22 WAIS stands for wide area information server.

2.23 Text can be inserted anywhere on the slide.

2.24 Character size is measured in points.

2.25 Output from the printer is called soft copy.

2.26 The mouse may be classified as Mechanical mouse or Optical mouse.

2.27 A computer can talk to persons through a device known as speech synthesizer.

2.28 Linux is a proprietary software.

2.29 The kernel is a program that constitutes the central core of a computer operating system.

2.30 The Print command is used to print a text file on printer in the background mode.

2.31 Data stored on magnetic disk can be accessed directly.

2.32 Ctrl+B is used to make the text bold in MS Word.

2.33 The key strokes Ctrl+; are used to enter current time in Excel.

2.34 Re-writable compact disks are now available.

2.35 Laser printers and plotters are graphics device.

2.36 In Word, the most easiest approach to resize a photo is by dragging its edges to match the size and shape you need.

2.37 In MS Excel, all formula use relative cell references.

2.38 The greatest capacity for data transmission happens in voice band devices.

2.39 Railway Ticket Reservation System is not an examples of on-line processing system.

2.40 Computer software is normally classified as system software and application software.

2.41 You can receive higher interest rate by engaging in various scheme offered by the bank.

2.42 If you do not want carrying cash with you because of safety issues, you can carry debit card or credit card provided by bank.

2.43 Once you establish good relationship with bank, you can apply for personal loans (cars, houses or education, business loans).

2.44 Rates of interest of savings account does not depends on how much you saved.

2.45 PMJJBY scheme will be linked to the bank accounts opened under the PMJDY scheme.

2.46 Business purpose website must be on .com domain.

2.47 Cheque or Demand draft (DD) is a valid document for the transfer of money.

2.48 A blank line is also called as a paragraph. It is called as an empty paragraph.

2.49 Digital financial services do not expand the delivery of basic financial services to the people through new technologies like Internet.

2.50 Parts of an e-mail address is separated by @ symbol.

Answers

1.

1.1	d	1.2	a	1.3	b	1.4	b	1.5	c
1.6	c	1.7	c	1.8	a	1.9	d	1.10	c
1.11	b	1.12	a	1.13	d	1.14	d	1.15	d
1.16	a	1.17	b	1.18	d	1.19	d	1.20	b

	1.21	b	1.22	a	1.23	b	1.24	c	1.25	b
	1.26	b	1.27	b	1.28	d	1.29	d	1.30	b
	1.31	c	1.32	d	1.33	d	1.34	b	1.35	c
	1.36	d	1.37	d	1.38	c	1.39	a	1.40	a
	1.41	c	1.42	a	1.43	b	1.44	b	1.45	a
	1.46	d	1.47	d	1.48	c	1.49	b	1.50	d
2.	2.1	F	2.2	F	2.3	T	2.4	T	2.5	T
	2.6	T	2.7	T	2.8	T	2.9	T	2.10	F
	2.11	F	2.12	T	2.13	F	2.14	T	2.15	F
	2.16	F	2.17	T	2.18	T	2.19	F	2.20	T
	2.21	T	2.22	T	2.23	T	2.24	T	2.25	F
	2.26	T	2.27	T	2.28	F	2.29	T	2.30	F
	2.31	T	2.32	T	2.33	F	2.34	T	2.35	T
	2.36	T	2.37	F	2.38	F	2.39	F	2.40	T
	2.41	T	2.42	T	2.43	T	2.44	F	2.45	T
	2.46	T	2.47	T	2.48	T	2.49	F	2.50	T

SOLVED SAMPLE PAPER – 3

Basic Computer Course

Total Time : 90 Minutes *Total Marks: 100*

PART – ONE

(Answer all questions; each question carries one mark)

1. **Multiple choice**

1.1 A CPU is also known as the:
a. Microprocessor c. Primary storage
b. Random Access Memory d. Micro unit

1.2 Clock speed is measured in
a. bit per second c. bytes
b. baud d. Hertz

1.3 Digital means that computer information is discrete and countable/subdivided into:
a. digits c. analog units
b. input d. bytes

1.4 A bit can have two values
a. bit and byte c. 0 and 1
b. 2 and 4 d. 1 and 2

1.5 Alignment means position of the text about:
a. Margins c. Header
b. Paragraphs d. Footer

1.6 Magnetic Tape used _______ access method?
a. Random c. Sequential
b. Direct d. None of the above

1.7 The ALU works on the instructions and data held in the _______
a. Notebook c. Copy pad
b. Registers d. I/O devices

1.8 The ability to combine name and addresses with a standard document is called ________.
a. document formatting c. mail merge
b. database management d. form letters

1.9 Which of the following component displays the contents of active cell?
a. Name box c. Inset tab
b. Formula bar d. Design tab

1.10 What do you call a collection of character and paragraph formatting commands?
a. The defaults c. A style
b. A template d. None of the above

1.11 Which PowerPoint 2010 feature adds special effects to modify the appearance of the slides and the timing between each slide?
a. Color Schemes c. Transition Settings
b. Animation d. Handouts

1.12 An affordable technology that uses existing telephone lines to provide high-speed connection is called
a. ISDN c. Cable modem
b. Microwave d. DSL

1.13 This address changes temporarily as the applications connect to the Internet?
a. Static IP address c. Dynamic IP address
b. Unique IP address d. None of the above

1.14 Which of the following is not a financial function?
a. FV() c. SUM()
b. NPV() d. PMT()

1.15 Left justify is the same as _________ .
a. Align Left c. Align right
b. Align centre d. None of the above

1.16 If a new device such as printer or scanner is attached to a computer its _______ must be installed before the device can be used.
a. Driver c. Manager
b. Platform d. Kernel

1.17 Which type of software is created and updated by a worldwide community of programmers and available for free?
a. Software packages c. Outsourced
b. Proprietary software d. Open Source

1.18 _________ allows LAN users to share computer programs and data.
a. Communication server c. File server
b. Print server d. Application servers

1.19 An error occurs in computer data is called as
a. Chip c. CPU
b. Bug d. Storage Device

1.20 The cell labelled F5 refers to _______.
a. row F column 5 c. functions available in cells
b. column F row 5 d. function key F4

1.21 The functions of Windows Explorer is to __________.
a. Organize files and folders
b. Change the settings
c. Add new programs
d. All of these

1.22 Which of the following option is included in E-learning?
a. Computer-based training c. Both (a) and (b)
b. Web-based training d. None of these

1.23 The settings to wrap text in a cell & to merge cells are found in the Format cells dialog on the _______ tab.
a. Number c. Font
b. Alignment d. Border

1.24 A technique that takes hard copy of an image/document and converts it into a digital format is known as _______.

a. Document imaging c. Document typing
b. Document printing d. None of the above

1.25 To select multiple non adjecent cells in a worksheet you will click them holding
a. Ctrl key c. Shift key
b. Alt key d. Ctrl + Shift key

1.26 After choosing a predefined template/_______ option is chosen to change a background color.
a. Design template c. Color scheme
b. Animation scheme d. Color Effects

1.27 What would you use for immediate, real-time communication with a friend?
a. e-mail c. Usenet
b. IRC d. Mailing List

1.28 When a user subscribes to a newsgroup?
a. All new posts are e-mailed to the user automatically.
b. The user must agree with everything said in that newsgroup.
c. The user is billed annually for the subscription.
d. The user is arranged with spam.

1.29 Which key is used to increase left indent?
a. Ctrl+I c. Alt+I
b. Ctrl+M d. F10

1.30 E-mail is _______.
a. Mail concerning electronic devices
b. Transaction of letters, messages, and memos over a communication network
c. Transaction of messages within a computer
d. None of the above

1.31 Which one is not the language of Internet?
a. Perl c. HTML
b. XML d. COBOL

1.32 Which of the following is/are true about rulers and guides?
a. Rulers and guides can be turned on or off
b. Rulers and guides help place objects on the slide
c. Both (a) and (b)
d. None of these

1.33 Slide Sorter of PowerPoint 2010 is available on _______ tab.
a. View c. Design
b. Reiew d. Home

1.34 What is e-commerce?
a. Buying and selling of international goods
b. Buying and selling of products and services over the Internet
c. Buying and selling of products having to do with the computers
d. Buying and selling of electronic goods

1.35 To undo the last work, press
a. Ctrl+U c. Ctrl+Z
b. Ctrl+Y d. Ctrl+W

1.36 The software that allows user to surf the Internet is called a/an ________.
a. Search engine c. Internet surfing provider
b. Internet Service Provider d. Browser

1.37 Choose the odd one out.
a. Web page c. Index page
b. Home page d. Cover page

1.38 NPS is a defined-contribution pension system, which is operated by _________ of India.
a. Prime Minister c. Government
b. President d. Home Minister

1.39 Which of the following technique is best suited for bank cheques?
a. OCR c. BAR
b. OMR d. MICR

1.40 To put text on the right of the page use the _________.
a. Align left button c. Justify button
b. Align center button d. Align right button

1.41 Fixed Deposit can
a. not be withdrawn before maturity
b. paid only after maturity
c. withdrawn before maturity
d. All of above

1.42 What is a slide transition?
a. Overheads
b. Letters
c. A special effect used to introduce a slide in a slide show
d. The way one slide tools

1.43 KYC means
a. Know your customer c. Both (a) and (b)
b. Know your character d. None of above

1.44 Which of the following is used for modulation and demodulation?
a. Modem c. Gateway
b. Protocols d. Multiplexer

1.45 To install program from network which option of network places you will choose
a. My network c. Internet
b. Entire network d. None of these

1.46 What is meant by Aadhaar seeding?
a. Linking of Aadhaar with Bank account
b. Duplicate issuance of Aadhaar
c. Transfer of Aadhaar
d. None of above

1.47 Which is/are the main provisions of Information Technology (IT) Act, 2000?
a. Finalisation of contracts through electronic media.
b. Legal recognition to digital signatures and documents.
c. Making hacking with computer system an office
d. All of the above

1.48 Bank does not give loan against
a. Gold Ornaments c. Lottery ticket
b. LIC policy d. NSC

1.49 When was Internet started in India
a. 15 August 1995 c. 8 August 1995
b. 9 August 1995 d. 7 August 1995

1.50 Nomination can be done in
a. Savings Bank account
b. Recurring Deposit account
c. Fixed Deposit account
d. All of above

PART – TWO

2. Select TRUE or FALSE in Statements

2.1 Dial-up is NOT a type of Broadband Internet connection.

2.2 An icon in the desktop that represents a temporary holding place for files that are deleted is called as Recycle bin.

2.3 A series of specially designed documents, all linked together to be viewed on the Internet is World Wide Web.

2.4 IPv4 has 128 bits and IPv6 has 32 bits.

2.5 Pradhan Mantri Suraksha Bima Yojana (PMSBY), is an accidental death and a disability insurance scheme.

2.6 The memories which do not loose their content on failure of power supply are known as non-volatile memories.

2.7 CD-ROM players are more rugged and have error correction.

2.8 Default number format is currency.

2.9 Computer memory or primary memory is also known as ROM.

2.10 The tabs appearing below at the bottom on the worksheet carry the default labelling of Sheet1, Sheet2, Sheet3 etc. These tabs cannot be renamed.

2.11 Murdra is Micro Units Development and Refinance Agency Ltd.

2.12 The software used to control the computer and run programs is called system software.

2.13 Kishore covers a loans above Rs 50,000 and up to Rs 5 lakh.

2.14 A Linux is Similar to Unix OS.

2.15 Downloading is process of copying a file from local computer to a remote computer.

2.16 MS PowerPoint reduces the size of the font automatically if the size of the text exceeds.

2.17 Text can be selected in a document by using the mouse/keyboard.

2.18 Banks acts as a medium for the transfer of money.

2.19 The RFCs core topics are Internet and the TCP/IP protocol suites.

2.20 Absolute references in Excel is indicated by a hash sign (#).

2.21 VDU can be used both as an input and output devices.

2.22 To send e-mail to a large group at one time, a mail server can be use.

2.23 The E-commerce domain that involves business activity initiated by the consumer and targeted to businesses is known as Business to consumer.

2.24 In Excel, the delete and clear commands perform the same function.

2.25 Press the key Ctrl + Esc to display a start menu.

2.26 Multiple non adjacent ranges can be selected in Excel.

2.27 To publish a presentation to the web, you must have an active internet connection.

2.28 One can open a file or folder by double-clicking on it.

2.29 Coins are issued by NABARD.

2.30 If documents contain your address details, then it would be accepted as 'proof of address'.

2.31 The FTP protocol is used to transfer, access and manage files.

2.32 Email messages that can not be conveyed to the recipient due to temporary error are called soft bounces.

2.33 The act of exploring Web is known as surfing.

2.34 You can have different header and footer on each sheet of a workbook.

2.35 Telephone network is multi-cast network.

2.36 Dial-up connection is always better than leased line.

2.37 When you insert an Excel file into a Word document, the data are placed as an embedded object.

2.38 On the off chance if PC is on however it is not responding to a system reset, then it is called hang.

2.39 Internet Explorer stores the web pages you visit in the Internet list folder on the hard disk.

2.40 Lables are right-justified by default.

2.41 The ROUND function shows only the non-decimal portion of a number.

2.42 The formula =B5^2 represents the fifth power of number 2.

2.43 Excel has a spell checker which can be used to check the worksheet for spelling errors.

2.44 When you turn on background printing, you can keep working in PowerPoint while you print.

2.45 Indian Currency issued by Central government and gauranteed by the Reserve Bank of India (RBI).

2.46 Notes pane appears in the Normal view in PowerPoint.

2.47 The speed of the system clock has no effect on devices such as printer or disk drive.

2.48 MS PowerPoint allows to insert a sound clip into a PowerPoint presentation but not music.

2.49 Animation is creating the appearance of movement with drawn objects.

2.50 Through the Internet, information is sent in the form of files, audio and graphics.

Answers

1.	1.1	a	1.2	b	1.3	a	1.4	c	1.5	a
	1.6	c	1.7	b	1.8	c	1.9	b	1.10	c
	1.11	c	1.12	d	1.13	c	1.14	c	1.15	a
	1.16	a	1.17	d	1.18	b	1.19	b	1.20	b
	1.21	a	1.22	c	1.23	b	1.24	a	1.25	a
	1.26	a	1.27	b	1.28	a	1.29	b	1.30	b
	1.31	d	1.32	c	1.33	b	1.34	b	1.35	c
	1.36	d	1.37	d	1.38	c	1.39	d	1.40	d
	1.41	c	1.42	c	1.43	a	1.44	a	1.45	b
	1.46	a	1.47	d	1.48	c	1.49	a	1.50	d
2.	2.1	F	2.2	T	2.3	T	2.4	F	2.5	T
	2.6	T	2.7	T	2.8	F	2.9	F	2.10	F
	2.11	T	2.12	T	2.13	F	2.14	T	2.15	F
	2.16	T	2.17	T	2.18	F	2.19	T	2.20	F
	2.21	T	2.22	T	2.23	F	2.24	T	2.25	T
	2.26	T	2.27	T	2.28	T	2.29	F	2.30	T
	2.31	T	2.32	T	2.33	T	2.34	T	2.35	F
	2.36	F	2.37	T	2.38	T	2.39	F	2.40	F
	2.41	F	2.42	F	2.43	T	2.44	F	2.45	F
	2.46	T	2.47	T	2.48	F	2.49	T	2.50	T

UNSOLVED SAMPLE PAPER – 1

Basic Computer Course

Total Time : 90 Minutes *Total Marks: 100*

PART – ONE

(Answer all questions; each question carries one mark)

1. Multiple choice

1.1 Which of the following are the two main components of the CPU?
a. Control Unit and Registers
b. Registers and Main Memory
c. Control unit and ALU
d. ALU

1.2 A disadvantage of the laser printer is:
a. It is quieter than an impact printer
b. It is very slow
c. The output is of a lower quality
d. None of the above

1.3 In Analog computer
a. Input is first converted to digital form
b. Input is never converted to digital form
c. The output is displayed in digital form
d. All of the above

1.4 Which of the following is the latest version of MS Word?
a. Word 2000 c. Word 2010
b. Word 2007 d. Word 2011

1.5 Material consisting of text and numbers is best presented as
a. A table slide c. A title slide
b. A bullet slide d. All of the above

1.6 Standalone program which has been modified to work on a LAN by including concurrency controls is an example of ________.
a. LAN intrinsic software
b. LAN-aware software
c. Groupware
d. LAN ignorant software

1.7 Alignment command available in the __________ group of ____ tab.
a. Click the home tab of paragraph group.
b. Click the home tab of Font group.
c. Click ther insert tab of Ilustration group.
d. None of the above

1.8 If you have a PowerPoint show you created and want to send that using e-mail to another teacher. You can add the show to your e-mail message as a (an):
a. Inclusion c. Reply
b. Attachment d. Forward

1.9 In order to edit a chart, you can:
a. Triple click the chart object c. Double click the chart object
b. Click and drag the chart object d. Click the chart object

1.10 To exit the PowerPoint:
a. Click the application minimize button
b. Click the document close button
c. Double click the applications control menu icon
d. Double click the document control menu icon

1.11 A relatively new technology that allows wireless connectivity is called ________.
a. Bluetooth c. Blueband
b. Blacktooth d. Broadband

1.12 To select one hyperlink after another during a slide presentation, what do you press?
a. Tab c. Ctrl + H
b. Ctrl + K d. All of above

1.13 Special effects used to introduce slides in a presentation are called
a. Custom animations c. Present animations
b. Transitions d. Effects

1.14 The Internet is __________
a. A large network of networks
b. An internal communication system for a business
c. A communication system for the Indian government
d. A communication system for some states of India

1.15 What is the term used when you press and hold the left mouse key and move the mouse around the slide?
a. Highlighting c. Selecting
b. Dragging d. Moving

1.16 What is the full form of MUDRA?
a. Mantri Udhar Dhan Rashi Aayog
b. Macro Units Development and Refinance Agency Ltd
c. Micro Units Development and Refinance Agency Ltd
d. Minor Units Decreases and Reformity Agent

1.17 How can you create a uniform appearance by adding a background image to all slides?
a. Create a template c. Use the autocorrect wizard
b. Edit the slide master d. All of the above

1.18 How do you create speaker note pages that show the slides, related notes, and your company logo on each page?
a. Edit the notes master and add your company logy.
b. Edit the slide master and insert your company logo and notes pane.

c. Edit the handout master to include your company logo and one slide per page with additional note space.
d. All of the above

1.19 Tab scroll buttons are placed on Excel screen:
a. Towards the bottom right corner
b. Towards the bottom left corner
c. Towards the top right corner
d. Towards the top left corner

1.20 What was the department of the U.S. government that developed the initial stages of the Internet?
a. Department of Commerce
b. Department of Defense
c. Department of the Military
d. Judicial Department

1.21 The Name box on to the left of formula bar:
a. Shows the name of workbook currently working on.
b. Shows the name of worksheet currently working on.
c. Shows the name of cell or range currently working on.
d. None of above

1.22 Each Excel file is a workbook that contains different sheets. Which of the following cannot be a sheet in workbook?
a. Work sheet
b. Chart sheet
c. Module sheet
d. Data sheet

1.23 The collection of communication lines and routers is called
a. LAN
b. MAN
c. WAN
d. Communication Subnet

1.24 Who has launched Atal Pension Yojna Scheme?
a. Manmohan Singh
b. Pranab Mukharjee
c. Narendra Modi
d. Abdual Kalam

1.25 How can you show or hide the gridlines in Excel Worksheet?
a. Go to View tab >> of Show group and mark or remove the check box named Gridline.
b. Click Gridline tool on Home tab.
c. Both of (a) and (b) above
d. None of above

1.26 What happens when you press Ctrl + X after selecting some cells in Excel?
a. The cell content of selected cells disappear from cell and gets stored in clipboard.
b. The cells selected are marked for cutting.
c. The selected cells are deleted and the cells are shifted left.
d. The selected cells are deleted and cells are shifted up.

1.27 Which of the following options in Word 2010 is not available in Paste Special dialog box?
a. Paste
b. Display as icon
c. Paste Link
d. Insert Hyperlink

1.28 What symbol is used to enter number as text?
a. '
b. "
c. =
d. +

1.29 The key F12 opens a:
a. Save As dialog box
b. Open dialog box
c. Save dialog box
d. Close dialog box

1.30 What is the short cut key to open the Open dialog box?
a. F12
b. Shift F12
c. Alt + F12
d. Ctrl + F12

1.31 An expansion card that allows the computer to output sound through connected speakers is __________.
a. Video card
b. Network Interface card
c. PC card
d. Sound card

1.32 Where can you find the horizontal split bar on MS Word 2010 screen?
a. On the Review of changes group
b. On the View tab of Windows group
c. On the top of vertical scroll bar
d. On the bottom of vertical scroll bar

1.33 Which of the following is not available on the ruler of MS Word screen?
a. Tab stop box
b. Left Indent
c. Right Indent
d. Center Indent

1.34 What is place to the left of horizontal scroll bar?
a. Tab stop buttons
b. View buttons
c. Split buttons
d. Indicators

1.35 How many ways you can save a document?
a. 3
b. 4
c. 5
d. 6

1.36 PMJJBY scheme will be linked to the bank accounts opened under the ________ scheme.
a. PMSBY
b. PMJDY
c. PMJJBY
d. None of these

1.37 What is a portion of a document in which you set certain page formatting options?
a. Page
b. Document
c. Section
d. Page Setup

1.38 Borders can be applied to:
a. Cells
b. Paragraph
c. Text
d. All of above

1.39 What is the full form of PMJJBY?
a. Pradhan Mantri Jagriti Jyoti Bima Yojna
b. Pradhan Mantri Jyoti Jeevan Bima Yojna
c. Pradhan Mantri Jeevan Jyoti Bima Yojna
d. Pradhan Mantri Jagruk Jyoti Bima Yojna

1.40 What is the default left margin in Word document?
a. 1"
b. 1.25"
c. 1.5"
d. 2"

1.41 Portrait and Landscape are:
a. Page Orientation
b. Paper Size
c. Page Layout
d. All of above

1.42 Which of the following is not an option when printing handouts?
a. Six slides per page
b. Five slides per page
c. Three slides per page
d. Two slides per page

1.43 An Aero theme is the combination of one or more desktop backgrounds, ________ and ________ screen saver.
a. Window colour, scheme
b. Desktop icons, Gadgets
c. Windows colour, Gadgets
d. Sounds, Gadgets

1.44 The slide that is used to introduce a topic and set the tone for the presentation is called the:
a. Table slide
b. Graph slide
c. Bullet slide
d. Title slide

1.45 You can jump to the next column by:
a. Clicking with your mouse on the next column
b. Press Alt + Down arrow
c. Both (a) and (b)
d. None of the above

1.46 __________ is an electronic system which enables the customersto conduct transactions on a Website.

a. Retail Banking c. Internet Banking
b. Corporate Banking d. Institution Banking

1.47 If you need to change the typeface of a document, which menu will you choose?
a. Home tab c. Insert
b. View tab d. None of the above

1.48 Which of the following is the default page setup orientation for slides in PowerPoint?
a. Vertical c. Portrait
b. Landscape d. None of above

1.49 ____________ have a single communication channel that is shared by all the users on the network?
a. Point-to-Point c. Protocol
b. Broadcast Network d. PAN

1.50 Odd one out from Photo ID Proof and Address Proof
a. Passport c. Voter's Identity Card
b. Driving License d. Credit Card

PART – TWO

2. Select TRUE or FALSE in Statements

2.1 Micro computer is called micro because it consists of micro processor.
2.2 Personal Computer is a micro computer.
2.3 e-Learning is the best learning for distance eduction.
2.4 FCNR account is opened by the NRIs is designated currencies.
2.5 Wi-Fi can be used for connecting two machines without any cable.
2.6 PAN means Position Account Number.
2.7 ATM means Any Time Money.
2.8 64 MB is the minimum requirement of random access memory for internet access.
2.9 You cannot see Page Breaks in Excel Worksheet.
2.10 F11 key is the keyboard shortcut for creating chart from the selected cell range.
2.11 Virtual memory is memory on the hard disk that the cpu uses an extended RAM.
2.12 Ctrl+9 to hide entire row in a Excel worksheet.
2.13 To start a new line within the same paragraph press Shift+Enter.
2.14 The formula bar displays the constant value or formula used in the active cell.
2.15 OMR stands for Optical Mark Reader.
2.16 The first time you save a presentation, you must name it.
2.17 CPU is a method of accessing the web.
2.18 An advantage of using the formula palette is that you can see the result of the formula as you create it.
2.19 Ctrl+U selects the underline style for the selected text.
2.20 Money can either get stolen or by anybody if it is kept at home.
2.21 Generally, Dynamic RAM is used as main memory in a computer system as it has higher speed.
2.22 Paragraph mark is a non-printing character.
2.23 When you use the Merge and Center button to center a heading, the heading text remains in cell A1.
2.24 PowerPoint has twenty four slide layouts.
2.25 To make a cell address absolute, you must type a dollar sign before each row and column reference in the formula.
2.26 In Word, the search is case sensitive by default.
2.27 Laser printers are non-impact printers.
2.28 Pure black and white is not available in the print options.
2.29 LINUX is a multi-user, multitasking OS that can run on PCs and large system, as well.
2.30 Information is retrieved from CD-ROM using a laser beam.
2.31 You can draw objects in a presentation by using the Design toolbar.
2.32 In Word, you can set page numbers to appear in the header or footer region on the page.
2.33 END key marks the end of a paragraph.
2.34 A customer can utilize all its stored information by opening an app on their phone, entering a PIN, password and then selecting the information they need to access.
2.35 You can change the character spacing from the toolbar.
2.36 Click the new button to open already opened document.
2.37 With the help of Mobile Wallet, Consumer can pay for a wide range of services and digital or hard goods.
2.38 Formatting of text is an example of text processing.
2.39 A chart can only be placed on the worksheet with the data.
2.40 More than one window can be opened on the screen at one time. However, we can work in only one window at a time.
2.41 By default, the numbers are left aligned and text values are right aligned.
2.42 Cancel button can be used to undo a cell entry after it has been completed.
2.43 All formulas start with an = sign in Excel.
2.44 Once you copy data on to the Clipboard, it can be copied to multiple ranges even after pressing Enter key.
2.45 Internet is owned by United States of America.
2.46 PPF is a savings-cum-tax-saving instrument,which mobilizes small savings by offering an investment with reasonable returns and provides income tax benefits.
2.47 E-mail reaches its destination immediately.
2.48 Internet can be used to send only text from one country to another.
2.49 E-mail always used bridge to send messages in different networks.
2.50 WWW stands for World Wide Web.

UNSOLVED SAMPLE PAPER – 2

Basic Computer Course

Total Time : 90 Minutes *Total Marks: 100*

PART – ONE

(Answer all questions; each question carries one mark)

1. Multiple choice

1.1 Life insurance means
a. Insurance of human
b. Insurance of life of human and Cattle
c. Insurance of Life of Machines
d. All of above

1.2 Network formed between computers spread over large geographical area is called:
a. LAN c. WAN
b. Public network d. None of the above

1.3 In LAN, communication between different machines is:
a. Slow c. slow or fast depending on traffic
b. fast d. None of these

1.4 Modem is used to:
a. Convert digital signal to analog signal only.
b. Convert analog signal to digital signal only.
c. Convert digital signal to analog signal and vice versa.
d. None of these

1.5 A server in LAN is a:
a. Device offering service to user
b. NIC (Network Interface Card)
c. Workstation with huge secondary storage
d. None of these

1.6 E-mail:
a. Cannot address many users.
b. Does not provide protection given to first class mail.
c. Always uses bridge to send messages in different networks.
d. None of these

1.7 WWW stands for:
a. World Wide Web c. We Were in Web
b. Whole World in Web d. None of these

1.8 The shortcut key used for copying selected text into Clipboard is:
a. Ctrl+X c. Ctrl+V
b. Ctrl+C d. Ctrl+D

1.9 Which of the following applications is no longer a part of Windows 7?
a. Windows Media Player c. Windows Photo Gallery
b. Windows Media Center d. WinZip

1.10 General Insurance relates to insurance against
a. Fire c. Burglary
b. Theft d. All of above

1.11 A recently created additional top-level domain name is?
a. .pro c. .business
b. .plan d. .school

1.12 Which of the following provides information regarding the status of your document like page numbers, number of pages.
a. Status bar c. Home tab
b. Mailings tab d. View tab

1.13 Alignment buttons are available on the __________ tab.
a. Home c. Page Layout
b. Insert d. None of these.

1.14 Header is __________ .
a. Any text printed at the top of every page.
b. Any graphics printed at the top of every page.
c. Any text or graphics printed at the top of a particular page.
d. Any text or graphics printed at the top of every page.

1.15 __________ case converts first character of first word of selected sentence to capital.
a. Sentence c. Upper
b. Toggle d. Title

1.16 Bank Pass Book is
a. Issued by Bank
b. Contains transaction details of Bank account
c. Shows balance in account
d. All of above

1.17 Which of the following will you opt for saving a file?
a. Save button on Standard toolbar c. Save option from File menu
b. Pressing Ctrl+S d. Any of the above

1.18 Banks pays interest on
a. Deposits c. Both (a) & (b)
b. Loans d. None of above

1.19 To select a sentence, click anywhere on the sentence while holding the following key pressed:
a. Shift c. Ctrl
b. Alt d. Esc

1.20 To show/hide the grid lines in Excel 2010.
a. Page Layout -> Grid lines -> view
b. Insert -> Grid lines -> view
c. View -> Grid lines -> view
d. Edit -> Grid lines -> view

1.21 To delete the selected sentence, press the following key:
a. Del c. Both (a) & (b)
b. Backspace d. None of the above

1.22 Mark the most appropriate statement:
a. A paragraph can be enclosed in a box.

b. A paragraph can be enclosed in a box and the background shade of the box can also be controlled.
c. A paragraph can be enclosed in a shadow box.
d. All of the above

1.23 Can you set 0.5 inch left indentation for a cell in Excel?
a. Excel does not have indentation feature
b. You can specify indentation only if you turn the rulers on
c. Indentation can be set from Format cells dialog box
d. The indentation can be specified only when printing

1.24 A set of predesigned formats of text or color scheme is called:
a. Slide c. Presentation scheme
b. Template d. Schema

1.25 A combination of various colours used for text and other presentation elements is called:
a. Fill effect c. Template
b. Color Scheme d. C-set

1.26 For what purpose, can you use the shortcut key Ctrl+D in PowerPoint?
a. Duplicating the selected slides. c. Pasting the selected text or graphics
b. Cutting the selected slides. d. None of the above

1.27 You see a tab on the ribbon that you had not noticed before called Drawing Tools. What is it there for?
a. To help you work with shapes
b. To help you work with SmarkArt graphics such as org charts
c. To help you work with pictures
d. None of the above

1.28 You have finished the presentation and you want to run the spelling checker. Where is it on the ribbon?
a. Home tab c. Review tab
b. Slide show tab d. None of the above

1.29 PowerPoint presentations are given extension called:
a. XLS c. PPTX
b. DOC d. BMP

1.30 Internet banking refers to
a. Operation of account through internet
b. Opening of account through ATM
c. Both (a) & (b)
d. None of above

1.31 Which of the following can be used to create presentation from scratch?
a. Autocontent wizard c. Design templates
b. Sample presentation d. Blank presentation

1.32 Which of the following view can you use to show just the slide and its contents?
a. Normal c. Slide Show
b. Slide d. Notes Page

1.33 ATM can be used for
a. Cash withdrawal c. Statement of account
b. Account enquiry d. All of above

1.34 Aadhaar is
a. 12 digit number card c. Both (a) & (b)
b. Identity proof issued by UIDAI d. None of above

1.35 Which of the following provides a printed copy of your presentation?
a. Outline c. Audience handouts
b. Speaker notes d. All of the above

1.36 Mouse, trackball and joystick are the examples of:
a. Scanning devices b. Storing devices
c. Pointing devices d. Multimedia devices

1.37 Which of these is a quick way to copy formatting from a selected cell to two other cells on the same worksheet?
a. Use Ctrl to select all three cells, then click the paste button on the standard toolbar.
b. Copy the selected cell, then select the other two cells, click style on the Format menu, then click Modify.
c. Click format painter on the Formatting toolbar twice then click in each cell you want to copy the formatting to.
d. All of above

1.38 You can open the Sort dialog box by choosing Sort from the ________ menu:
a. Home c. View
b. Page Layout d. References

1.39 A factor which would strongly influence a business person to adopt a computer is
a. Accuracy c. Speed
b. Reliability d. All of the above

1.40 Which of the following tools enable you to add text to a slide without using the standard placeholders?
a. Text tool box c. Drawing tool
b. Line tool d. Auto shapes tool

1.41 Which of the following is Not a characteristic of multimedia presentation
a. Non-linear c. Integrity
b. Interactive d. None of the above

1.42 A business data processing cycle consists of:
a. 3 steps c. 5 steps
b. 4 steps d. 6 steps

1.43 1 Byte is equal to:
a. 6 bits c. 18 bits
b. 8 bits d. 28 bits

1.44 The ________ is a portion of the magnetic tape that is left blank for winding the tape on the other spool, with the help of hand.
a. Leader c. Trailer label
b. Header label d. None

1.45 IIS refers to ________
a. International Institute for Standards
b. Internet Information Server
c. Internal IP Scheme
d. Internet Information System

1.46 Select the incorrect statement regarding bar-code reader.
a. It is used for fast identification of items.
b. It consists of a series of small lines, called bars.
c. The actual coding of the bars is the width of the bars
d. None of the above

1.47 Select the incorrect statement:
a. RAM is a volatile memory.
b. An interpreter is nearly 5 to 25 times faster than a compiler.
c. The operating system is the first program loaded into the computer memory after the computer is switched on.
d. Secondary memory is employed for bulk storage.

1.48 Message travels over ________ physical path.
a. Protocol c. Signal
b. Medium d. All of the above

1.49 Which one of the following is a secondary storage device?
a. CD-ROM c. Both (a) and (b)

b. RAM
d. None of the above

1.50 A device that gives emergency energy to your PC is:
a. Power Supply Unit
b. Universal Surge Protector
c. Universal Power Protection and Supply
d. Uninterruptible Power Supply

PART – TWO

2. Select TRUE or FALSE in Statements

2.1 The output obtained on the VDU is called the soft copy.
2.2 Physically, a CD-ROM and a DVD-ROM disk are different.
2.3 Data typed into the computer is called the output.
2.4 Software represents the physical components of the computer.
2.5 An interpreter is faster than a compiler.
2.6 Software is not a necessary part of the computer.
2.7 Real time means, payment transaction is subjected to waiting period.
2.8 System software is a set of one or more programs that are basically designed to control the operation of a computer system.
2.9 A search engine is a program designed to find information stored on a computer.
2.10 Computer manipulate data in many ways, and this manipulation is called processing.
2.11 Selected text under Word documents can be copied or moved using drag-and-drop feature.
2.12 The Undo command is always the first command under the Edit menu of Word.
2.13 In Word, the last action can be reversed by Repeat command
2.14 You cannot copy or move text to a different location within the same document.
2.15 RTGS systems is used for high-value transactions which require an immediate clearing.
2.16 Font formatting applies to specific characters in word.
2.17 NEFT is a "net" transfer facility, executed in hourly batches.
2.18 Footer is the repetitive text or graphics printed at the top of pages in a document.
2.19 NEFT takes long time as it is done via electronic messages.
2.20 Headers and Footers are displayed in Normal view.
2.21 In Normal view you can see miniature slides called AutoLayouts.
2.22 PowerPoint has 12 pre-formatted slides called AutoLayouts.
2.23 Placeholder is a dotted rectangular box that can contain only text.
2.24 We cannot select more than one object at a time.
2.25 Telnet is a network protocol used on the Internet.
2.26 To select more than one object hold down the Shift key.
2.27 The SUM() function has more than one arguments.
2.28 To delete the selected objects press Alt key.
2.29 You cannot insert a sound in a PowerPoint presentation.
2.30 You can record your own sound or voice narration in a PowerPoint Presentation.
2.31 NEFT provides a facility to bank customers to transfer the funds easily and securely.
2.32 You can adjust the timings you have already set and rehearse the new ones in a PowerPoint Presentation.
2.33 One can share his internet banking password to anybody.
2.34 You can create a shortcut of your file on Desktop.
2.35 A worksheet consists of cells organized into rows and columns.
2.36 The default name of worksheet are sheet1, sheet2 and so on.
2.37 A new Excel workbook contains five worksheets by default.
2.38 MS Excel worksheet has 65,536 rows and 256 columns.
2.39 Three types of data can be entered in MS Excel.
2.40 All the formulas in Excel, begin with an equal (=) sign.
2.41 By using internet banking, user can view account balances, statement history, recent transactions and can transfer the fund!between the customer's linked accounts.
2.42 The sum function has more than one argument.
2.43 Excel does not make an exact copy of a formula.
2.44 The Excel function arguments are enclosed within a square bracket.
2.45 NOS means Network Operating System.
2.46 Main functions of the operating system is Memory Management.
2.47 Premium of Rs.330/- per annum per member, which will be deducted from the account holder's savings bank automatically.
2.48 You can use Explorer program to open a word document.
2.49 OCR is a device that scans written or typed text and transforms it into computer readable forms.
2.50 You cannot hide a sheet in Excel, if it is the only sheet in a workbook.

UNSOLVED SAMPLE PAPER – 3

Basic Computer Course

Total Time : 90 Minutes *Total Marks: 100*

PART – ONE

(Answer all questions; each question carries one mark)

1. Multiple choice

1.1 A group of 8 bits is known as
a. kilobyte c. binary digit
b. byte d. megabit

1.2 The use of information and communication technologies in all facets of the operations of a government organization can be termed as:
a. e-gov c. e-biling
b. e-banking d. None of the above

1.3 Which key deletes the character to the left of the cursor?
a. End c. Home
b. Backspace d. Delete

1.4 An Excel Workbook is a collection of __________ .
a. Workbooks c. Charts
b. Worksheets d. Worksheets and Charts

1.5 How many sheets are there in Excel Workbook by default?
a. 2 c. 4
b. 3 d. 5

1.6 The spelling dialog box can be involved by choosing spelling from _________ tab.
a. Review c. Home
b. Insert d. Page Layout

1.7 A URL can specify the IP address of the Web __________ that houses a Web page?
a. Server c. Client
b. Page d. E-mail recipient

1.8 What is the difference between Memory and Storage?
a. Memory is temporary and storage is permanent
b. Memory is permanent and storage is temporary
c. Memory is slow and storage is fast
d. None of the above

1.9 The binary system use powers of
a. 10 c. 2
b. 8 d. 16

1.10 Which of the following is not one of the benefits of e-commerce to sellers?
a. E-commerce offers greater flexibility in meeting customer needs.
b. E-commerce can help to reduce costs.
c. E-commerce is a powerful tool for customer relationship building.
d. E-commerce increases the net cost per contact.

1.11 S/MIME in Internet technology stands for?
a. Secure Multipurpose Internet Mail Extension.
b. Secure Multimedia Internet Mail Extension.
c. Simple Multipurpose Internet Mail Extension.
d. Simple Multimedia Internet Mail Extension.

1.12 Name a technique __________ is used for creating Web pages.
a. Rich Text Format (RTF) c. BCD
b. ASCII d. Hyper Text Markup Language

1.13 Desktop in GUI OS is
a. Directory c. Screen
b. Device d. File

1.14 What are the tabs that appear at the bottom of each workbook called?
a. Reference tabs c. Location tabs
b. Position tabs d. Sheet tabs

1.15 _________ is a stage at which a customer makes a payment to the merchant in exchange of goods or service.
a. ATM c. Micro-ATMs
b. Point of sale d. None of these

1.16 A _________ is a data communication system within a building, plant, or campus, or between nearby buildings.
a. MAN c. WAN
b. LAN d. None of the above

1.17 DVD stands for
a. Decoded Video Disk c. Digital Virtual Disk
b. Digital Versatile Disk d. None of these

1.18 __________ are those individuals, who act as an agent of bank at those places where it is not possible to open a branch of bank.
a. Bank c. Bank Agent
b. Bank Mitra d. Bank Manager

1.19 LCD stands for __________.
a. Liquid Colour display c. Lithium Crystal display
b. Light Colour display d. Liquid Crystal display

1.20 The _________ is also called as letter quality printer.
a. Dot Matrix Printer c. Ink Jet Printer
b. Daisy Wheel Printer d. Laser Printer

1.21 You want to insert a new slide and pick a lyout for it, first?
a. Click the slide icon on the Home tab
b. Click the arrow under the slide icon on the Home tab, next to New slide
c. Click the slide icon on the Insert tab
d. None of the above

1.22 The latest DVD technology uses
a. Magneto-Optical c. Protein Molecules
b. Optical d. None of the above

1.23 ______ is a collection of many separate networks
a. A WAN c. A LAN
b. An Internet d. None of the above

1.24 What is the full form of PIN?
a. Private information Number c. People Identification Number
b. Personal information Number d. Personal Identification Number

1.25 When the text automatically goes onto the next line this is called ________.
a. Text wrap c. Word wrap
b. Page wrap d. Wrap word

1.26 An interface where facility is provided for entering commands is ________.
a. Menu-driven c. Command-driven
b. Graphic-driven d. None of these

1.27 What allows the user to run two or more applications on the same computer so that he/she can move from one to the other without closing the application?
a. Virtual Storage c. Multi-processing
b. Multi-tasking d. Multiprogramming

1.28 What is the full form of CVV?
a. Customer verification value c. Card verification value
b. Card value verification d. Customer verified value

1.29 To permanently delete a file or folder from the computer, which of the following keys must be pressed?
a. Ctrl+Delete c. Delete+Enter
b. Alt+Delete d. Shift+Enter

1.30 Which of the following is not an option in Taskbar and Start menu properties dialog box?
a. Lock the taskbar c. Auto Hide the taskbar
b. Shut down d. Show Quick Launch

1.31 The type of memory that can be erased by simply exposing the device to a strong source of ultraviolet light for a certain amount of time is
a. PROM c. EPROM
b. Flash Memory d. EEPROM

1.32 If you type a word that is not in Word's dictionary, a _______ way underline appears below the word.
a. Green c. Red
b. Blue d. Black

1.33 __________ branch is a retail location where a bank offers a wide range of face-to-face and automated services to its customers.
a. Bank c. College
b. Company d. Post Office

1.34 What is the Thesaurus used for?
a. Spelling options
b. Grammar options
c. Synonyms and Antonyms
d. None of these

1.35 Primary memory stores
a. Data alone c. Results alone
b. Programs d. All of these

1.36 Memory unit is one part of
a. Input device c. Output device
b. Control unit d. Central Processing unit

1.37 A multi-user OS allows more than one user to use computer
a. One by One
b. At a time
c. Simultaneously but CPU attends only one user at a time
d. More than one process are executed at the same time

1.38 A _________ is a grid with labeled columns and rows
a. Dialog box c. Clipboard
b. Worksheet d. Toolbar

1.39 ______ allows user to obtain information in another document by clicking on a word linked to another document.
a. Hypertext c. Cross-reference
b. Footnote d. None of the above

1.40 Which of the following files and folders does Recyle Bin store?
a. Hidden files and folders c. Deleted files and folders
b. Files and folders in Floppy drive d. None of these

1.41 In MS Excel the intersection of a row and a column is called _______
a. Square c. Cubicle
b. Worksheet d. Cell

1.42 The Internet is owned by ___________
a. The US government
b. The IETF
c. A consortium of telecommunications companies
d. None of the above

1.43 The forum formed for the discussion on a particular subject through the use of the Internet is known as _________.
a. News forum c. News guide
b. Newsgroup d. News channel

1.44 Which of the following is not a type of Internet connection?
a. ISDN c. Leased line
b. Dial up d. ISP

1.45 What is the full form of PAN?
a. Present Account Number c. Primary Account Number
b. Premature Account Number d. Permanent Account Number

1.46 What is the full form of RBI?
a. Reserve Bank of India
b. Reverse Bank of India
c. Reserve Bank of Insurance
d. Reserve Branch of India

1.47 ____________ is the official currency of the Republic of India.
a. Foreign Currency c. Indian Currency
b. Dollar d. Dirham

1.48 Which of the following options is present in the Display Properties dialog box?
a. Desktop c. Appearance
b. Themes d. All of these

1.49 Odd one out in filling of Cheques
a. Put your sign above your name to approve the transaction
b. Do not sign on the MICR (Magnetic Ink Character Recognition) Band
c. Do not forget to put the date
d. Can overwrite/cutting on the cheque

1.50 __________ also known as BIOS

a. Basic Internet Operating Setting
b. Basic Input Output System
c. Balanced Input Output Selection
d. Biased Interface Output Signal

PART – TWO

2. Select TRUE or FALSE in Statements

2.1 Modem is an expansion card that allows two computers to communicate over ordinary phone lines.

2.2 When you hide a slide it remains in your file, even though it is hidden when you run the presentation.

2.3 You cannot change the position of the slide images on the Handout master.

2.4 Loan against PPF /insurance policy/bonds/shares are kept as a security by the bank.

2.5 In a multi-page document, the dotted line that extends on a page is called as soft page break.

2.6 Even and odd pages can have different footers in Word.

2.7 In order to fill a cheque, person needs to mention the date, name of the person/ company (Payee), amount to be paid in words and in figures.

2.8 To fill a formula into a range, select the cell that contains the formula and then drag the fill handle downward, upward, right or left far as you need.

2.9 In Word, the easiest way to resize a picture is by dragging its edges to match the size and shape you want.

2.10 1 MHz CPU can process one million instruction in a second.

2.11 Magneto-optical disk is a hybrid of magnetic and optical technologies.

2.12 Keyboard, mouse and scanner are output devices.

2.13 Networking such as LAN, WAN started from third generation.

2.14 RW/RAM is the type of memory for information that does not change on your computer.

2.15 Ctrl+W is the shortcut key to close an active tab of a browser.

2.16 Mouse and light pen are examples of input/output devices.

2.17 Using an ATM, customers can withdraw cash, check balances and deposit money.

2.18 Web browser refers to a software application that allows you to interact with the information on the WWW.

2.19 When you copy a formula in Excel, relative cell references do not change.

2.20 Home loan is a type of Loan taken by people for a variety of home-related purposes.

2.21 You cannot move or copy sheets from one workbook to another.

2.22 Ctrl + End moves the last cell containing contents in the worksheet in Excel.

2.23 Each Web page has a unique address, called IP address that identifies its location on the Internet.

2.24 MS Excel ignores manual page breaks when you use the Fit to option of the Page Setup.

2.25 If required, a hidden slide can also be shown during a slide show.

2.26 Unwanted, unsolicited junk e-mail sent to a large number of recipients is not called spam.

2.27 Bounced e-mails always result in messages being sent back to the sender.

2.28 Recurring deposits is used to spend a certain amount of money regularly for a particular period and earn a higher interest rate on open recurring deposits.

2.29 Both, Now() and Today() can be used to display the current time.

2.30 MICR stands for magnetic ink character recognition.

2.31 Education loan is given on providing gold as security to a bank.

2.32 Objects on a PowerPoint slide that hold text are called placeholders.

2.33 User name and domain name are two parts of an E-mail address.

2.34 To delete unknown e-mail attachments because the person could track you down and hurt you.

2.35 Amount provided for a fixed tenure at the applicable interest rate, like 10-15 years for Short term loans.

2.36 AltaVista, Google and HotBot are examples of search engines.

2.37 A program that manages all other programs in a computer is called Operating system.

2.38 Firewall is not useful for preventing unauthorized users from accessing internal networks.

2.39 By default, the taskbar in Windows XP is located at the right of the desktop.

2.40 In Linux, error messages are place in a standard byte stream called the standard error.

2.41 A system can have more than one web browser installed at the same time.

2.42 A set of rules is known as protocol.

2.43 Spiders are the computer programs that are used by search engines to roam the World Wide Web via the Internet.

2.44 A non-impact printer that forms an image by spraying ink from a matrix of tiny jets is called Dot matrix.

2.45 OS is a program which acts as a mediator between the user and the hardware.

2.46 More money you keep in the bank for longer duration, the higher the interest will be.

2.47 Refresh button returns to home page.

2.48 The domain name with an extension .com describes a company or commercial organization.

2.49 Submenu is an additional set of commands that the computer displays after you make a selection from the main menu.

2.50 Mobile wallet is a payment services which are operated under financial regulation and performed via a mobile devices.

Specimen Answer sheet for Writing Answers to Objective Questions

PAPER CODE [ ] DATE [ ]

PART ONE : Multiple Choice										PART TWO: True/False					
[Put mark (✓) to your Choice]										[Put mark (✓) to your answer]					
Ques.	A	B	C	D	Ques.	A	B	C	D	Ques.	T	F	Ques.	T	F
1					26					1			26		
2					27					2			27		
3					28					3			28		
4					29					4			29		
5					30					5			30		
6					31					6			31		
7					32					7			32		
8					33					8			33		
9					34					9			34		
10					35					10			35		
11					36					11			36		
12					37					12			37		
13					38					13			38		
14					39					14			39		
15					40					15			40		
16					41					16			41		
17					42					17			42		
18					43					18			43		
19					44					19			44		
20					45					20			45		
21					46					21			46		
22					47					22			47		
23					48					23			48		
24					49					24			49		
25					50					25			50		